INTERNATIONAL ENVIRONMENTAL LAW

IN A NUTSHELL®

FIFTH EDITION

LAKSHMAN D. GURUSWAMY, Ph.D.,
Nicholas Doman Professor of
International Environmental Law
University of Colorado School of Law

MARIAH ZEBROWSKI LEACH
BA, MS., J.D.

WEST
ACADEMIC
PUBLISHING

Nutshell Series, In a Nutshell and the Nutshell Logo are trademarks registered in the U.S. Patent and Trademark Office.

PREFACE

There have been significant changes in International Environmental Law (IEL) since the fourth edition of this book. In this fifth edition, we have attempted to come abreast of these changes. Climate change has emerged as the greatest environmental issue of our time, and treaty law has changed. Consequently, we have focused attention on the 2015 Paris Agreement on Climate Change, but not the Kyoto Protocol, which is effectively moribund. We have continued to follow some of the difficult international environmental challenges arising from the Deepwater Horizon explosion and oil spill in the Gulf of Mexico, and the nuclear meltdown in Fukushima, Japan. There have been changes to some of the treaties and other instruments of international environmental law and policy, and we have attempted to incorporate these changes in the fifth edition.

The objectives of this book remain the same. The fifth edition continues to be a primer on IEL addressed to students, practitioners, teachers, decision-makers, policymakers, and the disquisitive generalists, who wish to obtain a functional, as distinct from a theoretical, introduction to the subject.

The core of this book attempts to distill the socio-scientific evidence confronting law-makers as they negotiate the form and content of substantive IEL. The *raison d'etre* for the development and creation of

IEL is the need for new laws that address the phenomena of environmental degradation in a way that existing laws are unable to do. In responding to this challenge, negotiators and lawmakers in all major treaties have adopted an approach that assimilates and incorporates the findings of the physical, natural, social, and political sciences within an interdisciplinary framework.

International environmental lawyers in their law-making or law-applying roles act as the gatekeepers of international society. They are constantly confronted with competing theories, ideas, and conclusions that clamor for admission into the law. Lawyers engaged in real life law making or interpretation do not have the luxury of ignoring the science or the politics surrounding them. They are compelled to make hard decisions about concepts and ideas. In light of this reality, an early introduction to the socio-scientific context equips them to better understand the tasks they will confront. Students and practitioners, in whose hands the future of IEL lies, need to appreciate that law is shaped by socio political, economic, and behavioral predicates. Unfortunately, these foundational premises of international environmental problems have not received the academic and scholarly attention they deserve.

A review of contemporary theoretical and academic legal writing addressing the global environment quickly reveals the extent to which IEL has been treated as an autonomous subject. But this is not particular to the discipline of law. Other disciplines also remain insular in their outlook. Whether emanating from the physical, natural, social or political sciences, or law, the tendency is for writers to address those within their own discipline. The result is a narrow outlook that contributes little toward the fuller understanding of IEL.

We have tried to remedy this shortcoming and have provided a more extensive review of relevant socio-scientific findings and their causal importance to substantive law. The page constraints of this book, and the changing legal character of the European Union (EU) as it evolves from an international organization into a confederation, restraints us from exploring the substantive corpus of EU environmental laws.

ACKNOWLEDGMENTS

The Fifth edition of this work, was written in the incomparable environs of Boulder.

The University of Colorado Law School is hugely enriched by our Research Librarian, Jane Thompson. We are most grateful to her for the generous and abundant help she provided this project.

Finally, we are grateful for the summer research grants made available to Lakshman Guruswamy by the University of Colorado, Law School.

LAKSHMAN GURUSWAMY
MARIAH ZEBROWSKI

2017

TABLE OF TREATISE AND OTHER SELECTED INSTRUMENTS

Bamako Convention on the Ban of Import into Africa and the Control of Transboundary Movement and Management of Hazardous Wastes Within Africa (Bamako Convention), Jan. 29, 1991, 30 I.L.M. 773

Barcelona Convention for the Protection of the Marine Environment (Barcelona Convention), Feb. 16, 1976 (entered into force Feb. 12, 1978) UNTS 1102

Basel Convention on the Control of Transboundary Movements of Hazardous Wastes and their Disposal (Basel Convention), Mar. 22, 1989 (entered into force May 5, 1992), 28 I.L.M. 657

Basel Protocol on Liability and Compensation for Damage Resulting from Transboundary Movements of Hazardous Wastes and their Disposal (Basel Protocol), (10 Dec. 1999) DOC.UNEP/CMW.1/WG/1/9/2

Brussels Convention Supplementary to the 1960 Convention of Third Party Liability in the Field of Nuclear Energy, Jan. 31, 1963, 2 I.L.M. 685

Canada-U.S. Agreement Concerning the Transboundary Movement of Hazardous Waste, Oct. 28, 1986 (amended in 1992), 11099 T.I.A.S. 496

Cartagena Protocol on Biosafety (Cartagena Protocol), Jan. 29, 2000, 39 I.L.M. 1027

Comprehensive Nuclear Test Ban Treaty (Sept. 10, 1996), 35 I.L.M. 1439

TABLE OF ACRONYMS

CERCLA	Comprehensive Environmental Response, Compensation and Liability Act
CFCs	chlorofluorocarbons
CIA	Chemical Industry Association
CITES	Convention on International Trade in Endangered Species and Wild Fauna and Flora
CL	civil liability
CO_2	carbon dioxide
COP	Conference of the Parties
CRAMRA	Convention on the Regulation of Antarctic Mineral Resource Activities
CRC	Convention on the Rights of the Child
CRIC	Committee for the Review of the Implementation of the Convention
CSD	Commission on Sustainable Development of the United Nations
CTBT	Comprehensive Nuclear Test Ban Treaty
DDT	dichlorodiphenyltrichloroethane
DSB	Dispute Settlement Body
DTRA	Defense Threat Reduction Agency
ECOSOC	Economic and Social Council of the United Nations

EEC	European Economic Community
EEZ	exclusive economic zone
EPA	Environmental Protection Agency
EU	European Union
EURATOM	European Atomic Energy Community
FAO	Food and Agricultural Organization
FIFRA	Federal Insecticide, Fungicide, and Rodenticide Act
GATT	General Agreement on Tariffs and Trade
GDP	gross domestic product
GEF	Global Environment Facility
GESAMP	Joint Group of Experts on the Scientific Aspects of Marine Environmental Protection
GHGs	greenhouse gases
GMOs	genetically modified organisms
GPA	Global Program of Action
GPGs	global public goals
HBFCs	hydrobromofluorocarbons
HCFCs	hydrochlorofluorocarbons
HFCs	hydroflurocarbons
IAEA	International Atomic Energy Agency

IBRD	International Bank for Reconstruction and Development
IBWC	International Boundary and Water Commission
ICJ	International Court of Justice
ICPD	International Conference on Population and Development
ICRW	International Convention for the Regulation of Whaling
IEL	international environmental law
IFC	International Finance Corporation
IJC	International Joint Commission
IL	international liability
ILA	International Law Association
ILC	International Law Commission
ILO	International Labor Organization
IMF	International Monetary Fund
IMO	International Maritime Organization
IPCC	Intergovernmental Panel on Climate Change
IPRs	intellectual property rights
ITER	International Thermonuclear Experimental Reactor
ITLOS	International Tribunal for the Law of the Sea

ITOPF	International Tanker Owners Pollution Federation
IUCN	World Conservation Union
IUU	illegal, unreported, and unregulated
IWC	International Whaling Commission
LDCs	least developed countries
LMOs	living modified organisms
LRTAP	Convention on Long-Range Transboundary Air Pollution
MARPOL	International Convention for the Prevention of Pollution from Ships
MDGs	Millennium Development Goals
MOP	Meeting of the Parties
MOU	Memorandum of Understanding
NAAEC	North American Agreement on Environmental Cooperation
NAFTA	North American Free Trade Agreement
NAP	National Action Programmes
NDC	nationally determined contribution
NEPA	National Environmental Policy Act
NGOs	non-governmental organizations
NOx	nitrous oxides
NPT	Non-proliferation of Nuclear Weapons
NRC	National Research Council

ODA   official development assistance

OECD   Organization for Economic Cooperation and Development

OPRC   International Convention on Oil Pollution Prepardenes, Response and Co-operation

OSHA   Occupational Safety and Health Act

PCBs   polychlorinated bipheneyls

PCIJ   Permanent Court of International Justice

PIC   Prior Informed Consent

POPs   persistent organic pollutants

RCPs   Representative Concentration Pathways

RCRA   Resource Conservation and Recovery Act

RIAs   Regional Implementation Annexes

RMP   Revised Management Procedure

RMS   Revised Management Scheme

SBI   Subsidiary Body for Implementation

SBSTA   Subsidiary Body for Scientific and Technological Advice

SD   sustainable development

SDGs   sustainable development goals

SDR   Special Drawing Rights

SFSA	Agreement for the Implementation of the Provisions of UNCLOS Relating to the Conservation and Management of Straddling Fish Stocks and Highly Migratory Fish Stocks
SO_2	sulfur dioxide
SPREP	South Pacific Regional Environmental Programme
SR	State responsibility
SRES	Special Report on Emission Scenarios
START	Strategic Arms Reduction Talks
TSCA	Toxic Substances Control Act
UARS	Upper Atmosphere Research Satellite
UN	United Nations
UNCCD	United Nations Convention to Combat Desertification
UNCED	United Nations Conference on Environment and Development (Earth Summit)
UNCLOS	United Nations Convention on the Law of the Sea
UNCSD	United Nations Conference on Sustainable Development
UNCTAD	United Nations Conference on Trade and Development

OUTLINE

INTERNATIONAL ENVIRONMENTAL LAW

IN A NUTSHELL®

FIFTH EDITION

CHAPTER ONE

SOURCES AND FORMS OF INTERNATIONAL ENVIRONMENTAL LAW

International Environmental Law (IEL) bears a name that reflects its content. At its substantive core, IEL endeavors to control pollution and the depletion of natural resources within a framework of sustainable development (SD). Although the presence of both the terms "international" and "environmental" in its name suggests parity between national and international laws, IEL is formally a branch of public international law—a body of law created by States for States to govern problems that arise between States.

IEL possesses some features that distinguish it from traditional international law. First, its creation and vigorous, if uneven, growth owe much to national environmental laws and policies. States frequently have been driven into landmark international agreements and practices by the momentum of law, regulation, and policies applicable to their own environmental challenges, and not necessarily because of the gravity of international problems. Second, national environmental regulatory laws and the conceptual frameworks of environmental sciences have been inevitably, albeit asymmetrically, infused into the corpus of IEL.

Third, in the past, the law-making in IEL was often shaped primarily by biophysical and not geopolitical forces. At times, this communal foundation sheltered IEL from the disfiguring political dissention found in other areas of international law. But today the foundational norm of IEL is SD, which is a political concept that will be more fully dealt with in Chapter 2. SD has re-engineered IEL into a triangle consisting of economic growth, social development, and environmental protection. SD has also led to the creation of established principles such as common but differentiated responsibilities (CBDR) and to a number of other putative principles, such as the polluter pays principle, the preventive and precautionary principles, and various principles of good neighborliness and cooperation.

As a result, IEL, while remaining a division or tributary of international law, possesses its own characteristics and attributes arising as much from its *relatively* non-political subject matter (at least when dealing with the environmental side of SD) as from the greater influence of domestic law. It is a measure of IEL's stature and recognition that it sits shoulder to shoulder, albeit uncomfortably, with other principles of public international law developed over the last 50 years, including those controlling the use of force, self-determination, permanent sovereignty over natural resources, and human rights.

Whether casting a gentle glance or a hard look at IEL, it is difficult to avoid its substantive corpus and powerful presence, or the vigor and fast rate of its expansion. It already has spawned over 1,190 multilateral, 1,500 bilateral, and 250 other instruments in addition to a host of declarations and United Nations (UN) General Assembly resolutions, some of which express "soft" IEL, while others articulate and restate existing rules of customary law [International Environmental Agreements (IEA), *Database Project of the University of Oregon, available at* http://iea.uoregon.edu (last visited Apr. 2017)]. Moreover, it boasts a small but growing body of judicial decisions (case law) and general principles of law. A look at the substantial document supplements to course books and treatises, for example, offers ample evidence of this growing corpus of IEL [*see, for example*, David Hunter, et al., INTERNATIONAL ENVIRONMENTAL POLICY, Fifth Edition (2015); Pierre-Marie Dupuy & Jorge E. Viñuales, INTERNATIONAL ENVIRONMENTAL LAW (2015); Philippe Sands & Jacqueline Peel, PRINCIPLES OF INTERNATIONAL ENVIRONMENTAL LAW (2012); Jonathan Carlson, Geoffrey Palmer, & Burns Weston, INTERNATIONAL ENVIRONMENTAL LAW AND WORLD ORDER, THIRD EDITION, (2012)].

Treaties, customary law, general principles of law, and judicial decisions are usually referred to as "sources of law." Article 38(1) of the Statute of the International Court of Justice (ICJ), confirms that:

The Court . . . shall apply:

a. international conventions. . . ;

b. international custom, as evidence of a general practice accepted as law;

c. the general principles of law recognized by civilized nations;

d. . . . judicial decisions and the teachings of the most highly qualified publicists of the various nations, as subsidiary means for the determination of rules of law [*Statute of the International Court of Justice,* Jun. 29, 1945 (entered into force Oct. 24, 1945), 59 Stat. 1031 at art. 38(1) (hereinafter Statute of ICJ)].

While these are all sources of law in one sense, they are also differing forms in which IEL is expressed or cast.

A. TREATIES

Over the last 50 years, international law has become a dynamic instrumentalist social force addressing a wide range of socioeconomic, sociopolitical, and biophysical challenges through bilateral, regional, and global treaties. International law now includes a formidable corpus of treaties dealing, for example, with labor, human rights, health, intellectual property, taxation, the environment, and energy. Many of these treaties establish articulated and implied goals and objectives, and some of them create new institutions.

While we have just referred to four major sources and forms of IEL, substantive IEL overwhelmingly consists of principles and rules creating preventive, precautionary, or remedial norms embodied in treaties. Treaties are written agreements between two or more States, governed by international law, creating or restating legal rights and duties. They are also described as conventions, agreements, protocols, covenants, pacts, etc. A question that needs to be answered before we commence our summary of the sources and forms of law is: why are treaties the principle source of IEL?

The preeminence of treaties is largely attributable to the nature of environmental problems. These problems range over a wide spectrum of factual situations. Moreover, they demand continuous observation and monitoring, as well as quick legal action and implementation in response to ongoing and relatively rapid changes in scientific knowledge and conclusions. The socio-scientific context calls for substantive IEL that is able to deal with wide and varied kinds of investigations, scientific monitoring, assessments, and findings. The law should be capable of responding to complex international environmental problems with a mix of generality, specificity, and adaptability. None of the four sources of IEL can fulfill all of these requirements, although treaties are best able to satisfy at least some of them.

For example, customary law, as we shall see, is made up of state practice and *opinio juris*, which usually takes time to crystallize, one issue at a time, and is carefully restricted to the specific facts. General principles of law take even longer to identify and ascertain. Even where customary rules or general principles are clear, these sources do not provide mechanisms for inducing compliance or considering infractions. Treaties, on the other hand, offer a superior framework for dealing with environmental issues by allowing for targeted laws, flexibility of law-making, machinery for inducing compliance, and non-compliance and dispute resolution mechanisms—all of which can be tailored to the problems at hand. Finally, treaties are reduced to writing and are therefore more accessible and applicable. This is particularly important when dealing with a developing system of law, like international law, that may lack clarity and certainty.

The Vienna Convention on the Law of Treaties (Vienna Convention) deals comprehensively with a number of complex questions concerning treaties [*Vienna Convention on the Law of Treaties*, May 23, 1969, 115 U.N.T.S. 331 (hereinafter Vienna Convention)]. Of these, we refer only to those of particular importance to IEL. The first concerns the entry into force of a treaty, or the date on which it officially binds the parties. Even though signed, a multilateral treaty typically does not enter into force until a stipulated minimum number of States have deposited their ratifications. Ratification is the process by which the respective national governments give legal force to the signatures entered by their representatives. For example, a signature by a U.S. diplomat does not bind the U.S. to an agreement until the Senate ratifies the treaty. The Convention on Biological Diversity (Biodiversity Convention) (*see* Ch. 5) required 30 ratifications [*The Convention on Biological Diversity*, Jun. 5, 1992 (entered into force Dec. 29, 1993), 31 I.L.M 818 at art. 36 (hereinafter Biodiversity Convention)], and the UN Framework Convention on Climate Change (UNFCCC) (*see* Ch. 6) required 50 ratifications [*United Nations Framework Convention on Climate Change*, Dec 31, 1992 (entered into force Mar. 21,

1994), 31 I.L.M. 849 at art. 23 (hereinafter
UNFCCC)].

Upon ratification, a party to a treaty may enter
reservations to the extent that they are not
prohibited. Reservations allow parties to agree to all
of the provisions of a treaty except those specified in
the reservation. Recent environmental treaties frown
on reservations, and conventions such as the
Montreal Protocol on Substances that Deplete the
Ozone Layer (Montreal Protocol), (*see* Ch. 7)
[*Montreal Protocol on Substances that Deplete the
Ozone Layer*, Sept. 16, 1987 (entered into force Jan.
1, 1989), 26 I.L.M. 1550 (hereinafter Montreal
Protocol)], the Biodiversity Convention (*see* Ch. 5),
and the UNFCCC (*see* Ch. 6) disallow reservations
altogether. Parties have attempted to get around this
ban on reservations by making "interpretive
declarations," such as those entered by Fiji, Kiribati,
Nauru, and Tuvalu to the UNFCCC, and by the
United Kingdom to the Biodiversity Convention, but
the legal effect of such declarations is undetermined.

Treaties may also be amended where allowed by
their provisions. The Vienna Convention for the
Protection of the Ozone Layer (Vienna Ozone
Convention), for example, has a number of innovative
procedures relating to the amendments of its
protocols and annexes that do not require unanimous
approval [*Vienna Convention for the Protection of the
Ozone Layer,* Mar. 22, 1985 (entered into force Sept.
22, 1988), 26 I.L.M. 1529 at art. 9 & 10 (hereinafter
Vienna Ozone Convention)]. However, treaty
amendments generally do not enter into force unless

ratified or accepted by all the parties. This formal, very demanding treaty amendment procedure has proved to be anachronistic, preventing existing treaty regimes from keeping abreast of new developments and technologies or incorporating new and essential scientific findings.

In order to meet this deficiency, a number of environmental treaties are now using the framework approach to international law-making. Also known as the convention-protocol approach, this method splits treaty development into two or three parts consisting of: (1) a "framework treaty" which usually functions as a constituent instrument containing general principles; (2) "protocols" that supplement or implement the framework treaty; and (3) technical and scientific "annexes" containing details that may need quick amendment according to changing needs.

1.   INTERPRETATION OF TREATIES

Like other areas of international law, many principles of IEL embodied in treaties are vague and nebulous for a number of reasons. Among the more important of these reasons is that treaties are drafted not by gods, but by humans who are unable to anticipate and provide for every factual or legal contingency that might arise in the future. To meet unforeseen contingencies, resort is made to abstractions and concepts of wide scope, which almost by definition lack specificity and exactitude and require interpretation before they can be applied to the facts of a case. When a novel case arises, the extent to which it might be covered by existing provisions   through   interpretation   may   be contentious.

In addition, there is a tendency for drafting conferences to resort to aspirational and hortatory expression when they cannot agree upon specific obligations. Furthermore, and conversely, when parties to a treaty want to move beyond the aspirational to the obligatory, but are unable to agree on the formulation of such an obligation, they sometimes leave it to be resolved by interpretation on a later occasion.

Consequently, treaties are replete with a variety of verbal formulations that do not amount to obligations of effect. These include: aspirational norms, general norms containing inchoate and open-textured obligations, and formulations of rules or principles that codify contentious or competing rules. Illustrations of aspirational and inchoate obligations abound in environmental treaties. For example, according to the UNFCCC (*see* Ch. 6), parties taking into account their undefined "common but differentiated responsibilities" shall include climate change considerations "to the extent feasible" [UNFCCC at art. 4(1)(f)]. The Biodiversity Convention (*see* Ch. 5) is choked by obligations of aspiration, such as "as far as possible and as appropriate" [Biodiversity Convention at arts. 5, 6, & 7] and "in accordance with its particular conditions and capabilities" [*Id*. at art. 6]. The Basel Convention on the Control of Transboundary Movements of Hazardous Wastes and their Disposal (Basel Convention) (*see* Ch. 9) requires each party to take "appropriate measures" to minimize the generation of hazardous wastes and also requires that parties manage wastes in an "environmentally sound" manner [*The Basel Convention on the Control of Transboundary Movements of Hazardous Wastes and their Disposal*, Mar. 22, 1989 (entered into force May 5, 1992), 28 I.L.M. 657 at art. 4(2)(a) & 4(2)(d) (hereinafter Basel Convention)]. The Protocol to the 1979 Convention on Long-Range Transboundary Air Pollution Concerning the Emissions of Nitrogen Oxides or Their Transboundary Fluxes (Sofia Protocol) (*see* Ch. 14) requires parties to "act as soon as possible" and "without undue delay" [*The Protocol to the 1979 Convention on Long-Range Transboundary Air Pollution Concerning the Emissions of Nitrogen Oxides or Their Transboundary Fluxes*, Oct. 31, 1988 (entered into force Mar. 16, 1983), 22 I.L.M. 212 at art. 2(1) & 7 (hereinafter Sofia Protocol)].

While the previous citations serve as examples of aspirational norms and inchoate or open-textured obligations, other provisions, embodying general duties and competing norms that remain undefined, further compound the difficulty of interpretation. A possible variation, perhaps even conflict, in the way a general duty is expressed may be found by comparing corresponding provisions of the Biodiversity Convention and the UN Convention on the Law of the Sea (UNCLOS) [*United Nations Convention on the Law of the Sea*, Dec. 20, 1982 (entered into force Nov. 16, 1994), 21 I.L.M. 1261 (hereinafter UNCLOS)]. Article 3 of the Biodiversity Convention (*see* Ch. 5) strikes a balance between the sovereign rights of States over natural resources and their duty toward the international environment by requiring that States "not cause damage" to areas outside their jurisdiction. This duty is formulated somewhat differently by Article 193 of UNCLOS (*see* Ch. 13), which requires States "to protect and preserve" the marine environment. Such a divergence between the more onerous duty of "protecting and preserving" in contrast to the less exacting duty "not to cause damage" can create an interpretive problem when trying to ascertain the meaning and import of the general obligation of preventing transboundary damage. It also invokes the need to reconcile the conflicting norms found in cognate treaties.

Two interconnected questions concerning treaty interpretation require further attention: (1) who is empowered to interpret a treaty? And (2) how, or according to what rules, is the law interpreted? Interpretation in IEL operates in a manner similar to national legal systems in which the interpretive task is undertaken by courts and judicial tribunals, as well as administrative agencies charged with implementing the statute in question.

The ICJ is perhaps the best known among international courts, but it depends on the acquiescence of the parties for its jurisdiction [Statute of ICJ at art. 36]. Judicial or arbitral tribunals created by treaties such as UNCLOS or the UNFCCC are also empowered to interpret the law. Moreover, there are a plethora of new judicial bodies consisting of courts as well as quasi-judicial tribunals of different kinds that are empowered to interpret IEL. This could lead to jurisdictional conflicts [Lakshman Guruswamy, *Jurisdictional Conflicts between International Tribunals: A Framework for Adjudication and Implementation*, BRINGING NEW LAW TO OCEAN WATERS, D. Caron & H. Scheiber, eds. (2005) at 297–347]. Interpretation may further be rendered by the declarations of diplomatic conferences such as the 1972 Stockholm Conference on the Human Environment (Stockholm Conference), the 1992 UN Conference on Environment and Development (UNCED or Earth Summit), and the General Assembly of the UN. Increasingly, interpretation is done by the institutions created by environmental treaties, including the permanent annual conferences of international regimes or even expert organizations such as those mentioned in the Appendix.

The Vienna Convention outlines basic rules of treaty interpretation. Article 31 stipulates that a treaty shall be interpreted in good faith, in accordance with the ordinary meaning given to the terms in context and in the light of the treaty's object and purpose. Article 32 allows for supplementary means of interpretation where interpretation according to Article 31 leaves the meaning ambiguous or obscure, or leads to a result that is manifestly absurd or unreasonable. While these appear to be reasonably objective rules, they are not self-executing and need to be applied by an interpreter. The process of applying the rules creates an unavoidably subjective human element and can result in demonstrable differences in opinion.

For example, the ICJ in a recent decision denied the World Health Organization (WHO) standing to request an Advisory Opinion on the legality of the threat or use of nuclear weapons (WHO Advisory Opinion) [*Legality of the Use by a State of Nuclear Weapons in Armed Conflict,* (Request for an Advisory Opinion by the WHO of Sept. 13) 1993 I.C.J. 467 (hereinafter WHO Advisory Opinion)]. The majority decision of the ICJ was based on a very narrow and restricted interpretation of the mandate of the WHO (*see* Ch. 17). On the other hand, as we see below, the Meeting of the Parties (MOP) under the Montreal Protocol interpreted some of its provisions in an expansive and even non-textual fashion.

2. CONFLICT WITH OTHER TREATIES

Like the body politic of civil society within States, the international community is also subject to interest group politics, and commits itself through treaties to a variety of objectives and goals which are not integrated, or even harmonized, and do not operate in unison. The clash of goals and objectives is vividly illustrated by the conflict between environmental protection and free trade (*see* Ch. 18). For instance, a number of environmental treaties such as the Montreal Protocol (*see* Ch. 7), the Basel Convention (*see* Ch. 9), and the Convention on International Trade in Endangered Species and Wild Fauna and Flora (CITES) (*see* Ch. 5) mandate trade restrictions to achieve their environmental goals [*Convention on International Trade in Endangered Species and Wild Fauna and Flora*, Mar. 3, 1973 (entered into force Jul. 1, 1975), 12 I.L.M. 1085 (hereinafter CITES)]. It is arguable that many of these trade restrictions could be justified under UNCLOS. Such trade restrictions, however, conflict with the General Agreement on Tariffs and Trade (GATT)/ World Trade Organization (WTO) regime that was restructured in 1994 [*General Agreement on Tariffs and Trade, Final Act Embodying the Results of the Uruguay Round of Multinational Trade Negotiations,* Apr. 15, 1994, 33 I.L.M. 1153 (hereinafter GATT)].

The Vienna Convention provides some guidance on how to interpret conflicting treaties dealing with the same "subject matter" [Vienna Convention at art. 30]. Where the parties to both treaties are common, there are two rules: (1) a treaty that is later in time prevails; however, (2) where a treaty either states that it is subject to, or not incompatible with another treaty, that other treaty prevails. Where there is a conflict between a treaty to which both States are parties and another to which only one State is a party, the treaty to which both are parties will prevail [*Id.* at art. 30(4)(b)].

With regard to the Montreal Protocol, CITES, and the Basel Convention, the last in time rule appears to give precedence to GATT/WTO, which was adopted more recently. However, in the event of a clash between GATT/WTO and UNCLOS, the advantage swings to UNCLOS, which came into force even later. The potential clash between GATT/WTO and UNCLOS was highlighted in the Chile Swordfish case [World Trade Organization, *Dispute Settlement: Dispute Ds193 Chile—Measures Affecting the Transit*

and Importing of Swordfish www.wto.org/english/
tratop_e/dispu_e/cases_e/ds193_e.htm (last visited
Apr. 2017)]. This case involved proceedings both at
the Dispute Settlement Body (DSB) of the WTO and
the International Tribunal for the Law of the Sea
(ITLOS). At the WTO, the European Union (EU)
asserted a right to access Chilean ports on the
grounds of the 1994 GATT freedom of transit. At the
ITLOS Chamber, Chile contended that the EU had
violated UNCLOS Article 64 (calling for cooperation
in ensuring conservation of highly migratory
species), Articles 116–119 (relating to conservation of
the living resources of the high seas), Article 297
(concerning dispute settlement), and Article 300
(calling for good faith and no abuse of right). Chile
further asserted that the EU failed to enact and
enforce substantive conservation measures on its
vessels fishing in the area, that the EU failed to
report its captures to the relevant international
organization (in this case the Food and Agriculture
Organization), and that the EU failed to cooperate
with the coastal state in ensuring the conservation of
highly migratory species.

In 2010, the EU and Chile informed the DSB and
ITLOS that they were withdrawing their respective
cases pursuant to an agreement between the parties
based on a fisheries and conservation program. The
issues presented by the parties on the clash of two
international regimes (WTO and UNCLOS) and
divergent conclusions reached by their respective
tribunals remain unanswered.

So do a number of other questions. For example, does the Basel Convention deal with the same subject matter as the GATT/WTO? If not, will the rule in Vienna Convention Article 30(4)(b) apply? Can it be argued that the Basel Convention deals with a specialized area and takes precedence over a more general treaty dealing with trade in the round? What if an environmental treaty were to say that its provisions would take priority over other treaties dealing with the same subject matter? Although one might be tempted to answer these questions in favor of the Basel Convention, there are as yet no conclusive answers to such problems.

B. CUSTOM

Customary law, or custom, refers largely to unwritten law inferred from the conduct of States, undertaken in the belief that they were bound to do so by law. In the words of the Statute of the ICJ, custom is "evidence of a general practice accepted as law" [Statute of ICJ at art. 38(1)(b)]. Customary international law, therefore, is created by the fusion of (1) an objective element: practice; and (2) a subjective element: *opinio juris*.

Suppose Country A asserts that customary law establishes the right to take countermeasures with respect to an environmentally wrongful act. In order to establish such a claim, it must first be proved that previously nations have resorted to such countermeasures following a pattern of conduct that is consistent, extensive, uniform, and general. Practice in IEL takes a number of forms, and the evidence necessary to establish it may be gathered, *inter alia,* from the following materials drawn from the legislative, executive, judicial, and administrative branches of a government: (1) national legislation; (2) diplomatic notes and correspondences; (3) statements and votes by governments in international organizations and forums of varying kinds; (4) ratification of treaties containing the obligations in question; (5) opinions of legal advisers; and (6) restatements of the law by scholars and jurists like the International Law Commission (ILC). Evidence gathered from these sources will testify to what States actually do and how they react when faced with a particular problem.

The next question is whether such practice was undertaken by a State in the belief that what they were doing was compelled or mandated by law. This subjective element is referred to as *opinio juris*. If a practice is regarded as discretionary, or simply convenient or self-serving rather than obligatory, it is an example of usage that does not possess the critical element of *opinio juris* and therefore is not considered customary law. In modern times, evidence of the *opinio juris* of States has been gathered from their declarations or admissions in international forums like the ILC and the General Assembly of the UN, in addition to the other more traditional sources used to gather evidence of practice.

The unwritten, uncodified form of custom remains among its chief weaknesses. One way to remedy this shortcoming is to codify or restate customary law, such as the restatements of customary law codified by the ILC, writings of scholars and jurists, courts, legal tribunals, conference declarations, and treaties. A restatement or codification, by the ILC for example, serves the important purpose of reducing the law's uncertainty, but leaves open the extent to which it is accepted as accurate. Questions may arise as to whether the codification of a particular rule is a faithful and true reflection of existing customary law, as distinct from the development of it. Such doubts weaken the authority of any restatement of customary law.

Customary law is sometimes codified during a law-making conference, where it may take the form of a draft treaty, which may be adopted in a law making assembly and become binding as a treaty. For example, as we will see in Chapter 2, it is possible to assert that the 15-year process of negotiating UNCLOS led to the crystallization of customary IEL, and that Part XII, relating to the protection of the marine environment, is a codification of existing customary rules of law [*see* Jonathan I. Charney, *Entry into Force of the 1982 Convention on the Law of the Sea,* 35 VA. J. INT'L. L. 381 (1995); Louis Sohn & Kristen Gustafson, THE LAW OF THE SEA IN A NUTSHELL (1984)]. In such a situation, the text of the treaty expresses both conventional and customary law, giving it a dual jural status. It is activated as a treaty only when signed and ratified, but it possesses the authority of customary law so long as the community of nations accepts it as law.

Important duties under customary IEL have been codified or restated in treaties and conference declarations as "principles" rather than "rules." In ordinary legal analysis, rules typically embody standards that are definitively applied to a specifically described state of affairs, and the application of such a rule frequently determines a particular controversy. Principles, on the other hand, are more abstract general norms from which specific rules or standards are derived; they embody reasons that argue for moving in a particular direction, rather than arriving at a specified result. Consequently, principles—unlike rules—do not themselves postulate obligations of result. Instead, principles are the foundations upon which rules incorporating obligations of result are built. One principle may also be offset by another, and thus a principle may be seen as only one among a number of considerations to be taken into account in reaching a decision [Ronald Dworkin, TAKING RIGHTS SERIOUSLY (1978) at 24–26].

While many principles and rules have been espoused, only a few have been accepted into the corpus of customary IEL. The biggest impediment to the formation of customary law lies in the element of generality, which requires that the practice be widespread among at least a majority of States. This is difficult to establish in a world divided along cultural, economic, social, and religious lines. There are a number of principles that aspire to the status of customary law, but have not as yet attained that designation. They include the polluter pays principle, the preventive and precautionary principles, and various principles of good neighborliness and cooperation. These are found in treaties, conference declarations, UN General Assembly resolutions, and the documents of various other international organizations and fora. These instruments of "soft," embryonic customary law play an important role in the development of IEL. They may not amount to customary law *per se*, but they do constitute a presence and a backdrop that facilitates the creation and interpretation of IEL in general (*see* Ch. 18).

In addressing the limited corpus of "hard" customary IEL, we first turn to the prohibition against transboundary harm. The obligation prohibiting transboundary harm is perhaps the most established of customary IEL obligations, and creates an obligation of effect—or a rule—premised on the broader principle of *sic utere tuo ut alienum non laedus* (use your own property in such a manner as not to injure that of another). It has been supported by the practice and *opinio juris* of States.

Nonetheless, this obligation has generally been described as a principle, not a rule. It is codified in Principle 21 of the Stockholm Conference Declaration and is now entrenched in numerous provisions of treaties and declarations. It has been included as a "principle" in the Biodiversity Convention, according to which: "States have . . . the sovereign right to exploit their own resources pursuant to their own environmental policies, and the responsibility to ensure that activities within their jurisdiction or control do not cause damage to the environment of other States or areas beyond the limits of national jurisdiction" [Biodiversity Convention at art. 3]. A variation was also articulated as a principle at the

Earth Summit in the Rio Declaration on Environment and Development (Rio Declaration) [*Rio Declaration on Environment and Development*, Jun. 13, 1992, 31 I.L.M. 874, principle 2 (hereinafter Rio Declaration)].

UNCLOS expresses the general duty, under customary international law, to preserve and protect the marine environment and its natural resources— including the obligation to prevent, reduce, and control pollution of the marine environment [UNCLOS at arts.192–96]. This set of obligations meshes with others dealing with State responsibility (SR). In the result, "[s]tates are responsible for the fulfillment of their international obligations concerning the protection and preservation of the marine environment" [*Id.* at art. 235]. It could also be argued that there is a customary law principle of notification and consultation before embarking on potentially damaging environmental activities (*see* Ch. 15). Finally, the principle of SD (*see* Ch. 2 & Ch. 18) lies at the foundations of modern IEL.

C. GENERAL PRINCIPLES OF LAW

It is to be noted that Article 38(1)(c) of the Statute of the ICJ refers to general principles of law recognized by civilized nations, not international law, and it is clear that these general principles cannot be equated with principles of customary law. But given the prominence afforded to these general principles, we might expect Article 38(1)(c), dealing with sources of international law, to be interpreted in accordance with its ordinary or plain meaning, in context, and in light of its object and purpose [*see* Vienna Convention at art. 31]. When so interpreted, "the general principles of law recognized by civilized nations" enjoy a parity of status with treaties and custom. Such a view is reinforced by its context in which a contrasting source of law, "judicial decisions," is relegated to the status of a "subsidiary" source [Statute of the ICJ at art. 38(1)(d)]. A persuasive case can therefore be made that the courts, not States, now possess the power and discretion to enunciate relevant general principles of law by induction [Antonio Cassese, INTERNATIONAL LAW IN A DIVIDED WORLD (1986) at 170–172].

The inductive task of ascertaining general principles from legal systems around the world falls to the comparative lawyer, and involves the gargantuan task of studying all major legal systems to discover and distill general principles of law (note that the search is all-inclusive and not limited to "civilized nations"—an embarrassingly anachronistic phrase of the 1940s). The systematic study of all legal systems has been fitfully attempted, and is by no means complete, though it is possible to garner general principles from some areas of national law such as contract, criminal, and environmental law. International courts, however, have not yet acknowledged that general principles of national law constitute a significant source of law that should be incorporated into international law. On the contrary, general principles have never been considered a major source of law, and have only been used in an interstitial manner to fill in very small gaps in procedural—not substantive—law.

The ICJ and other judicial bodies appear to have reasoned that general principles of domestic or "municipal" jurisprudence should be followed only so far as they are specifically applicable to relations between States [James Crawford, BROWNLIE'S PRINCIPLES OF PUBLIC INTERNATIONAL LAW, EIGHTH EDITION (2012) at 34–37]. National or domestic laws, which on the whole are applicable to parties within a State, as distinct from inter-state relations, have fallen short of this standard and have largely been ignored.

General principles have the potential for assuming a new role under IEL. In Chapter 18, The Future of IEL, we envision IEL's merger with national environmental laws to become part of the common law of humankind. Environmental protection, like justice, may be found within Natural law, Islamic, Buddhist, and Confucian jurisprudential lineages. [Lakshman Guruswamy, GLOBAL ENERGY JUSTICE: LAW AND POLICY (2016)]. A successful merger of IEL and national environmental laws that creates a common law of humankind demands that general principles of national environmental law be recognized and woven into the fabric of international law.

D. JUDICIAL DECISIONS

As we have noted, the Statute of the ICJ restricts the role of judicial decisions to a "[s]ubsidiary means for the determination of rules of law" [Statute of ICJ at art. 38(1)(d)]. One reason is that judicial decisions, including those of the ICJ, have no binding force "[e]xcept between the parties and in respect of that particular case" [*Id*. at art. 59]. In national common law systems, the best known of which developed in England, the common law is the customary law that is developed, modified, and sometimes fundamentally redirected by the judges, the legal profession, and the courts. The common law system grew through judicial decisions recorded by lawyers. Judicial decisions form the foundations of law and theoretically constitute the background against which statutes are introduced. Even civil law systems that repudiate the common law method of judge-made law possess hierarchical legal systems in which judicial decisions play a part and possess value because they contain principles of law that may be binding on subsequent courts.

It is evident that the international legal process lacks a hierarchical system of courts and/or a machinery of justice and cannot, therefore, adopt a strict doctrine of binding precedent. International judicial decisions are binding only on the parties. But it is also clear that judicial decisions play an important role in any system of customary law by restating, codifying, and clarifying the often uncertain and usually unwritten customary law. In a judicial decision, we find an analysis of the evidence supporting the law, an articulation or declaration of what the law is, and a demonstration of how law should be applied to the facts. As such, a court or tribunal performs the difficult and valuable duty of collecting, examining, and assessing the evidence and arguments, deducing rules from amorphous general concepts, reducing them into written form, and arriving at conclusions derived from the application of law to facts. The art of judging is a strenuous, costly, and time-consuming job, requiring training, discipline, diligence, and expertise.

Where a court exercises its responsibilities and decides a case, it is a perfectly natural for subsequent courts to learn from what has been achieved, and to avoid duplication. Moreover it is foolish, for example, to embark upon repeated investigations to rediscover the wheel whenever we need to use one. The judicial use of precedents by international tribunals, therefore, reflects a practical habit of mind that avoids duplication and looks to past history for guidance. Not surprisingly, subsequent international courts and tribunals have given earlier decisions a persuasive authority that shades into a form of precedent, albeit not of the strictly binding kind.

Judicial decisions have become part of the substantive corpus of IEL. Influential cases include: the Trail Smelter Arbitration (*see* Ch. 14) [*Trail Smelter Arbitration,* (U.S. v. Can.) 3 R.I.A.A. 1938 (1949)]; the Corfu Channel Case [*Corfu Channel* (U.K. v. Alb.) 1949 I.C.J. 4]; the River Oder Case [*Case Relating to the Territorial Jurisdiction of the International Commission of the River Oder* (Czech., Den., Fr., Ger., Swed., U.K., Pol.) 1929 P.C.I.J. (ser. A) No. 23 at 5]; the Lake Lanoux Arbitration (*see* Ch. 15) [*Lake Lanoux Arbitration* (Sp. v. Fr.) 12 R.I.A.A. 281 (1957)]; and Nuclear Test Case (I) (*see* Ch. 17) [*Nuclear Test Case (I)* (N.Z. v. Fr.) 1974 I.C.J. 253]. In 1993, the ICJ created a new chamber for environmental law, and a cluster of new IEL cases began to reach the ICJ. Examples include: the Gabcikovo-Nagymaros Project Case (*see* Ch. 3) [*Case Concerning the Gabcikovo-Nagymaros Project* (Hung. v. Slov.) ICGJ 66 (1997)]; Pulp Mills on the River Uruguay [*Pulp Mills on the River Uruguay,* (Ar. v. Uy.) ICGJ 425 (2010)]; and Construction of a Road in Costa Rica along the San Juan River [*Construction of a Road in Costa Rica along the San Juan River* (Ni. v. CR) ICJGJ 488 (2015)].

Four decisions of the court have forced the ICJ to take a more active role in IEL. Those decisions are: (1) Nuclear Test Case (II) [*Request for an Examination of Situation in Accordance with Paragraph 63 of the Court's Judgment of 20 December 1974 in Nuclear Tests* (N.Z. v. Fr.) 1995 I.C.J. 288 (Sept. 22)]; (2) the WHO Advisory Opinion; (3) the UN Advisory Opinion [*Legality of the Use of Nuclear Weapons,* (Request for an Advisory Opinion by the UN General Assembly of Feb. 1) 1995 I.C.J 3]; and (4) the Legality of the Use by a State of Nuclear Weapons in Armed Conflict [*Legality of the Use by a State of Nuclear Weapons in Armed Conflict,* 1996 I.C.J. 93 (July 8)]. Ambiguities in the decisions in Nuclear Test Case (II) and the WHO Advisory Opinion raise doubts as to whether this is a challenge the ICJ is willing to accept in the future (*see* Ch. 17).

E.   OTHER SOURCES OF LAW

Other subsidiary sources of international law include the writings of "the most highly qualified publicists" or scholars, again "as subsidiary means for the determination of rules of law" [Statute of the

ICJ at art. 38(1)(d)]. The most influential example of this source would be the work of the ILC, empowered by Article 13 of the UN Charter to "initiate studies and make recommendations for the purpose of encouraging the progressive development of international law and its codification" [*Charter of the United Nations*, 1 UNTS XVI (1945) at art. 13].

Further sources include resolutions, declarations, action plans, and agendas of the UN and other inter-governmental organizations, such as the Stockholm Conference and Earth Summit. We have already adverted to the way in which international organizations can interpret the law. In addition, it is possible for governments to create customary law by how they vote within international organizations. Where, for example, a nation votes in favor of a resolution affirming that it is illegal to build a nuclear reactor without consulting those who might be affected by an accident, that nation's supporting vote may demonstrate both practice and *opinio juris*. It would show *opinio juris* if the vote for the resolution was premised upon the assumption that there was no option but to vote for it because it embodies established law, or because the State now accepts that it is the law.

The possibility exists for such resolutions to assume a quasi-legal or "soft law" character in which the evidence surrounding a resolution does not give birth to law as of its passing, but takes it into a gray zone between gestation and labor. Although the terms "hard law" and "soft law" do carry fairly specific meanings, the underlying realm of international agreements defies such a clear dichotomy, rendering the terms somewhat deceptive. To begin with, the terms themselves refer to the type of *instrument*. Hard law is explained as treaties and custom, whereas soft law instruments include declarations of principle, codes of practice, recommendations, guidelines, resolutions, and standards [Patricia W. Birnie & Alan E. Boyle, INTERNATIONAL LAW AND THE ENVIRONMENT (2002)].

The criterion that is most commonly used to distinguish hard and soft law is that only hard law instruments are legally binding. International law scholars, particularly in the area of customary international law, have long recognized the importance of States' *recognition* that a particular instrument or rule is legally binding (*opinio juris*) [*see* Lakshman Guruswamy, *International Environmental Law: Boundaries, Landmarks, and Realities*, 10 FALL NAT. RESOURCES & ENV'T. 43 (1995) at 77]. However, when comparing hard and soft law sources, it is important to remember that *opinio juris* is only one factor out of many that compel States to meet the obligations each type of instrument creates. States may feel just as bound by provisions of soft law instruments for a variety of other reasons. Soft law instruments are negotiated in a political climate, implicating an intrinsic pressure to live up to their terms [Geoffrey Palmer, *New Ways to Make International Environmental Law*, 86 A.J.I.L. 259 (1992) at 270]. For example, when New Zealand and other Pacific countries sought a UN resolution banning driftnet fishing in the South Pacific, the earlier Langkawi Declaration on the

Environment of 1989, a soft law instrument, gave them leverage to align support from the parties to that agreement, even though they never meant to be legally bound [*Langkawi Declaration on the Environment of 1989,* U.N.Doc. A/44/673]. Also, States might choose to adhere to soft law norms out of concern for reciprocity—to ensure that the other parties to the agreement do likewise [Richard B. Bilder, MANAGING THE RISK OF INTERNATIONAL AGREEMENT (1981)]. Nations also seek to maintain an image of trustworthiness amongst other nations, both generally and for the purpose of preserving other nations' willingness to enter into further agreements [*Id.*]. Additionally, there often exists the threat of retaliation and other sanctions from other States in the event of noncompliance [*Id.*]. These and other pressures also operate to motivate States' compliance with hard law obligations.

The distinction between hard and soft law instruments is further clouded by the nature of compliance mechanisms in international law. There is no means of enforcing international legal obligations, even legally binding treaties, suggesting not that compliance is voluntary, but that political pressure, reciprocity, and other influences weigh more heavily on States than a sense of legal obligation, even for hard law. Furthermore, within supposedly "hard" treaties, the language used to create some of the obligations reveals that they are purely aspirational and not meant to be legally binding at all. So, while the terms "hard" and "soft" law are useful for distinguishing between two different sets of documents, this classification is not particularly instructive as to what extent a particular document affects the behavior of the party States. A treaty, even one whose provisions are worded in an effort to create binding obligations on the parties, may be largely ignored following its entry into force. Likewise, a soft law instrument intended largely to be a political instrument may receive vigorous adherence by its member parties.

A second, less commonly used criterion for distinguishing between hard and soft law instruments is the degree of specificity of their provisions. In general, the norms embodied in soft law instruments lack the precision and specificity of those found in treaties. Because of their elasticity, soft law norms may succeed in securing at least a preliminary consensus amongst nations with competing interests and views. By contrast, it is much more difficult to obtain consensus for legally binding treaty obligations in a politically, culturally, and economically diverse world of States. Any form of agreement is valuable in and of itself, and the flexibility of soft law instruments permits nations, often with contradictory interests, to reach agreements which they might have balked at in more formal and demanding treaty instruments [Palmer, *supra* at 269].

The preliminary consensus reflected in soft law agreements can serve as a catalyst to producing more binding agreements. The Helsinki Declaration on the Protection of the Ozone Layer sought successfully to reach a consensus that would ensure that meetings in London the following year would yield hard amendments to the Montreal Protocol [*Helsinki Declaration on the Protection of the Ozone Layer,* May 2, 28 I.L.M. 1335 (1989)]. The UN Environment Programme (UNEP) Cairo Guidelines and Principles for the Environmentally Sound Management of Hazardous Waste [*Cairo Guidelines and Principles for the Environmentally Sound Management of Hazardous Waste,* U.N. Doc U.N.E.P./GC.13/17 (1987)], both soft law instruments, saw many of their provisions incorporated into the Basel Convention; and the Berlin Mandate [United Nations Framework Convention on Climate Change (UNFCCC), *Report of the Conference of the Parties on its First Session,* FCCC/CP/1995/7/Add.1 (1995)] acted as a precursor to the Kyoto Protocol of the UNFCCC [*Kyoto Protocol to the UN Framework Convention on Climate Change,* 2303 UNTS 148, Dec. 11, 1997 (entered into force Feb. 16, 2005) (hereinafter Kyoto Protocol)]. Furthermore, Agenda 21 principles increasingly appear in new international agreements and judicial decisions [Craig H. Allen, *Protecting the Oceanic Gardens of Eden: International Law Issues in Deep-Sea Vent Resource Conservation and Management,* 13 GEO. INT'L ENVT'L L REV 563 (2001) at 600].

Consequently, it is no longer possible to confine the corpus of IEL to the formal and traditional sources of international law such as treaties, custom, general principles, and judicial decisions. As we have seen from the forgoing discussion, IEL has witnessed the growth of a significant and increasing body of declarations and resolutions of international conferences that will continue to play an even more important role in influencing its new contours.

Chapter 3 presents a case study of the implementation of the Millennium Development Goals (MDGs), which though not embodied in a treaty, is a good example of how soft law is implemented without the formal procedures used in the implementation of treaties.

F. VOLUNTARY AGREEMENTS

In addition to international treaties, recent years have increasingly given rise to numerous types of voluntary international agreements, such as partnership agreements involving countries and private sector entities, pledges found in political resolutions, codes of conduct, and declarations, agendas, programs, and various other non-binding instruments (*see* Ch. 3). Nomenclature can be misleading. For example the EU's Voluntary Partnership Agreement on illegal logging of timber [European Commission, *FLEGT Briefing Note Number 06: Voluntary Partnership Agreements* (2007)] is actually a legal treaty. The title voluntary is misleading because the agreement is formally signed, ratified, and becomes legally binding— committing parties to trade only in legal timber [EU FLEGT Facility, *EFI Policy Brief 3—What Is a Voluntary Partnership Agreement?* (2009)].

Voluntary instruments express commitments, of varying degrees and in different ways, relevant to the domain of IEL. For example, the Chemical Industry Association's Responsible Care program agrees to adhere to a set of six guiding principles, all of which aim to ensure that the companies present an acceptably high level of protection for the health and safety of employees, customers, the public, and the environment. The entire Association membership of roughly 200 companies has signed on to the program, and new firms must accept its principles if they wish to join the association [Peter Simmons & Brian Wynne, *Responsible Care: Trust, Credibility and Environmental Management*, in Kurt Fischer & Johan Schot, eds., ENVIRONMENTAL STRATEGIES FOR INDUSTRY, Washington, DC: Island Press (1993)].

Another form of voluntary regulation is an agreement negotiated between a government and a firm or industry. The ability of governments and industries to make binding commitments through contractual means appears to depend on the nature of governments and the corporate culture in particular countries. Negotiated agreements have been used extensively in the Netherlands, Germany, Japan, and Colombia and with somewhat lesser frequency in other European countries [Thomas P. Lyon, *The Pros And Cons Of Voluntary Approaches To Environmental Regulation,* Reflections on Responsible Regulation Conference (2013)].

It is important to appreciate the extent to which such voluntary agreements contribute to the context of IEL. Voluntary agreements could be used as evidence of practice, both with regard to the interpretation of treaties under Article 31(3)(b) of the Vienna Convention, as well as to establish customary law. They could also form the *fons et origio* (source or origin) of norms that could evolve from soft to hard law.

Moreover, the rise of voluntary agreements in an area of international relations that, hitherto, has almost exclusively been occupied by formal and binding international treaties, presents an important new doctrinal and functional dimension that implicate, *inter alia*: (1) the manner and extent to which voluntary agreements influence the operation and development of instruments of IEL; (2) the extent to which voluntary agreements alter the complexion of IEL by enhancing the profile, status, and normative role of non-state actors with respect to international environmental issues; (3) the conceptual and practical coherence of treating voluntary, non-binding instruments as a discrete corpus of norms to be treated differently than traditional IEL; (4) the possibility that a continued proliferation of voluntary instruments of international environmental cooperation will radically diminish or otherwise alter the future role and efficacy of binding international environmental instruments; and (5) the effectiveness of using voluntary agreements, as opposed to binding treaties, as instruments addressing international environmental challenges.

Voluntary agreements, as understood here, are not restricted to the realm of what is commonly referred to as "soft law." Just as the distinction between what is "hard" and "soft" law is not a binary one (*see* Ch. 3), so too the distinction between "soft law" and purely political arrangements is often beset by conceptual overlaps and definitional infirmities [*see* Kal Raustiala, *Form and Substance in International Agreements,* 99 AM. J. OF INT'L LAW 581 (2005);

Kenneth Abbott & Duncan Snidal, *Hard and Soft Law in International Governance*, 54 INTERNATIONAL ORGANIZATION (2000) at 421]. Such distinctions can often be useful as heuristic devices, and are also often indispensible for separating contractual documents from pledges.

In functional terms, however, a question that arises is the extent to which such voluntary agreements or pledges are effective instruments for finding answers to the environmental problems of the world. The extent to which voluntary agreements are found to be more effective or ineffective, and/or have a greater or lesser impact on environmental problems, will determine whether international society is embarking on parallel—i.e., legal and non-legal—paths toward environmental solutions. But evidence on the performance of voluntary as opposed to legal agreements is still not available.

CHAPTER TWO

INTERNATIONAL ENVIRONMENTAL LAW: THE HISTORICAL CONTINUUM

The present form and substance of International Environmental Law (IEL) did not serendipitously arrive in full bloom. Instead it developed over a period of years, and was substantially framed by the evolution of sustainable development (SD). This chapter will examine how IEL and SD were shaped by historical landmarks and socio-political events.

A. 1972 UNITED NATIONS CONFERENCE ON HUMAN ENVIRONMENT (STOCKHOLM CONFERENCE)

Over a period stretching nearly half a century, an important segment of laws and policies governing international society have crystalized into the concept of SD. The 1972 United Nations (UN) Conference on the Human Environment (Stockholm Conference) [United Nations Conference on the Human Environment, Stockholm, Swed. (June 5–16, 1972), *Report of the United Nations Conference on the Human Environment*, U.N. Doc. A/CONF.48/14/ Rev.1 (1973) (hereinafter Report of the Stockholm Conference)] primarily intended as a conference about the international environment, may well have been the chrysalis from which SD emerged as an international concept.

The themes articulated in Rachel Carson's book, *Silent Spring* (1962), Barry Commoner's book, *The*

Closing Circle (1971), and Kenneth Boulding's *Spaceship Earth* (1966) [*see generally* Kenneth Boulding, *The Economics of the Coming Spaceship Earth*, in ENVIRONMENTAL QUALITY IN A GROWING ECONOMY 3 (H. Jarret ed., 1966)] resonated from the U.S. into the thinking of other industrial nations. Many of these and other themes were melded and expressed with crusading cogency in an international context in *Limits to Growth* [Donella H. Meadows, et al., LIMITS TO GROWTH (1972)], a computer modeled study sponsored by the Club of Rome, a private group of industrialists and world leaders. *Limits to Growth* painted an apocalyptic picture of the growth of population, pollution, and the exhaustion of natural resources, leading to a breakdown of the carrying capacity of the earth. Along with a growing awareness of environmental phenomena, such as acid rain and the poisoning of Japanese fisherman in Minamata Bay, these publications led to a realization of the frailty of the planet Earth and created a ferment of apprehension among a cross section of common people, influential elites, and decision makers in the industrial world.

In the face of these concerns, the UN moved to convene a special international environmental conference to discuss the human environment in 1972. Sweden, which had begun to experience transboundary acid rain, volunteered to host the conference in Stockholm. The overall sense of crisis crying out for global action was brilliantly captured in the book by Rene Dubos and Barbara Ward, specially commissioned for the Stockholm Conference [*see generally*, Rene Dubos & Barbara

Ward, ONLY ONE EARTH: THE CARE AND MAINTENANCE OF A SMALL PLANET (1972)].

While concern about the environment motivated many rich, industrialized countries, the poor, developing countries did not share the view that environmental degradation was the biggest threat facing the planet. For developing countries, poverty and the alleviation of misery remained a more poignant and real problem. In the preparatory meetings leading to the Stockholm Conference, the developing countries—which called themselves the Group of 77 (their original number)—sharply and forcefully articulated the view that the worst pollution was caused by poverty.

Developing countries believed that greater development leading to material prosperity far outweighed any damage that might be caused by resource use and pollution. They were particularly scornful of the claim that industrialized countries were genuinely trying to steer them away from pitfalls into which the industrialized countries had already fallen. Developing countries also expressed resentment over the fact that industrialized countries—whose drive toward wealth had already consumed a great part of the earth's resources and led to devastating pollution—were now asking the developing countries to remain poor, and, more gallingly, to pay for the clean up, restoration, and conservation of the earth. Moreover, many developing countries feared that new environmental standards adopted by industrialized countries would effectively bar the entry of their goods into industrial markets.

This ideological impasse presented a formidable challenge to international environmental diplomacy. Consequently, nearly all the regional seminars and special meetings convened prior to the Stockholm Conference were focused on the interrelationship between development and the environment [Report of the Stockholm Conference at 38]. The question was resolved, as best it might be, by way of a compromise worked out in a meeting at Founex, near Geneva, Switzerland, in 1971. The compromise reached was that economic development was not necessarily incompatible with environmental protection and that environmental considerations should be an integral part of the development process. The essence of that understanding was summed up in the Preamble to the Stockholm Declaration of the UN Conference on the Human Environment (Stockholm Declaration) [*Stockholm Declaration of the United Nations Conference on the Human Environment*, Jun. 16, 1972, 11 I.L.M 1416 at pmbl. (hereinafter Stockholm Declaration)]. It stated "[i]n the developing countries most of the environmental problems are caused by under-development" and that industrialized countries must "direct their efforts to development, bearing in mind their priorities and the need to safeguard and improve the environment" [*Id*. at ¶ 4]. Similarly, the industrialized countries were exhorted to make efforts to reduce the developmental gap between themselves and the developing countries.

In sum, the developing countries successfully thwarted potential environmental laws and policies from damaging their efforts to develop and grow economically, whether by industrial progress or trade. The developing countries did not, however, obtain substantial bankrolling for environmentally conscious development nor did they pledge to protect the global environment. This early declaration also did not meaningfully advance the doctrine of "common but differentiated responsibilities" (CBDR) later accepted at the 1992 UN Conference on Environment and Development (UNCED), also known as Earth Summit, as a means of recognizing the different needs of developing and industrialized countries.

However, for a number of other reasons, the Stockholm Declaration may also be considered the cocoon of SD. First, the biosphere, or the planet, was identified as a subject and placed on the agenda of national and international policy and law in a way that had never been done before. Second, the Stockholm Conference was widely attended, with 114 of the then 131 UN members participating (the Soviet bloc abstained from attending, not because it rejected the purpose or mission of the conference, but because of the status accorded to East Germany). Third, the Stockholm Conference resulted in the creation of the United Nations Environment Programme (UNEP) the first international organization with an exclusively environmental mandate. Fourth, it produced the Stockholm Declaration, which sought to strike a balance between economic and social development and the improvement of the environment. The Stockholm Conference also created an action plan containing recommendations for future implementation [Report of the Stockholm Conference at 67].

The nature of the balance struck at Stockholm was weighted in favor of the environment. A number of specific principles of the Stockholm Declaration bear mention. Principles 1, 2, and 5, dealing with responsibilities to future generations, were undergirded by an obligation to conserve. Principle 1, albeit counterbalanced by Principle 11, recognized a nascent right to ". . . an environment of a quality that permits a life of dignity and well-being" [Stockholm Declaration at Principle 1]. Principle 21 referred to the right of a state to exploit its resources pursuant to its environmental (not developmental) policies, and affirmed its obligation not to cause transboundary injury. By holding states responsible for their transnational damage, Principle 21 may have crystallized or generated customary law. Lastly, Principle 22 posited that states should cooperate to develop international law regarding liability and compensation for transboundary harm.

These Principles have been re-institutionalized in many post-Stockholm agreements. For example, Principle 21 has been incorporated in a wide range of treaties including the United Nations Framework Convention on Climate Change (UNFCCC) [UNFCCC at prmbl.], the Convention on Biological Diversity (Biodiversity Convention) [Biodiversity Convention at art. 3], the Vienna Convention for the Protection of the Ozone Layer (Vienna Ozone

Convention) [Vienna Ozone Convention at art. 2], the Convention on Long-Range Transboundary Air Pollution (LRTAP) [Convention on Long-Range Transboundary Air Pollution, Nov. 13, 1979, 18 I.L.M. 1442 at arts. 1 & 2 (hereinafter LRTAP)], and the United Nations Convention on the Law of the Sea (UNCLOS) [UNCLOS at arts 1(4), Part X11]. Furthermore, the post-Stockholm world has spawned a prolific number of environmental treaties. Over 2,000 post-Stockholm treaties mirror almost every concern that has been the subject of national laws or regulations including acid rain, hazardous waste, ozone depletion, sea pollution from land and vessels, toxics, resource conservation, and climate change.

B.   1982 UNITED NATIONS CONVENTION ON THE LAW OF THE SEA (UNCLOS)

Negotiations about the law of the sea had commenced even before the Stockholm Conference. Those negotiations lasted until 1982, when UNCLOS was opened for signature. UNCLOS finally came into force on November 16, 1994. It is the strongest comprehensive environmental treaty now in existence or likely to emerge for quite some time [Letter of Submittal of the Secretary of State to the President of the United States, Sept. 23, 1994. reprinted in *Special Supplement: Message from the President of the United States and Commentary Accompanying the United Nations Convention on the Law of the* Sea,7 GEO. INT'L ENVT'L L. REV. 77 (1994)]. UNCLOS may be seen as a constitution for the oceans. The character and reach of its 59 provisions obligating environmental protection and conservation, out of 320 provisions in all, arguably possess such a fundamental and overarching character. Moreover, UNCLOS functions not only as a treaty, but also as a codification and articulation of customary international rules applicable to oceans. It is therefore binding on its parties as a treaty, while nonparties are bound by it because it is a codification of customary law [Jonathan I. Charney, *Entry Into Force of the 1982 Convention on the Law of the Sea,* 35 VA. J. INT'L. L. 381 (1995); Louis Sohn & Kristen Gustafson, *The Law of the Sea in a Nutshell* (1984)].

It is worth remembering, in this context, that the oceans occupy over 70% of the surface area of the earth and are, in many ways, a proxy for the global environment. Most pollution released into the environment from land-based sources is eventually deposited into the oceans through direct and indirect pathways. Moreover, notable areas of oceanic governance, such as conservation of wetlands, coastal areas, and biodiversity, are of critical significance to international environmental protection in general.

UNCLOS contains at least 59 environmental provisions, ranging from the global to the specific, spread out over several parts of the text including: The Territorial Sea and Contiguous Zone (Part II), Exclusive Economic Zone (Part V), High Seas (Part VII), Enclosed or Semi-Enclosed Areas (Part IX), The Area (Part XI), Protection and Preservation of the Marine Environment (Part XII), and Marine Scientific Research (Part XIII). The environmental provisions deal with: the conservation and management of living resources; pollution prevention, reduction, and control; vessel pollution; and environmental management. As an umbrella convention, UNCLOS brings other international rules, regulations, and implementing bodies within its canopy. At the substantive level of obligation and implementation, many of its provisions are of a constitutional or general character and must be augmented and supplemented by specific regulations, rules, and implementing procedures formulated by other international agreements and states. While UNCLOS does not use the term "sustainable development," the two elements of SD (as then conceived) dealing with economic development and environmental protection or conservation, are embodied in it. Within their 200-mile exclusive economic zones (EEZ), UNCLOS confers both rights and duties on States to explore, economically exploit, conserve and manage the natural resources [UNCLOS at art. 56(a)]. In the high seas beyond national jurisdiction states are required to maintain or restore harvested species at levels that can produce maximum yield [*Id.* at art. 119(1)(a)]. Moreover Part XII on the Protection and Preservation of the Marine Environment deals with the various ways in which States are obliged to protect and preserve the marine environment [*Id.* at arts 192–237]. In sum, UNCLOS attempted to balance economic development and environmental protection, and in doing so established the importance of SD as embracing not only the atmosphere and land but also the oceans.

C.   1983 WORLD COMMISSION ON ENVIRONMENT AND DEVELOPMENT (BRUNDTLAND COMMISSION)

Despite the uneasy truce at Founex reflected in the Stockholm Declaration, the persistent clash of two worldviews, one asserting environmental protection and the other economic development, continued to impede the progress of SD. In order to resolve this problem, the World Commission on Environment and Development (also called the Brundtland Commission) was created by the General Assembly of the UN in 1983 and charged with proposing long-term environmental strategies for SD, though the UN did not define that elusive term. After four years of deliberation and worldwide consultation, *Our Common Future* (Brundtland Report) [World Commission on Environment and Development, *Our Common Future* (1987), *available at* http://www.un-documents.net/our-common-future.pdf (last visited Apr. 2017) (hereinafter Brundtland Report)] articulated the paradigm on which Earth Summit, and indeed SD, has since been based. In essence, it rejected the despairing thesis that environmental problems were past repair, spiraling out of control, and could only be averted by arresting development and economic growth resulting in a policy of no growth. Instead, it argued that economic growth was both desirable and possible within a context of SD.

Although SD was not clearly defined and continues to elude canonical definition, some of its seminal attributes are identifiable. SD calls for developmental policies and for economic growth that can relieve the great poverty of the developing countries, while simultaneously protecting the environment from further damage. Such development and growth should be based on policies that sustain and expand the environmental resource base in a manner that meets the needs of the present generation without compromising the ability of future generations to meet their own needs.

In order to draw up a global plan for SD, the Brundtland Commission called for an international conference to act as the successor to the Stockholm Conference and carry forward its legacy. The UN General Assembly complied by convening the 1992 Earth Summit and directing it to further develop SD, taking account, *inter alia*, of the Stockholm Declaration. An ambitious agenda was drawn up for Earth Summit that included the following three endeavors: (1) an Earth Charter that would be the successor to the Stockholm Declaration; (2) an action plan for the planet called Agenda 21; and (3) the ceremonial signing of two conventions on biodiversity and climate change.

D.   1992 UNITED NATIONS CONFERENCE ON ENVIRONMENT AND DEVELOPMENT (EARTH SUMMIT)

Earth Summit, held in Rio de Janeiro, Brazil in June 1992, was attended by over 180 countries and 100 heads of State, and heralded as the greatest summit level conference in history. It departed somewhat from its original agenda, but resulted in five international instruments, predicated on SD: (1)

the Rio Declaration on Environment and Development (Rio Declaration); (2) Agenda 21 [United Nations Conference on Environment and Development, Rio de Janeiro, Braz., Jun. 3–14, 1992, *Agenda 21*, Jun. 13, 1992, *available at* https://sustainabledevelopment.un.org/content/docu ments/Agenda21.pdf (last visited Apr. 2017) (hereinafter Agenda 21)]; (3) the Global Consensus on Sustainable Development of Forests [United Nations Conference on Environment and Development, Rio de Janeiro, Braz., Jun. 3–14, 1992, *Non-Legally Binding Authoritative Statement of Principles for a Global Consensus on the Management, Conservation and Sustainable Development of All Types of Forests*, U.N. Doc. A/CONF.151/26 (Vol. III), Annex III (Aug. 14, 1992)]; (4) the UNFCCC; and (5) the Biodiversity Convention.

We very briefly advance some conclusions about the environmental dimensions of the 1992 Earth Summit, dealing first with the legally binding treaties and then moving on to the non-legally binding instruments. To begin, it is worth emphasizing a premise reiterated and reaffirmed in all the documents (legal and otherwise) emerging from Earth Summit. It is that the right of developing countries to economic advancement cannot be divorced from the pursuit of environmentalism and climate change.

We start with the UNFCCC, which is the most important treaty dealing with climate change because it is a treaty to which all nations of the world including the U.S., are parties. The objective of the UNFCCC is to ". . . prevent dangerous anthropogenic interference with the climate system" [UNFCCC at art. 2]. The parties make commitments to mitigate climate change by addressing anthropogenic emissions and adapting to the impacts of climate change [*Id*. at arts 4(1)(b) & (e)]. It is important to understand the rationale behind this objective. Parties agreed to mitigate (cut down or reduce) human emissions of carbon dioxide (CO_2) and other greenhouse gases (GHGs) in order to address the environmental problems arising from the greenhouse effect. The greenhouse effect occurs because GHGs act like a blanket, absorbing some of the heat that reaches the Earth and preventing it from escaping into outer space. This results in global climate change that can lead to the melting of ice packs in Greenland, a global rise of sea levels, and alteration in weather patterns.

The UNFCCC is a treaty addressing climate change that lays the foundation for climate action within the framework of SD. Commencing with its Preamble, the UNFCCC makes abundantly clear that responses to climate change should be coordinated with social and economic development ". . . taking into full account the legitimate priority needs of developing countries for the achievement of sustained economic growth and the eradication of poverty" [*Id*. at pmbl.]. Moreover, the UNFCCC stipulates that the parties have a right to and should promote SD policies, taking into account that economic development is an essential component of action against climate change [*Id*. at art. 3(4)].

Furthermore, the UNFCCC coalesced with the other widely accepted treaty adopted at Earth Summit, the Biodiversity Convention, by forcefully and unequivocally expressing the developmental priority of SD. Article 4(7) of the UNFCCC and Article 20(4) of the Biodiversity Convention reaffirm in unison that parties "will take fully into account that economic and social development and poverty eradication are the first and overriding priorities of the developing country Parties" [UNFCCC at art. 4(7); Biodiversity Convention at art. 20(4)].

The importance of economic development and the eradication of poverty are also affirmed in the nonbinding agreements or declarations embodying "soft law" norms. Treaties and custom generally create binding obligations on nations, while soft law sources are largely aspirational. Among the non-binding instruments, the Rio Declaration on Environment and Development (Rio Declaration) continues to emphasize the importance of economic development while pursuing environmental protection. For example, the nascent right to a wholesome environment, embodied in the Stockholm Declaration, was replaced by a right to development [Rio Declaration at Principle 2]. The Rio Declaration refers to "developmental and environmental needs of present and future generations" [*Id.* at Principle 3].

This re-formulation impliedly negates or weakens the obligation to conserve expressed in the Stockholm Declaration. In similar vein, the obligation to *conserve*, implied by the duty to protect the environment for the benefit of future generations, found in the Stockholm Declaration, is displaced in the Rio Declaration by a right to *consume* or develop. Furthermore, the obligation not to cause transboundary damage, contained in Principle 21 of the Stockholm Declaration, was weakened in the Rio Declaration by the addition of crucial language authorizing States "to exploit their own resources pursuant to their own environmental and *developmental* policies." [*Id.* (emphasis added)]. Thus, the Rio Declaration incorporated several allowances for nations' developmental needs, perhaps at the expense of more environmentally protective provisions found in the Stockholm Declaration.

Agenda 21 was a second institutional result of Earth Summit. Similar to the Rio Declaration, Agenda 21 was also shaped by the tension between development and environmental protection, and calls for the integration of environment and development concerns [Agenda 21 at Chapter 1.1]. While committing to the conservation and protection of resources, Agenda 21 mirrors the Rio Declaration in acknowledging and affirming the priority of political and social challenges in developing nations [*Id.* at Chapter 1.5]. Specifically, Chapter 3.2 gives substantial deference to the use of natural resources to combat poverty. Chapter 39, which deals with the review and development of international environmental policy, stresses the importance of participation by developing countries in drafting new legal instruments, but reaffirms the need to weigh their developmental needs against the obligations that might be imposed by those instruments. This is not to gloss over the significant environmental dimension of Agenda 21. Chapters 9 through 22 are devoted to and deal, *inter alia*, with the protection of the atmosphere, combating of deforestation, an integrated approach to land management, managing fragile ecosystems, conserving biodiversity, managing toxic chemicals, and the management of hazardous, solid, and radioactive wastes.

In assessing the individual strands that together comprise the braided rope of SD today, it is important to understand the conceptual evolution of these strands. In 1992, SD remained a syncopated concept consisting of economic development and environmental protection. By contrast, the present concept of SD possesses three elements: economic development, social development, and environmental protection. When the various documents emerging from Earth Summit were being negotiated, the social dimension of SD was in fact recognized and expressly articulated, as we have noted, by Article 4(7) of the UNFCCC, and Article 20(4) of the Biodiversity Convention. Social development was not, however, institutionalized as one of the three formal components of SD until the World Summit on Sustainable Development in 2002.

E.   2000 MILLENNIUM SUMMIT AND THE MILLENNIUM DEVELOPMENT GOALS (MDGs)

The Millennium Summit held in 2000 was the largest gathering of world leaders in history as of that date. The Millennium Summit adopted the UN

Millennium Declaration, committing nations to a new global partnership to reduce extreme poverty and setting out a series of time-bound targets, with a deadline of 2015, which become known as the Millennium Development Goals (MDGs).

The MDGs distilled the results of a wide array of global processes involving diverse actors over several years. Apart from conferences on SD and the environment, many international goals and targets were established through a series of other major subject-specific conferences in the 1990s. The agendas spanned education (Jomtien, 1990), children (New York, 1990), population (Cairo, 1994), social development (Copenhagen, 1995), and the status of women (Beijing, 1995). In 1995 and 1996, the Organization for Economic Cooperation and Development (OECD) development assistance committee set out to summarize the disparate agreements into a shorthand set of international development goals that could help motivate donors [John W. McArthur, *The Origins of the Millennium Development Goals,* XXXIV (2) SAIS REVIEW (Summer–Fall 2014), *available at* http://john mcarthur.com/wp-content/uploads/2015/01/SAIS review2014mcarthur.pdf (last visited Apr. 2017)]. The MDGs were time-bound and quantified targets for addressing extreme poverty in its many dimensions, including income poverty, hunger, disease, and lack of adequate shelter, while promoting gender equality, education, environmental sustainability, and social development [Millennium Project, *What They Are,* *available at* http://www.unmillenniumproject.org/

goals/index.htm (last visited Apr. 2017)]. They are expressed as individual benefits, granting each person on the planet the right to health, education, shelter, and security.

All 189 United Nations member states at the time (there are 195 currently), and at least 23 international organizations, committed to help achieve the following MDGs by 2015:

1.   To eradicate extreme poverty and hunger

2.   To achieve universal primary education

3.   To promote gender equality

4.   To reduce child mortality

5.   To improve maternal health

6.   To combat HIV/AIDS, malaria, and other diseases

7.   To ensure environmental sustainability

8.   To develop a global partnership for sustainable development by 2015 [*Id.*]

1.   EVALUATING THE MDGs

An important inter-agency UN evaluation of the MDGs in 2015 demonstrates what the MDGs have achieved or failed to deliver [United Nations, *The Millennium Development Goals Report* 2015 4–7 (2015), *available at* www.un.org/es/millenniumgoals/pdf/2015/mdg_2015_rev(july1).pdf (last visited Apr. 2017)]. What follows is a progress report of each MDG, as summarized in the report.

Goal 1:   Eradicate Extreme Poverty and Hunger.

Extreme poverty has declined significantly over the last two decades. In 1990, nearly half of the population in the developing world lived on less than $1.25 a day; that proportion dropped to 14% in 2015.

Globally, the number of people living in extreme poverty has declined by more than half, falling from 1.9 billion in 1990 to 836 million in 2015. Most progress has occurred since 2000.

The proportion of undernourished people in the developing regions has fallen by almost half since 1990, from 23.3% in 1990–1992 to 12.9% in 2014–2016 [*Id.* at 4].

Goal 2:   Achieve Universal Primary Education

The primary school net enrollment rate in the developing regions has reached 91% in 2015, up from 83% in 2000.

The number of out-of-school children of primary school age worldwide has fallen by almost half, to an estimated 57 million in 2015, down from 100 million in 2000.

Sub-Saharan Africa has had the best record of improvement in primary education of any region since the MDGs were established. The region achieved a 20 percentage point increase in the net enrolment rate from 2000 to 2015, compared to a gain of 8 percentage points between 1990 to 2000.

The literacy rate among youth aged 15 to 24 has increased globally from 83% to 91% between 1990 and 2015. The gap between women and men has narrowed [*Id.*].

Goal 3: Promote Gender Equality and Empower Women

Many more girls are now in school compared to 15 years ago. The developing regions as a whole have achieved the target to eliminate gender disparity in primary, secondary, and tertiary education.

In Southern Asia, only 74 girls were enrolled in primary school for every 100 boys in 1990. Today, 103 girls are enrolled for every 100 boys.

Women now make up 41% of paid workers outside the agricultural sector, an increase from 35% in 1990.

Between 1991 and 2015, the proportion of women in vulnerable employment as a share of total female employment has declined 13 percentage points. In contrast, vulnerable employment among men fell by 9 percentage points.

Women have gained ground in parliamentary representation in nearly 90% of the 174 countries with data over the past 20 years. The average proportion of women in parliament has nearly doubled during the same period. Yet still only one in five members are women [*Id.* at 5].

Goal 4:   Reduce Child Mortality

The global under-five mortality rate has declined by more than half, dropping from 90 to 43 deaths per 1,000 live births between 1990 and 2015.

Despite population growth in the developing regions, the number of deaths of children under five has declined from 12.7 million in 1990 to almost 6 million in 2015 globally. Since the early 1990s, the rate of reduction of under-five mortality has more than tripled globally.

In sub-Saharan Africa, the annual rate of reduction of under-five mortality was over five times faster during 2005–2013 than it was during 1990–1995.

Measles vaccination helped prevent nearly 15.6 million deaths between 2000 and 2013. The number of globally reported measles cases declined by 67% for the same period.

About 84% of children worldwide received at least one dose of measles-containing vaccine in 2013, up from 73% in 2000 [*Id.*].

Goal 5:   Improve Maternal Health

Since 1990, the maternal mortality ratio has declined by 45% worldwide, and most of the reduction has occurred since 2000.

In Southern Asia, the maternal mortality ratio declined by 64% between 1990 and 2013, and in sub-Saharan Africa it fell by 49%.

More than 71% of births were assisted by skilled health personnel globally in 2014, an increase from 59% in 1990.

In Northern Africa, the proportion of pregnant women who received four or more antenatal visits increased from 50% to 89% between 1990 and 2014.

Contraceptive prevalence among women aged 15 to 49, married or in a union, increased from 55% in 1990 worldwide to 64% in 2015 [*Id.* at 6].

Goal 6: Combat HIV/AIDS, Malaria and Other Diseases

New HIV infections fell by approximately 40% between 2000 and 2013, from an estimated 3.5 million cases to 2.1 million.

By June 2014, 13.6 million people living with HIV were receiving antiretroviral therapy (ART) globally, an immense increase from just 800,000 in 2003. ART averted 7.6 million deaths from AIDS between 1995 and 2013.

Over 6.2 million malaria deaths have been averted between 2000 and 2015, primarily of children under five years of age in sub-Saharan Africa. The global malaria incidence rate has fallen by an estimated 37% and the mortality rate by 58%.

More than 900 million insecticide-treated mosquito nets were delivered to malaria-endemic countries in sub-Saharan Africa between 2004 and 2014.

Between 2000 and 2013, tuberculosis prevention, diagnosis, and treatment interventions saved an estimated 37 million lives. The tuberculosis mortality rate fell by 45% and the prevalence rate by 41% between 1990 and 2013 [*Id.*].

Goal 7:   Ensure Environmental Sustainability

Ozone-depleting substances have been virtually eliminated since 1990, and the ozone layer is expected to recover by the middle of this century.

Terrestrial and marine protected areas in many regions have increased substantially since 1990. In Latin America and the Caribbean, coverage of terrestrial protected areas rose from 8.8% to 23.4% between 1990 and 2014.

In 2015, 91% of the global population is using an improved drinking water source, compared to 76% in 1990.

Of the 2.6 billion people who have gained access to improved drinking water since 1990, 1.9 billion gained access to piped drinking water on premises. More than half the global population (58%) now enjoys this higher level of service.

Globally, 147 countries have met the drinking water target, 95 countries have met the sanitation target, and 77 countries have met both.

Worldwide, 2.1 billion people have gained access to improved sanitation. The proportion of people practicing open defecation has fallen almost by half since 1990.

The proportion of urban population living in slums in the developing regions fell from approximately 39.4% in 2000, to 29.7% in 2014 [*Id.* at 7].

Goal 8: Develop a Global Partnership for Development

Official development assistance from developed countries increased by 66% in real terms between 2000 and 2014, reaching $135.2 billion.

In 2014, Denmark, Luxembourg, Norway, Sweden, and the United Kingdom continued to exceed the United Nations official development assistance target of 0.7% of gross national income.

In 2014, 79% of imports from developing to developed countries were admitted duty free, up from 65% in 2000.

The proportion of external debt service to export revenue in developing countries fell from 12% in 2000 to 3% in 2013.

As of 2015, 95% of the world's population is covered by a mobile-cellular signal.

The number of mobile-cellular subscriptions has grown almost tenfold in the last 15 years, from 738 million in 2000, to over 7 billion in 2015.

Internet penetration has grown from just over 6% of the world's population in 2000, to 43% in 2015. As a result, 3.2 billion people are linked to a global network of content and applications [*Id.*].

The progress appears remarkable, even though some of the claims of this report appear to be inaccurate, self-validating, and even misleading. For example, the claim that the improvement of the ozone layer resulted from the MDG 7 is misleading. The MDGs are political, not legal, commitments and the improvement in the ozone layer primarily resulted from the implementation of the legally binding Vienna Ozone Convention, the Montreal Protocol on Substances that Deplete the Ozone Layer (Montreal Protocol), and their various Adjustments and Amendments (*see* Ch. 7). Similarly, improvements in terrestrial and marine protection may more fairly be attributed to the implementation of two legally binding treaties: UNCLOS (*see* Ch. 13) and the Biodiversity Convention (*see* Ch. 5), and not MDG 7.

MDG 4 called for the reduction of child mortality, and the report gives MDG 4 credit for improved child mortality. But, the implementation of the legally binding Convention on the Rights of the Child (CRC) [*Convention on the Rights of the Child*, Nov. 20, 1989, G.A. Res. 44/25, Annex, U.N. GAOR, 44th Sess., Supp. No. 49, U.N. Doc. A/44/49, at 167 (1989) (hereinafter CRC)], ratified by 192 countries in 2000, may well be the stronger reason for the drop in child mortality. CRC Articles 6 and 24 clearly established a child's right to survival, development, and health. Parties to the CRC are required to implement it. Article 24(1) and (2) obliges States parties to recognize the right of the child to the enjoyment of the highest attainable standard of health and to ensure that no child is deprived of his or her right of access to health care services. At least a significant component of the reduction of child mortality should be attributed to the CRC and not merely MDG 4.

With regard to MDG 6, the Gates Foundation, which is not a party to the MDGs, has played a pivotal role in the fight against malaria [Bill & Melinda Gates Foundation, *Malaria Strategy Overview, available at* http://www.gatesfoundation. org/What-We-Do/Global-Health/Malaria (last visited Apr. 2017)] and against HIV/ AIDs [Bill & Melinda Gates Foundation, *HIV Strategy Overview, available at* http://www.gatesfoundation.org/What-We-Do/ Global-Health/HIV (last visited Apr. 2017)]. In fact, a joint report by the UN and the Gates Foundation showed that global investment in malaria has jumped in recent years by 2,000% annually, from just $130 million in 2000 to $2.7 billion in 2013. The extent of the investment by the Gates Foundation, which has committed more than $500 million, fundamentally transformed the fight against the disease [UN News Centre, *Report by UN and Gates Foundation Presents Vision for Eradicating Malaria by 2040*, (Sept. 28, 2015), *available at* http://www.un. org/apps/news/story.asp?NewsID=52006 (last visited Apr. 2017); South China Morning Post, *Gates*

Foundation to Spend US $500m Stopping Malaria and Other Diseases, (Mar. 4, 2016), *available at* http://www.scmp.com/news/world/article/1631289/ga tes-foundation-spend-us500m-stopping-malaria-and-other-diseases (last visited Apr. 2017)]. It is, therefore, inaccurate to primarily credit MDG 6 for successes in the fight against malaria. Doubts about this claim are supported by the fact that official development assistance (ODA) over the period amounted in total to $134 billion for all 8 MDGs. The Gates Foundation alone has invested billions of dollars in arresting malaria and HIV/AIDS, and must lay claim for a significant part of the progress made. Attributing such success to the MDG 6 alone is misleading.

Notwithstanding these caveats about a few of the MDGs, the overall progress made by MDGs is very impressive. The fact that the MDGs obtained a large increase in ODA to meet the additional funds required is particularly significant. It is important in this context to point out that many poverty reduction goals, similar to the MDGs, have been embraced by civil society entities, such as the Gates Foundation. The extent to which civil society groups contribute toward energy justice bears examination.

2.   CIVIL SOCIETY CONTRIBUTIONS

The MDGs were adopted and implemented by governments and international inter-governmental organizations. The ODA is an international fund set up under the auspices of the OECD to provide the aid necessary to meet the MDGs. But there are numerous groups outside the government sector that have adopted and worked toward achieving antipoverty objectives similar to the MDGs. Nongovernmental organizations (NGOs), like the Gates Foundation, mentioned above, are one among many civil society groups. They are many other nonprofit associations operating independently of government, working toward worthy social or political objectives. They may provide humanitarian relief and development assistance, like the International Committee of the Red Cross [International Committee of the Red Cross (ICRC), *available at* https://www.icrc.org/ (last visited Apr. 2017)], OXFAM International [OXFAM International, *available at* https://www.oxfam.org (last visited Apr. 2017)], and CARE [CARE, *available at* http://www.care-international.org (last visited Apr. 2017)], or engage in environmental analysis and advocacy like Greenpeace [Greenpeace, *available at* http://www.greenpeace.org/ (last visited Apr. 2017)], the World Wildlife Fund (WWF) [World Wildlife Fund, *available at* http://wwf.org (last visited Apr. 2017)], and the International Union for Conservation of Nature (IUCN) [International Union for Conservation of Nature, *available at* http://www.iucn.org/ (last visited Apr. 2017)]. These NGOs may be financed by private donations, international organizations, governments, or charitable foundations. Some, like the Gates Foundation, are privately endowed while others, such as Greenpeace or the WWF, depend on grass roots member support.

Partnerships are another kind of civil society entity. Partnerships consist of voluntary multi-stakeholder or multi-institutional initiatives, organized around a common purpose, and administered as their own entity, distinct from their constituent partners. The Renewable Energy and Energy Efficiency Partnership (REEEP) [Renewable Energy & Energy Efficiency Partnership (REEEP), *available at* http://www.reeep.org/ (last visited Apr. 2017)] and the Renewable Energy Network for the 21st Century (REN21) [Renewable Energy Network for the 21st Century, *available at* http://www.ren21. net (last visited Apr. 2017)] are two examples. Partnerships have become a recognized fixture in the international development arena and differ in size, agenda, and organization. They are also increasingly recognized as an essential mechanism for promoting and implementing SD in all its dimensions, and as a central element of contemporary sustainability governance [UN-DESA/DSD, *Multi-Stakeholder Partnerships in the Post-2015 Development Era: Sharing knowledge and expertise to support the achievement of the Sustainable Development Goals,* (Jun. 16, 2015) *available at* https://sustainable development.un.org/content/documents/7366Partner ships_Knowledge_BackgroundPaper_final.pdf (last visited Apr. 2017)].

Private for-profit corporations spanning manufacturers, agribusinesses, mining, banks, hotels, and others have likewise increased their role in international development. In industrialized and developing countries alike, the private sector has often become a key partner in international development [Bradford Strickland, Creative Associates International, *Survey of Trends in Private*

Sector Partnerships for International Development and Modalities for Engagement (Mar. 2014), *available at* http://www.creativeassociatesinternat ional.com/wp-content/uploads/2014/08/Survey_Of_ Trends.pdf (last visited Apr. 2017)].

Faith groups are also part of civil society. It has been found that religious leaders and institutions are often the most trusted institutions in developing countries. Faith groups can inspire confidence and trust and are often seen as more embedded in, and committed to, local communities. They are often the first groups that people turn to in times of need and contribute to in times of plenty [Department for International Development, *Faith Partnership Principles: Working Effectively With Faith Groups To Fight Global Poverty* (2012), *available at* https:// www.gov.uk/government/publications/faith-partner ship-principles-working-effectively-with-faith- groups-to-fight-global-poverty (last visited Apr. 2017)]. For example, Caritas Internationalis is one among several faith groups operating across the world. Caritas follows the mission of the Catholic Church to serve the poor, promote charity and justice throughout the world, and act on behalf of the world's most vulnerable people [Caritas Internationalis, *available at* http://www.caritas.org (last visited Apr. 2017)].

F.   2002 WORLD SUMMIT ON SUSTAINABLE DEVELOPMENT (WSSD)

The first major UN conference on SD, so titled, was organized in 2002, ten years after Earth Summit.

The World Summit on Sustainable Development (WSSD) was held in Johannesburg, South Africa. As originally envisioned, WSSD was intended primarily to stimulate implementation of the environmental aspects of Agenda 21. The focus of WSSD, however, as reflected in the deliberations and in the two documents produced by it, was more clearly on the problems created by poverty, as distinct from environmental degradation. The conference gave birth to just two documents: a political Declaration, the Johannesburg Declaration on Sustainable Development (Johannesburg Declaration) [*Johannesburg Declaration on Sustainable Development*, U.N. Doc. A/CONF.199/20 (Sept. 4, 2002) (hereinafter Johannesburg Declaration)] and an Implementation Plan, the WSSD Implementation Plan [*Plan of Implementation of the World Summit on Sustainable Development*, U.N. Doc. A/CONF.199/20 (Sept. 4, 2002) (hereinafter WSSD Implementation Plan)].

The WSSD Implementation Plan incorporated several important new goals to be reached within the next 20 years, including meeting people's basic sanitation needs, producing and using non-harmful chemicals, restoring the world's fish stocks, and reducing the rate of loss of biodiversity [*Id.*]. More importantly, the Johannesburg Declaration articulated a new dimension to SD by affirming "a collective responsibility to advance and strengthen the interdependent and mutually reinforcing pillars of sustainable development—economic development, social development, and environmental protection—

at the local, national, regional, and global levels."
[Johannesburg Declaration at ¶ 5].

The same principles were endorsed in the WSSD
Implementation Plan [WSSD Implementation Plan
at ¶ 2.]. As noted above, this re-statement of SD
confirms the third element in the definition of SD
introduced at the Millennium Summit. Social
development, which hitherto had been subsumed
under the rubric of economic development, is now
treated as a separate concept. This is a significant
development to the extent that SD—which hitherto
consisted of two legs (economic development and
environmental protection)—has now been given a
third   (social   development).   Consequently,
environmental protection, which had enjoyed rough
parity with economic development, has now been
reduced to a third part of a tripartite concept.

The WSSD also represented a step forward in
implementation of Agenda 21's focus on non-state
actors. Section III of Agenda 21 sets forth a novel,
hands-on approach with an emphasis on the
importance of major social groups in implementing
new   environmental   policies.   Unlike   previous
conferences on SD, in which delegates were
exclusively from States, delegates to WSSD included
not only 10,000 government delegates, but also some
8,000   delegates   from   civil   society,   including
representatives from NGOs, corporate interests, and
other areas. In addition, parallel events incorporated
conferences between interested parties representing
NGOs: women, indigenous people, youth, farmers,
trade unions, business leaders, the scientific and

technological community, local authorities, and Chief Justices from various countries.

G. 2012 RIO+20 UNITED NATIONS CONFERENCE ON SUSTAINABLE DEVELOPMENT (UNCSD)

The Rio+20 United Nations Conference on Sustainable Development (UNCSD) [United Nations Conference on Sustainable Development, Rio de Janeiro, Braz., Jun. 20–22, 2012, *Report of the United Nations Conference on Sustainable Development*, U.N. Doc. A/CONF.216/16 (Jun. 20–22, 2012)] was held 20 years after Earth Summit. UNCSD did not result in any treaties or legally binding documents. Instead, it produced a political UNCSD Outcome Document: *The Future We Want* [United Nations General Assembly, *Resolution adopted by the General Assembly on 27 July 2012: 66/288 The future we want,* G.A. Res. 66/288, U.N. Doc. A/RES/66/288 (Jul. 27, 2012)], consisting of 283 paragraphs. This largely hortatory UNCSD Outcome Document spanned the gamut of international concerns, and contained a long list of objectives. The resulting smorgasbord of something for everyone was patched together by the host country, Brazil, to obtain consensus on a final document [International institute for Sustainable Development (IISD), *Summary of the United Nations Conference on Sustainable Development: 13–22 June 2012,* 27(51) Earth Negotiations Bulletin 1 (Jun. 25, 2012)] that contrasted with the dissension that prevailed at the 2009 Copenhagen UN Climate Change Conference [Copenhagen Accord, Copenhagen, Den., Dec. 7–19, 2009, *Report of the*

Conference of the Parties, Part Two: Action Taken by the Conference of the Parties at its Fifteenth Session, U.N. Doc. FCCC/CP/2009/11/Add.1 (Mar. 30, 2010)]. In order to find the real needles buried in the UNCSD Outcome Document's haystack of aspirations, it is necessary to examine the conference negotiations. Such an examination reveals that the UNCSD focused on three issues: the green economy, a new iteration of SD in the form of sustainable development goals (SDGs) to replace the MDGs, and better institutional support for the envisioned SDGs.

Discussions about the green economy sought to lay the foundations for an effective transition to a low-carbon economy. A few matters relevant to the green economy are worthy of mention. First, economic and social development had hitherto been premised on conventional economic growth measured by gross domestic product (GDP). A green economy calls for broader metrics and measures of progress, and takes into account environmental and social considerations not typically included in the GDP. Given that national accounting systems are based on monetary values in dollars, discussions sought to give monetary or economic value to environmental and social factors by placing economic or dollar values on environmental services provided by nature. There was some resistance to these ideas by those who felt that such an approach diminished the ethical and aesthetic essence of nature by giving dollar values to qualities that could not be reduced to dollars [Suan Ee Ong, et al., *Examining Rio+20's Outcome*, Council On Foreign Relations (Jul. 5, 2012), *available at* http://www.cfr.org/world/examining-rio20s-outcome/

p28669 (last visited Apr. 2017)]. But the prevailing wisdom was that a green economy would need to express some environmental and social values in dollars.

Second, it became clear during UNCSD discussions that the green economy could not be established by governments alone, and required the backing of the private sector. Consequently, the conference saw a need to increase the role of civil society and the private sector in promoting SD policies. Third, the need for a green economy drew attention to the fact that a green economy must be established at national and local levels. Therefore, the responsibility for ushering green economics would need to be shifted primarily to developing countries.

On setting the foundations for an institutional framework for SD, UNCSD negotiations were directed toward the importance of launching a process to develop universal and inclusive SDGs applicable to all countries and to all three dimensions of SD [Frederico Ramos de Armas, *Rio+20—Start of a Process*, Our Planet—The Magazine of the United Nations Environment Programme (Feb. 2013) at 5–6]. The envisioned SDG topics would extend momentum in international development work beyond the poverty-eradicating mission of the MDGs, which lapsed in 2015. In order to reinforce governance, it was decided to create a "high-level" political forum that would replace the existing Commission on Sustainable Development.

It is important to emphasize the extent to which the conceptualization of the SDGs and the green economy in the UNCSD Outcome Document is radically different to SD as hitherto accepted. Up to this time, every formulation of SD in legal and political documents had given primary emphasis to eradicating poverty through economic and social development. A dramatically different picture now emerges. First, there is a new iteration of SD emphasizing global public goals (GPGs), discussed below, as distinct from the eradication of poverty based on individual economic growth. Second, developing countries assume greater responsibility for SD. Previously, SD had been premised on the legal and political principle of CBDR, decreed in the UNFCCC. CBDR declared that it was the overriding responsibility of developed countries to help developing countries. The UNCSD Outcome Document, however, appears to shift the onus by placing significant responsibility for the SDGs, and the green economy, on national States, the large majority of whom are developing countries.

H.   2015 SUSTAINABLE DEVELOPMENT GOALS (SDGs)

Based on the UNCSD Outcome Document, the 2015 SDGs were developed with input from the UN's 193 member states and an array of NGOs. They are embodied in a large document [United Nations General Assembly, *Resolution adopted by the General Assembly on 25 September 2015—70/1 Transforming Our World: the 2030 Agenda for Sustainable Development*, A/RES/70/1 (Sept. 25 2015)] that consists of 17 goals, including 169 targets and indicators [United Nations General Assembly, *Draft Outcome Document Of The United Nations Summit For The Adoption Of The Post-2015 Development Agenda,* (Aug. 12, 2015) A/69/L.85]. The SDGs replaced the MDGs in January 2016, and deal with the following:

1. **Poverty**—End poverty in all its forms everywhere.

2. **Food**—End hunger, achieve food security and improved nutrition, and promote sustainable agriculture.

3. **Health**—Ensure healthy lives and promote well-being for all at all ages.

4. **Education**—Ensure inclusive and equitable quality education and promote lifelong learning opportunities for all.

5. **Women**—Achieve gender equality and empower all women and girls.

6. **Water**—Ensure availability and sustainable management of water and sanitation for all.

7. **Energy**—Ensure access to affordable, reliable, sustainable and modern energy for all.

8. **Economy**—Promote sustained, inclusive, and sustainable economic growth; full and productive employment; and decent work for all.

9. **Infrastructure**—Build resilient infrastructure, promote inclusive and sustainable industrialization, and foster innovation.

10. **Inequality**—Reduce inequality within and among countries.

11. **Habitation**—Make cities and human settlements inclusive, safe, resilient, and sustainable.

12. **Consumption**—Ensure sustainable consumption and production patterns.

13. **Climate**—Take urgent action to combat climate change and its impacts.

14. **Marine ecosystems**—Conserve and sustainably use the oceans, seas, and marine resources for sustainable development.

15. **Ecosystems**—Protect, restore, and promote sustainable use of terrestrial ecosystems; sustainably manage forests; combat desertification; halt and reverse land degradation; and halt biodiversity loss.

16. **Institutions**—Promote peaceful and inclusive societies for sustainable development; provide access to justice for all; and build effective, accountable and inclusive institutions at all levels.

17. **Sustainability**—Strengthen the means of implementation and revitalize the global partnership for sustainable development [*Id.*].

I.   EVALUATING MODERN SUSTAINABLE DEVELOPMENT (SD)

1.   MILLENIUM DEVELOPMENT GOALS (MDGS)

The MDGs were written and institutionalized to mobilize support from the donor countries and their citizens primarily through ODA, a term coined by the Development Assistance Committee of the OECD to measure aid. The Development Assistance Committee is an international forum of many of the largest funders of aid, which includes twenty-nine members. The World Bank, the International Monetary Fund (IMF), and United Nations Development Programme (UNDP) participate as observers [Organization for Economic Cooperation and Development (OECD), *Development Assistance Committee (DAC), available at* http://www.oecd.org/dac/developmentassistancecommitteedac.htm (last visited Apr. 2017)].

The MDGs focus largely on the symptoms of underdevelopment and reducing poverty. MDGs 1 through 7 refer to improvements in private welfare through reduction of poverty and hunger, access to education, improving child mortality, better maternal care, proving safe drinking water and sanitation, and combating diseases such as malaria and HIV/AIDS. According to the UNDP's Human Development Report of 2005, the MDGs created incentives for donors and governments to favor quick impacts rather than addressing underlying complex social systems. This was advanced in the "quick wins" strategy outlined in the report on investing to advance the MDGs. The strategy calls for funding for "high potential, short-term impact" initiatives that can yield "breathtaking results within three or fewer years . . ." and "start countries on the path to the [MDGs]" [United Nations Development Programme (UNDP), *Human Development Report 2005* (2005) ISBN 0-19-530511-6].

These measures include, for example, mosquito bed-nets for malaria protection, MDG model villages, immunizations, school meals, and water purification devices. Such investments have two kinds of payoff: they begin to drive down key indicators for the MDGs and they offer the prospect of quick impact that can mobilize donors' aid funds. Most of the measures deliver individual health and education benefits, rather than systemic change. These "quick win" strategies made them central to the campaign and to the call for "scaled-up" investment in development assistance. Because MDGs are attractive to donor agencies and their domestic constituencies, they attract aid funds and therefore the attention of poor-country governments. Pragmatically, this feature can be seen as a strength of the MDGs: the goals establish benchmarks with attainable levels of progress, and they rely on interventions that can be accomplished without even attempting to address the thorny social and political causes of inequality and deprivation. Accomplishing the MDGs would mean real improvement in quality of life for some of the world's poor.

MDG strategies visualize the eradication of poverty and envision development and investment in measures benefitting individuals and households as a means of supplying individual material wants from a utilitarian perspective. Poverty is depicted as a multidimensional human material deprivation that arises from lack of income, water, food, education, and health services [Sakiko Fukudua-Parr, *Recapturing the Narrative of International Development*, in *The Millennium Development Goals And Beyond: Global Development After 2015*, 42 Rorden Wilkinson & David Hulme ed. (2012)]. The seven MDGs were calculated to maximize individual welfare gains by supplying material wants from a utilitarian perspective. The MDGs envisioned the alleviation of poverty, and the lack of water, food, education, and health as human needs that can be met in a pragmatic manner. They did not extend to GPGs, which are an extension of the concept of national goods to the global level.

National public goods have been part of the economic theory of government for centuries [William D. Nordhaus, *Paul Samuelson and Global Public Goods, available at* http://www.econ.yale.edu/ ~nordhaus/homepage/PASandGPG.pdf (last visited Apr. 2017)]. The idea that society needs government to overcome the failures of the market in achieving efficiency and equity in the allocation and distribution of resources is well established. It is widely understood that national public goods and services, such as environmental protection, health services, social security, and transportation infrastructure, are fundamental to the well-being of people, and that governments and markets must work together to provide them. Public goods have two key properties: non-rivalry and non-excludability. They are commodities for which the cost of extending the service to an additional person is zero, and for which it is impossible or expensive to exclude individuals from enjoying [*Id.*].

In a globalized world, problems and solutions reach across national borders, resulting in a growing need for international collective action. Inge Kaul, who pioneered the concept of GPGs, extended the concept of "public goods" from the national level to the global level. Her book, *Global Public Goods: International Cooperation in the 21st Century* [Inge Kaul, Isabelle Grundber, & Marc Stern, eds., *Global Public Goods: International Cooperation in The 21st Century* (1999)] convincingly argues that the two tests of a public goods, non-rivalry and non-excludability, can be applied at the global level to such things as environment, health, culture, and peace. GPGs are goods whose benefits reach across borders, generations, and population groups, and the concept of GPGs has become an increasingly important part of international policy making. A clean environment, climate stability, health, knowledge, property rights, peace, and security are all examples of public goods that could be made global.

2. SUSTAINABLE DEVELOPMENT GOALS (SDGs)

In stark contrast to the MDGs, the SDGs decisively address the problems of GPGs. As enumerated in the table below, nine of the SDGs—Goals 9 to 17—embrace GPGs.

MDG	Type	SDG	Costs	Type
1. Eradicate Extreme Poverty and Hunger	Individual Private Good/Welfare	End Poverty and Hunger		Individual Private Good
2. Achieve universal primary education	Individual Private Good/welfare	2: End hunger, achieve food security, nutrition and sustainable agriculture	$44 bn. per year [EurActiv]*	Individual Private Good
3. Promote gender equality and empower women	Individual Private Good/welfare	3: Good health and well-being		Individual Private Good
4. Reduce child mortality	Individual Private Good/welfare	4: Quality education		Individual Private Good
5. Improve maternal health	Individual Private Good/welfare	5: Gender equality		Individual Private Good
6. Combat HIV /AIDS, malaria and other diseases	Individual Private Good	6: Clean water and sanitation	$27bn per year [EurActiv]*	Individual Private Good

MDG	Type	SDG	Costs	Type
7. Ensure environmental sustainability	Global Public Good	7: Affordable and clean energy	$50bn per year [EurActiv]*	Individual Private Good
8. Develop a global partnership for development	Global Public Good	8: Decent work and economic growth		Individual Private Good
		9: Industry, innovation, infrastructure		Global Public Good
		10: Reduced inequalities		Global Public Good
		11: Sustainable cities and communities		Global Public Good
		12: Responsible consumption, production		Global Public Good
		13: Climate action	$1,100 bn. per year [EurActiv]*	Global Public Good
		14: Life below water		Global Public Good
		15: Life on Land	$430 bn. per year [EurActiv]*	Global Public Good

MDG	Type	SDG	Costs	Type
		16: Peace, justice and strong institutions		Global Public Good
		SDG 17: Partnerships for the goals		Global Public Good

Disquietingly, a number of the SDGs appear to violate international law. Goal 13 of the SDGs deals with the GPG of climate action and the need to take urgent action to combat climate change and its impacts. The explanation accompanying Goal 13 states that the "... UNFCCC or Framework Convention is a universal convention of principle, acknowledging the existence of anthropogenic (human-induced) climate change and giving industrialized countries the major part of responsibility for combating it." [UNFCCC COP 21/ CMP 11, Div. For Sustainable Dev., Un-Desa, *21st Session of the Conference of the Parties and 11th Session of the Conference of the Parties Serving as the Meeting of the Parties to the Kyoto Protocol,* (2015), *available at* https://sustainabledevelopment.un.org/ index.php?page=view&type=13&nr=1359&menu=16 34 (last visited Apr. 2017)]. The responsibility placed on developed countries is indubitably correct. Article 3(1) of the UNFCCC, institutionalizing CBDR, required developed countries to pay for climate action. But having acknowledged the legal obligation placed on developed countries by CBDR, the SDGs then renounces CBDR by placing the primary responsibility for climate change action on developing countries. In doing so, SDG 13 violates the UNFCCC, which draws a clear distinction between the GPG addressing climate change and the humanitarian goals of economic advancement and the eradication of poverty.

The Objective embodied in Article 2 of UNFCCC is ". . . to achieve in accordance with the relevant provisions of the Convention, the stabilization of greenhouse gas concentrations in the atmosphere at a level that could prevent dangerous anthropogenic interference with the climate system. Such a level should be achieved within a time-frame sufficient . . . to enable economic development to proceed in a sustainable manner" [UNFCCC at art. 2]. It is to be observed that the stabilization of greenhouse concentrations is to be achieved in conjunction, first, with the other relevant provisions of the Convention, and second, in a manner that enables SD. The other relevant provisions of the Convention make it abundantly clear that climate stabilization is not an unalloyed GPG to be sought at the expense of sustainable economic development and its corollary of humanitarian assistance. The preamble to the UNFCCC asserts that the parties should take into full account ". . . the legitimate priority needs of developing countries for the achievement of sustained economic growth and the eradication of poverty" [UNFCCC at pmbl]. The preamble then recognizes that in order to achieve sustainable social and economic development, the energy consumption of developing countries will need to grow. The body of the UNFCCC continues to emphasize the extent to which economic and social development tempers the quest for climate stability.

Article 3(4) on UNFCCC Principles, states that "The Parties have a right to and should promote sustainable development. Policies and measures to protect the climate system against induced change should be appropriate for the specific conditions of each Party . . . taking into account that economic development is essential for adopting measures to address climate change" [UNFCCC at art. 3(4)]. Article 4(7) is even more emphatic in asserting that economic and social development and poverty eradication are the overriding priorities of the developing country parties. These legal provisions are found in a treaty whose objective is to stabilize climate change. The compelling extent to which even the most important treaty dealing with climate change is qualified and modified by the reiteration of the primary importance of economic and social development cannot be ignored.

Article 4(3) of the UNFCCC is unequivocal in asserting and stressing that developed countries shall provide "*new and additional financial resources* to meet the agreed full costs incurred by developing countries Parties in complying with their obligations" [UNFCCC at art. 4(3) (emphasis added)]. The degree to which such new financial and technology transfers are crucial to the implementation of the UNFCCC is further highlighted by Article 4(7). The language of Article 4(7) emphasizes that the extent to which developing countries will effectively be able to implement their commitments under the UNFCCC will depend on the effective implementation of developed country commitments. In sum, implementing the GPG of climate stabilization would need new, fresh, and additional financing. The financial and other resources needed to advance climate change should not be funneled or siphoned from ODA, which is intended for individual human advances through economic and social development.

The cardinal importance of developed countries finding additional financing for promoting climate stabilization is further affirmed by UNFCCC Article 3(1), incorporating the Principle that parties should protect the climate system ". . . on the basis of equity and in accordance with their common but differentiated responsibilities and respective capabilities. Accordingly, the developed country Parties should take the lead in combating climate change and the adverse effects thereof" [UNFCCC at art. 3(1)]. Furthermore, as we have noted, the UNFCCC aligned with the other widely accepted treaty adopted at Earth Summit in 1992, the Biodiversity Convention. Both treaties forcefully and unequivocally expressed the developmental priority of SD. Article 4(7) of the UNFCCC and Article 20(4) of the Biodiversity Convention reaffirm in unison that parties "will take fully into account that economic and social development and poverty eradication are the first and overriding priorities of the developing country Parties" [UNFCCC at art. 4(7); Biodiversity Convention at art. 20(4)].

3.   THE LEGAL AND POLITICAL STATUS OF SUSTAINABLE DEVELOPMENT (SD)

The commitment to GPGs raises a number of interconnected questions. First, will the SDGs diminish, depreciate, and devalue the individual human development goals of the MDGs? Second, who will pay the very high price tag of the SDGs? Third, will ODA be diverted from the human developmental goals of the MDGs to the GPGs of the SDGs? Fourth, what effect will the transfer of resources from the MDGs to GPGs have on the poorest of the poor, especially the least developed countries (LDCs)?

In answering these questions it should be noted at the outset that the UNFCCC is a legal document that creates legal norms. By contrast, the SDGs express political norms. However, legal norms such as the right to SD, the need for economic and social development, and the principle of CBDR are general legal norms that need practical clarification. The SDGs offer this practical clarification and establish political norms that interpret the legal rules found in the UNFCCC. Consequently, the meaning of the legal norms found in the UNFCCC has been supplied by the political norms of the SDGs.

Second, the SDGs, particularly those aiming at GPGs, require enormous new amounts of additional funding. It is not clear how, and from where, the required additional finances might be found. Therefore, the answers to the questions raised will depend on the responses of the various national and civil society stakeholders.

CHAPTER THREE
IMPLEMENTATION AND COMPLIANCE

Most international treaties require implementation and compliance within individual States. When referring to "implementation" and "compliance" of a treaty, both terms convey several layers of meaning. They must be viewed in the broader context of the degree to which a treaty correctly diagnoses the problem it confronts, embodies prescriptions that institutionalize tough and serious objectives (as distinct from shallow, inadequate, or inconsequential ones), and directs compliance-eliciting measures toward changing State behavior.

A. THE LAYERED MEANING OF IMPLEMENTATION AND COMPLIANCE

There are a number of facets to the broad concept of *implementation*. The first and primary meaning refers to the process by which a treaty is incorporated into domestic law through legislative, judicial, or executive action. This will hereinafter be referred to as *formal implementation*. The second meaning of implementation is included in the concept of *compliance,* or the extent to which a party has adhered to its treaty obligations by deploying the formal implementing machinery established by the treaty [*see* Dinah Shelton ed., COMMITMENT AND COMPLIANCE: THE ROLE OF NON-BINDING NORMS IN THE INTERNATIONAL LEGAL SYSTEM (2000); E. Brown

Weiss & Harold K. Jacobson, ENGAGING COUNTRIES: STRENGTHENING COMPLIANCE WITH ENVIRONMENTAL ACCORDS (1998)]. This will be referred to as *formal compliance*.

The third aspect of implementation goes beyond formal implementation and compliance and focuses on a party's effective implementation on the ground. This aspect is referred to as *effectiveness*, and encompasses both the extent to which a treaty has achieved its goals as well as the costs of doing so [*see* Malgosia Fitzmaurice & C. Redgwell, *Non-Compliance Procedures and International Law*, 31 NETH, Y.B. INT'L L. (2000) at 35]. A treaty that aims low and achieves little could, nonetheless, be effectively implemented even though it may embody shallow commitments, contain inadequate goals, or fail to address tough issues [*see* George W. Downs, et al., *Is the Good News About Compliance Good News About Cooperation?*, 50 INT'L ORG. 379 (1996) at 383]. Alternatively, a treaty aiming high and containing demanding prescriptive remedies may be adjudged ineffective because it falls short of achieving its goals.

The chimerical nature of "effectiveness" is illustrated by treaty "X" that may not have a significant impact on the problem, nor result in behavioral changes. Treaty "X" may reiterate what States would have done anyway, or require only minimal changes that do not significantly affect the underlying problem. Nonetheless, once it is negotiated and comes into force, treaty "X" becomes part of the corpus of international law even if it fails the test of good prescription. This kind of treaty could be implemented effectively despite its flawed vision and very limited or modest goals. Effectiveness, unlike impact, is not based on the evaluation of a treaty as a problem solving institution, nor is it based on the depth of its commitments, nor the extent to which it addresses the problem that calls for legal remediation.

Perhaps the most important criterion for determining the success or failure of treaty implementation is the treaty's *impact*, or the extent to which the implementation of a treaty has solved, or made significant steps toward solving, the challenge or problem the treaty sought to address [*see* Kal Raustiala, *Compliance & Effectiveness in International Regulatory Cooperation*, 32 CASE W. RES. J. INT'L L. 387 (2000) at 393–394]. It is necessary to inquire about the depth of treaty goals, because it is possible that shallow commitments and modest goals could reflect what parties are already doing, rather than change that is needed to address the problem at hand.

It is important, therefore, to understand a treaty not only in terms of its *effectiveness* in achieving stated goals, but also in terms of its *impact* as a satisfactory response to the challenge addressed and in changing behavior. Where results, garnered from empirical data and evidence, show that goals have not been met, or point to the inadequacy of those goals, it is important to question the reasons for such shortfalls. Such an inquiry must traverse institutions, compliance methods, and enforcement, as well as the socioeconomic, political, or cultural context that might explain the gaps between the goals of a treaty and the inability to meet them, or the meagerness of the goals and the ease with which they were met.

There is a substantial body of literature on effectiveness [*see*, for example, Oran R. Young, et al., *Regime Effectiveness: Taking Stock*, THE EFFECTIVENESS OF INTERNATIONAL ENVIRONMENTAL REGIMES, Oran R. Young, ed. (1999) at 249; Harold Hongju Koh, *Why Do Nations Obey International Law?*, 106 YALE L.J. 2599 (1997) at 2603; Downs, et al., *supra*; Abram Chayes & Antonia Handler Chayes, THE NEW SOVEREIGNTY: COMPLIANCE WITH INTERNATIONAL REGULATORY AGREEMENTS (1995); Thomas M. Franck, FAIRNESS IN INTERNATIONAL LAW AND INSTITUTIONS (1995)]. However, these theoretically illuminating contributions do not include any authoritative conclusions based on a comprehensive empirical examination of the effectiveness or impacts of energy and environmental agreements [*see* David G. Victor, et al., eds., THE IMPLEMENTATION AND EFFECTIVENESS OF INTERNATIONAL ENVIRONMENTAL COMMITMENTS: THEORY AND PRACTICE IX (1998)]. This is primarily because of the absence of comprehensive and organized empirical evidence or data on such treaties. To a great extent, therefore, implementation, effectiveness, and impact are being judged without actual empirical evidence, and this is a gap that needs to be filled.

B.   INSTITUTIONS AND ORGANIZATIONS

At the normative level, the implementation of treaty obligations is hampered by the fact that the vertical command and control power structure governing domestic politics within States is conspicuously absent within the international legal order. In international society, power or authority rests on a horizontal base made up of co-equal sovereign States, and can be built into a pyramidal structure only if these States consent to and join in such an endeavor. While piecemeal building upon the base has resulted in the substantial corpus of international environmental law (IEL) (*see* Ch. 1), there is no overarching pyramid of authority consisting of law-making, law-interpreting, law-implementing, or law-enforcing institutions in IEL.

However, the absence of institutions equivalent to those within States does not signify a complete void in international implementing institutions. On the contrary, what we have are international implementing agencies and mechanisms serving the international society in which we live. They merit examination, and we begin with the many international organizations that facilitate the implementation of IEL and follow this by examining compliance mechanisms, diplomatic avenues, and judicial remedies.

Despite the impressive growth of IEL and its expanding domain, there is still no single institution or organization that serves environmental protection in the way the World Trade Organization (WTO) advances, interprets, implements, and enforces the concept of free trade. The institutions and organizations enlisted to advance IEL are fractured, fragmented, and divided along functional, regional, bureaucratic, and geopolitical lines. It is useful to take note of the more important of these entities, and a fuller description of them is found in the Appendix. They are classified as global organizations, regional organizations, treaty specific organizations, and non-governmental organizations (NGOs).

1.   GLOBAL ORGANIZATIONS

The United Nations (UN) was founded in 1947—before the dawn of environmental awareness. Its Charter creates seven principal organs, including the General Assembly, the Security Council, the Economic and Social Council (ECOSOC), and the International Court of Justice (ICJ) [*Charter of the United Nations*, Oct. 24, 1945, 1 U.N.T.S. xvi at art. 7]. The UN Charter neither creates an environmental organ nor specifically mandates the protection of the environment.

A number of international organizations created by treaty or agreement have been brought into a familial relationship with the UN pursuant to Charter provisions. These are known as Specialized Agencies of the UN. They enjoy juridical personality and may exercise rights and duties as subjects of international law. A number of them have broadly interpreted their constituent treaties to adopt an environmental competence. Those presently assuming environmental responsibilities include the Food and Agricultural Organization (FAO); the

International Labor Organization (ILO); the World Health Organization (WHO); the World Meteorological Organization (WMO); the International Maritime Organization (IMO); and the UN Educational, Scientific, and Cultural Organization (UNESCO).

While the International Atomic Energy Agency (IAEA) does not possess Specialized Agency status, it also plays a role in advancing environmental protection along with other semi-autonomous UN bodies, such as the UN Development Programme (UNDP), the UN Institute for Training and Research (UNITAR), and the UN Conference on Trade and Development (UNCTAD). After the United Nations Conference on Environment and Development (UNCED), also known as Earth Summit, the UN General Assembly created the Commission on Sustainable Development (CSD) as a functional commission of ECOSOC.

Perhaps the most important of the UN organizations, the UN Environment Programme (UNEP), was also created by a General Assembly resolution, not by treaty or agreement. UNEP acts as a focal point for environmental action and coordination, but possesses no executive power. All UNEP programs are financed directly by member States. Consequently, its mission is to persuade and convince States of the need for environmental action; to provide information, expertise, and advice; and to sponsor treaties. It has carried out these limited objectives credibly [Alexandre Kiss & Dinan Shelton,

INTERNATIONAL ENVIRONMENTAL LAW, Third edition (2004) at 112].

Increasingly, incentives, financial mechanisms, and technology transfers have become part of the architecture of IEL, so it is also necessary to take note of the more important of the institutions involved. The World Bank group consists of the International Bank for Reconstruction and Development (IBRD), the International Development Bank, and the International Finance Corporation (IFC). The World Bank has developed a bad record by encouraging environmentally damaging developments, but, under growing pressure from activists and NGOs, appears to be mending its ways. In 2001, it released its Environmental Strategy, which was a comprehensive pledge to consider environmental factors while pursuing its overarching goals of poverty reduction and social growth [The World Bank, *Making Sustainable Commitments: An Environment Strategy for the World Bank,* (2001) Washington, D.C.]. The Environmental Strategy also acknowledged the environmental shortcomings of its past decision-making. The World Bank has also attempted to incorporate the participation of key stakeholders through its Strategic Environmental Assessment, "giving voice to those affected by policy, programs, and plans" [World Bank, *Strategic Environmental Assessment, Concept, and Practice,* WORLD BANK ENVIRONMENTAL STRATEGY NOTE NO. 14 (2005)].

In addition, the Global Environment Facility (GEF) was established in 1990 on an experimental basis to provide financial and technical assistance to developing countries to promote environmental protection. It was restructured permanently in 1994 as an independent financial organization that provides grants to developing countries for projects that benefit the global environment and promote sustainable livelihoods in local communities. GEF grants support projects related to biodiversity, climate change, international waters, land degradation, the ozone layer, and persistent organic pollutants (POPs).

Lastly, a review of global environmental institutions would not be complete without a reference to two legal institutions: (1) the ICJ, and (2) the International Law Commission (ILC). The ICJ is the principal judicial organ of the UN system, and exercises jurisdiction by consent. It has now set up an environmental chamber and demonstrated in its *Legality of the Use by a State of Nuclear Weapons in Armed Conflict* that it possesses the authority to address vexing environmental issues and apply the law to changing situations [*Legality of the Use by a State of Nuclear Weapons in Armed Conflict*, (Request for an Advisory Opinion by the WHO of Sept. 13) (1993 I.C.J 467 (hereinafter Legality of the Use of Nuclear Weapons)]. The ILC was created by the UN General Assembly to work toward the codification and development of international law, and it has reported on subjects of great importance to IEL, such as State responsibility (SR) and international watercourses.

2.   REGIONAL ORGANIZATIONS

A number of regional organizations are playing an important role in developing IEL. The most important of these is the European Union (EU), formerly known as the European Community and the European Economic Community (EEC). The EU is the most advanced form of international organization in the world and is evolving into a continent-wide political confederation. It possesses three key attributes lacking in other international organizations: (1) law-making agencies; (2) law-interpreting and enforcing agencies; and (3) a court with compulsory jurisdiction. Clothed with explicit environmental jurisdiction, the EU has enacted a large number of environmental laws over a wide range of subject areas.

Other regional bodies of note are the Council of Europe, the Organization for Economic Cooperation and Development (OECD), the Organization of American States (OAS), and the South Pacific Regional Environmental Programme (SPREP).

3.   SPECIFIC TREATY ORGANIZATIONS

Many treaties set up institutional arrangements (or rudimentary international organizations) for their implementation. They range from *ad hoc* conferences to more permanent institutional structures. A number of them are called Conferences Of the Parties (COP), which include a permanent secretariat and a budget, and, in some cases, special science advisory bodies. Representative examples include the sporadic COPs under the Vienna

Convention for the Protection of the Ozone Layer (Vienna Ozone Convention) and regular COPs under the Montreal Protocol on Substances that Deplete the Ozone Layer (Montreal Protocol) (*see* Ch. 7). Additionally, the UN Framework Convention on Climate Change (UNFCCC) (*see* Ch. 6) institutes an annual COP, and the Convention on Biological Diversity (Biodiversity Convention) (*see* Ch. 5) provides for a COP on regular intervals. Finally, the Convention for the Protection of the Marine Environment of the North East Atlantic (OSPAR Convention) requires regular COPs [*Convention for the Protection of the Marine Environment of the North East Atlantic*, Sept. 22, 1992, 32 I.L.M. 1069 (hereinafter OSPAR Convention)] (*see* Ch. 10), while the Convention on International Trade in Endangered Species and Wild Fauna and Flora (CITES) (*see* Ch. 5) sets up a COP that meets at least every two years.

4.   NON-GOVERNMENTAL ORGANIZATIONS (NGOs)

Global NGOs are playing an increasingly important role in IEL. We referred to NGOs in the context of MDGs in Chapter 2, and now mention three out of hundreds to illustrate their diversity and spread. The World Conservation Union (IUCN) is a unique hybrid comprised of non-governmental conservation groups, States, and public law entities such as universities and research institutes (*see* Appendix § S). The World Wildlife Fund (WWF) is a non-governmental conservation group whose goals parallel those of IUCN (*see* Appendix § W). WWF finances conservation strategies throughout the world. A third is the Earth Council, endorsed by Earth Summit in 1992, which assists grassroots organizations pressing for the implementation of sustainable development (SD). The changing role of NGOs in shaping IEL is reflected by the substantial extent to which NGOs participated in the 2002 World Summit on Sustainable Development (WSSD) (*see* Ch. 2). Historically, only representatives of States attended UN Conferences, but WSSD offered extensive opportunities for NGO involvement. The role of NGOs in IEL continued to solidify in 2015 at the UN Sustainable Development Summit, including the development of partnerships for meeting sustainable development goals (SDGs).

NGOs have become established actors in the implementation of environmental law for a number of reasons. To begin, they are closer to the people affected by environmental degradation, and thus may have the ability to represent them more faithfully and diligently than their governments. Second, NGOs have played a major role in organizing the once invisible colleges of scientists for the purpose of studying the effects of various environmental problems, and have participated, unofficially but visibly, in the making of treaties. Not surprisingly, NGOs profess a legitimate and well-founded interest in the implementation of IEL. Third, the international character of NGOs embraces the concept of a global civil society committed to environmental protection, and their large and vocal membership have given them undeniable international political standing.

However, although NGOs exert pressure on States and international organizations to comply with IEL, they have not yet attained the status of States as subjects of international law. There are fundamental conceptual problems in their achieving theoretical parity with States within a legal system comprised of sovereign States alone. Some NGOs have made claims to the moral high ground of politics, however these claims have been criticized on the basis that NGOs are not significantly different from other self-seeking units of civil society. Critics point out that churches, civic groups, trade unions, and corporations seek to advance the interests of their members in the same way that NGOs do. They further argue that the self-interested propagation of false or inflated environmental claims, and alarm mongering resorted to by some NGOs to increase membership, is morally opprobrious. At the very least, such tactics are a far cry from the unsullied virtue claimed by some NGOs, and do not entitle NGOs to any preferential standing than other civic groups.

These critiques, however, do not prevent NGOs from participating in IEL altogether. States and international organizations have allowed environmental NGOs to perform the role of private attorney generals, empowered to protect the international environment. Some treaties also embark in this direction. For example, the IAEA has granted consultative status to NGOs having special competence in the nuclear field [International Atomic Energy Agency, *Rules on Consultative Status of NGOs with the Agency*, IAEA Doc. INFCIRC/14

(1959)]. The Convention on the Protection of the Environment between Denmark, Finland, Norway and Sweden (Nordic Convention) goes further and grants all legal persons, including individuals and NGOs, the right to protest and vindicate environmental rights and duties in the legal systems of the parties [*Convention on the Protection of the Environment between Denmark, Finland, Norway, and Sweden*, Feb. 9, 1974 (entered into force Oct. 5, 1976), 1092 U.N.T.S. 279 at art. 2 (hereinafter Nordic Convention)]. So, too, does the EU [*Treaty Establishing the European Community*, Mar. 25, 1957 (as amended), 1997 O.J. (C 340) 173–308 at art. 173; *see also Stitching Greenpeace, et al. v. Commission*, 695 B.O. 219 (Ct. First Instance 1995)]. The OSPAR Convention goes even farther by granting NGOs observer status—a role which entitles them to actually participate in COPs and to submit reports, but not to vote [OSPAR Convention at arts. 11(1) & (2)].

The Convention on Access to Information, Public Participation in Decision-making and Access to Justice in Environmental Matters (Aarhus Convention) is a regional treaty negotiated under the auspices of the UN Economic Commission for Europe (UNECE) [*Convention on Access to Information, Public Participation in Decision-making and Access to Justice in Environmental Matters*, Jun. 25, 1998, 38 I.L.M. 517 (hereinafter Aarhus Convention)]. The manner in which it provides citizens and NGOs access to information and allows their participation in its implementation makes it the most ambitious venture in "environmental democracy." Among its more remarkable features are the powers conferred on NGOs to nominate experts for election to the Aarhus Convention's Compliance Committee, the requirement that all members of the Committee be independent experts rather than representatives of State parties, and the right of citizens and NGOs to file a communication alleging non-compliance by State parties. The Compliance Committee has also promulgated the view that a party cannot demand those seeking environmental information pursuant to the Aarhus Convention provide a reason [*see* Svitlana Kravchenko, *The Aarhus Convention and Innovations in Compliance with Multilateral Environmental Agreements*, 18 COLO. J. INT'L ENVTL. L. & POL'Y 1, 5 (2007)].

Formal treaty provisions are not the only means of obtaining NGO input. For example, the CSD is required to accept input from NGOs relating to the implementation of Agenda 21 [United Nations General Assembly, *UNGA Res. 47/91* (1992) at ¶ 3 (h)]. The CSD invited extensive participation by NGOs at WSSD, including opportunities for representative groups to address the plenary. NGOs are sometimes invited to attend and participate as non-voting observers at the negotiations for international agreements, such as the Stockholm Convention on Persistent Organic Pollutants (Stockholm POPs Convention) [*Stockholm Convention on Persistent Organic Pollutants*, May 22, 2001, 40 I.L.M. 532 (hereinafter Stockholm POPs Convention)]. The World Bank has even created an Inspection Panel to provide an independent forum for private citizens or NGOs that believe their interests have been, or could be, directly harmed by a project financed by the World Bank. In a number of cases the World Bank has taken action pursuant to the reports of the Inspection Panel. In fact, since 1999, every Inspection Panel recommendation for a full investigation has been agreed to by the World Bank's Board of Executive Directors, which has thus allowed the Inspection Panel to examine any of the World Bank's records and employees [World Bank, THE INSPECTION PANEL ANNUAL REPORT 2005–2006 (2006); David Hunter, *Using the World Bank Inspection Panel to Defend the Interest of Project-Affected People*, 4 CHI. J. INT'L L. 201 (2003) at 206].

C. NON-LEGAL NORMS

In addition to legally binding obligations, legally non-binding norms and voluntary commitments are also playing a role in changing international environmental behavior. These norms may take the form of embryonic or putative obligations, sometimes called "soft law," as opposed to the legally binding treaties and established body of customary law referred to as "hard law" (*see* Ch. 1). Such norms may also be created by voluntary agreements or commitments that are non-contractual in nature. These agreements can take the form of multilateral, bilateral, or even unilateral pledges, and can include participation from a whole range of non-state or civil society actors, such as corporations, NGOs, churches, trade unions, or other groups (*see* Ch. 1).

These soft law and voluntary agreements are being included in the discussion of implementation because they sometimes embody more flexible forms and methods for compliance that could create synergies with the more difficult implementing mechanisms of hard law. Moreover, the interface between the implementation of legal and non-legal norms could generate and foster a spirit of cooperation that facilitates better compliance.

D.   COMPLIANCE MECHANISMS WITHIN TREATIES

International organizations and soft law mechanisms are unable to exercise the power and authority of national legislative, executive, and judicial bodies that supervise and enforce the implementation of laws within States. Thus it is important that the substantive rules of international law first possess an internal force or dynamic that makes sense to the parties and invokes an attitude of compliance, rather than non-compliance. We have discussed some of the factors inducing voluntary compliance in Chapter 1. Treaty negotiators try to formulate substantive rules with some compliance-generating character, based on an eclectic mix of self-interest, inducements, promises, embarrassment, and threats that promote implementation without the need for external supervision. Additionally, treaties also create institutions and techniques that induce compliance, while conferring power on appropriate authorities to deal with non-compliance, within the provisions of the treaties themselves.

Consequently, treaties display a variety of processes, procedures, and techniques that encourage compliance. As we have seen, some set up their own institutions while others delegate power to existing international organizations. Individual treaties contain varying baskets of measures addressing such tasks, and provide, *inter alia*, for the following:

1.   Interpretation;

2.   Research;

3.   Data collection and/or dissemination;

4.   Assessments (monitoring and/or reporting) and reviews of performance;

5.   Rule-making by experts subject to differing types of confirmation;

6.   Management by international organizations; and

7.   Enforcement.

1.   INTERPRETATION: THE EXAMPLE OF THE MONTREAL PROTOCOL ON SUBSTANCES THAT DEPLETE THE OZONE LAYER (MONTREAL PROTOCOL)

In Chapter 1, we referred to the importance of interpretation as a method of implementing a treaty. The Montreal Protocol provides a good example of how interpretation and other processes can be used as compliance techniques [*see* T. Ghering, *International Environment Regimes: Dynamic Legal Systems*, 1 Y.B. INT'L ENVT'L L. 35 (1990) at 47–54]. The First Meeting of the Parties (MOP-1) under the

Montreal Protocol clarified and interpreted various treaty obligations, including those in Annex A, which expressly stated that the Ozone Depletion Potential figure for one of the halons was "to be determined." Inserting an Ozone Depletion Potential figure technically required amending the Annex of the Protocol, which involved a circuitous procedure plus ratification by two thirds of the parties. To circumvent these cumbersome amendment procedures, the parties inserted an Ozone Depletion Potential figure into the Annex of the Protocol by way of interpretation.

MOP-2 continued further along these lines, as parties adopted a comprehensive "Amendment" to the Montreal Protocol that came into force upon ratification by one third of the parties, even though the explicit language of the Protocol itself required amendments to be ratified by two thirds of the parties. The parties also established an Interim Multilateral Fund to support ozone-friendly technology in developing countries, even though there was no provision in either the framework convention or the Montreal Protocol that authorized such a step. MOP-2 also adopted a "non-compliance procedure," not provided for in the Montreal Protocol, which allowed for the amicable resolution of disputes to be finally determined not by a judicial body but by a decision of the MOP. Finally, the "non-compliance procedure" also set up an "Implementation Committee" to deal with non-compliance and report to the MOP.

2. RESEARCH

In addition to interpretation, ongoing research to ascertain the true environmental impacts and effects of activities identified in a treaty is crucially important to enable the parties to comply with treaty provisions. This is particularly true when dealing with a framework treaty that requires later protocols to deal with unfolding facts. Thus, treaties are replete with references to research. For example, the parties to the Vienna Ozone Convention (*see* Ch. 7) undertake to carry out research and scientific assessments on a variety of activities that may affect the ozone layer. These assessments include research into the physics and chemistry of the atmosphere, health and biological effects, and effects of a variety of chemicals that might have a potentially deleterious consequence on the ozone layer [Vienna Ozone Convention at arts. 2, 3 & annex 1]. The UNFCCC (*see* Ch. 6) calls for research on the causes, effects, magnitude, and timing of climate change, and the economic and social consequences of various response strategies [UNFCCC at arts. 4(g) & 5], and sets up a subsidiary body for scientific and technological advice [*Id.* at art. 9]. The Biodiversity Convention (*see* Ch. 5) seeks to promote research that, *inter alia*, contributes to the conservation and sustainable use of biodiversity [Biodiversity Convention at art. 12] and sets up a subsidiary body on Scientific, Technical, and Technological Advice [*Id.* at art. 25].

3.   DATA COLLECTION AND DISSEMINATION

The three treaties mentioned above also call for data collection and the dissemination of research and data in order to facilitate compliance. Reporting requirements may include information obtained from research and data collection. They may take the form of reports by a particular international treaty organization to the parties, or, more often, reports by the parties to the international organization or the other parties. Again, the objective of reporting is to bring compliance into the light of scrutiny by other parties and by the treaty machinery.

The importance of reporting as a technique to secure compliance is illustrated in the UNFCCC. All parties are obliged to communicate to the COP a general description of steps taken to implement the UNFCCC, including a detailed description of anthropogenic emissions by sources and removal by carbon reservoirs known as sinks [UNFCCC at arts. 4(1)(a), 4(1)(j), 12(1)(a) & 12(1)(b)]. The reporting responsibilities of industrialized countries are even more onerous [*Id.* at art. 12(2)].

4.   ASSESSMENTS AND REVIEWS

Assessments and reviews of performance are tied to reporting. On the basis of the reports and research made available, the parties of a specific treaty organization may assess the extent of implementation and the progress made towards objectives. The UNFCCC entrusts this responsibility of implementing the objectives of the treaty to the COP [*Id.* at art. 7(e)], while the Montreal Protocol requires assessment and review of control measures based on the reports submitted by a panel of experts at least every four years [Montreal Protocol at art. 6].

5.   RULE-MAKING BY EXPERTS

Where a framework treaty institutes an objective or final goal, the task of approaching it is usually undertaken in steps and requires interim measures. The task of making these rules and drawing up other measures, or recommending what they should be, is sometimes delegated to a group of scientific experts. We have seen that panels of experts have been set up under the Montreal Protocol, while the UNFCCC and the Biodiversity Convention have each created special scientific bodies. In our discussion on the amendment of treaties (*see* Ch. 1), we noticed how the use of protocols and scientific annexes is directed at avoiding the tortuous process of treaty amendment. We have also noted above how annexes under the Montreal Protocol are amended.

6.   MANAGEMENT BY INTERNATIONAL ORGANIZATIONS

Chapter 8 on Antarctica will offer examples of how the Commission under the Convention on the Conservation of Antarctic Marine Living Resources (CCAMLR) is possessed of management powers that will help States comply with that treaty regime [*Convention on the Conservation of Antarctic Marine Living Resources*, May 20, 1980 (entered into force Apr. 7, 1982), 19 I.L.M. 841 (hereinafter CCAMLR)].

7. ENFORCEMENT

International treaty rules populate a consensual legal order and the implications of non-compliance with such rules stand in sharp relief to the comparable non-implementation of statutory rules within national legal systems. In the absence of bodies empowered to enforce compliance, the pressing goal of the parties to a treaty is to persuade the defaulter to comply. A medley of diplomatic and administrative measures is employed to secure such compliance. Judicial supervision leading to court-type decisions are available but are resorted to only in rare instances, and many environmental treaties provide for negotiation, conciliation, and arbitration as alternatives or preconditions to court litigation.

E. DIPLOMATIC AVENUES

Many environmental treaties require that parties employ diplomatic or other means of settling their differences before resorting to judicial or quasi-judicial settlement of disputes. Such treaties include the following: CITES [CITES at art. XVIII]; the International Convention for the Prevention of Pollution from Ships (MARPOL) [*International Convention for the Prevention of Pollution from Ships*, Nov. 2, 1973, 12 I.L.M. 1319 at art. 10 (hereinafter MARPOL)]; the 1972 Convention on International Liability for Damage Caused by Space Objects (Space Liability Convention) [*Convention on International Liability for Damage Caused by Space Objects*, Mar. 29, 1972, 961 U.N.T.S. 187 at art. IX (hereinafter Space Liability Convention)]; the Vienna

Ozone Convention [Vienna Ozone Convention at art. 11(1)]; the UNFCCC [UNFCCC at art. 14]; and the Biodiversity Convention [Biodiversity Convention at art. 27(1)]. These provisions signal the importance of diplomatic means for securing treaty compliance. A number of treaties in fact institutionalize consultation between parties: the Convention for the Prevention of Marine Pollution from Land-Based Sources (1974 Paris Convention) [*Convention for the Prevention of Marine Pollution from Land-Based Sources*, Jun. 4, 1974, 13 I.L.M. 352, at art. 9(1) (hereinafter 1974 Paris Convention)]; the Nordic Convention [Nordic Convention at art. 11]; and the Convention on Long-Range Transboundary Air Pollution (LRTAP) [LRTAP at art. 5]. Thus, diplomatic pressures and consultations are part of the implementing architecture of IEL. So, too, is the preventive regime, being developed by the ILC (discussed *infra).*

F.   JUDICIAL REMEDIES

Apart from regulatory regimes supervised by agencies that are established by treaty, judicial enforcement provides another avenue for securing compliance with IEL. Judicial remedies may be used to obtain specific acts of compliance and can act as deterrents by bringing embarrassment, and perhaps ignominy, to bear on wrongdoing States. In a community of nations, where good standing and reputation are important, judicial remedies may have some use even though they lack mechanisms for enforcement.

It is necessary, at the outset, to point out that a few environmental treaties have instituted a system of civil liability (CL) that allows private individuals to prosecute claims for breaches of the treaty within national courts [*see,* Nordic Convention at art. 3; *Convention on Third Party Liability in the Field of Nuclear Energy,* Jul. 29, 1960 (entered into force Apr. 1, 1968), 956 U.N.T.S. 251 at art. 3 (hereinafter Paris Nuclear Liability Convention); *Vienna Convention on Civil Liability for Nuclear Damage,* May 21, 1963 (entered into force Nov. 12, 1977), 7 I.L.M. 727 at art. II (hereinafter Vienna Nuclear Liability Convention); *International Convention on Civil Liability for Oil Pollution Damage,* Nov. 29, 1969 (entered into force Jun. 19, 1975), 9 I.L.M. 45 at art. III (hereinafter 1969 CLC)]. This type of judicial remedy is more fully described under the rubric of CL (discussed *infra*). In Chapter 18, we refer to the potential for developing national remedies for implementing international treaties.

More commonly, judicial or quasi-judicial remedies within IEL are invoked through inter-state litigation, and are based on the grievance-remedial principle of SR or international tort law that enables one State to demand *ex post* compensation and other relief for harm caused to it by another State (*see* "Accountability for Transboundary Environmental Harms" *infra*). Typically, international courts, tribunals, and arbiters, rather than national courts or institutions, handle questions arising under international law. The ongoing efforts to enlarge the domain of public international law by giving standing to injured persons other than States, such as NGOs, corporations, and private citizens, received weak institutionalization in the United Nations Convention on the Law of the Sea (UNCLOS), where the Sea Bed Dispute Chamber may exercise limited jurisdiction over non-state parties [UNCLOS at art. 187]. However, apart from narrow exceptions, the actors in public IEL remain confined almost exclusively to State parties.

1.   JURISDICTION

If a State decides to take the traditional grievance-remedial judicial route, it can demand reparations from the wrongdoing State and ask for a termination of the specific harmful conduct. However, this kind of *ex post* judicial remedy is a flawed way of dealing with an endemic problem because international judicial bodies suffer from an underlying constitutional infirmity: lack of compulsory jurisdiction. The lack of jurisdiction becomes evident when dealing with the more serious problems of the global commons like climate change, ozone depletion, or biodiversity loss. These problems require concerted and coordinated action by all relevant State actors, and judicial supervision must extend to all affected parties. Unfortunately, some States will not consent to being brought within the compulsory and binding jurisdiction of courts or tribunals established under the treaties addressing these problems.

The settlement of disputes by way of compulsory and binding judicial proceedings is optional under the UNFCCC [UNFCCC at art. 14(2)], the

Biodiversity Convention [Biodiversity Convention at art. 26(3)], and the Vienna Ozone Convention [Vienna Ozone Convention at art. 11(3)]. UNCLOS, on the other hand, does establishes a system of compulsory dispute settlement, but it remains to be seen how vigorously it will be used [UNCLOS at art 286–296]. The ICJ also possesses some level of compulsory jurisdiction, but as of 2017 only 72 States had signed (and not withdrawn) the so-called "optional clause," giving the court general jurisdiction [Statute of the ICJ at art. 36(2)]. Even where States have signed the optional clause, 75% have entered reservations. Several reservations are self-judging, and allow a State to decline jurisdiction where it determines that a case involves questions of domestic jurisdiction or national defense.

Thus, jurisdiction can prove to be a difficult obstacle. In the *Legality of the Use of Nuclear Weapons*, the ICJ defined the concept of jurisdiction to include legal capacity or status, and held that it lacked jurisdiction in that case because the WHO was unable to demonstrate legal capacity. The WHO, a specialized agency of the UN, sought an Advisory Opinion from the ICJ. The Constitution of the WHO commits it to the attainment by all peoples of the highest possible level of health, and the WHO is required to take all necessary action to attain this objective [*Constitution of the World Health Organization*, Jun. 19, 1946 (entered into force Apr. 7, 1948) at art. 1 & 2(v)]. The question posed to the ICJ was: "In view of the health and environmental effects, would the use of nuclear weapons by a State in war or other armed conflict be a breach of its obligations under international law including the WHO Constitution?" [Legality of the Use of Nuclear Weapons at ¶ 1].

In its majority opinion, the ICJ admitted that the WHO's Constitution authorized the WHO to deal with the effects of the use of nuclear weapons, or any other hazardous activity, and to take preventive measures aimed at protecting the health of populations in the event of such weapons being used [*Id.* at ¶ 21]. Despite this, the ICJ determined that preventive action, including asking the ICJ for the present Advisory Opinion, was not of the kind that fell within the scope of the WHO's activity [*Id.* at ¶ 22]. Furthermore, the authority to take preventive actions did not confer upon the WHO "[a] competence to address the legality of the use of nuclear weapons . . . or to ask the Court about them" [*Id.* at ¶ 21].

According to the ICJ, questions affecting the legality of nuclear weapons are matters of arms control and disarmament, not the concern of a "specialized agency" such as the WHO, whose authority is restricted to the sphere of public health. Questions of arms control and disarmament are matters for the UN itself, not the specialized agencies [*Id.* at ¶ 26]. Because the question posed to the ICJ was not one that fell within the scope of the WHO, the ICJ declared that it lacked jurisdiction to entertain the case [*Id.* at ¶ 31].

This decision highlights a number of more general issues concerning the concept of jurisdiction, which enables judicial forums like the ICJ to widen or narrow access to justice. The granting of an Advisory

Opinion is a discretionary remedy [Statute of ICJ at art. 65], and the ICJ could have assumed jurisdiction and declined to grant an opinion because, for example, the petitioning party lacked standing, status, capacity, or authority. Instead, it broadened the concept of jurisdiction to include questions of standing, status, or authority of a party to bring an action, and thereby widened the opportunities for denying jurisdiction and restricting access to the ICJ.

Even if there is no jurisdictional challenge to a case, judicial remedies addressing non-compliance suffer from other defects. Judicial remedies are confined to the facts of a specific dispute, and cannot deal with the whole or look at an individual case as part of a broader environmental problem. Furthermore, there is no mechanism for enforcing or systematically monitoring the implementation of the order of an international court. This is particularly unsatisfactory because most environmental problems occur on a continuous or recurrent basis. Finally, typical judicial decisions are restricted to containing damage after the fact, rather than preventing it from happening in the first place.

Despite these defects, judicial remedies can prove to be an effective way of implementing the law if they are administered by a tribunal with compulsory and binding jurisdiction, like the UNCLOS tribunals, and if the tribunals assume a more activist role in interpreting and applying the substantive law. Such tribunals ought not to model themselves on the ICJ. The WHO case gave the ICJ an admirable opportunity to demonstrate its willingness to grapple with difficult issues of IEL. Instead, as Judge Christopher Weeramantry pointed out in his powerful separate opinion, the ICJ took a peculiarly obtuse view of the scope of the WHO, and, in so doing, signaled its unwillingness to play a more vigilant role within IEL to those who might invoke its intervention.

2.   ACCOUNTABILITY FOR TRANSBOUNDARY ENVIRONMENTAL HARMS

The ILC shouldered the burden of codifying the law dealing with accountability for transboundary harms in 1955. The first of their three volumes of work, the *Draft Articles on Responsibility of States for Internationally Wrongful Acts* (Draft Articles on SR) was finalized in 2001, and it laid the conceptual foundations and provided an authoritative re-statement of state responsibility [*Articles on Responsibility of States for Internationally Wrongful Acts*, (2001) 2 Y.B. Int'l L. Comm'n 26, U.N. Doc. A/CN.4/SER.A/2001/Add.1 (hereinafter Draft Articles on SR)]. This final draft was submitted to the UN General Assembly, which commended it on numerous occasions, and decided in 2007 to consider the question of a convention on the basis of the Draft Articles on SR. This has not happened as yet. However, the authority of the Draft Articles on SR was confirmed by the ICJ in the case of the *Application of the Convention on the Prevention and Punishment of the Crime of Genocide (Bosnia case)* [*Application of the Convention on the Prevention and Punishment of the Crime of Genocide (Bosn. & Herz. v. Serb. & Mont.)* 46 I.L.M. 188, 233–35 (Feb. 26,

2007) (hereinafter *Bosnia case*)]. The ICJ found that Articles 4 and 8 were a codification of customary international law [*Id.* at 283–84, 287].

This first work was followed by the ILC's Draft Articles: *Prevention of Transboundary Harm from Hazardous Activities* also completed in 2001 [*Prevention of Transboundary Harm from Hazardous Activities*, (2001) 2 Y.B. Int'l L. Comm'n 146, U.N. Doc. A/CN.4/SER.A/2001/Add.1], and their *Draft Principles on the Allocation of Loss in the Case of Transboundary Harm Arising out of Hazardous Activities*, completed in 2006 [*Draft Principles on the Allocation of Loss in the Case of Transboundary Harm Arising Out of Hazardous Activities, in Report of the International Law Commission*, 61 U.N. GAOR Supp. (No. 10) ¶ 66]. These two volumes are of variable quality and have not received the international consensus commanded by the first. The UN General Assembly, to which the ILC is required to report its concluded work, confirmed the greater standing of the Draft Articles on SR. It decided in 2007 that the question of drafting a treaty based on the Draft Articles should be confined only to the Draft Articles on SR and not the others.

a. Application of State Responsibility (SR)

When one nation brings another to court, it relies on SR, a form of international tort law. Before examining the main features of SR, it is relevant to note that the considerable theoretical attention given to the concept stands in stark contrast to its conspicuous absence in environmental treaties. The stubborn fact is that questions of how to claim compensation for the breach of international environmental obligations, either in national or international forums, have been deliberately neglected or omitted in treaties. Cases where compensation is obtained are the exceptions, not the rule, and the absence of a willingness among States to develop principles of SR is yet another reason why judicial enforcement of environmental treaties can prove elusive.

The foundational principle of SR, as of tort law, is the concept of an internationally "wrongful" act. A State commits an internationally wrongful act when it violates or acts in breach of an existing international obligation, found in treaty or customary law. As such, an act's classification as "wrongful" depends not on its being morally unacceptable *per se*, but instead on the wrongfulness of breaching international law. In theory, all obligations, whether general or specific, contained in treaties as well as in customary law, have the potential to give rise to SR. An obligation may be very general and fail to specify exactly what a State should do. One such general obligation is to supply security or to implement CL mechanisms as required by the nuclear treaties discussed below. On the other hand, some obligations are very specific, such as those relating to timetables for reduction of ozone-damaging chemicals, and monitoring or reporting of ozone levels, which could also give rise to SR [Draft Articles on SR at arts. 20 & 21].

According to the Draft Articles on SR completed in 2001, "[e]very internationally wrongful act of a State entails the international responsibility of that State" [*Id.* at art. 1], and "there is an internationally wrongful act of a State when [the] conduct . . . [i]s attributable to the State under international law; and . . . constitutes a breach of an international obligation of the State" [*Id.* at art. 2(a) & (b)]. Questions then arise about the nature of an international wrong, particularly as to whether such wrongs should be based on fault, as distinguished from objective wrongs that give rise to SR despite the absence of any negligence or intent.

i. Fault Liability

The ILC's commentary to the Draft Articles on SR raises the question whether fault constitutes a necessary element of the internationally wrongful act of a State. They answer that:

> This is certainly not the case if by "fault" one understands the existence, for example, of an intention to harm. In the absence of any specific requirement of a mental element in terms of the primary obligation, it is only the act of a State that matters, independently of any intention [*Id.* at art. 2, ¶ 10].

The ILC, therefore, has divorced any fault component from its use of the term "wrongful." The approach of the ILC is consistent with general principles of interpretation. It makes eminent sense to examine the primary obligations created by treaties on a case-by-case basis to determine if fault is an ingredient or element of the breach giving rise to a wrong. If fault is an element or ingredient of a particular primary obligation, then it is a requirement of SR for the breach of that obligation. If not, we should imply fault only if there are other reasons for so doing. If, for example, the obligation we are examining is the one restated in Article 21 of the Stockholm Declaration of the United Nations Conference on the Environment (Stockholm Declaration), the fact that it does not require the transboundary harm to be caused intentionally or negligently suggests that fault is not a requirement [*Stockholm Declaration of the United Nations Conference on the Environment*, 16 Jun. 1972, 11 I.L.M. 1416 at art. 21].

ii. Strict and Absolute Liability

The concepts of strict and absolute liability have not been authoritatively defined, but standards of strict liability are less rigorous than absolute liability. Strict liability may constitute no more than a reversal of the burden of proof, allowing a defending State to establish circumstances precluding wrongfulness or liability. Absolute or objective liability, on the other hand, is more conclusive and prohibits, or very severely limits, evidence of circumstances precluding liability. For example, the Space Liability Convention illustrates absolute liability under a SR regime. Where damage is caused to the surface of the earth or to an aircraft in flight, it asserts that, "[a] launching State shall be absolutely liable to pay compensation for damage caused by its space object" [Space Liability Convention at art. II]. The Space Liability

Convention also draws a distinction between absolute liability [*Id.* at art. II] and fault liability [*Id.* at art. III]. While absolute liability is imposed for damage to the surface of the earth [*Id.* at art. II], damage resulting elsewhere can result in liability only where fault is established [*Id.* at art. III].

Other examples are taken from regimes dealing with CL (*see below*), but are illustrative of the common distinction between absolute and strict liability. The 1969 CLC, as amended by the Protocol of 1992, demonstrates strict liability. It places liability for oil spills on the owner of the ship, subject to exceptions in limited circumstances, such as war, hostilities, certain kinds of natural phenomena, and acts of a third party [1969 CLC at art. III(2)]. Four conventions on nuclear liability implement a system of absolute liability, even though that term is not expressly mentioned: (1) the Convention on Third Party Liability in the Field of Nuclear Energy (Paris Nuclear Liability Convention); (2) the Vienna Nuclear Liability Convention; (3) the 1962 Convention on the Liability of Operators of Nuclear Ships (not in force); and (4) the Convention Relating to Civil Liability in the Field of Maritime Carriage of Nuclear Materials (Maritime Carriage of Nuclear Materials Convention) [*Convention Relating to Civil Liability in the Field of Maritime Carriage of Nuclear Materials*, Jul. 15, 1975, 974 U.N.T.S. 255 (hereinafter Maritime Carriage of Nuclear Materials Convention)]. Like the 1969 CLC, they allow for certain very limited exceptions based on armed conflict and civil war.

iii. Attribution, Reparation, Causation, and Exhaustion of Local Remedies

Apart from proving the breach of an obligation, with or without fault, a wrongful act must be attributed to a State for SR to arise. In the case of environmental wrongs, the acts resulting in the wrong must be laid at the feet of the State or an agency of the State. The Draft Articles on SR state that the legislative, executive, or judicial conduct of any State organ shall be considered an act of the State [Draft Articles on SR at art. 6].

Because private parties often commit transboundary environmental harms, it is necessary to attribute the wrong to the agency or government department that authorized, mandated, or failed to prevent the wrongful action. The Draft Articles on SR state that the actions of private parties shall be attributed to the State where they are acting under "the direction or control" of a State [*Id.* at art. 8]. Thus, for example, if an industrial plant owned by a private corporation but subject to the regulatory direction or control of a State causes transboundary harm, could the conduct of the corporation be attributed to the State?

Attributing the actions of a corporation to a State under Article 8 is very difficult because it involves proving a direct agency relationship. Furthermore, it must be demonstrated that the State gave specific directions, or exercised explicit control over the actions of the corporation. In their commentaries to the Draft Articles on SR, the ILC concluded that, as a general rule, the conduct of private persons and corporations is not attributable to the State under public international law [*Id.* at Part 2].

In dealing with Article 8, the ILC considered the example of a State-owned and controlled enterprise. They concluded that *prima facie* the conduct of even such an enterprise is not attributable to the State. Given the opinion of the ILC, it is going to be substantially more difficult to attribute the conduct of a private corporation to a State. In sum, this means that the actions of a private corporation can only be attributed to a State under Article 8 in very exceptional circumstances. Such circumstances should demonstrate explicit control and direction exercised by the State over the impugned actions of a corporation.

The ICJ confirmed this strict interpretation of Article 8 in the *Bosnia case*. In that case, Serbia and Montenegro alleged that the former Yugoslavia (now Bosnia and Hertzgovania) was responsible for committing genocide. The ICJ discussed the question of whether, although not organs of Serbia in general, the perpetrators were acting under Serbian "direction and control" "in carrying out the conduct" under Article 8. The decision of the ICJ followed the reasoning and "effective control" test it used in the earlier case of the *Military and Paramilitary Activities* (*Nicaragua case*) [*Military and Paramilitary Activities (Nicar. v. U.S.),* 1986 I.C.J. 14, 110 (Jun. 27) (hereinafter *Nicaragua case*)].

Applying the "effective control" test from the *Nicaragua case* to the *Bosnia case,* the ICJ concluded that the State will be responsible for non-state actors to the extent that "they acted in accordance with that [S]tate's instructions or under its effective control" [*Bosnia case* at 287]. This responsibility requires direction or control by Serbia over specific, identifiable events of the genocide. General control over the direction of operations is inadequate; there must have been specific control over the international wrongful act. The ICJ explained that, "[i]t must however be shown that this 'effective control' was exercised, or that the State's instructions were given, in respect of each operation in which the alleged violations occurred, not generally in respect of the overall actions taken by the persons or groups of persons having committed the violations" [*Id.*].

A State found responsible for an internationally wrongful act is first obligated to cease a continuing wrong, and, having done so, to offer assurances and guarantees of non-repetition if the facts so warrant [Draft Articles on SR at art. 30]. Second, it is required to make full reparation for the injury the wrongful act caused [*Id.* at art. 31]. Reparation takes the form, either singly or in different combinations, of three remedies: restitution, compensation, and satisfaction [*Id.* at art. 34].

Restitution is the obligation to establish the situation that existed before the wrongful act was committed. Such a reinstatement of pre-existing conditions is subject to the proviso that it is not materially impossible, or "out of all proportion to the benefit deriving from restitution instead of compensation" [*Id.* at art. 35]. Where restitution is not feasible, a State responsible for an international wrong is under an obligation to compensate. Compensation covers any financially assessable damage [*Id.* at art. 36]. Where an injury cannot be made good by restitution or compensation, an aggrieving State is under an obligation to give satisfaction that may take the form of "an acknowledgement of the breach, an expression of regret, a formal apology or another appropriate modality" [*Id.* at art. 37].

In addition, a claimant for judicial remedies, whether based on SR, CL, or international liability (IL) (*see* below) must prove causation. This can present difficulties, particularly where there is more than one source of the impugned pollutant, as illustrated by the case of acid rain. Sweden, for instance, had to resort to very elaborate monitoring and measuring devices to trace the source of acid rain to a particular suspect country, whether it was the United Kingdom or Germany, or both.

As to whether there is an additional requirement of damage, the ILC in its commentary states:

It is sometimes said that international responsibility is not engaged by conduct of a State in disregard of its obligations unless some further element exists, in particular, "damage" to another State [*Id.* at art. 2(9)].

But whether such further event must occur depends on the content of the primary obligation, and there is no general rule in this respect. For example, the obligation under a treaty to enact a uniform law is breached by the failure to enact the law, and it is not necessary for another State party to point to any specific damage it has suffered by reason of that failure. Whether a particular obligation is breached forthwith upon a failure to act on the part of the responsible State, or whether some further event must occur, depends on the content and interpretation of the primary obligation and cannot be determined in the abstract.

There is also a procedural rule, subject to exceptions, regarding the exhaustion of local (national) remedies before instituting an international action. According to the Draft Articles on SR, the responsibility of a State may not be invoked if "the claim is one to which the rule of exhaustion of local remedies applies and any available and effective local remedy has not been exhausted" [*Id.* at art. 44(b)].

iv. Trail Smelter Arbitration

Trail Smelter, a well-known public international law case dealing with transboundary pollution, is invariably cited in any discussion of SR (*see* Ch. 14) [*Trail Smelter Arbitration,* (U.S. v. Can.) 3 R.I.A.A. 1938 (1949)]. The facts of that case also serve the double purpose of illustrating how a CL system under national law could have dealt with the transboundary wrongs suffered in that case. In *Trail Smelter*, sulfur dioxide fumes from a Canadian smelter were causing damage in the state of Washington in the U.S. Farmers who suffered damage were prevented from bringing an action in U.S. courts because they would have encountered jurisdictional difficulties. The first of these jurisdictional problems arose from the fact that the company owning the smelters had its place of business and was registered in Canada. A second jurisdictional problem arose from the *locus delicti,* or the fact that the act that initiated the damage, and therefore the tort, occurred in Canada.

Even if the plaintiffs had been able to overcome this difficulty and persuade a U.S. court to assume jurisdiction on the basis that the harm inflicted or damage suffered was in the U.S., they still faced other difficulties. Another problem was the proper law to be applied by the court. Should it be Canadian or U.S. law? If the applicable law were Canadian, to what extent did Canadian law permit recovery of damages in cases where the harm suffered was in a jurisdiction different from that in which it originated? The doctrine of *forum non conveniens,* or the appropriate forum for an action, raised a different question: were the U.S. courts an appropriate forum for deciding a case such as this?

These were among the reasons that it was necessary for the U.S. to espouse and advocate the claims of the Washington farmers and negotiate a treaty (known as the *Convention for the Settlement of Difficulties arising from Operations of Smelter at Trail, B.C.* (1935)) in which Canada accepted responsibility for provable damage. An arbitral tribunal was created under that treaty to find a solution that was just to all parties. The principles articulated by that arbitral tribunal in deciding this case have become one of the pillars of SR. The arbitrators determined that:

> Under the principles of international law, . . . no state has the right to use or permit the use of its territory in such a manner as to cause injury by fumes in or to the territory of another, or properties or persons therein when the case is of serious consequence and the injury is established by clear and convincing evidence [*Id.*].

It went on to conclude that:

> [The] Dominion of Canada is responsible in international law for the conduct of the Trail Smelter. Apart from the undertakings in the Convention, it is, therefore, the duty of the Government of the Dominion of Canada to see to it that this conduct should be in conformity with the obligation of the Dominion under international law as herein determined [*Id.*].

b. International Liability (IL)

As we have noted, the ILC's SR regime limits the application of SR to wrongful acts (i.e. those cases where a State causes injury through an act prohibited by treaty or custom). In reality, however, the conduct of one State can give rise to injury within the territory of other States without violating any such rule of treaty or customary law. Responding to this challenge, the ILC drafted a set of Draft Articles aimed at defining a State's liability for damages caused by acts that are not violations of international law. It should be noted from the outset that IL deals primarily with "non-wrongful" acts. The terms wrongful and non-wrongful can be deceptive because their usage typically invokes a moral component. But, as we have noted, non-wrongful means only that the act in question does not happen to violate an existing rule of international law. The more difficult and largely unresolved task lies in defining the non-wrongful acts to which IL attaches.

The ILC's work on IL has been plagued by conceptual difficulties since its inception. Critics have argued that the division between SR and IL creates unnecessary complication, and rests on an infirm conceptual basis [*see,* for example, Alan E. Boyle, *State Responsibility and International Liability for Injurious Consequences Not Prohibited by International Law: A Necessary Distinction?* 39 INT'L & COMP. L.Q. 1 (1990)]. Such critics suggest that it would have been simpler to consider all injurious acts (whether wrongful or not) under the single rubric of SR. In their view, SR could form a continuum, giving rise to a spectrum of liability, depending on the gravity of the injury. An injured State would thereby be free to invoke a suite of remedies that included reparation as well as compensation.

In practical terms, the forging of a new rubric called IL, as distinct from SR, may not have created significant new difficulties. This is because the real challenge is to define the non-wrongful acts (or acts not prohibited by international law) to which IL attaches. This is a ubiquitous difficulty that remains problematic whether encountered under the rubric of IL (as the ILC would have it) or under the heading of SR (as the critics prefer.) However, the ILC's separate treatment of wrongful and non-wrongful acts affirms the "legal" character of international law by emphasizing the difference between acts that violate international law and those that do not.

The twin objectives of the ILC in undertaking the codification of IL for non-wrongful acts was to provide compensation to injured States (liability) as well as to deter or prevent putatively liable States from undertaking the actions in question, or at least take adequate measures to minimize the risk of potential harms (prevention). The ILC focused primarily on the prevention objective, reasoning "pride of place would be given to the duty to avoid or minimize injury, rather than to the substituted duty to provide reparation for the injury caused" [International Law Commission, *Yearbook of the International Law Commission 34th Session,* U.N. Doc. A/CN.4/SER.A/1982/Add.1 (Part 2) (1983) at 86]. Impelled by the force of this logic, the ILC further divided IL into two topics: prevention and liability, and focused on the former rather than the latter. Pursuant to this decision, the ILC's work on prevention led to a set of Draft Articles on the Prevention of Transboundary Harm from Hazardous Activities (Draft Articles on Prevention) [International Law Commission, *Draft Articles on Prevention of Transboundary Harm from Hazardous Activities,* (2001) A/56/10 (hereinafter Draft Articles on Prevention)].

Under the current Draft Articles on Prevention, the ILC has come up with a procedure by which a State must notify, consult, arbitrate, and negotiate with potentially affected States before engaging in non-wrongful acts "which involve a risk of causing significant transboundary harm" [*Id.* at art. 1]. So far, the ILC has not compiled a more specific list of acts falling under the scope of their prevention Articles.

The ILC submitted the current Draft Articles on the Prevention to the UN General Assembly at its 56th session in 2001, with the recommendation that a convention be held to produce a treaty concerning them. The General Assembly has not yet done so.

The work on liability for injurious activities that do not constitute a violation of international law, commenced in 1997, and after much deliberation the ILC adopted a new set of Articles in 2006: Draft Principles on the Allocation of Loss [International Law Commission, *Draft Principles on the Allocation of Loss in the Case of Transboundary Harm Arising out of Hazardous Activities* (2006) A/61/10]. These Articles are based on the recognition that incidents involving hazardous activities might arise despite State compliance with obligations relating to preventive measures. It also underscores the harm that might arise in such circumstances. The principles provide for prompt and adequate compensation for the victims of harm. Significantly, these remedies are based on a primary regime of operator-based CL, with the State being responsible to ensure that adequate financial resources are made available for compensating victims [*Id.* at Principle 4]. These principles offer a bridge to CL.

c. Civil Liability (CL)

While States painfully and slowly struggle to set up rules of compensation under SR, or prevention of transboundary harm under the rubric of IL, they have also set up a third set of rules and regimes based on CL, which channels responsibility for an environmental wrong to the polluter rather than the State. CL regimes are usually established by treaty and place only residual duties upon States (which could give rise to SR). Regimes of CL have the potential to be expanded into more effective vehicles of environmental protection than those based on SR or IL.

It is worth considering the extent and manner in which the farmers in *Trail Smelter* case could have been compensated through other legal procedures. For example, the U.S. and Canada could have entered into a treaty in which their respective courts were granted jurisdiction to hear cases where damage occurred outside their ordinary jurisdiction. This approach might follow the recommendations of the OECD, which provides for access to domestic courts and remedies by national and foreign entities on a non-discriminatory basis [Organization for Economic Cooperation and Development (OECD), *Recommendation of the Council for the Implementation of a Regime of Equal Access and Non-discrimination in Relation to Transfrontier Pollution,* May 17, 1977, 16 I.L.M. 977 (1977)]. It could also have ensured that an order by a court vested with jurisdiction under the treaty could be enforced in either country.

This principle of non-discrimination has now been incorporated into the Convention on the Law of the Non-Navigational Uses of International Watercourses (Convention on International Watercourses) [*Convention on the Law of the Non-Navigational Uses of International Watercourses*, 21 May 1997 (entered into force 17 Aug. 2014), 36 I.L.M. 700 (hereinafter Convention on International Watercourses)] Article 32 avers that watercourse States shall not discriminate against injured parties on the basis of nationality, residence, or place where the injury occurred in granting persons access to judicial or other areas of remedial justice [*Id.* at 32].

Claims based on CL enjoy substantial advantages over those originating in SR or IL. To begin with, an individual victim of environmental damage has direct access to justice, whether courts or administrative agencies, and does not have to await espousal or adoption by his/her country. As we have seen, decisions to prosecute claims based on SR are taken only in rare circumstances and victims are often held hostage to the politics of their own country. Second, even where States premise their case on SR, the time taken in doing so often is inordinately long because the machinery of States is notoriously slow. Third, in SR, the victim is forced to rely upon the State, not an advocate or attorney of his/her choosing, to present and argue the case. Fourth, the absence of a liability regime in SR makes recovery of damages very difficult. Admittedly, a victim who files an action in a foreign State faces some obstacles arising from the differences of legal systems, language, procedure, and execution. But a constitutive treaty establishing a CL regime can address these difficulties. The constitutive treaty could place duties on the contracting parties relating to non-discrimination, access to justice, and security for payment of damages, and thereby remove or ameliorate these difficulties.

i. Treaty Overlay

Where CL regimes are created, the primary responsibility for environmental harm is usually placed on the polluter and not the State. It is important to note that this places the burden of compensation on private corporations and individuals. Such modalities for doing justice to the aggrieved parties have in fact been created by a number of treaties. UNCLOS, which is emerging as a "constitution" for the oceans, requires States to "ensure that recourse is available in accordance with their legal systems for prompt and adequate compensation or other relief in respect of damage caused by pollution of the marine environment by natural or juridical persons under their jurisdiction" [UNCLOS at art. 235(2)]. CL remedies against private and corporate entities are also underscored by a number of other treaties.

The Convention on International Watercourses, following the OECD recommendation, expressed the principle that domestic or national courts can and should grant environmental relief and compensation as one of "non-discrimination." Where a person suffers or is under a serious threat of suffering significant transboundary harm, the State in which the harm originated should grant the injured person "in accordance with its legal system, access to judicial or other procedures, or a right to claim compensation or other relief" [Convention on International Watercourses at art. 32].

The same principle is embodied in a cluster of other treaties dealing with a range of activities, including the peaceful use of nuclear energy, the operation of nuclear ships, maritime carriage of nuclear materials, oil pollution, and the carriage of dangerous goods by road, rail, and inland navigation vessels [Bjorn Sandvik & Satu Suikkari, *Harm and Reparation in International Treaty Regimes: An Overview,* HARM TO THE ENVIRONMENT: THE RIGHT TO COMPENSATION AND THE ASSESSMENT OF DAMAGES, Peter Wetterstein, ed., (1997) at 57–58; *North American Agreement on Environmental Cooperation* (1993), 32 I.L.M. 1480 at arts. 5 & 6 (hereinafter NAAEC); *Convention on the Regulation of Antarctic Mineral Resource Activities* (CRAMRA), Jun. 2, 1988, 27 I.L.M. 859 (not in force) at art. 8 (hereinafter CRAMRA)]. For example, the Vienna Nuclear Liability Convention places liability on the operator of the nuclear installation alone [Vienna Nuclear Liability Convention at art. II (5)], and restricts jurisdiction solely to the courts of the State where the accident occurred [*Id.* at art 11]. Rather than being held responsible for the actions of the operator according to the principles of SR, the State is under a more limited duty to ensure that any claims against the operator are satisfied through the availability of funds and the necessary security [*Id.* at art. 9]. Failure to fulfill this limited duty, however, could give rise to SR.

The field of oil pollution is governed by a cluster of treaties, including the 1969 CLC, the Protocol to Amend the 1969 CLC [*Protocol of 1992 to Amend the International Convention on Civil Liability for Oil Pollution Damage of 29 November 1969,* Nov. 26, 1992, AST 1996 No. 2 (hereinafter Protocol to Amend the 1969 CLC)], the International Convention on the Establishment of an International Fund for Compensation for Oil Pollution Damage (Fund Convention) [*International Convention on the Establishment of an International Fund for Compensation for Oil Pollution Damage,* Dec. 18, 1971 (entered into force Oct. 16, 1978), 1971 U.N. Jur. Y.B. 103 (hereinafter Fund Convention)], and the Protocol to the Fund Convention [*International Maritime Organization Protocol of 1992 to amend the International Convention on the Establishment of an International Fund for Compensation for Oil Pollution damage of 18 December 1971,* Nov. 27, 1992, AST 1996 No. 3 (hereinafter Protocol to the Fund Convention)]. Like the treaties dealing with civilian nuclear power, these oil pollution treaties place liability for oil pollution damage on the owner of the oil, or other individuals or corporations involved in the enterprise of the carriage of oil from one location to another [Gotthard Gauci, OIL POLLUTION AT SEA: CIVIL LIABILITY AND COMPENSATION FOR DAMAGE (1997) at 89–119].

Again, these treaties do not establish a regime of SR under public international law.

The Nagoya-Kuala Lumpur Supplementary Protocol On Liability And Redress To The Cartagena Protocol On Biosafety (Nagoya Protocol) [*Nagoya-Kuala Lampur Supplementary Protocol on Liability and Redress* (2010), BS-V/11 (hereinafter Nagoya Protocol)] also offers a template for CL. The Nagoya Protocol applies to damage resulting from living modified organisms that find their origin in a transboundary movement. It sets up a system of CL, under which the parties shall provide, in their domestic law, for rules and procedures that address damage. To implement this obligation, parties may apply their existing domestic law, including, where applicable, general rules and procedures on CL; apply or develop CL rules and procedures specifically for this purpose; or apply or develop a combination of both.

In drawing up their laws the parties are required to address: damage; standard of liability, including strict or fault-based liability; channeling of liability, where appropriate; and the right to bring a claim. The parties may provide for financial limits to the CL claims. The Nagoya Protocol explicitly states that it shall not affect the rights and obligations of States under the rules of general international law with respect to the responsibility of States for internationally wrongful acts.

The North American Agreement on Environmental Cooperation (NAAEC) also provides national remedies of a more limited nature. This environmental side agreement to the North American Free Trade Agreement (NAFTA) obligates each party to ensure that judicial, quasi-judicial, and administrative proceedings are available under its laws to sanction or remedy violations of its environmental laws [NAAEC at art. 5(2)]. It grants access to and empowers interested private persons to seek relief by way of damages or injunctions in the courts of that State party where the laws of that party have been broken [*Id.* at art. 6(2) & (3)]. While NAAEC opens the door to persons other than those within the jurisdiction of the State party concerned, the cause of action is limited to the breach of the laws of that party. Unlike the regimes dealing with civilian nuclear power or oil pollution, the agreement does not create a new regime of environmental laws that can be vindicated in the national courts of any of the State parties.

ii. Civil Liability (CL) Litigation

A CL case from Europe, in which the plaintiffs claimed environmental damages based on tort, illuminates the extent to which national courts can deal with cases of transboundary environmental injury, provided they are vested with appropriate jurisdiction by international agreement. The international agreement that enabled this case to proceed was the Convention on the Jurisdiction and the Enforcement of Judgments in Civil and Commercial Matters (Enforcement of Judgments Convention), [*Convention on the Jurisdiction and the Enforcement of Judgments in Civil and Commercial Matters*, Sept. 27, 1968, 15 1972 O.J. (L 299) at 32 (hereinafter   Enforcement   of   Judgments Convention)]. The Enforcement of Judgments Convention established uniform jurisdictional rules for national courts in the Member States of the then EEC, now the EU, regarding disputes between parties domiciled in different Member States.

In *Bier v. Mines de Potasse d'Alsace SA*, a French company in Alsace discharged massive amounts of chlorides into the Rhine [*Bier v. Mines de Potasse d'Alsace SA* (1976) ECR 1735]. The chlorides allegedly damaged nursery gardens in Holland, and the Dutch Supreme Court upheld the assertion of jurisdiction by a Dutch court, despite the argument that releasing the chlorides into the Rhine was lawful at the points of discharge in Alsace, France. The European Court of Justice affirmed, basing its jurisdiction on the Enforcement of Judgments Convention. Subsequently, a Dutch court applied Dutch law concerning environmental damage, and found for the complainants, rejecting the defense that the conduct was lawful [Andreas F. Lowenfeld, INTERNATIONAL LITIGATION AND THE QUEST FOR REASONABLENESS (1996) at 30].

In another case from Europe, the case of the *Sandoz fire*, complainants also pursued CL claims instead of SR [*see* Hans Ulrich Jessurun d'Oliveira, *The Sandoz Blaze: The Damage and the Public and Private Liabilities,* INTERNATIONAL RESPONSIBILITY FOR ENVIRONMENTAL HARM, Francesco Francioni & Tullio Scovazzi, eds. (1991) at 434–443]. In October 1986, a fire broke out in a chemical warehouse belonging to Sandoz, a major chemical manufacturer in Switzerland. The warehouse, also located on the banks of the Rhine, contained large quantities of pesticides and other harmful chemicals, and firefighters employed unsophisticated fire fighting methods, using huge quantities of water to extinguish the fire. Ten to fifteen thousand cubic meters of water, containing over 30 tons of toxic chemicals—including insecticides, herbicides, and fungicides—flowed directly into the Rhine due to the absence of a catchment area, which is customarily built as a precautionary measure to prevent this kind of direct discharge from chemical plants. The runoff seriously damaged fisheries, killed eels, and severely damaged the fauna and flora of the Rhine. It also posed grave threats to human health in France, Germany, and particularly Holland, where the Rhine constituted the primary source of drinking water.

There are a number of treaties protecting the Rhine against pollution to which Switzerland was a party. Moreover, the facts disclosed that numerous provisions of these treaties, relating to the care, storage, auditing, and emergency measures pertaining to the chemicals in the warehouse, had been violated. Despite this evidence, there were no claims based on SR, and none of the injured States made any direct claims against the Swiss Confederation for damages suffered.

Professor Hans Ulrich Jessurun d'Oliviera has commented that the German, French, and Dutch governments privatized their claims by seeking reparations against Sandoz, rather than the Swiss government. His observations reinforce the political reality that States will not litigate issues based on SR for good reason. The majority of claims were settled out of court, with the help of the Swiss government, within three years.

This contrasts to the fourteen years taken over the *Mines de Potasse d'Alsace* case, and the ten years for the *Amoco-Cadiz* litigation [*Id.* at 440–41]. The *Amoco Cadiz* was a very large crude oil carrier, owned by Amoco and carrying over 1,600,000 thousand barrels of crude oil, that ran aground about three miles from the coast of Brittany, France in 1978, and ultimately split in three and sank. The resulting oil spill was the largest of its kind to that date. While the riparian States did not pursue actions based on SR in the *Sandoz fire* case, it is open to conjecture whether the possibility of an action based on SR induced the Swiss government to exert pressure on Sandoz to settle the cases.

d. Conclusions on Accountability for Transboundary Environmental Harms

The last ten years have yielded remarkable developments in the regimes of SR and IL. The Draft Articles on SR have illuminated and clarified the complex and complicated laws dealing with SR, and have established the foundation on which the regime of SR can continue to be built. At the same time, the new directions in which IL has developed augur well for IEL. In restating the rules governing the prevention of transboundary harm from hazardous activities, the ILC has set the stage for the transformation of IEL from an *ex post* to an *ex ante* law.

These developments have been complemented by the emergence of new international laws based on CL, which break away from the inherited system of state-controlled law that gave rise to SR and IL. We live in a world in which national and international laws and regulations governing corporations and individuals in matters of trade, commerce, health, communications, and the environment have become more important than those controlling States. This necessarily means that SR and IL will lose their primacy as the principal legal instruments for governing environmental protection. CL opens the door to NGOs and other private parties to use the legal system to protect the environment in a way not permitted by SR or IL.

In judging the success or failure of the CL treaties, the importance of empirical evidence backing any such claims cannot be overemphasized. The absence of such data renders any judgment more impressionistic than objective. There is little empirical data on which to judge the real impact of existing CL regimes. Even on the formal level the present state of ratification of the nuclear liability treaties is patchy. The Vienna Nuclear Liability Convention has by far the widest participation, with 40 parties, compared to the Paris Nuclear Liability Convention's 16 parties, with only two ratifications of the 2004 Protocol. Six states—the U.S., Argentina, India, Morocco, Romania, and the United Arab Emirates—have ratified the Convention on

Supplementary Compensation for Nuclear Damage [*Convention on Supplementary Compensation for Nuclear Damage,* Sept. 12, 1997, 36 I.L.M. 1473]; and 17 States have ratified or become parties to Maritime Carriage of Nuclear Materials Convention.

The new developments discussed above do not mean that remedies based on SR and IL completely lose their utility or their importance. Instead, SR and IL assume new significance and vitality when used as interlocking remedies in conjunction with CL. Many CL regimes are established by treaties that place subsidiary, but nonetheless important, duties on States. For example, the Vienna Nuclear Liability Convention, as amended, makes the operator, and not the State, liable for injuries and damage caused by any accident, but it also requires the State to provide adequate security to ensure that the operators will pay up. A State that does not provide such security will be violating an obligation that may be actionable under SR. Again, in the *Sandoz fire*, the fact that SR could have given rise to actions against Switzerland may have prompted the Swiss government to pressure Sandoz into settlement. There can be little doubt that SR and IL will continue to play an important role in IEL.

G.   INSTITUTIONAL CONCERNS

Thousands of international treaties have established scores of rules, along with some institutional machinery for securing compliance and supervising non-compliance. Sometimes, as we have seen, the treaties also provide judicial remedies. Do all these legal measures make a difference to the way States, corporations, and individuals behave? Much legal analysis centers on the jural nature of treaties, their interpretation and implementation, making the *a priori* assumption that treaties do shape and change the behavior of the relevant parties.

There is, however, a substantial body of *realist* thinking, subscribed to by some of the world's most eminent states-persons, which defines international behavior and practice in terms of geopolitical power rather than law. According to the realists, States agree to treaties, and the rules therein embodied, only because they codify the existing or intended behavior or practice of the parties [*see* Kenneth Thompson, ed., POLITICS AMONG NATIONS: THE STRUGGLE FOR POWER AND PEACE (1993)]. Realists argue that States conform their behavior to treaty provisions because it is in their self-interest to do so, and not because they are obliged to so by law, and thus it would be a mistake to equate this spurious correlation with true causation, as international lawyers tend to do [*see* Ronald B. Mitchell, INTENTIONAL OIL POLLUTION AT SEA (1994) at 28–29].

Despite the strenuous exhortations and exertions of many international lawyers, the core of realist thinking is alive and well, now backed by critical legal studies adherents [Philip Trimble, *International Law, World Order, and Critical Legal Studies*, 42 STAN. L. REV. 811 (1990) at 833–834]. For critical legal studies adherents, the distinction between law and politics exists as an illusion [*see* David Kennedy, *A New Stream of International Law and Politics*, 7 WIS. INT'L. L. J. 1 (1988)]. Legal language—whether embodied in rules, treaties, or aspirational principles—like all language, simply operates in the service of persuasion towards some practical end. As Martii Koskenniemi has suggested, international law is the "practice of attempting to reach the most acceptable solution in the particular circumstances of the case. It is not the application of ready-made, general rules or principles but a conversation about what to do, here and now" [Martii Koskenniemi, *From Apology to Utopia* (1989) at 486].

In response to these realist claims, other scholars have attempted empirical studies to show a statistical connection between treaty provisions and modification of State behavior. In one well known study, a political scientist evaluated the evidence drawn from the control of intentional oil pollution, and concluded that the empirical evidence "unequivocally demonstrates that governments and private corporations have undertaken a variety of actions involving compliance, monitoring, and enforcement that they would not have taken in the absence of relevant treaty provisions" [Ronald Mitchell, INTENTIONAL OIL POLLUTION AT SEA (1994) at 299]. In response, a critical legal studies proponent would argue that the "relevant treaty provisions" simply exist as a political arrangement, and that whatever "compliance, monitoring and enforcement" results from such an arrangement does so out of further political expediency.

Finally, though debate continues as to causal impetus, it is worth reiterating that international law remains a social force that commands respect in the form of compliance. Despite its renowned asymmetry with domestic law, and its publicized defects in lacking a law-making and law-enforcing sovereign, international law does invoke compliance because it governs a law-abiding community of very politically minded States, not a gang of bandits or bank robbers [*see* Roger Fisher, IMPROVING COMPLIANCE WITH INTERNATIONAL LAW (1981) at 16]. Nonetheless, we have already pointed to the difficulties of assessing the true extent of implementation and compliance in the absence of empirical data.

H.   THE RELATION BETWEEN INTERNATIONAL ENVIRONMENTAL LAW (IEL) AND DOMESTIC LAW

A proper grasp and clear understanding of the relationship between national law and international law is of crucial importance to the study of IEL, particularly when clarifying the law of treaties, which impinges so frequently on the domain of national law. While it is unnecessary to explore the theoretical complexities of this discussion, it is important to understand some of the difficulties in the implementation of international obligations arising from the absence of any vertical power structure in the international community.

There are various approaches to the relationship between international and national law, reflected in the texts of the different types of national constitutions around the world. The two principal theories are known as *monism* and *dualism*. According to monism, international law and the national law of States are concomitant aspects of one unified legal system. An example of a monist approach, prevalent in Civil Law States, is reflected in the German legal system:

The general rules of public international law are an integral part of federal law. They shall take precedence over the laws and shall directly create rights and duties for the inhabitants of the federal territory [*Basic Law for the Federal Republic of Germany,* May 23, 1949 at art. 25].

Alternatively, dualism holds that international law and national law represent two entirely distinct legal systems, in which international law possesses a character intrinsically different to national law. The dualist approach is prevalent in Common Law States, such as New Zealand, where the official government policy establishes that treaty-making power is an executive function, but the performance of New Zealand's obligations requires the legislative action of Parliament, which may or may not give its sanction. The document quotes in part:

Once [obligations undertaken in treaties] are created [by the national executive], while they bind the State as against other contracting parties, Parliament may refuse to perform them and so leave the State in default. . . . Parliament will either fulfill or not treaty obligations imposed upon the State by its executive. The nature of the obligation does not affect the complete authority of the Legislature to make them law if it so chooses [*Legislative Change: Guidelines on Process and Content* (rev. ed. 1991) at ¶ 44, appendix E].

The U.S. adopts a mixed dualist-monist approach to the interrelation of national and international laws, and the mottled status of international law in the U.S. illustrates some of the difficulties surrounding these issues. We examine the U.S. approach in greater detail below.

1.   TREATIES AND U.S. DOMESTIC LAW

Although treaty negotiations between States may culminate in the actual signing of the treaty, most States require a domestic ratification procedure before the signature may be given any legal effect. For example, the U.S. Constitution effectively, but not explicitly, deals with the ratification of a treaty in Article II, Section 2, which provides that the President "shall have the Power, by and with the Advice and Consent of the Senate, to make Treaties, provided two-thirds of the Senators present concur" [*United States Constitution* at art. II, sec. 2]. Thus, in the U.S., though the President can sign a treaty, ratification can only occur with a two-thirds vote of approval by the Senate. This separate ratification procedure offers some evidence of the dualist character of international law in the U.S.

While treaties constitute law within the international legal system their status within the realm of U.S. domestic law is more dubious:

This Constitution, and the Laws of the United States which shall be made in Pursuance thereof; and all Treaties made, or which shall be made, under the Authority of the United States, shall be the supreme Law of the Land; and the Judges in every State shall be bound thereby, any Thing in the Constitution or Laws of any State to the Contrary notwithstanding [*Id.* at art. VI, § 2].

The Constitution makes treaties automatically part of the "supreme Law of the Land," however they are afforded parity of status, not supremacy, with the Constitution and acts of Congress. The Constitution does not limit the treaty power explicitly, and no treaty or treaty provision has ever been held unconstitutional, but it is generally agreed that such limitations exist. For example, the Supreme Court held in *Reid v. Covert* that treaties may not contravene any constitutional prohibition, such as those of the Bill of Rights or in the Thirteenth, Fourteenth, and Fifteenth Amendments [*Reid v. Covert*, 354 U.S. 1 (1957)].

The case of *Missouri v. Holland* is especially worthy of note because it concerned the constitutionality of an environmental treaty between the U.S. and Great Britain (for Canada) for the protection of migratory birds [*Missouri v. Holland*, 252 U.S. 416 (1920)]. The treaty provided that the U.S. and Canada would enact legislation prohibiting the "killing, capturing, or selling" of birds except in accordance with regulations promulgated by the federal government. The State of Missouri then brought suit to enjoin enforcement of a federal regulation enacted pursuant to the treaty on the grounds that the powers reserved to it under the Tenth Amendment had been invaded. Prior to this case, Congress had attempted to regulate the hunting of migratory birds through the interstate commerce clause, but the effort was voided on the ground that this was a subject matter left to the separate states under the Tenth Amendment. Thus, as the State of Missouri saw it, the treaty approach, granting Congress power that Congress did not have without the treaty, represented a usurpation of the power of the separate states and, consequently, a subversion of federal-state relations as envisioned by the Framers of the Constitution.

The U.S. Supreme Court largely disposed of the argument that the Tenth Amendment limits the subject matter of treaties. The court asserted that whilst the great body of private relations usually falls within the control of the state, a treaty may override its power where the national interest is at stake. The court held that the national interest of very nearly the first magnitude is involved [*Id.* at 435]. It can be protected only by national action in concert with that of another power. However, it remains possible, as the Court hinted in *DeGeofroy v. Riggs,* that the treaty power may be limited by "restraints . . . arising . . . from the nature . . . of the states" [*DeGeofroy v. Riggs*, 133 U.S. 258 (1890)].

In addition to granting the power to make and enter into treaties, the Framers of the Constitution provided that resulting treaties, together with the duly enacted laws of the U.S., should constitute part of the "supreme Law of the Land." Thus, as well as giving rise to international legal obligations, ratified treaties have force as domestic law, to be applied as federal statutes and, consequently, to prevail at all times over inconsistent state laws (assuming no conflict with the Constitution).

Still, not all treaties are automatically binding on the U.S. Aside from the general constitutional requirement, two additional conditions must exist for treaties to have effect domestically. First, a treaty must not conflict with a subsequent act of Congress. This is in keeping with the judiciary's interpretation of the Supremacy Clause, ranking treaties and acts of Congress equally, and therefore ruling that the law later in time prevails. With the sole exception of *Cook v. United States*, cases in this area have involved conflicts between an earlier treaty and a later statute, with the latter prevailing [*Cook v. United States*, 288 U.S. 102 (1933)]. The courts presume, however, that Congress does not intend to supersede treaties, and consequently the courts are disposed toward interpretations that will achieve compatibility between treaties and federal statutes on the same subject.

Second, for a treaty to bind courts it must be "self-executing" or, alternatively, "non-self-executing" but supported by enabling legislation. Such was the holding in *Foster v. Neilson* [*Foster v. Neilson*, 27 U.S. 253 (1829)]. Judicial decisions vary widely in their application of this requirement, however. The distinction between "self-executing" and "non-self-executing" treaties is more easily stated than applied. A determination that a treaty fits one category or the other may be shown to depend on subjective, or even political, considerations.

Although the Constitution is silent on the question of who has the power to suspend or terminate treaties and under what circumstances, it is generally accepted that the President has such power without the advice and consent of the Senate, based on the President's established constitutional authority to conduct the foreign affairs of the U.S. A challenge to the President's authority in this connection has thus far arisen only in the one case of *Goldwater v. Carter*, and that case was decided, on purely jurisdictional grounds, against the challenge [*Goldwater v. Carter*, 481 F. Supp. 949 (D.D.C. 1979)].

2.   CUSTOM AND U.S. DOMESTIC LAW

The status of customary international law within U.S. domestic law is even less certain than the position of treaties. One major reason for its dubious status arises from the omission of custom from such clauses of the Constitution as the Supremacy Clause, quoted above. While the Supremacy Clause unequivocally includes treaty law within the realm of federal law, it does not overtly afford such parity of status to customary law.

The famous case of *The Paquete Habana* offers a baseline from which to assess the place of international custom in U.S. law [*The Paquete Habana,* 175 U.S. 677 (1900)]. In that case, the U.S. President ordered a naval blockade of the Cuban coast "in pursuance of the laws of the U.S., and the law of nations applicable to such cases" [*Id.* at 712]. Two small Cuban fishing vessels were captured and sold in the U.S. as prize vessels. The original owners bought suit to recover those proceeds and the U.S. Supreme Court, sitting as a prize court wrote:

> International law is part of our law, and must be ascertained and administered by the courts of justice of appropriate jurisdiction, as often as questions of right depending upon it are duly presented for their determination. For this purpose, where there is no treaty, and no controlling executive or legislative act or judicial decision, resort must be had to the customs and usages of civilized nations [*Id.* at 700].

Relying upon the first sentence cited above, some commentators argue that this case gives custom an equal status with statutes and treaties [*see*, for example, L. Henkin, *International Law as Law in the United States,* 82 MICH. L.R. 1555 (1984) at 1556]. But such an argument faces a major analytical and legal difficulty. We noted in Chapter 1 that the establishment of customary international law is established by evidence of state practice and *opinio juris*. This means that proponents of an alleged rule of custom may need to rely upon the statements made by various heads of state, including the President, as evidence of practice and *opinio juris*. The President's statements, therefore, can become powerful tools for creating binding international obligations in the form of custom. If that were the case, and custom enjoyed *inter pares* status with treaties, without even the safeguard of Senate approval required for treaties, the door may well be opened for the President unilaterally to create domestically binding law by executive action and even overturn congressional legislation.

The more plausible possibility, that customary international law cannot supersede other sources of federal law, is supported by the second sentence from *The Paquete Habana* cited above. International rules of customary law became relevant in that case because the President had incorporated customary law into his order. The court, therefore, was relying on customary law to the extent that the President adopted it. In fact, U.S. courts will not give effect to customary norms whose existence is denied by the political branches. Moreover, U.S. courts will give special weight to the views of the executive branch in interpreting customary law [*see* Restatement (Third), § 112, cmt. c].

I. CONCLUSIONS

We have tried to identify how the implementation of IEL, be it treaty or custom, can be influenced by the manner and form in which it is incorporated into the domestic laws of states. U.S. law illustrates some of the difficulties surrounding this issue, while accentuating the extent to which customary law may be treated differently from treaty law.

CHAPTER FOUR
POPULATION

A. NATURE OF POPULATION GROWTH

When the first edition of this book was written, approximately 6.88 billion people inhabited our planet [U.N. Population Division, WORLD POPULATION PROSPECTS: THE 2008 REVISION (2008) (hereinafter WPP 2008)]. By July 2015, the world's population had reached 7.3 billion people [United Nations, Department of Economic and Social Affairs, Population Division; *World Population Prospects: The 2015 Revision, Key Findings and Advance Tables,* (2015) Working Paper No. ESA/P/WP.241 at 8 (hereinafter 2015 Revision)]—as previously predicted by the United Nations' (UN) medium variant based projections.

While it took until approximately 1804 for the global population to reach one billion, this figure doubled to two billion by 1927—a span of only 123 years. The global population then reached three billion in 1960 (33 years), four billion in 1974 (14 years), and five billion in 1987 (13 years). A mere 12 years passed for the global population to reach approximately six billion people in 1999 [WPP 2008]. At the current figure of 7.3 billion people, this indicates that the global population has increased by one billion since 2003 [2015 Revision at 8].

While world population continues to grow, the rate at which it is currently growing is slower than in the recent past. Ten years ago world population was growing by approximately 1.24% per year—today it is growing by approximately 1.18% per year [*Id.* at 2]. Still, despite a reduction in the overall rate of population growth, in 2016 it is expected that 83 million people will be added to the world's population [*Id.* at 8]. The UN's medium variant based projections now estimate that global population will reach 8.5 billion in 2030, 9.7 billion in 2050, and 11.2 billion in 2100 [*Id.*].

A great deal of the overall increase in global population is expected to occur in either high-fertility countries, mostly located in Africa, or in countries that already have large populations [*Id.* at 4]. Between now and 2050, half of the world's population growth is projected to occur within just nine countries: India, Nigeria, Pakistan, Democratic Republic of the Congo, Ethiopia, United Republic of Tanzania, the U.S., Indonesia, and Uganda, listed according to the size of their contribution to total future growth [*Id.*].

Africa is the fastest growing major area, experiencing a growth rate of 2.55% annually between 2010 and 2015 [*Id. at 3*]. While Nigeria currently has the seventh largest population in the world, it is growing more rapidly than any other country [*Id.*]. Nigeria's population is predicted to surpass the U.S. by about 2050, whereupon it will become the third largest country in the world [*Id.*].

After Africa, the second largest contributor to future population growth is likely to be Asia, adding an estimated 0.9 billion people between 2015 and 2050 [*Id.*]. The population of China, however, is expected to remain fairly constant until the 2030s, after which it may even decrease slightly [*Id.* at 4]. North America, Latin America, and the Caribbean and Oceania are projected to have much smaller increments of growth—while Europe is actually projected to have a smaller population in 2050 than it does in 2015 [*Id.*] Several countries may even see their populations decline by more than 15% by 2050, including Bosnia and Herzegovina, Bulgaria, Croatia, Hungary, Japan, Latvia, Lithuania, Republic of Moldova, Romania, Serbia, and Ukraine [*Id.*].

Despite the slowed rate of growth on the global scale, population growth rates still remain especially high in the group of 48 countries designated by the UN as least developed countries (LDCs), 27 of which are in Africa [*Id.*]. While growth rates in LDCs may slow slightly in the future, the population of this group is still projected to double in size from 954 million people in 2015 to 1.9 billion people by 2050, with a further increase to 3.2 billion by 2100 [*Id.*]. Between 2015 and 2100, populations in many LDCs have a high probability of at least tripling; and the populations of Angola, Burundi, Democratic Republic of Congo, Malawi, Mali, Niger, Somalia, Uganda, United Republic of Tanzania, and Zambia are projected to increase by at least five-fold by 2100 [*Id.*]. Continued population growth in LDCs will create challenges for these governments in addressing hunger and undernourishment, eradicating poverty, scaling up water and sanitation infrastructure, and improving the provision of basic services of health and education [United Nations,

Department of Economic and Social Affairs, Population Division, *Population 2030: Demographic opportunities for sustainable development planning,* (2015) ST/ESA/SER.A.389 at 1 (hereinafter Population 2030)]. It will also increase the challenge of protecting the environment and implementing the other elements of a sustainable development (SD) agenda.

Lastly, while international migration represents a much smaller component of population change than births or deaths, it is worth noting that the impact of migration on population size can be significant in countries that send or receive proportionately large numbers of economic migrants or in those affected by refugee flows [Revision 2015 at 6].

B.   DECREASING RESOURCES

Even over the short term, it can be very difficult to predict rates of economic growth and technological change. Economic forecasts carefully developed by the World Bank and the International Monetary Fund (IMF) extend no more than a few years into the future and are often subject to a high degree of uncertainty [Population 2030 at 1]. Still, the rate of economic and industrial growth has generally kept pace with population increases [United Nations, Department of Economic and Social Affairs, *World Population Monitoring 2001: Population Environmental and Development,* (2001) U.N. Doc. ST/ESA/SER.A/203 at 70 (hereinafter WPM 2001)].

In stark contrast to the uncertainty of economic projections, the future of global population is relatively certain as these estimates are based on demographic processes, such as fertility, that have already taken place in the past [Population 2030 at 1]. Future shifts in demographic characteristics will shape the demand for goods and services as well as the production and consumption patterns that characterize the economy [*Id.*]. In general, as national populations and economies expand, basic resources are dwindling.

Any environmental assessment of population growth must therefore evaluate the extent to which larger numbers of people consuming larger quantities of resources and energy cause damaging environmental impacts leading to the depletion, even the exhaustion, of scarce natural resources. While resources can be grouped in different ways, the classification of resources as non-renewable versus renewable enables us to understand that resources are exhaustible, and that unlimited growth cannot be supported perpetually.

The impact of global population growth on a diminishing natural resource base may be analyzed from a neo-Malthusian perspective (*see* below). For example, it is possible to assess the relationship between rates of population growth and resource depletion primarily in terms of the per capita consumption of these resources in select populations [WPM 2001 at 71]. While this analysis presents a gloomy prospect, there are other ways of analyzing the same phenomena. While population growth certainly poses challenges to SD, some developmental experts think the demographic changes projected to take place over the coming years may present additional opportunities to facilitate the financing and delivery of services, such as health and education, and to accelerate economic growth and poverty reduction [Population 2030 at 1–2].

The type of solutions offered to the problem of population growth and resource depletion will often depend on the rigidity with which an assessment adheres to a particular focus. Thus, while the following offers a brief summation of assessments using the perspectives more fully discussed below, it is important to keep in mind that no single perspective fully encapsulates the problems surrounding resource depletion and global population.

On the whole, human impact on the environment is determined by three intersecting factors: (1) population growth; (2) economic growth, which shapes production and consumption demands; and (3) technological advancements, which influence the efficiency and impact of the human consumption of resources [B. Commoner, M. Corr, & P.J. Stamler, *The causes of pollution*, (1971) Environment, vol. 13 no. 3 at 2–19; Ehrlich, P., and P. Holdren, *Impact of population growth*, (1971), Science, vol. 171 at 1212]. Thus, the impact of population growth on natural resources will depend on consumption and production patterns and the degree to which technological advancements can reduce humanity's global environmental footprint [Population 2030 at 1].

It is abundantly clear that richer countries consume more natural resources than poorer countries. To illustrate this point, compare the electricity usage of the U.S. and Nigeria. The U.S. is one of the largest and richest countries in the world, with a gross domestic product (GDP) of 14,451.51 billion dollars as of 2013 (in 2005 U.S. dollars) [International Energy Agency, *Key World Energy Statistics,* (2015) at 56–57 *available at* www.iea.org (last visited Apr. 2017)]. In 2013, the U.S. consumed 4,109.84 Terawatt-hours (TWh) of electricity (when considering gross production and imports minus exports and losses) [*Id.*]. This amounts to 12,987 kilowatt-hours (kWh) per person in the U.S. [*Id.*]. Alternatively, Nigeria, which we have already identified as the fastest growing country that will soon surpass the population of the U.S., had a GDP of only 183.31 billion dollars as of 2013 [*Id.* at 54–55]. Nigeria consumed 24,53 TWh of electricity in 2013— which is only 141 kWh per person [*Id.*].

A similar disparity is found when comparing the carbon dioxide (CO_2) emissions from fuel combustion in the U.S. and Nigeria. As of 2013, the U.S. emitted 5,199.70 megatons (Mt) of CO_2—which is 16.18 tons per capita [*Id.* at 56–57]. Nigeria, on the other hand, emitted only 61 Mt of CO_2—which is merely 0.35 tons per capita [*Id.* at 54–55]. The data clearly indicates that industrialized countries, which comprise a small segment of the total global population, consume a much larger proportion of global energy resources and produce a great deal more emissions than developing countries. Many LDCs contribute negligibly to global CO_2 emissions. From this perspective, overpopulation in the industrialized countries is the most important population problem.

At the same time, one cannot dismiss the actual impact of rapidly increasing numbers of human beings in developing countries. Larger numbers of people consuming larger quantities of resources leads to damaging environmental impacts and to the over-utilization of natural resources. Regardless of how one measures the current and future rate of global population growth, it is apparent this growth will have adverse environmental consequences [WPM 2001 at 71].

In a seminal examination of natural resource policy, researchers from the Massachusetts Institute of Technology found that at least 19 important natural resources were seriously depleted and would be exhausted in the foreseeable future [Meadows, et al. LIMITS TO GROWTH (1972)]. Though wrong about some conclusions, their original thesis about the finite nature of resources is buttressed by the fact that the physical environment is itself a resource. Climate change, loss of biodiversity, and depletion of the ozone layer are all related to consumption rates and growing populations, whose demands for material needs must be supplied by industry. Industry, in turn, uses natural resources and causes pollution in a way that endangers the planet itself. Thus, an essential kernel of *Limits to Growth*, if not its entire thesis, remains true even today.

C. ENVIRONMENTAL THREATS

The environmental impacts of population growth are ubiquitous and universal. For instance, population growth has lead to a greater reliance on oil, gas, and coal for energy, which leads to increased emissions of CO_2 and brings with it the environmental threats of climate change (*see* Ch. 6). Population growth also has a direct impact on agricultural resources, particularly in developing countries where increasing population has lead to environmentally damaging agricultural practices, such as deforestation and poor irrigation methods. While the intent of these practices is often to meet the sustenance needs of growing populations, the end result is often a reduction in the agricultural yield the land is capable of producing. Biodiversity also suffers as a result of this cycle of diminishing returns.

Land degradation is defined as a long-term decline in ecosystem function and it is measured in terms of net primary productivity. According to a report published by the UN Food and Agricultural Organization (FAO) in 2008, 24% of the world's land surface has been degraded [Bai ZG, Dent DL, Olsson L & Schaepman ME, *Global assessment of land degradation and improvement. 1. Identification by remote sensing*, (2008) Report 2008/01, ISRIC—World Soil Information, Wageningen at i]. Not only is this an increase in the overall percentage since the 15% measurement in the 1991 report, but the recent report also shows that the areas of currently degraded land hardly overlap with the previous report, which means that new areas of land are still being degraded [*Id.*]. Conversely, some areas of historical land degradation have become so degraded that they are now considered stable, albeit at very low levels of productivity [*Id.*].

To increase agricultural productivity, scientists have developed high-yield varieties and modified certain crops to be more resistant to adverse conditions, but have typically ignored genetic diversity. The use of irrigation, chemical pesticides, and fertilizers has increased production, but has also contributed to the depletion of arable land suitable for cultivation [*see* Lakshman Guruswamy, *Sustainable Agriculture: Do GMOs Imperil Biosafety?*, 9 IND. J. GLOBAL LEGAL STUD. (2002) at 461; Laura Jackson, *Agricultural Industrialization and the Loss of Biodiversity*, PROTECTION OF GLOBAL BIODIVERSITY: CONVERGING INTERDISCIPLINARY STRATEGIES, Lakshman Guruswamy & Jeffrey McNeely, eds. (1997); Robert Horsch & Robert Fraley, *Biotechnology Can Help Reduce the Loss of Biodiversity*, PROTECTION OF GLOBAL BIODIVERSITY: CONVERGING INTERDISCIPLINARY STRATEGIES, Lakshman Guruswamy & Jeffrey McNeely, eds. (1997)]. The use of pesticides and fertilizers has poisoned soil and water resources, while vermin have become resistant. Overuse of irrigation has resulted in salinization of the soil (build-up of salts and minerals) and waterlogging.

However, while older studies from the FAO showed global food production lagging behind population growth, recent reports present a more optimistic face. Global population growth is the main driver of increases in demand for food, but as population growth slows the demand growth for food is also expected to slow progressively over the next ten years [OECD & Food and Agriculture Organization of the United Nations, *OECD-FOA Agricultural Outlook 2016–2025,* (2016) OECD Publishing, Paris at 17]. In the meantime, continuing increases in food demand are projected to be satisfied through productivity gains and yield improvements [*Id.*]. There is also the potential to increase agricultural area sustainably, mainly in parts of Latin America and Sub-Saharan Africa [*Id.*]

These increases in productivity are projected to reduce the global proportion of people who are undernourished from 11% to 8% over the next ten years, with the total number of undernourished people declining from 788 million to less than 650 million [*Id.*]. However, undernourishment is still a growing issue in Africa, particularly in the Sub-Saharan region. Due to the rapidly growing populations in that area, in ten years the region will account for more than one third of the global total of undernourished individuals, compared with just over a quarter today [*Id.*]

Many countries that have made the least amount of progress in addressing undernourishment have experienced rapid population growth since 1990 [*Id.* at 5]. For example, in the United Republic of Tanzania the population more than doubled between 1990 and 2015, while the proportion of undernourished people increased by 33% [*Id.*]. In 26 countries, more than one in five children are currently severely underweight—and in ten of those countries the number of children under five years of age is projected to increase by more than 20% between 2015 and 2030 [*Id.* at 14]. Thus, achieving progress towards reducing hunger depends not only on feeding the children who currently lack adequate nutrition, but also on meeting the nutritional needs of additional children in the coming years [*Id.* at 14–15]. The implications of population growth present real challenges to progress towards eradicating undernourishment and extreme poverty [Population 2030 at 4].

The extent to which population and hunger are interlinked is underlined by the sustainable development goals (SDGs) that are more fully referenced in Chapter 2. The goal of SDG 1 is to end poverty in all its forms everywhere [United Nations, *Goal 1: End poverty in all its forms everywhere,* Sustainable Development Goals (2015), *available at* http://www.un.org/sustainabledevelopment/poverty/ (last visited Apr. 2017)], and SDG 2 is to end hunger and achieve food security and improved nutrition [United Nations, *Goal 2: End hunger, achieve food security and improved nutrition and promote sustainable agriculture,* Sustainable Development Goals (2015), *available at* http://www.un.org/sustainabledevelopment/hunger/ (last visited Apr. 2017)]. Globally, one in nine people in the world today (795 million) are undernourished, and the vast majority of the world's hungry people live in developing countries, where 12.9% of the population is undernourished [*Id.*]. These are also the countries in which population is growing.

Population growth also impacts the use of freshwater resources. Many countries with a shortage of arable land also have a shortage of freshwater. Over 97% of the water on the earth is salt water (oceans). Of the 3% of earth's water that is freshwater, slightly over two thirds is frozen in glaciers and polar ice caps. The remaining unfrozen freshwater is mainly found as groundwater, with only a small fraction present above ground or in the air [United States Geological Survey, *Earth's Water Distribution* (Feb. 8, 2011)].

SDG 6 specifically relates to water, with a goal of ensuring availability and sustainable management of water and sanitation for all [United Nations, *Sustainable Development Goal 6: Ensure availability and sustainable management of water and sanitation for all,* Sustainable Development Knowledge Platform (2015), *available at* https://sustainable development.un.org/sdg6 (Apr. 2017)]. While only one SDG relates specifically to water, water underpins or is associated with almost all of the other goals due to its multiple impacts on economic growth, environmental health, and human wellbeing. A question arising is to what extent the need to produce more food for a growing population is limiting water availability.

A recent report from the International Water Management Institute in 2014 indicates that population growth may not be the determining factor in water demand projections as previously thought. The review shows that water demand projections from prior to 1990, which considered population as the main driver of change, over-predicted current water use by 20% to 130% [U.A Amarasinghe & V. Smakhtin, *Global water demand projections: past, present and future,* (2014) Colombo, Sri Lanka: International Water Management Institute (IWMI) 10.5337/2014.212 at vii]. Water demand projections made since 1990 have used more sophisticated frameworks, integrating many additional exogenous and endogenous drivers of food and water supply and demand [*Id.*]. However, these methods have yet to be perfected, as the post-1990 water demand projections now show substantial underestimation of water use globally [*Id.*]. For example, the average per capita domestic water withdrawals when the report was written in 2014 already exceeded the projections made in the business as usual scenarios for 2025 [*Id.*]. The results demonstrate that while population growth is a necessary driver of freshwater use, it is not alone sufficient for making accurate projections, and many other drivers must be considered determine water demand [*Id.* at 5]. Still, despite inaccuracies, global water supply and demand studies have a number of benefits, including highlighting areas with physical or economic water scarcity or unsustainable water use where there is a need for immediate action and change [*Id.* at 20].

While there have been significant areas of improvement in global environmental quality during the past decades, this progress has been countervailed by conspicuous deterioration in other areas. Some experts believe that population growth is the major cause of such environmental deterioration [Paul Ehrlich & Anne Ehrlich, THE

POPULATION EXPLOSION (1990); Paul Ehrlich & Anne Ehrlich, EXTINCTION: THE CAUSES AND CONSEQUENCES OF THE DISAPPEARANCE OF SPECIES (1981) at 74]. Others believe that the most powerful factor in determining environmental quality is the technology used to produce goods and services, and that any chosen technology may cause either environmental degradation or improvement [Barry Commoner, *Rapid Population Growth and Environmental Stress*, 21 INT'L J. HEALTH SERVICES (1991) at 199]. It is difficult to deny, however, that population growth, even if not the single most important factor, does have a dramatic impact on the environment [Partha Dasgupta, AN INQUIRY INTO WELL BEING AND DESTITUTION (1995) at 269–96].

D. THEORIES ON POPULATION GROWTH

Experts disagree on how to balance population and economic growth, but almost all agree that current usage rates of essential resources, and the attendant rates of environmental degradation caused by this usage, are not infinitely sustainable. As a corollary to this position, most experts also agree that without a substantial reduction in population growth, or the development of resources capable of significantly attenuating its impact, population growth will eventually exceed the earth's carrying capacity—the maximum number of individuals that can be sustained by the earth's natural resources year after year without diminution in quality of life or resources. In general terms, contemporary theories of population growth can be grouped into three categories: (1) neo-Malthusian theories; (2) economic transition theories; and (3) redistributional theories. Prior to discussing these contemporary theories, however, it may be helpful to briefly canvass what is often considered the first modern theory of population growth expounded by Thomas Malthus.

1. MALTHUSIAN APOCALYPSE THEORY

An Essay on the Principle of Population, published by Malthus in 1798, made two fundamental points [Thomas Malthus, *An Essay on the Principle of Population,* (1798) printed for J. Johnson, in St. Paul's Church-Yard]. First and most obviously, food is necessary to human survival; second, that human reproduction will persist at a consistent rate with only minor variations. Under the conditions assumed by these two postulates (and relying on census data obtained from the recently formed U.S. government), Malthus argued that population growth increases geometrically, while the food resources necessary to sustain the population increase only arithmetically. In Malthusian terms, the inability of subsistence resources to match the rate of population growth ensured that a large portion of humanity would inevitably experience severe difficulties in meeting their basic needs. Not only did the lack of resources operate as a consistent and powerful restraint on population growth, it rendered impossible the Utopian ideal of a world free of hunger and poverty.

History has revealed the errors in the Malthusian view of population growth. Malthus, who wrote prior to the industrial revolution, did not foresee the dramatic impact technological advancements would have on food production. Increased crop yields, refrigeration, pesticides, mechanized farm equipment, and genetically modified organisms (GMOs) are just a few examples of the technological advancements that have allowed the world to move beyond the doom prophesied by Malthus [D. Lam, *How the world survived the population bomb: lessons from fifty years of extraordinary demographic history,* (2011) Demography, vol. 48, no. 4]. However, as noted above, undernourishment does still remain a significant problem in many parts of the world.

2.   NEO-MALTHUSIAN, ECONOMIC TRANSITION, AND REDISTRIBUTIONAL THEORIES

Neo-Malthusian theories predict disaster if population growth is not drastically reduced, but these theories also predict a technically and economically sustainable society if the rate of population growth is significantly reduced [David Pearce & R. Kerry Turner, ECONOMICS OF NATURAL RESOURCES AND THE ENVIRONMENT (1990) at 6]. These predictions are premised upon the neo-Malthusian theory that population growth will exceed food supply because the availability of arable farmlands sets a limit to agricultural expansion. These experts believe that even technologies providing unlimited resources and reduced pollution will be insufficient to counteract the effects of land overuse that lead to decreased food production and shortages [Robert Cassen, et al., POPULATION AND DEVELOPMENT: OLD DEBATES, NEW CONCLUSIONS (1994)].

Other theories are more optimistic and reject the alleged alarmism and panic sown by the neo-Malthusians. The proponents of developmental theory point to the continuing increases in food production and output throughout the developing world, arguing that these developments repudiate the neo-Malthusian predictions of famine [Amartya Sen, *Fertility and Coercion*, 63 U. CHI. L. REV. 1035 (1996) at 1050].

One class of developmentalists believes that economic and social development, technical innovation, better management of resources, and market substitutes can overcome the limits of natural resources and accommodate continued population growth [Pearce & Turner, *supra* at 45–53]. They reject the position that economic development resulting in improved living standards causes rapid population growth *per se*. Instead, these developmentalists subscribe to a two-stage theory of demographic transition. In the first stage, improved living standards reduce the death rate without creating sufficient economic security. A second stage follows in which the birth rate falls because of education, delayed marriage, and cultural changes. Some of these theorists point to prices of resources as indicators of scarcity, arguing that when prices become too high, a technology-driven market substitutes an equivalent but cheaper resource.

However, this theory depends on natural resources being owned while, in fact, many resources, such as water and the atmosphere, are "common goods," not personal property. For example, Garrett Hardin's

Tragedy of the Commons theorizes that the market price of common goods will not reflect the true social opportunity costs of over-use, pollution, and exploitation [Garrett Hardin, *The Tragedy of the Commons,* (1968) Science 162: 1243–1248]. As a result, others reject the developmentalists' price theories and argue that there are often no incentives to conserve or protect such common and essential resources. In fact, according to some, the market has built-in incentives for the destruction of the environment [Robin Hahnel, ECONOMIC JUSTICE AND DEMOCRACY: FROM COMPETITION TO COOPERATION (2005) at 69].

As distinct from the neo-Malthusians and developmentalists, redistributionists blame the problems of unsustainable growth and environmental depletion on the inequities of consumption and unequal distribution of rights among the States and peoples of the world [Cassen, et al. *supra*]. This group also believes in SD, but maintains that the major cause of environmental depletion lies in a consumption explosion by the industrialized world, rather than a population explosion in the developing world. This is illustrated by the fact that 15% of the world's population enjoys 80% of the world's income. To redistributionists, the problem is poverty rather than scarcity; and poverty is seen as "intimately related" to inequality [United Nations Development Program, *Human Development Report 2005: International cooperation at a crossroads,* (2005) *available at* www.undp.org (last visited Apr. 2017)]. Redistributionists argue that resources must be distributed more fairly between industrialized countries and developing countries. As such, the population problem is not about an increase in the number of humans, but in a lack of human rights. They emphasize the right to a decent standard of living and the right for women to control their own reproduction.

E.   LEGAL RESPONSE

1.   1994 INTERNATIONAL CONFERENCE ON POPULATION AND DEVELOPMENT (ICPD)

The above theories and corresponding practical problems jostle for recognition within the international framework of SD. The approach fashioned and proclaimed at the United Nations Conference on Environment and Development (UNCED), also known as Earth Summit, and the 2002 World Summit on Sustainable Development (WSSD) started a path towards integrating economic development, social development, and environmental protection without compromising the needs of present and future generations (*see* Ch. 2).

A related approach allowed for input from more than just governments. Taking into account input from experts, non-governmental organizations (NGOs), and international agencies, the UN International Conference on Population and Development (ICPD) took place in Cairo, Egypt in 1994. At the conference, 179 governments agreed that the proper focus of population policy should be on quality of life, as opposed to focusing purely on the quantity of people in the world. The result of this agreement was the ICPD Programme of Action, which set out a 20-year plan to provide everyone, especially women and girls, with environments in which they can make free and informed decisions about their lives and family formation. The plan highlighted the relationship between gender inequality and poverty, poor health, poor educational attainment, and SD. In particular, the ICPD Programme of Action recognized a need for countries to focus on human rights and the needs of women and young people [U.N. International Conference on Population and Development, *Programme of Action of the International Conference on Population and Development,* (1994) U.N. Doc. A/CONF. 171/13 Annex (hereinafter ICPD Programme of Action)].

However, while the ICPD Programme of Action was adopted by consensus, it also created a great deal of controversy. Many strongly objected to its ideas, particularly the assertion of reproductive rights and sexual health services. A handful of Islamic States were so opposed that they withdrew completely in protest. Parts of the document were also strenuously opposed by a number of States led by the Vatican [United Nations, *Report of the International Conference on Population and Development*, U.N. Doc. A/CONF.171/13 (1994) at 146–149]. Therefore, the ICPD Programme of Action, as a whole, cannot be seen as a crystallization of customary international law, and may possess dubious value even as soft law.

The lack of agreement over population growth may seem surprising. All States of the world, including the Vatican, recognize the environmental dangers of burgeoning populations. There is international consensus, falling short of unanimity, that coercion should be eschewed as a method of family planning [ICPD Programme of Action at ¶ 7(3)]. However, upon closer examination, a number of entrenched reasons exist to block the creation of an international population regime. For example, the Catholic Church advocates population control only through "natural family planning" [Gregory M. Saylin, *The United Nations International Conference on Population and Development: Religion, Tradition and Law in Latin America*, 28 VAND. J. TRANSNAT'L L. 1245 (1995) at 1270].

Another reason for the lack of consensus is differing perceptions of the population issue. Neo-Malthusians fear that increasing populations will inexorably lead to shortages of food and natural resources, resulting in failure of the carrying capacity of the planet. They demand immediate government intervention, in the form of family planning programs, to defuse this time bomb.

Developmentalists and redistributionists counter this view. In general, developmentalists see overpopulation as a symptom of underdevelopment, while the redistributionists argue that better distribution, more international equity, and less profligate consumption by the industrialized world would enable increasing populations to be sufficiently fed by an already adequate resource base. Developmentalists and redistributionists agree that the neo-Malthusians unwisely sow panic by ignoring strong evidence to the contrary. They also agree on the need for economic development and international equity. On social development, they agree on gender equity and the need for women to have improved health care. But the agreement stops there.

Disagreements between developmentalists and redistributionists are compounded by the tenets of western feminism, such as the empowerment of women through accessibility to abortion, contraception, and education, and the assertion that "women are crippled by unbridled fertility" [Conference on Population and Development, *Draft Programme of Action of the International Conference on Population and Development*, U.N. Doc. A/CONF. 171/L.1 (1994)]. At ICPD, western feminists and most industrialized countries saw empowerment of women as a critical step in the move toward population control. For them, it is absolutely essential to give women reproductive freedom and emancipate them from anachronistic customs that bind women to the home, deny them an education, force unwanted children upon them, and then commit them to a lifetime of unrelenting labor of caring for those children. However, for many religious traditionalists, whether Roman Catholic or Islamic, such a view insults the dignity of women. Religious traditionalists argue that western feminism seeks to limit a woman's freedom to bear children, denigrates motherhood, propagates immorality, promotes abortions, and assails the concept of a nurturing family which is the very foundation of society.

A political reason also militates against an international legal regime controlling population growth. In brief, such a regime may be seen as violating national sovereignty and encroaching on cherished notions of individual State control. With such colossal issues, the ICPD Programme of Action appears to have institutionalized, rather than resolved, deep controversies between feminist organizations, conservatives, environmentalists, religious traditionalists, and family planners.

Despite these problems, it is possible to point to some features of the ICPD Programme of Action that may amount to a crystallization of customary law. For example, the sixth principle set out in Chapter II, which even religious traditionalists accepted, endorses the concept of SD and requires the following:

> [S]tates should reduce and eliminate unsustainable patterns of production and consumption and promote appropriate policies, including population-related policies, in order to meet the needs of current generations without compromising the ability of future generations to meet their own needs. [ICPD Programme of Action at Chapter II, Principle 6].

This may be viewed as a restriction on unfettered consumption by industrialized countries, which, according to some commentators, significantly contributes to the population problem [Judith E. Jacobson, *Population, Consumption, and Environmental Degradation: Problems and Solutions*, 6 COLO. J. INT'L ENVT'L L. & POL'Y 255

(1995)]. Furthermore, even though the community of States may disagree as to the means, a consensus exists that population growth should be controlled.

Despite the disagreement over the ICPD Programme of Action, member states have re-affirmed their commitment to the plan every five years since 1994. Twenty years after the original commitment, in September 2014, governments gathered again at the UN General Assembly to analyze the findings of a three-year comprehensive review of data on progress, gaps, and challenges in delivering the original commitments. The results of this meeting will be discussed in more detail below.

2.   2000 UNITED NATIONS MILLENNIUM SUMMIT

Although not specifically focusing on population, the 2000 UN Millennium Summit addressed several related issues. Many of the population and development goals identified in the ICPD Programme of Action were incorporated into the resulting documents, the UN Millennium Declaration and the UN Millennium Development Goals (MDGs). In the MDGs, all UN member states at the time and at least 23 international organizations committed to a set of eight goals that sought to promote poverty reduction and education, improve maternal health and gender equality, reduce child mortality, combat HIV/AIDS and other diseases, ensure environmental sustainability, and develop a global partnership for development—all by the year 2015 [United Nations, *The Millennium*

Development Goals, (2000) *available at* www.un.org/
millenniumgoals (last visited Apr. 2017)].
Interestingly, reproductive health was specifically
excluded from the MDGs.

At the end of the MDG period in 2015, the MDGs
can be credited with saving millions of lives and
improving conditions for many more [*Id.*].
Nevertheless, there have been uneven achievements
and shortfalls in many areas, so work on these issues
must continue into the new development era [*Id.*].

3. 2005 WORLD SUMMIT

In September 2005, world leaders from more than
150 countries convened at the 2005 World Summit—
a high-level plenary meeting designed to produce a
collective agreement to address critical global issues
such as peace and security, development, human
rights, and the rule of law. The summit yielded the
World Summit Outcome, which resolved to achieve
universal access to reproductive health, promote
gender equality, and end discrimination against
women by 2015 [United Nations General Assembly,
2005 World Summit Outcome, A/RES/60/1 (Oct. 24,
2005)]. It also established a Human Rights Council,
charged with "promoting universal respect for the
protection of all human rights and fundamental
freedoms for all, without distinction of any kind and
in a fair and equal manner" [*Id.* at ¶ 159]. Adopted at
the 60th session of the UN General Assembly in
October 2005, the World Summit Outcome sets forth
a commitment to achieve "universal access to
reproductive health by 2015, as set out at [ICPD]"

[*Id.* at ¶ 57(g)]. The World Summit Outcome further declares a commitment to promote gender equality and eliminate pervasive gender discrimination by "[e]nsuring equal access to reproductive health" [*Id.* at ¶ 58(c)].

Within the context of these commitments, it is important to bear in mind that the ICPD Programme of Action defines "reproductive health" as a state of "well-being" in which people have the "capability to reproduce and the freedom to decide if, when and how often to do so" [ICPD Programme of Action. at 7.2]. Implicit in this understanding is the "right of men and women to be informed and to have access to safe, effective, affordable and acceptable methods of family planning of their choice, as well as other methods of their choice for regulation of fertility which are not against the law" [*Id.*]. The definition also includes the "right to make decisions concerning reproduction free of discrimination, coercion and violence" [*Id.* at 7.3].

The inclusion of the commitment to reproductive health in the World Summit Outcome is noteworthy for two related reasons. First, despite strenuous resistance to its adoption from the U.S. and the Vatican, it is a prominent renewal of the commitment to reproductive health first made in the ICPD Programme of Action. Second, the commitment can be seen as the development of a very strong, albeit not uniform, consensus on an international legal right to reproductive health.

Reproductive health is particularly important in the population context, because relatively small changes in fertility behavior can generate large differences in total populations when projected over several decades [2015 Revision at 8]. But despite these commitments, there is still substantial progress to be made in the area of reproductive health. As of 2015, the use of modern contraceptive methods in LDCs was estimated at only 34% among women of reproductive age who were married or in union [Id.]. A further 22% of such women had an unmet need for family planning, meaning they were not using any method of contraception despite expressing a desire to avoid or delay childbearing [Id.]. Advances in reproductive health could also address high adolescent fertility, which remains a concern in certain parts of the world [Id. at 10]. Ensuring that women and girls have access to reproductive health care is also critical to continued progress towards numerous other development goals [Population 2030 at 25].

4.   2014 UNITED NATIONS GENERAL ASSEMBLY REVIEW OF THE INTERNATIONAL CONFERENCE ON POPULATION AND DEVELOPMENT (ICPD)

Achievements since the ICPD Programme of Action was originally adopted 20 years ago have been remarkable, including gains in women's equality, population health, life expectancy, educational attainment, and human rights protection systems, as well as an estimated 1 billion people moving out of extreme poverty. Fears about the dangers of population growth have continued to ease as the population growth rate declines and the expansion of human capability and opportunity leads to additional economic development.

In September 2014, governments gathered at the UN General Assembly to continue discussions on population and development. The result was the ICPD Beyond 2014 Framework of Action, an agenda based on robust and comprehensive data gathered from governments, civil society, the UN system, and global partners. It provides a forward looking plan of action for governments and communities that identifies what still needs to be done to deliver a world of equality, opportunity, and freedom to all of the 7.3 billion people who share it—and who will someday be added to it [United Nations, *Framework of Actions for the follow-up to the Programme of Action of the International Conference on Population and Development Beyond 2014*, (2014) A/69/62].

The ICPD Beyond 2014 Framework continues to emphasize the need for the fulfillment of human rights. It reaffirms that sexual and reproductive health and rights, as well as an understanding of the implications of population dynamics, are foundational to SD [*Id*. at iii]. The ICPD Beyond 2014 Framework argues that the path to sustainability demands better leadership and greater innovation to address critical needs. These needs include extending human rights to protect all persons from discrimination and violence, investing in young people to assure future growth and innovation, strengthening health systems to provide universal access to sexual and reproductive health, building sustainable cities that enrich urban and rural lives alike, and transforming the global economy to one that will sustain the future of the planet [*Id.*].

5. 2015 UNITED NATIONS SUSTAINABLE DEVELOPMENT SUMMIT

In September 2015, more than 150 world leaders attended the UN Sustainable Development Summit to formally adopt the 2030 Agenda for Sustainable Development. The agenda includes SDGs that build on the MDGs discussed above. However, the SDGs are even more ambitious than the MDGs, seeking to completely eliminate poverty as well as setting more demanding targets on health, education, and gender equality. The agenda also includes issues that were not addressed in the MDGs, such as climate change, sustainable consumption, innovation, and the importance of peace and justice for all [United Nations General Assembly, *Transforming Our World: The 2030 Agenda for Sustainable Development*, (2015) A/RES/7-/1] (*see also* Ch. 2). Population trends that unfold during the implementation period for the 2030 Agenda for Sustainable Development will almost certainly hold significant implications for achieving the SDGs [Population 2030 at 47].

F.   CONCLUSIONS

Population issues demonstrate the intersection of three realities. First, those in the developed world consume resources at a much greater rate than the people of the developing world. Second, the population of the developing world is increasing, and more people are consuming larger resources and causing greater pollution. Third, the principle of common but differentiated responsibilities (CBDR) requires the developed world to take the lead in advancing SD, and helping the social and economic advancement of the developing world. The unresolved issue is whether these three intersecting realities call for population control and halting the growth of population in the developing world.

CHAPTER FIVE
BIODIVERSITY

A. NATURE OF THE PROBLEM

The term "biodiversity" encompasses three concepts: (1) the genetic diversity within each species; (2) the diversity between species; and (3) the diversity of ecosystems within a region. The greater a region's biodiversity, the greater its capacity to support life and adapt to changing conditions [E.O. Wilson, ed., BIODIVERSITY (1988) at 21]. Our anxiety over the loss of biodiversity may be based on the "use-value" of species and ecosystems, within economic, ecological, and aesthetic frameworks.

Biological resources and ecosystems provide a variety of services. These services include: *provisioning services* such as food, water, timber, and fiber; *regulating services* that affect climate, floods, disease, wastes, and water quality; *cultural services* that provide aesthetic and spiritual benefits; and *supporting services* such as soil formation, photosynthesis, and nutrient cycling [Millennium Ecosystem Assessment, ECOSYSTEMS AND HUMAN WELL BEING, SYNTHESIS (2005)]. A study concludes that approximately 25% of the total wealth of developing countries is derived from the environment and ecosystem services, as opposed to less than 4% within industrialized countries belonging to the Organization for Economic Cooperation and Development (OECD) [Biodiversity Convention, YEAR IN REVIEW 2006 (2007) at 5].

A cost-benefit figure can be calculated for preserving species with known economic value, and can even be estimated for those with unknown economic value, because if a species is lost the possibility of deriving use from it is also lost [Bryan G. Norton, WHY PRESERVE NATURAL VARIETY? (1987) at 27]. However, the services provided by ecosystems are so diffuse and untraceable that actual economic value for those services often cannot be attributed to individual species, as each species is interrelated and interdependent upon other species in the ecosystem. Thus, the value of preserving biodiversity is ultimately based on the incalculable value of ecosystem services.

It should also be remembered that an ecosystem is vulnerable to the weaknesses of its species. For example, loss of genetic diversity within plant and animal species leads to uniformity, which makes species more susceptible to diseases and pests. This weakness renders species less able to adapt to a changing physical environment, and in turn makes the ecosystem itself less stable [Paul Ehrlich & Anne Ehrlich, EXTINCTION, THE CAUSES AND CONSEQUENCES OF THE DISAPPEARANCE OF SPECIES (1981) at 74].

Biological resources also have aesthetic value as sources of recreation and beauty. Like economic and ecological values, aesthetic values are based on the uses provided by species and ecosystems. The value of nature is difficult to quantify, but can be assigned based on the value of a similar experience. For example, the ability to visit a pristine North Slope in

Alaska or a preserved tropical rain forest can be assigned based on what a person would be willing to pay for the experience or, alternatively, what he or she would accept for being denied that opportunity. According to this reasoning, even the aesthetic value of nature's spiritual effect on humans may depend on its "use-value."

In contrast, our concern for preserving biodiversity may also be premised on ethical value, which is different than use-value, and arises from a belief in the intrinsic worth of a species, independent of its other values. Ethical reasons for preserving biodiversity are based, quite simply, on the right of species and ecosystems to exist. Arguably, their enduring existence denotes the right to continued existence, which in turn carries responsibilities for humans. As the dominant species on earth, humans have a moral responsibility as caretakers or trustees to preserve other species.

B.   ENVIRONMENTAL IMPACTS

In 2005, the Millennium Ecosystems Assessment was conducted by over 2,000 scientists under the auspices of the United Nations (UN) system and a representative sample of other stakeholders from civil society. The Millennium Ecosystems Assessment was a response to government requests based on information received under the Convention on Biological Diversity (Biodiversity Convention), the Convention on Wetlands of International Importance, Especially as Waterfowl Habitat (the Ramsar Convention) [*Convention on Wetlands of*

International Importance, Especially as Waterfowl Habitat, Feb. 2, 1971, 1976 U.N.T.S. 245 (hereinafter Ramsar Convention)], the Convention on the Conservation of Migratory Species of Wild Animals (Bonn Convention) (*see* below) [*Convention on the Conservation of Migratory Species of Wild Animals,* Jun. 23, 1979, 19 I.L.M. 11 (hereinafter Bonn Convention)], and the UN Convention to Combat Desertification (Desertification Convention) (*see* Ch. 16) [*United Nations Convention to Combat Desertification in Those Countries Experiencing Serious Drought and/or Desertification, Particularly in Africa,* Jun. 17, 1994, 33 I.L.M. 1328 (hereinafter Desertification Convention)]. The objective of the Millennium Ecosystems Assessment was to assess the consequences of ecosystem damage and how it might be repaired. It produced the most authoritative statement on the state of the world's ecosystems and biodiversity.

According to the Millennium Ecosystems Assessment, over the past 50 years humans have changed ecosystems more than any other comparable period in history. Over two-thirds of the services performed by ecosystems were found to be in decline, including fresh water supplies, marine fishery production, pollination, habitats for indigenous peoples, natural hazard regulation, the ability of the atmosphere to purify itself, and the capacity of agricultural ecosystems to provide pest control. These ecosystem services continue to decline [Millennium Ecosystem Assessment, ECOSYSTEMS AND HUMAN WELL BEING (2005)].

The richest remaining areas of biodiversity are rainforests, coral reefs, and coastal wetlands. Tropical rainforests contain 50% to 90% of the approximately 10 million total species that live on Earth. They also contribute significantly to the global environment and human health. As the lungs of the planet, rainforests turn carbon dioxide (CO_2) into oxygen, thereby reducing the negative impacts of climate change. And, since they contain many species that have not been thoroughly identified and studied, tropical rainforests are also havens for potential medical research [National Academy of Sciences, ONE EARTH, ONE FUTURE (1990)].

Unfortunately, rapid population growth (*see* Ch. 4), increased need for agricultural land and fuel wood, and world markets for tropical hardwoods and animal products have contributed to the demise of global rainforests. Tropical deforestation to clear agricultural land is often accomplished by a *slash and burn* method, which releases CO_2 and other gases that contribute to climate change and deplete the ozone layer. Slash and burn can also lead to the degradation of soil fertility and changes in regional hydrology, as watersheds are destroyed and precipitation patterns change. However, the most serious long-term impact of tropical deforestation may be the loss of plant and animal species. Overall, more than 31 million hectares of rainforest are destroyed every year. The loss of primary tropical rainforest, the most diverse type, has been estimated at six million hectares annually since 2000 [Biodiversity Convention, YEAR IN REVIEW (2007) at 5].

Coral reefs cover only 0.17% of the sea floor, yet they contain 25% of all known marine species. They are created in tropical saltwater by animals called stony-coral polyps. With the aid of symbiotic algae living in their tissues, the corals secrete limestone reefs over thousands of years. These fragile ecosystems are vulnerable to natural environmental threats, such as disease and predation, as well as human activities that pollute or physically destroy the reefs [*Id.* at 7]. The reefs are disappearing at an alarming rate due to pollution and destruction by humans. Some 30% of reefs are severely damaged and experts say 60% may be destroyed by 2030 if left unchecked [United Nations Environment Programme (UNEP), et al. IN THE FRONT LINE: SHORELINE PROTECTION AND OTHER ECOSYSTEM SERVICES FROM MANGROVES AND CORAL REEFS (2006) at 5]. When managed well, these reefs provide all of the forms of ecosystem services mentioned at the beginning of this chapter [*Id.*] However, reefs are threatened not only through overfishing and direct pollution into the water and on the sea bed by humans, but also by climate change and warming water resulting in bleaching [*Id.*]

Coastal wetlands provide vital habitat, breeding, nursery, and feeding areas for marine species and waterfowl. They also provide the valuable ecosystem services of water purification and flood control. However, pollution pressure from expanding human populations increasingly threatens coastal wetlands, as six out of 10 people now live within 40 miles of the coast. Rising sea levels, predicted to result from climate change, and subsidence also negatively affect wetlands. Global shipping and development has taken a great toll on the world's coastal ecosystems, and over half of the wetlands in the contiguous U.S. have been dredged or developed [Walter V. Reid & Mark C. Trexler, DROWNING THE NATIONAL HERITAGE: CLIMATE CHANGE AND U.S. COASTAL BIODIVERSITY (1991) at 8].

Rainforests, coral reefs, and coastal wetlands are not the only ecosystems that human activity damages; nor are they the most fragile. Many polar ecosystems are so intricately and delicately created that even slight human interference can be extremely damaging. Human interference in the Antarctic, for example, has begun to affect those ecosystems in ways we do not yet fully understand (*see* Ch. 8).

C. CAUSES

The primary cause of biodiversity loss is habitat destruction from the expansion of human populations and activities. Growing human populations result in greater demand for food, water, timber, fiber, and fuel (*see* Ch. 4). Among terrestrial ecosystems, the expansion of agriculture and commercial harvesting has led to the conversion of forests to croplands, while overgrazing has significantly altered many other natural habitats. Industrial agriculture techniques that use fewer varieties of plants to increase productivity have created an increased susceptibility to pests. Livestock waste and fertilizers have contaminated many aquatic ecosystems with nitrogen and phosphorus. Dams have destroyed large sections of freshwater habitat, while coastal development is responsible for damaging mangrove swamps and coral reefs.

Almost all other causes of biodiversity loss are also related to the expanding influence of humans over the environment. The introduction of exotic predators, competitors, and pathogens by humans into isolated ecosystems, either purposely or accidentally, poses serious threats to the survival of native species. Humans have also over-exploited forest, marine, and wildlife resources, sometimes to the point of extinction, not only for food but also for commodities, such as elephant ivory. In addition, pollution of the air, water, and soil has led to the reduction, and even extinction, of some sensitive species, which can, in turn, lead to the destruction of entire ecosystems. Finally, many species and ecosystems may not be able to successfully adapt to predicted global climate changes.

D.   REMEDIAL OBJECTIVES

The primary goal of biodiversity conservation is to meet human needs for the variety of services provided by biological resources while ensuring that those resources last indefinitely. Earlier treaty regimes attempted to deal with biodiversity loss as a self-contained problem. However, subsequent geo-political developments demanded a different approach governed by two systemic principles that have become a foundational part of modern international environmental law (IEL). As we shall see, remedial actions need to be based within the global frameworks of (1) equity and resource transfers, and (2) sustainable development (SD). International equity demands that the endemic problems of global poverty must constitute the bedrock of any discussion of other global predicaments, such as environmental protection. SD, endorsed by the 1992 UN Conference on Environment and Development (UNCED), also known as Earth Summit, generally allows for the use and exploitation of resources subject to environmental restraints (*see* Ch. 18).

Consistent with a pattern established during the negotiations at the 1972 Stockholm Conference on the Human Environment (Stockholm Conference), the protection of biodiversity has become part of the debate on equity and SD between industrialized and developing countries, traversing issues of economic growth and global poverty. The experience of the Biodiversity Convention, signed at Earth Summit has demonstrated the near impossibility of segregating or surgically isolating the environmental and scientific problems of biodiversity from its socio-political milieu.

E. LEGAL RESPONSE

1. 1992 CONVENTION ON BIOLOGICAL DIVERSITY (BIODIVERSITY CONVENTION)

In 1987, the UN Environment Programme (UNEP) Governing Council asked an ad hoc working group to explore the desirability and possible form of an umbrella convention to rationalize current activities concerning biodiversity [Francoise Burhenne-Guilmin & Susan Casey-Lefkowitz, *Introduction,* THE CONVENTION ON BIOLOGICAL DIVERSITY: AN EXPLANATORY GUIDE, IUCN ENVIRONMENTAL LAW CENTRE/DRAFT TEXT (Oct. 1992) at 2. *Quoted in* Kal Raustiala, *Global biodiversity protection in the United Kingdom and United States,* THE INTERNATIONALIZATION OF ENVIRONMENTAL PROTECTION, Miranda A. Schreurs & Elizabeth C. Economy, eds. (1997) at 45]. By umbrella convention, the Governing Council meant a treaty that would consolidate existing treaties into a workable whole, eliminating jurisdictional overlap and filling perceived gaps. When this proved politically unattainable, the international community settled for the current Biodiversity Convention, a framework treaty that contains primarily aspirational provisions, with matters of substance left to future development by Conferences of the Parties (COPs).

As a framework treaty, the Biodiversity Convention possesses only the power to seek "appropriate forms of cooperation" with the executive bodies of other conventions [Biodiversity Convention at arts. 22(1) & 23(4)(h)]. There has been a great deal of criticism over the treaty's lack of substantive provisions, as even its most general obligations contain heavily qualified language. But others have defended the Biodiversity Convention by noting its resolution of long-standing issues, such as access to biological resources, while reminding detractors of the forward-looking framework approach in setting the stage for future solutions when faced with political difficulties.

In summarizing the provisions of the Biodiversity Convention, for analytical purposes, we return to the two overriding principles of (1) equity and resource transfers and (2) SD. Of course, these two principles are conceptually bound together. One way that the Biodiversity Convention addresses that connection is by applying an underlying, if not expressly articulated, third principle known as common but differentiated responsibilities (CBDR). CBDR links equity and SD by contemplating resource transfers where industrialized countries "acknowledge the responsibility that they bear in the international pursuit of sustainable development in view of the pressures their societies place on the global environment and of the technologies and financial resources they command" [Rio Declaration at Principle 7]. In our analysis, we locate the specific commitments, including those based on CBDR, within a general discussion of the issues.

a. Equity and Resource Transfers

When reviewing the outcome of equity issues in the Biodiversity Convention, we must notice the differences in the background positions of the richer States in the industrialized world as compared to the poorer States in the developing world (*see* Ch. 1). The industrialized world has already consumed a substantial degree of its own biological resources. Since most remaining biodiversity exists within developing countries, the developing world understandably felt possessive about those resources. Thus, the developing world favored conservation projects that did not compromise their sovereignty over their natural resources. In addition, since many of these States experience conditions of real poverty, they viewed cordoning off large tracts of land from development as an impediment to alleviating deprivation through economic progress. The developing world argued that equity required the industrialized world to embrace the costs of curtailing their development in the name of biodiversity.

On the other hand, the industrialized world tended to view the protection of biodiversity less from the point of view of past sins and more as a present global problem that entailed shared sacrifice. Consequently, the industrialized world placed restrictions on development in its own States— creating a series of protected areas such as parks, preserves, and wilderness—and believed the developing world should do the same. Although the industrialized world recognized that the developing world should receive some financial help with its efforts to protect biodiversity, the industrialized world saw protection as an outright obligation of each member of the global community, independent of financial transfer and ability to pay. Furthermore, in transferring financial resources to developing countries, the industrialized world wanted to retain control over exactly where that money would go; in other words, they wanted targeted and efficient use of their contributions.

i. Common Concern of Humankind

One outcome of the conflict between the industrialized and developing countries is expressed in the preamble of the Biodiversity Convention, which affirms "the conservation of biological diversity is a common concern of humankind" [Biodiversity Convention at Preamble]. Early in the negotiating process the parties dropped the phrase "common heritage" from consideration because of its connotation of community access to, and the sharing of proceeds from, the development of biological resources. The parties rejected the formulation of the UN Food and Agricultural Organization (FAO), which had earlier confirmed "plant genetic resources are a heritage of mankind . . . [which] consequently should be available without restriction" [Food and Agricultural Organization (FAO), INTERNATIONAL UNDERTAKING ON PLANT GENETIC RESOURCES (1983) at art. 1]. Previously, both the UN Convention on the Law of the Sea (UNCLOS) and the Treaty on Principles Governing the Activities of States in the Exploration and Use of Outer Space, Including the Moon and other Celestial Bodies (Outer Space Treaty) employed the "common heritage" language calling for the sharing of proceeds from resources lying outside the area of national jurisdiction [*Treaty on Principles Governing the Activities of States in the Exploration and Use of Outer Space, Including the Moon and Other Celestial Bodies,* (1967) 6 I.L.M. 386 (hereinafter Outer Space Treaty)]. However, these agreements were concluded at a time when developing countries would benefit from such a concept. By contrast, in the case of biodiversity, developing countries were dealing with resources within their own borders—resources to which they were reluctant to surrender sovereignty. Needless to say, due to its linguistic history, the "common heritage" term did not gain favor. Even so, the "common concern" formulation—though less broad in scope—does recognize the loss of biodiversity as a major problem that the international community must attend to on a global basis.

ii. Access to Genetic Resources

Though annexes to the FAO Undertaking, referred to above, make it clear that "free access" does not mean "free of charge," the principle of free access to genetic resources maintained the right of an industrialized country to obtain and freely use the genetic material of a developing country. In the Biodiversity Convention, the international community made a clean break from the original concept of free access, deciding that "the authority to determine access to genetic resources rests with the national governments and is subject to national legislation" [Biodiversity Convention at art. 15(1)].

Instead, the Biodiversity Convention adopts the principle of Prior Informed Consent (PIC), now a standard concept with regard to environmental transactions between industrial and developing countries [*Id.* at art. 15(5)]. A developing country party can negotiate with private companies or other parties on the "mutually agreed" price of access to genetic material [*Id.* at art. 15(4)] (*see* Ch. 9 for a discussion of PIC concerning hazardous waste transfers). Genetic resources taken from the State of origin before the Biodiversity Convention entered into force—such as those now held in gene banks throughout the world—are excluded from the present access provisions. COP-10 took up the question of such resources at its meeting in October 2010, agreeing to the Nagoya-Kuala Lumpur Supplementary Protocol on Liability and Redress to the Cartagena Protocol on Biosafety (Nagoya Protocol) governing access to genetic resources and sharing of profits among countries involved [Biodiversity Convention, REPORT OF THE TENTH MEETING OF THE CONFERENCE OF THE PARTIES TO THE CONVENTION ON BIOLOGICAL DIVERSITY (2010) UNE/CBD/COP/10/27].

iii. Biotechnology

Biotechnology, as considered in the Biodiversity Convention, means "any technological application that uses biological systems, living organisms, or derivatives thereof, to make or modify products or processes for specific use" [Biodiversity Convention at art. 2]. This ranges from the ancient practice of selective breeding of animals and plants to sophisticated DNA technology and genetic engineering. The Biodiversity Convention addresses two important and controversial areas with regard to biotechnology: the transfer of technology and the transfer of the benefits of biotechnology.

First, the Biodiversity Convention makes explicitly clear that "technology includes biotechnology," so any reference to the transfer of technology also includes the transfer of biotechnology [*Id.* at art. 2]. Access to and transfer of technology is dealt with in Article 16, a convoluted article with a number of overlapping and cross-referenced provisions. As a first requirement, Article 16 mandates that all parties, industrialized and developing countries alike, must "provide and/or facilitate" the access to and transfer of biotechnology [*Id.* at art. 16(1)]. In particular, the transfer of technology to developing countries must be made on "fair and favorable terms, including concessional and preferential terms where mutually agreed," and such transfer can occur by way of the financial mechanism [*Id.* at art. 16(2)]. Making the transfer available through the financial mechanism means that technology transfer qualifies as a fundable enterprise under the Biodiversity Convention. Finally, Article 16(2) also provides that technology protected by intellectual property rights (IPRs) in an industrialized country, if transferred, must receive "the adequate and effective protection" of that right in the developing country [*Id.* at art. 16(2)].

The controversy involving transfer of biotechnology again reflects fundamental differences of opinion between the industrialized and developing worlds. First, most biotechnology remains in the hands of private corporations in industrialized countries. As market players within market economies, these corporations demand some remuneration for their investment. Second, biotechnology generally is protected under IPRs in the industrialized world, and corporations insist on similar protection in developing countries. Without such protection, even payment for the technology will not suffice, as the technology might be copied and pirated in the developing country.

In contrast, developing countries see the transfer of biotechnology as a main incentive for participation in the Biodiversity Convention, enabling them, over time, to expand their own biotechnology industries and develop the wealth of their own biodiversity. In addition, the developing world views IPRs as an impediment to technology transfer, making the protected technology more expensive and thus more restrictive. Developing countries maintain that the level of IPRs protection required should be commensurate with an individual State's level of economic development, and thus a matter for national determination.

Resolution of the impasse concerning IPRs now rests with the new Trade-Related Aspects of Intellectual Property Rights of the WTO [WTO Agreement, Uruguay Round, Annex 1C, TRIPS Agreement at 319–351]. In effect, under this agreement, developing countries must generally respect IPRs, but have a number of years in which to implement protective legislation. As for the channeling of resources to developing countries (who then might remunerate corporations involved in the transfer), the Biodiversity Convention makes clear in Article 16(2) that such projects are fundable by the financial mechanism—either for the cost itself and/or for the cost of the IPRs foregone [*see* Biodiversity Convention at art. 19]. In fact, the first COP listed the matter as a program priority for the financial mechanism to consider, giving emphasis "[i]n accordance with Article 16 of the Convention . . . [to] projects which promote access to, transfer of and cooperation in joint development of technology" [Biodiversity Convention COP, *Decisions Adopted by the First meeting of the Conference of the Parties*, U.N. DOC. UNEP/CBD/1/17 (1994) at annex I(III)(4)(f)].

As previously mentioned, the Biodiversity Convention also provides for negotiations between industrialized country entities (usually corporations) and developing country parties concerning the price of access to genetic resources [Biodiversity Convention at art. 15(4) & 15(7)]. In this way, a mechanism is created by which the developing countries might: (1) negotiate the acquisition of biotechnology developed from genetic resources [*Id.* at art. 16(3)]; (2) participate in research projects connected to genetic resources [*Id.* at art. 19(1)]; and (3) gain priority access to the results and benefits (such as royalties) arising from biotechnologies based upon genetic resources [*Id.* at art. 19(2)]. The governments of industrialized countries must facilitate the above outcomes, but, on the whole, negotiations will take place between private corporations and developing countries. Again, Article 15(7) of the Biodiversity Convention makes allowance for use of the financial mechanism to fund projects that share the research, development, and benefits of genetic resources.

iv. Financial Transfers

Under the Biodiversity Convention, industrialized countries must also pay "to enable developing country parties to meet the agreed full incremental costs to them of implementing measures which fulfill the obligations of this Convention" [*Id.* at art. 20(2)]. Again, as stated above, this provision enshrines the principle of CBDR, as noted in Principle 7 of the 1992 Rio Declaration, in which industrialized countries acknowledge their greater financial responsibility in addressing global environmental degradation. Industrialized countries, listed in an annex adopted at the first meeting of the COP, will channel their contributions through the newly restructured interim financial mechanism, the Global Environment Facility (GEF) (*see* Appendix § C). Following the Programme Priorities laid down by the COP, the GEF will fund individual projects put forth by the developing countries—the "incremental cost" to be determined by individual negotiations between the GEF and the respective applicant. Also, industrialized countries may bypass the GEF through regional, bilateral, and multilateral channels under Article 20(3), but the extent to which such funding might meet an industrialized country's financial obligations under the Biodiversity Convention remains an open question for the COP.

b. Sustainable Development (SD)

As our second operating principle, SD functions as a prevailing focus within the Biodiversity Convention, as well as its ultimate objective.

Although direct reference to SD is made only once in the treaty, it is repeatedly circumscribed within two of its common terms: "conservation" and "sustainable use." These concepts may be seen as the twin poles of SD. On the one hand, "sustainable use" acknowledges the necessity of utilizing biological resources but directs parties to use the components of biodiversity in a way that maintains biodiversity's potential to meet the needs of present and future generations [*Id.* at art. 2]. On the other hand, although "conservation" is not specifically defined in the treaty, its usage clearly speaks to the preservation of biodiversity. For example, the treaty does define "*in situ* conservation" as "the conservation of ecosystems and natural habitats and the maintenance and recovery of viable populations of species in their natural surroundings" [*Id.* at art. 2]. Thus, in combining the development connotation of "sustainable use" with the preservation connotation of "conservation," the Biodiversity Convention strikes the balance of SD.

The treaty imposes various obligations with regard to SD, weaving these through a myriad of overlapping provisions. In summarizing these commitments, however, one is immediately confronted with the qualifying language "as far as possible" and "as appropriate" that accompanies nearly every obligation. These qualifications severely limit the strength of very important provisions. In particular, as most remaining biodiversity lies within the borders of developing countries, qualifications that reduce the commitments of developing countries have led to a perception of the Biodiversity Convention as an empty treaty. On the other hand, no treaty can go beyond the political realities of the time, and the framework approach used in the Biodiversity Convention provides a flexible method to institute stronger measures in the future.

Indeed, the international community's approach to biodiversity has changed over the past ten years. Conservation and development are no longer seen as conflicting goals but as mutually interdependent, and biodiversity is considered an essential part of efforts to eradicate poverty and achieve SD. This change has been in large part due to the Biodiversity Convention and its process of international consensus building, inherent strengths of near universal membership, a comprehensive and science-driven mandate, international financial support for national projects, world-class scientific and technological advice, and the political involvement of governments. By bringing together people with very different interests for the first time, the process initiated under the Biodiversity Convention offers hope for the future by forging a new deal between governments, economic interests, environmentalists, indigenous peoples, local communities, and the concerned citizen.

Additionally, through the Biodiversity Convention, most States have become more aware of the complex issue of biodiversity loss and necessary institutional mechanisms have been put in place to address it. More than 170 States have developed a national biodiversity strategy and action plan, the fundamental tool for the implementation of the Biodiversity Convention at the national level. In

April 2002, the parties committed themselves to achieve a significant reduction of the current rate of biodiversity loss at the global, regional, and national level by 2010 as a contribution to poverty alleviation and to benefit all life on earth. This target was subsequently endorsed by the World Summit on Sustainable Development (WSSD) and the UN General Assembly and was incorporated as a new target under the Millennium Development Goals (MDGs) [Secretariat of the Convention on Biological Diversity, GLOBAL BIODIVERSITY OUTLOOK 3 (2010) at 5 (hereinafter GLOBAL BIODIVERSITY OUTLOOK)]. An official report by the Biodiversity Convention Secretariat makes it abundantly clear that the target was not met [*Id.* at 9]. It also makes clear that much work needs to be done to protect all the services diversity of species provides to humans [*Id.*]

i. Commitments of All Parties (Including Developing Countries)

In implementing SD under the Biodiversity Convention, the focus is on national action. In general, all parties must develop "national strategies, plans or programmes for the conservation and sustainable use of biodiversity" [Biodiversity Convention at art. 6(a)]. National goals for biodiversity must then be integrated into other relevant national programs, such as forestry and agricultural planning [*Id.* at art. 6(b)]. As part of this process, each State must also conduct studies to identify the components of biodiversity and monitor those components most in need of conservation, as well as those "which offer the greatest potential for sustainable use" [*Id.* at art. 7(a)–(b)].

More specifically, with respect to the conservation of *in situ* biodiversity, or biodiversity in its natural setting, the Biodiversity Convention makes a number of important mandates, including the establishment of protected areas, the management of biological resources within or outside of such protected areas, the protection of ecosystems, and the maintenance of viable species populations [*Id.* at art. 8]. Furthermore, recalling Articles 8(g, 17) and 19(3–4), the parties adopted the Cartagena Protocol on Biosafety to the Convention on Biological Diversity (Cartagena Protocol) at an extraordinary meeting in 2000 [*Cartagena Protocol on Biosafety,* Jan. 29, 2000, 39 I.L.M. 1027 at art. 4 (hereinafter Cartagena Protocol)]. The Cartagena Protocol addressed transboundary movement, transit, handling, and use of living modified organisms (LMOs). This was done to reduce the adverse impacts of biotechnology on the environment. The Cartagena Protocol required 50 countries to ratify before it entered into force, and it received the last required ratification in 2003 [*Id.* at art. 37(1)]. Although the Biodiversity Convention stresses *in situ* conservation as the primary means of protecting biodiversity, a number of *ex situ* provisions also exist. *Ex situ* conservation includes gene banks, captive breeding programs, and zoos. Parties must adopt measures to promote *ex situ* conservation through the establishment of appropriate facilities and the development of appropriate species rehabilitation programs [Biodiversity Convention at art. 9].

Parties have also agreed to incorporate a consideration of SD into their national decision-making, protect traditional cultural uses of biological resources, and encourage cooperation between the public and private sectors [*Id.* at art. 10]. On a related issue, parties must also consider the implementation of environmental impact assessment procedures for proposed projects that are likely to have significant adverse impacts of biodiversity, clearly a step forward in achieving the overall goal of SD [*Id.* at art. 14].

Nevertheless, all of these critical provisions remain qualified with the phrases "as far as possible" and "as appropriate," except for the simple duty to create "national strategies, plans or programmes," which receives the arguably less evasive escape clause "in accordance with [a State's] particular conditions and capabilities" [*Id.* at art. 6(a)]. In overseeing the implementation of these requirements, the COP will receive reports from each party concerning its fulfillment of the provisions and objectives of the convention [*Id.* at art. 26]. One significant area about which the COP received recent reports was the measures each country took to achieve the 2010 biodiversity target. It then released individual country reports and a general report on the progress made by all of the parties [*see* Convention on Biological Diversity, *Country Profiles, available at* www.cbd.int/countries (last visited Apr. 2017)]. Unfortunately, the goal was not met [GLOBAL BIODIVERSITY OUTLOOK at 9].

ii. Commitments of Industrialized Countries

Following the concept of CBDR, the Biodiversity Convention creates additional commitments for industrialized countries. These separate obligations primarily involve funding and technology transfer, as outlined above. In fact, the obligations of developing countries depend on the "effective implementation" of industrialized country parties "of their commitments under the Convention related to financial resources and transfer of technology" [Biodiversity Convention at art. 20(4)]. In other words, one might see the qualifying language of developing country commitments, such as "as far as possible" and "as appropriate," as contingent on the contributions of industrialized countries. In this way, the industrialized world controls just how "qualified" the commitments actually are. If the industrialized world wants real action by developing countries on sustainable use and conservation of biodiversity, it need only contribute a commensurate amount.

Of further note, the Biodiversity Convention also distinguishes between OECD members and former Soviet bloc States. The latter, those "countries undergoing the process of transition to a market economy," can voluntarily assume the obligations of developing countries over time [*Id.* at art. 20(2)]. At the first meeting of the COP, a list of parties that assume the obligations of developed countries was officially adopted [Biodiversity Convention, COP-1, Decision I/2, Annex II]. This list had no parties on it [*Id.*]. There has been no effort by recent COPs to update this list [Yibin Xiang and Sandra Meehan,

FINANCIAL COOPERATION, REIO CONVENTIONS AND COMMON CONCERNS, RECIEL 14(3) (2005) at 30].

c. Institutions

The Biodiversity Convention offers the typical institutional arrangement of a framework treaty. The COP acts as the "all-powerful" legislative organ, which makes decisions on a range of substantive, administrative, and procedural matters. The COP, which meets annually, also votes on amendments, protocols, and amendments to protocols. The method for adopting informal or "everyday" decisions, whether administrative or substantive, is subject to the decisions of future COPs. Procedural questions are resolved by a simple majority vote. Amendments to the convention or to protocols are by at least a two-thirds majority of parties present and voting [Biodiversity Convention at art. 29].

The Secretariat functions as the administrative arm of the COP, working year round to coordinate action with other international bodies, and preparing reports and material for the next conference. The Subsidiary Body on Scientific, Technical, and Technological Advice provides expertise to the COP, creating scientific and technical assessments of both the status of biodiversity and the effects of measures taken to implement the Biodiversity Convention [*Id.* at art. 25]. Significantly, the first meeting of the COP also established a Clearing-House Mechanism for Technical and Scientific Cooperation, an institution that will act as a catalyst for collaborative research and joint projects under the Biodiversity Convention

[*Id.* at art. 18(3)]. Currently, full functionality of the Clearing-House Mechanism is still a goal, but COP-10 has confidence in its ability to provide valuable assistance in the next decade [Biodiversity Convention, COP-10, Decision X/15, Annex, Goal 1.3].

d. Relationship to Other Agreements

As we shall see, the international community has already created a number of international and regional treaties on specific subjects concerning biodiversity. Significantly, however, the Biodiversity Convention would trump all other treaties, including the World Trade Organization (WTO), formerly the General Agreement on Tariffs and Trade (GATT), where the exercise of rights and obligations under those treaties "would cause serious damage or a threat to biological diversity" [Biodiversity Convention at art. 22(1)]. The one exception to this is in regard to the marine environment, in which the rights and obligations of the Biodiversity Convention may not conflict with those created by UNCLOS. Thus, in effect, we now have two dominant environmental treaties dealing with biodiversity: the Biodiversity Convention for terrestrial biodiversity and UNCLOS for marine biodiversity.

As the preeminent treaty with respect to terrestrial biodiversity, the Biodiversity Convention directs the Secretariat to seek "appropriate forms of cooperation" with the executive bodies of other biodiversity treaties [*Id.* at art. 23(4)(h)]. The goal is to (a) facilitate the exchange of information, (b) harmonize reporting procedures, (c) coordinate respective programs of work, and (d) consult on how such conventions can contribute to the implementation of the Biodiversity Convention. To this end, the Secretariat has entered into Memoranda of Cooperation with a number of executive bodies of other treaties, including the Ramsar Convention, the Convention on International Trade in Endangered Species and Wild Fauna and Flora (CITES), and the Bonn Convention (*see below*). The Secretariat has similar memoranda with international organizations, such as: the Center for International Forestry Research; the International Tropical Timber Organization; the Intergovernmental Oceanographic Commission; the Pan-European Biological and Landscape Diversity Strategy; the UN Conference on Trade and Development (UNCTAD); the UN Educational, Scientific, and Cultural Organization (UNESCO); the World Conservation Union (IUCN); and the FAO. Significantly, there is no memorandum with GATT/WTO [Biodiversity Convention, *Cooperation and Partnerships* (2011), *available at* http://www. cbd.int/cooperation/ (last visited Apr. 2017)].

2. SUPPLEMENTARY AGREEMENTS TO THE BIODIVERSITY CONVENTION

a. 2000 Cartagena Protocol on Biosafety (Cartagena Protocol)

The Cartagena Protocol governs the movements of LMOs resulting from modern biotechnology from one country to another. It was adopted on January 29,

2000 as a supplementary agreement to the Biodiversity Convention and entered into force on September 11, 2003. In adopting this supplementary convention the COP paid special regard to Article 19(3) of the Biodiversity Convention, which stipulated:

> The Parties shall consider the need for and modalities of a protocol setting out appropriate procedures, including, in particular, advance informed agreement, in the field of the safe transfer, handling and use of any living modified organism resulting from biotechnology that may have adverse effect on the conservation and sustainable use of biological diversity [Biodiversity Convention at art 19(3)].

i. Advance Informed Agreement (AIA)

The Cartagena Protocol's Advance Informed Agreement (AIA) procedure places obligations on exporters of genetically modified organisms (GMOs). A particular procedure must be followed, unless expressly waived by the party of import. The exporter must provide a detailed, written description of the GMO to the importing State in advance of the first intentional transboundary shipment. The importing State must acknowledge receipt of the information within 90 days, and then explicitly authorize the shipment within 270 days or state its reasons for rejecting it. The absence of a response does not imply consent. The purpose of this procedure is to ensure that importing States have both the opportunity and the capacity to assess risks that may be associated with GMOs before agreeing to their import [Cartagena Protocol at art. 7].

However, a number of GMOs are specifically excluded from the AIA procedure. These are: GMOs in transit [*Id.* at art. 6]; GMOs destined for contained use [*Id.* at art 6]; and GMOs intended for direct use as food or feed or for processing [*Id.* at art 7(2)]. The Meeting of the Parties (MOP) to the Cartagena Protocol may also decide to exempt additional GMOs from the AIA procedure in the future. Nevertheless, while these categories of GMOs are excluded from the Cartagena Protocol's specific AIA procedure, this does not imply that States may not regulate their import.

Additionally, the COP has adopted requirements for labeling shipments of GMOs. Labels must state that the shipment carries GMOs, identify the organism, provide handling and storage requirements, and provide a contact for further information [Biodiversity Convention, REPORT OF THE FIRST MEETING OF THE CONFERENCE OF THE PARTIES SERVING AS THE MEETING OF THE PARTIES TO THE PROTOCOL ON BIOSAFETY (2004) at 88–89 (hereinafter Biosafety COP-1)]. The labeling requirements differ slightly depending upon whether the organism is intended for contained use or if it is to be intentionally introduced into the destination's environment. The COP imposed further labeling requirements for GMOs intended for use as food, feed, or for processing at COP-3 in March 2006 [Biodiversity Convention, REPORT OF THE THIRD MEETING OF THE CONFERENCE OF THE PARTIES TO THE

CONVENTION ON BIOLOGICAL DIVERSITY SERVING AS THE MEETING OF THE PARTIES TO THE CARTAGENA PROTOCOL ON BIOSAFETY (2006) at 60–61]. In October 2010, COP-5 decided to affirm its commitment to the control of GMOs and authorize the use of online means to gather and disseminate information necessary to that end [Biodiversity Convention, FIFTH MEETING OF THE CONFERENCE OF THE PARTIES TO THE CONVENTION ON BIOLOGICAL DIVERSITY SERVING AS THE MOP TO THE CARTAGENA PROTOCOL ON BIOSAFETY (2010), BS-V/9].

ii. Biosafety Clearing-House

The Cartagena Protocol also established a Biosafety Clearing-House in order to facilitate the exchange of scientific, technical, environmental, and legal information concerning GMOs, and to assist parties in implementing their commitments [Cartagena Protocol at art. 20(1)]. In 2003, the Secretariat released Guidelines for National Participation in the Biosafety Clearing-House, which gave technical guidance to parties and other governments on how to register and submit data to the Clearing-House. The COP set a minimum level of information to which the Clearing-House should provide access [Biosafety COP-1 at 35–37]. The COP also established goals for improving the efficacy of the Clearing-House [Biodiversity Convention, REPORT OF THE SECOND MEETING OF THE CONFERENCE OF THE PARTIES TO THE CONVENTION ON BIOLOGICAL DIVERSITY SERVING AS THE MEETING OF THE PARTIES TO THE CARTAGENA PROTOCOL ON BIOSAFETY (2005) at 33–36]. Recent COPs have made significant efforts to streamline the process and make it more widely available online and offline. The Biosafety Clearing-House Advisory Committee recommended a study of users and potential users and training for current users to advance to a second phase of technology [FIFTH MEETING OF THE INFORMAL ADVISORY COMMITTEE OF THE BIOSAFETY CLEARING-HOUSE (2009), UNEP/CBD/BS/BCH-IAC/5/2].

For GMOs intended for direct use as feed or food or for processing, the Cartagena Protocol establishes a special procedure that requires States to exchange information at an early stage through the Biosafety Clearing-House. For example, States must give notice to the Clearing-House of domestic authorizations of GMOs, and make available copies of national laws and regulations concerning these GMOs [Cartagena Protocol at art. 11].

iii. Precautionary Approach

The Cartagena Protocol contains references to a precautionary approach, reaffirming the precautionary language in Principle 15 of the Rio Declaration [Rio Declaration at Principle 15]. According to the Cartagena Protocol, States will decide whether or not to accept imports of GMOs on the basis of risk assessments, which are to be undertaken in a scientific manner based on recognized risk assessment techniques [Cartagena Protocol at art. 15]. However, where there is insufficient relevant scientific information, a State may decide to apply the precautionary approach and refuse the import of the GMO into its territory [*Id.* at art. 10(6)]. The Cartagena Protocol also recognizes the right of importing States to take into account socio-economic considerations, such as the value of biodiversity to its indigenous and local communities, in reaching a decision on the import of GMOs [*Id.* at art. 26(1)].

iv. Compliance

While the Cartagena Protocol concentrates on international action, it recognizes that national measures are vital to making its procedures effective. Consistent with the emphasis on civil society, parties commit themselves to promoting public awareness, ensuring public access to information, and consulting the public in decisions concerning GMOs and biosafety. Parties must also take national measures to prevent illegal shipments and accidental releases of GMOs, and they must notify affected or potentially affected States in the event that an unintentional release occurs. The COP has established a working group charged with developing rules and procedures for a liability and redress regime to deal with damages resulting from transboundary GMO shipments, but only recently has a binding regime been put in place [Biosafety COP-1 at 104–05]. The 2010 Nagoya Protocol authorizes countries to use their domestic law to grant redress within a liability regime [Nagoya Protocol at art. 3].

v. Relationship to Other Agreements

The commercialization of biotechnology and the proliferation of GMOs have spawned multi-billion-dollar industries for foodstuffs and pharmaceuticals that continues to grow at a dramatic pace. Advocates of GMOs have argued that GMOs offer one practical way of feeding the poor and advancing SD. However, as we have noted, the Cartagena Protocol permits restrictions and even the banning of imports of GMOs.

On the other hand, the WTO's Agreement on Sanitary and Phytosanitary Measures (SPS Agreement) also addresses trade in GMOs [GATT Uruguay Round General Agreements on Tariffs and Trade, *Agreement on Sanitary and Phytosanitary Measures,* 1994, Annex 1A (hereinafter SPS Agreement)]. The SPS Agreement forms part of the GATT regime institutionalizing free trade. The proponents of GATT contend that free trade is the most important international machinery for advancing economic growth and SD. To the extent that a decision to ban GMOs obstructs free trade, the SPS Agreement requires that such decisions be justified on principles of sound scientific knowledge based on scientific risk assessments [*Id.* at art. 5]. However, as we have previously seen, the Cartagena Protocol focuses on environmental protection, not free trade, and allows States pursuing biosafety to ban GMOs by using the precautionary principle, even where strict scientific proof may be lacking.

Any judicial dispute over this issue will fall within the jurisdiction of the Dispute Settlement bodies of the WTO, because neither the Biodiversity Convention nor the Cartagena Protocol creates binding dispute settlement procedures. Environmentalists, including the present authors, have justifiably been suspicious about the judicial machinery of the WTO. To assuage such fears, it is necessary that any decisions taken by the judicial bodies of the WTO be based on the international customary law principles of fairness and reasonableness [*see* Lakshman Guruswamy, *Sustainable Agriculture: Do GMOs Imperil Biosafety?* 9 IND. J. GLOBAL LEGAL STUD. 461 (2002)].

b. 2010 Nagoya-Kuala Lumpur Supplementary Protocol on Liability and Redress to the Cartagena Protocol on Biosafety (Nagoya Protocol)

The Nagoya Protocol was adopted on October 15, 2010, and opened for signature on March 7, 2011. It will enter into force on the ninetieth day after the date of deposit of the 40th instrument of ratification, acceptance, approval, or accession [Nagoya Protocol at art.18]. It has not yet come into force at the time of writing.

The new supplementary Nagoya Protocol provides international rules and procedure on liability and redress for damage to biodiversity resulting from LMOs. From the point of view of accountability for wrong, the Nagoya Protocol leaves intact the rule of State responsibility (SR) for internationally wrongful acts [*Id.* at art.11]. What is more significant is the establishment of a regime of civil liability (CL) of the kind referenced in Chapter 3.

Article 12 requires the parties to provide, in their domestic law, for rules and procedures that address damage. This would include applying their existing domestic law, including rules and procedures on CL; applying or developing CL rules and procedures specifically for this purpose; or applying or developing a combination of both. When developing their CL law, parties shall, as appropriate, address, *inter alia*, the elements of damage; standard of liability, including strict or fault-based liability; channeling of liability, where appropriate; and the right to bring claims.

3. INTERNATIONAL INSTRUMENTS ADDRESSING HABITAT DESTRUCTION

The primary cause of the loss of biodiversity is habitat destruction resulting from the expansion of human populations and activity. Several international legal instruments attempt to address the problem of habitat destruction.

a. 1971 Convention on Wetlands of International Importance, Especially as Waterfowl Habitat (Ramsar Convention)

The Ramsar Convention, signed in Ramsar, Iran in 1971, is the oldest international treaty created solely for the protection of ecosystems. This treaty specifically attempts to safeguard wetlands, with an emphasis in protecting areas of "international importance to waterfowl" [Ramsar Convention at art.

2(2)]. The Ramsar Convention establishes a list of protected sites called the List of Wetlands of International Importance, or the Ramsar List. As of this writing, the Ramsar List contains 2,260 entries [Ramsar Convention on Wetlands, *The Ramsar List of Wetlands of International Importance, available at* http://www.ramsar.org/sites/default/files/documents/ library/sitelist.pdf (last visited Apr. 2017)]. The Ramsar COP has also created a Record of Ramsar Sites, which includes Ramsar List sites most in need of conservation.

Once parties designate sites for inclusion on the Ramsar List, the Ramsar COP votes for approval (and removal) of listed sites [Ramsar Convention at art. 6(2)(b)]. To become a full party to the convention, each contracting State must designate at least one wetland for protection on the Ramsar List [*Id.* at art. 2(4)]. Unfortunately, this requirement has often acted as an impediment to the accession of developing countries, which often cannot meet the expense of creating a reserve. To assist developing countries with this issue, the Ramsar Convention established the Ramsar Wetland Conservation Fund in 1990. This move has attracted new parties from the developing world, and total membership now consists of 169 parties.

i. Conservation

For listed sites, the parties must inform the managing "Bureau" of any change in ecological character [*Id.* at art. 3(2)]. If a party must delete or restrict the boundaries of a designated site, it should compensate for any net loss through the creation of additional reserves [*Id.* at art. 4(2)]. The parties shall also "endeavor through management to increase waterfowl populations on appropriate wetlands" [*Id.* at art. 4(4)]. Finally, by recommendation of the Ramsar COP, each party must inventory and monitor its national wetlands. In addition to designating at least one wetland for inclusion on the Ramsar List, the parties must promote the general conservation of wetlands by establishing and maintaining nature reserves, whether included on the Ramsar List or not [*Id.* at art. 4(1)].

ii. Wise Use

In potential conflict with its obligation to conserve, the Ramsar Convention also mandates that parties "formulate and implement their planning so as to promote . . . as far as possible the wise use of wetlands in their territories" [*Id.* at art. 3(1)]. By juxtaposing conservation and wise use, the Ramsar Convention offers an early example of the protection versus development schism found in the Biodiversity Convention.

In 1987 the Ramsar COP defined "wise use" in terms of "sustainable utilization," and since has promulgated a number of requirements toward this end. Most notably, parties must adopt and apply the Ramsar COP's Guidelines for Implementation of the Wise Use Concept, including the establishment of National Wetlands Policies. Additionally, each party must develop management plans for each Ramsar site. Recent monitoring procedures require parties to file annual reports concerning the health of threatened areas on the Record of Ramsar Sites. The Ramsar COP has also instituted the rule of environmental impact assessment prior to any proposed development of national wetlands.

iii. Consultations

The Ramsar Convention further mandates that the parties "consult with each other about implementing obligations arising from the Convention," especially emphasizing this requirement with regard to transboundary wetlands [*Id.* at art. 5]. The preamble also makes the general point "that the conservation of wetlands and their flora and fauna can be ensured by combining far-sighted national policies with coordinated international action" [*Id.* at pmbl.].

Though wetlands continue to deteriorate worldwide due to development and population pressures, the Ramsar Convention has achieved a significant amount given its limited budget and its only recent growth in developing country membership. With greater resources channeled to developing country parties—and with increased coordination of its efforts with other treaty regimes such as the Biodiversity Convention—the Ramsar Convention can undoubtedly increase its contribution to the global effort of protecting wetland biodiversity. Historically, the Bureau of the Ramsar Convention and the Secretariat of the Biodiversity Convention have worked together very closely, beginning with their Memorandum of

Understanding (MOU) in 1996 and continuing to joint work toward the 2010 biodiversity goals [Convention on Biological Diversity COP 3, 1996, UNEP/CBD/COP/3/Inf.38].

b. 1972 UNESCO Convention Concerning the Protection of the World Cultural and Natural Heritage (World Heritage Convention)

Another early environmental treaty, the 1972 UNESCO Convention Concerning the Protection of the World Cultural and Natural Heritage (World Heritage Convention) plays a small but important role in the conservation of biodiversity by recognizing and protecting examples of "cultural" and "natural" heritage [*UNESCO Convention Concerning the Protection of the World Cultural and Natural Heritage*, Nov. 16, 1972, 1037 U.N.T.S. 151 (hereinafter World Heritage Convention)]. Like the Ramsar Convention, the World Heritage Convention maintains a list of protected sites called the World Heritage List. For a site to be included on the World Heritage List, individual States nominate a domestic site and then the World Heritage Committee, an elected group of 21 parties, judges the request with the help and expertise of the IUCN. Examples of "natural heritage" must fit within one of the following categories:

Natural features consisting of physical and biological formations or groups of such formations, which are of outstanding universal value from the aesthetic or scientific point of view; geological or physiographical formations and precisely delineated areas which constitute the habitat of threatened species of animals and plants of outstanding universal value from the point of view of science or conservation; natural sites or precisely delineated areas of outstanding universal value from the point of view of science, conservation or natural beauty [*Id.* at art. 2].

As of April 2017, 203 "natural" and 35 "mixed" cultural/natural sites are listed on the World Heritage List, including developing country sites and Everglades and Yellowstone National Parks in the U.S. [UNESCO, *World Heritage List, available at* http://whc.unesco.org/en/list (last visited Apr. 2017)]. Analogous to the Record of Ramsar Sites most in need of conservation, the World Heritage Committee also administers a List of World Heritage in Danger, which consists of sites "threatened by serious and specific dangers, such as the threat of disappearance caused by accelerated deterioration" [World Heritage Convention at art. 11(4)]. As of this writing there are 55 sites designated as "in danger." The World Heritage Convention also creates a World Heritage Fund, which helps developing countries in the establishment and maintenance of sites on both lists [*Id.* at arts. 15–26].

As a matter of international law, the World Heritage Convention creates obligations at both the national and international level. Domestically, it recognizes a duty for each party, "to the utmost of its own resources and where appropriate," to identify, conserve, protect, and transfer to future generations the natural heritage located within its jurisdiction [*Id.* at art. 4]. As this provision suggests, a party must fulfill this duty for every site it designates as natural heritage—regardless of whether the site actually is approved for the World Heritage List. Furthermore, each party must undertake specific actions to meet this obligation, such as legal and administrative reforms [*Id.* at art. 5]. The parties must also submit reports on the efforts that they have expended to comply with the World Heritage Convention [*Id.* at art. 29].

At the international level, while reaffirming territorial sovereignty, the World Heritage Convention recognizes that natural heritage "constitutes a world heritage for whose protection it is the duty of the international community as a whole to co-operate" [*Id.* at art. 6(1)]. This is an early example of the "common heritage" concept, which was downgraded in the Biodiversity Convention to "the common concern of humankind." In addition, the World Heritage Convention imposes a collective obligation on the parties to assist poorer developing countries, at the latter's request, in their efforts to fulfill the substantive obligations of the treaty [*Id.* at art. 6(2)].

Though the effectiveness of the World Heritage Convention remains limited by its narrow definition of "natural heritage"—in practice constraining its application to the establishment and protection of national parks—it has proven a helpful tool in the global effort to conserve biodiversity. To multiply its effect in the future, the treaty administration must closely coordinate its activities with the Biodiversity Convention.

c. 1979 Convention on the Conservation of Migratory Species of Wild Animals (Bonn Convention)

The Bonn Convention, signed in Bonn, Germany in 1979, covers the entire spectrum of migratory animal species, including birds, mammals, reptiles, and fish. After a slow start, the Bonn Convention has recently made considerable strides in effecting cooperation. As of this writing the Bonn Convention has 120 parties, and while previously the bulk of its parties were European, membership now includes countries from Africa, Central and South America, Asia, and Oceania [United Nations Environment Programme, *Parties to the Convention on the Conservation of Migratory Species of Wild Animals* (2011)].

Still, many States have not signed the Bonn Convention, presumably because they consider migratory species sufficiently protected under other conventions, often bilateral in nature. For example, neither Canada nor the U.S. is a party due to their own bilateral treaty, which arguably defends the flyways of most ducks and geese, particularly since the treaty now includes Mexico [*Protection of Migratory Birds Agreement,* 1916, 12 Bevans 375]. Such a stance, however, does little to protect the numerous other species listed in the Bonn Convention's annexes, and fails to recognize the continued threat to all migratory species. Nevertheless, despite unequal participation, the

Bonn Convention continues to gain adherents in its effort to protect migratory species.

The Bonn Convention adopts an interesting wrinkle to the usual framework approach to international law-making. Rather than relying on the adoption of protocols, the convention facilitates the creation of cooperative arrangements among States. This strategy is employed for species listed in Appendix II, and is described more fully below. At a more general level, the Bonn Convention contains perhaps the most evocative plea for intergenerational equity in international law, proclaiming "that each generation of man holds the resources of the earth for future generations and has an obligation to ensure that this legacy is conserved and, where utilized, is used wisely" [Bonn Convention at pmbl.]. The treaty then leaves its specific requirements for actions undertaken with regard to the two appendices.

Appendix I lists endangered species, creating broad duties for parties whose territory comprises any part of a listed species' range, or whose flagships hunt the species [*Id.* at art. I(1)(h)]. "Endangered" under the Bonn Convention "means that the migratory species is in danger of extinction throughout all or a significant portion of its range" [*Id.* at art. I(1)(e)]. For Appendix I species, parties must endeavor to conserve and restore habitats, to minimize the adverse effects of activities or obstacles impeding migration, and to reduce or control further endangerment [*Id.* at art. III(4)]. Parties must also prohibit "takings" of Appendix I species, except in exceptional circumstances [*Id.* at art. III(5)]. To monitor progress in protecting both Appendix I and Appendix II species, the treaty requires each party to submit reports on measures taken to implement their commitments [*Id.* at art. VI(3)].

Appendix II contains those species with an "unfavorable conservation status," a broad term which suggests all threatened migratory species [*Id.* at art. I(1)(c) & (d)]. Rather than general protection duties, however, the Bonn Convention requires that parties strive to enter into cooperative Agreements to promote conservation and restoration of selected species [*see Id.* at arts. IV & V]. Any Agreement should attempt to cover the entire migratory route of the species, and should remain open to accession by all States, including those not party to the Bonn Convention [*Id.* at art. V(2)]. To date, several Agreements have been concluded under the auspices of the Bonn Convention. Three of them entered into force in 1994: the Conservation of Bats in Europe; the Conservation of Small Cetaceans (whales and dolphins) of the Baltic and North Seas; and the Conservation of Seals in the Wadden Sea. These three Agreements have successfully attracted a significant number of States as parties. Since then there have been four additional Agreements: the Agreement on the Conservation of African-Eurasian Migratory Waterbirds (entered into force in 1999); the Agreement on the Conservation of Cetaceans in the Black Sea, Mediterranean Sea and contiguous Atlantic Area (entered into force in 2001); the Agreement on the Conservation of Albatrosses and Petrels (entered into force in 2004); and the

Agreement on the Conservation of Gorillas and Their Habitats (entered into force in 2008).

One criticism of the Bonn Convention is that it has not fostered more Agreements for Appendix II species, but at least part of the problem rests with the formal quality of such arrangements. As structured under the Bonn Convention, Agreements for the protection of Appendix II species are themselves binding legal instruments, necessitating long and often politically exhausting periods of negotiation and ratification. In lieu of such formal agreements, the Bonn Convention COP has recommended that parties first develop informal MOUs, a practice that might allow substantial cooperation until more formal arrangements come into being. To this end, the parties (and non-parties) have recently developed several new MOUs: the High Andean Flamingos MOU (effective in 2008); the West African Aquatic Mammals MOU (effective in 2008); the MOU on the Conservation of Migratory Sharks (effective in 2010); and the MOU on the Conservation of Migratory Birds of Prey in Africa and Eurasia (54 signatories as of 2016, still awaiting sufficient signatories from appropriate territories).

The Bonn Convention therefore has dramatically improved its record over the last five years, with a number of additional Agreements and MOUs in the development stage. The convention has also created a strong working relationship with the Biodiversity Convention, the Ramsar Convention, and CITES. With increased party recruitment, especially in the

Americas and Asia, it can continue to enhance its performance.

4.   1973 CONVENTION ON INTERNATIONAL TRADE IN ENDANGERED SPECIES OF FAUNA AND FLORA (CITES)

Trade has greatly contributed to the decline of wild species that possess some commercial viability, including the high profile mammals of Africa. The 1973 CITES convention, one of the largest international environmental treaties in the world boasting 183 parties as of this writing, attempts to protect endangered plant and animal species through restrictions on international trade. Ratified by most States involved in this type of commerce, CITES creates a number of bureaucratic hurdles that prevent particularly harmful exchanges and establishes a paper trail for all allowable trade in protected species. Any trade without proper documentation is considered illegal under the treaty.

CITES protects literally thousands of species, a large number of which have their primary habitats in the developing world. To keep track of such a high volume of trade, the CITES COP has established both a Plants Committee and an Animals Committee. The membership of both these committees was recently reconfigured to allow for greater representation by developing countries, or "producers." In addition to protecting both plant and animal specimens, either alive or dead, CITES also covers "any recognizable part or derivative thereof" [CITES at art. I(b)]. This provision restricts legal trade in coveted items such as rhino horns and elephant tusks, though a great deal of illegal traffic still occurs.

a. Commitments

CITES creates only a few substantive duties for the parties. To begin, each party must establish both a "Management Authority" and a "Scientific Authority," whose collective job it is to administer the permit system as detailed below. Each party must also submit annual reports to the Secretariat documenting the number and types of permits granted, and biannual reports on the legislative, regulatory, and administrative measures taken to enforce the convention [*Id.* at art. VIII]. Finally, each party must follow the procedures of documentation regarding the three appendices of protected species.

Appendix I "includes all species threatened with extinction which are or may be threatened by trade" [*Id.* at art. II(1)]. To engage in commerce involving an Appendix I species, a trader must obtain both an export and import permit. An importing State will grant an import permit only after its Scientific Authority advises that the import will not be "detrimental to the survival of the species involved" and that the recipient can suitably care for the specimen, if living [*Id.* at art. III(3)]. In addition, the importing nation's Management Authority must confirm that the proposed use of the specimen is not "for primarily commercial purposes" [*Id.* at art. III(3)].

Similarly, the exporting State may grant an export permit only after its Scientific Authority finds the exchange non-threatening to the survival of that species [*Id.* at art. III(2)]. Furthermore, its Management Authority must (1) discover no violation of its domestic species protection laws; (2) believe that the transfer will minimize the risk of injury, damage to health, or cruel treatment; and (3) confirm the previous granting of an import permit [*Id.* at art. III(2)]. Thus, the CITES regime disallows most harmful trade in Appendix I species, and generates an intricate paper trail for permissible exchanges.

Appendix II of the convention includes species that may become threatened in the future without trade controls [*Id.* at art. II(2)]. For this category, CITES requires only an export permit, not the additional burden of an import permit. Following the exact model for Appendix I, the exporting party may grant the permit only after its Scientific Authority deems the exchange non-threatening to the survival of the species, and after its Management Authority finds the specimen both legally obtained and safely transferable [*Id.* at art. IV(2)]. Therefore, though less involved for the parties than Appendix I exchanges, CITES still generates a considerable paper trail for all legal trade in Appendix II species.

Appendix III includes those species "which any Party identifies as being subject to regulation within its jurisdiction for the purpose of preventing or restricting exportation" [*Id.* at art. II(3)]. To trade in a species on this list in a State listing such species in

Appendix III, one must obtain an export permit and a Certificate of Origin. In this case, the export permit dispenses with the need for any determination by the exporting State's Scientific Authority, requiring only satisfaction by the Management Authority that no domestic laws were violated in the taking of the specimen, and that the transfer would not involve undue harm [*Id.* at art. V(2)]. CITES requires a Certificate of Origin for all trade in Appendix III species, even if the transaction involves parties that have not listed species in Appendix III [*Id.* at art. V(3)].

To amend either Appendix I or II requires a two-thirds majority of parties present and voting at a meeting of the COP [*Id.* at art. XV]. This includes transfers of a species from one appendix to another, as occurred with the "uplisting" of the Cuvier's Gazelle from Appendix III to Appendix I in 2007. In practice, this super-majority voting procedure provides the COP with a dynamic tool, allowing it to alter the protections of the regime as circumstances change. An amendment to Appendix III occurs simply by the communication of any party that it wishes to designate a species as such [*Id.* at art. XVI].

b. Continued Trade in Listed Species

Despite the commitments listed above, legal trade under CITES—not to mention illegal trade outside the treaty—still takes place in several different ways. A major loophole of the CITES regime lies in the ability of parties to file reservations against the listing of a species in Appendix I, II, or III—or in any parts and derivatives of Appendix III species [*Id.* at art. XXIII]. A reservation completely avoids the permit system with regard to that species, in effect placing the objecting party in the position of a non-party who can freely trade with other non-parties.

A second problem involves the ability of parties to continue engaging in trade with non-parties (or an objecting party for a particular species), when the non-party issues "comparable" documentation that "substantially conforms" to CITES permits and certificates [*Id.* at art. X]. This is a practice which remains open to fraud by traders and non-parties.

CITES also authorizes certain exemptions for listed species. For example, specimens that are acquired within an owner's usual State of residence and deemed "personal or household effects" generally are not covered by CITES [*Id.* at art. VII(3)]. The convention also exempts specimens documented by an exporting State's Management Authority as acquired before that particular species became listed [*Id.* at art. VII(2)]. Of greatest significance, CITES also excuses from its restrictions species "bred in captivity" if the trader obtains a certificate of captive breeding from the State of export [*Id.* at art. VII(5)]. However, to prevent fraud in this exemption, the COP oversees a register of all operations that breed Appendix I species worldwide, and has successfully urged parties not to receive certificates of captive breeding from unregistered facilities. The COP also oversees a list of scientific institutions entitled to a CITES exemption for "non-commercial loan, donation, or exchange between scientists or scientific institutions" [*Id.* at art. VII(6)].

In addition, the COP allocates quotas for certain species—including Appendix I species such as the leopard, various crocodilians, and the cheetah—when it determines that trade within set limits will not be detrimental to the survival of that species [*see* CITES, *Ninth Meeting* (1994) at Res. 9.21]. The COP has recommended that States with a population of African elephants establish quotas for the export of raw ivory [*Id.* at Res. 9.16]. This reinstitutes the quota system for raw ivory that was discontinued when the African elephant was "uplisted" to Appendix I in 1989. Again, the quotas should function so as to manage the resident population and not to the detriment of the species as a whole. In this way the CITES regime has acted to promote the principle of SD, rewarding those parties and local communities which have successfully protected their herds, by endorsing a managed and limited cull.

Overall, the CITES regime has performed well given its limited resources and broad scope. As the COP acknowledges, however, illegal trade in the most sought after species still continues at an alarming rate. Whether the treaty proves ultimately successful will depend on the industrialized world's greater financial commitment in promoting diligent enforcement in the developing world.

c. Relationship to Other Agreements

The provisions of the Bonn Convention dealing with takings of species helps to address the issue of over-exploitation of biological resources, particularly for migratory species. Under the Bonn Convention, States must prohibit takings of CITES Appendix I species, except in exceptional circumstances [Bonn Convention at art III(5)]. Parties to Bonn also must reduce and control further endangerment of CITES Appendix I species [*Id.* at art. III(4)]. By disallowing takings of CITES Appendix I species, and by requiring reduction of endangerment, obligations under the Bonn Convention arguably require States to make sure that Appendix I species are not over-exploited.

5. REGIONAL TREATIES AND AGREEMENTS RELATED TO BIODIVERSITY

In addition to the above international environmental treaties, a number of regional agreements have emerged over the years. These include a cluster of treaties protecting the Antarctic (*see* Ch. 8) such as the 1959 Antarctic Treaty, [*Antarctic Treaty,* Dec. 1, 1959 (entered into force Jun. 23, 1961), 19 I.L.M. 860 (hereinafter Antarctic Treaty)]; the Convention for the Conservation of Antarctic Seals (CCAS) [*Convention for the Conservation of Antarctic Seals,* Feb. 11, 1972 (entered into force Mar. 11, 1978), 11 I.L.M. 251 (hereinafter CCAS)]; and the Protocol on Environmental Protection to the Antarctic Treaty (1991 Antarctic Environmental Protocol) [*Protocol on Environmental Protection to the Antarctic Treaty,* Oct. 4, 1991 (entered into force Jan. 15, 1998), 30 I.L.M. 1461 (hereinafter 1991 Antarctic Environmental Protocol)]. Among the more

important of other regional treaties are the
Convention on Nature Protection and Wildlife
Conservation in the Western Hemisphere
[*Convention on Nature Protection and Wildlife
Conservation in the Western Hemisphere,* Oct. 12,
1940, 161 U.N.T.S. 193]; the African Convention for
the Conservation of Nature and Natural Resources
[*African Convention for Conservation of Nature and
Natural Resources,* Sept. 15, 1968, 1001 U.N.T.S. 3];
the Convention on Conservation of European Wildlife
and Natural Habitats (Berne Convention)
[*Convention on Conservation of European Wildlife
and Natural Habitats,* Sept. 19, 1979, Bern
19.IX.1979 (hereinafter Berne Convention)]; and the
1985 Agreement on the Conservation of Nature and
Natural Resources adopted by the Association of
South East Asian Nations (1985 ASEAN Convention)
[*Agreement on the Conservation of Nature and
Natural Resources,* Jul. 9, 15 1985, E.P.L. 64
(hereinafter 1985 ASEAN Convention)].

Members of the EU also remain bound by Council
Directive 92/43 on the Conservation of Natural
Habitats and of Wild Fauna and Flora [European
Union, *Council Directive 92/43 on the Conservation
of Natural Habitats and of Wild Fauna and Flora,*
1992 O.J. (L 206/7 1)], as well as the more specific
Council Directive 79/409 on the Conservation of Wild
Birds [European Union, *Council Directive 79/409 on
the Conservation of Wild Birds,* 1979 O.J. (L 103) 1].
More recently, the EU Biodiversity Strategy, adopted
in 1998, has become a framework for action. The
Strategy focuses specifically on the integration of
biodiversity concerns into relevant sectoral policies,

in particular: conservation of natural resources, agriculture, fisheries, regional policies, spatial planning, forests, energy, transport, tourism, development, and economic cooperation. In 2006, the Commission of the European Communities reiterated its commitment to the framework and set forth a plan to preserve European and global resources better by 2010, in concert with the Biodiversity Convention's goals [HALTING THE LOSS OF BIODIVERSITY BY 2010—AND BEYOND, COM (2006) 216 final]

F. CONCLUSIONS

This proliferation of agreements, some effective and some not, has compounded the need for coordination and cooperation among these various entities in order to effectively protect global biodiversity. As stated above, the Biodiversity Convention was originally intended to be an umbrella treaty that would consolidate the present cacophony of treaties into a workable whole. Hopefully, the existing Biodiversity Convention, though lacking any direct power over the other conventions, can still play a significant part in coordinating the diverse activities within the field.

CHAPTER SIX
GLOBAL CLIMATE CHANGE

A. ATMOSPHERIC FACTS

The earth receives constant solar radiation from the sun, which not only maintains temperatures but also drives the earth's climatic systems through a complex process of heat exchange. About a third of the incoming solar radiation is immediately reflected back by clouds, the atmosphere, and the earth's surface. The remaining two-thirds warms the earth's surface, which in turn reradiates part of the heat upwards into the atmosphere and back into space. To maintain a stable climate on earth, a balance between incoming and outgoing solar radiation is required.

The earth's atmosphere contains a mixture of gases. Nitrogen and oxygen are by far the most prevalent, accounting for approximately 78% and 21% respectively by volume. The remaining 1% consists of a variety of gases, among which argon is most voluminous. Greenhouse gases (GHGs) comprise a very small part of the atmospheric mix, yet they play a critical role in maintaining the balance of solar radiation. GHGs are largely transparent to incoming solar radiation, thereby allowing solar energy to reach the earth's surface. However, as energy is reradiated from earth, GHGs absorb most of the outgoing radiation. Then GHGs reradiate the absorbed energy uniformly in all directions, including back towards the earth's surface. This mechanism allows GHGs to trap some of the outgoing energy, thereby increasing the equilibrium temperature of the earth. This process is also known as the "greenhouse effect," drawing on the metaphor of glass in a greenhouse.

In the right quantities, GHGs help support life and ecosystems on earth by ensuring a relatively constant surface temperature of about 60°F (degrees Fahrenheit). However, a build-up of GHGs can upset this important equilibrium, resulting in a rise in surface temperatures [*see e.g.*, F. Sherwood Rowland, *Atmospheric Changes Caused by Human Activities: From Science to Regulation*, 27 ECOLOGY L.Q. 1261 (2001) at 1287]. Where GHGs are not present, as on Mars, the average surface temperature can fall to around minus 80°F; and where GHGs are present in relative excess, as on Venus, that average rises to an extreme high of 890°F.

Water vapor and carbon dioxide (CO_2) are the two most common GHGs. Water vapor comprises a highly variable 1% to 4% of atmospheric gases by volume. In comparison, CO_2 equals approximately 0.04% of the earth's atmosphere. Other less common yet stronger GHGs—as measured in terms of their efficacy in contributing to the greenhouse effect—include methane (CH_4), nitrous oxide (N_2O), ozone (O_3), and halocarbons (human made compounds that contain chlorine or bromine and carbon atoms) [*see* Environmental Protection Agency (EPA), INVENTORY OF U.S. GREENHOUSE GAS EMISSIONS AND SINKS 1990–2005 (2007)].

B. INCREASING GREENHOUSE GAS (GHG) EMISSIONS

Since the beginning of the industrial revolution in about 1750, the atmospheric concentration of CO_2 has increased by about 40%—primarily as the result of fossil fuel combustion, while methane levels have increased by 150%, and nitrous oxides by 20% [*see* Intergovernmental Panel on Climate Change (IPCC), *Climate Change 2014: Synthesis Report*, Contribution of Workings Groups I, II and III to the Fifth Assessment Report of the IPCC (2014) at 44 (hereinafter IPCC 2014)]. The present concentration of atmospheric CO_2, 390 parts per million (ppm), has not ever been exceeded in the past 650,000 years—the span of time measurable in ice cores [*Id.*].

Each year, human activities continue to discharge over 30 billion tons of CO_2 and significant quantities of other GHGs, such as methane and nitrous oxides, further altering the natural distribution of atmospheric gases that blanket the earth. From 2007 to 2035, global CO_2 emissions are expected to grow over 43% and rise to 45 billion tons per year. Much of this increase is expected to come from developing countries, where CO_2 emissions are projected to grow by an average of 3% per year between 2007 and 2035. In total, a full 86% of the projected increase in global CO_2 emissions by 2030 is expected to come from developing countries [U.S. Energy Information Administration, INTERNATIONAL ENERGY OUTLOOK 2010 (2010)].

C. GREENHOUSE GAS (GHG) EMISSIONS AND CLIMATE CHANGE

In response to growing scientific and political concern over GHG emissions, the Intergovernmental Panel on Climate Change (IPCC) was formed jointly by the World Meteorological Organization (WMO) (*see* Appendix § V) and the United Nations Environment Programme (UNEP) in 1988 (*see* Appendix § P). The IPCC was directed to assess the risk of human-induced climate change. Since its inception, the IPCC has issued five assessment reports on climate change in 1990, 1995, 2001, 2007, and 2014. The news and media are awash with predictions and forecasts about climate change. Many of them claim to be "scientific" and emerge from a variety of research bodies and non-governmental organizations (NGOs) concerned about climate change. The reports of the IPCC render it unnecessary to undertake the difficult task of tracking these studies, or determining their credibility. The IPCC is the officially, credentialed, and most authoritative global agency charged with studying climate change, and this book will primarily rely on the findings and reports of the IPCC.

Climatic records have been kept for nearly 125 years, although systematic climatic instrumental recording only began in the 1950s. The IPCC Fourth Assessment Report in 2007 (IPCC 2007) posited for the first time that "warming of the climate system is unequivocal" [Intergovernmental Panel on Climate Change (IPCC), *Climate Change 2007: Synthesis Report*, Contribution of Workings Groups I, II and III to the Fifth Assessment Report of the IPCC (2007) at 2 (hereinafter IPCC 2007)], and that human activity is "very likely" the cause of most of the increase in globally averaged temperatures since the mid-20th century [*Id.* at 8]. The term "very likely" was used to indicate greater than 90% certainty. The IPCC Fifth Assessment Report issued in 2014 (IPCC 2014) is now 95% certain that humans are the main cause of current global warming [IPCC 2014 at V].

The IPCC has not always been so certain of its conclusions. Initially, scientists were reluctant to causally attribute the recent warming trend to anthropogenic activities—cautioning that a number of uncertainties constrained them from coming to a more certain conclusion. For instance, the IPCC's original assessment report in 1990 declared that the "unequivocal detection of the enhanced greenhouse effect from observations is not likely for a decade or more" [Intergovernmental Panel on Climate Change (IPCC), FIRST ASSESSMENT REPORT: CLIMATE CHANGE (1990)]. Five years later in 1995, the IPCC cautiously advanced this conclusion by stating the "balance of evidence . . . suggests a discernable human influence on global climate" [Intergovernmental Panel on Climate Change (IPCC), 1995 ASSESSMENT: CLIMATE CHANGE (1995) at 15 (hereinafter IPCC 1995)]. And in 2001 the IPCC noted there "is new and stronger evidence that most of the warming observed over the last 50 years is attributable to human activities" [Intergovernmental Panel on Climate Change (IPCC), CLIMATE CHANGE 2001: THE SCIENTIFIC BASIS—SUMMARY FOR POLICYMAKERS (2001) at 10 (hereinafter IPCC 2001)].

The "very likely" language from IPCC 2007 represents a strong (though not absolute) consensus among the majority of the scientific community that anthropogenic global climate change is real and will have increasingly negative impacts on the earth's environment unless some action is taken to limit or reduce GHG emissions.

However, not everyone agrees that climate change is an anthropogenic phenomenon. Scientists and non-scientists alike have challenged the scientific basis of climate change and the predictions of the IPCC. In addition to highlighting the present limitations of climate models in representing phenomena such as cloud formation [*see* Richard A. Kerr, *Greenhouse Forecasting Still Cloudy*, 276 SCIENCE 1040 (1997)], skeptics argue that a number of non-GHG related factors have not been given sufficient attention. For example, climate change could be caused by such astronomical variations as a change in solar output or a shift in the inclination or eccentricity of the earth's orbit [*see* Richard A. Kerr, *Upstart Ice Age Theory Gets Attentive But Chilly Hearing*, 277 SCIENCE 183 (1997)]. Although the world's science academies posit that these factors have been properly studied [*see* Judith Lean & David Rind, *Climate Forcing by Changing Solar Radiation*, 11 J. OF CLIMATE 3069 (1998)], such arguments still serve as a basis for discounting human culpability for climate change [*see* Richard A. Kerr, *A New Dawn for Sun-Climate Links,* 271 SCIENCE 1360 (1996)].

Despite the strenuous assertions of the IPCC that ". . . warming of the climate system is unequivocal, and since the 1950s, many of the observed changes are unprecedented over decades to millennia" [IPCC 2014 at 40], skeptics rely upon the fact that atmospherics temperatures have actually decreased during the period 1998 to 2012. The drop in global temperature significantly undermines the conclusion that global warming is caused by CO_2. *The Economist* magazine reported in 2013, that the world added roughly 100 billion tonnes of carbon to the atmosphere between 2000 and 2010. That is about a quarter of all the CO_2 put there by humanity since 1750. Yet, no warming occurred during that time [Peter Ferrara, "To The Horror Of Global Warming Alarmists, Global Cooling Is Here," *Forbes*, May 16, 2013].

The IPCC's response does not offer a conclusive explanation or one with a 90% degree of certainty. Instead its explanation is offered in qualitative terms, with only a "medium high" degree of confidence. According to the IPCC, the drop of temperature between 1998 and 2012 is due in ". . . roughly equal measure to a reduced trend in radiative forcing and a cooling contribution from natural internal variability, which includes a possible redistribution of heat within the ocean" [IPCC 2014 at 43]. The strength of this explanation, however, is weakened by the fact that the IPCC is only able to support its radiative forcing explanation with "low confidence" [*Id.*].

For the most part there is very little debate as to the *existence* of climate change. Even skeptics are willing to concede this point [*see* Richard Lindzen, *Is*

There a Basis for Global Warming?, YALE CENTER FOR GLOBALIZATION (Oct. 21, 2005)]. The controversy has instead shifted to questions of severity and potential ramifications [*Id.*]. The majority of the controversy now surrounds the accuracy of the mathematical models used to predict climatic changes. At issue is the fact that even the best climate change models cannot perfectly account for the awesome complexity of the earth's atmospheric mechanisms [Intergovernmental Panel on Climate Change (IPCC), CLIMATE CHANGE 2001: THE SCIENTIFIC BASIS (2001) at 94–95].

The IPCC admits that accurate quantitative projections of future climate change can only be undertaken where models simulate all of the important processes governing climate. However, it is clear that the models currently employed do not entirely do so. IPCC 2007 makes it clear that there are at least four important anthropogenic climatic variables that are poorly understood: (1) stratospheric water vapor from methane, (2) surface albedo, (3) aerosols, and (4) linear contrails (as well as the additional non-anthropogenic factor of solar irradiance) [IPCC 2007 at 16]. IPCC 2014 shows improvements in the models [Gerald Meehl, *IPCC AR5: Projections, predictions and progress since the AR4*, IPCC AR5 Working Group 1 (2013)], but does not contradict the shortcomings of models referred to in IPCC 2007. The question raised by critics is whether these mechanisms have the ability to cancel or exacerbate some or all of the effects of anthropogenic GHG emissions.

So can we expect a 50°F or a 15°F rise in temperatures over the next century? The answer to this question is arguably much less certain than whether humans are culpable, yet perhaps far more important. Predicted degree changes and potential ramifications thereof will strongly influence what steps the international community should or will take towards mitigating the problem, and for this reason climate change models are of central importance.

D.   EXTENT AND CONSEQUENCES OF CLIMATE CHANGE

1.   INTERGOVERNMENTAL PANEL ON CLIMATE CHANGE (IPCC) SCENARIOS

In their laudable attempt to depict possible futures in the face of evolving dynamics based on changing social, economic, technological, and political facts, the IPCC, after a five-year study, completed a Special Report on Emission Scenarios (SRES) in March 2000, presenting a cluster of scenarios based on differing "story lines." The report posited six possible emission scenario groups, which were in turn included in IPCC 2007. The six scenarios each represent a different combination of population growth, energy intensity, and alternative energy adoption. These factors help determine future GHG emissions, and therefore the possible severity of future climate change. The SRES scenarios were replaced by the Representative Concentration Pathways (RCPs) for four greenhouse gas concentration (not emissions) trajectories adopted by IPCC 2014 [Richard Moss, et al. *Towards*

New Scenarios for Analysis of Emissions, Climate Change, Impacts, and Response Strategies, Geneva: Intergovernmental Panel on Climate Change at 132. 2024].

The four RCPs: RCP2.6, RCP4.5, RCP6, and RCP8.5, describe four possible climate futures, all of which are considered possible depending on GHG emissions peaking and decline. RCP2.6 assumes GHG emissions peak between 2010–2020, with emissions declining substantially thereafter. RCP4.5 peaks around 2040, then declines. RCP6 peaks around 2080, then declines. In RCP8.5 emissions continue to rise throughout the 21st century [*Id.*].

2.   RISING TEMPERATURES

Based on these RCPs, IPCC 2014 arrived at conclusions that were more measured, balanced, and tempered than those found in IPCC 2007. In dealing with rising temperature, IPCC 2014 found that the global mean surface temperature change for the period 2016–2035 is similar in all four RCPs, and will likely be in the range 0.3°C (degrees Celsius) to 0.7°C [IPCC 2014 at 75].

The projected increases in temperature after 2035 would depend on the particular RCP. For the period up to 2100, for example, the increases under RCP2.6 amount to less than 1°C, but continue to rise under the other scenarios to a possible 4°C under RCP8.5 [*Id.* at 76]. It is worth observing that these projections of the IPCC do not justify some of the apocalyptic forecasts of imminent danger and devastation attributed to it.

The scenario groups are meant as a look at possible variations of a business-as-usual trajectory. What these scenarios emphasize is the excruciating complexity facing decision-makers when deciding how to address the consequences of climate change. Moderate climate change will have both beneficial and adverse impacts on human and natural systems. However, all modeling scenarios indicate that more severe climate change brings an increased likelihood of adverse effects, and the IPCC is confident that we will face significant adverse impacts should we continue to experiment with the earth's delicate balance.

3.   CHANGES IN PRECIPITATION AND WATER STRESS

Climate change is also likely to result in many changes in precipitation patterns, creating floods in some parts of the world and droughts in others. IPCC 2014 says that extreme precipitation events over most mid-latitude land masses and over wet tropical regions will "very likely" become more intense and more frequent as global mean surface temperature increases [*Id.* at 77]. General increases in the amount of precipitation are also "very likely" in high latitudes, while decreases are "likely" in most subtropical regions [*Id.*]. Future tropical cyclones (typhoons and hurricanes) are also "likely" to become more intense [*Id.*].

IPCC 2014 did not confirm the unsubstantiated assertion of the IPCC 2007 summary for policy makers that climate change will expose hundreds of millions to increased water stress [IPCC, *Summary for Policy Makers,* CLIMATE CHANGE 2007: IMPACTS, ADAPTATION AND VULNERABILITY (2007) at 13]. In fact, the full report of IPCC 2007 does not support this assertion. According to the IPCC 2007 full report, "an analysis of six climate models . . . and the SRES scenarios . . . shows a likely increase in the number of people who could experience water stress by 2055 in northern and southern Africa . . . In contrast, more people in eastern and western Africa will be likely to experience a reduction rather than an increase in water stress" [IPCC 2007 at *9.4.1*].

Water stress occurs when the demand for water exceeds the available amount during a certain period, or when poor quality restricts its use. Lack of supply is often caused by contamination, drought, or a disruption in distribution. Water stress causes deterioration of fresh water resources in terms of quantity, by aquifer over-exploitation and dry rivers, and quality, leading to eutrophication, organic matter pollution, and saline intrusion.

Credible official research from the United Kingdom also confirms that even more millions will experience reduced water stress [*see* Martin L. Perry, et al., *Effects of Climate Change on Global Food Production Under SRES Emissions and Socio-Economic Scenarios,* 14 Global Environmental Change 53 (2004)]. This is because climate change will increase precipitation, and although some areas will have less water, there will be increased rain in the more populated parts of the world [Oki T and

Kanae S, *Global Hydrological Cycles and World Water Resources*, 313 SCIENCE 1068–1072 (2006)].

Nonetheless, there is no doubt that water stress presents a huge problem in sub-Saharan Africa. A report of the Council on Foreign Relations points out that while water stress occurs throughout the world, no region has been more afflicted than sub-Saharan Africa [Christopher W. Tatlock, *Water Stress in Sub Saharan Africa, Council on Foreign Relations* (2006)]. The report goes on to attribute water stress to weak governments, corruption, mismanagement of resources, poor long-term investment, and lack of environmental research and urban infrastructure. Climate change is not mentioned. One of the primary conclusions of this report is that economic development incorporating water infrastructure is necessary to end the severe problems caused by water stress, and to improve public health and advance the economic stability of the region [*Id.*]. Consequently, what is required for the people who inhabit sub-Saharan Africa is more development within the framework of sustainable development (SD). Cutting down CO_2 emissions seems largely irrelevant to their present plight.

4.   SEA LEVEL RISE AND ICE MELT

The possible consequence of sea level rise has received popular press and cinematic attention, and sea level rise serves as a proxy for the most certain and most damaging consequences of climate change. According to IPCC 2007's Physical Science Basis Report, rising sea levels have corresponded with rising temperatures, and seas have risen by an average of 1.8 millimeters per year (mm/yr) between 1961 and 2003. IPCC 2014 predicts sea levels rising at a rate of 3.2 mm/yr (2.8 to 3.6) consistent with contributions from observed thermal ocean expansion due to rising temperatures, glacier melt, Greenland ice sheet melt, Antarctic ice sheet melt, and changes to land water storage. Based on improved understanding of sea level rises since IPCC 2007, IPCC 2014 predicts future year-round reductions in Arctic sea ice based on all four RCP scenarios. This rise will very likely exceed the observed rate of 2.0 mm/yr (1.7–2.3) during 1971–2010 [IPCC 2014 at 79]. However, such a prediction is significantly less than the IPCC 2007 forecast of 18 to 58 centimeters. This conclusion of the IPCC must be placed in the context of the incontrovertible record increase in Antarctic ice, and the disputed increase in Arctic ice discussed below.

While the Greenland ice pack has obviously melted at its fringes, contributing to sea level rise, the extent to which it has done so has been the subject of numerous studies, models, and predictions. IPCC 2007 says it is also "very likely" (more than 90% confidence) that ice sheet losses from Greenland and Antarctica have already contributed to higher sea levels between 1993 and 2003, although they cannot say by how much [IPCC 2007 at 5–6]. The IPCC estimates that Greenland is expected to contribute 35 millimeters over the century by itself. IPCC 2014 estimated the Greenland ice sheet melt at 0.33 mm/yr (0.25 to 0.41). Other models indicate a lower estimate of 10 mm and a higher estimate of 150 mm

[J. Gregory & P. Huybrechts, *Ice-sheet Contributions to Future Sea-level Change*, 364 PHILOSOPHICAL TRANSACTIONS OF THE ROYAL SOCIETY A: MATHEMATICAL, PHYSICAL AND ENGINEERING SCIENCES 1709 (2006)].

The importance of Greenland ice melt in sea level rises have been graphically demonstrated by former Vice President Al Gore's Academy Award winning apocalyptic film: An Inconvenient Truth. The film suggests that Greenland could melt or break up and slip into the sea, and shows how the resulting sea level rises would inundate large parts of Florida, including all of Miami, flood San Francisco Bay, wipe out the Netherlands, submerge Beijing and then Shanghai, make Bangladesh uninhabitable for 60 million people, and even deluge New York City and its World Trade Center Memorial.

But this scary scenario is not actually corroborated by existing scientific studies. Bjorn Lomborg, who believes that the consequences of climate change have been "vastly exaggerated," relies on the Greenland studies to point out that none of them posit rises higher than 3 mm/yr by the end of the century, whereas Gore's claim would need to raise sea levels by 120 mm—40 times higher than the very highest model estimate [*see* Al Gore, *Testimony Before a Joint Meeting of U.S. House Subcommittees on Energy and Air Quality, and Energy and Environment* (March 21, 2007)]. IPCC 2007 stated "abrupt changes, such as the collapse of the West Antarctic Ice Sheet, the rapid loss of the Greenland Ice Sheet, or large scale changes of ocean circulation systems, are not considered likely to occur in the 21st century based on currently available model results" [IPCC 2007 at 818]. IPCC 2014 did not contradict this prediction.

Two important matters relevant to ice melt and rising sea temperatures and levels have not received adequate attention. First, there is no doubt that the Antarctic Sea ice reached a new record high in 2014. According to NASA, ice covers more of the southern oceans than it has since scientists began a long-term satellite record to map sea ice extent in the late 1970s [National Aeronautics and Space Administration (NASA), Antarctic Sea Ice Reaches New Record Maximum (Oct. 7, 2014), *available at* https://www. nasa.gov/content/goddard/antarctic-sea-ice-reaches-new-record-maximum (last visited Apr. 2017)]. NASA, however, claims that the increase in Antarctic ice is only about a third of the magnitude of the rapid loss of sea ice in the Arctic Ocean [*Id.*]. This conclusion is disputed by other scientists who, using NASA's own figures, show that the loss of ice is now being reversed. They state that the Arctic ice cap has expanded for the second year in succession—with a surge, depending on how you measure it, of between 43 and 63% since 2012 [David Rose, *Myth of Arctic meltdown: Stunning satellite images show summer ice cap is thicker and covers 1.7 million square kilometres MORE than 2 years ago . . . despite Al Gore's prediction it would be ICE-FREE by 2014*, Daily Mail, (Aug. 30, 2014)]. According to these scientists, by May 2015, the updated NASA data show polar sea ice is approximately 5% above the post-1979 average [James Taylor, *Updated NASA*

Data: Global Warming Not Causing Any Polar Ice Retreat, FORBES, (May 19, 2015)].

The second fact is just now receiving patchy discussion. According to IPCC 2014, it is very likely that the Atlantic Meridional Overturning Circulation (AMOC) will weaken over the 21st century. AMOC is more popularly identified as the Gulf Stream. This global conveyor belt of water is critical to the world's climate [Robinson Myer, *The Atlantic Ocean and an Actual Debate in Climate Science*, Atlantic (Jan. 17, 2017)]. This weakening may range from 11 to 34%. A weakening of AMOC leads to global cooling.

The extent to which such cooling competes with global warming has long been a topic for speculation, but has not been addressed using definitive and conclusive climate models. One author who used a model ensemble concludes that global cooling due to a collapsing AMOC "obliterates" global warming for a period of 15–20 years [Sybren Drijfhout, *Competition between global warming and an abrupt collapse of the AMOC in Earth's energy imbalance*, Scientific Reports 5, Article number: 14877 (2015)].

E.   LEGAL RESPONSE

The current international legal response to the threats posed by climate change is found in the United Nations Framework Convention on Climate Change (UNFCCC) and its progeny the Paris Agreement of 2015 [*Paris Agreement, December 12, 2015*, 37, ILM 743 (2016)]. The Kyoto Protocol to the UNFCCC is moribund, and is essentially an expired treaty. The Kyoto Protocol's first commitment period started in 2008 and ended in 2012. A second commitment period was agreed on in 2012, known as the Doha Amendment. The Doha Amendment establishes the second commitment period of the Kyoto Protocol, which began on January 1, 2013 and will end on December 31, 2020. It is intended to cover the period between the end of the Kyoto Protocol's first commitment period in 2012 and the formal implementation of the Paris Agreement in 2020. The Doha Amendment will enter into force after three-fourths of the parties to the Kyoto Protocol have deposited their instruments of acceptance [United Nations Climate Change Secretariat, *Frequently asked questions relating to the Doha Amendment to the Kyoto Protocol* (Nov. 21, 2014), *available at* http://unfccc.int/files/kyoto_protocol/doha_amendme nt/application/pdf/frequently_asked_questions_doha _amendment_to_the_kp.pdf (last visited Apr. 2017)].

It is highly unlikely that the Doha Amendment will be accepted by 75% of the parties to the Kyoto Protocol. In the absence of the Doha Amendment coming into force, the Kyoto Protocol will remain a moribund treaty. The decision of the Conference of the Parties (COP) adopting the Paris Agreement to undertake enhanced action prior to 2020 and to agree on a work plan for the 2016–2020 period, confirms that interim actions under the Paris Agreement may well have taken the place of the Kyoto Protocol [United Nations Framework Convention on Climate Change (UNFCCC), *Adoption Of The Paris Agreement, Conference of the Parties Twenty-first session Paris, 30 November to 11 December 2015* (Dec. 2015), FCCC/CP/2015/L.9]. For the foregoing reasons, we will examine the UNFCCC and the Paris Agreement, but not the Kyoto Protocol. We will first identify the key features of these two treaties, and then address some outstanding issues of interpretation and implementation. The table below provides a brief summary of some of the key developments in the international climate change regime from 1979 to the present.

Timeline: The International
Climate Change Regime

1979   WMO convenes First World Climate Conference

1985   UNEP & WMO convene Villach Conference

1988   Toronto Conference and Declaration

1988   IPCC established, first IPCC Session convenes

1989   Noordwikj Conference and Declaration

1990   IPCC releases First Assessment Report

1990   Second World Climate Conference recommends framework convention

1990   First Session of the Intergovernmental Negotiating Committee

1992   UNFCCC signed at Earth Summit

1994   UNFCCC enters into force

1995   COP-1 & Berlin Mandate

1995   COP-2 & Geneva Declaration

1995   IPCC Second Assessment Report

1997 COP-3 & the Kyoto Protocol

1998 COP-4 in Buenos Aries

1999 COP-5 in Bonn

2000 COP-6 initiated in The Hague

2000 IPCC Third Assessment Report

2001 U.S. repudiates Kyoto Protocol

2001 COP-6 resumed in Bonn & Bonn Agreement

2001 COP-7 & Marrakech Accords

2002 World Summit on Sustainable Development (WSSD)

2002 COP-8 & Delhi Ministerial Declaration

2003 COP-9 in Milan

2004 COP-10 in Buenos Aries

2005 Kyoto Protocol enters into force after Russian ratification

2005 EU Emissions Trading Scheme comes online

2005 COP-11/MOP-1 & Montreal Action Plan

2006 COP-12/MOP-2 in Nairobi

2007 COP-13/MOP-3 & Bali Roadmap and Action Plan

2008 COP-14/MOP-4 in Poznan

2009 COP-15/MOP-5 & Copenhagen Accord

2010 COP-16/MOP-6 in Cancun

2011 COP-17 in Durban & Durban Mandate

2012 COP-18 in Doha & Doha Amendment

2013 COP-19 in Warsaw

2014 COP-20 in Lima

2015 COP-21 in Paris & Paris Agreement

1. 1992 UNITED NATIONS FRAMEWORK CONVENTION ON CLIMATE CHANGE (UNFCCC)

a. History and Overview

The UNFCCC came into existence after an accelerated process of negotiation. As scientific concern over climate change increased in the late 1980s, international attention focused rapidly on the issue. In 1990, the United Nations (UN) General Assembly created the Intergovernmental Negotiating Committee, calling for the adoption of a global convention on climate change at the United Nations Conference on Environment and Development (UNCED), also known as Earth Summit. At the time there was a substantial political base that desired long-term quantitative emission limits, but eventually a "go slow" approach prevailed. The short negotiating period, combined both with the enormous economic stakes and a substantial amount of scientific uncertainty, resulted in the adoption of only cautious controls in the final version of the treaty.

The UNFCCC, however, is not an empty framework treaty whose substantive details entirely await further elaboration. Instead, it is a framework convention with a number of built-in requirements. First, industrialized countries must strive to reduce their overall emissions of GHGs to 1990 levels by the year 2000 [UNFCCC at art. 4(2)(a) & 4(2)(b)]. Second, industrialized countries have a general commitment to make financial and technological transfers to developing countries [*Id.* at art. 3(2), 4(1)(c), & 4(2)–(4)]. Third, all parties—both industrialized and developing countries—must create inventories of GHGs, as well as national mitigation and adaptation programs, though different timetables are specified for each type of party [*Id.* at art. 4]. In mandating different requirements for industrialized and developing countries, the UNFCCC explicitly embraces the concept of common but differentiated responsibilities (CBDR) [*Id.* at art. 3(1)]. As we shall see, however, the exact application of CBDR remains controversial.

b. Remedial Objectives

A cluster of remedial objectives have been set forth in the UNFCCC. First, Article 2 states that the ultimate objective is to achieve:

> stabilization of greenhouse gas concentrations in the atmosphere at a level that would prevent dangerous anthropogenic interference with the climate system. Such a level should be achieved within a time frame sufficient to allow ecosystems to adapt naturally to climate change,

to ensure that food production is not threatened and to enable economic development to proceed in a sustainable manner [*Id.* at art. 2].

It is noteworthy that the UNFCCC specifies that the human interference must be "dangerous," not simply human interference that might impact the environment. This makes ample sense, because the first law of thermodynamics states that matter and energy are only transformed, never destroyed. Thus, any wastes that are not recycled or absorbed by man-made industrial and economic systems necessarily have at least some kind of impact on the environment. The question then becomes: to what extent do these wastes constitute a *dangerous* interference with complex climatic systems? To answer this question, the UNFCCC stipulates "where there are threats of serious or irreversible damage, lack of full scientific certainty should not be used as a reason for postponing such measures" provided the measures are cost effective [*Id.* at art. 3(3)].

Second, it is equally important that economic development is to proceed in a sustainable manner. Article 3(4) underlines the importance of economic development by asserting, "the Parties have a right to, and should, promote sustainable development" [*Id.* at art. 3(4)]. As we have seen in Chapter 2, SD has become the foundational norm of IEL, and its contours have been redefined by the World Summit on Sustainable Development (WSSD). While SD began as a two-sided concept, based on environmental protection and economic development, it has now been enlarged to become a triangle based on economic, environmental, and social development (*see* Ch. 2).

Third, climate change policies and laws should be based on equity and in accordance with the principle of CBDR [*Id.* at art. 3(1)]. This principle recognizes that only international cooperation will help to resolve a problem of the magnitude of climate change, but that in responding to the problem different states have different social and economic conditions that affect their response capabilities. CBDR also incorporates the equitable notion that industrialized countries, which have the largest share of historical emissions of GHGs, should take the first actions to ameliorate the problem. It deserves emphasis, however, that in the UNFCCC developing countries accepted their "common" responsibility for addressing climate change. The UNFCCC refers to the CBDR of *all* States, and does not define such responsibilities as the sole and exclusive obligation of industrialized countries.

Fourth, the measures taken to deal with climate change could range from actions taken to mitigate or arrest climate change to actions that seek to adapt to the consequences of climate change [*Id.* at art. 3(3)]. Mitigation, according to the UNFCCC, should be directed to the sources and sinks of GHGs [*Id.* at art 4(1)(b)], and is defined by the IPCC as "anthropogenic intervention to reduce the sources of greenhouse gases or enhance their sinks" [IPCC 2001 at 294]. Accordingly, mitigation would be directed toward reductions in the emission and accumulation of CO_2

and other GHGs, either by cutting down on emissions or by increasing the role of sinks, such as forests or oceans, that absorb GHGs. Adaptation, on the other hand, would seek to adjust natural and human systems to the consequences of climate change. Such adjustments could range over a spectrum of socioeconomic policies including the building of sea walls, moving cities, variations of crops, and changes in clothing, housing, and infrastructure. The UNFCCC states that adaptation requires integrated plans for coastal zone management, water resources, agriculture, and rehabilitation [UNFCCC at art. 4(1)(e)].

Finally, it is inescapable that the call for reductions of GHG emissions must be accompanied by monumental efforts to increase alternative sources of energy. It seems almost hopeless to demand fossil fuel cuts without creating new sources of fuel, dramatically increasing fuel efficiency, and improving conservation.

c. The Comprehensive Approach

In negotiating the appropriate response to be taken by industrialized countries, the parties struggled with a number of possible strategies. One such point of contention involved the "Comprehensive Approach" to GHG emissions, a discussion of which we have included here to show both the complexity of the problem and the difficulty of available solutions.

Since CO_2 is the primary GHG and its sources and sinks were better understood, the international community generally agreed that controlling CO_2 seemed the prudent place to start. Late in the negotiating game, however, the U.S. presented a different approach. Under this strategy, each GHG received a scientifically based value that measured its contribution to climate change relative to CO_2. Under the Comprehensive Approach, parties could then choose any mix of GHG reductions and removals by sinks—not just CO_2 reductions—in reducing their net contributions to climate change.

In the end, the UNFCCC adopted language that approved the Comprehensive Approach. The treaty refers to the reduction of "anthropogenic emissions of carbon dioxide and other greenhouse gases," which, though singling out CO_2, also includes the full panoply of GHGs [*Id.* at art. 4(2)(a) & (b)]. The ambiguity of this language actually provided the COP with real latitude in attempting to develop quantifiable emissions limits in the future [*Id.* at art. 4(2)(d)]. As to the inclusion of sinks, again the phrasing of the UNFCCC endorses the Comprehensive Approach [*Id.* at art. 4(2)(a),(b) & (c)]. Thus, a party is free to subtract any appropriate sinks in its calculation of total emissions of GHGs, and the COP has developed methodologies that industrialized countries should follow in making this important calculation.

d. Commitments

In implementing the concept of CBDR, the UNFCCC creates several classes of parties through annexes. Annex I includes the wealthier

Organization for Economic Cooperation and Development (OECD) States, as well as the former Eastern Bloc States "undergoing the process of transition to a market economy." Annex II includes only the OECD States. By omission, therefore, all remaining parties are developing countries. At several junctures, which will be noted below, the UNFCCC makes further special provisions for "least developed countries" and "small island States."

i. All Parties (Industrialized and Developing Countries)

All parties, including developing countries, have a number of general commitments under the UNFCCC. These include a duty to "promote and cooperate in the conservation and enhancement, as appropriate, of sinks and reservoirs of all greenhouse gases" [*Id.* at art. 4(1)(d)]. Significantly, this commitment omits any special protection for forests—the most important GHG sink—due to the concern of developing countries that the treaty not impinge on their freedom to develop forest resources. The parties must also cooperate in preparing for adaptation to the impacts of climate change [*Id.* at art. 4(1)(e)] and promoting research and development [*Id.* at art. 4(1)(g)], exchange of information [*Id.* at art. 4(1)(h)], and education, training, and public awareness [*Id.* at art. 4(1)(i)]. To the extent feasible, each party must also take climate change considerations into account in domestic policies and actions, employing appropriate methods of environmental impact assessment [*Id.* at art. 4(1)(f)]. Furthermore, each party must create national programs to mitigate climate change by addressing GHG emissions, which would also contain measures to "facilitate adequate adaptation to climate change" [*Id*. at art. 4(1)(b)].

More specifically, all parties must undertake certain reporting requirements. To begin, all parties must "[d]evelop, periodically update, publish and make available . . . national inventories of anthropogenic emissions by sources and removals by sinks of all greenhouses gases" [*Id*. at art. 4(1)(a)] and communicate these to the COP [*Id*. at art. 12(1)(a)]. In the creation of inventories, the treaty lightens the burden on developing countries, qualifying the requirement by the phrase "to the extent [their] capacities permit" [*Id*. at art. 12(1)(1)]. In these national communications, the parties must also include a general description of steps taken or envisioned so as to implement the UNFCCC, such as progress on the creation of national mitigation and adaptation programs [*Id*. at art. 12(1)(b)]. In addition, as stated above, the COP has established different guidelines for industrialized and developing countries in making the required national communications, and most developing countries were given until 1997 to meet this requirement (assuming that industrialized countries provided the necessary financial resources to create such reports), while "least developed countries" may submit their first reports "at their discretion" [*Id*. at art. 12(5)].

ii. Annex I Parties (OECD and Former Eastern Bloc Parties)

For Annex I parties the UNFCCC stipulates limited targets and timetables, requiring that all such parties "aim" to return to 1990 emissions levels for all GHGs by the year 2000 [*Id.* at art. 4(2)(a) & (b)]. This obligation—qualified by the word "aim" rather than "must"—created some confusion as to its binding quality. However, the Kyoto Protocol cleared this confusion, and now all Annex I parties, or industrialized countries, must reduce their emissions of CO_2 to approximately 5% below 1990 levels by 2012.

e. Institutions and Implementation

i. Conference of the Parties (COP)

As is the general case with framework conventions, the COP functions as "the supreme body" of the UNFCCC. It possesses the legislative power to create additional protocols and amendments to the convention, as well as the authority to make any other "decisions necessary to promote the effective implementation of the Convention" [*Id.* at art. 7(2)]. This last mandate, though not rising to the formal character of amendments and protocols, allows the COP broad authority to interpret or clarify vague treaty provisions without embroiling itself in the complicated political process of formal law-making. It also provides the COP with implied power to make any other "necessary" decisions, even if such decisions are not specifically delegated to the COP by the convention. This ongoing process of informal law-making—when coupled with the majority voting procedures outlined below—exists as a dynamic tool of the UNFCCC [*see* Brent Hendricks, *Postmodern Possibility and the Convention on Biological Diversity*, 5 N.Y.U. ENVT'L. L. J. 1 (1996)].

Regarding formal protocols, the voting procedure for adoption remains unstated in the UNFCCC, but the practice is that protocols are adopted by consensus—although only parties who actually voted to adopt the instrument are bound by its provisions. As for amendments, the UNFCCC requires the agreement of a three-fourths majority of parties "present and voting at the meeting" [UNFCCC at art. 15(3)], but again only those parties who voted to adopt the amendment will be bound. Annexes, limited to "lists, forms and any other material of a descriptive nature that is of a scientific, technical, procedural or administrative character," require a similar three-fourths majority as amendments. In a burden-shifting move, however, even opposing parties are presumed bound by annexes unless they file a "notification of non-acceptance" [*Id.* at art. 16(3)].

With respect to the informal decision-making process noted above, the UNFCCC states that the COP "shall, at its first session, adopt its own rules of procedure ... which ... may include specified majorities" [*Id.* at art. 7(3)]. Nonetheless, the COP failed to do so at both its first and second meetings, and the majority voting procedures concerning such matters remain unsettled. In general, parties who fear the tyranny of the majority—those who perceive themselves as having the most to lose if the UNFCCC imposes strict emissions limits or substantial financial transfers—have attempted to block the implementation of majority voting. Thus, until the COP reaches agreement on the subject, it will continue to employ the consensus approach regarding such informal decision-making.

The UNFCCC also provides several noteworthy and specific requirements for the COP. First, the COP must help "facilitate" the development of joint implementation projects between parties [*Id.* at art. 7(2)(c)]. Second, the COP must continue to monitor the individual obligations of the parties and to assess the cumulative effect of their implementation [*see generally Id.* at art. 7(2)(a) & (b), & art. 12]. Third, where appropriate, the COP must seek the help of competent international organizations and NGOs [*Id.* at art. 7(2)(*l*)]. In fact, the UNFCCC mandates that qualified NGOs have access to meetings of the COP "unless at least one-third of the Parties present object" [*Id.* at art. 7(6)]. Such participation by NGOs is generally the rule for framework conventions, and, although NGOs have no voting rights, they typically do have the right to speak and to distribute literature.

ii. Secretariat

The Secretariat of the UNFCCC serves as the administrative arm of the COP [*Id.* at art. 8]. It works to organize new meetings of the COP, to compile and transmit reports submitted by the parties, and to help find assistance for developing countries in compiling their respective reports. In addition, the Secretariat undertakes any further tasks as designated by the COP. The Secretariat is institutionally linked to the UN and is administered under its rules and regulations.

iii. Subsidiary Body for Scientific and Technological Advice (SBSTA)

The UNFCCC also creates a Subsidiary Body for Scientific and Technological Advice (SBSTA), whose primary function is to advise the COP on technical matters [*Id.* at art. 9]. Given the high degree of scientific complexity regarding climate change, the SBSTA plays an important informational role. It must continually assess the state of scientific knowledge concerning climate change, as well as the effects of measures taken to curb climate change under the UNFCCC. Its mandate is to draw "upon existing competent international bodies"—ranging from the IPCC to qualified NGOs such as the World Conservation Union (IUCN)—in summarizing, compiling, and synthesizing information for the COP [*Id.* at art. 9(2)].

iv. Subsidiary Body for Implementation (SBI)

An innovative body created by the UNFCCC, the Subsidiary Body for Implementation (SBI), assists the COP in evaluating the implementation of the convention [*Id.* at art. 10]. In particular, the SBI considers the in-depth review reports of the national communications and makes broad assessments and recommendations concerning the overall aggregated effects of the steps taken by the parties. The SBI does not evaluate the individual efforts of parties, but it looks at the total picture of compliance. However, in developing the in-depth review reports, the Secretariat and nominated experts may critically evaluate an individual party's performance.

v. *Financial Mechanism*

The UNFCCC names the Global Environment Facility (GEF) as the "interim" financial mechanism [*Id.* at art. 21(3)]. This status was extended by the first meeting of the COP, where the parties adopted initial guidance procedures for the GEF, entrusting it with the task of meeting "the agreed full costs of relevant adaptation activities" undertaken in formulating national communications. These may include "studies of the possible impacts of climate change, identification of options for implementing the adaptation provisions . . . and relevant capacity building" [*Id.*]. The status of the GEF was subsequently reaffirmed at COP-4 in 1998, where parties assigned operation of the financial mechanism to the GEF on an on-going basis, subject to review every four years (*see* the general discussion of the GEF in Appendix § C).

As the financial mechanism for the UNFCCC, the GEF is entrusted with the operation and maintenance of two special funds: the Special Climate Change Fund and the Least Developed Countries Fund. The Special Climate Change Fund is designed to finance projects relating to adaptation, technology transfer, capacity building, energy, transportation, industry, agriculture, forestry, waste management, and economic diversification. The Least Developed Countries Fund is a development-focused fund that seeks to provide financial support to the poorest States, which are the most vulnerable to climate change impacts. It provides support to these States as they prepare National Adaptation Programs of Action to identify their most urgent adaptation needs. A third implementation fund, the Adaptation Fund, was established in 2001 to finance concrete adaptation projects and programs in developing countries that are parties to the Kyoto Protocol. However, as of this writing, the GEF is not entrusted with the operation and maintenance of this fund—a matter that still provokes some controversy.

In managing the funds, the GEF conforms to the criteria that the financial mechanism should have an "equitable and balanced representation of all parties within a transparent system of governance" [*Id.* at art. 11(2)]. To summarize, the GEF has both a Council and an independent Secretariat. The Secretariat (under the authority of the World Bank) approves individual projects, submits them to the Council, and the projects become final unless four Council members wish to put the project before a full vote of the Council. The Council employs a voting method known as "the double-weighted majority," in which affirmative decisions require a 60% majority of the total number of participants as well as a 60% majority of the total contributions. In effect, the Council only possesses a veto power over individual projects.

As for the relationship between the GEF and the UNFCCC, the GEF functions "under the guidance of and [is] accountable to the Conference of the Parties" [*Id.* at art. 11(1)]. Significantly however, the COP cannot recommend individual projects to the GEF, but only specifies "policies, programme priorities and eligibility criteria" [*Id.* at art. 11(1)]. Nevertheless, as the 1996 Memorandum of Understanding (MOU) between the COP and GEF makes clear, the COP does retain the power to have a specific project reconsidered for funding [*Id.* at art. 11(3)(b)].

f. Technology Transfers and Financing

Achieving the ultimate objective of the UNFCCC— "stabilization of greenhouse gas concentrations in the atmosphere at a level that would prevent dangerous anthropogenic interference with the climate system" [*Id.* at art. 2]—will require more than simply enacting emission reduction targets, however ambitious or comprehensive they might be. Global energy demand is surging at an unprecedented rate. Today's current primary global power consumption of about 19 terawatts (TW) is expected to reach 30 TW by 2040 [*see* Martin I. Hoffert et al., *Advanced Technology Paths to Global Climate Change: Energy for a Greenhouse Planet*, 298 SCIENCE 981 (2002)]. Situated in the context of population growth, efforts to grow national gross domestic products (GDPs), increasing per capita energy intensity, and increasingly tight global energy markets, achieving the UNFCCC's goal will necessarily involve technological innovation and the rapid and widespread transfer of environmentally sound technologies from the industrialized world to developing countries.

Moreover, ensuring the efficacy of such technology transfer will require more than merely transporting and implementing technologies from one locale to another. For such transfers to prove meaningful over the long-term, developing countries will require assistance with building human capacity, developing appropriate institutions and networks, and acquiring and adapting specific hardware. Importantly, while technology transfers should operate within a SD framework, SD is a contextually driven concept. It is thus critically important that transferred technologies meet local needs and priorities—ensuring greater likelihood of success—and that there is an appropriate enabling environment for promoting environmentally sound technologies. The transfer of technology for adaptation to climate change is also a critical element of reducing vulnerability to climatic impacts [*see generally* Intergovernmental Panel on Climate Change (IPCC), METHODOLOGICAL AND TECHNOLOGICAL ISSUES IN TECHNOLOGY TRANSFER: SUMMARY FOR POLICYMAKERS (2000)].

Under the UNFCCC, Annex II parties (OECD members only) must pay for all the reporting requirements undertaken by developing countries [UNFCCC at art. 4(3)]. This includes the developing countries' obligation to create national inventories of GHGs [*Id.* at art. 4(1)] and to communicate such information to the COP [*Id.* at art. 12]. In addition to the full costs of reporting, the Annex II parties must pay for the full incremental costs of projects undertaken by developing countries to fulfill the latter's general commitments [*Id.* at art. 4(1)]. However, these projects—such as designating and maintaining sustainable rainforest preserves—must be approved via the financial mechanisms as outlined above.

With regard to technology transfer, the UNFCCC stipulates the rather weak commitment that industrialized countries "shall take all practicable steps to promote, facilitate and finance, as appropriate, the transfer of, or access to, environmentally sound technologies" [*Id.* at art. 4(5)]. This commitment was essentially echoed in the Kyoto Protocol [Kyoto Protocol at art. 10(c)]. However, notwithstanding the distinctly tepid nature of the above language, the UNFCCC does require all Annex II parties to include measures taken for the transfer of technology in their national communications to the COP. Furthermore, at each COP, parties have taken up the issue of technology transfer. The resulting decisions, discussed below, have sought to apply a number of different approaches to facilitating the transfer of environmentally sound technologies. However, the impact of these decisions remains uncertain at best and, at worst, they have had little to no meaningful effect.

Pursuant to the agreement negotiated at COP-4 in 1998, parties to the UNFCCC called on Annex I parties (largely OECD States) to provide lists of environmentally sound technologies that were publicly owned. Developing countries were asked to submit prioritized technology needs, especially related to key technologies for addressing climate change. All parties were urged to create an enabling environment to stimulate private sector investment and to identify projects and programs on cooperative approaches to technology transfer. Perhaps most importantly, the agreement at COP-4 called for a consultative process to be established to consider a list of 19 specific issues and associated questions, and for the process to generate recommendations on how the issues and questions should be addressed.

As part of the Marrakech Accords adopted at COP-7 in 2001, parties advanced the consultative process begun at COP-4 and agreed upon a "framework for meaningful and effective actions" [United Nations Framework Convention on Climate Change (UNFCCC), *The Marrakesh Accords & The Marrakesh Declaration,* COP-7 at art. C(5)(a)]. Parties further agreed to collaborate on a set of technology transfer activities grouped under this framework, which would focus on five main themes: (1) technology needs and needs assessments; (2) technology information; (3) enabling environments; (4) capacity building; and (5) mechanisms for technology transfer.

The Marrakech Accords also provided for the creation of an Expert Group on Technology Transfer, nominated by the parties. Consisting of 20 experts, including three members from each of the developing country regions (Africa, Asia and the Pacific, and Latin America and the Caribbean), one from the small island developing countries, seven from Annex I parties and three from relevant international organizations, the goals of the Expert Group on Technology Transfer are to enhance the implementation of Article 4(5) of the UNFCCC, to facilitate and advance technology transfer activities, and to make recommendations to this end to the SBSTA.

2.   2015 PARIS AGREEMENT ON CLIMATE CHANGE

a. Legal Status

The analysis of the Paris Agreement will generally follow the rubrics used in examining the UNFCCC. We will begin by answering questions pertaining to the legal status of the Paris Agreement, and specifically whether it is a treaty under international law.

It was asserted by then Secretary of State John Kerry during its negotiation that the Paris Agreement was "definitively not going to be a treaty . . ." [*Paris climate deal must be legally binding, EU tells John Kerry*, The Guardian, *available at* https://www.theguardian.com/environ ment/2015/nov/12/paris-climate-deal-must-be-legall y-binding-eu-tells-john-kerry (last visited Apr. 2017)]. This statement of Secretary Kerry was immediately and forcefully repudiated [*Id.*]. The reason Secretary Kerry denied the treaty status of the Paris Agreement was because a treaty requires approval by two-thirds of the Senate under Article

11, Section 2 of the U.S. Constitution. It was impossible to achieve this given the composition of the Senate, and Secretary Kerry was trying to ensure that whatever emerged from Paris was not considered a treaty under the U.S. Constitution [Aurelien Breeden, *France Says Climate Talks Must Produce Binding Deal*, New York Times (Nov. 12, 2015)]. Given the different meanings of a treaty under international and U.S. law, we will deal with the status of the Paris Agreement under both these legal systems.

There is no doubt that the Paris Agreement is a treaty under international law. It was negotiated as a treaty in the manner and form required by the Vienna Convention on the Law of Treaties (Vienna Convention). It was adopted by consensus on December 12, 2015, was opened for signature on April 22, 2016, received the ratifications required, and entered into force on November 4, 2016 [United Nations Framework Convention on Climate Change (UNFCCC), *The Paris Agreement, available at* http://unfccc.int/paris_agreement/items/9485.php   (last visited Apr. 2017)].

The history of the Paris Agreement confirms it was negotiated as a treaty. In 2011, the Durban Platform provided a mandate for the Paris Agreement to develop "a protocol, another legal instrument or an agreed outcome with legal force under the Convention applicable to all parties" [Decision 1/CP.17, *Establishment of an Ad Hoc Working Group on the Durban Platform for Enhanced Action* (Mar. 15, 2012) UN Doc. FCCC/CP/2011/9/Add.1]. An informed commentator provides evidence that an unspoken presumption had emerged by the beginning of 2015 that the Paris Agreement would be a treaty. He concludes that this emerging consensus was not seriously challenged in the run-up to Paris Agreement, and that all of the iterations of the negotiating text made sense only if the Paris Agreement was to be a treaty [Daniel Bodansky, *The Legal Character of the Paris Agreement*, Review of European, Comparative, and International Environmental Law (Mar. 22, 2016)].

It is important to clarify in this context that a treaty under international law does not consist only of binding provisions that create obligations of effect. This means that not all provisions of a treaty create legal rights or duties that call for implementation, or application. Some may do so, while others do not.

In Chapter 1 we have offered examples drawn from the UNFCCC, the Convention on Biological Diversity (Biodiversity Convention), and numerous other environmental agreements to illustrate how treaties are replete with aspirational norms, general norms containing inchoate and open textured obligations, and formulations of rules or principles that codify contentious or competing norms. While these provisions are found in treaties, they do not create hard legal duties or specific rules.

The Vienna Convention defines a treaty as "an international agreement concluded between States in written form and governed by international law . . ." [Vienna Convention at art. 2(1)(a)]. Conspicuously, the Vienna Convention does not define a treaty as writing containing substantive, legally binding rules or principles. What controls its treaty status is not its substantive content, but the fixed verbal form of a written agreement between States, demonstrating an intention to create legal relationships under international law. The argument of some commentators that the Paris Convention is not a treaty because it lacks legally binding emissions reduction duties [*see* e.g. Anne-Marie Slaughter, *The Paris Approach to Global Governance*, Project-Syndicate (Dec. 28, 2015), *available at* https://www.project-syndicate.org/commentary/paris -agreement-model-for-global-governance-by-anne-marie-slaughter-2015-12 (last visited Apr. 2017)] confuses the legal form of a treaty as defined by the Vienna Convention, with the obligations or norms within it which may or may not create legal rights or duties.

Despite the protestations of the Obama administration, the Paris Convention is also a treaty under U.S. law. First, both its parent treaty the UNFCCC, and its sister treaty, the Kyoto Protocol, were treated by the Bush and Clinton administrations as Article 11 treaties that required the Advice and Consent of the Senate.

Second, the Paris Agreement is a treaty according to the State Department's own Handbook on Treaties and Other International Agreements (U.S. Department of State, *The C-175 Handbook* (Jan. 2001) *available at* https://www.state.gov/e/oes/rls/ rpts/175/1319.htm (last visited Apr. 2017)]. It satisfies six of the eight criteria suggested for determining whether an international agreement is a treaty or an executive agreement. A prominent criterion is whether the agreement involves commitments or risks affecting the nation as a whole. The Paris Agreement clearly creates national commitments.

The new obligations created by the Paris Agreement extend far beyond those found in its parent treaty, the UNFCCC, and affect the nation as a whole. The Paris Agreement's many legal obligations relating to emissions targets, domestic implementation commitments, and procedural commitments entail significant financial expenditures not embodied in the UNFCCC. For example, the U.S. is required to undertake and communicate a nationally determined contribution (NDC) for reducing emissions of GHGs every five years [Paris Agreement at art 4(2), (3) & (9)]. The U.S. is further required to "... pursue domestic mitigation measures, with the aim of achieving the objectives of such NDCs" [*Id.* at art 4(2)], and to undertake economy-wide, absolute emission targets [*Id.* at art 4(4)].

Furthermore, the U.S. is then required to ratchet down on this initial NDC by creating more onerous NDCs with increased reductions of GHGs every five years. The increased reduction of GHGs demanded by these subsequent NDCs is to be based on a "global stocktake" commencing 2023, repeated in five-year cycles, that assesses the collective progress toward achieving the object and purpose of the Paris Agreement [*Id.* at art 14].

The Obama administration formally submitted its emission reduction targets, or interim NDCs, to the body administering the Paris Agreement. The U.S. committed to reducing its GHG emissions by 26 to 28% below 2005 levels by 2025, and to make best efforts to reduce it by 28% [The White House: Office of the Press Secretary, *Fact Sheet: U.S. Reports its 2025 Emissions Target to the UNFCCC* (Mar. 31, 2015). *available at* https://www.whitehouse.gov/the-press-office/2015/03/31/fact-sheet-us-reports-its-2025-emissions-target-unfccc (last visited Apr. 2017)].

In addition, the U.S. will roughly double the pace of its carbon pollution reduction from 1.2% per year on average during the 2005–2020 period to 2.3 to 2.8% per year on average between 2020 and 2025. The U.S. will do so by a Clean Power Plan containing regulations that will reduce power plant emissions by 30% below 2005 emissions. There will be similar regulations setting standards for heavy-duty vehicles, energy efficiency standards, and other GHGs like methane [*Id.*]. The Paris Agreement also requires the U.S. to provide financial resources to assist developing country parties with both mitigation and adaptation [Paris Agreement at arts. 4(5), 7(13) & 9(1)].

The other criteria enumerated by the State Department include: past U.S. practice as to similar agreements; the preference of the Congress as to a particular type of agreement; the degree of formality desired for an agreement; the proposed duration of the agreement; and the general international practice as to similar agreements. When these criteria are applied, what clearly emerges is that the Paris Agreement is a treaty not an executive agreement.

b. Objectives

A number of objectives are enumerated in the Paris Agreement. The most important and primary objective is undertake mitigation measures that hold the increase in the global average temperature to well below 2°C above pre-industrial levels and to pursue efforts to limit the temperature increase to 1.5°C above pre-industrial levels [*Id.* at art. 2(1)(a)].

The mitigation objective is supplemented by those relating to adaptation [*Id.* at art. 2(1)(b)], and reinforced by the finance flows facilitating low GHG emissions and climate resilient development [*Id.* at art. 2(1)(c)]. The Paris Agreement also re-states Article 3 of the UNFCCC by requiring that it should be implemented to reflect equity and the principle of CBDR [*Id.* at art. 2(2)].

c. Commitments

NDCs form the substantive core of the Paris Agreement. All parties are required to undertake and communicate NDCs [*Id.* at art. 3]. These NDCs will be successive, and to be prepared, renewed and communicated every five years [*Id.* at art. 4(2) & art. 4(9)]. Each successive NDC will represent progress beyond the current NDC to reflect the highest possible ambition [*Id.* at art. 4(3)], and provide information necessary to track the progress of the

NDCs [*Id*. at art. 13(7)]. What this means is that the parties are required to ratchet down their NDCs.

The NDCs are not hollow vessels. They are recorded in a public registry [*Id*. at art. 4(12)] and the parties are required to pursue domestic mitigation measures with the aim of achieving the objective of holding emissions to 2°C above pre-industrial levels. Parties are further required to provide a national inventory report of sources and sinks of GHGs, as well as information necessary to track down progress toward achieving NDCs [*Id*. at art 13(7)]. This information will enable the COP to assess the individual and collective progress towards achieving its objectives. The COP is then required to undertake a global stocktake in 2023 to be repeated every five years [*Id*. at art. 14].

The commitments relating to NDCs are not free floating obligations. They are interwoven and nested within a cluster of other obligations that secure the implementation and ratcheting down of NDCs. One set of these other obligations require developed countries to provide financial resources to developing countries pursuant to their obligations under the UNFCCC [*Id*. at art. 9]. The reference here is to the principles of equity and CBDR, which as we have seen, are re-affirmed in Article 2(2) of the Paris Agreement. The Paris Agreement itself does not refer to the figure of 100 billion per year from 2020 through 2025. This figure is used in the decision of the parties adopting the Agreement and does not constitute a binding obligation.

Every two years developed countries are required to convey qualitative and quantitative data relating to the transfer of financial resources, as well as providing transparent and consistent information supporting their actions [*Id.* at art. 9(5) & 9(7)]. Developed countries are also required to provide financial support to developing countries to support technology development [*Id.* at art. 10(6)] and to provide information about such support [*Id.* at art. 13(9)].

It is important to evaluate the substantive legal commitments made by the parties. First, it is clear that NDCs are not required to incorporate pre-determined emission reduction standards. Many developing countries, like India and China, would not have agreed to such standards. This gives parties latitude in defining the stringency of their NDCs. Second, it is equally clear that the standards in the first NDCs will be succeeded by others at five year intervals. These successive NDCs must contain greater emission reductions than the earlier ones. Thus, the obligation or duty of parties to progressively reduce their emissions of GHGs through successive NDCs means they cannot get off the bus of GHG reductions once they have boarded it. Third, there are clear reporting obligations, and the global stocktaking is designed to tighten restrictions on GHG emissions through successive NDCs. Fourth, the ratcheting down of GHG emissions is tied to legally binding resource and technology transfers that will enable developing countries to participate. Finally, the Paris Agreement continues with some institutions for implementation created by the

UNFCCC, but also adds additional institutions for implementation.

3.   SUSTAINABLE DEVELOPMENT (SD) AND THE PARIS AGREEMENT

We have noted the extent to which the UNFCCC institutionalized SD and the principle of CBDR. The Paris Agreement represents the culmination of a paradigm shift away from the UNFCCC's iteration of SD and CBDR that began with the Rio + 20 Conference.

a. 2012 Rio+20 Conference

The first major step toward a different rendition of SD was taken at the Rio + 20 United Nations Conference on Sustainable Development in 2012 [*United Nations Conference on Sustainable Development*, Rio de Janiero, Braz., June 20–22, 2012, Report of the United Nations Conference on Sustainable Development, U.N. Doc. A/CONF.216/16 (June 20–22, 2012)]. The new thinking was embodied in its Rio + 20 Outcome Document: *The Future We Want* [United Nations General Assembly, *Resolution adopted by the General Assembly on 27 July 2012: 66/288. The Future We Want*, (Jul. 27, 2012) A/RES/66/288]. First, the Rio + 20 Outcome Document concluded that a green economy must be established at national and local levels, and arrived at the extraordinary position that ushering the new green economy would need to be shifted primarily to developing countries. Second, in creating the foundations of the new sustainable development goals (SDGs) that would replace the old millennium development goals (MDGs), the Rio + 20 Outcome Document envisioned that the new SDGs would extend international development work beyond the poverty-eradicating mission of the MDGs.

It is important to emphasize the extent to which the conceptualization of the SDGs and the green economy in the Rio + 20 Outcome Document is different to SD as hitherto accepted. Up until to this time, every formulation of SD in legal and political documents had given primary emphasis to economic and social development that eradicated poverty. A dramatically different picture now emerges. First, there is a new iteration of SD emphasizing global public goals (GPGs), discussed below, as distinct from the eradication of poverty based on individual economic growth. Second, developing countries now must assume greater responsibility for SD. Previously, SD had been premised on the legal and political principle of CBDR embodied in the UNFCCC, insisting on the overriding responsibility of developed countries to help developing countries. The Rio + 20 Outcome Document, however, shifted the onus by placing significant responsibility for the SDGs and the green economy on national States, the large majority of whom consist of developing countries.

b. Sustainable Development Goals (SDGs)

Based on the Rio + 20 Outcome Document, the 2015 SDGs were developed with input from the UN's 193 member states and an array of NGOs. Embodied in a larger document, they consist of 17 goals, including 169 targets and indicators, that replaced the MDGs in January 2016 [United Nations General Assembly, *Resolution adopted by the General Assembly on 25 September 2015: 70/1. Transforming our world: the 2030 Agenda for Sustainable Development* (Sept. 25, 2015), A/RES/70/1].

Nine of the 17 SDGs deal with GPGs that cover: infrastructure, inequality, habitation, consumption, climate, marine environment, institutions, and the partnership for SD. The reasons for incorporating GPGs are worth outlining. In a globalizing world, problems and solutions reach across national borders, resulting in a growing need for international collective action. Inge Kaul, who pioneered the concept of GPGs, extended the concept of "public goods" from the national level to the global level. Her book, *Global Public Goods: International Cooperation in the 21st Century,* convincingly argues that the two tests of a public goods, non-rivalry and non-excludability, can be applied at the global level to such things as environment, health, culture, and peace. GPGs are goods whose benefits reach across borders, generations, and population groups, and the concept of GPGs has become an increasingly important part of international policy making. A clean environment, climate stability, health, knowledge, property rights, peace, and security are all examples of public goods that could be made global.

SDG 13 specifically calls for urgent action to combat climate change and its impacts. Climate action is a developed country priority, because developed countries are the primary proponents of GPGs pertaining to climate change and these countries derive utilitarian, ecological, and socio-biological benefit from these GPGs. Nonetheless, developing countries are also required to shoulder this burden. Developing countries that take action to mitigate climate change provide a valuable service for which they are entitled to claim compensation under the doctrine of CBDR. The payment for providing such a service could take the form of resource or monetary transfers.

Another development confirms the extent to which the earlier meaning of SD has been radically re-interpreted. The new GPGs require enormous amounts of additional funding, and the question of how they would be funded was discussed at the Third International Conference on Financing for Development. The Addis Ababa Action Agenda agreed to at that conference highlights the fact that each country, including those among the least developed countries (LDCs), will bear the main responsibility for its own SD [Third International Conference on Financing For Development, *Addis Abada Action Agenda* (Jul. 27 2015) GA/69/313]. Moving the responsibility for SD to the poor and even poorest countries of the world is an unabashed repudiation of the earlier consensus that developed countries shoulder this responsibility.

As noted above, SDG 13 deals with the GPG of climate action—the need to take urgent action to combat climate change and its impacts. The explanation accompanying SDG 13 correctly asserts that the UNFCCC gives industrialized countries the major part of responsibility for combating climate change. However, having referenced CBDR, SDG 13 then turns the principle on its head by placing the primary responsibility for climate change action on developing countries.

Unlike SDG 13, the UNFCCC draws a clear distinction between the GPG of addressing climate change and the humanitarian goals of economic advancement and the eradication of poverty. It is worth reviewing the relevant provisions of the UNFCCC that have been sidelined by SDG 13 and the Paris Agreement. The objective embodied in Article 2 of the UNFCCC is ". . . to achieve in accordance with the relevant provisions of the Convention, the stabilization of greenhouse gas concentrations in the atmosphere at a level that could prevent dangerous anthropogenic interference with the climate system. Such a level should be achieved within a time-frame sufficient . . . to enable economic development to proceed in a sustainable manner" [UNFCCC at art. 2]. This stabilization is to be achieved first in conjunction with the other relevant provisions of the UNFCCC, and, second, in a manner that enables SD. The other relevant provisions of the UNFCCC make it abundantly clear that climate stabilization is not an unalloyed GPG to be sought at the expense of sustainable economic development and its corollary of humanitarian assistance.

The Preamble to the UNFCCC asserts that the parties should take into full account ". . . the legitimate priority needs of developing countries for the achievement of sustained economic growth and the eradication of poverty" [*Id.* at pmbl.]. The Preamble then recognizes that in order to achieve sustainable social and economic development, the energy consumption of developing countries will need to grow. The body of the UNFCCC continues to emphasize the extent to which economic and social development tempers the quest for climate stability.

Article 3(4) dealing with Principles states "the Parties have a right to and should promote sustainable development" [*Id.* at art. 3(4)]. It continues to state that "policies and measures to protect the climate system against induced change should be appropriate for the specific conditions of each Party . . . taking into account that economic development is essential for adopting measures to address climate change" [*Id.*]. The importance of economic development is re-affirmed and emphasized by Article 4(7), which asserts that economic and social development and poverty eradication are the overriding priorities of the developing country parties. The compelling extent to which even the most important treaty dealing with climate change is qualified and modified by the reiteration of the primary importance of economic and social development is hugely consequential. Article 4(3) is unequivocal in asserting and stressing that developed countries shall provide additional financial resources to meet the full costs of the developing countries in complying with their obligations. The extent to which such new financial and technology transfers are crucial to the implementation of the UNFCCC is further highlighted by Article 4(7), which emphasizes that the extent to which developing countries will implement their commitments under the UNFCCC will depend on the effective implementation of developed country commitments. In sum, implementing the GPG of climate stabilization would need new, fresh, and additional financing.

The cardinal importance of developed countries finding additional financing for promoting climate stabilization is affirmed by Article 3(1), which states the principle that parties should protect the climate system ". . . on the basis of equity and in accordance with their common but differentiated responsibilities and respective capabilities. Accordingly, the developed country parties should take the lead in combating climate change and the adverse effects thereof" [*Id*. at art. 3(1)]. Furthermore, as we have noted, the UNFCCC coalesced with the other widely accepted treaty adopted at Earth Summit, the Biodiversity Convention, by forcefully and unequivocally expressing the developmental priority of SD. Article 4(7) of the UNFCCC, and Article 20(4) of the Biodiversity Convention, reaffirm in unison that parties "will take fully into account that economic and social development and poverty eradication are the first and overriding priorities of the developing country Parties" [*Id*. at art. 4(7); Biodiversity Convention at art. 20(4)].

F.   CONCLUSIONS

The Paris Agreement gives flesh and form to SDG 13, claiming that it is enhancing the implementation of UNFCCC and SD [UNFCCC at art. 2(1)] and will be implemented to reflect equity and the principle of CBDR [*Id.* at art. 2(3)]. However, the singular focus of the Paris Agreement on GHG mitigation and adaptation is inconsistent with the priority given to economic and social development in the UNFCCC. Moreover, despite its invocation of CBDR, developing country parties are required to take costly actions to reduce GHGs. The Paris Agreement does not contain any provisions similar to Article 4(3) of UNFCCC under which the developed countries agree to pay the full cost of climate action taken by developing countries, or those found in Article 4(7) of the UNFCCC, stating that its implementation would depend on the extent to which developed countries met their financial obligations.

The Paris Agreement does contain some provisions dealing with financial assistance and technology transfer. But, in contrast to the core of the UNFCCC in which economic and social development takes primacy, the core of the Paris Agreement gives primacy to GHG reductions, while the financial and technical assistance obligations are pushed out to the peripheries.

The costs of climate action required by the Paris Agreement raises a central question. One estimate states that the costs of implementing the Paris Agreement will amount to $1,100 billion per year [EurActiv, *Infographic: Not All SDGs Were Created*

Equal (Oct. 19, 2015), *available at* http://www.
euractiv.com/sections/development-policy/infograph
ic-not-all-sdgs-were-created-equal-318558   (last
visited Apr. 2017)]. Another commentator estimates
that the Paris Agreement will cost between $1 to 2
trillion per year and cost $100 trillion by the end of
the century [Marc Morano, *Statistician: UN climate
treaty will cost $100 trillion—To Have No Impact—
Postpone warming by less than four years by 2100*
(Jan 17, 2017), Climate Depot, *available at* http://
www.climatedepot.com/2017/01/17/danish-statistic
ian-un-climate-treaty-will-cost-100-trillion-to-post
pone-global-warming-by-less-than-four-year-by-
2100/ last visited Apr. 2017)]. This is many times
higher than the total costs of achieving all of the
SDGs (1 to 8) dealing with the economic and social
dimensions of SD. Given the massive expenditure on
climate action, the unanswered question is whether
these expenses will be incurred at the cost of poverty
reduction and economic and social development
[Lakshman Guruswamy, *Global Energy Justice: Law
& Policy* (2016) at 75–83]. In the absence of enormous
increases in assistance from developed to developing
countries, it appears that the answer is yes.

CHAPTER SEVEN
OZONE DEPLETION

When discussing ozone, it is important to differentiate between "good" ozone and "bad" ozone. Ozone in the troposphere, the layer of atmosphere closest to the earth's surface, is considered "bad" ozone. Tropospheric ozone can damage human health and vegetation, exacerbates the greenhouse effect, and is also a key ingredient of urban smog. By contrast, "good" ozone is located in the stratosphere, the layer of atmosphere six to 30 miles above the earth's surface. About 90% of all ozone is stratospheric ozone, which creates a necessary and beneficial shield against biologically damaging solar ultraviolet (UV) radiation.

Without the protective shield provided by stratospheric ozone, living organisms would be exposed to a range of adverse consequences. In humans, exposure to excessive UV radiation can cause melanoma and non-melanoma carcinomas of the skin and cataract and pterygium (a growth on the conjunctiva) of the eye [United Nations Environment Programme (UNEP), *Environmental Effects of Ozone Depletion and Its Interaction with Climate Change: 2014 Assessment,* SECRETARIAT FOR THE VIENNA CONVENTION FOR THE PROTECTION OF THE OZONE LAYER AND THE MONTREAL PROTOCOL ON SUBSTANCES THAT DEPLETE THE OZONE LAYER (Jan. 2015) at xvi (hereinafter UNEP 2014 Ozone Assessment)]. A decrease in the ozone layer has also been linked to changes in plant productivity; phytoplankton destruction with repercussions up the food chain; increased ground-level ozone pollution; and increased damage to materials such as PVC building products, wood, and textiles [*Id.* at xvii–xxi]. Furthermore, solar radiation has the potential to contribute to climate change by stimulating emissions of certain greenhouse gases and altering carbon storage patterns [*Id.*]. The present chapter deals with the depletion of stratospheric "good" ozone.

A. NATURE OF THE PROBLEM

Despite the importance of the ozone layer, the total amount of ozone in the stratosphere is exceedingly small. For every million molecules of air there are, on average, fewer than five molecules of ozone [United Nations Environment Programme (UNEP), *Action on Ozone* (2002) at 1 (hereinafter UNEP 2002 Action on Ozone)]. Ozone is created and destroyed continually as part of a natural process. When solar UV radiation interacts with oxygen molecules (O_2) in the stratosphere, these molecules fracture into single oxygen atoms (O), known as atomic oxygen, which then bond to nearby oxygen molecules to form ozone molecules (O_3). This process ensures that stratospheric ozone is continually being produced via the interaction of energy from the sun and oxygen molecules [F.S. Rowland, *Atmospheric Changes Caused by Human Activities: From Science to Regulation*, 27 ECOLOGY L.Q. 1261 (2001) at 1267–68]. On the other hand, a number of natural compounds containing elements such as nitrogen, hydrogen, and chlorine work to destroy stratospheric ozone. This natural equilibrium of ozone creation and destruction has protected life on Earth from harmful solar radiation for nearly a billion years [UNEP 2002 Action on Ozone at 1–3].

It was not until the past half century that human activity began disrupting this natural equilibrium. In 1985, British scientists first published findings on a localized thinning of ozone in the Antarctic [*see* J.C. Farman, et al., *Large Losses of Total Ozone in Antarctica Reveal Seasonal ClOx/NOx Interaction*, 315 NATURE 207 (1985)]. While ozone concentrations fluctuate naturally by season, latitude, and altitude, the British data showed that ozone levels over the Antarctic between September and November (springtime in the Antarctic) had fallen 50% compared with 1960s levels. The scientists found that this "Antarctic ozone hole" covered an area larger than the U.S.

In 1994, NASA researchers analyzed three years of data collected by the Upper Atmosphere Research Satellite (UARS) [DIALOG, *NASA Reveals New Evidence for Chemical Cause of Ozone Depletion*, GLOBAL ENV'T CHANGE REPORT File No. 1994 (Dec. 23, 1994)]. The data confirmed the British team's finding of a localized diminishment in ozone levels above the Antarctic during the springtime. NASA's data also provided "conclusive evidence" that human activities, rather than natural factors, were the cause of ozone depletion above the Antarctic, and identified anthropogenic chlorine as the chemical culprit. Based on measurements taken by UARS, NASA researchers calculated that natural (non-anthropogenic) sources accounted for only 17% of the total amount of chlorine in the stratosphere. Since that time, scientific evidence has clearly established that anthropogenic emissions are the dominant cause of observed deviations from the "optimal equilibrium" of ozone formation and destruction, thus weakening the ability of the ozone layer to protect life from harmful radiation [*see* World Meteorological Organization (WMO), *Twenty Questions and Answers About the Ozone Layer: 2014 Update* (2014), Montreal Protocol Scientific Assessment Panel (hereinafter WMO 2014 Twenty Questions); United Nations Environment Programme (UNEP), 2006 SCIENTIFIC ASSESSMENT OF OZONE DEPLETION (2006); United Nations Environment Programme (UNEP), EXECUTIVE SUMMARY: 2002 SCIENTIFIC ASSESSMENT OF OZONE DEPLETION (2002) at 13 (hereinafter UNEP 2002 Scientific Assessment); United Nations Environment Programme (UNEP), EXECUTIVE SUMMARY: 1998 SCIENTIFIC ASSESSMENT OF OZONE DEPLETION (1998) at 25–26].

B.   CAUSES OF THE PROBLEM

Factors such as changes in solar radiation and the formation of stratospheric particles after volcanic eruptions do influence the ozone layer, but neither factor can explain the average decreases observed in global total ozone over the last three decades [WMO 2014 Twenty Questions at 49]. By analyzing air trapped in snow and ice since the late 1800s, researchers have confirmed that non-industrial sources of ozone-depleting substances have been insignificant in terms of their depletive effect [UNEP 2002 Scientific Assessment at 2]. In contrast to the causal questions that exist more explicitly in the context of climate change (*see* Ch. 6), research data has largely settled the question of what role humans play in causing stratospheric ozone depletion: human activities are the predominant cause of the problem.

Ozone-depleting substances are manufactured halogen source gases that are emitted by certain industrial processes and consumer products [WMO 2014 Twenty Questions at 22]. Chlorofluorocarbons (CFCs) are an important example. CFCs were first produced in late 1928 as the result of efforts to find a nontoxic substance capable of serving as an effective and safe refrigerant. Freon, the DuPont trademark name for one of these substances, replaced ammonia as the standard cooling fluid in home refrigerators, and soon became the primary coolant in automobile air conditioners [*see* Rowland at 1287].

Since the invention of CFCs, millions of tons of anthropogenic chlorine have been added to the natural levels of stratospheric chlorine. But unlike chlorine from natural sources, such as volcanoes and ocean spray, CFCs are not water-soluble and thus do not "wash out" of the troposphere. Because they are chemically stable, they do not break down in the lower atmosphere and may have a lifetime in the troposphere of over 100 years. They inevitably reach the stratosphere through atmospheric circulation. The two most important ozone-depleting chlorinated substances are CFC-11 and CFC-12. More recently, scientists developed hydrochlorofluorocarbons (HCFCs) as a less destructive (though still problematic) substitute for CFCs. Halons, methyl bromide, and carbon tetrachloride also are ozone-depleting substances.

Halons contain bromine, which attacks ozone molecules in a similar fashion to chlorine but can destroy four to 16 times more ozone than CFC-11 during its atmospheric lifetime. Methyl bromide, unlike other controlled ozone-depleting substances, has both natural and human-made sources—including emissions from biomass burning and soil fumigation. The final culprit, carbon tetrachloride, is a non-chlorinated compound whose ozone-depleting potential is approximately equal to that of CFC-11.

Approximately 350,000 to 400,000 ozone-depleting metric tons of CFCs were contained in refrigeration equipment in 2002, while 450,000 metric tons of halon—1301 and 330,000 metric tons of halon—1211 were installed in fire fighting equipment [United Nations Environment Programme (UNEP), *Report of the Technology and Economic Assessment Panel (TEAP)*, PROGRESS REPORT, VOLUME ONE (2002) at 27]. However, as will be discussed below, since the Montreal Protocol on Substances that Deplete the Ozone Layer (Montreal Protocol) came into force, there have been substantial decreases in the use of the majority of ozone-depleting substances [UNEP 2014 Ozone Assessment at xv].

C.   ENVIRONMENTAL IMPACTS

By enabling more UV radiation to reach the surface of the earth, ozone depletion effectively increases both the probability that adverse consequences will result from UV radiation exposure and the degree of harm. Among these possible adverse consequences are immune system suppression in humans and animals, skin cancer and other forms of cancer, cataracts, changes in plant productivity, and damage to marine ecosystems.

More specifically, exposure of the skin to UV radiation induces systemic immune suppression that may have adverse effects on health, such as through the reactivation of latent viral infections [*Id.* at 49]. Solar UV radiation is also the major environmental risk factor for both melanoma and non-melanoma skin cancers [*Id.* at 50]. It is difficult to assess whether, and to what extent, alternations in the ozone layer or climate have contributed to the rising incidence of skin cancer globally, but it is clear that skin cancer is a growing concern. For example, the incidence of cutaneous malignant melanoma in fair-skinned populations has approximately doubled every ten to 20 years since the 1960s, and this trend is projected to continue for at least 20 more years [*Id.* at 51]. In 2012 it was estimated that there were around 230,000 new cases of cutaneous malignant melanoma, and that this type of cancer lead to 55,000 deaths [*Id.*].

Exposure to UV radiation also increases the risk for a number of ocular conditions. Pterygium, an invasive growth of the conjunctiva, is common in adults living in environments with high UV radiation [*Id.* 58]. Increased UV radiation is also correlated with an increased rate of cataracts, which, as of 2010, is the leading cause of blindness worldwide [*Id.* at 59].

On the other hand, while past research focused on the potential detrimental impacts of UV radiation on plants and ecosystems, recent evidence has shown that while some detrimental effects do occur, UV radiation is also key for plant signaling and can perhaps be usefully exploited for adding value to agricultural crops [*Id*. at 96]. However, UV radiation is still implicated as a possible contributor to global warming through its stimulation of volatile organic compounds (VOCs) and increased emissions of carbon dioxide (CO_2) from plant litter and soils [*Id*.] Regarding aquatic ecosystems, interactions between climate change and UV radiation are having strong effects that will continue to change in the future due to feedbacks between rising temperatures and levels of UV radiation and greenhouse gas concentrations [*Id*. at xviii].

D.   REMEDIAL OBJECTIVES

In order to restore the ozone layer and prevent further enlarging of the ozone hole, it is necessary to prohibit the use of ozone-depleting substances. Beginning with the Vienna Convention for the Protection of the Ozone Layer (Vienna Ozone Convention) and advanced by the Montreal Protocol, the international community has successfully instituted such controls. These actions have led to decreases in the atmospheric concentration of controlled ozone-depleting substances, enabling the return of the ozone layer toward 1980 levels [World Meteorological Organization, *Assessment for Decision-Makers: Scientific Assessment of Ozone Depletion: 2014* (2014) Global Ozone Research and

Monitoring   Project—Report   No.   56,   Geneva, Switzerland at ES-1].

The legal response to the problem of ozone depletion remains one of the most striking achievements of international environmental law (IEL). A number of factors contributed to this success: (1) a growing scientific consensus concerning the threat posed to the ozone layer by the release of anthropogenic ozone-depleting substances into the atmosphere; (2) the role played by bellweather States like the U.S., which began controlling CFCs well prior to the start of negotiations for the Vienna Ozone Convention; (3) the existence of a relatively small number of producing nations whose industries, after limited objections, eventually backed international controls; (4) incentives for industry experts and other private parties to participate in technology assessments and policy recommendations, thus enabling greater effectiveness through increased compliance; and (5) the development of innovative institutional mechanisms that have attracted reluctant parties and have allowed for more flexible decision-making [Edward A. Parsons, *The Technology Assessment Approach to Climate Change*, ISSUES IN SCIENCE AND TECHNOLOGY (2002) at 65].

E. Legal Response

1. 1985 VIENNA CONVENTION FOR THE PROTECTION OF THE OZONE LAYER (VIENNA OZONE CONVENTION)

Under the Vienna Ozone Convention, nations agreed to take "appropriate measures . . . to protect human health and the environment against adverse effects resulting or likely to result from human activities which modify or are likely to modify the Ozone Layer" [Vienna Ozone Convention at art 2(1)]. However, the measures to be taken are unspecified and there is no mention of any substances that might harm the ozone. CFCs appear only towards the end of the annex to the treaty, where they are mentioned as chemicals that should be monitored. Instead, the main thrust of the Vienna Ozone Convention was to encourage research, cooperation, and the exchange of information among States. What is most significant is that, for the first time, nations agreed in principle to tackle a global environmental problem before its effects were felt, or even scientifically proven.

The international ozone regime reflects the framework approach, or convention-protocol approach, to international law-making (*see* Ch. 1). In this case, the Vienna Ozone Convention attracted over 25 signatories in the first two years, including all the major producers of ozone-depleting substances except Japan. With the science still uncertain in 1985, the parties negotiated a treaty without specific controls that instead stressed cooperation and research [*see Id.* at arts. 2–4]. Of greatest significance, the treaty empowered its Conference of the Parties (COP) to adopt future protocols dealing with such controls [*Id*. at art. 6(4)(h) & art. 2(2)(c)]. This was achieved in 1987 with the Montreal Protocol. Today the Vienna Ozone Convention is one of the world's most widely accepted treaties, having been ratified by 197 States, including all of the United Nations (UN) members, the Holy See, and the European Union (EU).

2.   1987 MONTREAL PROTOCOL ON SUBSTANCES THAT DEPLETE THE OZONE LAYER (MONTREAL PROTOCOL)

After a series of demanding meetings and negotiations, the Montreal Protocol was finally agreed upon in 1987. It sets the "elimination" of ozone-depleting substances as its "ultimate objective" [Montreal Protocol at pmbl.]. The Montreal Protocol came into force, on time, on January 1, 1989, with ratification by 29 States and the European Economic Community (EEC), which together accounted for 82% of global consumption of ozone-depleting substances. As of this writing, the Montreal Protocol has been ratified by all 196 States in the world and the EU.

A milestone in the field of IEL, the Montreal Protocol creates mechanisms and incentives for institutional participation that are now included in virtually every environmental convention. It should also be seen as an example of the application of the precautionary approach. While scientists had linked CFCs and halons to potential global ozone depletion and had also identified the Antarctic ozone hole, the atmospheric models remained inconclusive, with no direct evidence of physical harm to humans or the environment. Yet, despite this uncertainty, in 1987 the parties adopted a Protocol with firm national commitments regarding specific regulatory controls on CFCs and halons. Pursuant to its original terms, the Montreal Protocol required parties to ensure that by 1999 their production and consumption levels of the five main CFCs were 50% of those same levels in 1986. The Montreal Protocol provided for this goal to be achieved through the use of interim reductions.

Originally, the Montreal Protocol dealt only with halons and certain CFCs. As updated through the 27th Meeting of the Parties (MOP) in 2015, the Montreal Protocol sets specific consumption and production controls for eight types of chemicals: (1) CFCs [Montreal Protocol at arts. 2A & 2C], (2) halons [*Id*. at art. 2B], (3) carbon tetrachloride [*Id*. at art. 2D], (4) methyl chloroform [*Id*. at art. 2E], (5) HCFCs [*Id*. at art. 2F], (6) hydrobromofluorocarbons (HBFCs) [*Id*. at art. 2G], (7) methyl bromide [*Id*. at art. 2H], and (8) bromochloromethane [*Id*. at art. 2I].

The Montreal Protocol also addresses the special needs of developing countries, which did not want the agreement to hinder their development. These nations generally have less stringent requirements under the Protocol, including later base level dates and longer phase-out periods. The Montreal Protocol also provides developing country parties with the security that phase-outs will not leave them lacking necessary chemicals, as both industrialized and developing countries in most cases may continue production beyond a chemical's reduction date so as to meet the "basic domestic needs" of developing countries [*Id.* at art 5 & 8(a)–(b)]. These provisions have helped to allay the fears of the developing world of being left without proper substitutes.

Additionally, all parties, not just developing nations, are allowed "essential use" exemptions after the 100% reduction phase-out date for most chemicals. These exemptions are granted by the parties under Annex VI and cannot be taken unilaterally. For example, parties decided at MOP-18 to adopt an exemption allowing methyl bromide to continue to be used in specific ways in a laboratory setting [United Nations Environment Programme (UNEP), *Laboratory and Analytical Uses* (2016), Ozone Secretariat].

In 1996, when CFC-based aerosols were phased out in developed countries, a temporary exemption was allowed for the use of CFCs in metered-dose inhalers for patients with asthma and chronic obstructive pulmonary disease. As affordable CFC-free alternatives for inhaled treatments have been developed over the last 20 years, 98% of the exempted CFCs have already been phased out. After 30 years of concentrated global action to phase out CFCs, the United Nations Environment Programme (UNEP) Ozone Secretariat reports that the small remaining amount of CFCs used in inhalers will be phased out in 2016. This marks a significant milestone for the success of the Montreal Protocol in protecting the ozone layer, and the CFC-free alternatives now in inhalers have also had additional benefits for patient health [United Nations Environment Programme (UNEP), *Montreal Protocol Parties Achieve Complete Phase-Out Of Ozone-Depleting CFCs*, (2016) Ozone Secretariat].

a. Adjustments and Amendments

A look at the difference between adjustments and amendments provides a window into the dynamic institutional machinery of the ozone regime. While the MOP may pass an amendment by a two-thirds majority, these amendments may not bind a party against its will [Vienna Ozone Convention at art. 9(3)–(4)]. Instead, following the traditional rule of consent in international law, each party must sign on to and ratify each amendment before becoming obligated [*Id.* at art. 9(5)]. Since it's initial adoption 30 years ago, the Montreal Protocol has been amended four times—London (1990), Copenhagen (1992), Montreal (1997), and Beijing (1999).

Once an amendment is adopted under the Montreal Protocol, however, each party relinquishes its ability to avoid "adjustments." Adjustments include changes in the reduction and/or phase-out schedules of all controlled chemicals described in Articles 2A–2H and listed in Annexes A–E, as well as changes in the ozone-depleting potentials of the chemicals listed in Annexes A–E [Montreal Protocol at art. 2(9)(a)(i)–(ii)]. Significantly, if the MOP passes an adjustment by a two-thirds majority vote, which represents separate majorities of both the industrialized and developing countries present, the adjustments become binding on all the parties [*Id.* at art. 2(9)(c)–(d)]. In this way, the Montreal Protocol commits parties to specific numerical controls, regardless of whether they have voted for or against a successful adjustment. Some scholars have perceived the effect of this decision-making system as being an end-run around the formal doctrine of consent in international law. Others have argued that the parties have simply consented in the Montreal Protocol to be bound against their consent to adjustments. Regardless, the MOP has made six such adjustments over the past 30 years—London (1990), Copenhagen (1992), Vienna (1995), Montreal (1997), Beijing (1999), and Montreal (2007).

The first amendment to the Montreal Protocol, the London Amendment, took place in 1990 and added methyl chloroform, carbon tetrachloride, and an additional range of CFCs to the original phase-out schedules. It also established the means for conveying financial and technical assistance to developing country parties [*Annex II: The London Amendment (1990): The amendment to the Montreal Protocol agreed by the Second Meeting of the Parties* (Jun. 29, 1990) Ozone Secretariat]. In 1992, the Copenhagen Amendment added HCFCs, HBFCs, and methyl bromide to the phase-out schedules, as well as formally recognizing the creation of the Multilateral Fund as the official means for conveying financial and technological assistance [*Annex III to the report of the Fourth Meeting of the Parties: The Copenhagen Amendment (1992): The amendment to the Montreal Protocol agreed by the Fourth Meeting of the Parties,* (Nov. 25, 1992) Ozone Secretariat]. The 1997 Montreal Amendment instituted a mandatory licensing system for exports and imports of controlled ozone-depleting substances, with the primary motivation being to discourage the growing illegal trade in the substances. The Montreal Amendment also banned imports and exports of methyl bromide with any State not party to the Montreal Protocol, and further banned exports (except for destruction) of used, recycled, and reclaimed ozone-depleting substances from parties that are in non-compliance with the control measures in the Montreal Protocol [*Annex IV to the report of the Ninth Meeting of the Parties: The Montreal Amendment (1997): The amendment to the Montreal Protocol agreed by the Ninth Meeting of the Parties,* (Sept. 17, 1997) Ozone Secretariat]. Lastly, the 1999 Beijing Amendment extended the regulatory controls on HCFCs for production and added bromochloromethane to the phase-out schedules. The Beijing Amendment also implemented mandatory data reporting for quarantine and pre-shipment uses of methyl bromide [*Annex V to the report of the Eleventh Meeting of the Parties: The Beijing Amendment (1999): The amendment to the Montreal Protocol agreed by the Eleventh Meeting of the Parties,* (Dec. 3, 1999) Ozone Secretariat]. These amendments and adjustments to the ozone regime are set out in the table below.

OZONE AGREEMENTS AND THEIR EFFECTIVE DATES

TREATY	MEETING WHEN TREATY WAS AGREED		ENTRY INTO FORCE
	TITLE	VENUE, DATE	
Vienna Convention	High-level Diplomatic meeting	Vienna 22 March 85	22 Sept 88
Montreal Protocol	High-level diplomatic meeting	Montreal, 14–16 Sept 87	1 Jan 89
London Adjustment	2nd MOP the Montreal Protocol	London, 27–29 June 90	7 March 91
London Amendment			10 Aug 92
Copenhagen Adjustment	4th MOP to the Montreal Protocol	Copenhagen, 23–25 Nov 92	23 Sept 93
Copenhagen Amendment			14 June 94
Vienna Adjustment	7th MOP to the Montreal Protocol	Vienna, 5–7 Dec 95	5 Aug 96
Montreal Adjustment	9th MOP to the Montreal Protocol	Montreal, 15–17 Sept 97	4 June 98

OZONE AGREEMENTS AND THEIR EFFECTIVE DATES

TREATY	MEETING WHEN TREATY WAS AGREED		ENTRY INTO FORCE
	TITLE	VENUE, DATE	
Montreal Amendment			10 Nov 99
Beijing Adjustment	11th MOP to the Montreal Protocol	Beijing, 29 Nov–3 Dec 99	28 July 00
Beijing Amendment			25 Feb 02
Montreal Adjustment	19th COP to the Montreal Protocol	Montreal, 17–21 Sept. 07	14 May 08

b. Transfers

The Montreal Protocol originally allowed small-producing parties to transfer or receive production in excess of the prescribed limits, as long as the combined levels of the two parties engaged in the transfer did not exceed production standards. The 1990 London Amendments extend this right to all parties, not just small producers, and for all controlled substances except HBFCs [Montreal Protocol at art. 2(5)]. Identified as industrial rationalization, this mechanism attempts to enhance efficiency between producers, allowing a shift of reduction and phase-out burdens from those least capable to those in the best position to do so. For those controls already at 100% reduction, this has the practical effect of allowing a transfer from one producer to another of that excess deemed necessary for the basic domestic needs of developing countries. With regard to HCFCs, the 1992 Copenhagen Amendments permit industrialized country parties that are small consumers to transfer excess consumption to other industrialized country parties [*Id.*]. Again, as with all the provisions for industrial rationalization, the nations involved must notify the Secretariat of the terms and period of the transfer.

In a further nod to economic efficiency, regional organizations such as the EU may also "jointly fulfill" their consumption obligations, as long as the combined levels remain within the mandated limits [*Id.* at art. 2(8)]. This resembles the notion of "joint implementation" developed under the United Nations Framework Convention on Climate Change (UNFCCC) (*see* Ch. 6), by which parties may more efficiently share the burden of compliance.

c. Trade Restrictions

Though in possible violation of the 1994 World Trade Organization (WTO) Agreement's prohibitions on import bans between countries, the Montreal Protocol is one of the first IEL treaties that includes trade restrictions to achieve the stated goals of the treaty. Negotiators justified the use of these restrictions because the problem of ozone depletion is most effectively addressed on a global level. Without trade restrictions, non-parties might have an economic incentive to continue production and use of ozone-depleting substances.

As augmented by the London and Copenhagen Amendments, the Montreal Protocol bans all import of controlled substances from non-parties, except HCFCs and methyl bromide [*Id.* at art. 4(1)]. In addition, the Montreal Protocol now bans all export of these substances to non-parties [*Id.* at art. 4(2)], and discourages the export of technology for their production or utilization [*Id.* at art. 4(5)]. The Protocol also bans the import from non-parties of products containing the above substances, though a party who makes a timely objection to the Annex listing of such products will not be bound [*Id.* at arts. 4(3)]. Finally, the parties through the MOP must in the future consider the feasibility of so-called "process" trade restrictions, which disallow the import of products produced with, but not containing, the above controlled substances [*Id.* at art. 4(4)].

d. Technological and Financial Assistance

By way of the 1990 London Amendments, the Montreal Protocol became the first environmental treaty to link the compliance of developing countries with the provision of technological and financial assistance by industrialized countries. Accordingly, the Montreal Protocol now operates a "financial mechanism," including a Multilateral Fund, to meet all "agreed incremental costs" of compliance by developing country parties [*Id.* at art. 10]. Although what constitutes "incremental cost" within a particular situation remains highly debatable, the term refers to the cost of compliance that a party would not incur but for its adherence to the Montreal Protocol. In this way, developing nations need not simply rely on the protections offered by Article 5, but have a new incentive both to sign on to the Protocol and to meet the relevant control provisions. Since 1991, the fund has approved activities—including industrial conversion, technical assistance, training, and capacity-building—worth over U.S. $3.1 billion as of 2014 [Achim Steiner, *Forward to the Handbook for the Montreal Protocol on Substances that Deplete the Ozone Layer,* available at www.ozone.unep.org (last visited Apr. 2017)]. Today, the Multilateral Fund remains under the ultimate control of the MOP, but the World Bank, the UNEP, and the United Nations Development Programme (UNDP) share in its administration.

F. CONCLUSIONS

The legal regime controlling ozone is one of the most successful achievements of IEL. There are a number of reasons for this assertion. First, in quantitative terms, Ozone-depleting substances in the atmosphere would have been approximately five times greater, if not for the treaties. It is estimated that such increases would have resulted in approximately 19 million more cases of non-melanoma cancer, 1.5 million cases of melanoma cancer, and 130 million more cases of cataracts. The production and consumption of the majority of harmful ozone-depleting substances—over 98%—has already been successfully phased out in both developed and developing countries [United Nations

Environment Programme (UNEP), Backgrounder: Basic Facts and Data on the Science and Politics of Ozone Protection (Sept. 2008)]. There are plans to phase out the remaining 2% of CFCs currently used in metered-dose inhalers in 2016 [Id.] The phasing out of anthropogenic ozone is expected to increase chemically-driven polar ozone. In other words, the Antarctic ozone hole is expected to "heal." Scientific observations and model calculations taken together indicate that this healing is already underway [Susan Solomon, et al., Emergency of healing in the Antarctic ozone layer, (Jun. 2016) Science].

Second, the Vienna Ozone Convention established a framework approach that was implemented by the Montreal Protocol and various Amendments and Adjustments. The Vienna Ozone Convention has achieved truly global participation—with universal participation by all 197 States in the world [Steiner, *supra*]. The manner in which the Amendments and Adjustments have been used to advance ozone reduction is quite unique. These legal techniques have allowed adjustments and amendments to avoid the convoluted and often risk fraught path of traditional treaty making and amendments. They point the way to future international environmental law-making.

Third, the ozone regime offers powerful evidence of how to implement SD. The regime recognized the special situation of developing countries and set up mechanisms to provide financial and technological assistance to developing countries. This ensured developing countries were bought into and worked to implement the various objectives of the regime.

Fourth, in discussing the impact of the ozone regime, it is essential to note that ozone-depleting substances are also extremely powerful greenhouse gases (GHGs). On a gram-for-gram basis, the ozone-depleting substances previously used as refrigerants have thousands of times the climate change impact of CO_2. A 2007 study published in the Proceedings of the U.S. National Academy of Sciences indicates that the reductions of ozone-depleting substances brought about by the Montreal Protocol have been far more effective in mitigating climate change than the 1997 Kyoto Protocol to the United Nations Framework Convention on Climate Change (Kyoto Protocol), which was specifically designed to address climate change [Velders et al., *The Importance of the Montreal Protocol in Protecting Climate*, 12 PROCEEDINGS OF THE NATIONAL ACADEMY OF SCIENCES 4814 (2007) at 4814–19]. According to the report, the Montreal Protocol has been approximately 5.5 times as effective as the Kyoto Protocol was intended to be in reducing emissions of GHGs [*Id.*]

Unfortunately, some of the substitutes used to replace the ozone-depleting substances that were phased out by the Montreal Protocol are themselves potent GHGs. For example, hydroflurocarbons (HFCs) have been increasingly used in the last decade as a non-ozone-depleting alternative in air conditioning, refrigeration, foams, and aerosols. However, HFCs are themselves potent GHGs and also have a long atmospheric lifespan. It now seems that phasing out HFC use, and careful collection and disposal of existing HFC refrigerants, may present a good option in the context of limiting the impact of climate change.

CHAPTER EIGHT
ANTARCTICA

Geographers had posited the existence of a large southern continent long before seafarers first spotted Antarctica in the early 19th century. The ancient Greeks reasoned that in order to balance the major landmasses of the northern hemisphere a great continent to the south must exist. Later, European explorers set out to find *Terra Australis Incognita*—the Unknown Southern Land—believing this fabled continent would prove hospitable to human settlement. However, the Antarctic continent, first reached by explorers during the late 19th and early 20th centuries, proved to be anything but hospitable [*see* Maria Pia Casarini, *Activities in Antarctica Before the Conclusion of the Antarctic Treaty*, INTERNATIONAL LAW FOR ANTARCTICA 627, F. Francioni & T. Scovazzi eds. (1996) at 631–32].

A. GEOPHYSICAL SKETCH

Antarctica is the coldest, windiest, iciest, driest, and highest major landmass on the earth. The fifth largest continent in the world, Antarctica comprises around 9% of the earth's continental (lithospheric) crust and is approximately twice the size of Australia. However, only a tiny fraction of the continent itself is visible, as 98% of Antarctica's 5.4 million square miles is buried beneath an immense sheet of ice. Over three miles thick in certain areas, the continental ice sheet has an average thickness of over a mile and contains 90% of earth's ice. Two-thirds of all the fresh water in the world is contained within the ice of Antarctica [U.S. EPA, PROPOSED RULE ON ENVIRONMENT IMPACT ASSESSMENT OF NONGOVERNMENTAL ACTIVITIES IN ANTARCTICA (2001) at 2–6 (hereinafter EPA 2001); National Science Foundation (NSF), THE U.S. IN ANTARCTICA—REPORT OF THE U.S. ANTARCTIC PROGRAM EXTERNAL PANEL (1997) at 9–25 (hereinafter NSF REPORT)].

Yet despite the abundance of fresh water in the form of ice, Antarctica is climatologically a desert. The interior of the continent averages less than two inches of precipitation per year, just slightly more than the Sahara Desert [EPA 2001 at 2–3]. While the average annual temperature of the continental interior is −70°F (degrees Fahrenheit) or −57°C (degrees Celsius), Antarctic temperature trends vary considerably according to region. For instance, in the northern regions of the Antarctic Peninsula, average annual temperatures range from 50°F to 60°F (10°C to 15°C) during the austral summer, while temperatures in the interior high altitude regions range from −112°F to −130°F (−80°C to −90°C) during the austral winter [*Id*. at 2–3]. Antarctica also holds the record for the lowest recorded surface temperature in the world at −129°F (or approximately −89.4°C), [National Climate Data Center, GLOBAL MEASURED EXTREMES OF TEMPERATURE AND PRECIPITATION (2008)].

Unlike the Arctic polar region of the North, Antarctica has no indigenous human population; the continent is the largest single region historically uninhabited by humans. Itinerant researchers and a small but growing number of tourists constitute the visiting human population [United Nations Environment Programme (UNEP), GLOBAL ENV'T OUTLOOK 2000 (1999)]. The terrestrial flora of Antarctica consists mostly of certain species of algae, mosses, and lichens—though two species of angiosperms (flowering plants) grow in the relatively warmer region of the continent's northern-most extension, called the Antarctic Peninsula [EPA 2001 at 2–15]. The Antarctic Peninsula region supports the greatest diversity of flora and fauna on the continent. It also has the highest concentration of research stations [*Id.* at 15]. There are no exclusively terrestrial vertebrates capable of surviving an Antarctic winter. Tiny invertebrates such as mites, midges, and springtails, as well as some 76 arthropod species (insects and the like), comprise the fauna that live exclusively on land. Scientists have also discovered a number of microbial species of bacteria and fungi native to Antarctica. Virtually all of these life forms—whether terrestrial flora, invertebrate arthropods, or microbial bacteria—have habitats found only in Antarctica [NSF REPORT at 11].

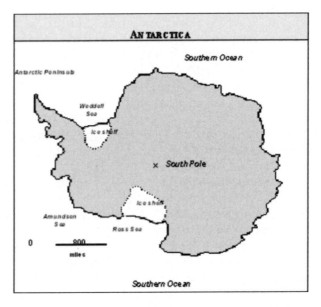

The continent of Antarctica is surrounded on all sides by the southern parts of the Pacific, Atlantic, and Indian Oceans, a region commonly referred to as the Southern Ocean. The Southern Ocean encompasses an area of approximately 13.9 million square miles—or about 10% of the earth's total ocean waters [EPA 2001 at 2–5]. In contrast to the biotic scarcity of the terrestrial environment, the waters of Antarctica have one of the highest concentrations of life in the world. The Southern Ocean is also home to numerous animal species whose survival depends upon their effective utilization of both the terrestrial and marine environments. In addition to an immense population of flying bird species, Antarctica is home to seven species of penguins—two of which breed exclusively in Antarctica—and six species of seals. The total bird population of Antarctica is estimated at 350 million, half of which are thought to be penguins. The aggregate weight of this prodigious bird population is estimated to be greater than 400,000 tons—more than the weight of all the seals and whales of Antarctica combined. Researchers have documented eight species of large cetaceans (whales) and nine species of small cetaceans (dolphins and porpoises) within the Southern Ocean, although none of these species are found exclusively within the region [*Id.* at 2–25].

Phytoplankton and zooplankton constitute the flora and fauna base of the Antarctic food chain— thus enabling the remarkable abundance of life within the Southern Ocean to exist. Within the dynamic of this food chain, zooplankton are an essential link between the region's primary producers (phytoplankton) and its major predators. Most prominent among the Antarctic zooplankton is the shrimp-like crustacean called the Antarctic krill (*Euphausia superba*). According to one study, krill comprise 75 to 90% of the marine invertebrate biomass within the Antarctic Peninsula region [*Id.* at 2–17].

B. SCIENTIFIC AND ARCHEOLOGICAL IMPORTANCE

Antarctica is an important location for globally significant scientific research that benefits virtually all scientific disciplines. Because it has been less affected by human activity than any other continent, its near-pristine environment provides baselines for measuring pollution in populated areas of the world [NSF REPORT at 1; *see also* Science Commission on Antarctic Research, *Info. Paper—Scientific Research in the Antarctic*, AGENDA ITEM 12, XXI ATCM]. Antarctic ice sheets also hold valuable records of past global climates, and help us to understand the effects of human activities on the global environment. Ice core samples, comprised of thin layers of ice deposited from yearly snows, can show evidence of industrial pollution and radioactive fallout, as well as volcanic eruptions from around the world. In addition, meteorites, valuable for their planetary information, are easier to find in Antarctica because they accumulate and are more noticeable on the ice sheets. The abundance and well-preserved nature of meteorite samples in Antarctica has proven more valuable in scientific research than any previously discovered source [Commission for Environmental Protection, *Antarctic Meteorites: SCAR Working Paper*, ANNEX 2 XXV/ATCM/IP (Sept. 2000)].

The continent also has terrestrial and freshwater ecosystems, unique in their simplicity, which provide valuable models for studying biological processes. As a result, many important global environmental problems, such as stratospheric ozone depletion and climate change, can be better studied in Polar Regions.

C. ECONOMIC CONCERNS

Based on their understanding of Antarctica's geological position, some scientists theorize that

Antarctica may contain rich oil and mineral resources similar to those found in Australia and South Africa. A number of different minerals have already been found within Antarctica by general geological surveys. Of the minerals Antarctica is known to possess, iron oxides and coal arguably comprise the list of those that could be extracted, processed, and distributed economically. However, scientific data also suggests the presence of oil and gas beneath Antarctica's continental shelf.

While economically attractive, the dangers and costs of exploiting Antarctic resources can be inhibitive. Drilling rigs and wellheads would have to withstand the most severe icebergs, high winds, and violent wave conditions in the world. This makes the prospect of oil or mineral development in Antarctica remote. Moreover, a lack of data, high financial costs, and technical obstacles introduced by increased conservation efforts has stymied mineral development.

The current international legal effort to prohibit oil and mineral exploration in Antarctica commenced almost 60 years ago. It sprang from the recognition that most drilling would occur on the continental shelf, in the very heart of Antarctica's biological productivity, and that an accident—made more likely by Antarctica's harsh climate—would have a disastrous effect on most Antarctic ecosystems [Frank G. Klotz, *America on the Ice*, ANTARCTIC POLICY ISSUES 87 (1990)]. The principle of non-degradation of the Antarctic environment was implied in the Antarctic Treaty of 1959, which dedicated Antarctica to scientific research and peaceful purposes. The principle has since been re-expressed in subsequent agreements. The 1991 Protocol on Environmental Protection to the Antarctic Treaty (1991 Antarctic Environmental Protocol) and various earlier conventions have committed the parties to a more comprehensive protection of the entire Antarctic environment.

Despite the constraints, there are additional economic draws to Antarctica. For example, Antarctica's tourism industry has rapidly expanded, although commercial tour operators work to minimize the industry's environmental impacts. Prior to 2000, there were generally less than 10,000 tourists visiting Antarctica each year. However, between 2010 and 2015 that number more than tripled, to approximately 34,000 tourists annually [International Association of Antarctica Tour Operators, *Tourism Statistics,* (2016) available at www.iaato.org (last visited Apr. 2017)]. In another example of economic potential, the ice sheet covering Antarctica contains 90% of the world's glacial ice (or 70% of the world's fresh water), and may be a potential supply of fresh water if and when technology makes this economically feasible.

D. ENVIRONMENTAL ISSUES

Antarctica is a microcosm of global environmental problems. For instance, Antarctica's coastal areas, where land is exposed, provide critical habitat and breeding grounds for mammals and seabirds. Human activities, in the form of scientific bases and support facilities, have sometimes contaminated the environment and disturbed these animals. Exposure to hydro-acoustic devices has increased the risk of damage to hearing in whales [Ulrich Kremser, et al., *Estimating the Risk of Temporary Acoustic Threshold Shift*, 17 ANTARCTIC SCIENCE 3 (2005)]. Seabirds have deserted their nests and breeding grounds, and altered their yearly breeding cycles. Research has also shown that Antarctic helicopter surveys have caused penguin stampeding and trampling, resulting in mass death, panicked fleeing, walking or running from nests and territories, and alert but nervous stationary behaviors [Colin Southwell, *Response Behavior of Seals and Penguins to Helicopter Surveys over the Pack Ice off East Antarctica*, 17 ANTARCTIC SCIENCE 328 (2005)].

Human activities can also lead to the introduction of foreign plant and animal species, which disrupt Antarctica's ecological balance by competing with and sometimes destroying native species [*see* David Walton, *Antarctic Biosecurity—Making it Happen*, 18 ANTARCTIC SCIENCE 161 (2006)]. Scientific vessels create novel and unnatural passageways for exotic species to reach the relatively secluded Antarctic continent and the surrounding Southern Ocean [*see* Patrick Lewis, et al., *Assisted Passage or Passive Drift: A Comparison of Alternative Transport Mechanisms for Non-indigenous Coastal Species into the Southern Ocean*, 17 ANTARCTIC SCIENCE 183 (2005)]. Additionally, the Antarctic ecosystem remains especially fragile in that just one species, the Antarctic krill, exists as the major food source of all higher species, such as whales, seals, fish, squid, penguins, and birds [*see* Stephen Nicol, *Antarctic Krill-Changing Perceptions of Its Role in the Antarctic Ecosystem*, ANTARCTIC SCIENCE: GLOBAL CONCERNS 144, G. Hempel ed. (1994) at 158].

The Antarctic continent also exerts a fundamental influence on the world's climate by regulating the average temperature of the earth. The immense Antarctic ice cap reflects up to 90% of the sun's energy, a primary reason Antarctica is so intensely cold. Oceanic and atmospheric currents work to carry this intense cold northward, thus cooling the waters of the Pacific, Atlantic, and Indian Oceans, and significantly impacting the earth's weather conditions. Antarctica is also the principal "heat sink" of the global climate system, causing the warmer air and ocean waters near the equator to move toward the colder air and waters at the southern pole, creating (in conjunction with the rotation of the earth) atmospheric and marine circulation patterns in the Southern Hemisphere.

Over the last half of the 20th Century, the Antarctic Peninsula region has grown warmer. Any major change in the reflective properties of the continent (its "albedo"), or the volume of the Antarctic ice sheet, could have dramatic effects on the rest of the world, including climate change and rising sea levels [Henry Phillpot, *Physical Geography—Climate*, KEY ENVIRONMENTS: ANTARCTICA 33, W. Bonner & D. Walton eds. (1985) at 36]. By one estimate, if the Antarctic ice (which comprises 90% of the world's ice) were to melt, sea level would rise some 200 feet—dramatically impacting humans and other forms of life across the entire planet [NSF REPORT at 14].

But, as of this writing, this does not appear likely. As we have noted in Chapter 6, Antarctic Sea ice reached a new record high in 2014. According to NASA, ice now covers more of the Southern Ocean than it has since scientists began a long-term satellite record to map sea ice extent in the late 1970s [NASA, *Antarctic Sea Ice Reaches New Record Maximum* (Oct. 7, 2014), *available at* https://www. nasa.gov/content/goddard/antarctic-sea-ice-reaches-new-record-maximum (last visited Apr. 2017)]. Climate models created in recent years have instead suggested a link between the lack of significant warming in Antarctica and the ozone hole over that continent. It is surmised, that as the ozone hole heals, all of Antarctica is likely to warm with the rest of the planet (*see* Ch. 6 & Ch. 7) [Peter Doran, *Cold, Hard Facts*, (Jul. 27, 2006) The New York Times].

Despite controversy about the effect of climate change in and around the Antarctic continent, the region has emerged as a significant player in the climate change debate. In addition to understanding the impact of melting ice and reduced albedo, ice cores harvested in Antarctica provide much of the key historical climatic and atmospheric data that are used to inform the debate about future climate change [Eric Wolff, *Understanding the Past Climate History from Antarctica*, 17 ANTARCTIC SCIENCE 487 (2005)].

E. GEOPOLITICAL SIGNIFICANCE

Protecting the Antarctic environment was made more difficult by the lack of recognized sovereignty over the entire continent. The primary international control strategies to protect Antarctica are collectively called the Antarctic Treaty System, which provides for cooperative international scientific projects, in which States exchange information, facilities, and personnel. Initially developed by 12 States that held conflicting views over the sovereignty of Antarctica, the Antarctic Treaty System is a remarkable accomplishment in international cooperation. It suspends conflicting territorial claims, prohibits military use, and preserves the continent for scientific research [*see generally* U.S. Department of State, HANDBOOK OF THE ANTARCTIC TREATY SYSTEM, NINTH EDITION, H. Kohen ed. (2002)].

F. LEGAL RESPONSE

1. OVERVIEW

As the forbidding continent of Antarctica gradually proved more accessible during the first half of the 20th century, questions arose as to its legal status. Given the potentially vast awards in the form of mineral and living resources, seven States made various and conflicting claims of sovereignty. The "claimant States," as these seven have become known, were the United Kingdom (1908), New Zealand (1923), Australia (1933), France (1939), Norway (1939), Chile (1940) and Argentina (1942).

The claimant States based their claims on a diverse assortment of theories, including the well-worn doctrine of "discovery" or "exploration," as well as "contiguity" or proximity to the Antarctic land mass. After World War II, another group of five States, each with extensive contacts on the continent, asserted that they would neither maintain nor acknowledge any territorial claims to Antarctica. Thus Belgium, Japan, South Africa, the U.S.S.R., and the U.S. became known as the "non-claimant States."

Throughout the 1950s, the dispute continued over who would control Antarctica. Finally, in 1959, the seven claimant and five non-claimant States all met to resolve their differences, eventually signing a compromise treaty. The result of these efforts, the Antarctic Treaty, has since given rise to a broader international regime for the continent. The Antarctic Treaty System now includes the 1972 Convention for the Conservation of Antarctic Seals (CCAS), the 1980 Convention on the Conservation of Antarctic Marine Living Resources (CCAMLR), the 1988 Convention on the Regulation of Antarctic Mineral Resource Activities (CRAMRA), and the 1991 Antarctic Environmental Protocol.

It should be noted, however, that from the outset, excluded States have questioned the legal basis of the original parties to contract on behalf of the entire world community. To these States, Antarctica still exists as part of the 'global commons,' and though the treaty parties may bind themselves, they may not bind other States by their private agreement. Though the number of parties to the Antarctic Treaty has grown from the original 12 to 53, it still remains unrepresentative of the entire international community, as only States who "conduct substantial scientific research" in the region achieve full voting status. Because of this exclusivity, some States have suggested that the Antarctic Treaty System operates more as a "club" than an internationally sanctioned authority. Still, the United Nations (UN) has not acted to co-opt or replace the present treaty system, and thus it remains the sole governing regime for Antarctica [*see* Lee Kimball, *The Antarctic Treaty System*, CONSERVATION AND MANAGEMENT OF MARINE MAMMALS 203, J.R. Twiss & R. Reeves eds. (1999)].

2.   1959 ANTARCTIC TREATY

The Antarctic Treaty considers several environmental matters, but only incidentally [*see* Kees Bastmeier, *The Antarctic Environmental Protocol and its Domestic Legal Implementation*, INT'L ENVTL L. & POL'Y SERIES, VOLUME 65 (2003)]. More significantly, the Antarctic Treaty places in abeyance the territorial claims of all contracting parties. It neither negates nor sustains the former claims. Instead, it provides that "[n]o new claim, or enlargement of any existing claim, . . . be asserted while the present Treaty is in force" [Antarctic Treaty at art. IV]. In addition to the 12 original "claimant" and "non-claimant" States, the Antarctic Treaty allows accession by any State, but, as mentioned above, only those who conduct "substantial scientific research activity" in Antarctica may achieve full voting status [*Id.* at art. IX(2)]. In effect, this system has created two classes of participants. As of this writing, there are 29 consultative parties (voting) and 24 non-consultative parties (non-voting).

Concerning the environment, the Antarctic Treaty does prohibit nuclear explosions and the disposal of radioactive wastes on the continent [*Id.* at art. V]. The treaty also names "preservation and conservation of living resources" as a possible topic of further measures by the parties [*Id.* at art. IX(1)(f)].

After the Antarctic Treaty went into force in 1961, the regime continued to advance through the adoption of recommendations from the Antarctic Treaty Consultative Meetings (ATCMs). These recommendations, which now number in the hundreds, include the 1964 Agreed Measures for the Conservation of Antarctic Fauna and Flora (1964 Agreed Measures) [*Agreed Measures for the Conservation of Antarctic Fauna and Flora*, Jun. 13, 1964, 17 U.S.T. 992 (hereinafter 1964 Agreed Measures)]. These measures designate the continent a "Special Conservation Area," and provide safeguards for both "specially protected species" and "specially protected areas" (these measures were later incorporated into the 1991 Antarctic Environmental Protocol). The 1964 Agreed Measures also prohibit the taking of all animals, except with a permit, and disallow the issuing of a permit for "specially protected species," except for a "compelling scientific purpose" that neither threatens the ecosystem nor the survivability of that species [*Id.* at art. VI]. Furthermore, the measures severely limit bringing into Antarctica any non-indigenous plant or animal species [*Id.* at art. IX], and require that, at all times, parties take precautions not to disturb or disrupt the animals living in Antarctica [*Id.* at art. VII].

Within specially protected areas, parties face more stringent requirements. In these areas, access is restricted and parties must not allow their nationals to collect plants or drive vehicles except with a permit [*Id.* at art. VIII]. In 1989, the consultative parties added multiple-use planning areas to the protections offered under the Antarctic Treaty, thereby establishing a larger zone for which parties must develop a management plan. In this way, and as altered and improved upon by the 1991 Antarctic Environmental Protocol, the Antarctic Treaty now requires the parties to work more closely in the coordination of all activities within a given locale.

3. 1972 CONVENTION FOR THE CONSERVATION OF ANTARCTIC SEALS (CCAS)

The Antarctic Treaty System originally grew through the adoption of ATCM recommendations, but in 1972 the regime was augmented by the first of three additional treaties. Although seals were afforded some protection under the 1964 Agreed Measures, CCAS improved upon these measures as a response to the near extinction of seal populations as a result of commercial exploitation.

Within regions addressed by the Antarctic Treaty, CCAS limits harvesting of three species of seals— Crabeater, Leopard, and Wedell—and prohibits harvesting of three others—Ross, Southern Elephant, and Southern Fur seals. In addition to the harvesting measures, CCAS creates a closed season and a sealing season, and stipulates sealing zones (which allow limited taking) and sealing reserves (which do not) for the harvestable species. However, a loophole exists. A party may issue a special permit that allows taking for reasons of scientific research or to provide specimens for museums, educational, or cultural institutions [CCAS at art. 4(1)(b)–(c)]. If a party issues such a permit, it must then report the number of seals killed or captured under these permits to the Scientific Committee on Antarctic Research [Id. at art. 4(2)]. The Committee also remains in charge of assessing the annual reports of the parties, as well as suggesting amendments to its technical provisions.

In point of fact, no commercial sealing has taken place in Antarctica since the inception of CCAS, though it is unclear whether driven by CCAS itself, politics, or economics. As a result, CCAS remains something of a "sleeping treaty," although that designation does not have the negative connotation that term usually implies. Should States ever decide to resume commercial sealing in Antarctica, the parties would have to reconcile the provisions of CCAS with those of the 1991 Antarctic Environmental Protocol (*see below*).

4.   1980 CONVENTION ON THE CONSERVATION OF ANTARCTIC MARINE LIVING RESOURCES (CCAMLR)

The objective of CCAMLR is the conservation of all living resources found south of the Antarctic Convergence, encompassing "fin fish, mollusks, crustaceans and all other species of living organisms, including birds" [CCAMLR at art. I(2)]. In effect, CCAMLR provides an early, rather rudimentary example of the ecosystem approach to conservation— an approach that aspires to protect the ecosystems as a whole rather than focusing on individual species. Although it does not define conservation, CCAMLR explains that the term "includes rational use" [*Id.* at art. II(2)]. It also lists "the following principles of conservation:

(a) prevention of decrease in the size of any harvested population to levels below those which ensure its stable recruitment. For this purpose its size should not be allowed to fall below a level close to that which ensures the greatest net annual increment;

(b) maintenance of the ecological relationships between the harvested, dependent and related populations of Antarctic marine living resources and the restoration of depleted populations to the levels defined in subparagraph (a) above; and

(c) prevention of changes or minimization of the risk of changes in the maritime ecosystem which are not potentially reversible over two or three decades, taking into account the state of available knowledge of the direct and indirect impact of harvesting, the effect of the introduction of alien species, the effects of associated activities on the marine ecosystem and of the effects of environmental changes, with the aim of making possible the sustained conservation of Antarctic marine living resources" [*Id.* at art. II(3)].

CCAMLR thus mandates a method of conservation that focuses on specific species, the interrelation between species, and the entire marine ecosystem. In addition, the mention of "sustained conservation" suggests an early move toward the concept of sustainable development (SD) in international law.

In order to implement these principles, CCAMLR creates two significant institutions: the Commission and the Scientific Committee. The Scientific Committee acts as the consultative body to the Commission, making recommendations concerning conservation matters [*Id.* at art. XV]. Here, CCAMLR makes an early gesture toward environmental impact assessment, requiring that the Scientific Committee gauge the "effects of proposed changes in the methods or levels of harvesting and proposed conservation measures" [*Id.* at art. XV(2)(d)]. The Commission then acts on the Scientific Committee's recommendations at its annual meeting, including the formulation of specific measures on the quantity of harvesting, method of harvesting, and the designation of protected species [*Id.* at art. IX].

Interestingly, CCAMLR binds its contracting parties to the important provisions of the Antarctic Treaty, whether or not they are parties to that treaty [*Id.* at arts. III & IV]. CCAMLR also requires its parties to adhere, "when appropriate," to the 1964 Agreed Measures [*Id.* at art. V(2)]. However, CCAMLR makes clear that it does not derogate from the rights and obligations under either the International Convention for the Regulation of Whaling (ICRW) [*International Convention for the Regulation of Whaling,* Dec. 2, 1946, 161 U.N.T.S. 366 (entered into force Nov. 10, 1948) (hereinafter ICRW)] or CCAS. CCAMLR also remains intact after the 1991 Antarctic Environmental Protocol, though the parties to both must cooperatively reconcile the differences between the two instruments.

5. 1988 CONVENTION ON THE REGULATION OF ANTARCTIC MINERAL RESOURCE ACTIVITIES (CRAMRA)

In contrast to CCAMLR, CRAMRA never received the full support of its own signing parties. CRAMRA was originally intended to establish a framework for ascertaining whether the wise utilization of Antarctic lands included the prospecting, exploration, and development of mineral resources. In its final form, CRAMRA set forth an extensive range of measures aimed at protecting the environment. In fact, CRAMRA's provisions concerning liability for environmental damage, environmental impact assessment, and dispute resolution will continue to serve as models for future IEL treaties. In the end, however, although 19 States signed the convention, none have ratified. Thus, CRAMRA never came into force and so remains a dead letter, presumably supplanted forever by the 1991 Antarctic Environmental Protocol.

6. 1991 PROTOCOL ON ENVIRONMENTAL PROTECTION TO THE ANTARCTIC TREATY (1991 ANTARCTIC ENVIRONMENTAL PROTOCOL)

As CRAMRA's prospects faded, and amid growing fears that Antarctica faced imminent environmental degradation, the Antarctic Treaty consultative parties chose to create an environmental protocol to the Antarctic Treaty. Broad and ambitious in scope, the 1991 Antarctic Environmental Protocol incorporates a number of progressive environmental ideals and principles, and currently has 37 parties. Most significantly, the 1991 Antarctic Environmental Protocol establishes Antarctica as a "natural reserve, devoted to peace and science" and commits the parties "to the comprehensive protection of the Antarctic environment and dependent and associated ecosystems" [1991 Antarctic Environmental Protocol at art. 2].

Though some States lobbied for the designation of the continent as a "World Park"—a designation which presumably would offer greater protection— the classification of Antarctica as a natural reserve marks a first for any substantial area within the global commons. Among other principles, the 1991 Antarctic Environmental Protocol places a premium on the planning and conducting of activities so as not to cause significant harm [*Id.* at art. 2]. This objective mandates prior assessment, effective monitoring, and cooperation among the parties. Furthermore, the parties acknowledge the intrinsic value of the continent, including its wilderness, aesthetic, and scientific values [*Id.* at art. 3(1)]. In fact, some critics see an over-emphasis on scientific value, worrying that the "priority" given to scientific research [*Id.* at art. 3(1) & (3)] could outweigh the prohibition against causing significant harm.

As for substantive requirements, the 1991 Antarctic Environmental Protocol adopts a 50-year moratorium on "any activity relating to mineral resources, other than scientific research" [*Id.* at art. 7]. Thus, it forbids all mineral exploration except that done for scientific purposes. While some parties sought a permanent ban on such activities, others, notably the U.S., preferred some flexibility to pursue mineral resources in the future. As a result, after 2048, any consultative party may call a Review Conference to amend the moratorium (or any other provision), at which time the parties may adopt any amendment accepted by a weighted majority [*Id.* at art. 25]. Otherwise, to change the moratorium before the expiration of the 50 year period, only the unanimous consent of the consultative parties will suffice [*Id.* at arts. 25(1), 12(1)(a) & (b)].

Other substantive provisions include the establishment of contingency plans in response to environmental emergencies [*Id.* at art. 15], and the requirement of annual reports filed by each party that outline the measures it has taken to comply with the protocol's various requirements [*Id.* at art. 17]. In this regard, the 1991 Antarctic Environmental Protocol creates no international authority to verify and enforce compliance, instead relying on the adoption of national measures by the individual parties. It does, however, create a Committee for Environmental Protection, the primary function of which is "to provide advice and formulate recommendations" to the ATCM on the specific operations of the protocol [*Id.* at arts. 11–12]. In general, the Committee for Environmental Protection must oversee, though not verify or enforce, the more detailed substantive requirements found in the protocol's annexes.

To date, six annexes to the 1991 Antarctic Environmental Protocol have been adopted on (I) Environmental Impact Assessment, (II) Conservation of Antarctic Fauna and Flora, (III) Waste Disposal and Waste Management, (IV) Prevention of Marine Pollution, (V) Area Protection and Management, and (VI) Liabilities Arising From Environmental Emergencies. The first four annexes were adopted with the Protocol in 1991, and entered into force in 1998. Annex V was adopted separately by the ACTM in 1991 and entered into force in 2002. Annex VI was adopted by the ACTM in 2005 and will enter into force once formally accepted by all States that were consultative parties at the time of its adoption.

The U.S. ratified the 1991 Antarctic Environment Protocol, passing implementing legislation in September 1996. The bill, The Antarctic Science,

Tourism, and Conservation Act of 1996, [*Antarctic Science, Tourism, and Conservation Act of 1996,* 16 U.S.C.A. §§ 2403a, 2413 (West 1997)], mandates the application of the National Environmental Policy Act (NEPA) [*National Environmental Policy Act,* 16 U.S.C.A. §§ 2401, et. seq. (West 1997)] procedures for all governmental and non-governmental activities on the continent.

a. Annex I: Environmental Impact Assessment

The 1991 Antarctic Environmental Protocol makes environmental impact assessment an integral part of each party's obligation to protect the ecosystem, subjecting all relevant activities to the assessment procedures set out in Annex I [1991 Antarctic Environmental Protocol at art. 8]. Though the procedures themselves are fairly detailed, the parties conduct the evaluations without international oversight. If an activity is determined to have "less than a minor or transitory impact," then no further assessment need take place, and the activity may proceed [*Id.* at Annex I, art. 1(2)].

Alternatively, if the party cannot make such a determination, then it must prepare an Initial Environmental Evaluation. Again, the purpose of the Initial Environmental Evaluation, which includes a consideration of alternatives and impacts, is to assess whether the activity will have "less than a minor or transitory impact" [*Id.* at Annex I, art. 2]. If the Initial Environmental Evaluation suggests the activity may have more than minor repercussions, the party must then prepare a much more extensive draft Comprehensive Environmental Evaluation. The draft Comprehensive Environmental Evaluation must contain very thorough investigations and conclusions about the possible impacts through the entire duration of the activity and beyond [*Id.* at Annex I, art. 3].

The party then must allow public comment for a period of 90 days, while simultaneously forwarding the draft Comprehensive Environmental Evaluation to the Committee for Environmental Protection for consideration [*Id.*]. If the Committee for Environmental Protection chooses, it may then pass the document on to the ATCM for further consideration [*Id.*]. In effect, the party always retains the right to go forward with its proposed activity, but only after intense public scrutiny at various levels. Finally, if the party does go forward after preparation of a final Comprehensive Environmental Evaluation, it must continue to monitor the activity, assessing and verifying the project's consequences [*Id.* at Annex I, art. 5].

b. Annex II: Conservation of Antarctic Fauna and Flora

The 1991 Antarctic Environmental Protocol also includes Annex II on the conservation of plants and animals. This Annex revises the relevant provisions of the 1964 Agreed Measures, and prohibits the taking of, or harmful interference with, both fauna and flora except with a permit [*Id.* at Annex II, art. 3]. However, in keeping with the Protocol's focus on national control, each party oversees its own endeavors and issues its own permits through an appropriate authority.

Annex II additionally contains an Appendix A, which lists "Specially Protected Species" that cannot be taken without a permit, and then only for a "compelling scientific purpose" that neither jeopardizes the species nor uses lethal force [*Id.* at Annex II, art. 3(5)]. Further, Annex II precludes the introduction of exogenous plants and animals for all species but those listed in Appendix B, except with a permit [*Id.* at Annex II, art. 4]. In actuality, Appendix B names very broad categories, such as "domestic plants" and "laboratory animals and plants including viruses, bacteria, yeast and fungi" [*Id.* at Appendix B]. Thus, the requirement remains primarily one of applying for a permit. Lastly, in a devastating blow to polar companionship, Annex II outlaws dogs from the continent, banning all canines from the Antarctic Treaty Area as of 1994 due to concerns that the dogs might transfer diseases to the seal population [*Id.* at Annex II, art. 4(2)].

c. Annex III: Waste Disposal and Management

In Annex III, the parties have attempted to deal with the difficult problem of waste from human activities in Antarctica. As a general obligation, each party must strive to reduce the amount of waste they create, to remove waste, and to clean up past and present disposal and work sites [*Id.* at Annex III, art. I]. More specifically, Annex III creates three categories of wastes requiring different disposal methods. First, the most hazardous wastes—such as radioactive materials, fuel, and acutely toxic wastes—must be removed by the generating party [*Id.* at Annex III, art. 2(1)]. Second, for less hazardous liquid wastes, sewage, and domestic liquid wastes, the generating party must work to remove these from the continent "to the maximum extent practicable" [*Id.* at Annex III, art. 2(2)]. Third, concerning other waste disposal on land, Annex III allows no disposal onto ice-free areas or into fresh water systems [*Id.* at Annex III, art. 4(1)] and, "to the maximum extent practicable," no disposal of Article 2(2) wastes onto ice-covered areas except by stations into deep-ice pits [*Id.* at Annex III, art. 4(2)]. On the other hand, a party may still discharge sewage and domestic liquid wastes directly into the sea in most circumstances [*Id.* at Annex III, art. 5].

d. Annex IV: Prevention of Marine Pollution

Annex IV creates rules for the prevention of pollution from ships in the Antarctic Treaty Area. It applies to all ships flying a party's flag, as well as any other ship engaged in Antarctic operations [*Id.* at Annex IV, art. 2]. However, Annex IV does not apply to warships or other ships owned and operated by a State party and used for government service [*Id.* at Annex IV, art. 11].

Annex IV contemplates four specific types of discharges: oil, noxious liquid substances, garbage, and sewage. For oil, Annex IV prohibits the release of oil or any oily mixture from a ship, except in cases permitted under Annex I of the International Convention for the Prevention of Pollution from

Ships (MARPOL) [*Id.* at Annex IV, art. 3] (*see* Ch. 11). The prohibition does not apply to discharge due to damage to a ship or its equipment. For noxious liquid substances, a category of more hazardous substances, Annex IV disallows discharge in any amount causing harm to the marine environment [*Id.* at Annex IV, art. 4]. Similarly, all garbage release remains prohibited, except for food wastes, which each ship must discharge at least 12 nautical miles from land or the nearest ice shelf [*Id.* at Annex IV, art. 5]. As for sewage, a ship may not dispose of any untreated wastes at sea within 12 nautical miles of land or ice-shelves, except where such a prohibition would "unduly impair" Antarctic operations [*Id.* at Annex IV, art. 6]. The qualifier "unduly impair" obviously allows flexibility on the part of each party's implementation of Article 6. Annex IV further states that it does not derogate from any specific rights and obligations under MARPOL [*Id.* at Annex IV, art. 14], and it requires the parties to develop contingency plans for combating marine pollution, including oil spills, from ships [*Id.* at Annex IV, art. 12].

e. Annex V: Area Protection and Management

Annex V, which entered into force in 2002, clarifies and updates the 1964 Agreed Measures (as well as later adoptions of the consultative parties) concerning area protection and management. It offers two types of designations: (1) Antarctic Specially Protected Areas and (2) Antarctic Specially Managed Areas.

An area may be approved as an Antarctic Specially Protected Area "to protect outstanding environmental values, scientific, historic, aesthetic or wilderness values, any combination of those values, or ongoing or planned scientific research" [*Id.* at Annex V, art. 3]. The primary protection afforded by an Antarctic Specially Protected Area designation, which includes areas formerly designated Specially Protected Areas and Sites of Special Scientific Interest, is to prohibit all access except by permit [*Id.*]. On the other hand an Antarctic Specially Managed Areas designation, which may include within it one or more Antarctic Specially Protected Areas, does not require a permit for entry but instead seeks to coordinate activities and improve cooperation among the parties [*Id.* at Annex V, art. 4]. Additionally, parties are also allowed to propose a site or monument of recognized historic value as a Historic Site or Monument [*Id.* at Annex V, art. 8]. The value of such a listing protects these locations from damage, removal, or destruction [*Id.* at Annex V, art. 8(4)].

To propose an area designation, any party (or certain institutions within the treaty system) must submit a detailed Management Plan to the ATCM [*Id.* at Annex V, art. 5]. The Management Plan should contain the necessary measures to protect each area as appropriate, and Annex V provides extensive guidelines in this regard. Thus, Annex V contains considerable potential protections, but again, potential pitfalls remain. Perhaps the most significant drawback (which is also an example of the emphasis on national enforcement throughout the

1991 Antarctic Environmental Protocol) exists in the reliance on each party's appointment of "an appropriate authority" to issue permits for access to the critical Antarctic Specially Protected Areas [*Id.* at Annex V, art. 7]. This, of course, leaves a great deal of discretion to the individual interpreter concerning what activities do and do not take place within the most fragile areas of the continent.

f. Annex VI: Liabilities Arising from Environmental Emergencies

Annex VI was adopted in 2005 and is still in the process of ratification. It addresses prevention and response to environmental emergencies in the Antarctic Treaty Area that are related to research activities and tourism, as well as other activities requiring notice pursuant to the Antarctic Treaty [*Id.* at Annex VI, art. 1].

Annex VI defines an "environmental emergency" as any accidental event that "results in, or imminently threatens to result in, any significant and harmful impact on the Antarctic environment" [*Id.* at Annex VI, art. 2(b)]. It goes on to require parties to develop preventative measures [*Id.* at Annex VI, art. 3] and contingency response plans [*Id.* at Annex VI, art. 4]. A vessel operator may be subject to strict liability if it fails to "take prompt and effective response action to environmental emergencies arising from its activities" [*Id.* at Annex VI, art. 6], although there are various exemptions and limitations [*Id.* at Annex VI, arts. 8–9]. Parties must also require operators to carry liability insurance [*Id.* at Annex VI, art.11]. Further, Annex VI creates a voluntary fund that can assist with reimbursement of costs associated with response actions taken [*Id.* at Annex VI, art. 12(1)].

G. CONCLUSIONS

The Antarctic continent and the Southern Ocean play a critical role in the global environmental system. The interactions between atmosphere, oceans, ice, and biota that take place in that region affect the entire global system, from bio-geochemical systems, to atmospheric and oceanographic circulation patterns, to the transport of energy and pollutants, to changes in sea level. The protection of the Antarctic is therefore a high priority [*see* UNEP, *Global Environmental Outlook Project*, GLOBAL ENV'T OUTLOOK 2000 (1999); UNEP, GEO YEAR BOOK 2006 (2006) at 31–38].

As we have noted, the principal environmental concerns in Antarctica are related to changes occurring at the global level rather than any changes originating from human activities within Antarctica itself. Those considered of most significance relate to the depletion of the ozone layer (*see* Ch. 7) and climate change (*see* Ch. 6).

In the recent past the Antarctic marine environment has also been subjected to uncontrolled, unsustainable, and profound disturbances by commercial exploitation of whale and seal stocks, leading to near-extinction of some species. While commercial exploitation is now prohibited, the impacts from this overexploitation are still evident in the marine ecosystem today. In comparison to these changes and the global changes noted, the environmental impacts of human activities occurring within Antarctica today are relatively minor and localized. Yet even these remain of concern because of the high scientific and aesthetic value to be derived by maintaining Antarctica as far as possible in a relatively undisturbed state.

The Antarctic Treaty reached its 50th anniversary in 2009. On that occasion, parties at the ATCM adopted a ministerial declaration "recognizing the historic achievements of the Treaty in promoting peace and international cooperation in the Antarctic region over the past half century" and reaffirming "continued commitment to the objectives and purposes of the Antarctic Treaty and the other elements of the Antarctic Treaty System" [Antarctic Treaty Consultative Meeting XXXII, *Washington Ministerial Declaration on the Fiftieth Anniversary of the Antarctic Treaty,* (2009) Washington]. The declaration also reaffirmed "it is in the interest of all humankind that Antarctica continue to be used exclusively for peaceful purposes" and that "freedom of scientific investigation is and continues to be a cornerstone of the Treaty" [*Id.*] The parties also reiterated the need to be sure that human activity in Antarctica, including tourism, is conducted in a manner that protects the Antarctic environment and minimizes any negative impacts.

CHAPTER NINE

TOXIC AND HAZARDOUS SUBSTANCES

A. NATURE OF THE PROBLEM

In large enough quantities, almost any chemical substance can harm humans and other living organisms. Toxic and hazardous substances, on the other hand, can cause significant damage in small, even minuscule, amounts. As we shall soon see, a precise definition of toxic and hazardous substances is difficult to elucidate. Generally, toxic and hazardous substances are those that have detrimental effects on organisms [Stanley E. Manahan, TOXICOLOGICAL CHEMISTRY AND BIOCHEMISTRY Section 97 (3d ed. 2002) (hereinafter Manahan, TOXICOLOGICAL)]. Toxic substances can include naturally occurring substances, such as certain heavy metals or volcanic pollutants, as well as anthropogenic pollutants, such as chemical pesticides and industrial wastes [*Id.*]. Toxic substances move through ecosystems in various ways. Some are added to the entire ecosystem from an external source, as with pesticides on grass. Others make their way through ecosystems internally through the bioaccumulation (or biomagnification) of toxins in the food chain (*see* below). The effects of toxic and hazardous substances can range from the minute to the widespread.

B. DEFINING THE ELEMENTS

Despite the fact that toxic and hazardous substances are often responsible for air, water, and land-based pollution, there is no universally adopted or accepted definition of a hazardous or toxic substance. The plethora of overlapping definitions and meanings attached to the terms has resulted in the terms toxic and hazardous being used interchangeably, hierarchically, conjunctively, and even disjunctively. Chemists define the terms differently than sociologists, environmentalists, and policymakers. This makes assessing and addressing toxic and hazardous substances difficult and often confusing.

In chemistry terms, the toxicity of a substance is identified by a number of factors including the length of time it will persist in the environment, how it tends to bioaccumulate in the tissues of lower species, the extent to which it reacts with other substances to form more harmful contaminants, and whether it produces a carcinogenic (cancer-causing), mutagenic (gene-altering), or teratogenic (birth defect-causing) effect in humans [G. Tyler Miller, LIVING IN THE ENVIRONMENT (14th ed. 2005) at 410–13]. Toxic substances that occur naturally are usually called toxins, while those that are created by humans are called toxicants [Manahan TOXICOLOGICAL at 117]. Toxic substances may be classified in several ways according to their chemical make-up, physical form, sources, uses, and effects on organisms [*Id.*].

A chemical substance is considered hazardous where it exhibits certain characteristics that can cause injury, disease, economic loss, or environmental damage [Miller, *supra* at 410–11]. Hazardous substances create a danger through many avenues including risk of explosion, corrosion, toxic contamination, and poisoning [Stanley E. Manahan, ENVIRONMENTAL CHEMISTRY, NINTH EDITION (2010) at Section 20.1]. Thus, from a scientific standpoint, a toxic substance is a type of hazardous substance.

However, definitions of toxic and hazardous substances tend to become blurred when the discussion is moved into the legal realm. The two terms have been variably defined even within national legal systems. For example, in the U.S. the term "hazardous" is defined differently for each class of pollutant and for differing regulatory schemes within a plethora of controlling statutes that include: the Occupational Safety and Health Act (OSHA) [*Occupational Safety and Health Act,* 29 U.S.C.A. §§ 651–678]; the Clean Air Act [*Clean Air Act,* 42 U.S.C.A. §§ 7401–7671 (hereinafter Clean Air Act)]; the Clean Water Act [*Clean Water Act,* 33 U.S.C.A. §§ 1251–1376]; the Federal Insecticide, Fungicide, and Rodenticide Act (FIFRA) [*Federal Insecticide, Fungicide, and Rodenticide Act,* 7 U.S.C.A. §§ 136–136(y)]; the Toxic Substances Control Act (TSCA) [*Toxic Substances Control Act,* 15 U.S.C.A. §§ 2601–2629 (hereinafter TSCA)]; the Hazardous Materials Transportation Act [*Hazardous Materials Transportation Act,* 49 U.S.C.A. §§ 5101–5127]; the Federal Hazardous Substance Act [*Federal Hazardous Substance Act,* 15 U.S.C.A. §§ 1261–1276 (hereinafter Federal Hazardous Substance Act)]; the Resource Conservation and Recovery Act (RCRA)

[*Resource Conservation and Recovery Act of 1976,* 42 U.S.C.A. §§ 6901–6991(k) (hereinafter RCRA)]; and the Comprehensive Environmental Response, Compensation and Liability Act (CERCLA, also known as Superfund) [*Comprehensive Environmental Response, Compensation and Liability Act,* 42 U.S.C.A. §§ 9601–9675].

Specifically, hazardous waste is defined by RCRA as any solid waste that because of concentration, quantity, physical, chemical, or infectious characteristics may cause or significantly contribute to an increase in mortality, or contribute to irreversible or incapacitating illness [RCRA at § 6903]. Hazardous air pollutants are defined by the Clean Air Act as air pollutants that may present a threat of adverse health effects, including those substances which may be carcinogenic, mutagenic, teratogenic, neurotoxic, or those that cause adverse environmental effects through bioaccumulation or deposition [Clean Air Act at § 7412 (b)(2)]. The Federal Hazardous Substances Act defines hazardous substances to include those that are toxic, corrosive, flammable, and radioactive [Federal Hazardous Substance Act at § 1261(f)(1)(a)–(c)]. The same Act defines "toxic" as any substance that causes injury or illness to humans "through ingestion, inhalation, or absorption" [*Id.* at § 1261(g)]. Interestingly, TSCA, which contains the word in the name of the act, does not specifically define "toxic" at all [TSCA at § 2602]. Gleaning a meaning for the terms "hazardous" and "toxic" can indeed be a frustrating task.

International definitions of hazardous and toxic substances are often an extension and conflation of different national definitions. For example, if a material is regulated domestically, it will also be treated as hazardous under the Basel Convention on the Control of Transboundary Movements of Hazardous Wastes and their Disposal (Basel Convention) and the Bamako Convention on the Ban of Import into Africa and the Control of Transboundary Movement and Management of Hazardous Wastes Within Africa (Bamako Convention). At first glance it might appear that these conventions defer to each individual State's definition of hazardous and toxic substances, but upon closer review one will see that the Basel Convention also seeks to posit its own definition for hazardous waste. The Basel Convention defines hazardous waste to include substances that are explosive, flammable, oxidizing, poisonous, infectious, corrosive, toxic, ecotoxic, or any substance capable of forming another material which possesses any of the previous characteristics after disposal [Basel Convention at Annex 3]. In addition to contaminants that possess these characteristics, a number of treaties, such as the Basel Convention, [*Id.* at art. 1 & Annex I] and the Bamako Convention [Bamako Convention at art. 2 & Annex I], contain a list of wastes that have previously been identified as hazardous by States, including medical waste, organic chemicals or hydrocarbons, radioactive wastes, and materials that contain traces of heavy metals.

C. SOURCES

About 95% of all hazardous pollutants are created by industries that generate four primary groups of toxic and hazardous chemicals: (1) toxic metals, (2) petrochemicals, (3) pesticides, and (4) radioactive materials (a discussion of radioactive materials is excluded from this chapter because it is dealt with in Chapter 17).

Metals are present in nearly all rock types and are concentrated in ores. Toxic metals include heavy metals and trace metals. Heavy metals are those such as mercury, cadmium, and lead whose densities are at least five times greater than water. Trace metals are those present in the environment or the human body in very low concentrations such as zinc, copper, and iron [John B Sullivan, Jr. & Gary R. Krieger eds., CLINICAL ENVIRONMENTAL HEALTH AND TOXIC EXPOSURE (2nd ed. 2001)]. Human activities have altered the natural cycle of metals and, in many instances, contributions from humans surpass those from natural sources.

Metals can contaminate our air, soil, and water. Toxic metals like mercury, cadmium, lead, and arsenic find their way into the air through burning coal and oil for energy, ore refining, trash burning, cement production, and the use of automobiles [Joseph A. Salvato, et al., ENVIRONMENTAL ENGINEERING (2003) at 900–901]. Arsenic and cadmium are found in pesticides and fertilizers and can enter our waters through agricultural run-off. Metal can also accumulate in atmospheric water as well and fall to earth as acid deposition [Manahan

TOXICOLOGICAL at 97–8]. Metal contaminants in soil and water are especially troublesome because of their tendency toward bioaccumulation (*see* below).

We use and find petrochemicals in goods as varied as food, medicine, cosmetics, lumber, household appliances, fuels, plastics, papers, and innumerable other manufactured products. Petrochemicals are divided into two groups: organic and inorganic. Organic compounds are based on carbon atoms usually in combination with hydrogen, and the better known include ethylene, methylene chloride, formaldehyde, benzene, dichloro-diphenyl-trichloroethane (DDT), and polychlorinated biphenyls (PCBs). Inorganic compounds are not based on carbon, and examples of such substances include sulfuric acid, aluminum, and chromium. Petrochemical products enter the environment in a number of ways. The principal among these are intentional use as in the case of pesticides, incidental and operational releases of liquid discharges and gaseous emissions during their manufacturing process, accidental spills, and waste disposal.

Most pesticides are produced by the petrochemical industry, but their importance as a source of pollution arising from individual and agricultural use calls for separate treatment. There are many different types of pesticide products in use, including: insecticides (insects), herbicides (plants), fungicides (molds and mildew), rodenticides (rats and mice), acaricides (mites and ticks), bactericides (bacteria), avicides (birds), and nematicides (roundworms). According to the most recent U.S. Environmental

Protection Agency (EPA) report on the subject, worldwide pesticide expenditure totaled $56 billion in 2012 [Donald Atwood & Claire Paisley-Jones, *Pesticides Industry Sales and Usage: 200–2012 Market Estimates,* (2017) U.S. Environmental Protection Agency at 12]. The U.S. accounted for 18-16% of total world pesticide expenditure, 14% of world insecticide expenditure, 21% of world herbicide expenditure, 10% of world fungicide expenditure, and 23% of world fumigant expenditure [*Id.*].

Pesticides contain both inert and active ingredients. The active ingredient is the portion of the chemical that actually kills or controls the target organism [T.S.S. Dikshith & V. Prakash, INDUSTRIAL GUIDE TO CHEMICAL AND DRUG SAFETY (2003) at 597]. Because pesticides are designed to kill a broad spectrum of organisms, they present a threat not only to the target organism but also to other animals, including humans [Stephen Crossley & Denis Hamilton, PESTICIDE RESIDUES IN FOOD AND DRINKING WATER: HUMAN EXPOSURE AND RISKS (2004) at 278]. Unfortunately, less than 0.1% of insecticides and only 5% of herbicides applied to crops by spraying actually reach the target organism. The remaining chemicals become toxic contaminants as they vaporize into air, run off into water, or leach into soil and groundwater [Miller, *supra*, at 507].

The most widely used pesticides fall into one of four chemical groups: organochlorines, organosphosphates, carbamates, and botanicals. The most dangerous of these are organochlorines (chlorinated hydrocarbons), which contain chlorine, carbon, and hydrogen. Examples of organochlorines include insecticides such as DDT, chlordane, lindane, aldrin/dieldrin, and heptachlor. Organochlorines are categorized as persistent pollutants because they do not readily break down in an ecosystem and can accumulate through the food chain in plant and animal tissues [David J. Hoffman, et al., HANDBOOK OF ECOTOXICOLOGY (2nd ed. 2003) at 12.1; Sullivan & Krieger, *supra*, at 1057–81].

Many of the organochlorine pesticides have now been replaced by organophosphorus and carbamate pesticides, which, while still highly toxic, are short-lived [*Id.* at 12.1]. However, the high toxicity of organophosphorus pesticides poses risks to organisms that come into contact with the substances, as these pesticides attack the nervous system and may be linked to changes in an animal's ability to cope with stresses, reproductive behavior, and migration patterns [*Id.* at 12.2.1]. Currently, one third of the world's registered pesticides are organophosphorus pesticides [*Id.*]. Carbamate pesticides are also relatively short-lived but still pose similar threats as organophosphorus. Carbamate pesticides are less widely used and constitute less than 25% of the world market [*Id.* at 12.2.2].

D.   ENVIRONMENTAL PATHWAYS AND IMPACTS

1.   PATHWAYS

Toxic substances often impact ecological food chains through the process of bioaccumulation, which begins when a toxic contaminant is present in soil or water and is absorbed by plants. While the contamination may affect the plants themselves, by stunting growth or making them more susceptible to other environmental damage, the toxin will also be passed on to herbivorous animals that consume the plants. When a carnivore then consumes that herbivore, the toxin moves up to the next trophic level. Toxins that are lipophilic (fat-seeking) cannot be easily metabolized and therefore persist in the fat deposits of carnivores. The effect is an accumulation and magnification of toxins toward the top of the food chain [Manahan, TOXICOLOGICAL at 100–102].

Toxic and hazardous wastes can take many forms: liquid, solid, semi-solid (sludge), and containerized gas. While there are hundreds of thousands of producers of small amounts of hazardous waste in the U.S., the top 50 producers create 85% of hazardous waste [U.S. Environmental Protection Agency (EPA). *The National Biennial RCRA Hazardous Waste Report (Based on 2011 Data)* (2011)]. The list of generators includes chemical manufacturers, the petroleum industry, metal fabricators, metal-related producers, and electrical equipment manufacturers [*Id.*].

Toxic wastes are neutralized or sequestered through various physical, chemical, and biological processes of treatment and disposal. A typical example of treatment is to place the waste in large surface impoundments such as pits, ponds, or lagoons where it is filtered, solidified, degraded, or neutralized. However, if not properly lined, the surface impoundment may leach into the groundwater. Also, the waste may simply run off into surface waters if the cap on the structure breaks down. And, because household and small-scale industrial waste is not generally treated as hazardous due to the small quantity, these wastes often end up in landfills that are not designed to contain them [Travis Wagner, IN OUR BACKYARD (1994) at 135–36].

Incineration is a more expensive method of treatment and disposal, in which wastes are burned at high temperatures. Depending upon the type of waste involved, incineration may offer a relatively safe disposal method, though the ash generated can itself contain toxic materials that require additional disposal. However, in some circumstances toxic gases and particulate materials may escape at harmful levels [Sullivan & Krieger, *supra*, at 628].

Wastes not successfully dealt with by any other means may be stored in waste piles or tanks and then disposed of in landfills, in surface impoundments, or in deep wells. Deep-well injection involves the pumping of liquid waste into a well or a geologic formation located below underground sources of drinking water. Unfortunately, injected hazardous wastes may eventually migrate into the groundwater through cracks or fissures [Salvato, et al., *supra*, at 884].

2. IMPACTS

When toxic and hazardous substances are introduced into our environment, there are impacts on ecosystems and human health hazards. Though these issues overlap, they will be discussed in turn in this section.

a. Ecosystem Effects

In the 1960s, U.S. scientists discovered that bald eagles, peregrine falcons, and other predatory animals were dying as a result of reproductive failure caused by excess DDT in their tissues. However, these birds did not feed on the farmlands where DDT had originally been applied. Instead, run-off had carried the DDT into lakes and ponds, where the pesticide passed from algae to plankton, eventually aggregating in fish through the process of bioaccumulation. Since the fish retained the poison, rather than excreting it, the birds that fed on these fish developed even higher concentrations of the deadly chemical. Thus, because ecosystems often consist of complex and intricate relationships between components, contamination of one component can easily affect others.

Toxins can affect ecosystems in two main ways. First, the toxic substance can spread through the ecosystem from component to component, as was the case with the bioaccumulation of DDT. Second, toxins can indirectly affect relationships between the organisms. For example, when populations of predatory birds declined due to DDT, the populations of their prey increased, changing the demands on vegetation and other resources. These two effects are not mutually exclusive.

In addition to potential reproductive harm, toxins can affect individual organisms in a variety of other ways. Some toxins can cause a direct decline in the number of juvenile organisms [Manahan, TOXICOLOGICAL at 5.10]. Carcinogenic toxins take time to accumulate and may alter the number of adult organisms in a population. Other toxins affect an organism's ability to cope with environmental stresses, a result which may not be apparent until environmental stresses reach a level beyond which the poisoned organism cannot function.

On a systemic level, toxins have both lethal and non-lethal effects. Lethal effects are evidenced by die-offs. While these are important, they are not the only type of effect toxins have on ecosystems. Non-lethal effects are also extremely important, and often harder to trace [*Id.*]. Reproduction, stress coping, and migratory changes can affect populations in very severe ways.

b. Human Health Hazards

We have dealt with the environmental movements of toxic substances through air, water, and land, as well as their advance up food chains through bioaccumulation and ecosystem effects. We now consider their points of entry into, and passage through, human bodies toward target organs, giving rise to disease and harm to human health. The tragedy that took place in the fishing village of Minamata, Japan in the 1950s offers a painful example. Japanese villagers were poisoned by mercury that had been discharged into the water by a nearby chemical company and bioaccumulated in fish consumed by the villagers. The incident resulted in approximately 50 deaths and several thousand cases of permanent nervous disorders.

When discharged into the environment, pollutants affect humans through three routes. A person may inhale a substance, ingest it through water or food, or absorb it through the skin. Once a toxin enters the bloodstream, it circulates to all of the organs in the body. However, the extent of harm depends on the concentration and type of toxin present. Some toxins are easily metabolized by the body and become detoxified. Other toxins—typically cancer-causing substances—become more toxic after metabolization. This is called bio-activation. The body may also reduce the toxic effect of a substance by storing it in fat tissue, but adverse effects may still occur if the body utilizes a large amount of fat for energy at one time. The acute effects of a toxin may disappear because a number of chemicals will naturally bind with proteins in the bloodstream, thereby reducing the amount free to attack a certain organ. Nonetheless, this process may result in a chronic effect because the chemical may stay in the body longer, becoming unbound and harmful at a later date.

All substances can become toxic if they impact humans in sufficient concentrations, and scientists engaged in ascertaining the risk posed by a chemical try to measure the linkage between exposure to a chemical and disease by employing both epidemiological and toxicological data. Epidemiology involves the study of human populations to discover the relationship between various risk factors and the occurrence of disease in that population. Toxicology uses data collected from laboratory experiments on animals, bacteria, and cell or tissue cultures to identify the mechanism of disease and the way that the contaminant causes harm.

Establishing linkages is particularly difficult for a number of reasons. The potency of a substance, the degree of exposure, and the fact that certain groups of people are more sensitive to particular toxic substances complicates such assessments. A fourth difficulty exists for toxicological data derived from high dosages administered to test animals. A researcher must extrapolate such high dosages onto a fact situation involving humans, who possess different metabolisms than animals, and whose contact occurs at a lower level of the suspect substance [Sullivan & Krieger, *supra*, at 49–51].

Real-life exposure to toxic and hazardous contaminants depend on the type of toxin and the organ involved and can result in both chronic and acute health effects in humans. Acute effects, such as skin burns, rashes, and kidney damage, appear shortly after introduction to a large dose or concentration of a contaminant. Chronic effects are those which do not appear initially, but tend to last for many years after long-term exposure to low concentration levels or short-term exposure to extremely high concentrations [Miller, *supra*, at 450]. Contact with certain types of toxic or hazardous contaminants can result in chronic health effects such as cancer, inheritable diseases, birth defects, heart and lung disease, and nerve or behavioral disorders.

Carcinogens remain extremely difficult to identify because of the complex nature of cancer as a disease and the broad range of chemicals and environmental factors encountered by humans. To date, common examples of carcinogens include asbestos, carbon tetrachloride, arsenic, and benzene. Mutagens, such as benzopyrene and ozone, can alter an organism's genetic code resulting in cancers or inheritable diseases like cystic fibrosis. Other chemicals and certain metals, including lead, cadmium, arsenic, and mercury, are classified as teratogens [Dikshith & Prakash, *supra*, at 402].

E.   REMEDIAL OBJECTIVES

Hazardous chemicals and wastes are the inevitable consequence of modern living. The lifestyle enjoyed in industrialized countries depends to a significant degree on the use of chemicals for a variety of purposes. So many of the goods taken for granted—ranging from simple articles like knives, forks, and instant food, to more complex machines such as cars or computers—involve the use of chemicals. Chemicals are used in the extraction and refining of raw materials needed for these products, as well as in the manufacturing and packaging process. They also find their way into the environment when these products are discarded.

The dangers associated with the use of hazardous chemicals, and the waste their use creates, can be controlled by a number of strategies. A primary goal should be to reduce demand for products that entail the use of such substances. Demand management exists as a painful but necessary step in any concerted attempt to find solutions. Second, it is necessary to adopt a comprehensive view of the problem by regulating and managing local, regional, and global material and energy flows in products, processes, and industrial sectors. Third, and this may be the more practicable of the objectives, integrated (as distinct from fragmented) pollution controls should be adopted. Many international conventions have attempted to control pollution within a particular environmental media (air, land, or water). However, while limitations on discharges in one medium, such as air, may correct the immediate air pollution problem, it often does little more than shift the pollution from air to land without recognizing the adverse impact of the transferred pollutant. Without an integrated strategy, pollutants eventually re-enter the flow of material within the environment.

This problem is evidenced by the massive quantities of sludge created by existing fragmented pollution controls in the U.S. For example, the provisions of the Clean Air Act directed at reducing sulfur dioxide in the atmosphere require the use of "scrubbers" in smoke stacks. Huge quantities of lime, limestone solution, and water are sprayed on exhaust gases as they flow up power plant smokestacks. Sulfur dioxide in the gas then reacts with the spray and forms a solution from which the sulfur dioxide is later removed, strained, and disposed of in the form of sludge. The EPA has estimated that three to six tons of scrubber sludge may be produced for each ton of sulfur dioxide removed from the flue gas. Consequently, the problem of sulfur dioxide in the air has been replaced by the problem of sludge disposal.

Such a fragmented approach also lacks economic efficiency. Pollution controls already in place ensure that wastes cannot be discharged according to the best environmental option. This may lead to inefficient use of the assimilative capacity of the environment. In the example previously considered we observed how implementation of the Clean Air Act leads to the creation of large quantities of sludge. Sludge can be disposed of in a number of ways: it can be discharged into a river or directly into the ocean, or it can be piped into a lagoon to settle and dry out as solid waste. What is germane is the possibility that current air pollution requirements might lead to water discharges or solid waste disposal problems that cause greater overall damage to the environment than might be the case if the air pollution standards had been cognizant of cross-media impacts. Furthermore, water pollution and land waste disposal laws also could prevent the discharges into water or disposal as solid waste without further treatment. Setting independent standards for each medium that ignore the assimilative capacity of the environment imposes unnecessary and unjustified costs on the manufacturing process.

A more efficient and cost effective method of pollution control would be to distribute the wastes between the three media of water, air, and land in a manner that makes optimum use of the environment and any special or particular assimilative capacity it might possess. This integrated policy would lead to a balanced approach to pollution control that would avoid the problems of standards that are overly stringent in some areas and unduly lax in others.

In the past, industrialized countries have either dumped hazardous waste directly into the ocean or buried it on the land. However, increased awareness of the dangers associated with these methods have led to strict regulation, forcing industries to look to developing countries for a solution. States with less stringent pollution control regulations, primarily located in Africa, Latin American, and the Caribbean, are usually more willing to accept hazardous wastes as a method to raise revenues. Also, the cost of disposing of wastes in these States is often significantly lower than instituting waste minimization techniques at the source or utilizing an approved disposal facility located in the waste-generating State.

Obviously, however, this practice is not a solution to the waste problem, as it merely transfers the environmental cost from industry to a group of people less qualified to bear it. Most States that import hazardous wastes lack information as to the risks these wastes pose to human health and the environment, and also may lack the knowledge and/or administrative capacity to manage the wastes properly. In fact, many States have accepted hazardous chemicals for use and disposal without knowing that the chemicals have been banned in the waste-generating State. Because of this overall lack of knowledge, developing countries may utilize disposal techniques that are not adequate to control the risks that hazardous wastes present to their citizens and their environment. In addition to the dangers posed by improper disposal techniques, the long distance transportation of hazardous wastes across land and water presents an increased risk of harm to transit States and the marine environment from accidental spillage.

Today, waste trade with developing countries continues to decline as industrialized countries have developed and utilized waste minimization techniques. Further, States have negotiated a number of treaties and regional agreements in order to deal with the problems associated with the trade of hazardous waste. As we shall see, both the Basel and the Bamako Conventions allow for trade between similarly situated party states, but only if the exporting State lacks the capacity to dispose of the waste in an environmentally sound manner and the importing State gives its Prior Informed Consent (PIC) (*see* below). The importing State must also possess the ability to dispose of the waste in an environmentally sound manner, and if an illegal trade occurs the exporting State must accept the waste for re-import [Basel Convention at arts. 6, 9; Bamako Convention at arts. 4, 6, 7, 9].

These conventions correctly seized the basic concepts underlying an integrated approach when they called upon all parties to reduce the generation of hazardous and toxic wastes to a minimum. This can only be done by reducing the sources of such wastes, which also means reducing demand for the products that require waste generation. The conventions also call for "environmentally sound management," which opens the door to integrated pollution control. Unfortunately, as detailed below, these requirements are left in the soft limbo of aspiration rather than that of hard legal duty.

The Bamako Convention calls for a prohibition on the importation of hazardous waste into their regions from non-parties, and attempts to regulate trade between parties to the convention. The right of States to ban imports is supported by other agreements, such as the Fourth Lome Convention (Lome Convention) [*Fourth Lome Convention,* Dec. 15, 1989 (entered into force Sept. 1, 1991), 29 I.L.M. 783 (hereinafter Lome Convention)], which prohibits exports of hazardous waste to African, Caribbean, and Pacific State parties from the European Union (EU). While the prohibitions on exports or imports of wastes express valuable, if controversial, aspects of international environmental law (IEL), it is well settled that the requirement of PIC codifies existing customary law (*see* below).

A number of international organizations, including the International Labour Organization (ILO), the Organisation for Economic Cooperation and Development (OECD), and the EU, have participated in the international effort to control the harmful effects of pesticides and other toxic chemicals. In addition, the World Health Organization (WHO) has developed important guidelines for classification, and works with both the United Nations Environment Programme (UNEP) and the ILO in promoting the International Programme in Chemical Safety.

Another significant contribution is made by the Codex Alimentarius Commission, which has developed regional and international standards regarding chemical residues in foods. The Codex standards, it should be noted, generally remain substantially less restrictive than those of industrialized States, and are relied upon by developing countries when alleging that industrialized country restrictions of trade are disguised as health and safety concerns. On the other hand, some domestic environmental organizations of industrialized countries have used the Codex standards as a rallying point against free trade agreements such as the North American Free Trade Agreement (NAFTA) [*North American Free Trade Agreement*, Dec. 17, 1992, 32 I.L.M. 289] and the General Agreement on Tariffs and Trade (GATT) and the World Trade Organization (WTO). The work of the Food and Agricultural Organization (FAO) and UNEP, however, has had the greatest impact on the behavior of States.

F.   LEGAL RESPONSE

1.   TOXIC AND HAZARDOUS SUBSTANCES IN GENERAL

Toxic and hazardous substances are ubiquitous, and many multilateral treaties and instruments deal with different manifestations of the global, regional, and bilateral challenges posed by them. These treaties and international instruments have been addressed in other parts of this book. For example, the Montreal Protocol on Substances that Deplete The Ozone Layer (Montreal Protocol) has been dealt with in Chapter 7; the Convention for the Protection of the Marine Environment of the North East Atlantic (OSPAR Convention) and others addressing land-based pollution will be discussed in Chapter 10; the Convention on Long-Range Transboundary Air Pollution (LRTAP) is analyzed in Chapter 14; and various oil pollution treaties responding to pollution from ships are covered in Chapters 11 and 12. In this chapter we are dealing with the aspects of toxic and hazardous substances that are not covered in these other chapters.

No international treaty controlled the distribution and use of hazardous substances prior to 1998. In the absence of such a treaty, the FAO and UNEP filled the gap with two sets of voluntary guidelines. These influential regulations—prime examples of "soft law"—predominantly focused on the relative obligations of industrialized and developing countries regarding trade. Both sets of rules adopted a regulated trade approach to the interaction between exporter and importer, allowing transfers of substances banned in another State under the principle of PIC.

In 1998, the Rotterdam Convention on the Prior Informed Consent Procedure for Certain Hazardous Chemicals and Pesticides in International Trade

(Rotterdam Convention) was adopted, making the principle of PIC legally binding [*Rotterdam Convention on the Prior Informed Consent Procedure for Certain Hazardous Chemicals and Pesticides in International Trade,* 10 Sept. 1998 (entered into force Feb. 24, 2004) 38 I.L.M. 1734 (hereinafter Rotterdam Convention)]. The Rotterdam Convention builds on earlier soft law voluntary guidelines. While States may still import hazardous substances, they may do so only if they have been notified of the potential hazards and the reasons for its ban in the exporting State.

This approach contrasts with that taken by the 1991 Bamako Convention, negotiated by the Organization of African States. The Bamako Convention, discussed in detail below, prohibits African States from importing *all* banned or restricted pesticides and chemicals from outside the continent.

2.   PRIOR INFORMED CONSENT (PIC)

a. FAO International Code of Conduct on the Distribution and Use of Pesticides (FAO Code)

As pesticide exports continued to accelerate during the 1980s, the FAO sought to limit the harmful effects of improper use in developing countries. The FAO International Code of Conduct on the Distribution and Use of Pesticides (FAO Code) offers guidance on pesticide management worldwide [Food and Agriculture Organization of the United Nations,

International Code of Conduct on the Distribution and Use of Pesticides, Revised Version, (2003), FAO Council Resolution 1/123 (hereinafter FAO Code)]. The FAO Code was originally adopted in 1985. However, following the adoption of the Rottedam Convention in 1998, and in view of the changing international policy framework, the FAO initiated an update and revision process of the FAO Code in 1999. In November 2002, the FAO approved the revised version.

The FAO Code seeks to "establish voluntary standards of conduct for all public and private entities . . . particularly where there is inadequate or no national law to regulate pesticides" [*Id.* at art. 1.1.1]. The FAO Code—which deals only with pesticides and does not address other hazardous substances—embraces the "necessary and acceptable use of pesticides," while striving to prevent "significant adverse effects on human health or the environment" [*Id.* at art. 1.1.3]. Non-binding in nature, the FAO Code consequently employs hortatory and sometimes vague aspirational language.

Under the FAO Code, governments retain ultimate responsibility for the distribution and use of pesticides in their States, but the pesticide industry—including manufacturers, marketers, and traders—also plays a significant role. Indeed, the revised FAO Code reflects more strongly than ever the responsibility of governments, the chemical and food industry, traders, pesticide users, public interest groups, and international organizations in reducing the health and environmental risks associated with pesticide use. The FAO Code also addresses the need for a cooperative effort between governments of pesticide exporting and importing States [*Id*. at art. 1.1.5)].

The FAO Code aspires to a number of laudable objectives, some of which are fleshed out in the body of the text, while others are not. For example, Article 1 seeks to promote integrated pest management [*Id*. at art. 1.7.6], but the exhortations in the body of the text do not contain a strategy or operational modalities for doing so [*see Id*. at art. 3.7, 3.8 & 3.9]. Alternatively, other objectives are backed by norms. The FAO Code deals with risk assessment and management of pesticides [*Id*. at art 6.1.3]. It requires the pesticide industry to carry out scientific testing [*Id*. at art. 4] and provide adequate data which governments can use to conduct risk assessments and undertake risk management [*Id*. at art. 6.2]. In order to receive and evaluate these reports, the governments of importing States should possess or have access to effective analytical facilities [*Id*. at art. 4.2]. Governments of exporting States, as well as international organizations, should strive to assist developing countries in establishing facilities capable of undertaking product and residue analysis [*Id*. at art. 4.3].

The FAO Code also requires the governments of importing States to develop necessary regulatory legislation for the control of pesticides, including registration [*Id*. at art. 6.1.2] and rules on availability and safe use [*Id*. at art. 7]. Additionally, all pesticide containers are required to be clearly labeled according to FAO guidelines on good labeling practice [*Id.* at art. 10.1]. In this regard, industry should use labels that include appropriate symbols and pictograms whenever possible in addition to written instructions, warnings, and precautions [*Id.* at art. 10.2]. Likewise, the packaging, storage, and disposal of pesticides should conform in principle to the applicable guidelines formulated by FAO and WHO, respectively [*Id.* at art. 10.3]. Industry is also encouraged to dispose of toxic pesticide waste in an environmentally sound manner [*Id.* at art. 10.6].

Undergirding the provisions of the FAO Code is the principle of PIC. This principle requires that no pesticide that is banned or severely restricted to protect human health or the environment in an exporting country can be imported into another country without the knowledgeable acquiescence of the importing State. The FAO Code's standards include reference to participation in information exchange and international agreements, particularly the Rotterdam Convention [*Id.* at art. 1.7.7] (*see* below). The FAO Code goes on to state that governments should facilitate the exchange of information regarding actions to ban or severely restrict a pesticide, as well as the exchange of scientific and legal information concerning pesticides [*Id.* at art. 9]. Additionally, governments are encouraged to develop their own legislation and regulations that allow information about pesticide risks to be available to the public, and to encourage public participation in the regulatory process [*Id.* at art. 9]. Lastly, all parties are to "encourage collaboration between public sector groups, international organizations, governments and other interested stakeholders to ensure that countries are provided with the information they need to meet the objectives of the Code" [*Id.* at art. 9.4.2].

As a soft law instrument that only provides voluntary standards of behavior, the FAO Code must rely on persuasion rather than the threat of legal consequences. Nevertheless, the FAO Code has steadily provided sound advice concerning the management of pesticides, and the institution has developed a considerable and well-respected expertise in the area. But despite the broad political acceptance of the FAO Code, non-governmental organizations (NGOs) have documented routine violations of its provisions in developing countries.

b. UNEP London Guidelines for the Exchange of Information on Chemicals in International Trade (London Guidelines)

The London Guidelines for the Exchange of Information on Chemicals in International Trade (London Guidelines) were originally adopted by the UNEP in 1987, then amended in 1989 to incorporate PIC procedure [United Nations Environment Programme (UNEP), *London Guidelines for the Exchange of Information on Chemicals in International Trade,* (1987) UNEP/GC/DEC/15/30)]. In substance, they closely resemble the voluntary standards of the FAO code (*see* above). Providing a broad definition of the term, the London Guidelines state that " 'chemical' means a chemical substance whether by itself or in a mixture or preparation, whether manufactured or obtained from nature and includes such substances used as industrial chemicals and pesticides" [*Id.* at art. 1(a)]. Concerning pesticides, however, the London Guidelines actually defer to the FAO Code, acknowledged as the primary source of guidance for the management of pesticides internationally [*Id.* at Intro. 7]. Thus, the London Guidelines seek in non-duplicative fashion to supplement and cooperate with the FAO Code regarding pesticides, while establishing the primary system of voluntary controls for other hazardous chemicals.

As an overriding principle, the London Guidelines state that both importing and exporting States should protect human health and the environment against potential harm by exchanging information on chemicals [*Id.* at art. 2(a)]. To this end, the amended London Guidelines also promote the principle of PIC and establish formal PIC Procedures. On the other hand, the London Guidelines make it clear that States may participate in information exchange procedures without participating in the more formal PIC Procedures [*Id.* at art. 7.1(a)].

The London Guidelines establish the International Register of Potentially Toxic Chemicals as the general information clearing-house, and require all States that have taken action to ban or severely restrict a chemical to notify the Register with information surrounding that action [*Id.* at art. 6]. Particularly, an exporting State having taken any action should provide the Designated National

Authority of the importing State with the relevant information through the Register [*Id.* at art. 8]. Additionally, an importing State participating in the PIC Procedures, when responding using the official PIC forms, "will have the opportunity to record their decisions regarding future imports of banned or severely restricted imports in a formal way" [*Id.* at art. 7.1]. For its part, the Register relays the decision to the exporting State, maintains a database of all important information, and provides such information for inclusion in the regular updates of the United Nations' (UN) Consolidated List of Products whose Consumption and/or Sale have been Banned, Withdrawn or Severely Restricted by Governments [*Id.* at art. 7.4].

Beyond the use of the clearing-house, exporting States should directly provide information, advice, and assistance to importing States regarding the sound management of hazardous chemicals [*Id.* at art. 13(b)]. Exporting States should, for example, as far as practicable, supply precautionary information in the principle language(s) of the importing State, accompanied by suitable pictorial aids and labels [*Id.* at art. 13(d)]. The London Guidelines require, in the absence of standards in the importing State, that the exporter employ classification, packaging, and labeling standards in conformity with internationally harmonized procedures [*Id.* at art. 14]. Importing States, on the other hand, have responsibilities with regard to their own citizens, and should take measures to ensure that users at all levels are given the necessary information, advice, and assistance to manage these chemicals safely [*Id.* at art. 13(c)].

The London Guidelines therefore closely follow the substantive standards offered by the FAO Code, with FAO and UNEP working jointly to implement the PIC procedure. In 1995, the Inter-Organization Programme for Sound Management of Chemicals was established to coordinate the efforts of all international and intergovernmental organizations involved in chemical safety. Even with such improvements, however, the distribution and use of hazardous substances remains one of the most under-regulated areas of IEL. As we shall see below, the world community has so far placed more energy and attention on the transboundary movement and trade in hazardous wastes.

c. Code of Ethics on the International Trade in Chemicals (Code of Ethics)

In 1994, the Code of Ethics on the International Trade in Chemicals (Code of Ethics) was concluded [United Nations Environment Programme (UNEP), *Code of Ethics on the International Trade in Chemicals,* (Jul. 1994) ISBN 9280716417 (hereinafter Code of Ethics)]. While the Code of Ethics is a complement to the London Guidelines, it is broader in scope. The Code of Ethics is a voluntary instrument aimed at private sector parties that are expected to help achieve the goals of the London Guidelines. Thus, these private sector parties seek to increase chemical safety through the exchange of information on chemicals in international trade. Specifically, these parties are to develop safer packaging and clear and concise labeling, end the production and trade in chemicals with unacceptable risks, reduce the use of hazardous chemicals, and take other steps to promote chemical safety through testing and assessment, quality assurance, providing safety information, and promoting education and training for safety purposes [*Id.*].

d. UNECE Convention on Access to Information, Public Participation in Decision-Making and Access to Justice in Environmental Matters (Aarhus Convention)

The United Nations Economic Commission for Europe (UNECE) adopted the Convention on Access to Information, Public Participation in Decision-Making and Access to Justice in Environmental Matters (Aarhus Convention) on June 25, 1998, and the Convention entered into force on October 30, 2001. As of July 2016 there are 47 parties to the Convention, which aims to improve public access to environmental information. The Aarhus Convention provides a forum for developing protocols to strengthen democratic interactions between the public and public authorities. It also addresses processes for public participation in the negotiation and implementation of international agreements [*Id.*].

The UNECE Kiev Protocol on Pollutant Release and Transfer Registers (Kiev Protocol) was adopted on May 21, 2003 and entered into force on October 8, 2009 [*Protocol on Pollutant Release and Transfer Registers to the Convention on Access to Information, Public Participation in Decision-Making and Access to Justice in Environmental Matters*, May 21, 2003 (entered into force Oct. 8, 2009) Doc.MP.PP/2003/1 (hereinafter Kiev Protocol)]. As of July 2016, the Kiev Protocol has 35 parties. It is the first legally binding international instrument on pollutant release and transfer registers, which are inventories of pollution released to all media by industrial sites and other sources. The Kiev Protocol covers releases and transfers of greenhouse gases, acid rain pollutants, ozone-depleting substances, heavy metals, and certain carcinogens (e.g. dioxins). Releases and transfers from certain types of major point sources (e.g. thermal power stations, mining and metallurgical industries and chemical plants) are covered. Under the Kiev Protocol, information is publicly accessible via the internet, free of charge [*Id.*].

e. Rotterdam Convention on the Prior Informed Consent Procedure for Certain Hazardous Chemicals and Pesticides in International Trade (Rotterdam Convention)

In the FAO Code and the London Guidelines, the FAO and UNEP developed and promoted voluntary international information exchange programs. However, officials attending the 1992 United Nations Conference on Environment and Development (UNCED), or Earth Summit, saw the need for mandatory controls. They adopted Chapter 19 of Agenda 21, which called for a legally binding instrument on the voluntary PIC procedure by the year 2000 [*Agenda 21*, (1992) U.N. Doc. A/CONF.

151/26 at Ch. 19]. Thus, the Rotterdam Convention was negotiated and entered into force on February 24, 2004.

The Rotterdam Convention seeks to promote shared responsibility and cooperative efforts among parties for the international trade of certain hazardous chemicals. The term "chemical" is defined in accordance with the London Guidelines, however the Rotterdam Convention does not defer to the FAO to determine how pesticides should be managed internationally. Thus, while the Rotterdam Convention builds on the existing voluntary PIC procedure, its provisions are legally binding on the parties independent of other soft law instruments.

The primary principle established by the Rotterdam Convention is that chemicals listed in Annex III can only be exported with the PIC of the importing party. The Conference of the Parties (COP) decides which chemicals to list in Annex III [*Id*. at art. 7(2)]. Initially, 22 pesticides and five industrial chemicals were listed in Annex III, with the possibility of additional chemicals being added with each meeting of the COP [*Id*. at art. 7(2)]. As of this writing, there are a total of 47 chemicals listed in Annex III; 33 pesticides and 14 industrial chemicals [*Id*. at Annex III].

Once a chemical is listed in Annex III, and is therefore subject to the PIC procedure, importing States receive a "decision guidance document," which contains information concerning the chemical and the regulatory decisions to ban or severely restrict it for health or environmental reasons [*Id*. at art. 7(3)].

The importing States must respond within nine months, with either a final decision or an interim response [*Id.* at art. 10(4)]. The final decision must contain the importing State's consent to import, refusal to import, or consent to import subject to specified conditions [*Id.* at art. 10(4)(a)]. The decisions of the importing States are then circulated to exporting parties, who must then ensure that exporters within its jurisdiction comply with the decisions [*Id.* at art. 11(1)(b)].

As for exchange of information, the Rotterdam Convention requires parties who have banned or severely restricted a chemical they wish to export to provide the importing party with information concerning said chemical [*Id.* at art. 12(1)]. The information the exporting party must provide includes the reasons for their regulatory action, a summary of the hazards and risks presented by the chemical to human health or the environment, and precautionary measures to reduce exposure to, and emission of, the chemical [*Id.* at Annex 5].

Additionally, the Rotterdam Convention provides that, as soon as practicable, the COP shall develop procedures for determining non-compliance as well as treatment of parties found to be in non-compliance [*Id.* at art. 17]. As of this writing, the COP has been unable to agree on the details of a compliance mechanism for the Rotterdam Convention, though substantive progress was made through negotiations at COP-7 in Geneva, Switzerland in May 2015.

3. HAZARDOUS WASTES AND THEIR MOVEMENT

a. Basel Convention on the Control of Transboundary Movements of Hazardous Wastes and Their Disposal (Basel Convention)

i. *The Ban Amendment*

In 1987, UNEP adopted the Governing Council Decision on Cairo Guidelines and Principles for the Environmentally Sound Management of Hazardous Wastes (Cairo Guidelines), [United Nations Environment Programme (UNEP), *Governing Council Decision on Cairo Guidelines and Principles for the Environmentally Sound Management of Hazardous Waste,* UNEP/GC/DEC/14/30, UNEP ELPG no. 8 (1987)]. The Cairo Guidelines function as soft law guidelines for the management of hazardous wastes, similar to the London Guidelines' management of chemicals (*see* above). The same UNEP working group then developed the text of the 1989 Basel Convention, which came into force in 1992. Like the Cairo Guidelines, the Basel Convention originally adopted a broad managed-trade approach to hazardous wastes—allowing all transboundary transfers of hazardous wastes based on the principle of PIC. African States were most vocal against the managed-trade approach of the Basel Convention and collectively in 1991 adopted the Bamako Convention—which strictly bans the import of hazardous wastes from outside the continent (*see* below).

Opponents complained that the Basel Convention did little to restrict trade, and instead functioned more as a tracking system for continued transfers to developing countries, in effect licensing the dumping of hazardous wastes in the developing world. The Ban Amendment was originally adopted as a decision at COP-2 in 1994 as a way to address this problem, and then adopted as an official amendment to the Basel Convention at COP-3 in 1995. The Ban Amendment now bans hazardous wastes exports for final disposal and recycling from Annex VII States (parties that are members of the EU, OECD, and Liechtenstein) to non-Annex VII States (all other parties to the Basel Convention) [Basel Convention at art. 4(a)].

For a number of years following COP-3, there was debate regarding the manner in which the Ban Amendment could legitimately enter into force. Article 17 of the Basel Convention states that amendments shall "as a last resort be adopted by a three-fourths majority vote of the parties" [Basel Convention at art. 17(3)]. Article 17(5), however, also states that "[a]mendments adopted in accordance [with the above] shall enter into force between Parties" when three-fourths of the *Parties having accepted them*" have ratified the amendment [*Id.* at art. 17(5), emphasis added]. The phrase "Parties having accepted them" has been interpreted to mean that amendments will enter into force after being ratified by three-fourths of the parties who were parties at the time of the amendment's adoption. However, it can also be interpreted to mean the parties at the time each ratification is deposited, rather than the parties at the time of the amendment's adoption. Thus, many considered Article 17(5) to be ambiguous.

After several COPs without agreement concerning this issue, the President of COP-9 in 2008 called on parties to create country-led initiatives as a possible way forward on the Ban Amendment. At COP-10 in 2011, the parties adopted the Indonesian-Swiss country-led initiative, which agreed to an interpretation of Article 17(5) and served as an important step for the development of the Basel Convention. A follow-up to the country-led initiative was also adopted at COP-11 in 2013. Though progress has been made, as of this writing the Ban Amendment has not yet entered into force.

ii. Environmentally Sound Management

The Basel Convention, though primarily dealing with the transboundary movement and trade in hazardous wastes, also contains general provisions regarding the environmentally sound management of such wastes. Under the convention, "hazardous waste" means those substances or objects included in the categories set out by Annexes I and III, as well as those defined or considered as hazardous wastes by the domestic legislation of the party of export, import, or transit [*Id*. at art. 1(1)]. Other substances or objects included in the categories of Annex II, such as those collected from households, are known as "other wastes" [*Id*. at art. 1(2)]. Under the Basel Convention, "environmentally sound management" is defined as "taking all practicable steps to ensure that hazardous wastes or other wastes are managed in a manner which will protect human health and the environment against the adverse effects which may result from such wastes" [*Id*. at art. 2(8)].

With environmentally sound management as the operative model, all parties must reduce the generation of hazardous and other wastes to a minimum—though the obligation remains qualified by the phrase "taking into account social, technological and economic aspects" [*Id*. at art. 4(2)(a)]. Each party also must strive to create adequate disposal facilities within its own boundaries [*Id*. at art. 4(2)(b)], and must require its management personnel to take the necessary steps to prevent pollution and minimize its consequences [*Id*. at art. 4(2)(c)]. The Basel Convention further mandates that the parties cooperate: (1) in the exchange of information; (2) in the monitoring of effects; and (3) in the development of environmentally sound technologies (ESTs) and its transfer [*Id*. at art. 10].

iii. *Transboundary Movement*

Concerning the transboundary movement of hazardous wastes, the Basel Convention creates a number of general obligations for parties. As a rule, the parties must reduce the transboundary movement of hazardous and other wastes to a minimum consistent with the environmentally sound and efficient management of such wastes [*Id*. at art. 4(2)(d)]. In this regard, the amended preamble of the Basel Convention now states, "transboundary movements of hazardous wastes, especially to developing countries, have a high risk of not constituting an environmentally sound management of hazardous wastes as required by this Convention" [*Id.* at pmbl.]. Parties additionally must not allow export to parties that have prohibited all imports, or which cannot manage the particular wastes in question in an environmentally sound manner [*Id.* at art. 4(2)(e)]. Likewise, importing parties must prevent import if the wastes cannot be managed in proper fashion [*Id.* at art. 4(2)(g)]. The Basel Convention also prohibits any transfers between parties and non-parties [*Id.* at art. 4(5)], except transfers that do not derogate from environmentally sound management and that are communicated to the Secretariat [*Id.* at art. 11]. This provision has enabled the U.S., a signatory that has not ratified the Basel Convention, to continue exporting hazardous wastes to parties.

The Basel Convention only allows transfers of hazardous wastes between parties in the following circumstances: (a) the State of export cannot dispose of the wastes adequately; (b) the wastes in question are required as raw material for recycling or recovery industries; or (c) the transfer is in accordance with other criteria to be decided by the parties [*Id.* at art. 4(9)]. When transboundary movement does take place, the parties must conduct such transfers in a manner protecting human health and the environment [*Id.* at art. 4(2)(d)]. In this regard parties must ensure that packaging, labeling, and transport conform to international rules and standards [*Id.* at art. 4(7)(b)]. More broadly, in no way may generating States transfer the duty to manage wastes in an environmentally sound manner to States of import or transit [*Id.* at art. 4(10)]. Finally, as remarked above, the amended Basel Convention prohibits all transboundary movements of hazardous wastes not designated for recycling from all OECD and EU States to all non-OECD and non-EU States [*Id.* at art. 4A(1)]. Hazardous wastes designated for recycling must likewise be phased out between the same States by the end of 1997 [*Id.* at art. 4A(2)].

In addition to these general obligations, the Basel Convention establishes a global paper trail for any transboundary movement of hazardous or other wastes. The State of export must notify (or require the generator or exporter to notify) any State of transit or import concerning the details of the transaction [*Id.* at art. 6(1)]. This is done by way of written instrument through each State's designated "competent authority" [*Id.* at art. 6(1)]. The written notification must contain all the declarations and information specified in Annex V [*Id.* at art. 6(1)]. Upon receipt, the State of import must respond in writing to the competent authority—consenting to the movement with or without conditions, denying the movement, or requesting additional information [*Id.* at art. 6(2)]. Until the competent authority has received written permission, as well as confirmation of an environmentally sound contract from the importing State, the exporting State may not allow shipment [*Id.* at art. 6(3)]. The State of export must also receive written consent from the State of transit, though provisions are made for a State of transit that is also a party to opt out of this requirement [*Id*. at art. 6(4)]. With written consent of all the States concerned, the State of export may use a less detailed general notification for regular shipments over a twelve-month period [*Id*. at arts. 6(6–8)]. Finally, if informed by the importing State that the contract cannot be completed as drawn, the State of export must receive the shipment back unless other arrangements can be made, and neither the State of export nor any party of transit may hinder that return [*Id*. at art. 8].

At COP-5 in 1999, the Ministers set out guidelines for the 2000–2010 decade. The guidelines place emphasis on creating partnerships with industry and research institutions to create innovative approaches to environmentally sound management, with the primary emphasis on minimizing hazardous waste. The guidelines also seek to achieve further reduction of the movement of hazardous and other wastes, the prevention and monitoring of illegal traffic, and active promotion and use of cleaner technologies and production methods.

Another development from COP-5 was the adoption of the Basel Protocol on Liability and Compensation for Damage resulting from Transboundary Movements of Hazardous Wastes and their Disposal (Basel Protocol) [*Basel Protocol on Liability and Compensation for Damage Resulting from Transboundary Movements of Hazardous Wastes and their Disposal,* (10 Dec. 1999) DOC.UNEP/CMW.1/WG/1/9/2 (hereinafter Basel Protocol)]. The objective of the Basel Protocol is similar to the International Convention on Liability and Compensation for Damage in Connection with the Carriage of Hazardous and Noxious Substances by Sea (HNS Convention) [*International Convention on Liability and Compensation for Damage in Connection with the Carriage of Hazardous and Noxious Substances by Sea,* May 3, 1996, 35 I.L.M. 1406 (hereinafter HNS Convention)] (*see* below) in that it addresses who is financially responsible for damage resulting from transboundary movement of hazardous wastes. The Basel Protocol addresses financial responsibility in relation to each phase of a transboundary movement, from the point at which the wastes are loaded on the means of transport to their export, international transit, import, and final disposal. As of this writing, the Basel Protocol has 11 ratifications and will enter into force after 20 ratifications.

As a framework treaty, the Basel Convention has benefited from the cooperative impetus and flexible decision-making power built into the framework approach. Informal decisions of the COP, meaning those that do not call for ratification or other formal approval by each State, have led to a number of innovative mechanisms. Such innovations include "Model National Legislation" for the transboundary movement and management of hazardous wastes, a "Manual for the Implementation of the Basel Convention," and "Draft Forms" for the identification and tracking of illegal trade. In addition, the COP has swiftly moved to implement specific provisions of the Basel Convention, including the establishment of regional and sub-regional centers for training and technology transfer regarding both the management of wastes and the minimization of generation. In short, under UNEP guidance, the Basel Convention has quickly evolved from a poorly ratified treaty into a relatively effective, if under-funded, hazardous waste regime.

In 2008, COP-9 took a significant step toward greater collaboration between the different international treaty regimes dealing with transboundary movements. It arrived at a decision on enhancing the cooperation and coordination among the Basel Convention, the Rotterdam Convention, and the Stockholm Convention on Persistent Organic Pollutants (Stockholm POPs Convention). The COPs of both the Rotterdam Convention and the Stockholm POPs Convention adopted substantially identical "synergies decisions." COP-12 in 2015 featured joint sessions to address cross-cutting issues of concern to these three Conventions.

b. Convention on the Ban of Imports into Africa and the Control of Transboundary Movement and Management of Hazardous Wastes Within Africa (Bamako Convention)

Though born out of disapproval with the Basel Convention's managed-trade approach, in reality the Bamako Convention closely follows its predecessor in most respects. It does, however, create more stringent rules for its African parties in several ways. The most significant difference from the original Basel Convention lies in the Bamako Convention's banning of all hazardous wastes into Africa from non-parties [Bamako Convention at art. 4(1)]. Of course, this difference narrows considerably when the Basel Convention's Ban Amendment is taken into account.

Additionally, "hazardous wastes" is defined more broadly in the Bamako Convention, and even includes banned or strictly regulated hazardous substances [*Id.* at art. 2(1)]. The Bamako Convention also provides for unlimited liability, as well as joint and several liability, on hazardous waste generators [*Id.* at art. 4(3)(b)]. Other differences include a stronger commitment to the precautionary approach that emphasizes clean production methods rather than permissible emissions [*Id.* at art. 4(3)(f-g)], and the repudiation of general notification procedures for regular shipments of the same wastes [*Id.* at art. 6(6)].

Though the Bamako Convention creates more stringent conditions than the Basel Convention, an African State may nonetheless become party to both. The Basel Convention clearly allows a party to impose "additional requirements . . . in order to better protect human health and the environment" [Basel Convention at art. 4(11)], and the Bamako Convention permits a party to enter into other agreements as long as these do not "derogate from the environmentally sound management of hazardous wastes" as required by the Bamako Convention [Bamako Convention at art. 11(1)]. Therefore, as long as an African party follows the strict procedures of the Bamako Convention, it may also benefit from the transfer of resources through the Basel Convention. Indeed, a number of African States have ratified both treaties as of this writing.

c. International Convention on Liability and Compensation for Damage in Connection with the Carriage of Hazardous and Noxious Substances by Sea (HNS Convention)

The HNS Convention was designed to compensate for damage caused in connection with the carriage of hazardous and noxious substances by sea. It provides for compensation on two fronts. First, the owner of the hazardous substance is liable for any damage caused by the carrying of such substances by sea [*Id.* at art. 7(1)]. Second, if the owner is either not liable or cannot compensate the injured for the entire amount, the HNS Convention establishes an HNS Fund that will then provide compensation [*Id.* at art. 14(1)]. The HNS Convention specifies the process by which the initial and annual contributions to the HNS Fund will be determined [*Id.* at art. 16–20]. Owners and the HNS Fund must compensate for "damage," which includes death or personal injury, loss of or damage to property, loss or damage by contamination of the environment, and the costs of preventive measures [*Id.* at art. 1(6)]. Since liable owners are required to provide compensation, each owner must have insurance or other financial security, such as the guarantee of a bank to cover liability [*Id.* at art. 12(1)]. If two or more ships, each carrying hazardous substances, are responsible for damage, then there is joint and several liability [*Id.* at art. 8(1)].

The HNS Convention requires ratification by 12 States, including four States that each possess registered fleets totaling two million tons or more. Due to an insufficient number of ratifications, a second international conference on the subject was held in April 2010. A Protocol to the HNS Convention (HNS Protocol) was adopted, designed to address practical problems that had prevented many States from ratifying the original HNS Convention [*Protocol of 2010 to the International Convention on Liability and Compensation for Damage in Connection with the Carriage of Hazardous and Noxious Substances by Sea, 1996,* Mar. 15 2000, IMO Doc. HNS-OPRC/CONF/11/Rev.1 (hereinafter HNS Protocol)]. The HNS Protocol places some limits on liability, both for shipowners and for the HNS Fund. Though the HNS Protocol is intended to supersede the HNS Convention, it too has not yet entered into force.

4.   ELIMINATION AND REDUCTIONS AT SOURCE

So far, we have dealt with voluntary guidelines and treaties focused primarily on the transboundary movement and trade in chemicals and hazardous wastes. The Stockholm POPs Convention is attempting to change this approach by requiring that certain hazardous pollutants be eliminated or reduced. This approach is more fully discussed below.

The Stockholm POPs Convention, which acknowledges the importance of precaution in its preamble, seeks to protect human health and the environment from persistent organic pollutants

(POPs) [Stockholm POPs Convention at art. 1]. It entered into force in 2004 and endeavors to achieve its objective by eliminating existing POPs, avoiding further production and use of POPs, and minimizing emissions of POPs that cannot be eliminated. The Stockholm POPs Convention calls for the parties to eliminate chemicals listed in Annex A [*Id.* at art. 3(1)(a)], unless the party has obtained an exemption [*Id.* at art. 4(3)]. Even if there is an exemption, however, the party must prevent or minimize human exposure and release into the environment [*Id.* at art. 3(6)]. Additionally, parties may only import chemicals listed in Annex A and B for the purpose of environmentally sound disposal or for a use permitted by Annex A or B [*Id.* at art. 3(2)(a)]. Such chemicals can only be exported to another party for the purpose of environmentally sound disposal or if the importing party is permitted to use the chemical under Annex A or B [*Id.* at art. 3(2)(b)]. If exporting to a State not party to the Stockholm POPs Convention, the exporting party must be sure that the importing State is committed to protecting human health and the environment and will comply with the measure to reduce or eliminate releases from stockpiles and wastes [*Id.* at art. 3(2)(b)(iii)].

Each party must submit an implementation plan within two years of the date on which the Stockholm POPs Convention enters into force [*Id.* at art. 7(1)]. Part of this implementation plan must include an action plan that pertains to the chemicals listed in Annex C [*Id.* at art. 5(a)]. The action plan must evaluate the current and projected releases of Annex C chemicals, evaluate the laws and policies of the party relating to the management of such releases, and contain strategies to minimize and ultimately eliminate releases derived from such chemicals [*Id.* at art. 5(a)]. Annex C designates certain chemicals which must have priority consideration in order to prevent formation and release of those chemicals, and also lists possible measures to achieve that goal [*Id.* at Annex C pt. V(A)].

The Stockholm POPs Convention also calls for "best available techniques" and "best environmental practices" for dealing with chemicals in Annex C [*Id.* at art. 5(d)]. "Best available techniques" is not meant to be any specific technique or technology, but rather is aimed at the consideration of the technical characteristics, its geographical location, and the local environmental condition of the installation [*Id.* at Annex C pt. V(B)]. The consideration of best available technique must bear in mind the likely costs and benefits of a measure as well as consideration of precaution and prevention [*Id.* at Annex C pt. V(B)]. "Best environmental practices" is defined as "the application of the most appropriate combination of environmental control measures and strategies" [*Id.* at art. 5(f)(v)].

Finally, regarding chemicals listed in Annexes A, B, or C, parties must develop strategies to identify and then reduce and ultimately eliminate releases of such chemicals from stockpiles and wastes [*Id.* at art. 6]. Such chemicals must be handled in an environmentally sound manner and disposed of in such a way that the POPs content is destroyed or irreversibly transformed [*Id.* at art. 6(d)].

Additionally, parties must ensure that upon becoming wastes, the POPs are not recycled or reused or allowed to cross international boundaries without taking into account the relevant international rules, standards, and guidelines [*Id.* at art. 6(d)]. Since the Stockholm POPs Convention came into force, the COP has amended it at several meetings. These amendments have included establishing arbitration and conciliation procedures and listing additional chemicals.

5.   OTHER REGIONAL AGREEMENTS

In North America, the U.S. has signed two pre-NAFTA agreements with its hemispheric trading partners. The Canada-U.S. Agreement Concerning the Transboundary Movement of Hazardous Waste allows the "export, import, and transit of hazardous waste" across the border [*Canada-U.S. Agreement Concerning the Transboundary Movement of Hazardous Waste,* Oct. 28, 1986 (amended in 1992), 11099 T.I.A.S. 496 at art. 2], and requires notification of the importing State for any planned transfers [*Id.* at art. 3]. In a twist on the principle of PIC, however, silence is deemed consent, and the exporter may proceed with the shipment if the importing State does not respond to the notification within 30 days [*Id.* at art. 3].

In a more traditional version of PIC, and one more in adherence with the relative positions of industrialized and developing countries, the Mexico-U.S. Agreement for Co-operation on Environmental Programmes and TransBoundary Problems prohibits transfer of hazardous waste without approval by the importing State [*Mexico-U.S. Agreement for Cooperation on Environmental Programmes and TransBoundary Problems,* Nov. 12, 1986 (entered into force Jan. 29, 1987), 26 I.L.M. 25 at art. III]. For its part, the importing party must respond within 45 days and may choose to accept, accept with conditions, or reject the planned shipment [*Id.* at art. III].

The Convention to Ban the Import into Forum Countries of Hazardous Waste and to Control the Transboundary Movement and Management of Hazardous Wastes within the South Pacific Region (Waigani Convention) is a multilateral regional treaty adopted in 1995 [*Convention to Ban the Import into Forum Countries of Hazardous Waste and to Control the Transboundary Movement and Management of Hazardous Wastes within the South Pacific Region,* Sep. 16, 1995 (entered into force 2001) (hereinafter Waigani Convention)]. The Waigani Convention establishes hazardous waste and radioactive waste import and export ban requirements for the South Pacific Region. It covers a broad range of hazardous wastes, excluding those derived from the normal operations of a vessel and some radioactive wastes.

Another significant regional instrument, the Lome Convention, prohibits all exports of hazardous wastes from EU States to African, Caribbean, and Pacific States [Lome Convention at art. 39(1)]. In fact the Lome Convention, which defines hazardous wastes according to Basel Convention standards [*Id.*

at art. 39(3)], mandates that African, Caribbean, and Pacific States prohibit the import of hazardous wastes from all States [*Id.* at art. 39(1)]. The obligations of Article 39(1), however, are without prejudice to other international obligations.

G.   CONCLUSIONS

In recent decades there has been a dramatic growth in chemical production and trade, which has raised concerns about the potential risks posed by pesticides, hazardous chemicals, and hazardous waste. Countries lacking adequate infrastructure to monitor the import and use of these chemicals, such as the least developed countries (LDCs), are particularly vulnerable. Under the present treaty architecture, legally binding procedures on PIC are now in place, but there is currently no arbitral or judicial mechanism dealing with non-compliance. Moreover, while international regimes address transboundary movement and trade in chemicals and hazardous wastes, they do not satisfactorily deal with the cause of such wastes or the need to reduce or eliminate the use of goods and services that result in the creation of such hazardous pollutants.

CHAPTER TEN
LAND-BASED POLLUTION

A. NATURE OF THE PROBLEM

In 2012, the Rio+20 United Nations Conference on Sustainable Development (UNCSD) developed the sustainable development goals (SDGs) to replace the millennium development goals (MDGs) as of January 2016. SDG14 accurately points out that oceans cover three quarters of the earth's surface, contain 97% of the earth's water, and represent 99% of the living space on the planet by volume. Rainwater, drinking water, weather, climate, coastlines, food, and even the oxygen in the air humans breathe are all ultimately provided and regulated by the oceans [United Nations Sustainable Development Goals, *Goal 14: Conserve and sustainably use the oceans, seas and marine resources, available at* http://www.un.org/sustainabledevelopment/oceans/ (last visited Apr. 2017)]. Thus, the health of our oceans reflect the health and safety of our planet.

Eighty percent of all oceanic pollution comes from land-based sources. Pollutants generated on land travel through numerous environmental pathways, such as the atmosphere, rivers, canals, underground watercourses, and outfalls, before eventually finding their way to the ocean. Urban expansion into coastal areas has also exacerbated the problem of land-based marine pollution. Half the world's population lives within 100 kilometers (km) of the ocean, and three-quarters of all large cities are located on the coast [United Nations Environment Programme (UNEP) &

United Nations Human Settlements Programme (UN-HABITAT), *Coastal Area Pollution: The Role of Cities,* (Sept 2005)]. Land-based pollution looms as problematic because urban growth has diverged from principles of sustainable development (SD), and because environmental protection has been ignored or minimized by economic growth.

Thus, land-based pollution is not confined to land. Much of what begins as land-based pollution is eventually discharged as waste into the ocean, estuaries, or rivers. In this chapter, we deal with land-based pollution from direct outfalls such as rivers, pipelines, and runoff as well as pollution of the oceans caused by atmospheric interface. We also follow the rationale of the Convention for the Protection of the Marine Environment of the North East Atlantic (OSPAR Convention), treating "dumping"—insofar as it originates on land—as a species of land-based pollution. In Chapter 12 we will discuss vessel-based dumping and marine pollution, and provide an overview of the international legal regime regarding dumping as a whole.

B.　SOURCES AND ENVIRONMENTAL IMPACTS

In general, there are eight groups of pollutants that are deposited into the ocean from land-based sources: (1) chemical nutrients; (2) sewage and bacterial agents; (3) oil; (4) organic chemicals; (5) metals; (6) litter and sediment; (7) radioactive substances; and (8) heat. Some pollutants are also deposited in the oceans through the air, and air pollution has been found to impact marine environments.

Chemical nutrients, such as phosphorus and nitrogen compounds, are introduced into marine environments by runoff from fertilized agricultural lands, discharges of domestic sewage, industrial effluents, and atmospheric emissions. Excessive nutrient concentrations can accelerate the naturally occurring process of eutrophication, by which waters are enriched with nutrients, and can lead to uncontrolled phytoplankton growth. Popularly known as a red tide, this uncontrolled growth can result in the creation of "dead zones," where the oxygen content of the water is so low that nothing can live, which can have a major impact on fishery production or quality of life for coastal communities. The United Nations Environment Programme (UNEP) has identified approximately 150 of these dead zones around the world. The largest dead zones at present are found in the Gulf of Mexico (70,000 square km, seasonally) and the Baltic Sea (up to 100,000 square km, permanent) [P.F. Sale, et. al, *Stemming Decline of the Coastal Ocean: Rethinking Environmental Management*, (2008) UNU-INWEH at 2]. Additionally, some species of phytoplankton emit toxins that, if present in high concentrations, will contaminate shellfish and damage certain types of fish. In the ocean, increased algal growth and a lack of dissolved oxygen may also have a detrimental effect on coral reefs, which function as important repositories of biodiversity (*see* Ch. 5).

Sewage and bacterial agents account for a large portion of all marine pollution. The principal pollutants contained in sewage include organic materials, nutrients, pathogens, and trace metals. In industrialized countries, sewage is usually treated to remove solids and is sometimes chemically or biologically treated to produce a less harmful effluent. However, in many developing countries, raw sewage is often discharged directly into watercourses. The pathogens present in raw sewage contaminate shellfish and may lead to serious gastrointestinal disorders if consumed. Recreational activities may also be affected in areas in which raw sewage discharge has led to high pathogen concentrations. Finally, the organic materials and nutrients in sewage contribute to accelerated eutrophication, as previously explained.

Historically, the release of oil from catastrophic spills or tanker accidents has received the greatest publicity, but this type of pollution is now relatively well regulated (*see* Ch. 11) [Joint Group of Experts on the Scientific Aspects of Marine Environmental Protection (GESAMP), *Protecting the Oceans from Land-Based Activities* (Jan. 2001) Rep. Stud. GESAMP No. 71 at 2.4.5 (hereinafter GESAMP REPORT)]. The bulk of oil pollution actually enters the marine environment from far less publicized land-based sources. These sources include industrial discharges, sewage disposal, river runoff, and atmospheric fallout from fossil fuel combustion. Natural seepages also have a significant impact.

Organic chemicals, such as dichlorodiphenyltrichloroethane (DDT) and polychlorinated bipheneyls (PCBs), are introduced into the marine environment through rivers, pesticide runoff from agricultural land, atmospheric deposition, and municipal and industrial discharges. Climate change may increase the concentration of organic chemicals, chemical nutrients, and sewage discharged into the ocean due to the convergence of a variety of factors. Warmer waters and alterations in freeze-thaw cycles may deplete or destroy coastal environments that currently act as pollution sinks, such as swamps, estuaries, kelp beds, and salt marshes. Rising water levels may also contribute to environmental damage as a result of additional coastal flooding. Increases in the frequency and intensity of precipitation and extreme weather events, such as hurricanes, will lead to flooding. Coastal erosion, damage to ecosystems that act as pollution sinks, and urban destruction all result in more discharge from land-based sources into the ocean. Climate change may also disrupt ocean currents that naturally dilute land-based pollution. Finally, warmer ocean temperatures may increase the threat of eutrophication and dead zones (*see* Ch. 6).

High concentrations of metals in the marine environment can be toxic to marine life and can also present dangers to human health. The principal sources of metals in the ocean are industrial and municipal discharges into rivers, coastal discharges, and atmospheric emissions. Concentrations of these metals tend to be greatest in industrial areas and estuaries. Metals are a particularly vexing pollutant because they are elements that do not degrade even when they are diluted, and thus they can bioaccumulate to toxic concentrations (*see* Ch. 9).

Litter and debris from human activities enter the ocean through rivers, municipal drainage systems, and coastal recreational areas. Plastics are the major type of litter present in marine environments, and marine fish and mammals are often injured or killed by plastics when they ingest or become entangled in the debris. In addition, debris often ends up in coastal areas where it mars the beauty of the natural environment. Soil sediments found in agricultural run-off can cover and destroy the bottoms of rivers, estuaries, bays, and even entire sections of ocean gulfs. An example of this phenomenon is found in the Chesapeake Bay on the eastern coast of the U.S., where agricultural sediments have damaged the Chesapeake Bay marshes, fisheries, and bottom ecologies [Environmental Protection Agency (EPA), EVALUATION REPORT: SAVING THE CHESAPEAKE BAY WATERSHED REQUIRES BETTER COORDINATION OF ENVIRONMENTAL AND AGRICULTURAL RESOURCES (2006)].

A percentage of the radioactive material in all nuclear power plants escapes into the environment during normal operation and finds its way to the ocean, just like other types of pollutants. Additionally, radioactive waste generated on land is often dumped into the ocean from ships, thus blurring the distinction between land-based pollution and dumping. The marine impact of radioactive waste disposal is illustrated by the case of the Savannah River Site, which straddles the border of South Carolina and Georgia. The facility produced tritium, plutonium, and other special nuclear materials for national defense and the space program. This resulted in disposal practices that caused pollution of the river and groundwater. The radioactive materials found in the water, sediments, and biota of the Savannah River are then carried into the Atlantic Ocean. A range of nuclear-related research and production operations are ongoing at the site, which is now a superfund site [U.S. Environmental Protection Agency (EPA), *Superfund Site: SAVANNAH RIVER SITE (USDOE), AIKEN, SC, available at* https://cumulis.epa.gov/supercpad/cursites/csitinfo.cfm?id=0403485 (last visited Apr. 2017)]. According to the U.S. Environmental Protection Agency (EPA), while considerable cleanup progress has been made since the 1980s, much additional cleanup work remains, which will likely take decades. Site cleanup completion is currently scheduled for 2065 [*Id.*].

The extent to which nuclear waste could also be deposited in the oceans by accidents is demonstrated by the nuclear disaster in Fukushima, Japan in 2011. The Fukushima I Nuclear Power Plant, which is located in close proximity to the ocean, was one of the 15 largest nuclear power stations in the world. The plant suffered major damage from a 9.0 earthquake and subsequent tsunami that hit Japan on March 11, 2011. The earthquake and tsunami disabled the reactor cooling systems, leading to nuclear radiation leaks. As of this writing, more than 760,000 tons of water has been contaminated and radioactive water continues to leak into the ocean, though at a lesser rate than it did early in the disaster. However, because of concerns about the health of marine life, fishing is still banned in waters just off the plant. The radioactive water leaks have slowed the process of plant decommissioning [The Associated Press, *5 years on, Japan nuke plant still leaking radioactive water*, (Mar. 8, 2016)].

Moreover, past nuclear bomb testing—particularly atmospheric testing—has introduced enormous quantities of radioactive material into the marine environment. Furthermore, climate change may alter Arctic currents, which could result in the spread of radioactive waste previously confined to the Arctic Ocean into other oceans [Lakshman Guruswamy, Geoffrey Palmer & Burns Weston, INTERNATIONAL ENVIRONMENTAL LAW AND WORLD ORDER (1999)] (*see also* Ch. 12).

The concept of heat pollution illustrates the need for a flexible, working definition of pollution. Electric power generation creates large quantities of excess heat. As a result, most power plants are located on or near large sources of water that can be used to cool the plant's equipment. However, when the heated water is expelled back into the ecosystem, the marine ecology surrounding the power plant can be severely impacted. For example, death of mangrove trees may occur with only a 3 to 5°C (degrees Celsius) increase in ambient water temperature, and the diversity and mass of associated fauna may diminish by 90% [GESAMP REPORT at 2.4]. Still, the dangers of heat discharge remain relatively unexplored and unaccounted for.

More recently, air pollution from land-based sources has been found to have dramatic impacts on the oceans. One example is the emergence of the Asian Brown Cloud in 2002, which still hangs over parts of South Asia and the Northern Indian Ocean. The Asian Brown Cloud is caused by large amounts of aerosols (such as soot and dust) produced in the combustion of fossil fuels and biomass across the region. It has been linked to decreases in summer monsoon rainfall in India since 1930, the southward shift of the summer monsoon in eastern China, declines in agricultural production, and increases in respiratory and cardiovascular problems in the people inhabiting the region [The Editors of Encyclopedia Britannica, *Asian brown cloud* (Jan. 9, 2015), *available at* https://www.britannica.com/science/Asian-brown-cloud (last visited Apr. 2017)]. It has also been found to adversely affect phytoplankton involved in the carbon-oxygen transfer and reduce the amount of nutrients in the ocean [United Nations Environment Programme and C[4], *The Asian Brown Cloud: Climate and Other Environmental Impacts*, UNEP/DEWA/RS.02–3 (2002)].

With any polluting substance, the impact on the marine environment depends on whether the pollutants are present in the open seas or in a semi-enclosed or coastal area. Pollutants in the open seas tend to have a less detrimental effect than pollutants in coastal areas because of the natural capacity of the open sea to assimilate and dilute large amounts of pollution [GESAMP REPORT at 2.4.1]. However, the ocean's assimilative capacity is not infinite, and it can take a considerable amount of time before the pollutant is dispersed, diluted, or sedimented. In addition, some pollutants, like heavy metals (*see* Ch. 9), are impossible to transform into less harmful substances and may bioaccumulate in marine animals. Coastal areas are usually more sensitive to pollution because they receive higher levels of pollutants from more concentrated sources and tend to be more biologically active [*Id.*].

C. REMEDIAL OBJECTIVES

For a number of reasons, the control of land-based pollution is one of the most daunting tasks facing the international community. First, land-based pollution is the direct result of domestic pollution, and can enter the environment via air, land, and water. Controlling land-based pollution thus exists as a proxy for controlling the sovereign rights of States to pollute their own territory—a restraint that States rarely accept. The problem stems from the extreme reluctance of States to surrender even a modicum of sovereignty with respect to actions within domestic boundaries, strongly preferring to retain control at the national level.

Second, environmental controls on the sources of land-based pollution—such as run-off from rivers, estuaries, and pipelines—generally require extremely expensive measures entailing significant economic sacrifice. States invariably balk at accepting such controls. In light of these difficulties, States have focused less on the remedial objective of solving land-based pollution, and more on maintaining the widest possible flexibility to adopt measures as they see fit.

Third, the scientific difficulties of demonstrating pathways and sources are immense, except in cases of single source direct outfalls and pathways. In situations with more than one set of contributors, apportioning responsibility to individual polluters is fraught with uncertainty. Uncertainties exist in the identification of sources of pollutants and their respective impacts, and in the creation of mechanistic, statistical, or stochastic models that are able to allocate pollutant reduction among sources. There is also uncertainty involved in developing a common understanding of such information that enables collective actions to be undertaken and monitored.

As an additional complication, chemicals released into air or water often interact with each other and give rise to synergistic reactions and effects. The impact of such synergistic effects can be greater than the sum of the individual effects, making it very difficult to establish cause-and-effect relationships. DDT, for example, is extremely soluble in oil, greatly multiplying the exposure risk for marine organisms in oil-polluted waters [Ruth A. Eblan & William R. Eblan eds., THE ENCYCLOPEDIA OF THE ENVIRONMENT (1994) at 686]. But where different States are responsible for land-based discharges of DDT and oil, respectively, they may resist control measures by arguing that another State is the more culpable agent. In sum, even where the political will to roll back or reduce land-based pollution is present, the implementation of such policies presents daunting scientific problems.

D. LEGAL RESPONSE

Although land-based sources contribute the highest percentage of marine pollution, the international commitment to controlling these wastes remains low. As it stands at the international level, there exists little more than a framework for future regulation of land-based marine pollution, with occasional calls for a legally binding instrument on the subject. The most effective agreements remain regional ones, despite the fact that they do not comply with the rigorous standards imposed both internationally and regionally on, for example, dumping and vessel-based pollution.

1.   1982 UNITED NATIONS CONVENTION ON THE LAW OF THE SEA (UNCLOS)

The United Nations Convention on the Law of the Sea (UNCLOS) defines pollution as:

The introduction by man, directly or indirectly, of substances or energy into the marine environment, including estuaries, which results or is likely to result in such deleterious effects as harm to living resources and marine life, hazards to human health, hindrance to marine activities, including fishing and other legitimate uses of the sea, impairment of quality for use of sea water and reduction of amenities [UNCLOS at art. 1(4)].

Despite this broad definition, UNCLOS provides only a general scheme for States to follow in attempting to reduce land-based marine pollution. UNCLOS requires States to adopt measures "to prevent, reduce and control" such pollution, "taking into account internationally agreed rules, standards and recommended practices and procedures" [*Id.* at art. 207(1)]. The mandate that States "take into account" international constraints has little normative value, as States need only consider, and not follow, such rules, and no formal standards exist at the global level for land-based pollution.

UNCLOS also provides that States "[s]hall endeavor to harmonize their policies . . . at the appropriate regional level" [*Id.* at art. 207(3)], and "shall endeavor to establish global and regional rules, standards and recommended practices and procedures" [*Id.* at art. 207(4)]. Again, however, the agreement that States "shall endeavor" does not mean that States must act to facilitate these ends. Moreover, the rules for enclosed or semi-enclosed seas—areas that tend to be the most susceptible to land-based marine pollution—only offer the slightly more forceful requirement that States "should cooperate" in coordinating protective action [*Id.* at arts. 122–123].

2.   1985 MONTREAL GUIDELINES FOR THE PROTECTION OF THE MARINE ENVIRONMENT AGAINST POLLUTION FROM LAND-BASED SOURCES (MONTREAL GUIDELINES)

The Montreal Guidelines for the Protection of the Marine Environment Against Pollution from Land-Based Sources (Montreal Guidelines) are a set of recommendations compiled by a Working Group of Experts under UNEP auspices [*Montreal Guidelines for the Protection of the Marine Environment Against Pollution from Land-Based Sources,* (1985) UNEP/GC.13/9/Add.3]. Adopted as a UNEP Governing Council Decision in 1985, they present a broad range of specific suggestions that States may adapt to national legislation, regional agreements, or any future global agreement on land-based pollution. As such, the Montreal Guidelines elaborate on the generalities of UNCLOS Article 207—providing for the basic obligations to protect the marine environment, to adopt control measures, to cooperate with other States, and to not cause transboundary harm [*Id.*]. The Montreal Guidelines also state the need to establish "specially protected areas" to protect marine sanctuaries from pollution [*Id.* at art. 7] and to assist developing countries in their efforts to combat pollution [*Id.* at art. 9]. Interestingly, in an early recognition of integrated pollution control, the Montreal Guidelines warn against simply preventing one type of pollution (i.e. land-based marine pollution) by creating another (e.g. hazardous waste landfills) [*Id.* at art. 6]. Additionally, the Montreal Guidelines echo UNCLOS' expansive definition of marine pollution referred to above [*Id.* at art. 1(a); *see also*, UNCLOS at art. 1(4)].

To give more specific advice to governments, the Montreal Guidelines provide fairly detailed information in the three Annexes attached to the document. Annex I, "Strategies for Protecting, Preserving and Enhancing the Quality of the Marine Environment," gives a substantial account of the three control strategies of environmental quality standards, emission standards, and environmental planning. In developing a program to combat marine pollution, Annex I suggests that governments individually tailor an approach combining all three strategies [Montreal Guidelines at Annex I]. Annex II, "Classification of Substances," provides an overview of the typical method of rating harmful substances, advising the creation of a "black list" for dangerous substances, and a "gray list" for less dangerous substances [*Id.* at Annex II]. Annex III, "Monitoring and Data Management," presents valuable recommendations toward the creation of effective technical programs, gleaned from the experiences of the better regulated States [*Id.* at Annex III].

3.   1995 GLOBAL PROGRAM OF ACTION FOR
      THE PROTECTION OF THE MARINE
      ENVIRONMENT FROM LAND-BASED
      ACTIVITIES (GPA) AND THE WASHINGTON
      DECLARATION ON PROTECTION OF THE
      MARINE ENVIRONMENT FROM LAND-BASED
      ACTIVITIES (WASHINGTON DECLARATION)

As discussed above, UNCLOS requires States to address land-based sources of marine pollution. But it was the recognition among the international community of the problems posed by land-based pollution, as well as the need to implement the strategic framework of UNCLOS and the Montreal Guidelines, that resulted in a 1995 meeting in Washington. This conference resulted in two instruments of soft law: the Global Program of Action for the Protection of the Marine Environment from Land-Based Activities (GPA) [*Global Program of Action for the Protection of the Marine Environment from Land-Based Activities,* (1995) UNEP (OCA)/LBA/IG.2/7 (hereinafter GPA)] and the Washington Declaration on Protection of the Marine Environment from Land-Based Activities (Washington Declaration) [*Washington Declaration on Protection of the Marine Environment from Land-Based Activities,* (1995) UNEP (OCA)/LBA/IG.2.6 (hereinafter Washington Declaration)].

The GPA calls on all parties to take action at the national, regional, and international levels. It is designed to serve as a source of conceptual and practical guidance for the parties in the development of these programs. It includes detailed recommendations for the regulation of sewage, persistent organic pollutants (POPs), radioactive substances, heavy metals, oils, nutrients, sediment mobilization, litter, and physical alteration and destruction of habitats. It also identifies steps for sharing knowledge and experience with respect to combating land-based sources of marine pollution. Chapter II of the GPA describes a methodology for problem identification and solution at the national level [GPA at Ch. II]. Chapter III addresses regional considerations [*Id.* at Ch. III], while Chapter IV contains approaches for dealing with numerous source categories of pollutants [*Id.* at Ch. IV].

The GPA identifies the sources of land-based pollution and prepares priority action programs of measures to reduce them. It concentrates not just on problems originating near the shores—such as discharges from mega-cities, other urban areas, harbors, or industrial enterprises in the coastal zone—but targets pollution from entire catchment areas, taking into account sources such as agriculture, forestry, aquaculture, and tourism. The GPA, although a global program, also addresses problems at regional, sub-regional, and national levels, and thus helps to guide the efforts of the individual Regional Seas programs to deal with land-based pollution (*see* below).

The other document resulting from the 1995 Washington Meeting is the Washington Declaration, which accords priority to the implementation of the GPA [Washington Declaration at art.13]. Like the GPA, the Washington Declaration identifies the common goal of dealing with all land-based impacts upon the marine environment, specifically those resulting from sewage, POPs, radioactive substances, heavy metals, oils, nutrients, sediment mobilization, litter, and physical alteration and destruction of habitat [*Id.* at art. 1]. The Washington Declaration also focuses on the development and implementation of national action programs. Priority is given to the treatment and management of wastewater through the installation of environmentally and economically appropriate sewage systems [*Id.* at art. 15]. Both the Washington Declaration and the GPA were endorsed by the United Nations (UN) General Assembly in December 1996 [U.N. GAOR 86th Plenary Mtg., U.N. Doc. A/RES/51/189 (1996)].

4. 2012 MANILA DECLARATION

The Third Intergovernmental Review Meeting on the Implementation of the GPA took place in Manila, the Philippines in January 2012. With the aim of delivering new policies and actions to improve the sustainable management of oceans and coasts, the meeting brought together environment ministers, marine scientists, non-governmental organizations (NGOS), and other representatives from 65 countries. The outcome of the meeting was the Manila Declaration, containing 16 provisions focusing on actions to be taken between 2012 and 2016 at international, regional, and local levels [*Manila Declaration,* (Jan. 2012) UNEP/GPA/IGR.3/CRP/1].

The Manila Declaration focuses on furthering the implementation of the GPA and recognizes, in particular, the vulnerability of low-lying coastal areas and small island developing nations. Signatories reaffirmed their commitment to develop policies to reduce and control wastewater, marine litter, and pollution from fertilizers. These commitments included a call for countries to develop better guidance on the sustainable use of fertilizers, such as nitrogen and phosphorous, and to mitigate runoff and the resulting creation of dead zones. The Manila Declaration also calls for collaborative action to reduce the vulnerability of coastal communities to contamination from POPs, the results of climate change (*see* Ch. 6), and the impact of biodiversity loss (*see* Ch. 5). The recommendations also include targeted financial support from governments for marine-based renewable energy projects, such as wind and wave power, in an attempt to harness opportunities for green job creation.

5.   REGIONAL TREATIES

a. Regional Seas Programmes

The Regional Seas Programme, launched in 1974, is perhaps one of the UNEP's most significant achievements. Today, more than 143 States have joined 18 Regional Seas Conventions and Action Plans for the sustainable management and use of the marine and coastal environment. Regional Seas Programmes administered under the auspices of UNEP include: Wider Caribbean; Mediterranean; East Asian seas; East Africa region; Northwest

Pacific; West and Central Africa region; and the Caspian Sea. Many of these programs have also adopted conventions [United Nations Environment Programme (UNEP), *Regional Seas Programme,* available at http://www.unep.org/regionalseas (last visited Apr. 2017)] (*see also* Ch. 13).

UNEP Regional Seas Conventions are the centerpiece of the oceans program and have spawned specific protocols dealing with land-based pollution. These protocols are concerned with both the consequences and the causes of environmental harm, and encompass a comprehensive approach to combating environmental problems [Daud Hassan, PROTECTING THE MARINE ENVIRONMENT FROM LAND-BASED SOURCES OF POLLUTION (2006) at 124]. They include: the Protocol for the Protection of the Mediterranean Sea Against Pollution from Land-Based Sources and Activities, [*Protocol for the Protection of the Mediterranean Sea Against Pollution from Land-Based Sources,* May 17, 1980 (entered into force Jun. 17, 1983; amended Mar. 1996), 19 I.L.M. 869]; the Protocol for the Protection of the South-East Pacific Against Pollution from Land-Based Sources [*Protocol for the Protection of South-East Pacific Against Pollution from Land-Based Sources,* Jul. 23, 1983 (entered into force Sept. 23, 1986), reprinted in 2 New Directions In The Law of the Sea, Doc. J. 18, at 25]; the Protocol on Protection of the Black Sea Marine Environment Against Pollution from Land-Based Sources (LBS Protocol) [*Protocol on Protection of the Black Sea Marine Environment Against Pollution from Land-Based Sources,* 1992 (entered into force 1994), 31

I.L.M. 1110 (hereinafter LBS Protocol)]; the Kuwait Region Protocol for the Protection of the Marine Environment against Pollution from Land-Based Sources [*Kuwait Region Protocol for the Protection of the Marine Environment against Pollution from Land-Based Sources*, 1990 (entered into force 1993)]; and the Protocol Concerning Pollution from Land-Based Sources and Activities to The Convention for the Protection and Development of the Marine Environment in the Wider Caribbean Region (WCR) [*Protocol Concerning Pollution from Land-Based Sources and Activities to the Convention for the Protection and Development of the Marine Environment in the Wider Caribbean Region,* 1999 (entered into force 2010), U.N. Doc. UNEP (WATER)/CAR WG.21/6 (hereinafter WCR)].

The LBS Protocol is perhaps the most significant agreement of its kind, with its inclusion of regional effluent limitations for domestic wastewater (sewage) and its requirement of specific plans to address agricultural non-point sources. Specific schedules for implementation have also been included. In addition, the LBS Protocol sets the stage for the development and adoption of future Annexes to address other priority sources and activities of pollution.

The protocols developed before 1995 typically apply only to the jurisdictional sea area covered by the convention and a land application area measured up to the freshwater limit. However, the more recent protocols, such as those adopted for the Mediterranean and the Wider Caribbean, take a more comprehensive approach. That is, these protocols extend the application area to the hydrologic basin, and they regulate more sources of pollution that affect the marine environment. Additionally, they contain obligations requiring national plans, programs, and specific measures for addressing land-based pollution, as well as other regional or sub-regional cooperative initiatives.

In addition to the UNEP administered Regional Seas Programmes, there are a number of independent regional treaties, not established under UNEP auspices, which also address the problem of land-based pollution, including those for the Antarctic (*see* Ch. 8), Baltic Sea, Caspian Sea, the North-East Atlantic Ocean, and the Arctic Ocean. As a general rule, these treaties have had a difficult time developing regional standards, and even when standards are developed they do not bind objecting parties. Furthermore, even when parties agree to regional standards, no higher authority exists to compel action because all enforcement power remains in the hands of the national governments. The regime dealing with the North East Atlantic (the OSPAR Convention) is the most promising of these regional approaches (*see* below).

b. Convention for the Prevention of Marine Pollution from Land-Based Sources (1974 Paris Convention)

The Convention for the Prevention of Marine Pollution from Land-Based Sources (1974 Paris Convention) was perhaps the most developed and comprehensive example of regional cooperation on the subject. Covering the area of the North-East Atlantic and the North Sea, the 1974 Paris Convention called for the elimination of pollution from a "black list" of dangerous substances, and the strict limitation of pollution from a "gray list" of less harmful substances [1974 Paris Convention at art. 4]. A supervisory body known as the Paris Commission amended the contents of both lists, binding parties who vote for its decisions but not others [*Id.* at art. 18]. Over the years, the Paris Commission adopted a considerable number of broadly accepted measures, including a phased-out reduction of PCBs and a strong endorsement of the precautionary principle as applied to integrated ecosystem protection [Philippe Sands et al., PRINCIPLES OF INTERNATIONAL ENVIRONMENTAL LAW, THIRD EDITION (2012)].

c. Convention for the Protection of the Marine Environment of the North East Atlantic (OSPAR Convention)

The 1974 Paris Convention and the 1972 Convention for the Prevention of Marine Pollution by Dumping from Ships and Aircraft (1972 Oslo Convention) [*Convention for the Prevention of Marine Pollution by Dumping from Ships and Aircraft,* Feb. 15, 1972 (entered into force Apr. 7, 1974), 932 U.N.T.S. 3 (hereinafter Oslo Convention)] were both replaced by the OSPAR Convention, which entered into force in 1998 (*see* Ch. 12). The OSPAR Convention consolidates efforts to combat land-based pollution with those controlling dumping—creating a single commission to oversee both activities. The OSPAR Convention also covers all sources of marine pollution, and addresses the adverse effects of human activities on marine environments, while strengthening regional cooperation [Hassan, *supra,* at 107].

Article 2 of the OSPAR Convention specifies the general obligations of the parties to comply with two principles: the precautionary principle and the polluter pays principle. The notoriously vague precautionary principle (*see* Ch. 12), as defined in the OSPAR Convention, means:

> . . . preventive measures are to be taken when there are reasonable grounds for concern that substances or energy introduced, directly or indirectly, into the marine environment may bring about hazards to human health, harm living resources and marine ecosystems, damage amenities, or interfere with other legitimate uses of the sea, even when there is no conclusive evidence of a causal relationship between the inputs and the effects [OSPAR Convention at art 2.2(a)].

According to the OSPAR Convention, the polluter pays principle requires that the "costs of pollution prevention, control and reduction measures are to be borne by the polluter" [*Id.* at art. 2.2(b)].

The OSPAR Convention also calls for the use of best available techniques, best environmental practices, and "clean" technology in the implementation of programs and measures aimed at meeting its objectives [*Id.* at art. 3]. To determine what constitutes best available technique and best environmental practices in a specific circumstance, the OSPAR Convention establishes a Commission that must first look to the guidelines provided in Appendix 1, with best available technique as state of the art technology and best environmental practices as the most appropriate mix of measures and strategies taking environmental, social, and economic factors into account [*Id.* at Appendix 1]. Next, in the setting of specific programs and time scales for the control of a specific substance, the Commission considers a series of criteria listed in Appendix 2, including persistency, toxicity, and tendency to bioaccumulate [*Id.* at Appendix 2]. In this way, the OSPAR Convention dispenses with the "black list—gray list" method by providing a single, non-exhaustive list of substances to be regulated. This approach appears to offer more flexibility in controlling any particular substance and consequently may lead to greater acceptance of the Commission's standards. Even so, objecting parties are still not bound by the Commission's official decisions with regard to the Annexes and Appendices [*Id.* at art. 13], or Amendments to the Annexes [*Id.* at art. 17] or Appendices [*Id.* at art. 19]. Without a doubt, however, the OSPAR Convention presents a better chance for more effective pollution control than the 1974 Paris Convention or the 1972 Oslo Convention.

The Commission continues to work within the framework of the OSPAR Convention as well as with six long-term strategies concerning: (1) protection and conservation of marine biodiversity and ecosystems; (2) eutrophication; (3) hazardous substances; (4) the offshore oil and gas industry; (5) radioactive substances; and (6) monitoring and assessment. In June 2003, the Commission committed itself to utilizing an "ecosystem approach" in managing the impact of human activities on the marine environment. As defined by the Commission, this approach requires "the comprehensive integrated management of human activities based on the best available scientific knowledge about the ecosystem and its dynamics" [First Joint Ministerial Meeting of the Helsinki and OSPAR Commissions, *Statement on the Ecosystem Approach to the Management of Human Activities*, (2003) at Agenda Item 6]. In 2010, in furtherance of the ecosystem approach, the OSPAR Convention established the Ecological Quality Objectives for specific aspects of the marine ecosystem [OSPAR, *Quality Status Report 2010*, (2010) OSPAR Commission, London].

d. The Arctic Council

There has also been some movement, albeit much less promising than the OSPAR Convention, towards protection of the marine environment from land-based sources of pollution in the Arctic. The governments of Canada, Denmark, Finland, Iceland, Norway, Sweden, Russia, and the U.S. are working together to protect the "Arctic Region," meaning the area north of 60° latitude, including Labrador and the region in northern Quebec known as Nunavik. The Arctic Council, established in 1996, functions as a partnership for SD.

In 1998, the Arctic Council adopted the Regional Programme of Action for the Protection of the Arctic Marine Environment from Land-Based Activities (RPA) [Arctic Council, *Regional Programme of Action for the Protection of the Arctic Marine Environment from Land-Based Activities* (Sept.1998) (hereinafter RPA)]. The RPA specifically notes the importance of working with the GPA [Id. at. art. 1.9] (*see* above). The RPA also adheres to GPA guidelines by considering the severity of land-based activities in relation to food security, public health, coastal and marine resources, ecosystem health, and socio-economic benefits [Id. at. art. 4.1]. The RPA lays out its priorities for regional action, with POPs and heavy metals as the highest concerns [Id. at. Table 2]. It then sets out specific objectives and strategies for each source [Id. at. art. 6], and calls for progress reports to be submitted to the Arctic Council Ministers [Id. at. art. 7.2].

In February 2003, a working group led by Iceland and Canada was assigned the task of developing a strategic plan for the Protection of the Arctic Marine Environment. The Protection of the Arctic Marine Environment Working Group addresses policy and non-emergency pollution prevention and control measures related to the protection of the Arctic marine environment from land-based activities and other sources [Arctic Council, ARCTIC MARINE STRATEGIC PLAN (2004)]. The same Working Group contributes to the regional and national implementation of the GPA (*see* above). The Working Group does this through further implementation and development of the Arctic Council Regional

Programme of Action on the same issues. In 2013, the Arctic Council adopted a "Vision for the Arctic," which committed the Arctic states to "pursue opportunities to expand the Arctic Council's roles from policy-shaping into policy-making" [Arctic Council, *Vision for the Arctic,* (May 15 2013) at 5]. The Arctic Council recognizes that much of the pollution in the Arctic Region is derived from sources outside the region, and thus is also working with UNEP for a global approach to the region's problems.

E. CONCLUSIONS

In conclusion, we see that the umbrella provisions of UNCLOS are being implemented, albeit slowly, through a variety of regional treaties. Of these, the OSPAR Convention best addresses the problem of land-based pollution in a comprehensive manner. The OSPAR Convention could prove to be a model for controlling land-based sources of marine pollution.

CHAPTER ELEVEN

POLLUTION BY VESSELS AND OFFSHORE OIL PLATFORMS

A. NATURE OF THE PROBLEM

Pollution caused by ships is regulated by well-established international laws dealing with different aspects of vessel-based pollution. With a few exceptions, mentioned below, these international treaties do not control pollution caused by offshore oil rigs and platforms. We begin with pollution from ships, which is extensively covered by a variety of treaties and calls for analysis commensurate with its legal status and import. By contrast, oil rigs and platforms are only sparingly dealt with under international law, and will not receive as much attention.

The primary source of vessel-based pollution is oil, but other physical and chemical pollutants are also discharged from ships, either deliberately or accidentally. Since the bulk of the world's oil resources are thousands of miles away from the primary markets for oil, giant oil tankers must crisscross the oceans of the world transporting massive quantities of oil. In 2015 just under 3,000 million tons of oil and gas were transported by ship Slightly smaller loads were carried from 2010 to 2014 [United Nations Conference on Trade and Development (UNCTAD), *Review of Maritime Transport 2016*, UNCTAD/RMT/2016 (hereinafter Review of Maritime Transport)]. Marine ecosystems are threatened by the deliberate release of oil in the course of routine shipping operations, oil spills caused by tanker accidents, air emissions from ships, the accidental release of other chemicals transported by ships, and the breaking up of ships [*see* Robert Clark, MARINE POLLUTION (5th ed. 2001) at 64–72]. Vessels may also deliberately discharge their garbage into the oceans, and plastic debris can present serious hazards to marine life. In addition to ecological concerns, human society may suffer impacts from vessel-based pollution, as one half of the world's population lives in coastal regions and depend on ocean resources for food, transportation, and their livelihoods [Alan Khee-Jin Tan, VESSEL-SOURCE MARINE POLLUTION (2006) at 11].

According to an authoritative report of the Joint Group of Experts on the Scientific Aspects of Marine Environmental Protection (GESAMP) in 1997, the estimated average annual inputs of oil entering the marine environment, from operational and accidental discharges amounted to 457,000 metric tonnes [Joint Group of Experts on the Scientific Aspects of Marine Environmental Protection (GESAMP), *Estimates of Oil Entering the Marine Environment from Sea-Based Activities*, IMO (2007)]. In a later review, the U.S. National Research Council (NRC) found that the transportation of crude oil and refined petroleum products results in the release of approximately 160,000 tons of petroleum per year into the world's oceans due to spills or operational discharges [U.S. National Research Council (NRC), COMM. ON OIL IN THE SEA: INPUTS, FATES, AND

EFFECTS, OIL IN THE SEA III (2003) at 78 (hereinafter NRC 2003)].

In fact, the gross volume of oil that is spilled into the sea is declining. In 1971, 6.3 million tons of oil was lost to the sea. In 1980 the figure was 3.2 million tons, and in 1989 the figure dropped further to 560,000 tons [Ronald Mitchell, INTENTIONAL OIL POLLUTION AT SEA (1994) at 70]. The NRC, which computed figures from 1990 to 1999, has made a best estimate of annual discharges of petroleum during transportation worldwide and puts this figure at 160,000 tons [U.S. National Research Council (NRC), *Oil in the Sea III: Inputs, Fates, and Effects* (2003) at Table 2–2]. Their estimate of all discharges is 1,300,000 tons [*Id.*]. The International Tanker Owners Pollution Federation (ITOPF) claims that the annual quantity of spilled oil dropped from 435,000 tons in 1991 to 10,000 tons in 2010 [International Tanker Owners Pollution Federation (ITOPF), *Tanker Spill Statistics* (2010)], and dropped further to 6,000 tons in 2016 [International Tanker Owners Pollution Federation (ITOPF), *Oil Tanker Spill Statistics* (2016) (hereinafter ITOPF 2016)]. It is to be noted that the ITOPF figures relate to spills while the NRC figures apply to operational discharges as well as spills.

If we accept the NRC figure, vessels are responsible for only 160,000 tons out of 1,300,000 tons, which amounts to 11.5% of the oil pollution in the oceans. As it turns out, 36% of the oil pollution in the world's oceans actually comes from land-based sources (*see* Ch. 10), while natural seepages account

for 46%, and extraction accounts for the balance [*Id.*].
However these sources generally do not attract much
attention because they are not visually graphic or
arresting. By contrast, the visual effect of vessel-
based spills is often dramatic because of the large
volume of oil released in a small area over a short
period of time.

GESAMP is an organization consisting of eminent
experts jointly sponsored and convened by the
International Maritime Organization (IMO), the
Food and Agricultural Organization (FAO), the
United Nations Educational Scientific and Cultural
Organization (UNESCO), the World Meteorological
Organization (WMO), the International Atomic
Energy Agency (IAEA), and the United Nations
Environment Programme (UNEP). The purpose of
GESAMP is to undertake authoritative studies of
marine pollution. The 2001 GESAMP Study cites the
Black Sea, where oil tanker traffic is heavy, to
illustrate the impact of vessel-based pollution. The
vast bulk of the total of 111,000 tons of oil entering
the Black Sea is attributable to land-based pollution,
with another 53,000 tons arriving via the Danube
River. A further 30,000 tons is derived from domestic
sources, plus 15,400 tons from industrial sources.
Even after considering unquantified inputs of oily
residue discharge from ships, GESAMP found that
only 136 tons could be attributed to accidental oil
spills [Joint Group of Experts on the Scientific
Aspects of Marine Environmental Protection
(GESAMP), PROTECTING THE OCEANS FROM LAND-
BASED ACTIVITIES (2001)].

Thus, land-based sources of oil pollution are likely to remain the most significant, even in areas with heavy tanker traffic like the Black Sea. Perhaps more significantly, GESAMP opines that vessel pollution may be of negligible importance on oceanic scales [*Id.* at 23]. The findings of the NRC that the majority of oil in the oceans comes from oil runoff from land and municipal and industrial wastes bolsters this conclusion. Accordingly, "chronic release from natural and anthropogenic sources (e.g., natural seeps and run-off from land-based sources) are responsible for the majority of petroleum hydrocarbon input to both North American waters and the world's oceans" [NRC 2003 at 65]. Catastrophic spills such as those from the *Amoco Cadiz,* the *Exxon Valdez*, and the *Prestige* will cause severe, if transient, problems within regional areas. But even these high-profile vessel discharges are of limited significance on spatial oceanic and long-term time scales.

While a few large spills are responsible for a high percentage of oil spilled, the majority of oil spills are actually relatively small. There has been a downward trend in numbers of large oil spills, i.e. greater than 700 tonnes, from tankers annually. The average number of tanker incidents involving large oil spills, has progressively been reduced since 2010, and stands at an average of 1.7 per year [ITOPF 2016]. Most spills from tankers are small ones that result from routine operations like loading, discharging, and bunkering in ports or at oil terminals, whereas large spills generally result from collisions at sea.

While vessel-based pollution may at times create more than a negligible risk, it is not the most dangerous form of marine pollution and does not present as large a risk to human health as compared to pollutants released by land-based activities or dumping. It is being treated as a separate subject in this book primarily to reflect the international attention given to it. There are a number of reasons that account for the international response to vessel-based pollution. Oil spills create dramatic and frightening visual effects and lend themselves to graphic photographs and media attention. For example, the oil tanker *Prestige*, which sank 150 miles off the coast of Spain in November 2002 and resulted in an estimated $1 billion dollar cleanup effort, was carrying 70,000 tons of oil. This is more than twice the amount of oil spilled by the *Exxon Valdez*, and the resulting spectacle received wide media publicity. Such publicity is heightened by the harm suffered by seabirds and other marine creatures, which provokes public indignation and tarnishes the image of the oil industry. Oil slicks also wash ashore and prevent the use of beaches, which further agitates public sentiment. In response, ship owners, operators of oil tankers, and oil companies—who do not cherish their tarnished environmental image—have been willing to take steps to control vessel pollution and to set up their own compensation schemes.

B.   IMPACTS OF OIL POLLUTION

1.   ENVIRONMENTAL IMPACTS

a. Harm Caused by the Physical Properties of Oil

Studies conducted over the last 20 years confirm that the physical properties of oil are harmful to marine life [NRC 2003 at 120]. Oil spilled or discharged at sea changes its composition as it spreads over the surface of the water in a thin layer called an *oil slick*. Some components evaporate or dissolve, while others break down and disperse as small droplets. Under some water conditions a thick, sticky mass may form on the surface of the water. The heavy residues of oil from the discharge of oily bilge and ballast water may form tar balls.

Oil that becomes stranded near shore smothers small marine animals and destroys plant life. Heavier oils and mousse-like emulsions clog the bodies of small marine animals, interfering with respiration, feeding, and movement. Seabirds, sea otters, and other small marine animals that spend much of their time on the surface of the water, and rely on the insulating properties of feathers or fur to survive, are particularly vulnerable [*see* Dwight Holing, COASTAL ALERT, ECOSYSTEMS, ENERGY, AND OFFSHORE OIL DRILLING (1990) at 28]. Oil destroys the water repellence of a seabird's plumage, causing it to become waterlogged and drown, or causing it to freeze to death from the loss of thermal insulation [Clark, *supra,* at 85–95]. Over 30,000 seabirds died as a result of the 1989 *Exxon Valdez* oil tanker accident in Alaska, but many more seabirds die each year from non-accidental releases of oil in the Northeast Atlantic. Sea otters, which rely on the trapped air in their dense fur for survival in the cold, are likewise vulnerable to floating oil. A sea otter will die of hypothermia if 20 to 30% of its body is covered with oil. The *Exxon Valdez* oil spill caused the deaths of over 1,000 sea otters. While oil disrupts the proper functioning of marine communities and ecosystems, it is difficult to determine the long-term effects of oil exposure at these biological levels over the long-term or at low doses [NRC 2003 at 120].

b. Harm Caused by the Toxic Properties of Oil

Crude oils as well as refined petroleum products contain toxic substances detrimental to the health of seabirds, plankton, and fish [Clark, *supra,* at 86–95]. Depending on the toxicity of the oil even small quantities swallowed by animals can prove deadly. Oils that are dissolved or dispersed in the water can easily penetrate the gills of fish, causing irritation and preventing respiration. Adult fish may be able to avoid areas of floating oil, but immature fish and planktonic fish eggs that inhabit surface waters cannot. Exposure to hydrocarbons at these developmental stages often results in death or decreased hatching rates. Oil that settles in ocean sediments reduces the production of aerobic bacteria, on which the benthic (bottom-dwelling) organisms depend for their diet, thus impacting the very base of marine food webs.

2.   FINANCIAL IMPACTS

Determining the financial cost associated with vessel-based pollution is not an easy task, and differs with each unique spill. The type of oil spilled affects the cost of the cleanup. In general, thicker and persistent oil is more difficult and costly to clean up. Refined products, such as gasoline and diesel, are generally easier to clean up, and in some instances do not require a cleanup effort at all due to their quick dispersal and evaporation rates. The geographic area in which the spill occurs can also significantly affect the cost of cleanup. The sensitivity of the shoreline ecology, the ease of access to the area, and tidal activity can all increase the cost of cleaning up a spill. The rate of spillage, the tonnage of oil spilled, and a variety of other factors can also impact the final cleanup cost. A quick glance at the cost statistics of oil spills can be misleading, however, as each spill engenders a different set of cost factors. Understanding the differences of these cost-factors, and their impact on the cleanup process, can provide a more informed and useful evaluation of the financial cost of vessel-based pollution.

The actual incurred financial cost of specific oil spills are difficult to determine. Much of the costs are confidential between the parties involved, and the burden is often shared between many different parties. While the International Oil Pollution Compensation Fund collects some of this data, the scope of the data collected is limited. The Fund becomes operational only once a spill has exceeded the costs incurred by the ship owner. Therefore, the data collected by the Fund only reflect the very largest spills.

It is very clear, however, that these spills can incur enormous financial costs. The *Exxon Valdez* disaster has proven to be one of the most expensive oil spills to date, accruing nearly $3 billion in associated costs [Richard T. Carson et al., *Contingent Valuation and Lost Passive Use: Damages from the Exxon Valdez Oil Spill*, 25 ENVTL. & RESOURCE ECON. 257 (2003) at 278]. Furthermore, costs associated with the 2002 *Prestige* disaster are expected to reach £8.5 billion in the long term [Xin Liu & Kai W. Wirtz, *Total Oil Spill Costs and Compensations*, 33 MAR. POL'Y & MGMT. 49 (2006) at 55]. These particularly expensive oil spills are not representative of oil spills in general; however, they do exemplify the potentially high cost of vessel-based pollution.

C. VESSEL-BASED OIL POLLUTION

1. CAUSES OF VESSEL-BASED OIL POLLUTION

Vessel-based pollution has declined impressively over the past three decades and continues to do so. These dramatic decreases in oil discharges have largely been the result of regulations under the International Convention for the Prevention of Pollution from Ships (MARPOL). Two authoritative reports of the NRC, the first issued in 1985 and the second in 2002, flag these dramatic changes. Accidental spills were estimated at 390,000 tons per year according to the 1985 report, and fell to 100,000 tons per year according to the 2002 report. Operational discharges, which accounted for 710,000 tons in the 1985 report, plummeted to 72,000 tons according to the 2002 report [U.S. National Research Council (NRC), STEERING COMM. FOR THE PETROLEUM IN THE MARINE ENV'T UPDATE, OIL IN THE SEA (1985) at 52–61; NRC 2003 at 69]. In addition, as we have noted, ITOPF has tracked vessel-based pollution since the 1970s and has reported a drastic reduction in the total number of large accidental spills. It is estimated that intentionally discharged tanker oil accounts for up to one fourth of all vessel-generated pollution [NRC 2003 at 76]. Tanker accidents, discharges from non-tankers, and escapes from pipelines and atmospheric depositions account for the rest. Tanker de-ballasting and cleaning previously constituted the major source of oil pollution. When a tanker delivers its cargo, a thin layer of oil remains in the tanks. On the return voyage, tankers fill empty cargo tanks with sea water as ballast to stabilize them. They also use seawater in high pressure cleaning procedures to wash down the tanks before receiving a new consignment of oil. Additionally, oil and lubricants from the ship's engines leak into the bilges (bottoms) of tankers and become mixed with seawater. Prior to their arrival at port, captains traditionally discharged the resulting oil/water solutions (or *slops*) at sea.

Much of this changed with the regulations made under MARPOL. Tankers whose deadweight is at least 20,000 tons are required to have segregated ballast tanks, dedicated clean ballast tanks, or crude oil washing systems. These are tanks completely separated from cargo and fuel oil systems, and are permanently allocated to the carriage of ballast water. Moreover, pursuant to MARPOL regulations, at least two thirds of the tanker fleet now has double-hull arrangements [NRC 2003 at 76]. The space between the two hulls is often used for storage of fuel or ballast water.

In addition to discharging oil-contaminated bilge and ballast water, ships also discharge garbage as part of routine operations [Clark, *supra,* at 6]. Non-biodegradable plastic debris is an especially serious problem because it may remain in the ocean for centuries [Richard C. Thompson et al., *Lost at Sea: Where Is All the Plastic?*, 304 SCIENCE 838 (2004)]. In the early 1990s, an estimated 6.5 million tons of plastic per year was discarded into the ocean by ships. This figure is now estimated at 5.6 million tons per year [Jort HANVOER et al., *Plastics in the marine environment: the dark side of a modern gift, 220,* REVIEW OF ENVIRONMENTAL CONTAMINATION AND TOXICOLOGY (2012) at 1–44]. Seabirds, fish, and mammals die from drowning or injury caused by entanglement in plastic packaging, such as six-pack rings and sheeting, or by swallowing plastic objects.

2.   REMEDIAL OBJECTIVES

In order to prevent future oil spills from occurring and to help mitigate damages after a spill, several remedial procedures and regulations have been developed. While they may not be sufficient in completely preventing vessel-based pollution, they have greatly decreased the total negative effect of such spills. Remedial objectives for routine operational discharges have included ship design changes, as well as port facilities for receiving *slops*. Most tanker accidents occur in high-risk areas near shore and close to port entrances where the high volume of shipping traffic multiplies the risk of a collision, and natural hazards such as reefs and rocks increase the risk of ships running aground. Accident prevention has concentrated on construction standards, such as double-hulled oil tankers, and safety standards that ensure seaworthiness and prevent navigational errors that might result in a collision or grounding. Ships should be prepared for emergencies, and provisions need to be made for intervention in case of an accident. As we shall see, there has been a positive legal response to these issues.

In an effort to control and contain spilled oil, several cleanup techniques have been developed. While these emergency procedures are not always effective, they can help mitigate the damage caused by oil spills. Floating booms, for example, can help contain the oil in a small, more manageable area. These large nets (similar to short curtains) can be used to both contain and deflect the flow of the oil away from coastlines. Unfortunately, the use of floating booms is a difficult and often ineffective procedure. Wind and tides spread oil very quickly. Therefore, booms are most effective immediately after a spill, before the sea current can disperse the oil over a large, unmanageable area. However, the deployment and movement of these large floating booms is a complex procedure, requiring the coordination of sea vessels and aircraft. Largely because of these difficulties, the use of floating booms has proven relatively ineffective, resulting in 10–15% recovery at best.

Another technique used in the cleanup process involves spraying chemicals called dispersants over the spill. Dispersants work by accelerating the natural process of biodegradation. Once they are sprayed onto an oil slick, the dispersants aid in mixing the oil and water, creating finely dispersed oil droplets. All the components of crude oil biodegrade with time, and chemical dispersants simply accelerate this process [see International Tanker Owners Pollution Federation (ITOPF), THE USE OF CHEMICAL DISPERSANTS TO TREAT OIL SPILLS (2005)]. Therefore, dispersants do not help to extract or contain the oil like floating booms. Rather, they spread it out, protecting sea life and vulnerable coastlines from floating oil.

Spraying dispersants onto an oil spill is often an effective technique, and given the challenges surrounding the use of floating booms, it is sometimes the only technique that can be used. However, there are many challenges and environmental costs associated with the application of dispersants. For example, dispersants do not work against highly viscous oils. In addition, the dispersants must be applied soon after the spill or they may prove ineffective. Environmental concerns have also been raised about the use of dispersants. Instead of attempting to extract the spilled oil, the use of dispersants encourages the introduction of oil into the surrounding ecosystem. In deeper seas, the toxicity level decreases quickly as the oil disperses out. However, in shallow waters with less water turbulence, the increased oil toxicity may severely affect the surrounding ecosystem. Both floating booms and chemical dispersants can be effective in certain situations but by no means do they solve the demands of oil spill cleanup projects. These techniques need to be improved and other techniques should continue to be explored.

Another technique sometimes utilized is called in-situ burning. This involves igniting and burning the oil floating on the surface. This process can often be very dangerous and poses significant environmental costs. As mentioned before, oil biodegrades over time into simple compounds such as carbon dioxide (CO_2), water, and biomass. Bioremediation is another cleanup technique used to stimulate and accelerate the growth of naturally occurring oil-degrading bacteria. Unfortunately, this process is slower than chemical dispersion and has proven to be problematic in some circumstances. As with booms and dispersants, these alternative techniques are limited. The proper cleanup technique for a given oil spill will depend on a variety of factors and should include a cost-benefit analysis. However, it is clear that these techniques are insufficient for the majority of large spills, and new techniques and laws are needed to prevent future damage to the oceans and coastlines from oil spills.

More progress is also needed in shore cleaning techniques, which have sometimes increased the damage and delayed recovery from oil spills affecting shorelines [U.S. National Research Council (NRC), COMM. TO REVIEW THE OIL SPILL RECOVERY INST.'S RESEARCH PROGRAM, THE OIL SPILL RECOVERY INSTITUTE: PAST, PRESENT, AND FUTURE DIRECTIONS (2003) at 60]. Beach cleaning techniques include the application of high-pressure water, steam, and dispersants. However, heat and cleaning-chemical toxicity may kill many naturally occurring organisms on the beach that have not already been killed by the effects of the oil. An alternative to these beach-cleaning techniques is the physical mopping of oil from the beach. However, this is only partially effective, because most of the oil spilled eludes recovery or cleanup. Moreover, cleanups are often more apparent than real, because the oil is not removed but drained away or forced to a few inches below the surface. Here, without oxygen to degrade the oil, it may remain for up to a year or more.

3.   LEGAL RESPONSE

The international response to vessel pollution has been more satisfactory than in many other areas of international environmental law (IEL). International law has responded to the two different causes of vessel pollution: (1) the general operation of commercial shipping; and (2) the occasional accident occurring at sea (*see also* Ch. 10).

a. Operational Pollution

As we have noted, most vessel pollution of the marine environment arises from the daily operation of ships, not from the highly publicized, but infrequent, catastrophe. The 1972 Convention on the Prevention of Marine Pollution by Dumping of Wastes and Other Matter (London Convention) prevents pollution by regulating the dumping of wastes [*Convention on the Prevention of Marine Pollution by Dumping of Wastes and Other Matter*, Dec. 29, 1972, (entered into force Aug. 30, 1975) 1046 U.N.T.S 120 (hereinafter London Convention)]. For other vessel-based operational pollution, the international community has developed two fundamental and related schemes of governance. The first is MARPOL, which sets out specific regulations for, among other things, the permissibility of pollution discharge as well as the construction requirements for ships. The second important legal regime is the United Nations Convention on the Law of the Sea (UNCLOS), which potentially alters the jurisdictional structure of MARPOL while generally deferring to its other provisions.

i. *1972 Convention on the Prevention of Marine Pollution by Dumping of Wastes and Other Matter (London Convention)*

Working in conjunction with MARPOL (*see* below), the London Convention was developed to control all sources of marine pollution, and prevents pollution by regulating the dumping of waste materials. The London Convention consists of 22 Articles and 3 Annexes. Annex I lists materials that may not be dumped at sea, Annex II lists materials that require "special care" before being dumped, and Annex III lays out general technical factors to be considered in establishing criteria for issuance of ocean dumping permits [London Convention at Annex I–III]. MARPOL and the London Convention are not duplicative, but rather work together. For example, the London Convention regulates waste from ships, but not accidental spills or other discharges resulting from ship operations. MARPOL does, however, control such losses from ships. In 1996, the London Protocol was adopted to further modernize the London Convention and, eventually, to replace it [*Protocol to the Convention on the Prevention of Marine Pollution by Dumping Wastes and Other Matters,* Nov. 8, 1996 (entered into force Mar. 24, 2006), 36 I.L.M. 7 (hereinafter London Protocol)]. The London Protocol establishes a "precautionary approach" under which all dumping is prohibited, with exceptions. That is, instead of prohibiting specific materials, parties must not dump any materials except those included in a "reverse list." The London Protocol entered into force in March 2006 (*see* Ch. 12).

ii. 1973 *International Convention for the Prevention of Pollution from Ships (MARPOL)*

MARPOL is the most important global treaty for the prevention of pollution from the operation of ships. It governs the design and equipment of ships, establishes a system of certificates and inspections, and requires States to provide reception facilities for the disposal of oily waste and chemicals. It covers all the technical aspects of pollution from ships, except the disposal of waste into the sea by dumping. It also applies to ships of all types, although it does not apply to pollution arising out of the exploration and exploitation of seabed mineral resources.

MARPOL and its Protocols, most significantly the Protocol of 1978 Relating to the International Convention for the Prevention of Pollution from Ships, supply general duties for parties, supplemented by the more detailed Annexes that are themselves supplemented by Appendices to Annexes. In this way, MARPOL creatively deals with the problem of balancing general duties with specific obligations. The regime also provides a flexible approach to law-making, as various combinations of a two-thirds majority in either the IMO or a convened Conference of the Parties (COP) can effectively amend MARPOL or its Protocols, Annexes, or Appendices [MARPOL at art. 16(f)(i)–(v)].

MARPOL currently includes regulations aimed at preventing and minimizing pollution from ships—both accidental pollution and that from routine operations—and also includes six technical Annexes: Annex I deals with prevention of oil pollution; Annex II deals with noxious liquid substances; Annex III with harmful substances in packaged form; Annex IV with sewage; Annex V with garbage; and Annex VI with air pollution from ships [*Id.* at Annex I–VI]. Parties to MARPOL must accept Annex I and II, but the rest are voluntary [*Id.* at art. 16].

Annex I entered into force in 1983 and covers the regulation of oil discharge from ships, mandating both construction requirements and release allowances. The technical requirements of construction and readiness are fairly intricate, and attempt to provide minimum safety standards with respect to tankers. Significantly, 1992 Amendments 13(f) and 13(g) call for "double-hulls" on all new oil tankers—a feature long sought by environmentalists to prevent spillage in case of hull rupture. In April 2005, Amendments to Annex I of MARPOL, adopted by IMO's Marine Environment Protection Committee in December 2003, entered into force for all MARPOL parties. The Amendments revise the existing Regulation 13(g), and add a new Regulation 13(h) on the prevention of oil pollution from oil tankers carrying heavy grade oil as cargo. Consequential Amendments to the Condition Assessment Scheme for oil tankers were also adopted. The revised Regulation 13(g) brings forward the phase-out schedule that was first established in 1992, and revised in both 2001 and 2003, for existing single-hull tankers. It requires that single-hull tankers be phased out or converted to a double-hull by the dates set out in the revised regulation. Annex I was amended again in 2006 to include a new Regulation 12(a), which requires a protected location for fuel tanks on tankers. With respect to release allowances, Annex I quantitatively limits discharge from all ships, limits the rate at which oil may be discharged to 60 liters per mile traveled, and prohibits discharge in most circumstances within 50 miles of the coastline [*Id.* at Reg. 9]. Annex I and its revisions also severely limit the release of oil in special environmentally sensitive areas, including the Baltic, Mediterranean, Black, Oman, and Red Seas, the Gulfs, areas off the coasts of southern Africa and northwestern Europe, and Antarctic waters [*Id.* at Reg. 10].

Annex II entered into force in 1987 and details the discharge criteria and measures for the control of pollution by noxious liquid substances carried in bulk. There were 250 substances included under MARPOL, and the discharge of their residues is allowed only to reception facilities. No discharge of residues containing noxious substances is permitted within 12 miles of the nearest land. Annex II was revised in 2004 to include a hierarchical categorization of substances based on the degree of hazard posed to the environment.

Annex III entered into force in 1992 as the first optional annex. It contains general requirements for the issuing of detailed standards on packing, marking, labeling, documentation, stowage, quantity limitations, exceptions, and notifications for preventing pollution by harmful substances. Annex IV contains requirements to control pollution of the sea by sewage, and entered into force in September 2003. The 2006 amendments to Annex IV grant inspection authorities to port States. Annex V entered into force in 1988 and deals with different types of garbage. A revised Annex V came into force in 2012. It also specifies the distances from land and the manner in which garbage may be disposed of. The most important feature of Annex V is the complete ban it imposes on dumping all forms of plastic into the sea. Annex VI (the Protocol of 1997 for the Prevention of Air Pollution) entered into force in May 2005. The regulations in Annex VI set limits on sulfur oxide and nitrogen oxide emissions from ship exhausts, and prohibit deliberate emissions of ozone-depleting substances.

In allocating responsibility for the monitoring of its regulations, MARPOL creates a role both for the flag State and the port State. To fulfill its obligations, the flag State must certify each ship's compliance with MARPOL's construction and readiness guidelines by issuing an International Oil Pollution Prevention Certificate for each vessel [*Id.* at Reg. 5(2)]. In addition, the flag State must update the certificate by conducting periodic surveys of each ship to ensure continued observance of the regulations [*Id.* at Reg. 4]. However, flag States may lack incentives to properly exercise their regulation powers [Tan, *supra,* at 24]. This is because many ships simply fly flags of "convenience" registries, creating attenuated connections between ships and registry States apart from the registration procedures. These ships may never even sail within the waters of their registry State, and thus these States have little need or access to ensure compliance with regulations.

The port State, for its part, may inspect any ship within its ports or offshore terminals in order to verify "that there is on board a valid certificate" [MARPOL at art. 5(2)]. If "clear grounds" exist for believing that the condition of the ship does not correspond to the certificate, the port State may then conduct a full inspection of the vessel [*Id.* at art. 5(2)]. If it finds a violation, the port State must prevent the ship from setting sail until the vessel "can proceed to sea without presenting an unreasonable threat of harm to the marine environment" [*Id.* at art. 5(2)].

Concerning the investigation of discharge violations, the port State has more latitude than in construction and readiness inspections. In this case, the port State does not need "clear grounds" upon which to proceed with an inspection, but in fact may examine any and all ships within its jurisdiction. When coupled with some reliable evidence, the port State may also investigate any violation alleged by another party to MARPOL, regardless of where the claimed illegal discharge occurred [*Id.* at art. 6(5)]. If an inspection indicates a violation of MARPOL discharge rules, the port State immediately submits a full report to the flag State [*Id.* at art. 6(4)]. The flag State must then institute appropriate actions against the violating ship, and must notify both the port State and the IMO of the disciplinary steps taken [art. 6]. In applying its own law, the flag State must not allow more lenient treatment of its flag ships, but must impose penalties "adequate in severity to discourage violations" of the MARPOL regime [*Id.* at art. 4(4)].

iii. United Nations Convention on the Law of the Sea (UNCLOS)

As previously discussed, UNCLOS significantly alters the jurisdictional scheme of the world's oceans. Concluded after MARPOL, UNCLOS makes potentially broad changes in the application of the former, especially in regard to coastal State power under the expanded exclusive economic zone (EEZ).

MARPOL does not compel extension of coastal State jurisdiction beyond the territorial sea, but neither does it forbid such an extension. Instead, MARPOL simply gives deference to future application of UNCLOS to its own provisions, stating "the term 'jurisdiction' . . . shall be construed in the light of international law in force at the time of application or interpretation of the present Convention" [MARPOL at art. 9(3); Patricia Birnie, et al., INTERNATIONAL LAW AND THE ENVIRONMENT, THIRD EDITION (2009) at 420–423)].

As a jurisdictional matter, the question arises as to when a coastal State may adopt stricter pollution provisions than those provided in MARPOL. Based on traditional notions of sovereignty, UNCLOS codifies a long-held customary rule that a coastal State may adopt more stringent discharge rules in both its internal waters and territorial sea [UNCLOS at arts. 211(3), 211(4)]. The rigor of these laws, however, must not interfere with a foreign vessel's right of innocent passage [*Id.* at art. 24]. Innocent passage remains a time-honored right, and UNCLOS defines the term as movement that is "not prejudicial to the peace, good order or security of the coastal State" [UNCLOS at art. 19(1)]. However, a coastal State may not adopt stricter construction or readiness requirements for foreign vessels traveling in its internal waters or territorial sea, as clearly this would dramatically hinder the right of innocent passage by limiting access to only certain types of vessels [*Id.* at art. 21(2)].

In the EEZ, by contrast, a coastal State may not adopt more exacting discharge rules than those already in place under MARPOL [*Id.* at art. 211(5)]. In this way, UNCLOS limits the sovereignty of a coastal State within its own jurisdiction. Even for environmentally sensitive areas, a coastal State must first seek approval of the IMO to adopt special pollution discharge rules and, if approved, the adopted rules must follow IMO recommendations [*Id.* at art. 211(6)(a)].

Concerning enforcement of discharge violations, UNCLOS offers several variations from the more limited MARPOL regulations, though States have yet to put these expanded powers into practice. Under UNCLOS, coastal States have a type of graduated authority in dealing with pollution violations. For example, if "clear grounds" exist for believing a vessel has committed a State or MARPOL violation in the territorial sea, the coastal State may undertake physical inspection of the ship, detain the vessel, and institute proceedings against it [*Id.* at art. 220(2)]. For minor violations in the EEZ, a coastal State may only require the ship to provide information concerning its identity as well as its last and next ports of call [*Id.* at art. 220(3)]. However, when "clear grounds" exist for believing a ship has committed "a substantial discharge causing or threatening significant pollution of the marine environment" in the EEZ, the coastal State may commence an inspection if the vessel fails to provide satisfactory information about the incident [*Id.* at art. 220(5)]. Finally, in the most egregious circumstances, if "clear objective evidence" exists that a vessel has committed a violation causing "major damage or threat of major damage to the coastline," the coastal State may then undertake a broader physical inspection of the ship, detain the vessel, and institute proceedings against it [*Id.* at art. 220(6)].

UNCLOS also gives expanded enforcement jurisdiction to the port State, but again in practice States have yet to employ these powers. Understandably, a port State may institute proceedings against any vessel voluntarily in port that has committed a violation within that State's territorial sea or EEZ [*Id.* at art. 220(1)]. Additionally, however, UNCLOS conveys a qualified universal jurisdiction on the port State, which may institute proceedings against any ship that has committed a MARPOL discharge violation on the high seas or within the jurisdiction of another State, if the latter so requests [*Id.* at art. 218]. The result is an expanded role for the port State, much beyond that bestowed by MARPOL. The universal jurisdiction remains limited only by that of the flag State, which always retains a right of preemption under Article 228, except in cases of "major damage" to coastal States. Whether the international community actually adopts the expanded jurisdictional powers of the port and coastal States under UNCLOS remains to be seen. In the meantime, the legal regimes of MARPOL and UNCLOS deserve significant credit for the fact that non-natural petroleum inputs into the marine environment have decreased substantially. Total petroleum input estimates fell from 43 million barrels per year in 1975 to 9 million barrels per year in 2002 [Minerals Management Service of the U.S. Department of Interior, OCS OIL SPILL FACTS: 2002 (2002) at 1].

iv. 2004 International Convention for the Control and Management of Ships' Ballast Water and Sediments (BWM)

Ballast water is routinely taken on by ships for stability and structural integrity. When ships take on ballast water, plants and animals that live in the ocean are also picked up. In the result, ballast water can contain thousands of aquatic microbes, algae, and animals, which are then carried across the world's oceans and released into ecosystems where they are not native.

Expanded ship trade and traffic volume over the last few decades has increased the likelihood of ballast water released at a ship's destination containing new invasive aquatic species. The introduction of harmful aquatic organisms and pathogens to new environments has been identified as one of the four greatest threats to the world's oceans [United Nations Conference on Trade and Development (UNCTAD), REVIEW OF MARITIME TRANSPORT, (2016) at 87].

The International Convention for the Control and Management of Ships' Ballast Water and Sediments (BWM) [*International Convention for the Control and Management of Ships' Ballast Water and Sediments*, Feb. 16, 2004 (entered into force Sept. 8, 2017), IMO Doc. BWM/CONF/36 (hereinafter BWM)] aims to prevent the spread of harmful aquatic organisms from one region to another, by establishing standards and procedures for the management and control of ships' ballast water and sediments.

Article 2 General Obligations requires parties to give full and complete effect to the provisions of BWM and the Annex in order to prevent, minimize, and ultimately eliminate the transfer of harmful aquatic organisms and pathogens through the control and management of ships' ballast water and sediments. Under BWM, all ships in international traffic are required to manage their ballast water and sediments to a certain standard, according to a ship-specific ballast water management plan. All ships will also have to carry a ballast water record book and an international ballast water management certificate. The ballast water management standards will be phased in over a period of time, eventually resulting in the installation of an on-board ballast water treatment system.

b. Accidental Pollution

Over the years, accidental pollution of the marine environment—especially in the form of oil spills—has given rise to an extensive system of international agreements for the prevention and containment of such disasters. At the most general level, UNCLOS provides a requirement that States notify other affected States in the case of imminent danger or damage to the marine environment [UNCLOS at art. 198]. It also mandates that States cooperate in the development of contingency plans to respond to these emergencies [*Id.* at art. 199]. To this end, States have added a number of safety protocols to the UNEP Regional Seas Conventions—providing a framework for collaboration and specific response plans. In addition to these protocols, the International Convention on Oil Pollution Preparedness, Response and Co-operation (OPRC) established a broader role for the IMO in coordinating action among parties [*International Convention on Oil Pollution Preparedness, Response and Co-Operation,* Nov. 30, 1990 (entered into force May 13, 1995), 30 I.L.M. 733 (hereinafter OPRC)].

i. 1969 International Convention Relating to Intervention on the High Seas in Cases of Oil Pollution Casualties (1969 Intervention Convention)

To clarify extra-jurisdictional powers of States, the international community created one of the earliest environmental pollution treaties with the 1969 International Convention Relating to Intervention on the High Seas In Cases of Oil Pollution Casualties (1969 Intervention Convention), [*1969 International Convention Relating to Intervention on the High Seas In Cases of Oil Pollution Casualties*, Nov. 29, 1969 (in force May 6, 1975), 26 U.S.T. 765 (hereinafter 1969 Intervention Convention)]. Developed in response to another major oil spill, the *Torrey Canyon* disaster, in which a tanker mishap caused massive damage to the coastlines of Britain and France, the 1969 Intervention Convention lays down the requirements for a coastal State's intervention during a high seas accident. Under the 1969 Intervention Convention, parties may take measures on the high seas as necessary "to prevent, mitigate, or eliminate grave and imminent danger to their coastline" [*Id.* at art. I(1)]. The 1969 Intervention Convention also provides mandatory notification and consultation procedures with regard to flag States and other interested parties, except in cases of extreme urgency [*Id.* at art. III]. All actions taken by an intervening coastal State must be proportionate to the actual or threatened damage, or the State may be liable to those unreasonably harmed [*Id.* at arts. V & VI].

In the 1973 Protocol Relating to the Intervention on the High Seas of Pollution by Substances Other Than Oil (1973 Intervention Protocol), the parties extended the rules of the original convention to cover other hazardous substances [*1973 Protocol Relating to the Intervention on the High Seas of Pollution by Substances Other Than Oil*, Nov. 2, 1973 (entered into force Mar. 30, 1983), 34 U.S.T. 3407 (hereinafter 1973 Intervention Protocol)]. The 1973 Intervention Protocol creates a list of such substances, but also allows action to control any accident involving "those other substances which are liable to create hazards to human health, to harm living resources and marine life, to damage amenities, or to interfere with other legitimate uses of the sea" [*Id.* at art. I(2)]. Concerning the latter group of unlisted substances, the burden of proof shifts to the intervening coastal State to prove a "grave and imminent danger" analogous to that of a listed substance [*Id.* at art. I(3)]. The 1973 Intervention Protocol was amended to include a revised list of substances in 1991, 1996, and 2002.

In dealing with intervention, UNCLOS drops the requirement of "grave and imminent danger" and allows a coastal State the right to take any measures proportionate to the actual or threatened damage [art. 221]. No reference is made here to the coastal State's EEZ. Therefore, UNCLOS appears to apply the same standard of proportionality to actions taken in the EEZ as to those taken on the high seas under the 1969 Intervention Convention and the 1973 Intervention Protocol. The only significant difference is that UNCLOS discards the "grave and imminent danger" threshold for both the EEZ and high seas.

ii. 1990 International Convention on Oil Pollution Preparedness, Response and Co-Operation (OPRC)

Parties to the OPRC are required to establish measures for dealing with pollution incidents, either nationally or in cooperation with other States. Under OPRC, each party must require its flagships to carry on board "an oil pollution emergency plan" that adheres to the criteria put forth in MARPOL Annex I, Regulation 26 [OPRC at art. 3(1)(a)]. These ships also remain subject to inspection by the port State in accordance with MARPOL Articles 5 and 6 [*Id.* at art. 3(1)(b)]. Moreover, operators of offshore units—such as drilling rigs—must have oil pollution emergency plans [*Id.* at art. 3(2)]. At the State level, each party must develop a "national contingency plan for preparedness and response" as part of a national and regional system designed to deal with major oil spills [*Id.* at art. 6]. Parties also have quite specific procedures for reporting oil pollution incidents [*Id.* at art. 4] and for acting on such reports [*Id.* at art. 5]. Buttressing each of these obligations, the OPRC provides a strong oversight role for the IMO—a function designed to foster efficient use of the organization's expertise, and to effect fairness and universal compliance with its provisions.

iii. 2000 Protocol on Preparedness, Response and Cooperation for Pollution Incidents by Hazardous and Noxious Substances (HNS Protocol)

The Protocol on Preparedness, Response and Cooperation for Pollution Incidents by Hazardous and Noxious Substances (HNS Protocol) was established to fill a gap left by the OPRC. The OPRC focuses purely on oil pollutants, while the HNS Protocol applies to any substance other than oil that, if introduced into the marine environment, is likely to create hazards to human health, harm living resources and marine life, damage amenities, or interfere with other legitimate uses of the sea. The HNS Protocol follows the principles of the OPRC, and was formally adopted by States party to the OPRC at a Diplomatic Conference held at the IMO headquarters in March 2000. The HNS Protocol, like OPRC, aims to provide a global framework for international cooperation in combating major incidents or threats to marine pollution. Parties to the agreement are required to establish measures for dealing with pollution incidents, and ships are required to carry a shipboard emergency plan to deal with incidents involving hazardous and noxious substances.

The HNS Protocol entered into force in June 2007, and will ensure that ships carrying hazardous and noxious liquid substances are covered, or will be covered, by regimes similar to those already in existence for oil incidents.

iv. *2003 Protocol on Civil Liability and Compensation for Damage Caused by the Transboundary Effects of Industrial Accidents on Transboundary Waters (Industrial Accidents Protocol)*

Though only a regional agreement, the United Nations Commission for Europe (UNECE) Protocol on Civil Liability and Compensation for Damage Caused by the Transboundary Effects of Industrial Accidents on Transboundary Waters (Industrial Accidents Protocol), which was adopted at Kiev on May 21, 2003, points the way to a broader and more inclusive treaty [*Protocol on Civil Liability and Compensation for Damage Caused by the Transboundary Effects of Industrial Accidents on Transboundary Waters*, May 21, 2003, IUCN TRE-OO1372]. The Industrial Accidents Protocol sets up a strict liability scheme in Article 4, and defines out exceptions such as damage resulting from armed conflict; "natural phenomen[a] of exceptional, inevitable, unforeseeable and irresistible character;" damage "wholly the result of compliance with a compulsory measure of a public authority of the party;" or damage "wholly the result of the wrongful intentional conduct of a third party" [*Id.* at art. 4(2)(a)–(d)]. In Article 5, the Industrial Accidents Protocol establishes a fault liability system that traces to the wrongful, intentional, reckless, and negligent acts of "persons," not States [*Id.* at art. 5]. Annexes to the Protocol define hazardous substances and threshold quantities thereof, and are remarkably specific for an international environmental legal document.

c. Noise Pollution

A different kind of pollution is also gaining attention: underwater noise pollution. The U.S. and its North Atlantic Treaty Organization (NATO) allies operate loud military sonar that has been linked to the fate of stranded whales and other species, led astray by the noise. UNEP scientists issued a report that examined the effects of ocean noise on small crustaceans [Mark Palmer, *UN Recognizes Dangers of Ocean Noise*, 21 EARTH ISLAND JOURNAL 14 (2006)].

In 2005, the International Ocean Noise Coalition successfully lobbied the United Nations (UN) to acknowledge the dangers of ocean noise to marine life, particularly its effect on whales. The UN passed a resolution encouraging "further studies and consideration of the impacts of ocean noise on marine living resources" [*Id.*] While the scope and severity of the problem pales in comparison to coral reef destruction, marine noise pollution is an important proxy of the visibility of marine life conservation measures in the international community. Indeed, because noise pollution does not cause property damage or economic losses to businesses, often the driving force in other "environmental measures," the fact that the UN is addressing it is an indication of genuine environmental concern. Moreover, because of the long reach of sonar and its widespread use on the open seas, it is a problem uniquely suited to an international solution.

d. Pollution from Trade Vessels

Several new treaties relating to the conservation of marine living resources deal with ship pollution from a uniquely environmental standpoint. The IMO developed the International Convention on the Control of Anti-Fouling Systems on Ships in 2001 [*International Convention on the Anti-Fouling Systems on Ships*, Oct. 18, 2001, IMO Doc. AFS/CONF/26] and the BWM in 2004. Both of these treaties are directed at protecting the marine environment from ship pollution, and are specifically focused on threats to marine biodiversity.

e. State Responsibility (SR)

The principle of State responsibility (SR) for wrongful actions affecting the marine environment remains a well-settled rule of international law. UNCLOS codifies the principle in Article 235(1), asserting "States are responsible for the fulfillment of their international obligations concerning the protection and preservation of the marine environment" [UNCLOS at art. 235(1)]. Therefore, both flag and coastal States may find themselves liable for actions taken or not taken in accordance with international law. As to the specific liability imposed, most commentators consider the standard "due diligence" rather than "strict liability" [Birnie, et al., *supra* at 217–219]. In fact, although several instances exist in which flag States have paid compensation for oil tanker accidents, injured parties have not targeted States concerning marine pollution. Instead, given the elaborate compensation scheme outlined below, nearly all claimants for oil pollution accidents have looked to private entities for a remedy.

f. Civil Liability (CL)

The two conventions that follow provide a two-tiered system of compensation. The primary responsibility for compensation rests with the tanker owner under the 1969 Intervention Convention Civil Liability for Oil Pollution Damage (1969 CLC). This is a regime of strict liability with a pre-determined ceiling on compensation. The 1971 International Convention on the Establishment of an International Fund for Compensation for Oil Pollution Damage (Fund Convention) offers a supplementary source of compensation based on a fund.

i. *1969 International Convention on Civil Liability for Oil Pollution Damage (1969 CLC) and the 1992 Protocol to Amend the Convention*

The 1969 CLC created a system for awarding compensation as well as limiting the liability incurred by the owner of a ship involved in an oil pollution accident. It placed the liability for damage on the owner of the ship from which the polluting oil escaped or was discharged. Subject to a number of specific exceptions, this liability is strict. In 1992, the Protocol to Amend the 1969 CLC clarified that "pollution damage" includes damage to the marine environment, though "compensation for impairment of the environment other than loss of profit from such impairment shall be limited to costs of reasonable measures of reinstatement actually undertaken or to be undertaken" [Protocol to Amend the 1969 CLC at art. I(6)(a)]. In other words, claimants will not receive speculative awards for environmental damage, but will only obtain compensation for actual restoration of the marine ecosystem.

According to an allocation procedure based on gross tonnage, the total compensation of a ship owner remains limited for any particular accident. In arriving at the right total some calculation is involved. For example, each "unit of tonnage"—computed in accordance with measurement regulations—corresponds to a certain number of "units of account." Under the Protocol to Amend the 1969 CLC, this translates into three million units of account for the first 5,000 units of tonnage, and 420 units of account for each unit of tonnage thereafter [*Id.* at art. V(1)]. A ceiling of 59.7 million units of account exists for any specific accident. To qualify for the ceiling, the owner must deposit funds with the appropriate court constituting the total amount of its liability—converting the specified units of account (or "Special Drawing Rights" (SDR) as defined by the International Monetary Fund (IMF)) into national currency according to IMF procedures. Claimants then receive compensation from the fund "in proportion to the amounts of their established claims" [*Id.* at art. V(4)].

Under the 1969 CLC, the owner cannot take advantage of the limit on liability if the owner's "actual fault or privity" caused the accident [1969 CLC at art. V(2)]. The Protocol to Amend the 1969 CLC changes this provision, only disallowing the limit on liability when the owner's actions or omissions intentionally or recklessly caused the pollution damage. Under both conventions, the owner of a tanker must hold insurance in the amount of its potential fund contribution, and the ship must carry a certificate attesting to that fact on board at all times [*Id.* at art. VII]. From May 16, 1998, parties to the Protocol to Amend the 1969 CLC ceased to be parties to the 1969 CLC due to a mechanism for compulsory denunciation of the "old" regime established in the Protocol to Amend the 1969 CLC. However, for the time being, the two regimes co-exist, since there are a number of States that are party to the 1969 CLC but have not yet ratified the Protocol to Amend the 1969 CLC—which is intended to eventually replace the 1969 CLC. Amendments made in 2000 raised the compensation limits by 50% compared to the limits set in the Protocol to Amend the 1969 CLC.

ii. 1971 International Convention on the Establishment of an International Fund for Compensation for Oil Pollution Damage (Fund Convention)

The Fund Convention creates a burden sharing system in which the owners of oil cargo, such as oil companies, contribute to the overall cost of a tanker accident. In this way ship owners do not shoulder the entire cost of such a catastrophe. The Fund Convention adopts most of the definitions of the 1969 CLC, and by protocol in 1992, incorporates the definitions of the Protocol to Amend the 1969 CLC. To date, much confusion has occurred under the Fund Convention concerning the application of the term "pollution damage" to environmental harm. However, in adopting the definition from the Protocol to Amend the 1969 CLC, discussed above, the 1992 Protocol to the Fund Convention will now allow compensation for "reasonable measures of reinstatement actually undertaken or to be undertaken" [Protocol to the Fund Convention at art. I(1)].

As was the case with the 1992 Protocol to Amend the 1969 CLC, the main purpose of the Protocol to the Fund Convention was to modify the entry into force requirements and increase compensation amounts. The scope of coverage was extended in line with the 1992 CLC Protocol. The 1992 Protocol to the Fund Convention also established a separate International Oil Pollution Compensation Fund, known as the 1992 Fund, which is managed in London by a Secretariat, as with the 1971 Fund. In practice, the Fund

Convention and its 1992 counterpart exist solely as additional sources of restitution for injured "persons"—whether individuals, corporations, or States. To this end, such persons have access to the Protocol to the Fund Convention only if "unable to obtain full and adequate compensation" under the Protocol to Amend the 1969 CLC for the following reasons: (a) the Protocol to Amend the 1969 CLC is inapplicable; (b) the owner or its insurance company cannot pay; or (c) the damage exceeds that allowed under the Protocol to Amend the 1969 CLC [*Id.* at art. 4(1)]. As in the Protocol to Amend the 1969 CLC, the Protocol to the Fund Convention itself establishes a limit on the total contribution the Fund might make to a particular accident, in most cases in the amount of 135 million "units of account," or SDR, as converted into national currency by the IMF [*Id.* at art. 4]. This limit was raised to 203 million SDR by the 2000 Amendments. An insurance mechanism that attempts to spread the cost of a single accident among all oil cargo owners, the 1992 Fund obtains its own contributions from these entities through the contracting parties, basing each assessment on the number of tons of oil cargo received during the preceding year. The 2003 Protocol established another fund to supplement the 1992 Fund with an additional tier of compensation. Participation in this Protocol is optional, and the total compensation for a single incident is limited to 750 million SDR.

iii. 2001 International Convention on Civil Liability for Bunker Oil Pollution Damage (Bunker Convention)

A significant gap in the international regime for compensating victims of oil spills from ships was found in the liability and compensation for pollution from ships' bunkers. To remedy this, the International Convention on Civil Liability for Bunker Oil Pollution Damage (Bunker Convention) was adopted by the IMO in 2001 "to ensure that adequate, prompt, and effective compensation is available to persons who suffer damage caused by spills of oil, when carried as fuel in ships' bunkers" [*International Convention on Civil Liability for Bunker Oil Pollution Damage,* Mar. 27, 2001, LEG/CONF.12/19 (hereinafter Bunker Convention)]. The Bunker Convention is designed to work with the 1969 CLC to broaden the scope of liability coverage. As with the 1969 CLC, a key requirement in the Bunker Convention is the need for the registered owner of a vessel to maintain compulsory insurance coverage. However, the Bunker Convention does not establish independent limits like many related agreements, instead relying on the regimes of relevant State parties.

iv. 2010 International Convention on Liability and Compensation for Damage in Connection with the Carriage of Hazardous and Noxious Substances and Protocol to the Convention (2010 HNS Convention)

In 1996, the IMO adopted the International Convention on Liability and Compensation for Damage in Connection with the Carriage of Hazardous and Noxious Substances by Sea (HNS Convention). The HNS Convention is based on the model of the 1992 CLC. In 2010, an International Conference adopted a Protocol to the 1996 HNS Convention (HNS Protocol), which was designed to address the practical problems that had been perceived to prevent many States from ratifying the HNS Convention. Together, these treaties constitute the 2010 HNS Convention [International Maritime Organization (IMO), *An Overview of the International Convention on Liability and Compensation for Damage in connection with the Carriage of Hazardous and Noxious Substances By Sea, 2010, available at* http://www.hnsconvention. org/fileadmin/IOPC_Upload/hns/files/HNS%20Conv ention%20Overview_e.pdf last visited Apr. 2017)]. The regime established by the 2010 HNS Convention is largely modeled on the existing regime for oil pollution from tankers set up under the 1969 CLC and the Fund Convention, discussed above.

The HNS regime is governed by the 2010 HNS Convention, the purpose of which is to provide adequate, prompt, and effective compensation for loss or damage to persons, property, and the environment arising from the carriage of hazardous and noxious substances by sea. The Convention covers both pollution damage and damage caused by other risks, e.g. fire and explosion. Under the 2010 HNS Convention, the ship owner is liable for the loss or damage up to a certain amount, which is covered by insurance (1st tier). A compensation fund (the HNS Fund) will provide additional compensation when the victims do not obtain full compensation from the ship owner or its insurer (2nd tier). The HNS Fund will be funded by those companies and other entities that receive hazardous and noxious substances after sea transport in a Member State in excess of the thresholds laid down in the HNS Convention.

As of writing, however, the 2010 HNS Convention has not come into force [International Maritime Organization (IMO), *IMO Secretary-General urges States to ratify 2010 HNS Protocol as signature period ends,* (Nov. 1, 2011), *available at* http://www.imo.org/en/MediaCentre/PressBriefings/Pages/53-hns-2010.aspx (last visited Apr. 2017)]. Consequently, it is not clear if and when the 2010 HNS Convention will enter into force and this remains an important gap in the global liability and compensation regime.

D.   POLLUTION CAUSED BY OFFSHORE INSTALLATIONS

1.   ABOUT OFFSHORE OIL PRODUCTION

Offshore oil production accounts for about 30% of total world oil production, and offshore gas production accounts for about half of the world production of natural gas. According to a report by the NRC, there were about 8,300 fixed or floating offshore platforms worldwide in 1999 [NRC 2003]. According to the UNEP's Offshore Oil and Gas Environment Forum, there are more than 6,500 offshore oil and gas installations worldwide, with about 4,000 in the U.S. Gulf of Mexico, 950 in Asia, 700 in the Middle East, and 400 in Europe [UNEP & OGP, *Environmental management in oil and gas exploration and production* (1997)].

Offshore drilling for oil and natural gas on the continental shelf is carried out in many waters and sometimes at large depths. Three different types of offshore platforms are found in waters of more than half the nations on earth: concrete, jack up, and floating platforms. They can float while being moved, and often while drilling. Further, offshore rigs have drilled in waters over 7,500 feet deep and as far as 200 miles from shore [National Ocean Industries Association (NOIA), *About offshore oil and gas*, *available at* http://www.noia.org/ (last visited Apr. 2017)].

2.   THE DEEPWATER HORIZON OIL SPILL

The Deepwater Horizon explosion and oil spill in April 2010 resulted in the largest accidental marine oil spill in the history of the petroleum industry [Campbell Robertson & Clifford Krauss, *Gulf Spill is the Largest of its Kind, Scientists Say,* NEW YORK TIMES (Aug. 2, 2010)]. The explosion killed 11 men working on the platform and injured 17 others. By the time the leak was stopped by capping the gushing wellhead, the spill released nearly 4.9 million barrels of crude oil, making it the largest accidental oil spill in history [Amanda Briney, *Geography of the World's Largest Oil Spills,* ABOUT.COM (Jan. 1, 2011)]. The 4.9 million barrels spilled amounts to about 585,000 tons, which is many times more than the oil that is spilled into the sea annually by tankers.

The spill has resulted in oil plumes, causing damage to ecosystems, fisheries, health, and tourism in the U.S. Researchers from the National Institute for Undersea Science and Technology identified oil plumes in the deep waters of the Gulf of Mexico including one as large as 10 miles long, three miles wide, and 300 feet thick in certain areas [Justin Gillis, *Giant Plumes of Oil Forming Under the Gulf,* NEW YORK TIMES (May 15, 2010)]. The deepest oil plume the researchers discovered was near the seafloor, at about 4,200 feet, while the shallowest oil plume was at about 2,300 feet [*Id.*]

While Cuba and some Caribbean States have expressed concern about the impact of the spill, as of this writing no nation had made claims against the U.S. for the oil plume. However, the path of an oil plume is difficult to predict, and its effects may still be unknown for many years [Jessica Gresko, *Cloudy with a Chance of Tar Balls,* WASHINGTON POST (Jul. 19, 2010)]. Unfortunately, the Deepwater Horizon oil spill is not an isolated example, and there have been numerous other accidents, collapses, explosions, and sunk oil rigs all over the world, which have discharged millions of barrels of oil into the oceans

[Alonso Soto, et al., *Timeline—Major offshore accidents in the global oil industry* (May 13, 2010) Reuters].

3.   ENVIRONMENTAL IMPACTS OF RIGS AND PLATFORMS

The impacts of oil on the marine environment have already been examined above, but rigs and platforms have other environmental impacts. These environmental impacts begin during the first stage of offshore oil operations with the geological surveying of the seabed. As already mentioned in the discussion of noise pollution, many marine animals possess hearing organs designed to detect low-frequency sounds [S. Patin, *Environmental Impact of the Offshore Oil & Gas Industry* (1999) at 3]. The intense seismic wave impulses used for geological surveying may harm or destroy the sound detection organs of marine animals, or alter their important behaviors involving sound production.

The most adverse environmental impacts of rigs and platforms usually occur during the exploration and production stages. Offshore activities, such as platform emplacement, dredging, pipe-laying, and construction of support facilities, cause physical disturbances and produce various emissions and discharges of pollutants into the oceans [Sakhalin Energy Investment Company, *Environmental Impact Assessment: Project Description,* OFFSHORE FIELD DEVELOPMENT (2003) at 2.2.3]. Pollution also occurs from disposing of sewage and garbage from offshore platforms, flaring natural gas, and discharging produced formation waters into the sea. However, the greatest pollution hazard comes directly from offshore drilling operations, which are always associated with discharges of drilling fluids, mud, and drill cuttings [C. Brown, *International Environmental Law in the Regulation of Offshore Installations and Seabed Activities: The Case for a South Pacific Regional Protocol,* AUSTRALIAN RESOURCES AND ENERGY LAW JOURNAL, vol. 17 (1998) at 110].

4.   LEGAL RESPONSE

The offshore petroleum industry is subject to sparse and fragmented international regulations, which appear to be dubiously enforced. There is no treaty overlay similar to that dealing with vessels that provides effective regulation for all aspects of offshore oil and gas activities. The foundation for a global framework for controlling offshore rigs and platforms is established by UNCLOS, however UNCLOS lacks standards and specific rules, and does not create machinery for implementation or enforcement. The 1990 OPRC does create rules dealing with accidents, but does not appear to be diligently or strenuously enforced. Despite this, the IMO has determined that there is no compelling need to develop a comprehensive international convention dealing with accidental or operational oil spills [International Maritime Organization (IMO), *Report of the Legal Committee on the work of its one hundred and second session,* (2015) LEG 102/12. London].

a. Operational Pollution

i. United Nations Convention on the Law of the Sea (UNCLOS)

UNCLOS creates a general obligation to protect and preserve the marine environment [UNCLOS at arts. 192 & 194], which applies to offshore installations [John Warren Kindt, *The Law of the Sea: Offshore Installations and Marine Pollution,* 12 PEPP. L. R. 381 (1985)]. In addition, UNCLOS specifically addresses offshore installations and authorizes States to build them in their EEZ [UNCLOS at art. 60] and the Continental Shelf [*Id.* at art. 80]. Furthermore, UNCLOS directs States to prevent, reduce, and control pollution from the operational aspects of:

> installations and devices used in exploration or exploitation of natural resources of the sea-bed and subsoil, in particular measures for preventing accidents and dealing with emergencies, ensuring safety of operations at sea, and regulating the design, construction, equipment, operation and manning of such installations or devices [*Id.* at art. 194(3)(c)].

UNCLOS further requires coastal States to adopt laws and regulations controlling pollution arising from seabed activities and artificial island installations and structures subject to their jurisdiction [*Id.* at art. 208(1)]. States are also required to establish global and regional rules, standards, and recommended practices and procedures to prevent, reduce, and control pollution of the marine environment [*Id.* at art. 208(5)]. However, UNCLOS fails to establish any specific rules or standards, or provide methods and procedures for internal compliance, implementation, and enforcement.

ii. 1972 Convention on the Prevention of Marine Pollution by Dumping of Wastes and Other Matter (London Convention)

The 1972 London Convention, discussed above, exists as the primary vehicle for international regulation of dumping. As defined by the London Convention, dumping includes the platforms or other man-made structures at sea, as well as the deliberate sinking of those structures as a method of disposal [London Convention at art. III(1)]. Dumping, however, does not include the discharge of oil and other harmful substances in the normal operation of those structures. What this means is that the London Convention does not control operational pollution.

iii. 1973 International Convention for the Prevention of Pollution from Ships (MARPOL)

MARPOL, which is discussed above, is primarily concerned with ships. However, it also applies to fixed and floating offshore platforms when they are in mobile configuration [MARPOL at Annex 1, reg. 21(a)]. MARPOL requires offshore structures to be equipped with the same pollution control devices required for ships of 400 gross tones and above, including oil discharge monitoring and controlling systems, as well as oily-water separating equipment and sludge tanks [*Id.* at Annex IV, reg. 8]. MARPOL prohibits the discharge of sewage into the sea, and the discharge of oil in mixtures greater than 15 parts per million (ppm) in certain areas [*Id.* at Annex 1]. Although MARPOL generally applies to offshore platforms in mobile configuration, it does not address many other operational aspects of offshore oil and gas exploration and production—such as geological surveying, exploration and production, and decommissioning—which may also cause harm to the marine environment.

b. Accidental Pollution

i. *1990 International Convention on Oil Pollution Preparedness, Response and Co-Operation (OPRC)*

OPRC, discussed above, sets out the pollution emergency plans for vessels, offshore drilling units, production platforms, and onshore facilities. OPRC defines offshore units comprehensively, to include both floating and fixed structures engaged in exploration, production, loading, and unloading of oil [OPRC at art. 4]. Parties to OPRC must require offshore unit operators to report discharges [*Id.* at art. 6]. OPRC encourages states to cooperate and establish national, as well as regional, systems for oil pollution preparedness and response [*Id.* at arts. 7 & 9]. It also covers requirements relating to mutual assistance and international cooperation in matters such as the exchange of information on the capabilities of states to respond to oil pollution incidents, preparation of oil pollution emergency plans, the exchange of reports on incidents of significance that may affect the marine environment, as well as research and development aspects of combating oil pollution. OPRC also contains very specific and detailed provisions that deal with the prevention of marine pollution from offshore installations, and it is probably the most important international legal document that regulates pollution of the marine environment resulting from offshore oil and gas activities [Mikhail Kashubsky, *Marine Pollution from Offshore Oil and Gas Industry: Review of Major Conventions and Russian Law*, MarStudies 31 (2006) at 151].

c. Liability

Most treaties dealing with the liability of ships, discussed above, do not apply to offshore installations. UNCLOS provides a partial exception, because it invokes SR and affirms the responsibility of states for the fulfillment of their international obligations (*see* Ch. 3). However, we have seen in Chapter 3 that SR is an anachronistic and inefficient way of holding States accountable, and that it is necessary to establish specific rules and standards and provide internal procedures for their enforcement. Not surprisingly, as of this writing there have been no claims made by States attempting to hold others responsible for the non-fulfillment of their UNCLOS obligations relating to offshore structures.

UNCLOS also calls for the establishment of a liability system. It requires States to ensure that recourse is available in accordance with their legal systems for prompt and adequate compensation, or other relief, in respect of damage caused by pollution of the marine environment by natural or judicial persons under their jurisdiction, and further requires States to cooperate for the purposes of doing so [UNCLOS at art. 235(2)(3)]. Again, there are no standards or deadlines for doing so, and such a liability system has not been established.

E.   CONCLUSIONS

Pollution caused by vessels offers a good example of how IEL should work. As we have noted, laws now cover all aspects of maritime transportation. We have also drawn attention to some areas, such as the transport of hazardous substances, which are not addressed by law. Despite these deficiencies, the extent to which ship owners, owners of oil, and States have agreed to treaties that are overseen by the IMO is remarkable.

The same approbative assessment cannot be made about the legal response to offshore oil. Offshore oil activities are usually carried out on the continental shelf of a coastal State, as happened in the Deepwater Horizons oil spill discussed above. In many such cases, coastal States are likely to be the victim of an oil pollution incident. In other cases, oil pollution from offshore installations can cross maritime boundaries. Offshore oil operations in some sea areas, like the semi enclosed South China Seas, are more prone to lead to multilateral, not merely bilateral, damage. Therefore, it behooves the oil community, and particularly the IMO, to step up to the plate and negotiate a multilateral CL regime, similar to those applicable to ships. It is baffling as to how the IMO can advance treaties dealing with pollution damage caused by ships, and ignore the extensive harm caused by offshore drilling operations.

CHAPTER TWELVE
DUMPING

A. NATURE OF THE PROBLEM

The wastes generated in today's world need to be neutralized or disposed of in a manner that is both effective and efficient. We have noted that optimal waste treatment includes conversion of wastes into less taxing forms that will better enable the environment to dilute, degrade, assimilate, or absorb them. Conversion of wastes also includes emission of gases and particles into the atmosphere, discharge of sludge and liquid effluent into the aquatic environment, and burial on land (*see* Ch. 9). To this list we must now add "dumping" wastes directly into the ocean. Approximately 12% of pollutants and toxic materials that enter the ocean do so through dumping [International Chamber of Shipping, SHIPPING AND THE ENVIRONMENT: A CODE OF PRACTICE (1999)].

"Dumping" is a term of art referring to a particular form of marine pollution that is not included in land-based (*see* Ch. 10) or vessel-based pollution (*see* Ch. 11, *infra* for a legal definition). Specifically, dumping is confined to a form of marine pollution in which wastes, often containing toxic materials, are taken by ship and dumped or incinerated on the high seas. Dumping does not, therefore, typically refer to land-based discharges of wastes into the ocean, estuaries, or rivers from direct outfalls, or to vessel-based pollution caused by accidental or deliberate discharges by oil tankers or other ships. However, since what is dumped is generated on land, it is difficult to refute the rationale of the Convention for the Protection of the Marine Environment of the North East Atlantic (OSPAR Convention), which treats dumping as a species of land-based pollution (*see* Ch. 10).

In the past, dumping hazardous waste into the ocean was seen as an acceptable method of disposal because of the relatively low economic costs and the perception that oceans could readily assimilate unlimited quantities of waste. Ocean dumping has become less favored as its effects on marine ecology have become apparent. Questions have also arisen concerning the reasonableness of allowing industrialized countries to utilize a shared resource (the oceans) without regard to the risks and costs imposed on future generations [Patricia Birnie, Alan Boyle and Catherine Redgwell, INTERNATIONAL LAW AND THE ENVIRONMENT, THIRD EDITION (2009) at 467].

B. SOURCES AND ENVIRONMENTAL IMPACTS

Many types of waste that are difficult to dispose of on land have traditionally been dumped directly into oceans and rivers without regulation. This includes many hazardous materials, such as sewage, industrial effluents, sludge, radioactive wastes, and polluted dredged spoils. A more detailed review of the characteristics and environmental impacts of these materials is provided in Chapters 9 and 10. Bulky but relatively harmless materials such as construction waste, wreckage, sand, and excavation debris have also been subject to widespread dumping. These activities have had significant repercussions in marine food chains and may impact deep-sea biodiversity and ecosystem health.

C.   REMEDIAL OBJECTIVES

As we have noted in Chapter 9, dumping is a symptom of the malaise of ever-spiraling wastes. Remedial objectives, generally, have largely failed to deal with the root source of toxic wastes, which lies in human demand for products that can only be met by generating such wastes. Moreover, the international environmental community has failed to adopt a truly integrated approach to waste disposal and pollution control.

We shall see that the United Nations Convention on the Law of the Sea (UNCLOS) and the 1972 Convention on the Prevention of Marine Pollution by Dumping of Wastes and Other Matter (London Convention) did not prohibit all ocean dumping. Instead, they attempted to control it by prohibiting the disposal of particular wastes based on their toxicity, persistence, bioaccumulation, and likelihood of widespread environmental exposure. Today, this regime has been expanded by the 1992 OSPAR Convention, which takes a more comprehensive view of waste management by including ocean dumping within land-based and other sources of pollution. In addition, the 1996 Protocol to the Convention on the Prevention of Marine Pollution by Dumping Wastes And Other Matters (London Protocol) incorporates crucial features of the OSPAR Convention and is more fully discussed below.

D. LEGAL RESPONSE

The international attitude toward ocean dumping has moved from an initial stage of acceptance, through a phase of stricter regulation, to the present general trend of prohibiting the dumping of particular kinds of wastes. Especially in recent years, the international community has tightened the rules related to dumping of hazardous substances by, for example, banning all ocean dumping of radioactive wastes. The general legal regime for dumping is defined by UNCLOS, which sets forth a framework of rules for States to follow. The London Convention and the London Protocol govern more specific actions, and a system of regional agreements facilitates compliance.

1. 1972 CONVENTION ON THE PREVENTION OF MARINE POLLUTION BY DUMPING OF WASTES AND OTHER MATTER (LONDON CONVENTION)

The 1972 London Convention is the primary vehicle for international regulation of dumping. As of 2017, 89 States have signed and ratified the treaty. With almost half of the world's States as parties to the London Convention, including nearly all of the largest waste-producing States, the treaty represents a significant step in the international regulation of dumping.

As defined by the London Convention, dumping includes the "disposal of wastes or other matter from vessels, aircraft, platforms or other man-made structures at sea" as well as the deliberate sinking of those structures as a method of disposal [London Convention at art. III(1)]. Dumping, however, does not include the discharge of oil and other harmful substances in the normal operation of those structures, which in general is covered by the International Convention for the Prevention of Pollution from Ships (MARPOL) (*see* Ch. 11).

In regulating the disposal of wastes, the London Convention employs a listing and permit system that is intended to cover the entire spectrum of dumping at sea. For substances listed in Annex I, or the "black list," dumping is prohibited except in emergency situations [*Id.* at arts. IV(1)(a) & V(2)]. In addition to dangerous substances such as mercury, cadmium, and crude oil, this list includes "netting and ropes" which may "interfere materially with fishing, navigation or other legitimate uses of the sea" [*Id.* at Annex I(4)]. In contrast, the London Convention allows the dumping of substances on Annex II, or the "grey list," but requires obtaining a "special permit" to do so [*Id.* at art. IV(1)(b)]. Materials on this list include trace amounts of the toxic substances listed in Annex I as well as less hazardous wastes such as chromium and nickel [*Id.* at Annex II(A)]. The London Convention allows the dumping of all other wastes at sea, requiring only that the vessel obtain a "prior general permit" [*Id.* at art. IV(1)(c)].

The responsibility for issuing these permits, and thereafter reporting the information to the International Maritime Organization (IMO), falls upon the appropriate authorities of a party for all wastes loaded in its territory [*Id.* at art. VI(2)(a)]. On the other hand, when a flag ship loads wastes in the territory of a State not party to the London Convention, the responsibility for permitting and reporting remains with the flag State [*Id.* at art. VI(2)(b)]. In considering whether to grant either type of permit, the designated authorities must look to the broad dictates of Annex III, which mandates that they take into account both the characteristics of the material dumped and the dump site, as well as such general considerations and conditions as possible effects on marine life and the availability of practical land-based alternatives [*Id.* at Annex III(A)–(C)].

Especially for an older treaty, the London Convention created an innovative and flexible rule-making system. Consultative Meetings of the parties may adopt an Amendment to the Convention by a two-thirds majority of those present, but such a change only comes into force for those parties who accept it [*Id.* at art. XV(1)(a)]. For an Amendment to any Annex—which must be based on scientific or technical considerations—again a two-thirds majority at the Consultative Meeting passes the change. Here, however, the burden shifts as only parties who denounce the Amendment within a certain time frame remain unbound [*Id.* at art. XV(2)].

In considering the special example of radioactive waste dumping, we can see the flexibility of the above system at work. For instance, the London Convention originally placed high-level radioactive wastes in Annex I, and low-level radioactive wastes in Annex II. In 1983, however, and then again in 1985, the Consultative Meeting passed a non-binding resolution that installed a moratorium on the dumping of all radioactive wastes, including low-level wastes. From then on the political and scientific debate concerning the potential harm of radioactive dumping intensified, culminating with the Russian admission that the former Soviet Union had repeatedly dumped both high- and low-level wastes for decades. As a final measure, in 1993 the Consultative Meeting amended Annex I to include all "radioactive wastes or other radioactive matter" [*Id.* at Annex I(6)]. In response, only Russia officially filed a declaration of non-acceptance with the IMO, in effect allowing it legally to continue the disposal of low-level radioactive wastes at sea. For all other parties, the dumping of radioactive material of any type remained illegal. In 2005 the issue was finally brought to a uniform conclusion, with the formal acceptance by the Russian Federation of the 1993 ban—thus finally bringing the prohibition into force for *all* contracting parties some 12 years after its adoption.

Thus, despite the ultimate resolution of the issue, the case of radioactive dumping, while reflecting the flexibility of the London Convention system, also reveals its limitations in controlling all dumping of an environmentally damaging nature. Furthermore, though in theory the permit and reporting system covers the entire spectrum of dumping at sea, States have had a difficult time in controlling illegal dumping by their own nationals [Philippe Sands & Jacqueline Peel, PRINCIPLES OF INTERNATIONAL ENVIRONMENTAL LAW, THIRD EDITION (2012) at 368]. Nonetheless, as a general rule, commentators point to the London Convention as one of the most successful environmental treaties to date for its significant role in the quantitative worldwide reduction of the disposal of wastes at sea [Birnie,Boyle and Redgwell, *supra*, at 472.

2.   1982 UNITED NATIONS CONVENTION ON THE LAW OF THE SEA (UNCLOS)

UNCLOS creates a comprehensive legal framework defining the features and extent of State jurisdiction for the implementation of IMO regulations. UNCLOS mandates that all States adopt measures "to prevent, reduce and control pollution of the marine environment by dumping" [UNCLOS at art. 210(1)]. However, in creating such measures, States may not establish standards that are "less effective" than global rules and standards [*Id.* at art. 210(6)]. In this way, UNCLOS establishes a "floor" of minimum protection that all States must follow, and that floor is the London Convention. Yet within its own territorial sea, Exclusive Economic Zone (EEZ) (*see* Ch. 13), or continental shelf, a State has the right to institute more stringent requirements than those of the London Convention [*Id.* at art. 210(5)]. Furthermore, in codifying customary international law, UNCLOS provides the coastal State with the right of prior approval to any dumping within its sovereign waters, which of course now includes both the EEZ and the continental shelf.

3.   1996 PROTOCOL TO THE CONVENTION ON THE PREVENTION OF MARINE POLLUTION BY DUMPING OF WASTES AND OTHER MATTER (LONDON PROTOCOL)

The London Protocol, which is intended to replace the 1972 London Convention, entered into force on March 24, 2006 after the requisite 26 States signed and ratified. As of 2016, 47 States have signed and ratified the treaty, representing approximately 38% of global shipping tonnage. The U.S. signed the London Protocol in 1998, and President George W. Bush submitted it to the Senate for advice and consent on September 4, 2007. However, the U.S. has not yet ratified the treaty.

The London Protocol marks a significant change in the approach to waste management. Substantively, the London Protocol replaces the selective restrictions on dumping imposed by the London Convention with a total ban on waste incineration, dumping of most materials, and exporting wastes to non-parties for the purposes of dumping or incineration at sea [London Protocol at arts. 5 & 6]. Even the limited exceptions to these bans, which may be granted in cases of serious, unavoidable threats to human health, safety, or the marine environment when there is no feasible less-harmful alternative, require substantial international consultation and oversight [*Id.* at art. 8]. The London Protocol joins a number of other international instruments such as the Stockholm Convention on Persistent Organic Pollutants (Stockholm POPs Convention) (*see* Ch. 9), the Cartagena Protocol on Biosafety (*see* Ch. 5), and the United Nations Framework Convention on Climate Change (UNFCCC) (*see* Ch. 6) in incorporating its own version of the elusive and ill-defined precautionary principle [Christopher D. Stone, *Is There a Precautionary Principle?* 31 ENVTL. L. REP. 10790 (2001) at 10799] (*see* Ch. 18 for fuller discussion of the precautionary principle). It also embodies the "polluter pays" principle and moves toward a more comprehensive strategy of waste reduction and prevention.

Unlike the London Convention that prohibits the dumping of specific listed materials, the London Protocol bans dumping of *any* material that is *not* listed in Annex 1 [London Protocol at art. 4(1)]. Materials currently listed are dredged materials; sewage sludge; industrial fish processing waste; vessels and offshore platforms; inert, inorganic geological material; organic material of natural origin; and bulky but not harmful materials like iron, steel, and concrete for which no waste disposal on land is possible [*Id.* at Annex 1(1)]. Dumping of radioactive materials, or of matter that could seriously impede fishing or navigation, is prohibited [*Id.* at Annex 1(3)].

While the London Convention permits the dumping of unlisted wastes, the London Protocol allows dumping permits to be issued only for listed substances. To list a new substance, the would-be polluter must conduct a scientific risk assessment of its probable impact on human health and the environment [*Id.* at Annex 2(7)], including complete information about the product's origins; physical, chemical, biochemical, and biological properties; toxicity; persistence; and tendency to accumulate or bio-transform in organisms or sediments [*Id.* at Annex 2(8)]. If this information is incomplete, the waste cannot be listed [*Id.* at Annex 2(7)].

The London Protocol adopts a proactive approach to the generation of wastes. Applicants for dumping permits are required to undertake an exhaustive self-evaluation of waste reduction and disposal strategies with a view toward avoiding dumping altogether by finding "environmentally preferable alternatives" [*Id.* at art. 4(1)]. To apply for a permit, a polluter must first conduct a "Waste Prevention Audit" to identify sources of the waste and find ways to reduce it at the source [*Id.* at Annex 2(2)]. This entails a complete evaluation of polluters' production systems, and a full assay of the feasibility of waste reduction via product reformulation, clean production technologies, process modification, input substitution, and recycling [*Id.* at Annex 2(3)]. If the audit reveals that one or more of these methods could feasibly reduce the amount of waste produced by the permit applicant, the applicant must formulate a general waste reduction strategy incorporating those methods, setting specific target reductions, and providing for future audits to ensure compliance.

Once the dumping permit applicant has conducted waste prevention analysis and implementation, the

London Protocol also requires it to submit a comparative risk assessment to demonstrate that it is unable to dispose of the waste in less environmentally harmful ways. In order of preference, disposal should be sought via reuse, recycling, destruction of hazardous materials, treatment to reduce or remove hazardous components, and disposal of the waste on land, into air, or in water [*Id.* at Annex 2(5)]. If the permitting authority finds that the permit applicant could utilize one of these less harmful alternatives without disproportionate cost, it may deny the permit. Similarly, the permit applicant must demonstrate that the specific dump site is the best feasible choice, taking into account factors like biological sensitivity of the area and the location of other possible uses of the sea [*Id.* at Annex 2(11)].

Finally, the London Protocol requires the permitting authority to conduct an assessment of the potential effects each disposal option could have on human health, its environmental costs, hazards, economics, and exclude the possibility of future uses of the waste, and issue or deny a permit based on that assessment [*Id.* at Annex 2(12)–(13)]. Extensive monitoring provisions are also incorporated to ensure compliance with the authority's guidelines and to verify that the environmental and health costs projected in the assessment were correct [*Id.* at Annex 2(16)].

For settlement of disputes, the London Protocol sets forth a detailed arbitration procedure paid for by the parties to the dispute [*Id.* at Annex 3]. This is a compulsory system of arbitration that significantly buttresses the role of arbitration, as distinct from judicial settlement, as a form of legal enforcement (*see* Ch. 3).

In 2006, parties to the London Protocol adopted an amendment regulating the sequestration of carbon dioxide (CO_2) in sub-seabed geological formations. With its entry into force on February 10, 2007, the amendment states that CO_2 streams may only be considered for permissible dumping if one of the following conditions is met: (1) disposal is into a sub-seabed geological formation; (2) it consists overwhelmingly of CO_2 (it may contain incidental associated substances derived from the source material and the capture and sequestration processes used); or (3) no wastes or other matter are added for the purpose of disposing of the CO_2. In effect, the amendment creates a basis under international environmental law (IEL) to regulate carbon capture and storage in sub-seabed geological formations for permanent isolation, as part of a suite of measures to tackle the challenge of climate change (*see* Ch. 6).

4.   REGIONAL TREATIES

A number of regional treaties have also dealt with the question of dumping, and in some cases these agreements have led to a tightening of standards beyond those of the London Convention. These regional treaties include: the Convention on the Protection of the Marine Environment of the Baltic Sea Area [*Convention on the Protection of the Marine*

Environment of the Baltic Sea Area, Apr. 9, 1992 (entered into force on Jan. 17, 2000), 13 I.L.M. 544]; the Convention on the Protection of the Black Sea Against Pollution [*Convention on the Protection of the Black Sea Against Pollution,* Apr. 21, 1992 (entered into force on Jan. 15, 1994), 32 I.L.M. 1101]; the accompanying Protocol on the Protection of the Black Sea Marine Environment Against Pollution by Dumping [*Protocol on the Protection of the Black Sea Marine Environment Against Pollution by Dumping,* Apr. 21, 1992 (entered into force on Jan. 15, 1994), 32 I.L.M. 1129]; the Convention for the Protection of the Natural Resources and Environment of the South Pacific Region (Noumea Convention) [*Convention for the Protection of the Natural Resources and Environment of the South Pacific Region,* Nov. 24, 1986 (entered into force Aug. 22, 1990), 26 I.L.M. 38 (hereinafter Noumea Convention)]; and the accompanying Protocol for the Prevention of Pollution of the South Pacific by Dumping [*Protocol for the Prevention of Pollution of the South Pacific by Dumping,* Nov. 24, 1986 (entered into force Aug. 22, 1990), 26 I.L.M. 38]. By far the most encouraging of the regional conventions is the OSPAR Convention, which takes an integrated approach and deals with land-based pollution and dumping together in one treaty (*see* Ch. 10).

E. CONCLUSIONS

The OSPAR Convention and the London Protocol demonstrate a more comprehensive ecosystem approach to protection. They more clearly define the strong presumption against dumping by disallowing the practice entirely—*except* for a small number of listed substances. These treaties point the way towards adopting an integrated approach to waste disposal and pollution control.

CHAPTER THIRTEEN
CONSERVATION OF MARINE LIVING RESOURCES

A. NATURE OF THE PROBLEM

Ninety percent of all marine life exists in ecosystems located in the shallow waters above continental shelves. While the oceans cover 70% of the earth's surface, continental shelves—the submerged extensions of the coastline at the edge of continents—form only a small fragment of the oceans. The proximity of these shallow waters to land and human populations exposes marine living resources and ecosystems to increasing environmental impacts from human activities (*see* Chs. 4 & 10).

As of this writing, approximately three billion people live within 200 kilometers (km) of a coastline, but that figure is likely to double by 2025 [Liz Creel, *Ripple Effects: Population and Coastal Regions,* POPULATION REFERENCE BUREAU (2011)]. Some 37% of the world's population lives within 100 km of the coast [United Nations Environment" Regional Seas, *Coastal Zone Management, available at* http://web. unep.org/regionalseas/what-we-do/coastal-zone-management (last visited Apr. 2017)], and three-quarters of all large cities are located on the coast [United Nations Environment Programme & United Nations Human Settlements Programme, *Coastal Area Pollution: The Role of Cities,* (Sept 2005)]. In the U.S., coastal regions make up only 17% of the nation's contiguous land area but are home to half the nation's population [NOAA Office for Coastal Management, *About the National Coastal Zone Management Program*, *available at* https://coast. noaa.gov/czm/about/?redirect=301ocm (last visited Apr. 2017); National Ocean Service, *Population Trends Along the Coastal United States: 1980–2008,* COASTAL TRENDS REPORT SERIES (Sept. 2004)]. Consequently, unless careful environmental management and planning are instituted, severe conflicts over coastal space and resource utilization are likely, and the degradation of natural resources will close development options [World Bank, GUIDELINES FOR INTEGRATED COASTAL STATE MANAGEMENT (1996)].

Burgeoning population and economic growth gives rise to oceanic over-exploitation and habitat destruction that threatens the health and bounty of the marine environment. Protecting marine living resources and ecosystems from this degradation is important not only for maintaining the world's ecological balance, but also for meeting the food needs of an increasing world population [*see* Daud Hassan, *International Conventions Relating to Land-Based Sources of Marine Pollution Control: Applications and Shortcomings,* 16 GEO. INT'L ENVT'L L.R. 657 (2004)] (*see also* Ch. 4).

B. SOURCES AND IMPACTS

In this section, we introduce and briefly canvass a few of the major human activities that adversely impact marine ecologies.

1. BIODIVERSITY DECLINE CAUSED BY OVER-EXPLOITATION OF FISH STOCKS

Over-exploitation of fish stocks has caused a serious decline in marine biodiversity in the world's fishing regions. Many modern fishing technologies yield a harvest rate exceeding the reproductive rate of fish, which results in the depletion or full exploitation of almost every commercial species of fish. Over-exploitation of commercially exported fish stocks continues to be a problem worldwide, particularly in many of Africa's fisheries, which also face issues of illegal, under-reported, and unregulated fishing [United Nations Environment Program, *Summary of the Sixth Global Environmental Outlook GEO-6—Regional Assessments: Key Findings and Policy Messages,* (May 2016) UNEP/EA.2/INF/17 at 3].

Driftnet fishing is a particularly devastating method of catching (or taking) fish, in which a single boat, or several boats working together, suspend a series of nylon nets up to 40 miles wide and 48 feet deep, catching everything in their wake [*see* Lakshman D. Guruswamy, et al. INTERNATIONAL ENVIRONMENTAL LAW AND WORLD ORDER, Second Edition (1999) at 747]. The result includes the illegal catch of undersized, pre-reproductive fish of the target species, as well as non-target species that are then thrown back into the ocean to die. Such illegal and unwanted fish, called "by-catch," may amount to as much as 30% of the legal catch. In addition, drowning or injury in fishing nets kills thousands of marine mammals, seabirds, and sea turtles each year. Dolphins are frequent victims because commercially valuable tuna often swim beneath them, and the dolphins become entangled in nets intended to catch the tuna. Driftnets are considered responsible for the near collapse of the Albacore tuna fishery in the South Pacific, and also contributed to the serious decline of the North American salmon fishery.

The 1989 Convention for the Prohibition of Fishing with Long Driftnets in the South Pacific entirely prohibits the fishing practice within a party's exclusive economic zone (EEZ) [*Convention for the Prohibition of Fishing with Long Driftnets in the South Pacific*, Nov. 23, 1989 (entered into force May 17, 1991), 29 I.L.M. 1454 at art. 3]. In the same year, the United Nations (UN) General Assembly recommended a moratorium on the use of large-scale pelagic driftnets in high seas fishing [UN, *Resolution on Large-Scale Pelagic Driftnet Fishing and its Impact on Living Marine Resources of the World's Oceans and Seas*, U.N.Doc. A/RES/44/225 (1989), 29 I.L.M. 1555, at 4(b)]. No official enforcement measures exist with the resolution, but the progressive development of soft law on the subject makes driftnet fishing on the high seas a politically unacceptable endeavor. Due to this legal pressure, Japan and Taiwan, two of the major driftnet fishing States, have ceased the practice altogether.

2.   EXPLOITATION OF MARINE MAMMALS

Prior to the international ban on whaling, whales were commercially hunted to the verge of extinction, exploited for their meat, oil, and baleen [Judith Berger-Eforo, *Sanctuary for the Whales: Will this Be the Demise of the International Whaling Commission or a Viable Strategy for the Twenty-First Century?,* 8 PACE INT'L L.R. 439 (1996) at 452]. Prior to the establishment of the whaling industry, it is estimated that more than 3.9 million whales swam in the world's oceans. By 1975, the whale population had shrunk to 2.1 million as a result of whaling [David S. Lessoff, *Jonah Swallows the Whale: An Examination of American and International Failures to Adequately Protect Whales from Impending Extinction,* 11 J. ENVTL. & LITIG. 413 (1996) at 419].

Additionally, sea otters and seals almost vanished during the 19th century, due to being hunted for their lush pelts. By 1911, the original sea otter population, estimated to be 150,000, was down to as few as 200 sea otters as a result of hunting [Michael Bhargava, *Of Otters and Orcas: Marine Mammals and Legal Regimes in the North Pacific,* 32 Ecology L.Q. 939 (2005) at 953]. Additionally, the killing of perhaps three or four million seals during the 19th century resulted in the serious depletion of seal populations, and led to international efforts to protect seals in the early 1900s.

Today, despite international efforts, whales and thousands of seals (including baby harp seals) are still killed illegally or under the guise of a legal taking for "scientific purposes." Furthermore, human demand for fish competes with the demand on those resources by other fish, seabirds, and marine mammals. Natural fishery environments are highly diverse, and fishing one or two commercial species causes imbalances in the many ecosystems in these environments. For example, commercial over-fishing of cod and haddock at New England's Georges Bank depleted a prime feeding area for whales. Similarly, the Antarctic marine food chain has been disrupted by fishing for krill—shrimp-like crustaceans that are an important food source for whales, seals, penguins, and seabirds [Stephen Savage, ENDANGERED SPECIES, DOLPHINS AND WHALES (1990) at 106] (*see also* Ch. 8).

3.   ECOLOGICAL DAMAGE RESULTING FROM HUMAN POLLUTANTS

Pollution threatens marine living resources by destroying habitats and adversely affecting the health of species that live there. Some land-based discharges are directly toxic to marine life. The effects of these toxins are worsened by their concentration in the surface layer of the sea containing the phytoplankton on which the marine food chain depends. This toxic pollution has resulted in thinner eggshells of seabirds that feed on contaminated marine life (decreasing their survival rate), impaired reproduction in some marine mammals, and physical deformities in other marine life. Other pollutants, though not toxic, contribute to rampant algae growth that kills fish by clogging their gills and depleting the water of oxygen (*see* Chs. 9 & 10).

Pollutants are deposited in the oceans by many mechanisms including atmospheric deposition, ocean dumping, and oil contamination from commercial activities. Atmospheric deposition is responsible for over 30% of marine pollution. Chlorinated hydrocarbons (including pesticides, such as dichlorodiphenyltrichloroethane (DDT) and polychlorinated bipheneyls (PCBs)) are released into the atmosphere by evaporation from the earth's surface and during crop spraying. They are also carried on wind-borne dust. These pollutants then precipitate into the marine environment as rain or fallout.

Ocean dumping (*see* Ch. 12) constitutes 12% of marine pollution [International Chamber of Shipping, SHIPPING AND THE ENVIRONMENT: A CODE OF PRACTICE (1999)]]. The most significant ocean dumping involves dredged spoils or sediments removed from shipping channels. Because shipping areas are often industrialized, dredged spoils can contain significant amounts of heavy metals, petroleum hydrocarbons, and chlorinated hydrocarbons. Other wastes dumped at sea include sewage sludge, garbage, and radioactive wastes. Overall, ocean dumping adversely affects marine habitat in two ways: the solid material settles to the bottom smothering bottom-dwelling marine life, and the toxic pollutants in the dredged spoils or wastes are released into the water. Oil pollution from tanker operations and accidents, coastal refineries, and offshore oil production also account for about 10% of all marine pollution (*see* Chs. 10, 11, & 12).

4. THE EFFECT OF DEVELOPMENT AND SOIL EROSION ON ESTUARINE AND COASTAL HABITATS

Estuarine and coastal habitats, such as coral reefs, mangrove forests, and coastal wetlands, are damaged not only by chemical pollution, but also by development and the accompanying soil erosion. Soil sediments clog and destroy estuarine and coastal habitats. Mangrove forests along the reef shores, which provide essential feeding and breeding habitat for young fish, also remain vulnerable to the deleterious impacts of sedimentation and erosion. Pressure from coastal development has led to rapid losses of mangrove forests—nearly 20% have disappeared since 1980 [Lauretta Burke, et al., *Reefs at Risk Revisited*, (2011) World Resources Institute at 23].

Additionally, human activities and subsidence destroy coastal wetlands. For example, the Mississippi Delta sustains the largest fishery by weight in the U.S. However, about one-quarter of the wetlands in the delta were lost during the 20th century, primarily as a result of human activities. Recent projections indicate that most of the remaining wetlands will disappear in this century if we continue current patterns of development and management [John W. Day, et. al, *Biophysical economics: The Mississippi Delta as a lens for global issues,* Earth Magazine (Nov. 24, 2009)].

5. THREATS TO CORAL REEF ECOSYSTEMS

By far the greatest sources of biodiversity in the ocean are coral reefs, which also serve as a main source of animal protein for over one billion people in the tropics. Unfortunately, coral reefs are especially susceptible to damage from overfishing, coastal development, agricultural runoff, and shipping—in addition to the global threat of climate change. More than 60% of the world's coral reefs are under immediate and direct threat, and these threat levels have been increasing dramatically [Burke, et. al, *supra,* at 3–4]. Because so many countries are highly dependent on coral reefs for resources and livelihoods, degradation and loss of these reefs will result in significant social and economic impacts [*Id.* at 6–7].

Even more so than the rocky inter-tidal substrate, coral reefs demonstrate complex inter-linkages—the disturbance of a key component can trigger devastating chain reactions. For example, when overfishing of a particular species occurs, such as parrotfish or sea urchins, opportunistic algae can smother reefs and kill coral polyps, which had previously been cleaned of algae by the parrotfish and urchins. The result is not just a reduction in the population of the species that was taken, but rather the collapse of an entire ecosystem.

Harmful and negligent fishing practices such as dynamite, cyanide, fine-meshed nets, and anchors dropped carelessly onto the reef continue to threaten reefs worldwide. Tanzania, which has an extensive network of coral reefs that support fishing and tourism industries, is the only country in Africa where dynamite fishing still occurs on a large scale. While efforts have been made to eradicate this devastating form of fishing, inadequate prosecution and minimal penalties have allowed this illegal practice to expand [*Id.* at 26].

Locally, some States have taken individual initiative in protecting their reefs: Australia's Great Barrier Reef Marine Park divides the 350,000 square km of reef into use zones. General zones prohibit only spearfishing, mining, and oil drilling; national park zones, mostly for divers, have a "look but don't touch" policy; and restricted zones are for scientific research only. Internationally, the U.S. spearheaded an initiative for coral reef protection in 1994, with Australia, France, Japan, Jamaica, the Philippines, Sweden, and the United Kingdom (UK) as partners. Together, these States launched the International Coral Reef Initiative, whose key principle is international action with local backing and the coordination of research efforts. While these efforts are not legal measures, it is important for the student of international environmental law (IEL) to understand the differing paradigms that exist in the international decision space.

6.   THE IMPACT OF POPULATION GROWTH

In the discussion above we identified a few of the major ecological impacts of human activities on the marine environment. However, to understand the growing problems presented by these impacts, we must not only investigate the human activities that precipitated them, we must also investigate the pressures behind these human activities. Population growth, urbanization, industrialization, and tourism in coastal areas are just a few of the many topical faces that such an investigation might reveal. As a more specific example of this point, consider that in 1997 an estimated 50% of the global population lived in coastal areas; and that by 2025 this percentage is expected to increase to 75%. The activities of this population profoundly impact the marine environment (and beyond), which in turn markedly affects that population (and beyond). When we see that 37% of the population in 1997 is far larger than the total number of people living on the planet in 1950, the phenomenon of population growth becomes apparent as an important factor in developing solutions to the problems created by human-induced damage to the marine environment (*see generally* Ch. 4).

C.   REMEDIAL OBJECTIVES

Marine living resources are an integral part of the biodiversity of the world, and the protection of marine biodiversity has to be approached in tandem with the preservation of terrestrial biodiversity under the Convention on Biological Diversity (Biodiversity Convention) (*see* Ch. 5). Responding to this reality, the parties to the Biodiversity Convention agreed on a program of action for implementing the Convention. The program, called the Jakarta Mandate on Marine and Coastal Biological Diversity (Jakarta Mandate), was adopted in 1995 [Conference of the Parties to the Convention on Biological Diversity, *Jakarta Mandate on Marine and Coastal Biological Diversity,* (1995)]. Through its program of work, adopted in 1998, the Biodiversity Convention focuses on integrated marine and coastal area management, the sustainable use of living resources, protected areas, mariculture, and alien species. In this endeavor, the Biodiversity Convention has many partners, including international organizations and initiatives, regional organizations such as the Regional Seas Conventions and Action Plans (*see* Ch. 10), local governments, research facilities, and non-governmental organizations (NGOs).

A twin challenge faces the protection of both marine and terrestrial living resources and ecologies: human population growth and economic development. IEL, on the whole, has attempted to deal with over-exploitation, pollution, and habitat destruction, rather than directly address the more intransigent issues of population growth and economic development that fall within the matrix of sustainable development (SD). This pragmatic attempt to address the more immediate issues can be seen as a necessary first step toward a more complete solution because the international community may not be willing to go further at this stage. It is important, however, that any serious attempt to address marine over-exploitation should at least open the door to a more explicit and concrete recognition of the demands of SD.

The first steps toward a more integrated approach to managing natural resources within the framework of SD have been taken at programmatic as well as treaty levels. In addition to the Jakarta Mandate under the Biodiversity Convention referred to above, marine living resources are also addressed in Chapter 17 of Agenda 21, a non-binding voluntary action plan of the UN with regard to SD. Chapter 17 is titled "Protection of the Oceans, All Kinds of Seas, Including Enclosed and Semi-Enclosed Seas, and Coastal Areas and the Protection, Rational Use and Development of Their Living Resources," and provides prescriptions for ocean and coastal management (*see* Ch. 2). Coastal States commit themselves to "integrated management and sustainable development of coastal areas and the marine environment under their jurisdiction" [Agenda 21 at Chapter 17, ¶ 17.5]. The text stresses the need to reach integration (e.g., identify existing and projected uses and their interactions and promote compatibility and balance of uses); the application of preventive and precautionary approaches (including prior assessment and impact studies); and full public participation. More recently, sustainable development goals (SDGs) were developed at the Rio+20 United Nations Conference on Sustainable Development (UNCSD) to replace the millennium development goals (MDGs) as of January 2016. SDG14 emphasizes the need to conserve and sustainably use the oceans, seas, and marine resources [United Nations Sustainable Development Knowledge Platform, *Sustainable Development Goal 14, available at* https://sustainabledevelopment.un. org/sdg14 (last visited Apr. 2017)].

In addition, under the UN Framework Convention on Climate Change (UNFCCC), parties commit themselves, inter alia, "to develop integrated plans for coastal zone management" [UNFCCC at art. 4]. Thus, the UNFCCC reinforces the more general prescriptions concerning integration contained in Chapter 17 of Agenda 21. Furthermore, under the Global Programme of Action on Protection of the Marine Environment from Land-Based Activities (GPA) (see Ch. 10), States agree to focus on sustainable, pragmatic, and integrated environmental management approaches and processes such as integrated coastal area management, harmonized, as appropriate, with river basin management and land use plans.

For both ecological and political reasons, it is important that the conservation of marine living resources be located within an integrated legal design for the oceans. Under a comprehensive approach what happens in the oceans is dependent on activities on land. A functional first step in implementing such an approach is Integrated Coastal Zone Management. At the UN Conference on Environment and Development (UNCED) in 1992, also known as Earth Summit, Chapter 17 of Agenda 21 globally introduced this concept (see Ch. 2). A major goal of Integrated Coastal Zone Management is to safeguard coastal resources by undertaking a holistic approach that interweaves terrestrial, atmospheric, and marine ecosystems with political institutions. This is because many oceanic problems like sewage, chemical pollution, habitat degradation and destruction, coastal development, marine debris, marine resource utilization, and overfishing are land-based activities subject to national laws and policies. Integrated Coastal Zone Management, therefore, involves the integration of biophysical, governmental, managerial and scientific interests, and stakeholders [Joint Group of Experts on the Scientific Aspects of Marine Environmental Protection, *The Contributions of Science to Integrated Coastal Zone Management*, Study No. 61 (1996)].

The UN Convention on the Law of the Sea (UNCLOS) has also responded to this challenge by initiating the beginnings of such a comprehensive regime. UNCLOS focuses on the protection of marine living resources as an intrinsic component of the oceanic environment, and contains a number of necessary, general obligations dealing with the protection of different marine resources. The comprehensive approach of UNCLOS to the oceans, which deals, inter alia, with land-based pollution, sets the stage for further coordination between UNCLOS and the Biodiversity Convention—as well as international legal regimes whose topical focus and substantive commitments are not that of environmental protection, such as the General Agreement on Tariffs and Trade/World Trade Organization (GATT/WTO) [*see also* Lakshman Guruswamy, *The Promise of the United Nations Convention on the Law of the Sea (UNCLOS): Justice in Trade and Environment Disputes*, 25 ECOLOGY L.Q. 189 (1998)].

D. LEGAL RESPONSE

1. 1982 UNITED NATIONS CONVENTION ON THE LAW OF THE SEA (UNCLOS)

a. Overview

Developed over a period of 30 years, including 15 years of active negotiation, UNCLOS is an example of the comprehensive approach to treaty-making, as opposed to the framework approach. UNCLOS combines a broad codification of international law and other substantive rules into a single authoritative source. It addresses a remarkably broad range of issues: e.g., navigational rights; territorial sea limits; economic jurisdictions; passage of ships through narrow straits; conservation, management and protection of the marine environment; a marine research regime; and, rather uniquely, a binding procedure for the settlement of disputes between States. UNCLOS could be described as a constitution for the oceans—a convention that incorporates other international rules, regulations, and implementing bodies, and which aspires to be the authoritative voice (with some specified exceptions) on these matters (*see also* Ch. 1).

b. Jurisdiction Zones

UNCLOS resolves a centuries-long debate concerning the jurisdictional boundaries of the world's oceans. In fact, its jurisdictional pronouncements have evolved from case law, particularly the International Court of Justice (ICJ) jurisdictional guidelines as set forth in the *Icelandic Fisheries Cases* in 1974 [*Fisheries Jurisdiction* (Federal Republic of Germany v. Iceland), 1974 I.C.J. 3; *Fisheries Jurisdiction* (United Kingdom of Great Britain and Northern Ireland v. Ice.), 1973 I.C.J. 302]. For the purposes of marine living resources, UNCLOS delineates four major areas: the territorial sea, the EEZ, the continental shelf, and the high seas.

i. Territorial Sea

In clear language, UNCLOS extends the sovereignty of a coastal State to 12 nautical miles from shore, an area known as the territorial sea [UNCLOS at arts. 2 & 3]. This means that specific utilization of the area remains subject to the laws and regulations of the coastal State. The coastal State can, for example, prohibit all fishing in its territorial sea unless otherwise provided by agreement. In effect, UNCLOS grants other States only the right of innocent passage through territorial seas, which the coastal State may strictly control through the adoption of laws and regulations with respect to "the conservation of the living resources of the sea" [*Id.* at art. 21(1)(d)].

ii. Exclusive Economic Zone (EEZ)

Potentially a major breakthrough for the preservation of marine living resources, the EEZ comprises a 200 nautical mile breadth as measured from the same baselines used to measure the territorial sea [*Id.* at art. 57]. UNCLOS grants sovereignty and jurisdiction over this area to the coastal State [*Id.* at art. 56(1)(a)], in return for which the coastal State must perform a number of obligations, including the conservation and management of marine living resources in the EEZ [*Id.* at art. 61(2)]. In this way, UNCLOS supersedes the former doctrine of "freedom of fishing," which now applies only in limited fashion on the high seas, and which has long contributed to over-exploitation of resources.

As part of its conservation and management duties, the coastal State must determine the "allowable catch of the living resources" in its EEZ [*Id.* at art. 61(1)] and must take measures to ensure that marine living resources are "not endangered by over-exploitation" [*Id.* at art. 61(2)]. In doing so, the coastal State must consider the effects of exploitation on any species related to the harvested species, which includes other species caught incidentally while trying to catch commercial species [*Id.* at art. 61(4)]. Further, the coastal State must "promote the objective of optimum utilization of living resources" [*Id.* at art. 62(1)], and strive "to maintain or restore populations of harvested species at levels which can produce the maximum sustainable yield" [*Id.* at art. 61(3)].

After setting an appropriate "allowable catch" for a commercial species, the coastal State may then take the entire catch if it desires. If, however, the coastal State cannot harvest the full allowable catch, then the coastal State may grant access to other States in order to harvest the surplus [*Id.* at art. 62(2)]. Contrary to the former freedom of fishing doctrine, other States may therefore only take certain designated species in the EEZ, and then only with permission of the coastal State. In considering which States to give permission to, a coastal State is obligated to first look to the needs of developing countries and landlocked States [*Id.* at arts. 62(2) & (3); 69 & 70].

By extending conservation and management duties to the 200-mile limit of the EEZ, UNCLOS provides a potentially effective mechanism to prevent over-exploitation of marine living resources and fisheries, 90% of which, according to recent figures, lie within EEZs. Nonetheless, in practice, developing countries have had technical difficulty in determining the allowable catch for all commercial species in their respective EEZs and in enforcing both their conservation laws and their exclusive rights to development. Organizations such as the Food and Agricultural Organization (FAO) and the UN Environment Programme (UNEP) have endeavored to assist developing countries in these efforts, but funds remain scarce. Much work still exists to fulfill this promising aspect of UNCLOS.

iii. Continental Shelf

The coastal State will, in all cases, have sovereignty over the natural resources of its continental shelf [*Id.* at art. 77(1)]. This means that the coastal State has exclusive rights to the "sedentary species" of the seabed—those "organisms which, at the harvestable stage, either are immobile on or under the seabed or are unable to move except in constant physical contact with the seabed or the subsoil" [*Id.* at art. 77(4)]. In most cases the continental shelf will exist within the EEZ, and so the rules pertaining to the waters above the shelf will be those of the EEZ. In the unusual case of a continental shelf extending beyond the 200-mile limit, however, a special situation arises. The waters above the seabed will remain subject to the rules of the high seas, while the natural resources of the seabed will still fall within the sovereignty of the coastal State [*Id.* at art. 77(1)]. Interestingly, UNCLOS includes no explicit duty to conserve the resources of the continental shelf, but most commentators agree that a duty is implied given the strong emphasis on conservation throughout the convention.

iv. High Seas

In the area beyond the EEZ the former doctrine of freedom of fishing still prevails, though in a qualified fashion. States do have the right for their nationals to engage in fishing on the high seas [*Id.* at art. 116], but certain duties of conservation and management also apply. For example, as necessary, States must adopt measures for their respective nationals regarding the conservation of living resources on the high seas [*Id.* at art. 117]. In addition, States have a duty to cooperate with each other concerning the conservation and management of these resources; as appropriate this may include the creation of regional fisheries [*Id.* at art. 118]. Furthermore, through such cooperative arrangements, States must endeavor to set "allowable catch[es]," again designed to maintain or restore harvested species at levels of maximum sustainable yield, and to take any other conservation measures regarding harvested species [*Id.* at art. 119(1)(a)]. In doing so States must also protect incidentally captured species from becoming "seriously threatened" [*Id.* at art. 119(1)(b)].

The above general obligations have been further defined by the 1995 Agreement for the Implementation of the Provisions of UNCLOS Relating to the Conservation and Management of Straddling Fish Stocks and Highly Migratory Fish Stocks (SFSA) [*Agreement for the Implementation of Provisions of UNCLOS Relating to the Conservation and Management of Straddling Fish Stocks and Highly Migratory Fish Stocks,* Dec. 4, 1995, (entered into force Dec. 11, 2001), 34 I.L.M. 1542 (hereinafter SFSA); *see also* G.A. Res. 57/143, 57th Sess., Agenda Item 25(c), A/RES/57/143 (2002) (regarding the relation between UNCLOS and 1995 SFSA)]. States whose vessels work the high seas must follow the regulations of the SFSA, outlined directly below, concerning these designated categories of fish stocks.

c. The Species Approach

In combination with the general obligations laid down for different jurisdictional zones, UNCLOS adopts special rules for several groups of species. This approach acknowledges the wide variety of marine living resources, as well as the commensurate difficulties in dealing with such variability. Unless otherwise noted in the treaty, the general obligations regarding the EEZ and the high seas still remain— such as setting allowable catches and adopting proper conservation and management measures. However, regarding "straddling stocks" and "highly migratory fish stocks," the SFSA provides more extensive protections.

i. Straddling Stocks

"Straddling stocks" are fish stocks located both in a coastal State's EEZ and an adjacent area of the high seas. In general, UNCLOS mandates that the coastal State and other States fishing the stocks on the high seas enter into agreed measures "necessary for the conservation of these stocks" [UNCLOS at art. 63(2)]. In practice, however, only some regional fisheries have been able to address this problem. The Northwest Atlantic Fishing Organization is using port and trade measures to discourage illegal fishing activity. Measures include not allowing vessels suspected of fishing illegally to dock or unload in a country's port; developing illegal, unreported, and unregulated (IUU) fishing lists of vessels taking part in illegal fishing activities; and scrapping vessels found guilty of multiple illegal fishing offences [Fisheries and Oceans Canada, *Illegal, Unreported and Unregulated (IUU) Fishing* (Mar. 2015), *available at* http://www.dfo-mpo.gc.ca/international/ isu-iuu-eng.htm (last visited Apr. 2017)].

In dealing with such difficulties, the SFSA compels greater cooperation between coastal States and distant-water flag States. Coastal States and States fishing on the high seas must "adopt measures to ensure the long-term sustainability of straddling fish stocks and highly migratory fish stocks and promote the objective of their optimum utilization" [SFSA at art. 5(a)]. In short, this means that both coastal States and flags States must cooperate to adopt compatible "conservation and management measures," such as catch limits for certain species [*Id.* at art. 7]. In most instances this negotiation will take place through the appropriate regional or sub-regional fishery, and all flag States fishing on the high seas must either join the relevant fishery or at least agree to abide by the measures established by that organization [*Id.* at art. 8].

The SFSA also provides for enforcement mechanisms on the high seas. This is a major step with regard to the management of high seas fishing. In effect, a member of a sub-regional or regional fishery organization may board and inspect a flag State ship on the high seas "for the purpose of ensuring compliance with conservation and management measures ... established by that organization" [*Id.* at art. 21(1)]. The inspecting State must notify the flag State of any alleged violation [*Id.* at art. 21(2)], such as failing to maintain accurate catch data or fishing for a prohibited stock, and the flag State must then respond within three working days [*Id.* at art. 21(6)]. In the meantime, inspectors may remain on board, and the flag State must choose either to inspect the matter itself or authorize the inspection by the inspecting State [*Id.* at art. 21(6)]. The result is a new approach to policing the high seas—one that requires all States to follow the rules adopted by regional and sub-regional fisheries organizations as these organizations attempt to protect straddling stocks and highly migratory fish stocks. (For a more recent, and potentially conflicting, perspective, see the *Southern Bluefin Tuna Case, below*)

ii. Highly Migratory Species

UNCLOS creates a special category for highly migratory species listed in Annex I of the treaty. This Annex includes some mammals, but the primary focus is on non-mammals such as marlin, swordfish, and tuna. Coastal and other fishing States must "co-operate" directly or through organizations "with a view to ensuring conservation and promoting the objective of optimum utilization of such species throughout the region, both within and beyond the exclusive economic zone" [UNCLOS at art. 64(1)]. In addition, States must work to establish appropriate cooperative organizations where none exist [*Id.* at art. 64(1)]. As made clear by Article 65, the treaty excludes marine mammals from the Article 64(1) requirement of promoting "optimum utilization" of such species if States, collectively or individually, opt for more stringent protection [*Id.* at art. 65]. Again, for non-mammals the SFSA creates further duties of cooperation between distant-water flag States and coastal States, with the focus of such cooperation taking place through relevant regional and sub-regional fisheries organizations.

iii. Marine Mammals

In singling out marine mammals, UNCLOS recognizes their especially fragile circumstances. Through loss of habitat, over-exploitation, and incidental taking, the mammals of the oceans have proved particularly vulnerable, and as a rule their populations do not recover as quickly as fish. UNCLOS allows coastal States, or any appropriate international organization, "to prohibit, limit or regulate the exploitation of marine mammals more strictly than provided for" in the general articles dealing with the EEZ [*Id.* at art 65]. UNCLOS Article 120 broadens the protections offered by Article 65 to include the high seas. Furthermore, States must "co-operate with a view to the conservation of marine mammals," and in the case of cetaceans (whales and porpoises), States must "work through the appropriate international organizations for their conservation, management and study" [*Id.* at art. 65]. This latter provision has led to some confusion, both as to the identity of the "appropriate international organizations" and as to the breadth of the phrase "work through." Canada, for example, has taken the stand that it should manage the small cetaceans found in its own EEZ, and that Northwest Atlantic Fishing Organization should play a limited consultative role. Others have argued that the International Whaling Commission (IWC) exists as the proper institution for all cetaceans, and that its role should be determinative rather than consultative. As it turns out, a number of States have instituted outright bans on the taking of many marine mammals, but small cetaceans especially remain at risk of continued depletion without a coherent framework of protection (for more on the role of IWC, *see below*).

iv. The Special Case of Seals

The extension of State jurisdiction under UNCLOS has largely supplanted international efforts to protect seals, as nearly all seals live within the 200-mile limit of the EEZ. Formerly, however, the conservation of seals for later exploitation purposes very much occupied the minds of fur industry States. As early as 1911, Japan, the U.S., Russia, and Canada signed a treaty to share in the taking of certain Pacific Ocean species [*Convention Between the United States of America, the United Kingdom of Great Britain and Northern Ireland and Russia, for the Preservation and Protection of Fur Seals*, Jul. 7, 1911 (entered into force Dec. 15, 1911), 214 C.T.S. 80]. With the expiration of this convention in 1941, the same parties (Russia replaced by the Soviet Union) concluded the Interim Convention on Conservation of North Pacific Fur Seals [*Interim Convention on Conservation of North Pacific Fur Seals,* Feb. 9, 1957 (entered into force Oct. 14, 1957), 314 U.N.T.S 105]. The parties amended and renewed this convention a number of times, though the last agreement of 1984 has now expired. In the Atlantic, two different instruments protect seals in the northeast and northwest Atlantic, respectively, though again their importance as conservation instruments has waned. The Agreement on the Conservation of Seals in the Wadden Sea, entered into force in 1991 between the Netherlands, Denmark, and Germany, takes an ecosystem approach to habitat protection and pollution control, while also prohibiting the taking of seals within the region [*Agreement on the Conservation of Seals in the*

Wadden Sea, Oct. 16, 1990 (entered into force Oct. 1, 1991)].

Therefore, though bilateral and small multilateral agreements may help in the coordination of regional protection of seals, the more wide-ranging and inclusive treaties of the past no longer possess their former appeal. In the future, more effective protection may be afforded by the listing procedures of both the Convention on International Trade in Endangered Species of Wild Fauna and Flora (CITES) and the Convention on Migratory Species (Bonn Convention). Finally, for the protection of seals living outside of national jurisdiction in the Antarctic, please see the Chapter 8.

v. *Anadromous Species*

Anadromous species are those species, such as salmon, which spawn in freshwater rivers, migrate to the high seas, and finally return to the same freshwater rivers to reproduce. UNCLOS allocates a dual role for the State of origin, which has both a "primary interest in and [a] responsibility for such stocks" [UNCLOS at art. 66(1)]. This means that the State of origin, after negotiations with other interested States, may set a total allowable catch for such species [*Id.* at art. 66(2)]. The State of origin therefore obtains the first right to exploit these species, and all taking should occur landward of the outer limits of its EEZ. However, other States that might experience economic dislocation without harvesting the species may, by agreement, receive special allowance to participate in the taking—either in the EEZ or on the high seas [*Id*. at art. 66(3)(a)]. In return for the right to utilize the species, the State of origin has the obligation to "ensure their conservation" by proper regulatory measures [*Id*. at art. 66(2)]. This includes the creation of conservation regulations for all takings landward of its EEZ and the good faith attempt to establish conservatory agreements for all takings beyond that limit.

vi. Catadromous Species

Catadromous species are species spawned on the high seas, such as eels, which then migrate to freshwater rivers and lakes. For these species, UNCLOS gives the coastal State—"in whose waters catadromous species spend the greater part of their life cycle"—the responsibility for "management" [*Id*. at art. 67(1)]. Harvesting by any party is prohibited on the high seas [*Id*. at art. 67(2)]. In waters landward of the outer limits of the EEZ, the coastal State assumes the rights and obligations generally allocated for other types of fishing in its EEZ. This means that the coastal State sets an allowable catch and other States may only participate in the harvest by agreement [*Id*. at art. 67(2)].

d. Dispute Settlement Under UNCLOS

The scope and authority of the dispute settlement machinery established by UNCLOS was canvassed in the *Southern Bluefin Tuna Case* in 1999. Australia, New Zealand, and Japan had signed a trilateral regional fisheries agreement known as the Convention for the Conservation of Southern Bluefin

Tuna (Bluefin Convention) [*Convention for the
Conservation of Southern Bluefin Tuna,* May 10,
1993 (entered into force May 10, 1994), 1819 U.N.T.S.
360; *see* Southern Bluefin Tuna Case (N.Z. v. Japan;
Austl. v. Japan), 1999 ITLOS Nos. 3 & 4 (Provisional
Measures Order of Aug. 27)]. The Bluefin Convention
allocated to each party a quota of allowable catches.
Australia and New Zealand alleged that Japan had
exceeded its quota by employing "research fishing."
When the three States failed to resolve the issue
under the Bluefin Convention, Australia and New
Zealand initiated an action before the International
Tribunal for the Law of the Sea (ITLOS), charging
Japan with violations of UNCLOS. In a decision
announced August 27, 1999, ITLOS required Japan
to provisionally cease its experimental fishing
program until an UNCLOS arbitration panel had the
opportunity to decide the issue of whether Japan's
actions violated UNCLOS on the merits.

However, in August of 2000, a five-member
international arbitral tribunal held that it lacked
jurisdiction to decide the issue on the merits
[Australia and New Zealand v. Japan, Award on
Jurisdiction and Admissibility, 39 I.L.M. 1359
(2000)]. Accordingly, the tribunal revoked the
provisional measures issued by ITLOS, which had
enjoined Japan's Bluefin experimental fishing
program. The core of Japan's argument before the
arbitral tribunal was that (1) the dispute arose solely
under the Bluefin Convention, (2) a provision of the
Bluefin Convention excluded compulsory settlement
procedures without the agreement of all the parties,
and (3) thus it could not *ipso facto* be compelled to

arbitrate the merits of the dispute. In the alternative, Japan argued (4) if the tribunal were to hold that the dispute arose under both conventions, a provision of UNCLOS that entitles parties to avoid compulsory dispute settlement where another treaty to which they are parties excludes such a settlement procedure governed this case and militated in favor of a decision by the tribunal against recognizing its jurisdictional authority.

The arbitral tribunal rejected Japan's argument that the dispute arose only under the Bluefin Convention as relying on an "artificial" distinction, and held that the dispute arose under both conventions. However, by a vote of 4 to 1, the tribunal sustained Japan's contention that a provision of the Bluefin Convention excluded compulsory jurisdiction over disputes arising both under it and UNCLOS. Under the logic of the arbitral tribunal, the Bluefin Convention had rejected compulsory jurisdiction, since Article 16(3) of the Bluefin Convention allows only for consensual, not compulsory, arbitration (so the argument goes). Accordingly, the tribunal held that compulsory adjudication under UNCLOS was unavailable to these parties [*Id.* at ¶ 57].

Curiously, while the arbitral tribunal ruled that the terms of Article 16(2) of the Bluefin Convention were determinative of the jurisdictional issue, it also stated that the provisions of Article 16 "do not expressly and in so many words exclude the applicability of any procedure, including the [compulsory procedures of UNCLOS]" [*Id.* at ¶ 56]. According to the tribunal's analysis, by providing for

other methods of dispute settlement, Article 16(2) of
the Bluefin Convention had excluded UNCLOS by
implication. As regarding the binding nature of
UNCLOS, the arbitral tribunal was of the view that
"UNCLOS falls significantly short of establishing a
truly comprehensive regime of compulsory
jurisdiction entailing binding decisions" [*Id.* at ¶ 62].
This view, however, is highly contentious and, as we
have seen, is based on dubious reasoning.

Since the *Bluefin Tuna Case*, ITLOS has
attempted to deal with two other cases relating to
environmental damage. The first, the *Swordfish
Stocks Case*, was repeatedly delayed from
adjudication by both parties and eventually resolved
by agreement of the parties out of court [*Swordfish
Stocks Case* (Chile v. European Community), 2005
ITLOS No. 7 (order 2009/1 of Dec. 16, 2009)]. The
MOX Plant Case is more substantive [*MOX Plant
Case* (Ireland v. UK), 2001 ITLOS No. 10 (hereinafter
MOX Plant)].

In the *MOX Plant Case*, Ireland instituted
arbitration proceedings against the UK under Article
287 of UNCLOS for the construction of a MOX plant
at Sellafield nuclear facility. Ireland designated that
an Annex VII arbitral tribunal would hear the merits
of the case, but stated that the UK had not, as
requested, ceased the authorization process or
international movements of radioactive materials
associated with the MOX plant in the intervening
period before the convening of the Annex VII arbitral
tribunal. It asked ITLOS to use its compulsory
jurisdiction under UNCLOS to halt the UK's actions

concerning the MOX plant. The issue is analogous to a preliminary injunction hearing in the Common Law tradition [*MOX Plant Case*, Request for Provisional Measures and Statement of Case of Ireland].

Flummoxed by the utter lack of agreement concerning the environmental effects of the MOX plant's approval and operation, ITLOS ordered the parties to cooperate in the sharing of information and determination of scientific findings, and gave the parties two weeks to comply. Specifically, Ireland and the UK were to consult in order to

> exchange further information with regard to possible consequences for the Irish Sea arising out of the commissioning of the MOX plant; monitor risks or the effects of the operation of the MOX plant for the Irish Sea; [and] devise, as appropriate, measures to prevent pollution of the marine environment which might result from the operation of the MOX plant [*MOX Plant Case*, Order of 3 December 2001 at 13].

A joint declaration by Judges Caminos, Yamamoto, Park, Akl, Marsit, Eiriksson, and Jesus compared this result with the *Bluefin Tuna Case*:

> Under these circumstances of scientific uncertainty, the Tribunal might have been expected to have followed the path it took in the *Southern Bluefin Tuna Cases* to prescribe a measure preserving the existing situation. In its wisdom, it did not do so. It decided, in the circumstances of the case, that, in the short period before the constitution of an arbitral

tribunal under Annex VII to the United Nations Convention on the Law of the Sea, the urgency of the situation did not require it to lay down, as binding legal obligations, the measures requested by Ireland [*MOX Plant Case*, Joint Declaration].

However, the forced cooperation prescribed by the tribunal also reveals a frustration with the "almost complete lack of cooperation between the Governments of Ireland and the UK with respect to the environmental impact of the planned operations" and a desire to see parties respect their fundamental duty to cooperate under UNCLOS [*Id.*].

Sadly, this victory of ITLOS is overshadowed by the painfully slow operation of the arbitral tribunal, which was to adjudicate the merits. Instead, Ireland formally notified the arbitral tribunal of the withdrawal of its claim against the UK on February 15, 2007. On June 6, 2008, the tribunal issued Order No. 6, terminating future proceedings on this case.

e. The Future of UNCLOS

As of 2017, 168 parties have ratified UNCLOS. In June 2006, the Seventh UN Open-ended Informal Consultative Process on Oceans and the Law of the Sea met to discuss "ecosystem approaches and oceans" [ABA Year in Review, INTERNATIONAL ENVIRONMENTAL LAW: 2005 ANNUAL REPORT (2006) at 77]. The group's report lists four areas of further discussion: (1) the social aspects of oceans; (2) maritime security; (3) flag State responsibility; and (4) oceans and climate change. The Seventeenth

Meeting of the Consultative Process took place in June 2016, and addressed marine debris, plastics, and micro-plastics.

In May 2006, the UN initiated a review conference of the SFSA [UN Division for Ocean Affairs and the Law of the Sea, *Review Conference on the Agreement for the Implementation of the Provisions of the United Nations Convention on the Law of the Sea of 10 December 1982 relating to the Conservation and Management of Straddling Fish Stocks and Highly Migratory Fish Stocks* (Sept. 24, 2010)]. The latest review session's report was released in 2016 and assesses "the effectiveness of the Agreement in securing the conservation and management of straddling fish stocks and highly migratory fish stocks" [REPORT OF THE RESUMED REVIEW CONFERENCE ON THE AGREEMENT FOR THE IMPLEMENTATION OF THE PROVISIONS OF THE UNITED NATIONS CONVENTION ON THE LAW OF THE SEA OF 10 DECEMBER 1982 RELATING TO THE CONSERVATION AND MANAGEMENT OF STRADDLING FISH STOCKS AND HIGHLY MIGRATORY FISH STOCKS, UNGA A/Conf.210/2016/5 (May 2016) at ¶ 1].

While these annual meetings show signs of progression in the management of marine resources, a reading of the meeting reports quickly makes clear the fact that these meetings consist mostly of bureaucratic updates and aspirational rhetoric. The 2016 Review Conference agreed that "future rounds of informal consultations should focus on specific issues," but as of this writing the choice of issues has not yet been made [*Id.* at ¶ 186].

2. UNITED NATIONS ENVIRONMENT PROGRAMME (UNEP) REGIONAL SEAS PROGRAMME

An umbrella program of UNCLOS, the Regional Seas Programme of the UNEP has evolved into an extremely broad system of marine protection. Covering a number of seas and coastal regions—a majority involving developing countries—the Regional Seas Programme often functions as the primary means for coordinating environmental action within the geographic area (*see* Ch. 10).

In implementing the Regional Seas Programme, UNEP made use of the convention-protocol approach to international law-making. First, UNEP developed an Action Plan for the region, which the potential parties then used to create a framework treaty. Subsequently, the parties negotiated protocols to the treaty dealing with specific areas of concern.

With regard to species conservation, though all the treaties contain general obligations to protect the marine environment, a handful also have generated protocols mandating the establishment of marine or coastal protected areas. For example, the Nairobi Protocol for the Eastern African Regional Sea Convention requires parties to cooperate in the creation of a network of protected areas with the aim of preserving both flora and fauna.

The UNEP Regional Seas Programme has proven successful in providing flexible mechanisms for the coordination of regional responses to marine problems. UNEP cites the Regional Seas Programme, as one of UNEP's most significant achievements in the past four decades [United Nations Environment, *Regional Seas, Overview, available at* http://web.unep.org/regionalseas/who-we-are/overview (last visited Apr. 2017)]. Currently there are 18 such programs [*Id.*]. Five Regional Seas Conventions currently include Areas Beyond National Jurisdiction under their geographical coverage: the OSPAR Convention; the Convention for the Protection of Natural Resources and Environment of the South Pacific Region (Noumea Convention); the Convention on the Conservation of Antarctic Marine Living Resources (CCAMLR); the Barcelona Convention for the Protection of the Marine Environment (Barcelona Convention) [*Barcelona Convention for the Protection of the Marine Environment,* Feb. 16, 1976 (entered into force Feb. 12, 1978) UNTS 1102 (hereinafter Barcelona Convention)]; and the Lima Convention for the Protection of the Marine Environment and Coastal Areas of the South-East Pacific (Lima Convention) [*Lima Convention for the Protection of the Marine Environment and Coastal Areas of the South-East Pacific,* Nov. 12, 1981 (entered into force May 19, 1986, IELMT 981:85] that include provisions dealing with the conservation of marine living resources.

3.   INTERNATIONAL CONVENTION FOR THE REGULATION OF WHALING (ICRW)

Signed in 1946, the International Convention for the Regulation of Whaling (ICRW) still exists as the controlling document for the regulation of whaling throughout the world. Created more as an exploitation rather than conservation treaty, the ICRW has since evolved into an ideologically strict and somewhat controversial preservation regime. This shift in attitude reflects the current anti-whaling makeup of the IWC—the supervising body of the convention.

The ICRW creates a relatively simple institutional system. Under the treaty, the IWC maintains a Schedule, which fixes "with respect to the conservation and utilization of whale resources" the following regulations:

(a) protected and unprotected species;

(b) open and closed seasons;

(c) open and closed waters, including the designation of sanctuary areas;

(d) size limits for each species;

(e) time, methods and intensity of whaling (including the maximum catch of whales to be taken in any one season);

(f) types and specifications of gear and apparatus and appliances which may be used;

(g) methods of measurement; and

(h) catch returns and statistical and biological records [ICRW at art. V(1)].

The IWC may amend the Schedule at any time, but any amendments must be "necessary to carry out the objectives and purposes" of the convention [*Id*. at art. V(2)(a)], and must be "based on scientific findings"

[*Id.* at art. V(2)(b)]. In addition, each party to the treaty has one vote on the IWC, and each amendment to the Schedule must carry a three-fourths majority for approval.

Originally comprised of predominantly pro-whaling States, the IWC consistently set catch limits too high, resulting in the continued depletion of commercial whale species throughout the 1970s. By 1982, however, as public outrage over whaling reached dramatic proportions, membership in the IWC came to include a majority of non-whaling States, and the commission passed a moratorium on all commercial whaling beginning three years later in 1985.

When the moratorium was introduced, the IWC asked the Scientific Committee to develop a new, safe, and practical approach to providing scientific advice on commercial catch limits. In 1994, the IWC adopted the Revised Management Procedure (RMP). As the first process to take into account the large levels of uncertainty inevitable in disciplines like cetacean science, the RMP is regarded as setting a precedent for provision of scientific management advice for marine and other living resources. However, the IWC decided that the RMP should not be implemented and used in the context of whaling until the accompanying Revised Management Scheme (RMS) was agreed, which is to cover the aspects of commercial whaling not related to setting catch limits. Unfortunately, the discussions on the RMS reached an impasse in 2006.

While the moratorium remains in place as of this writing, it contains a double loophole that allows some whaling to continue. First, parties can simply object to the moratorium (or any other amendment) within a timely fashion and the moratorium will not bind them [*Id.* at art. V(3)]. Norway, for example, immediately did object to the moratorium in 1982, and thus continues commercial whaling today. Alternatively, Iceland left the IWC in 1992 and returned in 2002 under a reservation. Using this reservation as backing, Iceland announced that it would begin commercial whaling again in 2006 [BBC News, *Iceland Begins Commercial Whaling* (17 Oct. 2006)]. Anti-whaling States claim that Iceland's return to the IWC under a reservation is illegal, because Iceland did not make the reservation at the time it left the IWC [*Id.*]. Thus, anti-whaling States claim Iceland's whaling is a violation of the moratorium, and therefore illegal [*Id.*]. A State "cannot step down from a convention and then rejoin it under a reservation—that is not possible under international law" [*Id.* (quoting Dutch whaling commissioner Guiseppe Raaphorst)]. The IWC, however, has not expressed a formal view on the issue.

The second loophole is that the ICRW allows continued whaling "for the purposes of scientific research"—with power to grant permits for such "scientific" action at the discretion of the flag State [*Id.* at Article VIII(1)]. Japan has continued to conduct its own "scientific" whaling, taking hundreds of minke whales in the Southern Ocean Whale Sanctuary—a sanctuary specifically created in 1994 to protect whales from exploitation in Antarctica. In March 2014, the ICJ ruled that the Japanese whaling program—called "JARPA II"—was not in accordance with the ICRW and was not for scientific purposes [International Court of Justice (ICJ), *Whaling in the Antarctic (Australia v. Japan: New Zealand intervening)*, (Mar. 31, 2014)]. The court ordered Japan to "revoke any extant authorization, permit or license to kill, take or treat whales . . . and refrain from granting any further permits" [*Id.* at 230]. As a result of the judgment, Japan ended the JARPA II program. However, rather than ceasing "scientific" whaling all together, Japan resumed their controversial hunt in late 2015 with a scaled down program [Elahe Izadi, "A Japanese fleet killed 333 whales for 'research,'" *The Washington Post* (Mar. 25, 2016)].

In June 2006, a slim majority of the members of the IWC voted in favor of the St. Kitts and Nevis Declaration, which states that the moratorium on whaling instituted 20 years previously was invalid [Whales and Dolphin Conservation Society, *A Huge Blow for the conservation of the world's whales*, (Jun. 18, 2006)]. This marks the end of an era in which whaling has been vehemently opposed by a majority of the States in the IWC. In recent years, many developing countries have sided with Japan, the strongest and wealthiest of the States that still strongly support whaling.

In April 2010, the IWC issued a draft proposal to lift the moratorium in favor of a progressive reduction and regulation approach. The draft proposal was not favorably received by environmental NGOs, who argued that the proposal helps preserve a dying industry rather than conserving the diminishing whale population. The proposal needed a three-quarters approval by IWC members at the 62nd Annual Meeting in June 2010. However, instead of adopting the draft proposal, the IWC postponed its decision on lifting the moratorium.

The present impasse reflects the political vulnerability of some international environmental institutions. Anti-whaling States, who so importantly voted the moratorium into place in 1982, now find it politically impossible to reverse their position—even when confronted with strong scientific evidence. Of course these States may simply want to ban whaling altogether for a variety of valuable reasons, including moral and aesthetic ones. Nevertheless, the IWC remains committed to conservation *and utilization*, and the international community remains committed to SD under Agenda 21. This case is a high profile example of the potential conflict between preservation on the one hand, and sustainable use on the other.

E. CONCLUSIONS

When considering the conservation of marine living resources, UNCLOS establishes a legal framework within which all activities in the oceans and seas must be carried out. Under UNCLOS, national governments of States and regional and global intergovernmental organizations are all given roles to play. However, each of the many players may be focused on their own sectoral needs, failing to take into account the ways in which their decisions may interact with others. For this reason, the World Summit on Sustainable Development (WSSD) recommended in 2002 that there be a regular process for global reporting and assessment of the state of the marine environment, including socioeconomic aspects. Since then, SDG14 seeks to conserve and sustainably use the oceans, seas, and marine resources for SD and emphasizes the importance of sustainable use and preservation of marine and coastal ecosystems and their biological diversity.

Additionally, the First Global Integrated Marine Assessment, also known as the first World Ocean Assessment, was released by the Group of Experts of the Regular Process under the auspices of the UN General Assembly in 2016 [United Nations, *The First Global Integrated Marine Assessment—World Ocean Assessment I,* (2016) Regular Process for Global Reporting and Assessment of the State of the Marine Environment]. The detailed examination conducted in the Assessment resulted in ten main themes, though the order in which they are presented does not represent any judgment on their priority. Those themes are: issues in the oceans presented by climate change; the exploitation of marine living resources; food security and food safety; preservation of marine biodiversity; increased use of ocean space; increasing inputs of material and excess nutrients into the ocean; adverse impacts on marine ecosystems from cumulative impacts of human activities; uneven distribution of ocean benefits around the world;

sustainable use of the ocean; and the degradation that occurs during the delay in implementing known solutions to problems which have already been identified. Regular integrated marine assessments of the ocean, similar to this, should advance SDG14 and facilitate better protection of marine living resources.

CHAPTER FOURTEEN
TRANSBOUNDARY AIR POLLUTION

A. NATURE OF THE PROBLEM

Human demands lead to a number of physical processes and activities that convert raw materials, energy, and labor into desired finished products. Unfortunately, diverse pollutants are introduced into the environment during almost every stage of these production and consumption cycles. We have noted in Chapter 9 that the environment is indivisible, interconnected, and interdependent, and contaminants can move within or beyond the original medium (air, water, or land) into which they are introduced.

The migration of air pollutants has created several major global problems that are discussed in other chapters of this book. Chapter 6 discussed climate change, Chapter 7 discussed ozone depletion, and Chapter 17 discusses nuclear fallout. Also, Chapter 9 discussed how pollutants transported through the air could cause human health and environmental problems. This chapter will focus on the residual transboundary air pollution problems that are not covered by regimes described elsewhere in this book. We will briefly discuss problems caused by ubiquitous pollutants such as sulfur dioxide (SO_2) and nitrous oxides (NOx)—including acid deposition—and how and why they have given rise to customary law and treaty regimes.

B. SOURCES AND ENVIRONMENTAL IMPACTS

Acid deposition, commonly referred to as acid rain, is a classic example of transboundary air pollution. Acid rain is created when industrial plants, principally fossil-fuel power stations and metal smelters with tall smoke stacks, emit SO_2 into the atmosphere. Mobile sources, such as automobiles, and industrial sources also discharge NOx. Once in the atmosphere, these emissions react with cloud water to form acids, the worst being sulfuric acid. Cloud water then falls to the earth as acid rain. Alternatively, these gases may also be deposited as dry deposition. When this pollution is high in the atmosphere there is great potential for the acid to travel long distances and across state or national boundaries [Fredric C. Menz & Hans M. Seip, *Acid rain in Europe and the United States: An Update,* ENVIRONMENTAL SCIENCE AND POLICY, Volume 7, Issue 4 (2004) at 253–54].

It is important to note that some acid in rain occurs naturally as part of the carbon cycle. Carbon dioxide (CO_2), for example, results from respiration, fires, and volcanoes. These emissions naturally react with rainwater forming carbonates, making a mildly acidic solution that actually "buffers" the rain. That is, it forms a solution with the water that can absorb new sources of acidity or basicity before the pH changes. The atmospheric transport of carbon places carbon in locations—such as rocky or nutrient poor habitats—where it might not otherwise be available [*Id.* at 254].

While some scientific uncertainties remain with respect to the effects of acid rain, the evidence unequivocally indicates that acid rain adversely impacts surface waters such as lakes and streams, as well as life in those aquatic ecosystems. Terrestrial ecosystems can also be damaged—particularly those at higher elevations. Materials such as bronze, marble, and limestone can be corroded and visibility damaged. Acid rain precursors can also form secondary pollutants, transforming the pollution into a more toxic chemical and exacerbating its effects. In addition, though acid rain is not directly harmful to human health, the constitutive elements of acid rain (SO_2 and NOx) do cause damage to human health. Numerous scientific studies have identified a causal relationship between elevated levels of fine particles and increased illness and premature death from heart and lung disorders, such as asthma and bronchitis [*Id.* at 254–56].

In the 1970s and 80s, coal and oil-fired power plants in the U.S. emitted significant amounts of SO_2 and NOx pollution, producing acid rain that eroded forests and created toxic lakes. The detrimental effects occurred primarily in the Northeast and Upper Midwest, but also crossed national boundaries into Canada. However, as a result of both technological improvements and international environmental law (IEL) agreements, which will be discussed below, emissions have decreased dramatically in the U.S. in recent years. The national composite average of SO_2 annual mean ambient concentrations has decreased 85% between 1980 and 2012 [United States Environmental Protection

Agency (EPA), *2012 Progress Report: Environmental and Health Results,* (2012) Acid Rain Program Historical Reports at 4].

Similarly, acid rain has crossed many national boundaries in Europe, with Scandinavian States sustaining the majority of the damage. For example, acid rain caused the loss of fish populations in thousands of lakes in Norway. However, the majority of European countries have now reduced their emissions by more than 60% between 1990 and 2004, and one quarter have already achieved SO_2 emission reductions higher than 80% [V. Vestreng, et. al, *Twenty-five years of continuous sulphur dioxide emission reduction in Europe,* (Jul. 12, 2007) ATMOSPHERIC CHEMISTRY AND PHYSICS 7 at 3663]. IEL has also played an important role in reducing these emissions, as will be discussed below.

Despite these successes, transboundary air pollution continues to be a problem in many parts of the world. In India, SO_2 and NOx emissions from coal power plants and smelters have increased by more than 100% and 50%, respectively, from 2005 to 2015 [Nickolay A. Krotkov, et al., *Aura OMI observations of regional SO2 and NOx pollution changes from 2005 to 2015,* (Apr. 13, 2016) ATMOSPHERIC CHEMISTRY AND PHYSICS 16 at 4605]. In 2014, India surpassed the U.S. to become the world's second largest SO_2 emitting country [*Id.* at 4621]. The world's largest emitter of SO_2 is China, a nation of 1.3 billion people, which generates most of its electricity by burning coal. The North China Plain has the world's most severe SO_2 and NOx pollution, with SO_2

emissions peaking in 2007, with a secondary peak in 2011. By 2015, China had experienced about a 50% reduction in SO_2 emissions due to an economic slowdown and government efforts to restrain emissions [Nickolay A. Krotkov, et al., *supra* at 4605]. However, China still remains the leader of SO_2 pollution.

C. REMEDIAL OBJECTIVES

Transboundary air pollution was recognized quite early as an international pollution problem. For example, the facts of the well-known *Trail Smelter Case* transpired in the 1920s and 30s. The principles derived from that case have become the bedrock of customary transboundary pollution law, although the arbitration itself, and the applicable law, was governed by an international agreement between Canada and the U.S.

The *Trail Smelter Case,* discussed below, presents the need for *ex ante* regulatory measures that prevent pollution and establish compliance procedures and enforcement mechanisms, as well as *ex post* grievance-remedial methods, such as arbitral and judicial proceedings that are able to assign responsibility and liability for wrongful actions. As we shall see, IEL dealing with transboundary pollution is an incomplete patchwork of customary law, interwoven with regional agreements of limited jurisdiction.

D.   LEGAL RESPONSE

1.   CUSTOM

No discussion of transboundary air pollution could begin without mention of the 1941 *Trail Smelter Case*. As observed in Chapter 3, *Trail Smelter* remains one of the most significant cases in IEL, and the only important international case dealing with air pollution. The facts of the case suggest an unusual transboundary air pollution scenario, without the usual causation problems due to multiple polluters and multiple delivery streams. In this situation, a single, identifiable smelting plant located in Trail, British Columbia in Canada was found to have caused air pollution damage to a region of the State of Washington in the U.S. In 1935, Canada accepted responsibility by a treaty between the U.S. and Canada for the provable damage (*see* Ch. 3). An arbitral tribunal was set up by the treaty to determine the extent of the damage caused. In doing so, the arbitral tribunal reiterated the customary law rule of State responsibility (SR) on which the treaty may have been based, and held as follows:

> The Tribunal, therefore, finds that the above [U.S. domestic] decisions, taken as a whole, constitute an adequate basis for its conclusions, namely, that, under the principles of international law, as well as of the law of the United States, no state has the right to use or permit the use of its territory in such a manner as to cause injury by fumes in or to the territory of another or the properties or persons therein,

when the case is of serious consequence and the injury is established by clear and convincing evidence [*Trail Smelter* at 1965].

This ruling has since become the basis for the general prohibition against transboundary environmental harm, reaffirmed by Principle 21 of the 1972 Stockholm Declaration of the United Nations Conference on the Human Environment (Stockholm Declaration) and, most recently, stated in the Rio Declaration on Environment and Development (Rio Declaration) in 1992:

> States have, in accordance with the Charter of the United Nations and the principles of international law, the sovereign right to exploit their own resources pursuant to their own environmental and developmental policies, and the responsibility to ensure that activities within their jurisdiction or control do not cause damage to the environment of other States or of areas beyond the limits of national jurisdiction [Rio Declaration at Principle 2].

Consequently, the basic premise of *Trail Smelter* has evolved into a well-accepted rule of customary IEL— restated in myriad international, regional, and bilateral agreements. Taking into account the sovereign right to development, one State may not cause significant transboundary environmental harm to another [*see* Thomas W. Merrill, *Golden Rules for Transboundary Pollution*, 46 DUKE L.J. 931, (1997) at 951].

2.   1979 CONVENTION ON LONG-RANGE TRANSBOUNDARY AIR POLLUTION (LRTAP)

a. Overview

In the absence of a global international treaty on transboundary air pollution, the 1979 Convention on Long-Range Transboundary Air Pollution (LRTAP)—a regional treaty—emerges as the most significant legal regime in this field. Created under the auspices of the United Nations Economic Commission for Europe (UNECE) in 1979, LRTAP counts most States in the Northern Hemisphere as parties, including the U.S., Canada, Russia, and the Holy See. It represents an early form of a framework convention, though its institutions lack the degree of flexibility and power inherent in more recent framework treaties. Still, LRTAP has evolved to meet the needs of its parties, adding seven protocols that require specific emission limitations for: SO_2 (1985, 1994); NOx (1988); volatile organic compounds (VOCs) (1991); heavy metals (1998); persistent organic pollutants (POPs) (1998); and emission ceilings for four pollutants by 2010: SO_2, NOx, VOCs, and ammonia (1999).

LRTAP, with its strong focus on combating acid rain, embraces the duty to not cause transboundary harm [LRTAP at pmbl. ¶ 5]. It mandates that the parties endeavor to limit, reduce, and prevent air pollution, including long-range transboundary air pollution [*Id.* at art. 2]. The latter phenomenon is defined as air pollution from one State "which has adverse effects in the area under the jurisdiction of another State at such a distance that it is not generally possible to distinguish the contribution of individual emission sources or groups of sources" [*Id.* at art. 1(b)]. As such, LRTAP attempts to deal with pollution problems beyond the facts of the original *Trail Smelter*, which identified a nearby Canadian polluter as the sole perpetrator of cross-border harm in the U.S.

In addition to promoting general calls for consultations, exchanges of information, and research and development on the issue, LRTAP endorses the existing "cooperative programme for the monitoring and evaluation of the long-range transmission of air pollutants in Europe" [*Id.* at art. 9]. Each party is asked to join in this program of scientific monitoring and evaluation, which is overseen by a Steering Committee. LRTAP also establishes a Secretariat, as well as an Executive Body, which resembles the Confrence of the Parties (COPs) of more recent framework treaties. However, unlike the newer versions of the framework approach, the Executive Body's powers remain general and un-enumerated, and LRTAP fails to create a formal dispute resolution procedure [*see Id.* at art. 13]. Still, as discussed below, LRTAP has given birth to a number of substantive protocols. The most recent of these, the 1999 Gothenburg Protocol to Abate Acidification, Eutrophication and Ground-level Ozone (Gothenburg Protocol), deals with SO_2, NOx, VOCs, and ammonia [*Protocol to the 1979 Convention on Long-Range Transboundary Air Pollution to Abate Acidification, Eutrophication and Ground-Level Ozone,* Nov. 20, 1999 (entered into force May 17, 2005) EB.AIR/1999/1 (hereinafter Gothenburg Protocol)]. While it thus addresses the various pollutant categories referenced below, we discuss the protocol separately on the basis of its unique "multi-pollutant" scope.

b. Sulfur Dioxide (SO₂)

Responding to increased anxiety over the threat of acid rain, the parties have made two efforts at controlling SO_2 emissions. The first attempt, the 1985 Protocol on Further Reduction of Sulfur Emissions or Their Transboundary Fluxes by at Least 30 Percent (1985 Sulfur Protocol), required parties to reduce their national annual SO_2 emissions by a flat-rate of at least 30% of their 1980 levels by the year 1993 [*Protocol to the 1979 Convention on Long-Range Transboundary Air Pollution on Further Reduction of Sulfur Emissions or Their Transboundary Fluxes by at Least 30 Percent,* Jul. 8, 1985 (entered into force Sept. 2, 1987), 27 I.L.M. 707 (hereinafter 1985 Sulfur Protocol)]. The 1985 Sulfur Protocol also mandated that each party develop a national program to this end, and report its national annual SO_2 emissions to the Executive Body [*Id.* at art. 4]. It should be noted that the parties in aggregate succeeded in achieving the goals of the 1985 Sulfur Protocol, surpassing the 30% target.

The second attempt, the 1994 Protocol on Further Reduction of Sulphur Emissions (1994 Sulfur Protocol), as its name implies, goes beyond the measures of the 1985 Sulfur Protocol [*Protocol to the 1979 Convention on Long-Range Transboundary Air*

Pollution on Further Reduction of Sulphur Emissions, Jun. 14, 1994 (entered into force Aug. 5, 1998), 33 I.L.M. 1540 (hereinafter 1994 Sulfur Protocol)]. The 1994 Sulfur Protocol required the parties not to exceed annual SO_2 ceilings as set forth in Annex II [*Id.* at art. 2(2)]. Annex II also created percentage emissions reductions that each party is required to meet for the years 2000, 2005, and 2010. However, unlike the 1985 Sulfur Protocol, the percentage of required reduction varies with each party—thus taking into account the different situations of individual States. The 1994 Sulfur Protocol also obligates parties to ensure, as far as possible and without excessive costs, that sulfur depositions do not exceed "critical loads"—defined as a "quantitative estimate of an exposure to one or more pollutants below which significant harmful effects on specified sensitive elements of the environment do not occur according to present knowledge" [*Id.* at art. 1(8)]. The essence of the "critical loads" approach is that emission reductions are negotiated according to the individualized effects of air pollutants, rather than requiring States to achieve equal flat-rate reductions. Put simply, this approach seeks to establish target-specific toxicity thresholds—a critical environmental level below which no harmful effects occur. The use of critical loads was seen as a way to overcome some of the infirmities associated with the flat-rate approach utilized in the 1985 Sulfur Protocol. For instance, while sensitivity to pollution and the cost of reducing emissions can vary widely throughout a given region, the flat-rate approach is not able to take these differences into account. However, while the critical loads approach does enable an emission reduction system to set emission targets based on localized variables, there are significant scientific and political problems associated with determining what actually constitutes a critical load.

The 1994 Sulfur Protocol also sets emission limitations for new stationary combustion sources, which existing sources must meet by 2004 [*Id.* at art. 2(5)]. However, it exempts Canada and the U.S. from these emission limitations, giving way to the 1991 U.S.-Canada Agreement on Air Quality [*United States-Canada Agreement on Air Quality,* Mar. 13, 1991, 30 I.L.M. 676 at art. 2(5) (hereinafter Agreement on Air Quality)] (*see below*). Regardless, as of this writing, the U.S. has yet to ratify the 1994 Sulfur Protocol.

c. Nitrogen Oxide (NOx)

In contrast to the relatively successful endeavor to reduce SO_2 emissions, the attempt to control NOx emissions has proved more difficult. The 1988 Protocol to the Convention on Long-Range Transboundary Air Pollution Concerning the Emissions of Nitrogen Oxides or Their Transboundary Fluxes (Sofia Protocol) has only slightly reduced overall emissions of NOx. Utilizing the type of flat-rate reduction approach employed by the 1985 Sulfur Protocol, the Sofia Protocol requires all parties to ensure that emissions of NOx, or their transboundary fluxes at the end of 1994, are not higher than those in 1987 [Sofia Protocol at art. 2(1)].

The Sofia Protocol also mandates that the parties apply national emission standards to major new stationary sources, based on the "best available technologies which are economically feasible" (BATEF) [*Id.* at art. 2(2)(a)–(c)]. The parties must likewise use the BETEF approach to apply national emission standards to mobile sources [*Id.* at art. 2(b)]. As a recommended guideline, the parties are encouraged to look at the Technical Annex for purposes of implementation [*Id.* at art. 10].

d. Volatile Organic Compounds (VOCs)

An additional effort under the umbrella of LRTAP involves the attempt to regulate VOCs through the 1991 Protocol Concerning the Control of Volatile Organic Compounds or Their Transboundary Fluxes (1991 VOCs Protocol), [*Protocol to the 1979 Convention on Long-Range Transboundary Air Pollution Concerning the Control of Emissions of Volatile Organic Compounds or Their Transboundary Fluxes,* Nov. 18, 1991 (entered into force Sept. 29, 1997), 31 I.L.M. 568 (hereinafter 1991 VOC Protocol)]. The 1991 VOCs Protocol provides parties with three different ways to meet the basic requirement of controlling and reducing VOCs emissions. First, a party may choose to reduce its national annual emissions "by at least 30% by the year 1999, using 1988 levels as the basis or any other annual level during the period 1984–1990" [*Id.* at art. 2(a)]. Second, if a party's damaging transboundary emissions only originate from a specified area listed in Annex I (known as a tropospheric ozone management area), then it need only stabilize its total annual emissions while reducing those particularly harmful emissions using the above 30% formula [*Id.* at art. 2(b)]. Third, a small polluter may simply choose to stabilize its national annual emissions by 1999, again using 1988 as the baseline [*Id.* at art. 2(c)].

The parties also must, within two years, apply national or international standards to new stationary and mobile sources, using BATEF and taking into consideration the respective technical annexes [*Id.* at art. 3(a)(i) & (iii)]. Within five years of entry into force, the parties must apply BATEF to existing stationary sources located in sensitive areas [*Id.* at art. 3(b)(i)].

The 1991 VOCs Protocol expands the concept of critical loads first introduced in the 1994 Sulfur Protocol to explicitly include damaging effects on human beings. As defined by the Protocol, a "critical level" is reached when "concentrations of pollutants in the atmosphere for a specified exposure time" are such that below that level "direct adverse effects on receptors, such as human beings, plants, ecosystems or materials do not occur according to present knowledge" [*Id.* at art. 1(8)].

e. A More Comprehensive Approach to Pollution Control: The 1999 Gothenburg Protocol

The Gothenburg Protocol, originally adopted by the LRTAP Executive Body in 1999, establishes national emission ceilings to be achieved by 2010 for four pollutants: SO_2, NOx, VOCs, and ammonia

[Gothenburg Protocol at art. 3]. Utilizing the critical loads approach first adopted in the 1994 Sulfur Protocol, the Gothenburg Protocol sets limits on specific emission sources—such as combustion plants, electricity production, dry cleaning, cars, paints or aerosols, and some specific ammonia sources—and requires best available techniques to be used to keep emissions down [*Id.* at Annex VI]. Importantly, however, in addition to employing the critical loads approach, the Gothenburg Protocol also endeavors to take into account the interdependencies of environmental effects, such as acidification, eutrophication, and ground ozone accumulation, in order to achieve effective reductions of environmental damages at the least cost [*Id.* at art 2].

As a kind of "multi-effect" and "multi-pollutant" instrument, the Gothenburg Protocol is significant for three key reasons. First, it is the only protocol within the LRTAP regime to utilize a comprehensive approach in addressing more than one pollutant. Second, the Gothenburg Protocol includes fuel and emission standards for both mobile and stationary sources. And third, it is the first LRTAP protocol to encompass agriculture through the introduction of mandatory ammonia emissions measures.

For the most part, the Gothenburg Protocol has delivered on its original goals in terms of emissions reductions and closing the gap between the 1990 acid deposition levels and the critical loads [Netherlands Environmental Assessment Agency & International Institute for Applied Systems Analysis, *Review of the*

Gothenburg Protocol: Report of the Task Force on Integrated Assessment Modelling and the Centre for Integrated Assessment Modelling, (2007) CIAM report 1/2007 at 39]. However, more recent scientific findings suggest that critical loads in the base year may be higher than previously thought, making even complete implementation of the original Gothenburg Protocol insufficient to solve problems like acidification, eutrophication, and health damages due to ground-level ozone [*Id.*].

Thus, the Gothenburg Protocol was amended in 2012 by the LRTAP Executive body to include national emission reduction commitments to be achieved by 2020 and beyond (amended Gothenburg Protocol) [*Protocol to Abate Acidification, Eutrophication and Ground-level Ozone to the Convention on Long-range Transboundary Air Pollution, as amended on 4 May 2012,* May 4, 2012 (not yet entered into force) ECE/EB.AIR/114 (hereinafter amended Gothenburg Protocol)]. The amended Gothenburg Protocol updates emission limit values for stationary and mobile sources and is the first binding agreement to include emission reduction commitments for fine particulate matter [*Id.*]. Parties to LRTAP have also broken new ground in IEL by specifically including the short-lived climate pollutant black carbon (or soot) as a component of particulate matter, which is a major step in reducing air pollution while simultaneously facilitating climate benefits. The amended Gothenburg Protocol also introduces flexibility mechanisms to encourage new parties to join and to allow current parties—under clearly defined circumstances—to propose adjustments to their commitments, which allows for scientific and methodological improvements [*Id.*]. The amendments to Annex I entered into force on June 5, 2013. However, as of this writing, the amendments to the text of the amended Gothenburg Protocol and Annexes II and IX, as well as the addition of new Annexes X and XI, have yet to be ratified by two thirds of the parties and have thus not entered into force.

3.   UNITED STATES—CANADA

On March 13, 1991, the U.S. and Canada signed the Agreement on Air Quality, creating a regional agreement on transboundary air pollution between just two States. The result of more than a decade of negotiations, the Agreement on Air Quality primarily attempts to engage the problem of acid rain. The treaty provides that the parties shall "establish specific objectives for emissions limitations or reductions of air pollutants and adopt the necessary programs and other measures to implement such specific objectives" [Agreement on Air Quality at art. 3(2)(a)]. As a framework agreement, the breadth of the accord allows the U.S. and Canada to confront both current problems and those that may arise in the future.

Annex I establishes emissions limitations for SO_2 and NOx, in a direct attempt to address the problem of acid rain. As agreed, the U.S. committed to reducing its annual SO_2 emissions attributable to power plants by 10 million metric tons relative to

1980 levels by the year 2000 [*Id.* at Annex I, art 1(A)(1)]. This obligation is in accordance with Title IV of the U.S. 1990 Clean Air Act Amendments (CAAA). The U.S. further pledged to cap such emissions at 8.9 million tons per year by the year 2010 [*Id.* at Annex I, art. 1(A)(2)]. Similarly, Canada committed to reducing its annual SO_2 emissions to 3.2 million tons annually by the year 2000 [*Id.* at Annex I, art. 1(B)(1)].

As for NOx emissions, by 2000 the U.S. was required to reduce its total annual emissions by approximately 2 million tons (again using 1980 as the baseline) [*Id.* at Annex I, art. 2(A)]. For its part, by 2000 Canada pledged to reduce its annual emissions of NOx from stationary sources by 100,000 tons below the forecast level of 970,000 tons [*Id.* at Annex I, art. 2(B)(1)]. Additionally, Canada was required to impose mobile source emissions limitations similar to those found in the U.S. CAAA [*Id.* at Annex I, 2(B)(2)].

The Agreement on Air Quality also establishes an Air Quality Committee to review progress on implementation [*Id.* at art. VIII]. The Committee compiles reports on such matters and presents these to the parties, as well as to the International Joint Commission (IJC) [*Id.* at art. IX], a body established under the Treaty Between Canada and the United States of America Relating to Boundary Waters and Questions Arising Along the Boundary Between the United States and Canada (*see* Ch. 15) [*Treaty Between Canada and the United States of America Relating to Boundary Waters and Questions Arising*

Along the Boundary Between the United States and Canada, Jan. 11, 1909 (entered into force May 5, 1910), 36 Stat. 2448 (1909–11), TS No. 548]. The IJC also investigates and makes general recommendations regarding transboundary air pollution. It then invites public comment on these progress reports and submits a synthesis of its findings back to the parties. In this way, the Agreement on Air Quality makes use of one of the oldest institutions in international law.

In 2000, the U.S. and Canada added the Ozone Annex to the Agreement on Air Quality, committing both countries to reducing emissions of NOx and VOCs, the precursors to ground-level ozone and a key component of smog [International Joint Commission, *Canada—United States Air Quality Agreement Progress Report 2014,* (2014) at 58]. The Ozone Annex has resulted in considerable progress in addressing transboundary ozone pollution, especially in the eastern border regions [*Id.*]. By joint scientific and technical analysis, both countries decided in 2013 that an annex regarding the transboundary transport of particulate matter was not yet necessary, but the situation continues to be monitored [*Id.*].

As reported by the IJC in 2014, the U.S. and Canada have updated and improved their emission inventories and projections on pollutants—including VOCs, NOx, and SO_2—to reflect the latest information available [*Id.* at 32]. As of 2012, the United States has had an overall trend of emissions reductions for SO_2 (78%), NOx (46%), and VOCs

(37%) [*Id.* at 34]. Canada's emissions reductions have been less extreme, due in part to the fact that Canada emitted far smaller amounts of these pollutants to begin with. For example, SO_2 emissions in Canada were 1.7 million tons/year in 2008 and have gone down to 1.3 million tons/year in 2012 [*Id.* at 33]. In comparison, despite a 78% reduction, U.S. SO_2 emissions for 2012 were 5.2 million tons/year [*Id.*]. Nevertheless, the IJC reports that the U.S. and Canada continue to successfully meet their commitments under the Agreement on Air Quality [*Id.* at 58].

4. UNITED STATES—MEXICO

In 1983, the U.S. and Mexico signed the Agreement to Cooperate in the Solution of Environmental Problems in the Border Area (La Paz Agreement) [*United States-Mexico Agreement to Cooperate in the Solution of Environmental Problems in the Border Area,* Aug. 14, 1983, 22 I.L.M. 1025 (hereinafter La Paz Agreement)]. The parties agreed to take measures "to the fullest practical extent . . . to prevent, reduce and eliminate" border pollution [*Id.* at art. II], and to coordinate their efforts to address the problems of air, land, and water pollution in the area [*Id.* at art. V]. The La Paz Agreement defines the border area as the region "situated 100 kilometers on either side of the inland and maritime boundaries between the Parties" [*Id.* at art. IV]. In effect, the La Paz Agreement functions as a framework for further action, providing for the creation of Annexes to deal with specific problems.

With respect to transboundary air pollution, the La Paz Agreement contains two separate Annexes. The first, Annex IV, deals with air pollution from all new copper smelters located in the border region. For both parties, SO_2 emissions from all new copper smelters in the area must not exceed .065% by volume during any six-hour period [*Id.* at Annex IV, art. I(1) & (3)]. To monitor compliance, smelter owners and operators must track emissions and report any violations exceeding maximum levels, while every six months an "air pollution working group" assesses the progress made in abating smelter pollution [*Id.*]. Based on this assessment, the working group then makes specific recommendations to national coordinators in both the U.S. and Mexico [*Id.*].

Annex V of the agreement intends to reduce pollution caused by urban development [*Id.* at Annex V]. It provides for the determination of air pollution causes in certain U.S. and Mexican border cities denominated as "study areas" [*Id.* at art. 1]. The Annex requires the U.S. Environmental Protection Agency (EPA) and the Mexican Social Development Secretariat to catalogue emissions from major stationary, mobile, and area sources [*Id.* at art. 2]. The two agencies must then ascertain measures necessary to bring identified pollutants within acceptable control levels, a task facilitated by ambient air quality monitoring and air modeling analysis. Such measures may include, but are not limited to, requiring a given polluter to implement pollution control technology or alter management practices [*Id.*]. As an ultimate goal, the parties shall "jointly explore" the harmonization of their air pollution control standards and ambient air quality standards—a process which the North American Free Trade Agreement (NAFTA) and its progeny may help to spur in the future [*Id.* at art. V].

In 2002, the U.S. and Mexico announced a program called Border 2012—an agreement to work jointly to develop a new bi-national 10-year plan to improve the environment and reduce the highest public health risks on the U.S.-Mexico border. Border 2012 had many successful accomplishments, including helping El Paso, Texas achieve U.S. pollution standards for ozone and carbon monoxide as well as retrofitting over 100 school buses to reduce air contamination [Carlos A. Rincon, *Border 2012 Accomplishments and Border 2020 Framework,* (9 Nov. 2012) U.S.-Mexico Border Environmental Program Legislative Conference at 5–6].

Based on these successes, the U.S. and Mexico have launched Border 2020, which has identified five long-term goals with specific objectives to address the most serious environmental and environmentally-related public health challenges in the border region [U.S. Mexico Border Environmental Program, *Border 2020* at Goal 1]. Goal 1 is to reduce air pollution, particularly since the border region includes a number of cities that share common airsheds. Goal 1 is to be accomplished through five specific objectives: (1) reduce the number of vehicles that do not comply with emissions standards by 2020; (2) reduce pollutant emissions to national ambient air quality standards in specific airsheds by 2020; (3) maintain effective monitoring networks and provide real-time access to air quality data in specific airsheds by 2018; (4) support completion of climate action plans in each of the six northern Mexican Border states by 2015; and (5) reduce emissions and associated impacts through energy efficiency and/or alternative or renewable energy projects by 2020 [*Id.*] Additional goals of Border 2020 include improving access to clean and safe water, promoting waste management, enhancing preparedness for environmental response, and enhancing environmental stewardship.

E.   CONCLUSIONS

The prohibition against transboundary environmental harm, including air pollution, has evolved into a well-accepted rule of customary IEL. In some instances, this rule has been incorporated into regional treaties that provide specific emissions reduction goals as well as enforcement mechanisms. In general, the international regime on transboundary air pollution remains an incomplete patchwork of regional agreements. In practice, these agreements have resulted in significant reductions in emissions—particularly SO_2 and NOx and aided in the reduction of acid deposition.

CHAPTER FIFTEEN
TRANSBOUNDARY WATER POLLUTION

A. NATURE OF THE PROBLEM

Water covers the face of the earth and the oceans occupy 70% of the planet's surface. In earlier chapters we noted how wastes and pollutants are emitted into the air; discharged or dumped into rivers, streams, and the sea; or disposed of on land (*see* Chs. 9, 10, 11, & 12). While direct discharges into the aquatic environment are obvious sources of pollution, we have also seen how indirect sources, such as the atmosphere, can significantly contribute to the problem.

Pollutants can be changed for better or worse within the aquatic environment. Water is a solvent with the ability to dissolve or dilute chemicals and make them harmless to human health or ecosystems. The capacity for "self-purification" of a given body of water will depend on hydrologic conditions such as the type, location, temperature, and pH level of a body of water; the nature of the pollution load; and the concentration and characteristics of the contaminants. Self-purification can occur through a variety of physical, chemical, and biological processes [M Lippmann, et. al, ENVIRONMENTAL HEALTH SCIENCE 39 (2003) at 132–7]. On the other hand, water can also react with contaminants to form more hazardous or more synergistic reactions, depending on the temperature, acidity, and oxygen level of the water [John G. Farmer & Margaret C. Graham, *Freshwaters,* UNDERSTANDING OUR ENVIRONMENT: AN INTRODUCTION TO ENVIRONMENTAL CHEMISTRY AND POLLUTION, THIRD EDITION (1999) at 73–74]. Furthermore, all the water on the earth (the hydrosphere) is continually recycled between the oceans, lakes, streams, and groundwater. This recycling process results in the movement of toxic chemicals from one water source to another [Dade W. Moeller, ENVIRONMENTAL HEALTH, FOURTH EDITION (2011) at 139–147].

As we have seen, the environmental health of the oceans is critical to humanity. Rivers and streams, though they constitute less than 0.5% of the water in the hydrosphere, are also essential to the proper maintenance of the global environment and human habitation [Lippmann, et al., *supra.* at 40]. The pollution of common pool resources such as the high seas (to which all States have open access) can create global problems, while the use or abuse of transboundary or international rivers and groundwater can cause harm to States sharing these resources. Since all of the oceans and over 200 large river basins are shared by two or more States, competition over the quality and quantity of shared waters can become very intense. In this chapter we concentrate on problems that arise when rivers, lakes, estuaries, coastlines, and groundwater are used in a manner that causes harm to other States.

B.   SOURCES OF ENVIRONMENTAL HARM

Pollution introduced into the rivers, watercourses, and coastal waters of one State can affect another State through transport, diffusion, or dispersion. As we have seen in our discussion in Chapter 9, chemicals are usually discharged into water as part of a waste stream from industrial sources such as pulp and paper mills, iron and steel works, petroleum refineries, petrochemical industries, fertilizer factories, and other chemistry-based production installations including pharmaceutical plants. Modern agricultural practices can contaminate water through the heavy use of pesticides and fertilizers, including nitrates and phosphates. All of these contaminants can be washed into nearby surface waters [G.M Robinson & F. Harris, *Food Production and Supply,* GLOBAL ENVIRONMENTAL ISSUES (2004) at 133]. Apart from chemicals, municipal waste, such as untreated or partially treated sewage, and other types of organic matter, such as waste from livestock, are also discharged into streams, lakes, and rivers [Ming-Ho Yu, et al, ENVIRONMENTAL TOXICOLOGY: BIOLOGICAL AND HEALTH EFFECTS OF POLLUTANTS, THIRD EDITION (2011) at 2.4]. In the case of transboundary rivers, these pollutants can be carried downstream into other States or into shared coastal waters or estuaries.

Indirect pollution, another major source of fresh water contamination, arises, for example, from the improper storage of hazardous waste that results in the leaching of hazardous substances into underground aquifers that lie beneath common borders. Such contamination may affect an entire State's source of drinking water. Additionally, emissions of toxic metals and gases from an industrial park can be transported thousands of miles by the wind and deposited directly in a body of water, or on the soil where they can then leach into the groundwater [John Harte, et al., TOXICS A TO Z (1991) at 77].

Changes in the quantity of water, like changes in the quality of water, can also cause transboundary damage. Water can be extracted in such quantities as to affect its ability to sustain marine life or the marine life-supporting ecosystems. The damage caused by the reduction of water volume is not restricted to the ecological health of a river or stream. The overuse of water by an upper riparian State may deprive a lower State of essential water, lead to increased soil salinity, and may even create deserts. Extracting, impounding, or diverting water into dams and reservoirs can certainly affect downstream settlements because these flow-regulating projects may restrict sources of potable or agricultural water and may also affect human health [P. Fradkin, A RIVER NO MORE: THE COLORADO RIVER AND THE WEST (1984) at 64]. In the water-deprived areas of the world, such as the Middle East, water conflicts may potentially bring States to the brink of war.

C.   ENVIRONMENTAL IMPACTS

The deleterious effects of water pollution vary significantly and range from chemical and biological damage, to physical damage to riverbeds and harbors, to pure economic loss. The chemical and biological effects of chemicals are more fully discussed in Chapter 9. We take note here of the specific attributes displayed by some of these pollutants in water. For example, organo-chlorines, like dichlorodiphenyltrichloroethane (DDT), dieldrin, aldrin, heptachlor, and mirex, are chemicals used as pesticides and insecticides that display three remarkable characteristics. First, they are all toxic or poisonous in small doses; at critical concentrations they can affect the marine life in a body of water and humans who drink or are exposed to such water. Second, they are persistent, or stable. This means that they are not readily broken down by microorganisms, enzymes, heat, or ultra-violet light, and thus have stable and long lives in aquatic environments. Third, they bioaccumulate. This means that they are water insoluble and not readily metabolized, so they accumulate in the fatty tissue of fish and animals upon ingestion. These contaminants then move up the food chain by aggregating in the body fat of predator fish and animals. DDT has been found, for example, to affect condors, osprey, falcons, golden eagles, sea gulls, pelicans, and even humans who have eaten such contaminated fish or mammals. A similar profile could be drawn of the impacts of industrial chemicals discharged into the aquatic environment [Harte, et al., *supra*, at 86–90].

Water polluted by sewage has substantial biological effects, including impacts on human health and on aquatic species. Microbial agents can affect people on contact by causing skin infections and respiratory illness, while the ingestion of water or seafood contaminated by pathogens from sewage can cause severe gastrointestinal and respiratory problems [Charles Goldman & Alexander Horne, LIMNOLOGY, SECOND EDITION (1994) at 470–471]. In ordinary circumstances, the microbial activity in water breaks down normal organic wastes by decomposition—a process that takes up oxygen. When large volumes of organic wastes, like sewage and agricultural runoff, are introduced into a body of water, the nutrients they provide can spur microbial growth and increase the amount of oxygen utilized in the decomposition process—the biochemical oxygen demand (BOD). The increase in BOD leads to a decrease in the dissolved oxygen content of the water, potentially to a level that is too low to support any type of life [D.B. Botkin & E.A. Keller, ENVIRONMENTAL SCIENCE (1998) at 417–19]. This process is often called "cultural eutrophication."

Rivers not only carry chemical and biological substances downstream, they also bring sediment caused by erosion, deforestation, agricultural run-off, and irrigation. Such sediment can clog up harbors and cause problems in shipping lanes. Moreover, the inflow of pollutants with attendant human health and environmental problems can adversely affect tourism, an industry upon which many developing countries are heavily dependent [D.A. Bigham, *Pollution from Land-Based Sources,* THE IMPACT OF MARINE POLLUTION (1980) at 203].

D.   REMEDIAL OBJECTIVES

We have observed in Chapters 9 and 10 that remedial measures should endeavor to reduce waste generation by addressing consumption demands. In order to achieve such a goal, the control of water pollution should become part of a more comprehensive attempt to integrate pollution control of atmospheric, terrestrial, and aquatic pollution. Without losing sight of this more comprehensive goal, remedial measures also need to address the more immediate problems posed by transboundary river pollution. These problems, which, as we shall see, have been considered by the International Law Commission (ILC), arise from the disputed rights and duties pertaining to the quality and quantity of water claimed by upper and lower riparian owners of international rivers. Furthermore, water pollution, not unlike other areas of international environmental law (IEL), primarily requires an *ex ante* approach, supplemented by *ex post* grievance remedial mechanisms. As discussed below, various regional conventions have attempted to address this challenge.

E.   LEGAL RESPONSE

1.   1997 CONVENTION ON THE LAW OF THE NON-NAVIGATIONAL USES OF INTERNATIONAL WATERCOURSES (CONVENTION ON INTERNATIONAL WATERCOURSES)

Cooperation concerning the use of transboundary watercourses is well established. As a number of rivers and lakes demarcate international boundaries, States have found it beneficial to arrive at cooperative relationships regarding utilization of these shared resources. As such, we can now confidently cite several broad-based rules of customary law with regard to the use of international watercourses.

In 1991 the ILC expounded and elaborated on these rules in the Draft Articles on the Law of the Non-navigational Uses of International Watercourses (Draft Articles on Watercourses) [*Draft Articles on the Law of the Non-navigational Uses of International Watercourses, U.N. GAOR, 46th Sess., Supp. No. 10 at 161, U.N. Doc. A/46/10 (1991)*]. Empowered by the Charter of the United Nations (UN) to "initiate studies and make recommendations for the purpose of... encouraging the progressive development of international law and its codification," [United Nations, *Charter of the United Nations*, (24 Oct. 1945) 1 UNTS XVI at 13(1)(a)], the ILC in its Draft Articles on Watercourses provided a roadmap both to extant law and the law as it "might be." This completed effort at codification and development was the first regarding watercourses since the Helsinki Rules on the Uses of the Waters of International Rivers [*Helsinki Rules on the Uses of the Waters of International Rivers,* Aug. 20, 1966, 52 I.L.A. 484 (1967)].

In 1994, the UN General Assembly called for an international framework convention to be negotiated based on the Draft Articles on Watercourses. Pursuant to this directive, on May 21, 1997, the General Assembly adopted the Convention on the Law of the Non-Navigational Uses of International Watercourses (Convention on International Watercourses). The Convention on International Watercourses pertains to the use of watercourses for purposes other than navigation, as well as to their protection, preservation, and management [Convention on International Watercourses at art. 1].

In light of its purposes and symbiotic relationship to customary law, the Convention on International Watercourses, which entered into force on August 17, 2014, can be used as a roadmap in traversing the customary law on the subject of transboundary water pollution. It is the first global framework on fresh water—and the world's only global framework for transboundary cooperation endorsed by the General Assembly of the UN. The Convention on International Watercourses attempts to standardize one set of criteria by which all countries with international river basins and transboundary waters will abide. Additionally, in the sections that follow, we shall also take note of the pronouncements of the International Court of Justice (ICJ) in the important case between Hungary and Slovakia regarding the Gabcikovo-Nagymaros Project [*Case Concerning the Gabcikovo-Nagymaros Project* (Republic of Hungary v. Slovak Federal Republic), International Court of Justice, Case No. 92, Sept. 25, 1997 (hereinafter *Hungary v. Slovakia*)].

a. Communication: Notification, Consultation, and Negotiation

The Convention on International Watercourses reinforces the need for communication by institutionalizing a general obligation to cooperate [Convention on International Watercourses at art. 8]. However, in discussing the type of cooperation arising from the obligation to cooperate, it would be helpful to clarify some of the relevant terms. Perhaps the best approach is to consider notification, consultation, and negotiation on a continuum of governmental interaction.

Notification, *per se,* simply requires providing information without a mutual exchange [*see Id.* at arts. 12, 13, 15, 16, & 18]. However, some types of notification under the Convention on International Watercourses are tied to a further requirement of consultation and negotiation. Consultations require a dialogue among participants without an obligation of reasonable compromise, or, therefore, of result [*see Id.* at arts. 4, 6, 7, 17, 18, 19, 24, 26, & 30]. Article 17 refers to a special situation where a notification relates to possible infractions of the principle of equitable distribution or the duty not to cause transboundary damage [*Id.* at art. 17]. A distinction is then drawn between consultation and negotiation by declaring that the notifying State "shall enter into consultations and if necessary, negotiations with a view to arriving at an equitable resolution of the situation" [*Id.* at art 17(2)]. Negotiation requires a dialogue with an obligation to compromise—if in good faith a reasonable actor would so compromise—but not necessarily an obligation of result [*see Id.* at arts. 4, 17, 18, 19, 30, & 33]. Of course, all three terms function within a political context in which the pressures to agree (or disagree) would both inform the terms and promote an outcome.

As an overriding objective, the Convention on International Watercourses mandates communication, and thus cooperation, between watercourse States, requiring that they "shall, at the request of any of them, enter into consultations concerning the management of an international watercourse" [*Id.* at art. 24(1); *see also* arts. 4(2), 5(2), 6(2), 8, & 11]. It thus requires the adoption of "watercourse agreements" among watercourse States, and further stipulates that "[e]very watercourse State is entitled to participate in the negotiation of and to become a party to any watercourse agreement that applies to the entire international watercourse, as well as to participate in any relevant consultations" [*Id.* at art. 4(1)].

Concerning the future use of a watercourse, the Convention on International Watercourses contains a high degree of specificity regarding States' obligations to communicate. The details—such as timeframes to respond—are pragmatic embellishments, but the basic obligations correspond to customary law. For example, before a watercourse State implements "planned measures" having a possibly significant adverse effect, it must provide a potentially harmed State with timely notification [*Id.* at art. 12]. The notifying State must allow the potentially harmed State six months in which to respond [*Id.* at art. 13(a)–(b)], and may not implement the planned measures without consent during this period [*Id.* at art. 14(b)]. If the notified State believes the planned measures to be unacceptable—that is, inconsistent with either the rules of equitable utilization or the duty not to cause harm (discussed below)—then the parties must "enter into consultations and, if necessary, negotiations with a view to arriving at an equitable resolution of the situation" [*Id.* at art. 17(1)]. Should the consultations and negotiations fail, the Convention on International Watercourses offers dispute settlement provisions for impartial fact-finding (if requested by one party), and mediation or conciliation (if agreed to by both parties) [*Id.* at art. 33(3)–(4)].

Given the extensive degree of cooperation found today concerning planned uses of international watercourses, the above requirements of notification, consultation, and negotiation appear to follow state practice. In the *Lac Lanoux Arbitration*, for instance, an arbitral tribunal stated that France could not ignore Spanish interests regarding a planned hydraulic construction project on the Carol River [*Lac Lanoux Arbitration,* (Spain v. France), 12 R.I.A.A. 281 (Nov. 16, 1957)]. The tribunal, however, did not go as far as the Convention on International Watercourses, explaining that "if, in the course of discussions, the downstream State submits schemes to it, the upstream State must examine them, but it has the right to give preference to the solution contained in its own scheme provided that it takes into consideration in a reasonable manner the interests of the downstream State" [*Id.*]. The tribunal also disavowed as a rule of law that only a prior agreement between riparian States would allow one State to utilize the hydraulic power of a watercourse [*Id.*].

Nonetheless, the mandate of the Convention on International Watercourses on consultations and negotiations (leading finally to impartial fact-finding and possibly mediation/conciliation) reflects contemporary practice. States nearly always settle these disputes among themselves. In this regard one need only look at the proliferation of regional and bilateral watercourse agreements discussed below to appreciate how the degree of communication—and the perception of that communication as a legal requirement—has significantly increased since the 1957 *Lac Lanoux Arbitration*.

The development of the law since *Lac Lanoux* is confirmed by the case of *Hungary v. Slovakia* in 1997. After protracted litigation, both parties were ordered by the ICJ to undertake good faith negotiations consistent with both international environmental norms (e.g. sustainable development (SD)) and the law of international watercourses to come up with a new management scheme in the context of the already constructed projects in Slovakia. Though Hungary and Slovakia have conducted a series of negotiations based on the ICJ ruling, as of this writing the dispute has still not been settled.

b. Equitable Utilization

The doctrine of equitable utilization enjoys a long lineage. In *in re the Territorial Jurisdiction of the International Commission of the River Oder*, the Permanent Court of International Justice (PCIJ), dealing with a navigable river, declared that each riparian State's "community of interest . . . becomes the basis of a common legal right, the essential features of which are the perfect equality of all riparian States in the use of the whole course of the river and the exclusion of any preferential privilege of any one riparian State in relation to the others" [*in re the Territorial Jurisdiction of the International Commission of the River Oder,* 1929 P.C.I.J. (Ser. A) No. 23 at 5]. In reference to non-navigational uses, the Convention on International Watercourses requires that "[w]atercourse States shall . . . utilize an international watercourse in an equitable and reasonable manner" [Convention on International Watercourses at art. 5(1)]. It further requires that the resource be used "with a view to attaining optimal and sustainable utilization thereof and benefits therefrom, taking into account the interests of the watercourse States concerned [and] consistent with adequate protection of the watercourse" [*Id.* at art. 5(1)].

The doctrine of equitable utilization has been confirmed by the ICJ as the fundamental law of international water law in the case of *Hungary v. Slovakia*. The ICJ found that Slovakia "failed to respect the proportionality . . . required by international law," by "depriving Hungary of its right to an equitable and reasonable share of the natural resources of the Danube . . ." [*Hungary v. Slovakia* at Sec. 85]. Even though the case did not directly apportion the Danube's flow, the ICJ's opinion firmly establishes that international rivers are shared resources, and all riparian States have equal rights to enjoy both the commodity and non-commodity ecological benefits of the river, hydrologically connected groundwater, and the riparian corridors.

On its face, this universally accepted rule seems incontrovertible. Who would disagree with a requirement that one State only use a shared river or lake in an equitable and reasonable manner? Problems of interpretation arise, however—as elsewhere in the law regarding standards of reasonableness—because of different operative contexts. Obviously, the very nature of a dispute means that one State does *not* consider another State's use "equitable" or "reasonable." In an effort to overcome this difficulty, the Convention on International Watercourses defines the "[u]tilization of an international watercourse in an equitable and reasonable manner" as "taking into account all relevant factors and circumstances, including:

(a) Geographic, hydrographic, hydrological, climatic, ecological, and other factors of a natural character;

(b) The social and economic needs of the watercourse States concerned;

(c) The population dependent on the watercourse in each watercourse State;

(d) The effects of the use or uses of the watercourse in one watercourse State on other watercourse States;

(e) Existing and potential uses of the watercourse;

(f) Conservation, protection, development and economy of use of the water resources of the watercourse and the costs of measures taken to that effect;

(g) The availability of alternatives, of comparable value, to a particular planned or existing use [Convention on International Watercourses at art. 6(1)].

These clearly remain helpful factors in backing up one's own position (State X's social and economic needs), but it is difficult to see how these do not equally aid an adversary's contrary position (State Y's social and economic needs). In other words, the list simply offers a language in which to continue the consultations and negotiations mentioned above; it does not, however, offer much help in the way of proposing solutions. The real benefit is that it may keep the conversation ongoing so that a mutually advantageous political settlement will arise over time. Additionally, should an outside arbiter be brought into the picture, that arbiter may use the listed factors to validate his/her own interpretation of "reasonableness."

One might also notice the dearth of environmental factors in the list of factors relevant to equitable and reasonable utilization. This lack is presumably balanced by the duty not to cause transboundary harm [*Id.* at art. 7(1)] and the provisions against ecosystem destruction [*Id.* at art. 20] and pollution [*Id.* at art. 21(2)]. The limited voice given to environmental factors in ascertaining equitable utilization, however, does show the continuing tension between development and environmental protection—a tension the Convention on International Watercourses can only attempt to broker and not to resolve.

In the case of *Hungary v. Slovakia*, the ICJ confirmed, inter alia, (a) that multipurpose river basin development treaties may establish a continuing (and environmentally sensitive) management regime that cannot be unilaterally abrogated, (b) that SD and ecological risk assessment are customary rules of international environmental and water law, and (c) that these customary rules can apply to treaties negotiated prior to the recognition of these emerging norms.

In the case, Hungary justified its 1989 suspension of a 1977 river basin treaty, involving the construction of a series of locks and dams, as an "ecological state of necessity" [*Hungary v. Slovakia* at

Sec. 44] To justify termination, Hungary invoked a number of familiar contract defenses (impossibility and changed circumstances) and asserted that the emerging precautionary principle imposed "an *erga omnes* obligation of prevention of damage" and thus precluded the continued performance of the treaty [*Id.* at Sec 97]. To defend its suspension, Hungary also invoked Article 33 of the ILC Draft Articles on the International Responsibility of States, which allows a State to avoid an international obligation when so doing is "the only way for the State to safeguard an essential interest against a grave and imminent peril" [International Law Commission (ILC), *Draft Articles on Responsibility of States for International Wrongful Acts* (2001) A/56/10 at art. 25].

In a significant expansion of the concept of State necessity, the ICJ agreed that the environmental risks were indeed related to an essential State interest. It interpreted Article 33 to require "that a real 'grave' and 'imminent' 'peril' existed in 1989" and that the State's response was "the only possible response" [*Hungary v. Slovakia* at Sec. 54]. While Article 33 embodies a limited precautionary principle, a State invoking it must demonstrate, by credible scientific evidence, that a real risk will materialize in the near future and is thus more than a possibility. The ICJ found that Hungary's evidence of risk, and the possible range of alternatives, did not meet these standards. In a separate opinion, Judge Weeramantry adopted the interrelated principles of SD and cautionary environmental assessment and management as *erga omnes* customary rules. In his view they command the same general applicability as the laws of human rights [Christopher Weeramantry, *Separate Opinion of Vice-President Weeramantry, Case Concerning the Gabcikovo-Nagymaros Project*, International Court of Justice, Case No. 92, Sept. 25, 1997].

c. Obligation Not to Cause Transboundary Harm

Like the rule of equitable utilization, the rule against causing transboundary harm has long been established for international watercourses. As early as 1937, in the case of *Diversion of Water from the River Meuse*, the PCIJ formulated the general rule that "each of the two states is at liberty, in its own territory, to modify [canals], to enlarge them, to transform them, to fill them in and even to increase the volume of water in them from new sources," provided that the discharge of water outside their respective territories remained at a normal level [*Diversion of Water from the River Meuse* (Netherlands v. Belgium), 1937 P.C.I.J. (Ser. A/B) No. 70, at 4]. This is an early formulation of Principle 2 of the 1992 Rio Declaration, which asserts that "States have . . . the sovereign right to exploit their own resources . . . and the responsibility to ensure that activities within their jurisdiction or control do not cause damage to the environment of other States . . ." [Rio Declaration at Principle 2].

The Convention on International Watercourses makes it clear that the harm must be "significant harm," and places a duty of due diligence upon watercourse States not to cause such harm [Convention on International Watercourses at art. 7(1)]. The difficulty is determining the proper relationship between "equitable and reasonable utilization" [*Id.* at art. 5] and the no-significant-harm rule [*Id.* at art. 7]. What happens if the two rules are perceived as being in conflict? Suppose, for example, a perceived equitable utilization in State A—such as a municipal power plant—causes significant harm to the watercourse in State B, despite State A's diligent efforts to prevent that harm? The Convention on International Watercourses offers this solution:

> 1. Watercourse States shall, in utilizing an international watercourse in their territories, take all appropriate measures to prevent the causing of significant harm to other watercourse States.

> 2. Where significant harm nevertheless is caused to another watercourse State, the States whose use causes such harm shall, in the absence of agreement to such use, take all appropriate measures . . . in consultation with the affected State, to eliminate or mitigate such harm and, where appropriate, to discuss the question of compensation [*Id.* at art. 7(1)–(2)].

And there is a further condition: "In the event of a conflict between uses of an international watercourse, it shall be resolved with reference to the principles and factors set out in Articles 5 to 7, with special regard being given to the requirements of vital human needs" [*Id.* at art. 10(2)].

Obviously, the Convention on International Watercourses does not convey an unequivocal priority of either rule, but it does soften the absolute prohibition against causing transboundary harm. In fact, it stresses an ad hoc consultative resolution of such conflicts, which follows the trend in state practice toward negotiated settlement of such disputes. Taking the articles together, we might suggest a new formulation of the customary rule: a use is not *per se* violative of international law if it causes significant transboundary harm, as long as the use is equitable and reasonable, and the parties involved have conducted informed consultations on the matter.

Skeptics, of course, might maintain that the Convention on International Watercourses simply offers another level of "reasonable" action in Article 7—in effect a tautology which attempts to balance reasonable harm against reasonable use, all in the name of reasonableness. But, to be fair, the Convention on International Watercourses has committed itself to promoting dialogue when conflicts do arise among watercourse States. It has not attempted to lay down the law rigidly with regard to specific and highly contextual problems, but instead has opted for an ongoing conversation among disputants. As long as the conversation is maintained, the chance for a political solution to a problem remains.

d. Further Protections

The Convention on International Watercourses provides a number of additional obligations for watercourse States that, unlike the basic rules regarding communication, equitable utilization, and the duty to not cause transboundary harm, do not so clearly follow state practice. As such, these may be seen as part of the "progressive development of the law," or at least as obligations less universally recognized as examples of customary international law. These include: (1) the duty to protect and preserve ecosystems of international watercourses [*Id.* at art. 20]; (2) the duty to harmonize pollution prevention policies [*Id.* at art. 21(2)]; and (3) the duty to take all appropriate measures to prevent or mitigate conditions that may be harmful to other watercourse States, such as flood or ice conditions, water-borne diseases, siltation, erosion, salt-water intrusion, drought, or desertification [*Id.* at art. 27]. The last duty, though moderated by the qualifier "where appropriate," especially expands the traditional no-significant-harm rule by holding States responsible for both "natural causes [and] human conduct" causing potential harm [*Id.*].

e. The Question of Groundwater

The ILC debated whether to include all types of transboundary groundwaters within the scope of its Draft Articles on Watercourses, the precursor to the Convention on International Watercourses. As the Convention now stands, "[w]atercourse means a system of surface waters and groundwaters constituting by virtue of their physical relationship a unitary whole and normally flowing into a common terminus" [*Id.* at art. 2(a)]. In adopting this definition of a watercourse, the Convention on International Watercourses applies only to those groundwaters that are (1) physically part of a system of surface and groundwater; (2) part of a unitary whole; (3) normally flow to a common terminus that is hydraulically linked to surface water; and (4) are part of a system located in different States [*Id.* art 2]. The Convention on International Watercourses thus excludes so-called "unrelated confined groundwaters," which by definition do not flow into a common terminus.

Though in 1994 the Special Rapporteur strongly recommended the deletion of the phrase "flowing into a common terminus" to the Draft Articles on Watercourses, and therefore the inclusion of confined transboundary groundwaters [Robert Rosenstock, *Second report on the law of the non-navigational uses of international watercourses,* (1994) A/CN.4/462 at Ch. 1, Sec. 7], the ILC as a whole rejected the proposal. For his part, the Special Rapporteur maintained that the ILC should include these transboundary waters to "encourage their management in a rational manner and prevent their depletion and pollution" [*Id.* at Annex, Sec. 38]. The ILC on the other hand, remained reluctant to extend the scope of its work because the Draft Articles on Watercourses had not been formulated with confined aquifers in mind. Instead, as a compromise, the ILC adopted a resolution stating its "view that the principles contained in the draft articles [on watercourses] ... may be applicable to transboundary confined groundwater" [International Law Commission (ILC), *Resolution on Confined Transboundary Groundwater,* (1994) 2 Y.B. Int'l L. Comm'n 135 at Sec. 40].

Thus, the protection and management of groundwater resources was somewhat neglected in IEL until 2006, when the ILC modified its position on the law on transboundary groundwaters by adopting the Draft Articles on the Law of Transboundary Aquifers (Draft Articles on Transboundary Aquifers) [International Law Commission (ILC), *Draft Articles on the Law of Transboundary Aquifers* (2008) UN Doc.A/CN.4/L.724]. At its 2008 session, the ILC completed its work on the Draft Articles and transmitted the draft to the UN General Assembly. The ILC recommended that the UN take note of the Draft Articles and, at a later stage, consider the elaboration of a framework convention based upon them.

The revised Draft Articles on Transboundary Aquifers adopt an "aquifer" or "aquifer systems" approach to regulating transboundary groundwaters. Only transboundary aquifers and aquifer systems are covered; domestic aquifers and aquifer systems are excluded from its scope. Thus, a domestic aquifer or aquifer system that is linked to an international watercourse would not be covered. However, the Draft Articles on Transboundary Aquifers note that domestic aquifers or aquifer systems linked to international watercourses could be covered by the Convention on International Watercourses.

The Draft Articles on Transboundary Aquifers also codify a number of general principles. Among the more important of them are the principles of sovereignty, "equitable and reasonable utilization," [*Id.* at art 4], and the obligation not to cause harm [*Id.* at art 6]. Each "aquifer State has sovereignty over the portion of a transboundary aquifer or aquifer system located within its territory" [*Id.* at art 3]. This recognition, however, is qualified by countervailing principles. Each State is required to exercise its "sovereignty in accordance with the present draft articles" [*Id.*]. Aquifer States must "utilize the transboundary aquifer or aquifer system in a manner that is consistent with the equitable and reasonable accrual of benefits therefrom to the aquifer States concerned" [*Id.* at art. 4(a)]. The question of whether or not a particular utilization is "equitable and reasonable" is to be answered by "taking into account all relevant factors," which include: populations that rely on the aquifer or aquifer system; present and future social and economic needs of the aquifer States concerned; natural characteristics of the aquifer or aquifer system; the impact of the utilization on the formation and recharge of the aquifer or aquifer system; the current and potential utilization of the aquifer or aquifer system; the impact of the utilization on other concerned aquifer States; the availability of alternatives to the utilization; the development and protection of the aquifer or aquifer system and the cost of related action; and the role of the aquifer or aquifer system in the surrounding ecosystem [*Id.* at art. 5(1)(a)–(i)]. Aquifer States are also required to take appropriate steps to prevent the causing of transboundary harm and to take all appropriate measures to protect ecosystems dependent on aquifers [*Id.* at art. 9].

With the promulgation of the Berlin Rules on Water Resources in 2004, the International Law Association (ILA) reached a similar but more sweeping conclusion, requiring the integrated management of *all* aquifers—including those that do not connect to an "international drainage basin" [International Law Association (ILA), *Report of the Seventy-First Conference* (Aug. 9, 2004) No. 2/2004 at art 36]. The Berlin Rules apply to renewable, non-renewable, domestic, and international groundwater. In addition, the Berlin Rules contain specific provisions, *inter alia*, for the precautionary and sustainable management of aquifers and their protection [*Id.*].

Given the evolution of the ILC's position on confined transboundary groundwaters and the pronouncement made by the ILA's Berlin Rules, one might plausibly extrapolate the rules regarding international watercourses to the special situation of confined transboundary groundwaters.

2. REGIONAL AND BILATERAL AGREEMENTS

The ratification of the Convention on International Watercourses in 2014 provides an important impetus to foster additional cooperation over transboundary waters at the global level. However, as this global regime continues to develop, there are still a number of regional and bilateral arrangements in place that provide an extensive body of state practice. We have tried to highlight those most important, but one should be aware that a long list of such agreements now exists. Among the agreements negotiated but not covered here include those for Lake Constance, the River Danube, the River Elbe, the Niger Basin, and the Zambezi River System.

a. 1992 ECE Convention on the Protection and Use of Transboundary Watercourses and International Lakes (ECE Convention)

In 1992, the UN Economic Commission for Europe (UNECE) codified basic regional rules for the protection and use of transboundary watercourses. The UNECE Convention on the Protection and Use of Transboundary Watercourses and International Lakes (ECE Convention) incorporates much of the customary law discussed above, while further developing the law by affirming the precautionary principle, the polluter pays principle, and environmental impact assessments [*ECE Convention on the Protection and Use of Transboundary Watercourses and International Lakes,* Mar. 17, 1992 (entered into force on Oct. 6, 1996), 31 I.L.M. 1312 (hereinafter ECE Convention)].

The ECE Convention defines "transboundary waters" to mean "any surface waters or ground waters which mark, cross or are located on boundaries between two or more States" [*Id.* at art. 1(1)]. As such, the ECE Convention provides broader coverage than the Convention on International Watercourses, which does not officially include isolated or "unrelated" groundwaters (*see* above). The ECE Convention also contains a broad definition of "transboundary impact" as meaning "any significant adverse effect on the environment" including "effects on human health and safety, flora, fauna, soil, air, water, climate, landscape and historical monuments . . . [and] effects on the cultural heritage or socio-economic conditions" [*Id.* at art. 1(2)].

Part I of the ECE Convention describes the provision relating to all parties, not just riparian parties, and creates the affirmative duty to take all appropriate measures to "prevent, control and reduce any transboundary impact" [*Id.* at art. 2(1)]. Clearly, this would preclude an upstream State from reducing the water supply to a downstream State if such a reduction would cause significant harm. More specifically, the parties must prevent, control, and reduce pollution, and ensure not only the conservation of water resources but also the conservation and restoration of ecosystems [*Id.* at art. 2(2)]. In guiding the obligations of the parties, the ECE Convention also strongly affirms the concept of SD.

Following customary law, the ECE Convention also imposes a duty of equitable and reasonable utilization for international watercourses. As discussed above, this principle is firmly ensconced in international law. The ECE Convention, however— like the Convention on International Watercourses— loosens the absolute prohibition against causing transboundary impact, in effect appearing to allow some transboundary harm perpetrated by an equitable use.

The parties to the ECE Convention shall, in particular, take all appropriate measures: "to ensure that transboundary waters are used in a reasonable and equitable way, taking into particular account their transboundary character, in the case of activities which cause or are likely to cause transboundary impact" [*Id.* at art. 2(2)(c)]. As the ECE Convention and the Convention on International Watercourses remain the most important pronouncements on the issue, we repeat again our understanding of the customary rule: a use is not *per se* violative of international law if it causes significant transboundary harm, as long as the use is equitable and reasonable, and the parties involved have conducted informed consultations on the matter.

Balanced against the heightened profile of equitable utilization is a detailed enumeration of obligations to prevent, control, and reduce transboundary impact. Among these is the requirement that each party set emission limits for discharges from point sources based on "best available technology" (BAT), and that the parties specifically tailor these limits to individual industrial sectors [*Id.* at art. 3(2)]. For diffuse sources, particularly from agriculture, the parties must develop and implement "best environmental practices" (BEP) to reduce the inputs of nutrients and hazardous substances [*Id.* at art. 3(1)(g)]. To aid in the formulation of both types of controls, the ECE

Convention defines BAT in Annex I, and provides guidelines for developing BEP in Annex II. The ECE Convention further requires parties to define water quality objectives and to adopt water-quality criteria [*Id.* at art. 3(3)], supplying guidelines for these actions in Annex III. As an additional general duty, parties must undertake environmental impact assessments to gauge any future level of harm [*Id.* at art. 3(1)(h)].

In Part II, the ECE Convention more specifically focuses on the duties of riparian parties, especially emphasizing the need for cooperation. Riparian parties, if they have not already done so, are required to enter into bilateral or multilateral agreements in order to prevent, control, and reduce transboundary impact [*Id.* at art. 9(1)]. These agreements must provide for the establishment of "joint bodies" to administer the agreement [*Id.* at art. 9(2)]. A joint body thus acts as the mechanism through which the parties can discharge numerous duties, including joint monitoring and assessment, exchange of information, and the establishment of warning and alarm procedures [*Id.* at art. 9(2)].

Regarding the standard customary obligations of notification and consultation, the ECE Convention mandates that consultations be held in good faith at the request of any riparian party [*Id.* at art. 10], and that each State give prompt notification concerning "any critical situation that may have transboundary impact" [*Id.* at art. 14]. Going beyond custom, the ECE Convention also requires that riparian parties provide mutual assistance upon request should a critical situation arise [*Id.* at art. 15].

At a joint special session held in 2001, the parties to the ECE Convention and the Convention on the Transboundary Effects of Industrial Accidents [*Convention on the Transboundary Effects of Industrial Accidents* (1992) (entered into force on Apr. 19, 2000), 31 I.L.M. 1333] decided that an intergovernmental negotiation process—within the scope of both conventions—should be entered into with the aim of adopting a legally binding instrument on civil liability for transboundary damage caused by hazardous activities. As a result of this decision on May 21, 2003, parties to the ECE Convention and the Convention on the Transboundary Effects of Industrial Accidents adopted the Protocol on Civil Liability and Compensation for Damage Caused by the Transboundary Effects of Industrial Accidents on Transboundary Waters (Industrial Accidents Protocol) [*Protocol on Civil Liability and Compensation for Damage Caused by the Transboundary Effects of Industrial Accidents on Transboundary Waters,* (21 May 2003) IUCN TRE-001372 (hereinafter Industrial Accidents Protocol)]. The Industrial Accidents Protocol provides individuals affected by the transboundary impact of industrial accidents on international watercourses a legal claim to compensation. Similarly, it renders operators of industrial installations, including tailing dams and pipelines, liable for damage depending on the risk they pose, i.e. the quantities of hazardous substances present and their toxicity. As of this writing, the Industrial Accidents Protocol has been signed by 24 States and ratified by one. The Industrial Accidents Protocol requires 16 ratifications in order to enter into force.

In 1999, parties to the ECE Convention adopted the Protocol on Water and Health [*Protocol on Water and Health to the 1992 Convention on the Protection and Use of Transboundary Watercourses and International Lakes,* Jun. 17, 1999 (entered into force Aug. 4, 2005), MP.WAT/2000/1/EUR/ICP/EHCO 020205/8Fin]. The overarching objective of the Protocol on Water and Health is to protect human health and well-being through improved water management, including the protection of water ecosystems, and by preventing, controlling, and reducing water-related diseases [*Id.* at art. 1]. The Protocol on Water and Health requires parties to establish national and local targets for the quality of drinking water and the quality of discharges, as well as for the performance of water supply and wastewater treatment [*Id.* at art. 6(2)(a)–(n)]. Parties are also required to reduce outbreaks and the incidence of water-related diseases. Importantly, the Protocol on Water and Health introduces a social component into cooperation on water management. It notes that "[w]ater has social, economic and environmental values and should therefore be managed so as to realize the most acceptable and sustainable combination of those values" [*Id.* at art. 5(g)].

b. Regional Agreements Concerning the Rhine River

The Rhine River regime offers an example of long-term regional cooperation with regard to an international watercourse. As early as 1950, the riparian European States of the Rhine created an international commission to oversee the waterway, and in 1963 reformed that institution in the Agreement Concerning the International Commission for the Protection of the Rhine Against Pollution (1963 Berne Convention) [*Agreement Concerning the International Commission for the Protection of the Rhine Against Pollution,* Apr. 23, 1963 (entered into force May 1, 1965), 994 U.N.T.S. 3 (hereinafter 1963 Berne Convention)]. Under this agreement, the primary function of the International Commission was to research the river's pollution problems and offer guidelines for improvement.

Only in 1976, however, did the riparian parties more effectively attempt to arrive at solutions. In that year the parties amended the 1963 Berne Convention and created two more treaties—the Convention for the Protection of the Rhine against Chemical Pollution (Rhine Chemicals Convention) [*Convention for the Protection of the Rhine against Chemical Pollution,* Dec. 3, 1976 (entered into force on Feb. 1, 1979), 1124 U.N.T.S. 375 (hereinafter Rhine Chemicals Convention)], and the Convention for the Protection of the Rhine against Chemical Pollution by Chlorides (Rhine Chlorides Convention) [*Convention for the Protection of the Rhine against Pollution by Chlorides,* Dec. 3, 1976 (entered into force on July 5, 1985), 16 I.L.M. 265 (hereinafter Rhine Chlorides Convention)].

The more general of the two, the Rhine Chemicals Convention, mixes international and national controls. For example, it mandates that the parties gradually eliminate the discharge of dangerous substances listed in Annex I and reduce the discharge of less dangerous substances listed in Annex II [Rhine Chemicals Convention at art. 1]. The parties must also draw up a national list of all Annex I substances discharged into the river [*Id.* at art. 2], and must grant prior national approval for any such discharge [*Id.* at art. 3]. In granting approval, the national authority must specify emissions standards that do not exceed the limits proposed by the International Commission [*Id.* at art. 3(2)]. Any discharge of Annex II substances must also receive prior authorization, but the emission standards are to be established by the national authorities and not the International Commission [*Id.* at art. 6].

The Rhine Chemicals Convention also contains a provision requiring the immediate notification of the commission and affected parties in case of an accident [*Id.* at art. 11]. Despite this requirement, the Swiss government failed to provide timely notice to either following a devastating fire at its Sandoz facility in 1986. The toxic effluent from this accident caused widespread damage to the entire ecosystem of the Rhine and led to the creation of the Rhine Action Programme in 1987 (*see* below).

The Rhine Chlorides Convention more specifically attempts to control pollution of the river by chloride ions [Rhine Chlorides Convention at art 2]. The Rhine Chlorides Convention has been supplemented by a 1991 Protocol, which further tightens the obligations of the parties. As it stands, each party is allocated certain discharge limits as set out in Annex IV under the 1991 Protocol [*Id.*]. The strongest measures apply to France, which must reduce its discharges where they exceed 200 milligrams per liter at the Netherlands-Germany border. The excess is to be stored on land and later discharged into the Rhine, pending favorable environmental conditions. The Rhine Chlorides Convention and the 1991 Protocol also provide for cost-sharing with regard to the major obligations of the parties, with percentage shares given to France, Germany, the Netherlands, and the Swiss Confederation.

Driving the measures of the 1991 Protocol was the 1987 Rhine Action Programme, which was adopted in the aftermath of the Sandoz incident. Though not a treaty, the Rhine Action Programme established as objectives: (1) the restoration of the ecosystem so as to accommodate the return of higher species; (2) the maintenance of the river as a source of drinking water supplies; and (3) the further reduction of pollution by harmful substances [International Commission for the Protection of the Rhine (ICPR), *Upstream: Outcome of the Rhine Action Programme,* (2000) ISBN 3-935324-46-4].

Since the inception of the Rhine Action Programme in 1987, significant progress has been made towards achieving these objectives. In particular, the water quality has improved considerably. A sharp reduction of the emissions of communities and industries has been realized. This is the result of the joint efforts of the International Commission for the Protection of the Rhine and the implementation of measures by the contracting parties. As some hundreds of salmon have ascended the Rhine, the ecological success of this program is evident. In addition to what has already been realized, more SD is expected as part of the International Commission for the Protection of the Rhine's "Rhine 2020" program, including thousands of salmon in the upper Rhine [*Id.*].

On April 12, 1999, the parties to the 1963 Berne Convention signed the Convention on the Protection of the Rhine (Rhine Convention) [*Convention on the Protection of the Rhine* (entered into force on Jan. 1, 2003), 2000 O.J. (L 289) 31 (hereinafter Rhine Convention)]. The Rhine Convention is designed to augment the parties' efforts towards improving the Rhine ecosystem. It replaced the 1963 Berne Convention and the Rhine Chemicals Convention [*Id.* at art. 19(1)]. However, any decision or arrangements made based on either of these conventions would require an explicit act of the International Commission to be repealed [*Id.* at art. 19(2)]. Some obligations from these conventions can also be found in the new Rhine Convention, such as the obligation to inform the Commission and the other parties in the event of an accident [*Id.* at art. 5(6)]. Alternatively, it may be posited that the Rhine Chlorides Convention and its 1991 Protocol were not affected by the Rhine Convention. The Rhine Convention applies to the river itself and to groundwater interacting with it [*Id.* at art. 2]. It invokes many common principles including the precautionary principle and the polluter pays principle [*Id.* at art. 4]. In the event of a dispute between the parties, the parties must first attempt to settle it through negotiation [*Id.* at art. 16(1)]. However, if negotiations are futile, an Annex to the Rhine Convention provides procedures for arbitration [*Id.* at art. 16(2); Annex].

c. United States—Canada

A very early example of cooperation between States with regard to shared water resources is provided by the U.S. and Canada. The 1909 Treaty Between the U.S. and Great Britain Relating to Boundary Waters, and Questions Arising between the U.S. and Canada (1909 Boundary Waters Treaty) deals primarily with issues of navigation and the construction of dams and other diversion projects [*Treaty Between the U.S. and Great Britain Relating to Boundary Waters, and Questions Arising between the U.S. and Canada,* Jan. 11, 1909 (entered into force May 5, 1910), X I.P.E. 5158 (hereinafter 1909 Boundary Waters Treaty)]. Importantly, however, the 1909 Boundary Waters Treaty also states that the "waters flowing across the boundary shall not be polluted on either side to the injury of health or property of the other" [*Id.* at art. IV]. As such, the document provides one of the earliest treaty commitments to control environmental pollution in international law.

The 1909 Boundary Waters Treaty also established the International Joint Commission (IJC), which is composed of six commissioners—three each from the U.S. and Canada [*Id.* at art. VII]. The IJC must approve any uses, obstructions, or diversions that change the level or flow of the boundary waters [*Id.* at art. III]. The IJC additionally acts as both an informal and formal arbiter of disputes, with the power to administer oaths and subpoena witnesses [*Id.* at arts. IX–XIII].

The Agreement Between the U.S. and Canada on the Water Quality of the Great Lakes (1978 Great Lakes Water Quality Agreement) further expands both the duties of the parties and those of the IJC [*Agreement Between the U.S. and Canada on the Water Quality of the Great Lakes,* Nov. 22, 1978 amended by protocol in 1987), 30 U.S.T. 1383 (hereinafter 1978 Great Lakes Water Quality Agreement)]. Its primary objective is the restoration and maintenance of the chemical, physical, and biological integrity of the waters of the Great Lakes basin ecosystem. The agreement is quite detailed, with numerous Annexes and Appendices, and creates "General" as well as "Specific Objectives." As "General Objectives," the parties agree that the Great Lakes System should be free from substances or materials that interfere with beneficial uses and/or cause harm to human, animal, or aquatic life [*Id.* at art. III]. So as to meet these goals, the 1978 Great Lakes Water Quality Agreement provides for "Specific Objectives" which "represent the minimum levels of water quality" for the Great Lakes System [*Id.* at art. IV]. These are set out in Annex 1 and mandate numerical concentration values for Persistent Toxic Substances, such as pesticides and metals, defined as any substance which has a half-life in water of greater than eight weeks.

Augmenting the General and Specific Objectives, the 1978 Great Lakes Water Quality Agreement requires both parties to develop and implement programs and measures covering a range of problems. The requirements of these provisions are then further detailed in accompanying annexes. As such, the parties must develop programs and measures to combat pollution from municipal sources, industrial sources, non-point sources, shipping activities, dredging activities, off-shore facilities, contaminated sediments, and contaminated groundwater and subsurface waters [*Id.* at art. VI]. In addition, the parties must reduce and control inputs of phosphorous and other nutrients which cause eutrophication, as well as other hazardous polluting substances [*Id.* at art. VI]. Emphasizing the ecosystem approach to coordinated action, the treaty further requires the parties to develop and implement both Remedial Action Plans and Lakewide Management Plans [*Id.* at art. VI].

To administer and oversee these obligations, the 1978 Great Lakes Water Quality Agreement places more responsibilities on the IJC. Now backed up by a Water Quality Board and a Science Advisory Board, the IJC must analyze and distribute information relating to both water quality in the Great Lakes System and pollution entering the system from outside waters [*Id.* at art. VII]. The IJC must also collect and analyze information concerning the General and Specific Objectives and the efficacy of adopted programs [*Id.* at art. VII]. To this end, the IJC is asked to provide biennial reports detailing its assessments, advice, and recommendations [*Id.* at art. VII]. The treaty also provides the IJC with the authority to verify independently the data and other information submitted by the parties [*Id.* at art. VII].

The most recent Biennial Report on Great Lakes Water Quality, the Sixteenth Report, was issued in 2013. The report data showed significant achievements in improved water quality, but also demonstrated the need for sustained investment and action to protect and restore the Great Lakes [International Joint Commission (IJC), *Assessment of Progress Made Towards Restoring and Maintaining Great Lakes Water Quality Since 1987: Sixteenth Biennial Report on Great Lakes Water Quality,* (15 Apr. 2013) E95-1/1-16E at iii]. The ICJ recommended sustained monitoring of a core set of ecosystem indicators and the development of goals, targets, or standards for each core indicator so that future policymakers can make informed and cost-effective judgments based on the best available scientific information [*Id.* at 33–34]. The 2013 report also recommends a revised treaty [*Id.*]

d. United States—Mexico

Another longstanding relationship of cooperation regarding transboundary waters exists between the U.S. and Mexico. Treaties drawn in the 1880s deal with navigation and the two States have also signed the 1944 Treaty between the U.S. and Mexico Relative to the Utilization of Waters of Colorado and Tijuana Rivers and of the Rio Grande from Fort Quitman to the Gulf of Mexico (1944 Colorado River Treaty), [*Treaty Between the U.S. and Mexico Relative to the Utilization of Waters of Colorado and Tijuana Rivers and of the Rio Grande from Fort Quitman to the Gulf of Mexico,* Feb. 3, 1944, 3 U.N.T.S. 314 (hereinafter 1944 Colorado River Treaty)]. The 1944 Colorado River Treaty considers utilization issues such as apportionment, dam construction, and flood control [*Id.*]. It also establishes the International Boundary and Water Commission (IBWC) (formerly known as the International Boundary Commission), and endows this body with a number of powers and duties. These include investigating and developing plans for construction works, overseeing the respective obligations of apportionment, and resolving any disputes between the parties [*Id.* at art. 24].

In addition, in making specific suggestions regarding improvements to the waterways, the IBWC proposes official instruments known as "Minutes" that the parties adopt through the diplomatic process. In formalizing a Minute, the IBWC publicly announces a written recommendation and the governments then bind themselves to that recommendation through an exchange of diplomatic Notes. An important example of these is Minute No. 242 (1973), which establishes specific responsibilities for both parties regarding the salinity of the Colorado River [International Boundary and Water Commission United States and Mexico, *English Text of Minute 242*, (30 Aug. 1973) Minute No. 242]. More recent examples include Minute No. 319 (2012), which extends humanitarian measures from a 2010 agreement to allow Mexico to defer delivery of a portion of its Colorado River allotment while it continues to make repairs to earthquake-damaged infrastructure and implements measures to address salinity impacts stemming from joint cooperative actions [International Boundary and Water Commission United States and Mexico, *English Text of Minute 319*, (20 Nov. 2012) Minute No. 319]. Minute No. 320 (2015) marks the first IBWC agreement focused on sediment and trash problems in the Tijuana River Basin, and establishes a framework of cooperation to address those issues [International Boundary and Water Commission United States and Mexico, *English Text of Minute 320*, (5 Oct. 2015) Minute No. 320].

Though the 1944 Colorado River Treaty does require the IBWC "to give preferential attention to the solution of all border sanitation problems" in providing for joint use of the international waters [1944 Colorado River Treaty at art. 3], this mandate by itself proved insufficient in protecting the common environment. To address this need more adequately, the parties adopted a separate agreement—the 1983 Agreement to Cooperate in the Solution of Environmental Problems in the Border Area (La Paz Agreement). The La Paz Agreement commits the two parties to cooperation in the field of environmental protection and conservation in the border area, obligating that they "undertake, to the fullest extent practical, to adopt the appropriate measures to prevent, reduce and eliminate sources of pollution" [La Paz Agreement at art. 1]. To this end the parties conclude Annexes that specify more detailed obligations, such as Annex I concerning the San Diego—Tijuana water sanitation problem [*Id.* at Annex I]. Annex I, the only addendum dealing exclusively with water pollution, requires that the parties continue appropriate consultations with regard to the construction, operation, and maintenance of disposal and treatment facilities [*Id.*].

In the La Paz Agreement, the parties agree to take measures, "to the fullest practical extent," to prevent, reduce, and eliminate border pollution [*Id.* at art. II], and to coordinate their efforts to address the problems of air, land, and water pollution in the area [*Id.* at art. V]. The agreement defines the border area as the region "situated 100 kilometers on either side of the inland and maritime boundaries between the Parties" [*Id.* at art. IV]. In effect, the La Paz Agreement functions as a framework for further action, providing for the creation of annexes to deal with specific problems.

The North American Free Trade Agreement (NAFTA) and its progeny, the North American Agreement on Environmental Cooperation (NAAEC) between the U.S., Canada, and Mexico, have prompted more extensive cooperation regarding transboundary water resources. The latter document—in addition to restating general objectives of environmental protection—establishes a Commission for Environmental Cooperation (CEC) that oversees the environmental status of the three North American States. The Council of the CEC considers and develops recommendations concerning pollution prevention techniques, conservation and other transboundary environmental issues [NAAEC at art. 10]. Recognizing water resources as a significant transboundary environmental issue, the CEC has initiated studies to improve the management of transboundary water resources along both the U.S.-Mexico border and the U.S.-Canada border.

Building on the goals and objectives of the Environmental Side Agreement, Mexico and the U.S. also created the Border Environment Cooperation Commission (BECC) in 1993 [*see Agreement Concerning the Establishment of a Border Environment Cooperation Commission and a North American Development Bank,* Nov. 16, 1993, 32 I.L.M. 1545]. The BECC works closely with the North American Development Bank and the IBWC with regard to environmental infrastructure projects, facilitating the construction and improvement of border sanitation facilities. The BECC was also part of the ten-year Border 2012 program, which used a community-based approach to fund a wide range of activities, including watershed cleanups and storm water harvesting [U.S.-Mexico Environmental Program, *Border 2012 Accomplishments Report (2010–2012),* (2012) U.S. Environmental Protection Agency at 2]. Based on the successes of Border 2012, a new bi-national program has been developed through extensive public input and participation. Border 2020 will continue the collaboration and cooperation between the U.S. and Mexico to improve the environment in the shared border region.

F.   CONCLUSIONS

About 60% of the world's freshwaters are transboundary, so a solid international legal framework for water cooperation is critical for preventing conflicts and ensuring sustainable management of shared resources. The entry into force of the Convention on International Watercourses is a breakthrough for transboundary water cooperation and international water law, as it provides a firm ground for cooperation in transboundary water basins around the world. However, it is still evident that the problems of transboundary water pollution form only a part of the larger picture of land-based pollution, toxics, and biodiversity. Our focus on transboundary river pollution has been based on political and legal developments, and should not obscure the importance of seeing this as one component of a more comprehensive challenge.

CHAPTER SIXTEEN
DESERTIFICATION

A. NATURE OF THE PROBLEM

The arid, semi-arid, and dry sub-humid regions of the world are generally referred to as "drylands," "plains," or "grasslands." Dryland areas naturally receive less water than forest regions, but more than deserts. These areas can be severely affected by climate change, and other human impacts, Climate change may be caused by severe short term droughts as well as long periods without rainfall. Human impacts arise from the removal of natural vegetation, over-cultivation, the exhaustion of surface water, and the mining of groundwater. Climate change and human impacts often destroy the life-supporting quality of drylands and cause erosion, loss of soil fertility, reduced ability to hold water, salinization of the soil and water (the accumulation of salts), exhaustion of groundwater, and diminution of surface water [Agenda 21, (1992) U.N. Doc. A/CONF. 151/26 at chs. 12.2 & 12.18]. This advanced stage of land degradation, in which the biological potential of the land is destroyed, is a called "desertification."

Drylands make up nearly 34% of the world's landmass and are particularly vulnerable to natural and human destruction due to the small water containment in the soil [United Nations Convention to Combat Desertification (UNCCD), *Desertification: The Invisible Frontline* May 2016 at 2–3 (hereinafter UNCCD Invisible Frontline)]. Agriculture on these lands makes up a major source of the world's food supply, particularly for populations living in poverty [*Id.* at 2]. Unfortunately, 70% of the world's drylands (equal to 3,600 million hectares) are degraded [United Nations Convention to Combat Desertification (UNCCD), *Fact Sheet 2: The Causes of Desertification* at 1]. Drylands continue to be degraded at an alarming rate—over 12 million hectares of productive land become barren every year due to desertification and drought, which is a lost opportunity to produce 20 million tons of grain [UNCCD Invisible Frontline at 2]. The impacts of desertification are far worse in developing countries, which have scant resources for rehabilitating degraded land [*see generally* William C. Burns, *The International Convention to Combat Desertification: Drawing a Line in the Sand?*, 16 MICH. J. INT'L L. 831 (1995) at 845–48].

B. IMPACTS OF DESERTIFICATION

Desertification of agricultural drylands jeopardizes ecosystem services globally, including crop yields, clean air, fresh water, disturbance regulation, climate regulation, recreational opportunities, and fertile soils [The Economics of Land Degradation (ELD), *The value of land: Prosperous lands and positive rewards through sustainable land management* (Sept 2015) at 8]. Estimates of the global value of lost ecosystem services range between $6.3 and $10.6 trillion [*Id.*]. Unfortunately, this impact is distributed unevenly across human populations, often with the greatest impact on the most vulnerable populations—the rural poor [*Id.* at 9]. This population depends on land for their sustenance, and desertification often forces them to migrate. Some may attempt to cultivate remaining marginally productive land, further enhancing the process of desertification. Others migrate to urban areas, where the added stress on urban resources has the potential to create social unrest. Moreover, in addition to the agricultural, economic, and social impacts, desertification also threatens the biodiversity of ecosystems by destroying plants and critical habitat for animals (*see* Ch. 5).

Desertification has its greatest impact in Africa, where two thirds of the continent is desert or drylands. Africa is home to extensive agricultural drylands, almost three quarters of which are already degraded to some degree [United Nations to Combat Desertification (UNCCD), *Fact Sheet 11: Combating desertification in Africa* at 1].

Desertification also comes in many different forms in Asia. Of the 4.3 billion hectares in Asia, almost 1.7 billion are dry sub-humid, semi-arid, and arid land. Highly degraded areas include the deforested and overgrazed highlands of Laos, the steeply eroded mountain slopes of Nepal, and the growing sand dunes of Syria [United Nations Convention to Combat Desertification (UNCCD), *Fact Sheet 12: Combating desertification in Asia* at 1].

Though better known for its rain forests, Latin America and the Caribbean are actually about one-quarter desert and drylands. The deserts of Latin America's Pacific Coast stretch from southern Ecuador along the entire Peruvian shoreline and well into northern Chile. Further inland, at altitudes between 3,000 and 4,500 meters, the high, dry plains of the Andean mountains cover large areas of Peru, Bolivia, Chile, and Argentina. The Caribbean States of the Dominican Republic, Cuba, Haiti, and Jamaica, amongst others, also contain arid zones, and erosion is noticeably intensifying in many East Caribbean islands [United Nations Convention to Combat Desertification (UNCCD), *Fact Sheet 13: Combating desertification in Latin American and the Caribbean* at 1].

The Northern Mediterranean region has been settled and cultivated for millennia by various cultures and civilizations. Most of the region is semi-arid and subject to high rainfall variability, resulting in seasonal droughts or sudden intense downpours. Soils often become salinized and unproductive in response to over-cultivation and overgrazing [United Nations Convention to Combat Desertification (UNCCD), *Fact Sheet 14: Combating desertification in the Northern Mediterranean* at 1].

Desertification and drought also affect many parts of Central and Eastern Europe. Much of the climate in this region is classified as dry sub-humid, although some areas, such as those along the northwest coasts of the Black Sea and the Caspian Sea, are even drier and are classified as semi-arid. Soil degradation, particularly due to water-induced erosion, is considered to be medium to very high in many countries in this region [United Nations Convention to Combat Desertification (UNCCD), *Fact Sheet 15:*

Combating   land   degradation / desertification   in Central and Eastern Europe at 1].

C. CAUSES OF DESERTIFICATION

Population growth and economic demand have led to over-cultivation—farming land beyond its sustainable fertility. Population growth has demanded increased food production, requiring the farming of marginally productive lands and encouraging the shortening of fallow periods. Over-cultivation also arises from economic pressures for revenue-generating cash crops that can be exported. These crops are usually land-intensive, nutrient-depleting, and reduce the land area available for food crops. The result of over-cultivation is that drylands, naturally poor in nutrients and organic content, become even more susceptible to erosion. Their topsoil is blown or washed away, exposing subsoil that is often infertile and less able to absorb water, thus leading to desertification.

In addition to over-cultivation, irrigation practices that do not properly drain the soil cause salinization, reducing soil fertility and stunting plant growth. It is a serious problem not only in Asia and the Middle East, but also in North America, where irrigation practices in the western U.S. have caused serious land degradation in California and Mexico [*see generally* Gary D. Weatherford & F. Lee Brown eds., NEW COURSES FOR THE COLORADO RIVER (1986)]. In order to fulfill its international obligations to Mexico, the U.S. has built a $260 million desalinization plant and improved its irrigation practices by lining water canals to reduce salt accumulation (*see* Ch. 15).

Overgrazing is also a problem, as one-half of the world's cattle graze in drylands [WRI 1994 at 296–7]. In developing countries, cattle are raised as a source of food for domestic consumption as well as for export. When land shortages lead to the unsustainable pasturing of livestock, native vegetation (such as grasses, which naturally help hold the soil) are often replaced with shrubs. At the same time, the pulverizing and compacting of soil by cattle hooves leads to soil erosion and contributes further to desertification.

Deforestation is another cause of desertification. Globally, around 2.8 billion people (the "Energy Poor") rely almost exclusively on wood and other types of biomass for cooking and heating [Lakshman Guruswamy, ed., *International Energy and Poverty: The Emerging Contours,* (2016) Routledge]. The lack of alternative sources of energy leads to difficulty meeting basic human needs—including cooking, heating, water, sanitation, illumination, transportation, and basic mechanical power—and also results in deforestation, as forests are cleared to provide fuel [*Id.*]. More than 95% of the Energy Poor live in either sub-Saharan Africa or developing Asia, which already have large areas of drylands [*Id.*]. Forests are also cleared for crop cultivation and livestock grazing. Deforestation often acts as a starting point for desertification because destroyed tree and plant roots no longer hold the soil together or provide the organic material necessary for soil to maintain its water absorbent qualities.

Some social policies are more responsible for desertification than others. For example, many States with severe desertification problems have land ownership and tenure systems that do not provide security of tenure for the farmers and ranchers who work the land. Consequently, these groups find no incentives to conserve soil or water. Some developing nations have even encouraged farmers to clear and settle in forests as a means of asserting national sovereignty over native tribes and appeasing demands for land ownership reform.

D.   REMEDIAL OBJECTIVES

Desertification raises questions common to other international environmental problems, and thus must be addressed within the conceptual framework of sustainable development (SD). In 1992, the United Nations Conference on Environment and Development (UNCED), also known as Earth Summit, adopted Agenda 21, a program for SD that recommended preventive measures for threatened or slightly degraded drylands, and rehabilitative measures for moderately or severely degraded drylands. Recommended activities included improved land- and water-use policies, improved agricultural and ranching technologies, soil and water conservation to restore and sustain productivity, reforestation, protection of special ecological areas, and development of alternative energy sources [Agenda 21 (1992), U.N. Doc. A/CONF/ 151/26 at Ch. 12].

In a global attempt to reduce extreme poverty, the Millennium Development Goals (MDGs) were adopted at the Millennium Summit in 2000. In 2012, sustainable development goals (SDGs) were adopted to replace MDGs at the United Nations Conference on Sustainable Development (UNCSD). SDG15 deals with life on land. It seeks to sustainably manage forests, combat desertification, halt and reverse land degradation, and halt biodiversity loss [Sustainable Development Knowledge Platform Report of the Secretary-General, *Progress towards the Sustainable Development Goals: Sustainable Development Goal 15.* E/2016/75, *available at* https://sustainable development.un.org/sdg15 (last visited Apr. 2017)]. While desertification is not the only focus of SDG15, it identifies issues such as biodiversity loss and land degradation that cause or result from desertification, and accentuates the need for a global legal response.

The United Nations Convention to Combat Desertification (UNCCD) is the sole legally binding international agreement linking environment and development to sustainable land management [*United Nations Convention to Combat Desertification*, 17 Jun. 1994 (entered into force 26 Dec. 1996) 33 I.L.M. 1328] (hereinafter UNCCD)]. The UNCCD specifically addresses drylands, where some of the most vulnerable ecosystems and peoples can be found. As of 2017, the UNCCD has 195 parties.

E. LEGAL RESPONSE

The UNCCD adopts an innovative "bottom-up" approach to an increasingly destructive environmental problem, seeking to combat desertification and mitigate the effects of drought, with the goal of promoting SD in affected areas [*Id.* at art. 2(1)]. It defines desertification as "[l]and degradation in arid, semi-arid and dry sub-humid areas, resulting from various factors, including climatic variations and human activities" [*Id.* at art. 1(a)]. In other words, desertification is not—as it is often misunderstood—the expansion of existing deserts. Instead, the UNCCD places significant emphasis on the human role in creating desertification, identifying causation as a "complex interaction among physical, biological, political, social, cultural and economic factors" [*Id.* at pmbl.]. Drought, on the other hand, is defined as a naturally occurring phenomenon brought about by below normal precipitation [*Id.* at art. 1(c)].

While requiring cooperation and coordination at the sub-regional, regional, and international levels, the UNCCD also establishes a strong mandate to involve local communities both in the decision-making and implementation processes. This dedication to a "bottom-up" approach reflects a growing consensus that only a decentralized strategy will work to control environmental degradation, a strategy that includes and rewards local people.

1. REGIONAL IMPLEMENTATION
ANNEXES (RIAs)

The emphasis of the UNCCD remains on Africa, where the problem is seen as most acute, but it also contains Regional Implementation Annexes (RIAs) that spell out specific provisions for Asia, Latin America and the Caribbean, the Northern Mediterranean Region, and Central and Eastern Europe. Still, the RIA for Africa is by far the most detailed and thorough. Its proposals for National Action Programmes (NAPs) (*see* below) benefited from early attention when parties adopted a Resolution on Urgent Measures for Africa, which entered into force in June 1994, some two and a half years before the UNCCD itself [*Id.* at Annex I].

The RIA for Africa recognizes the particular conditions of the African region, including the fact that nearly two-thirds of the African continent is desert or drylands. While this land is vital for agriculture and food production, nearly 75% of these lands are estimated to be degraded to varying degrees. All African countries are parties to the UNCCD, and most have developed and submitted NAPs. In order for these NAPs to be successfully implemented, they must be integrated into other national strategies for SD, such as the Poverty Reduction Strategy, and consultative processes must be launched with the intention of building partnerships across sectors [*Id.* at Annex I].

The RIA for Asia calls for activities at the national, sub-regional, and regional level in the form of coordinated and integrated action programs.

Integration of activities directly related to desertification into other environmental and SD strategies is meant to maximize the output and benefit for affected State parties. Therefore, action at the local level should combine the fight against desertification with efforts to alleviate rural poverty [*Id.* at Annex II].

The RIA for Latin America and the Caribbean strongly emphasizes the need for SD. Unsustainable practices include excessive irrigation, harmful agricultural practices (such as inappropriate use of soil, fertilizers, and pesticides), overgrazing, and intensive exploitation of forests. Along with these unsustainable practices, frequent droughts and forest fires lead to massive land degradation. Indeed, the sharp losses of ecosystem productivity reduce overall economic productivity and livelihoods [*Id.* at Annex III].

The RIA for the Northern Mediterranean Region calls on its members to cooperate with other regions and sub-regions, and particularly with the developing countries of Northern Africa. The RIA also stimulates action at the national level. By 2008, in order of submission, Portugal, Italy, Greece, Turkey, and Spain had all adopted their NAPs to combat desertification [*Id.* at Annex IV].

The RIA for Central and Eastern Europe is the youngest annex in the UNCCD, adopted by the fourth session of the Conference of the Parties (COP) in 2000 and entered into force on September 6, 2001. Characteristics of this region include the process of economic transition, the variety and forms of land degradation in the different ecosystems, agricultural productivity problems due to soil depletion in arable lands, and other stresses. A Regional Coordination Unit was established in 2011 by the UNCCD secretariat in order to support the countries in this region. This RIA also contains sub-regional activities aimed at managing drought in South Eastern Europe [*Id.* at Annex V].

2. COMMITMENTS

a. Developing Countries

For their part, affected developing country parties must prepare and implement NAPs that seek to meet the objectives of the UNCCD. The purpose of each NAP is to identify the factors causing desertification, as well as practical measures that might ameliorate both desertification and drought [*Id.* at art. 10(1)]. In creating a long-term plan, each developing country party must specify the roles of government, local communities, and landowners, while also allowing for changing circumstances at the local level [*Id.* at art. 10(2)]. Furthermore, each NAP must provide for participation by non-governmental organizations (NGOs) and "local populations, both women and men, particularly resource users, including farmers and pastoralists" at all levels of the decision-making and implementation processes [*Id.* at art. 10(2)(f)].

In addition to the creation of individual NAPs, the UNCCD requires affected parties to consult and cooperate, as appropriate, in the development of sub-regional and regional action programs [*Id.* at art. 11].

The RIA for Africa elaborates on these obligations, requiring, among other things, that affected parties establish sub-regional mechanisms both to manage shared natural resources and to deal with transboundary environmental problems [*Id.* at Annex I, art. 11]. At the regional level, the RIA for Africa requires a further action program that promotes regional cooperation through regular consultations, focusing particularly on capacity-building and the development and exchange of scientific and technological information [*Id.* at Annex I, art. 13].

At every level, the UNCCD sees the creation of partnership agreements as a means of elaborating and implementing the required action programs [*Id.* at arts. 9(3) & 14]. At the earliest juncture, developing countries should therefore seek the cooperation and involvement of industrialized countries, intergovernmental organizations, and NGOs. In the RIA for Africa, these partnership agreements should include both financial and technical assistance, whether attached to national, sub-regional, or regional action programs [*Id.* at Annex I, art. 18]. In this way the UNCCD—again in a "bottom-up" approach that begins at the field level—attempts to create a decentralized system of cooperation and commitment, involving a wide range of prospective donors at the first stages of design.

b. Industrialized Countries

The primary obligations of industrialized country parties remain the transfer of financial resources and technical assistance to developing countries [*Id.* at art. 6]. This means early involvement in partnership agreements, with a focus on addressing the physical, biological, and socio-economic aspects of the problem [*Id.* at art. 4]. As stated above, fulfillment of these obligations includes strategies for the eradication of poverty in the affected States [*Id.* at art. 4(2)(c)]. The RIA for Africa further elaborates on these general requirements, while also promoting institutional capacity-building in the areas of administration, science, and technology [*Id.* at Annex I, art. 5].

c. Implementation

The UNCCD created a number of institutional bodies that will help to implement it. The first is the COP, which was established as the supreme decision-making body of the UNCCD, comprising ratifying governments and regional economic integration organizations, such as the European Union (EU). One of the main functions of the COP is to review reports submitted by the parties detailing how they are carrying out their commitments and make recommendations based on the reports. The COP also has the power to make amendments or adopt new Annexes, such as additional RIAs. In this way, the COP can provide guidance as global circumstances and national needs change. To assist the COP, the UNCCD also provides for subsidiary bodies and allows the COP to establish additional ones if necessary. The implementation of the UNCCD was significantly advanced when the COP decided to set up a permanent secretariat in 1999 in Bonn, Germany.

The second institutional body is the Committee on Science and Technology, a subsidiary body of the COP. The Committee on Science and Technology provides the COP with information and advice on scientific and technological matters relating to combating desertification and mitigating the effects of drought, using the most up-to-date scientific knowledge. The Committee on Science and Technology is multi-disciplinary, open to the participation of the parties, and composed of government representatives with relevant expertise. It reports regularly to the COP on its work, including at each of the sessions of the COP.

Thirdly, a Global Mechanism helps the COP to promote funding for UNCCD-related activities and programs, though this mechanism was not conceived to raise or administer funds. Instead, the Global Mechanism encourages and assists donors, recipients, development banks, NGOs, and others to mobilize funds and to channel them to where they are most needed. It seeks to promote greater coordination among existing sources of funding, and greater efficiency and effectiveness in the use of funds. The Global Mechanism is under the authority of the COP, which periodically reviews its policies, operational modalities, and activities. The Global Mechanism is hosted by the International Fund for Agricultural Development.

Finally, the UNCCD has given NGOs a special place. It recognizes that one of the many strengths of the NGO community is that they are the voice of grassroots communities. To the extent that the

UNCCD aims to improve the livelihoods of marginalized populations, particularly those communities most threatened by drought and desertification, the COP has sought the assistance of the NGO community as part of the official program of work of the COP. As of COP-12 in 2015, 314 NGOs have been accredited with observer status to the COP [United Nations Convention to Combat Desertification (UNCCD), *Accreditation of intergovernmental and non-governmental organizations, and admission of observers,* Oct. 12–23, 2015, Conference of the Parties: Twelfth Session at 32]. The participation and contribution of NGOs is a necessary component of successful implementation of the UNCCD.

As with all international environmental regimes, the success of the UNCCD also rides on tangible contributions from the wealthier parties. In a recent review, it was found that the degree of progress made differs from State to State. For example, while most African parties have finalized their NAPs to combat desertification and are starting to implement them, the lack of adequate and predictable funding is an obstacle to implementation.

The Committee for the Review of the Implementation of the Convention (CRIC) assessed implementation in 2001 and found that the alignment of NAPs with national social and economic plans was not receiving "sufficient" priority from affected countries. They recommended that the Global Environmental Facility (GEF) simplify its procedures to allow easier access to funding to aid implementation. The CRIC applauded the creation of performance indicators and regulations on national monitoring systems for affected countries, but noted that there are problems with implementation and regulation. There was general concern that regional and sub-regional NAPs were not being implemented and a focus on improving the data submitted by affected countries—both in terms of standardizing national reports and for transfer of knowledge from NGOs. Developed countries were also encouraged to contribute more financial and technical assistance. At COP-12 in 2015, parties decided to make the next reporting exercise optional in light of the need to finalize the methodological approach to reporting. Thus, the special session of the CIRC in March 2017 will include only optional reporting.

3.   2007 10-YEAR STRATEGY

In 2007, parties to the UNCCD unanimously adopted a 10-Year Strategy to enhance the implementation of the UNCCD for 2008–2018. The Strategy further specified their goal:

"to forge a global partnership to reverse and prevent desertification/land degradation and to mitigate the effects of drought in affected areas in order to support poverty reduction and environmental sustainability" [United Nations Convention to Combat Desertification (UNCCD), *Report of the Conference of the Parties on its eighth session* (3–14 Sept. 2007) Madrid, Spain at Annex(II)(8)].

The 10-Year Strategy also contains the "strategic objectives" to be achieved by 2018 as well as the "operational objectives" that guide the actions of the short and medium-term effects. Since the adoption of the 10-Year Strategy, many affected countries have started the process of aligning their NAPs, sub-regional, and regional action programs with the 10-Year Strategy.

F.   CONCLUSIONS

Parties to the UNCCD are working together to improve the living conditions for people in drylands, maintain and restore land and soil productivity, and mitigate the effects of drought. Through its commitment to a bottom-up approach, the UNCCD encourages the participation of local people in combating deforestation and desertification. The UNCCD secretariat also works to facilitate cooperation between developing and industrialized countries. Two points need emphasis.

First, as we have noted in Chapters 2 and 6, and will emphasize in Chapter 18, the "bottom up" approach to SD has shifted the primary onus of taking action on desertification on developing countries. Prior to the SDGs, the primary responsibility for the alleviation of poverty and economic, social, and environmental action was placed squarely on the shoulders of the developed or industrialized countries. Developed countries accepted their legal obligation to do so under the principle of common but differentiated responsibilities (CBDR). The MDGs represented the practical expression of SD, and there was no doubt that the developed countries had undertaken the responsibility of financing the MDGs through overseas development assistance.

The bottom up approach and the SDGs reflect a different international ethos in which primary responsibility is place on those affected by the challenge: the developing countries. While the need for development assistance and CBDR is not abandoned, its role is clearly diminished. Development assistance has moved from its established position as the primary source of financing and action to an attenuated secondary source. The least developed countries (LDCs) are among the worst impacted by desertification, and this paradigm shift of SD can make their position very difficult because the UNCCD will be pushing against the tide of the new SD.

Second, the interconnected dynamics of land, climate, and biodiversity require an integrated approach. Thus, the UNCCD must collaborate with the other two Conventions from Earth Summit: the Convention on Biological Diversity (Biodiversity Convention) (*see* Ch. 5) and the United Nations Framework Convention on Climate Change (UNFCCC) (*see* Ch. 6), in pushing to implement whatever remains of CBDR.

CHAPTER SEVENTEEN
NUCLEAR DAMAGE

A. NATURE OF THE PROBLEM

The military use of nuclear bombs can lead to unparalleled suffering, while civilian deployment of nuclear energy has raised concerns about risks associated with exposure to radiation. Consequently, this chapter deals with military weapons production, use, and testing, as well as civilian nuclear energy applications such as power generation, medical uses, and nuclear waste disposal.

Radiation is a form of energy consisting of atomic particles and electromagnetic rays that are emitted from radioactive elements, such as uranium and plutonium. Radiation creates chemical changes, and when radiation strikes human tissue, it strips (or ionizes) the electrons or neutrons of the molecules, thereby killing or damaging human cells. The nature of the harm depends on the type and intensity of the radiation and the part of the body that is exposed. High-level radiation kills cells and can cause excruciating radiation sickness and death within days or weeks. In contrast, low-level radiation only damages cells, still allowing them to multiply, but the damaged cells may produce mutations that can lead to cancers and genetic defects years later. However, while radiation can be harmful, it is also important to remember that life evolved in the presence of natural radiation, called background radiation, and over time radiation has proven beneficial by facilitating adaptation and change in organisms and species [Martin S. Silberberg, CHEMISTRY: THE MOLECULAR NATURE OF MATTER AND CHANGE (2000) at 1060–1062].

The risk of exposure to radiation above the background level arises both from military and civilian uses of nuclear power. While the these figures conceal wide variations, it is estimated that 78% of worldwide human exposure to radiation arises from natural causes (i.e. background radiation), 14% from medical treatment and X-rays, and less than 1% from fallout, discharges, and occupational exposure resulting from nuclear weapons testing and power generation [R.B. Clark, MARINE POLLUTION, Fifth Edition (2001) 167–168]. Nonetheless, there is a strong public perception that radiation caused by nuclear power generation is dangerous, and the threat of mass destruction posed by the military use of the nuclear bomb is clearly etched in the public psyche. Such fear is reinforced by the reality of less catastrophic, but nonetheless devastating, accidents in nuclear power plants, such as the 1986 Chernobyl accident, which by one estimate caused thousands of cancer deaths [Silberberg, *supra*, at 1060], and the more recent 2011 incident in Fukushima, Japan. Moreover, it is a fact, as distinct from public sentiment or irrational fear, that some high-level nuclear wastes remain radioactive for many thousands of years, continuing to present the unresolved problem of nuclear waste disposal.

1. USE AND TESTING OF NUCLEAR WEAPONS

The detonation of a single nuclear bomb, or "warhead," would cause a local disaster on a scale that few people in the world have seen and survived. However, it pales in comparison with the effects of a nuclear war, in which many nuclear bombs explode. A conflict of that magnitude would likely cause the end of civilization in the States concerned, and perhaps over the whole world, as well as radioactive contamination of entire continents and terrible damage to the environment and ecology.

The effect of a single bomb would depend on its power, where it exploded (high in the air or at ground level), and whether it struck in a densely populated area, like a city, or in open country, like an isolated missile silo. The nuclear bombs available to the great military powers of the world (China, France, Israel, Russia, the United Kingdom, and the U.S.) range in power from several megatons down to a few kilotons, and some even smaller (a "megaton" is the explosive power of one million tons of TNT; a "kiloton" is the power of one thousand tons of TNT). Nuclear bombs likely to be available to terrorist organizations or governments other than the great military powers would likely be in the 10 to 100 kiloton range. Bombs made by amateurs might not explode with the full power they were designed for. The two bombs that have been exploded over cities, Hiroshima and Nagasaki in Japan in August 1945, were in the 10 to 20 kiloton range.

A one-megaton hydrogen bomb, hypothetically detonated on the earth's surface, would have about 80 times the blast power of the 1945 Hiroshima explosion. The devastation caused by such a nuclear bomb would begin at the core, with an intensive thermal wave causing pressure damage that creates a crater 200 feet deep and 1,000 feet in diameter, filled with highly radioactive soil and debris. Casualties from this initial impact decrease with distance from the core: within 1.7 miles of the core 98% of the people would be killed and only a few of the strongest buildings would remain standing, while 7 miles from the core only 5% of people would be killed instantly and 45% would be injured.

The initial blast and its shock waves would be followed by an equally destructive mass fire, which would accompanied by hurricane-force fire winds [Lynn Eden, *City on Fire*, BULL. OF THE ATOMIC SCIENTISTS (Jan/Feb 2004) at 33 & 37]. A great deal of radioactive earth and debris would be carried high into the atmosphere, forming a mushroom cloud. The material would drift downwind and gradually fall back to earth, contaminating thousands of square miles. Thus, the number of casualties caused by such a blast depends not only on the topography and density of the surrounding population, but also on the attendant weather conditions that would distribute the fission debris [John F. Ahearne et al., THE EFFECTS OF NUCLEAR EARTH-PENETRATOR AND OTHER WEAPONS (2005) at 75–76].

The extent to which radiation affects humans is usually measured in rems, a measurement that seeks to quantify the amount of radiation that will produce certain biological effects. However, because uncertainty continues to exist concerning the extent and nature of such biological effects, we will express effects in qualitative terms.

At a distance of 30 miles from the core, humans would be exposed to a greater-than-lethal dose of radiation. Death can occur within hours, and it would take about 10 years for radioactivity to drop to safe levels. At a distance of 90 miles, radiation exposure would cause death in 2 to 14 days. At 160 miles, humans would suffer extensive internal damage, including harm to nerve cells and the cells that line the digestive tract, loss of white blood cells, and temporary hair loss. Some 250 miles from the core, humans would suffer a temporary decrease in white blood cells and an uncertain increase in the risk of cancer and genetic diseases. Two to three years would need to pass before radioactivity levels in this area would drop enough to be considered safe by U.S. peacetime standards [Office of Technology Assessment, THE EFFECTS OF NUCLEAR WAR (1979)].

The explosion of numerous nuclear weapons of this magnitude could produce global environmental problems and climatic changes. Edible plants, livestock, and marine food sources could be destroyed or become contaminated, resulting in severe food shortages. Water could be contaminated by radioactivity and by pathogenic bacteria and viruses, especially if the initial explosions destroy sewage treatment and waste disposal facilities. Crop failures may also result from "nuclear winters" caused by the accumulation of soot in the atmosphere from explosion-induced fires. Finally, the ozone layer may be damaged by nitrogen oxides (NOx) released by fires caused by the bomb [John Harte, et al., TOXICS A TO Z (1991) at 153]. As we have seen, any damage to the ozone layer will expose the earth to harmful ultraviolet (UV) radiation (*see* Ch. 7).

Since 1945, there have been more than 2,000 nuclear test explosions. These have been primarily underground, but have also taken place in the atmosphere and underwater. Both the U.S. and the Soviets have conducted nuclear weapons tests in sparsely populated areas within their own borders, as well as outside of them [Geoscience Australia, *Query Nuclear Explosions Database, available at* http://www.ga.gov.au/oracle/nuclear-explosion.jsp (last visited Apr. 2017)]. Radioactive fallout from above-ground explosions cannot be contained within borders, and may be carried hundreds of miles downwind. For example, fallout from aboveground testing in northwest Russia during the Cold War was transported into air, land, and water throughout the Arctic [Environment and Health of Arctic Peoples, 2 L'AURAVETL'AN INFORMATION BULLETIN (Mar. 13, 1997)].

Underground testing also has potentially harmful effects on health and the environment. At the Nevada Test Site, used in 900 weapons tests between 1952 and 1992, underground nuclear explosions have caused serious radioactive contamination of the groundwater and soil, and the surrounding area suffers from increased incidents of cancer, thyroid disease, and birth defects [Jessica Barkas, *Testing the Bomb: Disparate Impacts on Indigenous Peoples in the American West, the Marshall Islands, and in Kazakhstan,* 13 U. BALT. J. ENVTL. L. 29 (2005) at 35–37]. The explosion of the first nuclear weapons at the end of the Second World War began the process of radioactive pollution of the sea, which was accelerated by conducting nuclear weapons testing until the Treaty Banning Nuclear Weapon Tests in the Atmosphere, in Outer Space and Underwater (Partial Test Ban Treaty) was signed, prohibiting all nuclear tests except for those carried out underground [*Treaty Banning Nuclear Weapon Tests in the Atmosphere, in Out Space and Underwater,* Aug. 5, 1963 (entered into force Oct. 10, 1963), 2 I.L.M 883 (hereinafter Partial Test Ban Treaty)]. French underground nuclear testing on atolls in the South Pacific produced fissures in the basalt bases, subsidence, and submarine slides. This has given rise to fears of a massive release of radioactive debris and concern about long-term containment of radioactive materials underground [testimony by Joshua Handler & Thomas W. Clements, *French Nuclear Testing and the South Pacific Nuclear Free Zone: Testimony on Nuclear Issues in the South Before the Subcomm. on Asia and the Pacific of the House Comm. on Int'l Relations,* 104th Cong. (1995), *available at Westlaw,* 1995 WL 12715828].

2.   CIVILIAN NUCLEAR ENERGY

The most recent report from the International Atomic Energy Agency (IAEA), in 2014, indicates that there are currently 435 operational nuclear power reactors in 30 countries around the world, with 72 more that were under construction in 15 countries [International Atomic Energy Agency (IAEA), *International Status and Prospects for Nuclear Power 2014*, (Aug. 4, 2014) GOV/INF/2014/12-GC(58)/INF/6 at 1]. In 2013, these plants generated less than 11% of world electricity production, the lowest value for nuclear energy since 1982 [*Id.*]. Still, all IAEA projections for global installed nuclear power capacity indicate an increase by 2030 [*Id.*]. The reasons for this increase include the need for carbon-free electricity, higher fossil fuel prices, and improved reactor designs.

In a nuclear power reactor, the chain reaction is controlled to prevent an explosion and the heat is used to generate power. Three risks of radiation leaks from civilian nuclear power generation arise: (a) during the operation of power plants; (b) by accidents; and (c) from waste disposal.

The routine operation of nuclear power plants generates radioactive materials in the form of stack gases, as well as radioactive liquid effluent. The IAEA has issued standards, regulations, codes of practice, guides, and other related instruments dealing with operational safety. Unfortunately, these are voluntary, not obligatory, standards. The continuing absence of universal standards of safety in the operation of nuclear power plants accentuates the dangers of accidents.

Unintentional releases of nuclear radiation, such as occurred at Three Mile Island, Chernobyl, and Fukushima, Japan, illustrate the perils of civilian nuclear use [*see generally* Shepard Buchanan et al., ENVIRONMENTAL COSTS OF ELECTRICITY (1991)]. The meltdown during the Three Mile Island accident in the U.S. in 1979 did not result in an explosion, and the amount of radiation released was far less than at Chernobyl. Still, abnormal radiation was detected 250 miles from the power plant and in Wales, England.

The Chernobyl accident took place in the former Soviet Union in 1986, where design flaws and operator error caused a meltdown and explosion that resulted in a massive release of radiation. Within two months of the accident, 31 people had died from severe radiation burns. However, the overall extent of the damage remains controversial. For example, a book authored by three notable Russian scientists, published in 2009 by the New York Academy of Sciences, puts the total Chernobyl death toll at 985,000 people between 1986 and 2004 [Alexey V. Yablokov, et al., Chernobyl, *Consequences of the Catastrophe for People and the Environment*, ANNALS OF THE NEW YORK ACADEMY OF SCIENCES, Volume 1181 (Dec. 2009)]. The book is based on health data, radiological surveys, and over 5,000 scientific reports detailing the spread of radioactive poisons following the explosion at Chernobyl. It reports that Chernobyl emitted hundreds of millions of curies of radiation, a quantity hundreds of times larger than the fallout from the atomic bombs dropped on Hiroshima and Nagasaki.

On the other hand, the United Nations (UN) Scientific Committee on the Effects of Atomic

Radiation came to a remarkably different conclusion. It found that, apart from the dramatic increase in thyroid cancer among those exposed at a young age and some indication of increased leukemia and cataract incidence among the workers, there is no clearly demonstrated increase in the incidence of solid cancers or leukemia due to radiation in the exposed populations. Neither is there any proof of other non-malignant disorders that are related to ionizing radiation. However, there were widespread psychological reactions to the accident, which were due to fear of the radiation, not the actual radiation doses received. This study estimates the total deaths reliability attributable to the radiation produced at Chernobyl at 62 [UN Scientific Committee on the Effects of Atomic Radiation, *Health Effects Due to Radiation from the Chernobyl Incident* (2008)].

More recently, a 9.0 earthquake in March 2011 created a tsunami that damaged a nuclear power plant in Fukushima, Japan. The accidents at Fukushima and Chernobyl were both given a severity rating of seven, the highest possible level on the international scale used to evaluate the seriousness of nuclear incidents. However, the accidents were starkly different in terms of their cause, the local government's response, and their health effects [Nuclear Energy Institute, *Fact Sheet: Comparing Fukushima and Chernobyl* (Mar. 2015)]. The authorities in the former Soviet Union were slow to take action to protect the supply of food and milk, which lead to a spike in thyroid cancers among children from consuming contaminated products. Conversely, the Japanese government moved rapidly to implement protective measures, evacuating people and halting food shipments from the area, as well as distributing potassium iodide to local residents to prevent their thyroid glands from absorbing radiation [*Id.*]. Though there is some controversy over how many deaths to attribute to Chernobyl, it is clear that some deaths did occur as a result. However, no deaths from radiation exposure have been attributed to the accident in Japan [*Id.*].

3.   NUCLEAR WASTE

Nuclear wastes are the by-products of nuclear weapons production, nuclear power generation, medical and dental uses, research, and other processes using radioactive elements. By volume, 99% of nuclear waste emits a low level of radiation. Low-level radioactive waste is solid by definition, and is usually disposed of by packaging it in leak-resistant containers and burying in shallow trenches. This creates the potential for environmental problems if radioactive contamination leaks from the waste repository. Disposal sites may have hydrological problems—such as erosion, accumulation of water in the trenches, and groundwater movement—that would allow the radiation to contaminate the ground and water, and thereby enter food chains. Contaminated groundwater is the most common pathway for human exposure to radiation from nuclear waste. In addition to waste in repositories, some low-level waste was dumped at sea by both the U.S. and the Soviets [Jeffrey L. Canfield, *Soviet and Russian Nuclear Waste Dumping in the Arctic Marine Environment:*

Legal, Historical, and Political Implications, 7 GEO. INT'L ENVTL. L. REV. 353 (1994)].

High-level radioactive wastes are defined as those that are sufficiently radioactive to generate heat, and are composed of spent nuclear fuel. Nuclear weapons production requires plutonium, which is extracted from the fuel of military production reactors, leaving large quantities of highly radioactive liquid waste and fuel rods. Nuclear power plant fuel is replaced about once a year, and the spent fuel rods are temporarily stored at the power plants to cool down in large ponds of water [*see* Harte, et al., *supra*, at 162–63]. The water thereby becomes radioactive. The spent fuel itself will remain radioactive for thousands of years. Long-term storage of such high-level waste has been attempted either by placing the waste in repositories in deep geologic formations or by ocean dumping [*see* Ronnie D. Lipschutz, RADIOACTIVE WASTE: POLITICS, TECHNOLOGY, AND RISK (1980)]; (*see* Ch. 9). With both methods, the concern is the possible effect of radioactive waste leaks and the effects of decay heat on the surrounding environment. As we have seen, the Convention on the Prevention of Marine Pollution by Dumping of Wastes and Other Matter (London Convention) banned the dumping of high-level waste in the oceans 1972, and all radioactive waste in 1994 (*see* Ch. 12).

In the U.S., despite several decades of preparations to make Yucca Mountain in Nevada the nation's first permanent nuclear waste repository, the project is still mired in intense controversy. According to experts, it would take more than another decade and cost at least $30 billion before the underground site could actually begin accepting shipments of highly radioactive waste [Keith Rogers, *Many obstacles remain before Yucca Mountain could accept first nuclear waste shipments,* (Nov. 18, 2016) Las Vegas Review-Journal]. The future of the Yucca Mountain site is unclear. As of this writing, President Donald Trump has declined to take a position for or against storing radioactive waste at Yucca Mountain [Sean Sullican, *Trump punts on Yucca Mountain, a major issue in key swing state of Nevada,* (Oct. 6, 2016) The Washington Post]. Alternatively, spent fuel can be reprocessed for additional uses, which reduces the quantity of nuclear waste requiring permanent disposal. Most States, apart from the U.S., are currently reprocessing their nuclear wastes.

B.   REMEDIAL OBJECTIVES

In the Advisory Opinion of the International Court of Justice (ICJ) on the *Legality of the Threat or Use of Nuclear Weapons*, the ICJ stated: "Nuclear weapons which cannot be contained in either space or time have the potential to destroy all civilization and the entire ecosystem of the planet" [*Legality of the Threat or Use of Nuclear Weapons,* 1996 I.C.J. 226 (July 8)]. Fear of such destruction has led the international community to seek ways of containing and eliminating the nuclear threat from both military and civilian sources.

The most obvious way to eliminate a nuclear threat is to remove the source: in the military case, this means banning nuclear weapons all together. In the

Legality of Nuclear Weapons Case, the ICJ appeared to endorse such a method by holding that States are under a legal obligation to pursue and conclude negotiations with a view to achieving nuclear disarmament.

However, the political problems confronting such a course are formidable. One such obstacle is that States in possession of nuclear weapons happen to include the most powerful States in the world, who are loath to relinquish weapons they see as fundamental to their international influence. A second, related roadblock to disarmament is the fact that nuclear deterrence and the "balance of terror" have been the linchpins of Western defense policy for over 50 years during the Cold War and its aftermath.

Nevertheless, the end of the Cold War has accelerated a sequence of unfolding conventional and judicial developments of great importance. These continuing changes, in the view of many commentators, have transformed the mirage of a nuclear weapons-free world into a foreseeable objective. Even if total nuclear disarmament were impossible, alternatives include non-proliferation of nuclear weapons and banning any further nuclear tests. Unfortunately, any of these options will still leave the problem of what to do with the huge quantities of existing nuclear wastes.

In the realm of civilian nuclear energy, an important question is the extent to which preventative and remedial legal responses have been successful. A preventative regime seeks to regulate the construction and operation of nuclear plants in a way that prevents pollution and accidents. It also provides for a system of warning and assistance if accidents do occur. At present, the IAEA is not empowered to impose obligatory international safety standards for reactor construction or operations: instead, a remedial regime facilitates the granting of compensation when damages have been caused. The details of how the international community has responded legally call for fuller discussions.

C. LEGAL RESPONSE

As the dangers of nuclear contamination have gradually become more apparent over the years, the international community has struggled to develop rules governing both the civilian and military uses of nuclear energy. In this section of the book, we first outline how the international community has addressed the intractable challenge of nuclear weapons, despite formidable political difficulties. We next outline the response of international environmental law (IEL) to the dangers of civilian nuclear power generation. Finally, we discuss the regime governing accidents at nuclear installations and the question of liability.

1.   USE AND TESTING OF NUCLEAR WEAPONS

a. Treaty Overlay

The arms control treaties took the first steps toward nuclear disarmament. The Treaty Between the U.S. and the U.S.S.R on the Elimination of Their

Intermediate-Range and Shorter-Range Missals [*Treaty Between the U.S. and the U.S.S.R on the Elimination of Their Intermediate-Range and Shorter-Range Missals*, Dec. 8, 1987, 27 I.L.M. 84] dealt with the reduction of nuclear missiles, while the Strategic Arms Reduction Talks (START) led to the Treaty Between the U.S. and the U.S.S.R. on the Reduction and Elimination of Strategic Offensive Arms, [*Treaty Between the U.S. and the U.S.S.R. on the Reduction and Elimination of Strategic Offensive Arms,* Nov. 25, 1991, 32 I.L.M. 246], which reduced the massive nuclear arsenals of the U.S. and Russia. Second, a cluster of treaties addressed the testing, deployment, possession, and use of nuclear weapons in a variety of locales and conditions. The most important of the treaties restricting nuclear testing are the Partial Test Ban Treaty and the Treaty on Principles Governing the Activities of States in the Exploration and Use of Outer Space, Including the Moon and other Celestial Bodies (Outer Space Treaty). Four significant regional treaties confine the deployment of nuclear weapons in Latin America, the South Pacific, South-East Asia, and Africa. The Treaty of Tlatelolco for the Prohibition of Nuclear Weapons in Latin America [*Treaty of Tlatelolco for the Prohibition of Nuclear Weapons in Latin America*, Feb. 14, 1967 (entered into force Apr. 22, 1968), 6 I.L.M. 52] prohibits the use of nuclear weapons by the contracting parties. The parties to the South Pacific Nuclear Free Zone Treaty [*South Pacific Nuclear Free Zone Treaty*, Aug. 6, 1985 (entered into force Dec. 11, 1986), 24 I.L.M. 1442], the Organization of African Unity: African Nuclear-Weapon-Free Zone

Treaty [*Organization of African Unity: African Nuclear-Weapon-Free Zone Treaty*, June 21–23, 1995, 35 I.L.M. 698], and the South-East Asia Nuclear Free Zone Treaty [*South-East Asia Nuclear Free Zone Treaty*, Dec. 15, 1995, 35 I.L.M. 635] undertake not to manufacture, acquire, or possess any nuclear weapons. These treaties must be read in the context of the Treaty on the Final Settlement with Respect to Germany [*Treaty on the Final Settlement with Respect to Germany*, Sept. 12, 1990, 29 I.L.M. 1186] and the Treaty on the Non-proliferation of Nuclear Weapons (NPT) [*Treaty on the Non-Proliferation of Nuclear Weapons,* July 1, 1968 (entered into force Mar. 5, 1970), 7 I.L.M. 809 (hereinafter NPT)].

The contours of a general prohibition on nuclear weapons began to take definite shape with the NPT in 1968. This treaty sought to control nuclear damage by prohibiting "horizontal" proliferation (the spread of nuclear weapons to non-nuclear States in a world of five declared nuclear States) and "vertical" proliferation (the further amassing and development of nuclear weapons by nuclear States). The nuclear States were obligated:

"to pursue negotiations in good faith on effective measures relating to cessation of the nuclear arms race at an early date and to nuclear disarmament, and on a treaty on general and complete disarmament under strict and effective international control" [*Id.* at art. VI].

In 1995, the NPT Review and Extension Conference indefinitely extended the NPT, endorsing an earlier UN Security Council resolution that reiterated and re-affirmed the need for "general and complete disarmament" called for by Article VI [United Nations, *Resolution 988* (1995)]. The Conference did so with a "politically binding" Final Document on Extension of the Treaty on the Non-proliferation of Nuclear Weapons that re-asserted the importance of fulfilling the legal obligation expressed in Article VI [*Final Document on Extension of the Treaty on the Non-proliferation of Nuclear Weapons,* May 11, 1995, 34 I.L.M. 959].

One problem facing the NPT is how to deal creatively with three States that remain outside the treaty: Pakistan and India, both holders of nuclear arsenals, and Israel, which maintains an official policy of ambiguity but is believed to be nuclear-weapons-capable. As the Director-General of the IAEA pointed out, none of these three is likely to give up its nuclear weapons or the nuclear weapons option outside of a global or regional arms control framework. The traditional strategy of treating such States as outsiders is no longer a realistic method of bringing these last few States into the fold [Mohamed ElBaradei, *Rethinking Nuclear Safeguards*, THE WASHINGTON POST (Jun. 14, 2006) at A23]. (One other UN member State—South Sudan—has also never joined the NPT. While it is the only African state that is not party to the NPT, South Sudan does not possess nuclear weapons.)

In 2006, however, India entered into an agreement with the U.S. called the U.S.-India Civil Nuclear Cooperation agreement, which was approved by the

Senate in November 2006 and implemented in the U.S. by the U.S.-India Peaceful Atomic Energy Cooperation Act of 2006 [*United States-India Civil Nuclear Cooperation Agreement* (2006), 46 I.L.M. 415]. Pursuant to the agreement, India will divide its nuclear facilities into two separate categories: military and civilian. The civilian installations will now be subject to safeguards, and India will develop a relationship with the IAEA. India has also agreed to a moratorium on nuclear testing. In return, the U.S. will provide India with nuclear fuel and technology for its civilian facilities. This is a groundbreaking pact, which brings India closer to the mainstream of the NPT, without actually joining. It is a realistic agreement that works around India's refusal to ratify the NPT. While the Director-General of the IAEA commended the agreement and its "outside-the-box thinking," he pointed out that the strong support of both India and the U.S.—as well as all other nuclear weapons states—is sorely needed to make this treaty a reality [ElBaradei, *supra*]. As of this writing, cooperation between the U.S. and India on this matter appears to be ongoing. In 2015 the IAEA sent a team to review India's regulatory framework for the safety of its nuclear power plants. The team both identified good practices and also provided recommendations and suggestions for improvement [International Atomic Energy Agency (IAEA), *IAEA Mission Concludes Peer Review of India's Nuclear Regulatory Framework,* (Mar. 27, 2015)].

b. Nuclear Testing

Even at the height of the Cold War, the nuclear powers recognized the environmental threat posed by nuclear explosions, and so negotiated the Partial Test Ban Treaty, which, not surprisingly, forbids all nuclear weapons tests in the atmosphere, outer space, and underwater. The agreement also prohibits any other nuclear explosion, such as an underground explosion, that causes a transboundary exchange of radioactive debris [Partial Test Ban Treaty at art. I(1)(b)]. The Partial Test Ban Treaty seeks to end the "contamination of man's environment by radioactive substances," and calls upon the parties to continue negotiations toward the banning of all nuclear testing, including underground explosions [*Id.* at pmbl.]. Originally, the treaty was signed by all the nuclear powers except France and China.

Since 1963 there has been considerable pressure to take the final step toward cessation of all nuclear testing. Of their own accord, the U.S. and the former Soviet Union forged two treaties controlling underground explosions in the 1970s—the Treaty Between the Soviet Union and the U.S. on the Limitation of Underground Nuclear Weapons Tests [*Treaty Between the Soviet Union and the U.S. on the Limitation of Underground Nuclear Weapons Tests,* July 3, 1974, 13 I.L.M. 906] and the Treaty on Underground Nuclear Explosions for Peaceful Purposes [*Treaty on Underground Nuclear Explosions for Peaceful Purposes,* May 28, 1976, 15 I.L.M. 891].

Efforts to halt nuclear testing took a dramatic step forward when the UN General Assembly responded to increased concern from non-nuclear States by calling for the development of a comprehensive ban on all nuclear testing. After many years of arduous negotiation, the Comprehensive Nuclear Test Ban Treaty (CTBT) was opened for signature in late 1996 [*Comprehensive Nuclear Test Ban Treaty* (Sept. 10, 1996), 35 I.L.M. 1439]. By prohibiting all nuclear testing, the CTBT effectively prevents the development of new nuclear weapons (although recent monumental advances in supercomputers have enabled scientists to test the reliability of current nuclear stockpiles through complex simulation runs). The five major nuclear States immediately signed the CTBT—the U.S., Russia, China, France, and the United Kingdom— as well as nearly one hundred other States. The Preparatory Commission for the CTBT began work almost immediately on the task of establishing the International Monitoring System and the International Data Centre, and developing operational manuals for on-site inspection, all of which will be implemented as soon as the treaty goes into effect.

However, the treaty must be ratified by the 44 presumptive nuclear powers before it comes into force, and this has presented substantial difficulties. Presently, eight of the required States refrain from ratifying the treaty, and three—North Korea, India, and Pakistan—have yet to sign it [Preparatory Commission for the Comprehensive Nuclear-Test-Ban Treaty Organization, *Status of Signature and*

Ratification, available at http://www.ctbto.org/the-treaty/status-of-signature-and-ratification/ (last visited Apr. 2017)]. Furthermore, the U.S., alone among its NATO partners, has thus far declined to ratify the CTBT. According to its critics, this places the U.S. in an ambiguous position vis-à-vis disarmament. In light of the fact that the U.S. has maintained a moratorium on testing for years and has promised to maintain that status at the present time, its abstention from the CTBT seems to serve no useful function.

Senate opponents of the CTBT have offered four reasons as to why it should not be ratified by the U.S. First, opponents argue that the CTBT would stop neither proliferation nor testing by current nuclear States. The fact is that States may develop nuclear weapons without testing—North Korea is a case in point. Iran may be close behind. Opponents reject the claim that in following the U.S. example of ratifying the CTBT, other States would stop testing as well. They noted that although the U.S. has observed a unilateral moratorium on nuclear testing since 1992, China, India, and Pakistan all subsequently tested nuclear weapons.

Second, opponents of the CTBT cite the need to keep the U.S.'s options open and note that the CTBT could limit future U.S. flexibility in the event that changed circumstances require new technologies or weapons to deal with unforeseen threats. For example, in light of the rise in terrorist and anti-American activities, the U.S. may want to test new, earth-penetrating nuclear weapons that can destroy underground compounds.

Third, opponents claim that the CTBT would have an adverse effect on the safety, reliability, and effectiveness of the U.S. nuclear deterrent. They raise concerns that the current stewardship program for the U.S. nuclear stockpile is inadequate to ensure the safety, security, and reliability of the weapons. In a related vein, they also hold that ongoing tests are necessary to warn off potential attackers, and that without further testing, confidence in the nuclear arsenal's deterrent capacity will be damaged.

Finally, opponents are concerned about the effectiveness of the CTBT's verification system. Small, low-yield nuclear tests could be used by advanced nuclear States to develop new weapons as well as verify old ones, and such tests may escape detection by the CTBT's monitoring system. Opponents of the treaty argue that there is no way to reliably differentiate between low-yield nuclear explosions and earthquakes, conventional explosions, or other "seismic events."

Proponents of the treaty note, however, that since the U.S. also conducts its own highly sensitive monitoring procedures, the risk of small tests escaping notice would be greatly reduced or eliminated by the two systems acting in concert. Proponents further point out that without ratifying the CTBT, the U.S. cannot receive the treaty's benefits, such as monitoring and on-site inspections, and its moral authority to press other States to disarm is substantially weakened.

In 1998, the prospects of the CTBT were further set back by news of nuclear weapons tests in India and Pakistan. Both States had been considered presumptive nuclear powers whose ratification was required for the CTBT to enter into force, but neither had signed or ratified prior to their testing. The UN Security Council swiftly passed a resolution condemning the tests, urging the cessation of testing in South Asia and the ratification of the CTBT, and calling upon other States to affirm their commitments to non-proliferation and disarmament [UN Security Council, *Resolution 1172* (Jun. 6, 1998) 37 I.L.M. 1243].

India and Pakistan both refuse to ratify the CTBT, citing three major objections. First, India, in particular, is wary of agreeing to disarm when the other nuclear States—including the U.S.—have thus far failed to agree to a schedule or timetable for total disarmament. A second but related objection is that the CTBT's moratorium on nuclear tests would freeze international nuclear capabilities at their present levels, so that States like the U.S. and Russia would have sophisticated technology and expansive arsenals that newer nuclear weapons programs would never be able to obtain. Finally, India cites the China-Pakistan alliance, which enabled the rapid development of Pakistani nuclear technology and the buildup of a substantial Pakistani arsenal, as a tangible nuclear threat on its borders justifying its own nuclear weapons program. Pakistan, of course, cites India's own armament as a similar threat. Relations between the two States are strained at the best of times, and an agreement on this issue does not appear to be forthcoming. Given this impasse, neither State is likely to sign or ratify the CTBT in the near future.

c. Nuclear Materials

Nuclear pollution of the world's oceans has been a problem since 1946, when the first sea dumping operation took place at a site in the North East Pacific Ocean, about 80 kilometers off the coast of California [Dominique P. Calmet, *Ocean disposal of radioactive waste: Status report,* (1989) IAEA Bulletin at 47]. This practice of dumping continued unabated until the advent of the environmental movement in the 1970s. It is estimated that since the 1940s, millions of curies of radioactive material, resulting from both civilian uses and military sources, have been dumped into the world's oceans [*Id.*]. The Cold War exacerbated the problem of nuclear pollution in the oceans, as it resulted in tens of thousands of steel drums of radioactive waste, which were dumped into the Atlantic and Pacific at dozens of sites off California, Massachusetts, and a handful of other states [John R. Emshwiller & Dionne Seacey, *Nuclear Waste Sits on Ocean Floor,* (Dec. 31, 2013) The Wall Street Journal].

i. Decommissioning Nuclear Submarines

Nuclear submarines are sophisticated machines powered by nuclear reactors, but they do not last forever. The lifespan of a nuclear submarine is typically 25 to 30 years, after which they must be decommissioned and their spent fuel and reactors disposed of. The START agreements for reducing nuclear stockpiles mandated the premature retirement of an additional 31 nuclear submarines. However, retired submarines with their spent fuel still on board give rise to considerable global concern, because they are at risk of leaking, rusting, and sinking before the waste they contain is properly processed. These risks were demonstrated in August 2003, when the Russian nuclear submarine K-159 sank as it was being towed to a scrapyard for decommissioning [Tom Parfitt, *Nuclear leak feared as second Russian sub is lost with nine crew*, (Aug. 31, 2003) The Telegraph].

Unfortunately, to decommission and de-fuel a nuclear submarine, several steps must be taken, each of which pose a significant risk of accident [Susan Kopte, NUCLEAR SUBMARINE DECOMMISSIONING AND RELATED PROBLEMS (1997)]. The decommissioning process begins with removing all weapons and explosive devices. Then, the submarine is towed to a decommissioning shipyard, where the reactor is shut down to allow short-lived isotopes to decay. The third step is de-fueling, which involves opening the hull to remove the top shield of the reactor and extract the nuclear fuel. The de-fueling process is quite similar to the refueling process, and unfortunately Russia has a poor refueling track record [*Id.* at 12]. To make matters worse, the Russian Navy has five nuclear submarines with damaged cores, which cannot be removed at all by presently available techniques [*Id.* at 13]. After the fuel is removed, it is placed in a shipping container to be transported to an interim spent fuel storage facility. Finally, spent fuel is either sent for reprocessing or treated as radioactive waste that requires permanent disposal.

Even after the fuel is safely removed, the highly radioactive reactor compartment of the submarine must also be safely disposed of. Unfortunately, and in contrast to the U.S. policy to bury its reactors, there are currently at least 50 Russian reactor compartments stored at Sayda Bay. The storage facilities are in poor condition and there is further danger of leakage into the Arctic [Environmental Rights Center Bellona, *Remediation of Nuclear and Radiation Legacy Sites In Russia's Northwest: An Overview of Projects Carried Out As Part of International Cooperation,* (2014) Bellona]. Overall, the Soviet Navy disposed of approximately 4 million Curies of nuclear waste in the Arctic's shallow Barents and Kara Seas between 1958 and 1992, which included six or seven fully-fueled nuclear reactors [*see* A.V. Yablokov et al., *Facts and Problems Related to the Dumping of Radioactive Waste in the Seas Surrounding the Territory of the Russian Federation: Materials from a Government Report on the Dumping of Radioactive Waste* (May 1993) Commissioned by the President of the Russian Federation, Oct. 24, 1992, Decree No. 613]. Not surprisingly, Russian nuclear pollution is the Arctic Ocean's heaviest source of impact.

Unfortunately, the Joint Convention on the Safety of Spent Fuel Management and on the Safety of Radioactive Waste Management (1997 Joint Convention), to which Russia is a party, does not apply to decommissioning naval submarines [*Joint*

Convention on the Safety of Spent Fuel Management and on the Safety of Radioactive Waste Management, Sept. 29, 1997, 36 I.L.M. 1431]. Nor does the 1997 Joint Convention apply to spent nuclear fuel or radioactive wastes from civilian nuclear power plants that are being held at reprocessing facilities as part of reprocessing activity. However, the 1997 Joint Convention does cover other civil nuclear power plants that are sources of spent fuel and radioactive waste, and Russia, along with all other parties, is obliged to file a comprehensive annual report with regard to this category of spent fuel and waste. Russia filed its first national report in 2006 [NATIONAL REPORT OF THE RUSSIAN FEDERATION ON COMPLIANCE WITH THE OBLIGATIONS OF THE JOINT CONVENTION ON THE SAFETY OF SPENT FUEL MANAGEMENT AND THE SAFETY OF RADIOACTIVE WASTE MANAGEMENT (2006) at § D 19 (hereinafter 2006 RUSSIAN NATIONAL REPORT)]. The fourth national report was filed in 2014, and describes in detail the obligations arising from the 1997 Joint Convention and compliance with them by the Russian Federation [FOURTH NATIONAL REPORT OF THE RUSSIAN FEDERATION ON COMPLIANCE WITH THE OBLIGATIONS OF THE JOINT CONVENTION ON THE SAFETY OF SPENT FUEL MANAGEMENT AND THE SAFETY OF RADIOACTIVE WASTE MANAGEMENT (2014) Moscow].

While accounts of Russian nuclear practices had previously been based on reports assembled by outside entities [*see* Environmental Rights Center Bellona, *supra*; Kopte, *supra*], the 2006 First Russian National report confirms questionable practices pertaining to the storage of spent fuel and radioactive wastes. According to the 2006 report, there was 18,000 tons of accumulated spent nuclear waste being held on site or in reactor storage facilities [2006 Russian National Report at appendix B1]. What is significant is that the report admits to a large quantity of accumulated waste that is neither connected to the navy nor part of a reprocessing facility. If the even larger quantities of military spent fuel and waste held in reprocessing facilities bordering the Arctic are brought into the picture, the situation of the Arctic looks exceedingly grim.

Nuclear dumping in the Arctic is a serious cause for future concern due to three major factors. First, existing stockpiles of waste present a disquieting quandary: roughly 1,680 fuel assemblies have already been dumped into the Arctic [*Id.* at 283], and 30,000 or more fuel assemblies still await disposal [*see* Lakshman D. Guruswamy & Jason B. Aamodt, *Nuclear Arms Control: The Environmental Dimension*, 10 COLO. J. INT'L ENVTL. L. & POL'Y 267 (1999) at 282]. Second, nuclear submarines that have yet to be retired will create 2,300 to 7,000 times more waste and spent nuclear fuel, but reports indicate that there is little or no space left for waste storage [*Id.*]. The third factor that may accelerate nuclear dumping in the Arctic is Russia's plan to grow its civilian nuclear industry, in which case nuclear pollution may reach the Arctic through land-based sources via rivers. Although some experts maintain that the threat of nuclear contamination from Russia's actions is slight, most States seem to recognize that decommissioning nuclear submarines represents a potentially serious threat to the global community.

ii. Cooperative Exchanges

In dealing with nuclear materials, science and technology agreements have led to greater involvement of technical agencies and private company experts, and a greater depth and complexity of cooperation among the States involved. These cooperative exchanges override ideological or national aims, and reduce future conflicts. For example, when nuclear weapons are disarmed, plutonium sequestered in weapons needs to be safely managed. One way of doing so is to stabilize and transform it into fuel for nuclear power reactors. In 1998, the U.S. and the Russian Federation formed a joint steering committee on plutonium management, intended to research and review scientific efforts to improve plutonium conversion capabilities [*U.S.-Russian Federation: Agreement on Scientific and Technical Cooperation in the Management of Plutonium that has been Withdrawn from Nuclear Military Programs*, Jul. 24, 1998, 37 I.L.M. 1296 (1998)].

Cooperative exchanges of this kind are currently also being facilitated by the Defense Threat Reduction Agency (DTRA) of the U.S. The Cooperative Threat Reduction Program, operated under the DTRA since its establishment in 1998, was created by the U.S. Congress to help Russia carry out its obligations under the START agreements. One aspect of this program is addressed to Chain of

Custody activities. These Chain of Custody activities enhance security, safety, and control of nuclear weapons and fissile material in Russia by assisting in centralizing fissile material in a limited number of storage areas and strengthening safety, security, and control during movement and interim storage. Projects provide assistance to enhance effective controls over nuclear weapons, and the fissile materials removed from them, throughout the drawdown and dismantling of these weapons. This includes providing safe and secure transportation of nuclear weapons from operational sites and storage areas to dismantlement facilities, improved security and accountability for weapons in transit, safer and more secure storage and transport of fissile material removed from nuclear weapons by providing storage containers, and designing, equipping, and assisting in construction of centralized fissile material storage facilities [*see generally* Cooperative Threat Reduction, ANNUAL REPORT TO CONGRESS: FISCAL YEAR 2009, (2009)].

However, DTRA's projects are aimed almost entirely at the reduction of military threats—not environmental ones. This has lead to tensions surrounding project prioritization, especially concerning the decommissioning of nuclear submarines [T. Jandl, *Proliferation Ahead of Remediation*, THE NUCLEAR CHRONICLE FROM RUSSIA (2000)]. One proposed solution is for the U.S. Congress to expand the scope to include environmental concerns when formulating and prioritizing plans. In this way, a single agency would share the twin objectives of arms control and environmental protection [*see generally* Lakshman D. Guruswamy & Suzette R. Grillot eds., ARMS CONTROL AND THE ENVIRONMENT (2001)].

d. Customary Law

i. *Nuclear Testing*

Until the total phase-out of nuclear testing occurs, the customary international law status of such explosions remains in doubt. The general international support for the CTBT, coupled with state practice in this area, support a strong claim that customary international law forbids the atmospheric, outer space, or underwater testing of nuclear weapons. This would appear to be the rule even in the absence of transboundary environmental harm. On the other hand, the status of underground testing remains problematic. Should the testing cause significant environmental damage, or a threat of such damage, to another State, the well-settled general prohibition against such damage would control. Without transboundary environmental harm, however, and until the CTBT comes into its own, it seems doubtful that underground testing *per se* would violate customary international law.

Though the *Nuclear Tests Cases* did not resolve the issues surrounding underground nuclear testing, they remain some of the most important cases in IEL for their discussion of important issues. And, as they dealt first with the issue of atmospheric testing and only more recently considered underground testing, they track the evolution in thinking concerning nuclear weapons testing. More generally, the cases also provide a glimpse into the evolution of IEL over a 20-year period. The cases also highlight the severe limitations of the ICJ—both real and self-inflicted—that continue to hamper the development of IEL. For all of these reasons, and to provide a window into the actual functioning of the ICJ, we offer an extended analysis of these decisions.

ii. The Nuclear Test Cases (Round One)

In 1973, both Australia and New Zealand brought separate, but similar, actions against France in the ICJ, complaining of France's imminent atmospheric tests on the Mururoa Atoll in the South Pacific [See *Nuclear Tests* (Australia v. France), 1973 I.C.J. 99 (Jun. 22); 1973 I.C.J. 320 (Jul. 12); 1974 I.C.J. 253 (Dec. 20); 1973 I.C.J. 338 (Aug. 28); 1974 I.C.J. 530 (Dec. 20); *Nuclear Tests* (New Zealand v. France), 1973 I.C.J. 135 (Jun. 22); 1973 I.C.J. 341 (Sep. 6); 1973 I.C.J. 324 (Jul. 12) 1974 I.C.J. 457 (Dec. 20); 1974 I.C.J. 535 (Dec. 20)]. From 1967 to 1972 France had conducted atmospheric tests within its own territory, and appeared about to begin another series of tests in 1973. In its application to the ICJ Australia claimed:

(i) The right of Australia and its people, in common with other States and their peoples, to be free from atmospheric tests by any country is and will be violated;

(ii) The deposit of radio-active fall-out on the territory of Australia and its dispersion in Australia's airspace without Australia's consent:

(a) violates Australia's sovereignty over its territory;

(b) impairs Australia's independent right to determine what acts shall take place within its territory and in particular whether Australia and its people shall be exposed to radiation from artificial sources;

(iii) The interference with ships and aircraft on the high seas and in the super-adjacent airspace, and the pollution of the high seas by radio-active fall-out, constitute infringements of the freedom of the high seas [*Nuclear Tests* (Australia v. France), 1973 I.C.J. 99, 103 (Jun. 22)].

New Zealand's claim was somewhat different, presenting a *jus cogens* argument and also referring to nuclear testing in general, not just atmospheric nuclear testing. According to New Zealand's application:

(a) [France's action] violates the rights of all members of the international community including New Zealand, that no nuclear tests that give rise to radio-active fall-out be conducted;

(b) It violates the rights of all members of the international community, including New Zealand, to the preservation from unjustified artificial radio-active contamination of the terrestrial, maritime and aerial environment and, in particular, of the environment of the region in which the tests are conducted . . .

(c) It violates the right of New Zealand that no radio-active material enter [its] territory . . . ; including [its] air space and territorial waters, as a result of nuclear testing;

(d) It violates the right of New Zealand that no radio-active material, having entered [its] territory . . . , including [its] air space and territorial waters, as a result of nuclear testing, cause harm, including apprehension, anxiety and concern to the people and government of New Zealand . . . ;

(e) It violates the right of New Zealand to freedom of the high seas, including freedom of navigation and overflight and the freedom to explore and exploit the resources of the sea and the seabed, without interference or detriment resulting from nuclear testing [*Nuclear Tests* (New Zealand v. France), 1974 I.C.J. 457, 512 (Dec. 20)].

Though it had previously accepted the compulsory jurisdiction of the ICJ under Article 36 of the Statute of the ICJ, France disavowed the ICJ's competence to hear the cases, denied jurisdiction, and declined to appear. In spite of France's rejection, the case remained on the ICJ's official docket.

iii. Interim Measures

The two petitioners also asked for interim measures, and the ICJ granted these requests in 1973, stating that "no action of any kind [should be] taken which might aggravate or extend the dispute

. . . in particular, the French Government should avoid nuclear tests causing the deposit of radio-active fall-out" on the respective territories of Australia and New Zealand [*Nuclear Tests* (Australia v. France), 1973 I.C.J. 99, 106 (Jun. 22); *Nuclear Tests* (New Zealand v. France), 1973 I.C.J. 135, 142 (Jun. 22)]. France, in turn, ignored the decision and actually conducted two nuclear tests.

iv. Jurisdiction

In 1974, the ICJ had to decide the question of jurisdiction. As this phase of the ICJ proceedings approached, however, the French government suddenly shifted direction—making a number of public declarations to the effect that it would discontinue its atmospheric nuclear tests and would move on to underground tests. These unilateral statements reassured neither Australia nor New Zealand, and both States continued to press their respective claims.

In the decision on its competence to hear the cases, the ICJ first had to deal with France's request that the ICJ remove the two cases from its list, based on the fact that France now did not accept the ICJ's jurisdiction. Without elaboration, the ICJ simply stated in both instances that "the present case was not one in which the procedure of summary removal from the list would be appropriate" [*Nuclear Tests* (Australia v. France), 1974 I.C.J. 253 (Dec. 20); *Nuclear Tests* (New Zealand v. France), 1974 I.C.J. 457, 460 (Dec. 20)].

In the next step, the ICJ focused on whether a present dispute still existed between France on the one hand, and Australia and New Zealand on the other. On this matter—though France's unilateral promise to stop atmospheric testing was not embraced as sufficient by either applicant—the ICJ decided that France had made a binding commitment. Therefore, with the objective of both applicants presumably met and the "dispute having disappeared," the ICJ dismissed both cases without reaching the merits [*Nuclear Tests* (Australia v. France), 1974 I.C.J. 253, 271 (Dec. 20); *Nuclear Tests* (New Zealand v. France), 1974 I.C.J. 457, 475 (Dec. 20)].

The environmental significance of the first round of the *Nuclear Tests Cases* primarily lies with the granting of interim measures. Though the ICJ did not base its decision on the merits of the Applicants' cases, it did admit that both had established *prima facie* cases of possible harm and that the rights of all parties needed to be preserved for later adjudication. The granting of interim measures thus lends support to the general rule that one State may not inflict transboundary environmental harm on another. On the other hand, the decision on jurisdiction shows how ready the ICJ is to dispose of cases on procedural grounds when faced with controversial substantive issues. Here the ICJ creatively and very narrowly dispensed with a case—following an outdated formalism—in which it might have made important pronouncements of law.

To its credit, however, the ICJ did provide an opportunity to reopen the cases, stating that "if the basis of this Judgment were to be affected, the Applicant could request an examination of the situation in accordance with the provisions of the statute" [*Nuclear Tests* (Australia v. France), 1974 I.C.J. 253, 271 ¶ 60 (Dec. 20); *Nuclear Tests* (New Zealand v. France), 1974 I.C.J. 457, 477 ¶ 63 (Dec. 20)]. This is the first time the ICJ has contemplated the possibility of noncompliance and made provisions accordingly [Thomas M. Franck, *World Made Law: The Decision of the ICJ in the Nuclear Test Cases*, 69 AM. J. INT'L L. 612 (1975) at 618]. It is this opening which led to round two of the dispute.

v. The Nuclear Test Cases (Round Two)

Two decades later, with a newly elected, conservative administration firmly in control, France declared its intention to conduct another series of underground tests in the South Pacific beginning in 1995. Outraged by what they perceived as the continued arrogance of France and the renewed threat of environmental harm, the South Pacific States loudly denounced the action. New Zealand swiftly moved to reopen its 1974 case against France, claiming that "the basis of the Judgment had been affected" by the new underground tests proposed by France [*Request for an Examination of the Situation in Accordance with Paragraph 63 of the Court's Judgment of 20 December 1974 in the Nuclear Tests (New Zealand v. France) Case*, 1995 I.C.J. 288, 298 ¶ 33 (Sept. 22)]. As France no longer accepted the compulsory jurisdiction of the ICJ under Article 36 of the ICJ Statute, New Zealand could not institute new proceedings but could only hope to gain access through the older case. Australia, it will be recalled, had based its original complaint more narrowly on atmospheric testing, and apparently for this reason did not try to reopen its own case. Instead, Australia later attempted to intervene in New Zealand's proceedings.

In its Application to the ICJ, New Zealand stated:

(i) that the conduct of the proposed nuclear tests will constitute a violation of the rights under international law of New Zealand, as well as of other States; further or in the alternative;

(ii) that is unlawful for France to conduct such nuclear tests before it has undertaken an Environmental Impact Assessment according to accepted international standards. Unless such an assessment establishes that the tests will not give rise, directly or indirectly, to radioactive contamination of the marine environment the rights under international law of New Zealand, as well as the rights of other States, will be violated [*Id.* at 290 ¶ 6].

New Zealand asked that the ICJ make a broad interpretation of the words "the basis of the Judgment"—that the phrase should not be restricted to France's atmospheric testing only, but that it referred more generally to the cessation of environmental contamination by nuclear testing [*Id.* at 293 ¶ 18]. According to New Zealand, as current scientific evidence now showed that the environmental risks of underground nuclear testing were greater than had been thought in 1974, the resumption of such tests would alter the underlying protection afforded by the judgment. Indeed, New Zealand's original Application in 1973 did not even mention atmospheric tests, but instead focused on the right to be free from nuclear damage.

In addition, through its application and oral argument, New Zealand now backed up its complaint with specific advances in IEL. First, it maintained that the duty not to cause transboundary harm—in an early stage of crystallization in 1974—was now a well-settled principle of customary international law. Second, it noted that the principle of intergenerational equity was at stake, that the 20,000-year by-product of nuclear testing invoked a consideration of the rapidly developing principle of intergenerational rights. Third, it claimed that the precautionary principle mandated a shift of the burden of proof to France, and that France should have to conduct an Environmental Impact Assessment before proceeding with its tests. Fourth, it stated that a number of treaties disallowed the introduction of radioactive wastes into the marine environment, and that France's action violated the high standard afforded that medium [*Id.*].

Once again, however, the ICJ adopted an extremely narrow interpretation of the law. By a vote of twelve to three, the ICJ refused to reopen the case, agreeing with France's argument that the "basis of the Judgment" in the 1974 adjudication had only to do with "atmospheric" testing. As New Zealand knew that France would begin conducting underground tests in 1974, it could not now complain of those tests, but only the threatened commencement of atmospheric tests. France, of course, was not proposing atmospheric tests, and New Zealand had no legitimate fears that pertained to the earlier case.

The significance of this second round of the *Nuclear Test Cases*, however, resides in the opinions of the dissenting judges. In dissent, Judge Christopher Weermantry, supported by Judge ad hoc Palmer, devastatingly criticized the unnecessary formalism of the decision, pointing out the dangers of strict construction. Judge Weermantry explained:

> If X should complain to the village elder that Y is threatening him with a sword in a manner causing reasonable apprehension of an intention to cause grievous harm, and the village elder orders Y to drop his sword, is that order to be construed as an order to refrain from causing bodily harm, whatever the weapon used? If Y thereafter proceeds to harm X with a club, Y would surely not be able to contend that the order issued on him related to the use of a sword and that he did not violate it in any way by using a club. Clearly, a larger reason lies behind the order than the mere prohibition against inflicting harm with a sword. The unexpressed rationale laying behind the order, namely, the desire to protect X from bodily harm, lies at the very heart of the order, if it is to be construed in the light of common sense [*Id.* at 334]

Clearly, according to Weermantry, the original decision back in 1974 had attempted to protect New Zealand from harm caused by nuclear weapons testing, not just the fall-out from atmospheric tests. If, at this juncture, progress in scientific knowledge reveals underground testing as causing greater harm than thought in 1974, then a *prima facie* case has been established. The case should then proceed to the merits and the ICJ should engage, rather than by-pass, the very important legal issues at hand.

Judge Weermantry argued against the narrow formalism of the majority, and showed a willingness to discuss all the important issues brought forward— including transboundary environmental harm, intergenerational equity, the precautionary principle, environmental impact assessment, and protection of the marine environment. Unfortunately, due to the reticence of the ICJ, a majority decision on these issues of general customary international law must await another day. And regarding the specific status of underground nuclear testing, in the near future it is unlikely that the ICJ will obtain jurisdiction over a seminal case. More probably, a ratified CTBT will provide primary guidance in this area.

vi. Use of Nuclear Weapons

The Advisory Opinion of the ICJ in the *Legality of the Threat of the Use of Nuclear Weapons*, requested by the UN General Assembly, forms an important part of the emerging customary law on nuclear weapons. The ICJ was urged by the U.S. and other nuclear powers to decline the question. Instead, the ICJ held, by a wafer-thin majority secured by the double vote of the president, that the threat or use of nuclear weapons would generally be contrary to the rules of international law applicable in armed conflict, and in particular the principles and rules of humanitarian law. The ICJ refrained from ruling unequivocally that the threat or use of nuclear weapons would be illegal under any circumstances. According to the majority, the inadequacy of facts at its disposal precluded the ICJ from concluding definitively that the threat or use of nuclear weapons would be lawful or unlawful in extreme cases of self-defense, where the very survival of the State would be at stake.

However, in light of the horrendous threats posed by nuclear weapons, and the growing consensus among the community of nations as evidenced in the treaties referred to above, the ICJ was of the unanimous opinion that these treaties foreshadowed "a future general prohibition of the use of such weapons," although not presently constituting a prohibition on the use or possession of nuclear weapons [Legality of the Use of Nuclear Weapons at 825 ¶ 62]. Addressing Article VI of the NPT, it concluded: "The legal import of that obligation goes beyond that of a mere obligation of conduct; the obligation involved here is an obligation to achieve a precise result—nuclear disarmament in all its aspects—by adopting a particular course of conduct, namely, the pursuit of negotiations on the matter in good faith" [*Id.* at 830]. This means that nuclear States are under a legal obligation—an "obligation of result"—to bring to a conclusion negotiations leading to nuclear disarmament in all its aspects under strict and effective international control.

Even though the ICJ did not declare every threat or use of nuclear weapons illegal, it carved out a rule of illegality and confined its exception to cases of extreme self-defense where the survival of the State is at stake. Judge Stephen Schwebel, the American judge, dissented, arguing that neither law, State practice, nor comity supported the conclusion that the use or threat of use of nuclear weapons are generally illegal. On the other hand, Judge Weermantry reasoned that the decision did not go far enough. He asserted that use or threat of use of nuclear weapons is illegal in any circumstances, and that self-defense did not constitute an exception. Nevertheless, the implications of this decision are noteworthy. First, it may assail and dismantle the legal foundations of nuclear defense policies premised on first use of nuclear weapons. Second, it confronts the permanent members of the Security Council (U.S., England, Russia, France, and China, all of which are nuclear powers) with the illegality of the threat or use of their nuclear weapons, except in self-defense when their very existence is at stake. Third, it directs all nuclear powers that they must enter into good faith negotiations to achieve total nuclear disarmament. While it is true that the last finding is not as imperative as it may seem, because good faith negotiations could go on indefinitely, it appears that the nuclear powers have not taken such a cynical view of their obligations.

2. CIVILIAN NUCLEAR ENERGY

a. International Atomic Energy Agency (IAEA) Standards

Concerning the uses of civilian nuclear energy, three international organizations have primary responsibility. The Nuclear Energy Agency, created by the Organization of Economic Cooperation and Development (OECD), has played a limited role in promoting common safety standards through national legislation in its member States, but its fundamental function remains that of disseminating information. The European Atomic Energy Community (EURATOM), an entity of the European Union (EU), has developed mostly health-related safety directives that member States must implement and enforce, but the organization has yet to expand into the area of siting, design, and operation. The most significant international organization is the IAEA, created by statute under the auspices of the UN in 1956, and supported by nearly all the States of the world as parties. According to its statute, the IAEA's principal objective is "to accelerate and enlarge the contribution of atomic energy"—though as a secondary function it is required to establish "standards of safety for protection of health and minimization of danger to life and property" [*Statute of the International Atomic Energy Agency*, Art. III (A)(6), Oct. 26, 1956, art. II, 276 U.N.T.S. 3 (entered into force Jul. 29, 1957)]. Thus the IAEA operates with the twin purposes of fostering the development of nuclear power and controlling its dangers.

Though undertaking the function belatedly, and to its critics at cross-purposes with its development function, the IAEA has gradually assumed the leadership role in health and safety standards through: (1) the transfer of nuclear technology, particularly to developing countries; (2) the advancement of nuclear safety; and (3) verification aimed at ensuring the peaceful use of nuclear technology and nuclear material. Over the years, the IAEA has generated a broad set of non-binding rules covering virtually every area of nuclear safety, including the siting, design, and operation of nuclear installations. While in practice many States rely on these in setting national requirements, and the IAEA itself remains bound by its own provisions, the standards legally exist as technical guidelines. Only if, by agreement, the IAEA helps establish a particular facility—through the providing of IAEA materials and expertise—do the standards, as well as follow-up inspections, become binding on that facility. As detailed below, the relatively recent adoption of the 1994 Convention on Nuclear Safety has raised the profile of the IAEA standards, but these still remain guidelines rather than obligatory measures.

b. 1986 IAEA Convention on Early Notification of a Nuclear Accident (Notification Convention)

Prompted by the Chernobyl accident, the 1986 IAEA Convention on Early Notification of a Nuclear Accident (Notification Convention), attempts to prevent delay by parties in reporting accidents to its neighbors [*Convention on Early Notification of a Nuclear Accident,* Sept. 26, 1986 (entered into force Oct. 27, 1986), 25 I.L.M. 1369 (hereinafter Notification Convention)]. Presently in force and signed by nearly all the nuclear capable States, the Notification Convention covers any civilian accident in which the "release of radioactive material occurs or is likely to occur and which has resulted or may result in an international transboundary release that could be of radiological safety significance for another State" [*Id.* at art 1]. In short, the Notification Convention encompasses present, as well as probable, nuclear accidents if they cause significant or potentially significant transboundary harm. Unfortunately, a major shortcoming of the Notification Convention exists in the broad discretion given to parties in interpreting the word "significance." In another important limitation, the Notification Convention does not mandate notification regarding accidents at military facilities. This problem has since been ameliorated by the declaration of the five nuclear States that they will extend the Convention's provisions to these incidents.

Faced with a significant nuclear accident, a party must "forthwith notify" either the IAEA or the potentially "physically" affected States as to the nature, time, and location of the accident [*Id.* at art. 2(a)]. Furthermore, the party must promptly provide any information that might minimize the radiological effects of the accident, such as the possible cause, general release characteristics, and any results of environmental monitoring [*Id.* at arts. 2(1) & 5]. A party also must "promptly" respond to any request for consultations by an affected State, when such consultations would seek to minimize the radiological consequences inside the latter's territory [*Id.* at art. 6].

c. 1986 IAEA Convention on Assistance in the Case of a Nuclear Accident or Radiological Emergency (Assistance Convention)

Complementing the Notification Convention, the 1986 IAEA Convention on Assistance in the Case of a Nuclear Accident or Radiological Emergency (Assistance Convention) creates a framework of cooperation that strives to facilitate aid among States in the event of a nuclear accident [*Convention on Assistance in the Case of a Nuclear Accident or Radiological Emergency,* Sept. 26, 1986 (entered into force Sept. 26, 1987), 25 I.L.M. 1377 (hereinafter Assistance Convention)]. The Assistance Convention situates the IAEA as the conduit of such assistance, but also encourages other bilateral or multilateral arrangements [*Id.* at art.1]. Though nothing in the Assistance Convention forces a party to request assistance, upon doing so it must "specify the scope and type of assistance required and, where practicable, provide the assisting party with such information as may be necessary for that party to determine the extent to which it is able to meet the request" [*Id.* at art. 2(2)]. In turn, the providing party must promptly respond concerning the availability, scope, and terms of any assistance [*Id.* at art. 2(3)]. For its part, the IAEA proactively collects and distributes information as to each party's available experts, equipment, and material in the event of a nuclear accident, and, if requested, assists parties in the preparation of emergency plans and the development of personnel training and radiation monitoring programs [*Id.* at art. 5(1)]. The Assistance Convention also provides for immunity from legal proceedings for the assisting party and its agents, though any party may at the time of accepting the convention declare itself not bound by these specific provisions [*see Id.* at arts. 8 & 10]. In short, the Assistance Convention seeks to expedite voluntary assistance by other States, removing administrative and legal roadblocks.

d. 1994 Convention on Nuclear Safety

In 1994 the international community—led by the G7, the group of finance ministers of the seven most powerful industrial and economic powers in the world—worked toward the adoption of a treaty on nuclear safety. As the preamble states, the 1994 Convention on Nuclear Safety, functions as an "incentive convention," mandating the creation of appropriate national standards for civil nuclear installations, but not requiring the use of IAEA provisions [*Convention on Nuclear Safety,* Sept. 20, 1994, 33 I.L.M. 1514 (hereinafter Convention on Nuclear Safety)]. To that end, the Convention on Nuclear Safety "entails a commitment to the application of fundamental safety principles for nuclear installations rather than of detailed safety standards" [*Id.* at pmbl. (viii)], and ensures that "there are internationally formulated safety guidelines which ... provide guidance on contemporary means of achieving a high level of safety" [*Id.*]. Hence, the 1994 Convention on Nuclear Safety is not based on sanctions, but, rather, on the common interest of the parties to achieve higher levels of safety through exchange of information and regular meetings. Though many non-nuclear States desired more stringent and specific standards, the requirements of the Convention remain largely hortatory, with the parties simply charged with taking "appropriate steps" at the national level [*Id.* at art. 6]. Entirely based on action at the national level, the treaty contains no provisions for enforcement or dispute resolution. The hope is that "appropriate" national standards will follow IAEA or other international standards, fostering an improved level of nuclear safety throughout the world.

Under the 1994 Convention on Nuclear Safety, each party must install "a legislative and regulatory framework to govern the safety of nuclear installations" [*Id.* at art. 7]. However, the Convention only covers power plants, and does not deal with nuclear fast breeder reactors or any other aspect of the nuclear fuel cycle, most notably radioactive waste. In addition to the establishment of national safety standards, each party must develop a competent regulatory authority that, unlike the IAEA itself, does not engage in the promotion of nuclear energy [*Id.* at art. 8]. As to general areas of action, each State must take "appropriate steps" to ensure emergency preparedness [*Id.* at art. 16], assessment and verification of safety [*Id.* at art. 14], quality assurance [*Id.* at art. 13], and radiation protection [*Id.* at art. 15]. More specifically, concerning the safety of installations, each party must develop "appropriate" standards and procedures regarding siting [*Id.* at art. 17], design and construction [*Id.* at art. 18], and operation [*Id.* at art. 19].

The 1994 Convention on Nuclear Safety is stricter regarding existing nuclear plants. Each party must make "all reasonably practicable improvements" of existing nuclear installations and, if upgrading cannot be undertaken, should close the nuclear installation "as soon as practically possible" [*Id.* at art. 6]. In considering the timing of any necessary shut-down, the party may weigh "the whole energy context and possible alternatives as well as the social, environmental and economic impact" [*Id.*].

The IAEA acts as the secretariat of the Convention, though as such it has little independent power. Instead, the 1994 Convention on Nuclear Safety relies on national implementation and oversight, requiring parties to submit compliance reports to the contracting parties at review meetings [*Id.* at arts. 5 & 20]. At these meetings, each party may discuss and seek clarification of another party's report, but no official dispute resolution machinery exists by which to challenge that report's content [*Id.* at art. 29]. Following the same logic, neither the IAEA nor any other institution created by the Convention possesses formal enforcement powers [*Id.* at art. 20].

e. Liability

i. State Responsibility (SR)

The legal fallout from Chernobyl has arguably undermined the strength of the customary law rule prohibiting States from causing transboundary environmental harm. In the specific area of liability for nuclear accidents, the necessary doctrinal component of State practice appears lacking, as no aggrieved State brought a formal claim against the former Soviet Union (though several reserved the right to do so). The result obviously questions whether States are legally responsible for this type of nuclear harm under customary international law. Simply put, if, in the face of widespread damage, no claims were filed and no compensation volunteered or awarded, then how can liability for nuclear accidents exist under international law?

The fact that States declined to press claims does not necessarily mean that they believed the claims legally unwarranted. It is perfectly feasible that States declined to press claims for fear of establishing precedents that could be used against them. The States harmed by Chernobyl fallout were themselves nuclear States and may have decided it was in their self-interest not to create a legal weapon that might be used against them. Moreover, in the particular case of Chernobyl, the harmed States may only have decided that the costs of pursuing compensation outweighed the benefits—especially given the inability to pay on the part of the former Soviet Union.

In fact, evidence of a liability regime applicable to radioactive contamination is supplied by another case. In 1979, Canada pressed a claim against the U.S.S.R. for damages caused by a nuclear-powered satellite that broke up over its territory. Canada made its claims both under general principles of international law and the 1972 Convention on International Liability for Damage Caused by Space Objects (Space Liability Convention). This time the U.S.S.R. agreed to pay Canada $3 million as compensation. As the legal basis for liability remained unnamed in the concluding document, the result permits an argument in favor of applying both custom and the 1972 Space Liability Convention. More recently, by resolution on December 14, 1992, the UN General Assembly adopted Principles Relevant to the Use of Nuclear Power Sources in Outer Space, which again provides for State responsibility (SR) for damage caused by outer space operations utilizing nuclear power [United Nations General Assembly, *Principles Relevant to the Use of Nuclear Power Sources in Outer Space,* (1992) at Principle 8].

Furthermore, the general rule against transboundary environmental harm—first provided in the *Trail Smelter Case*—continues to find universal support in international environmental treaties and declarations. Therefore, to carve out an exception to the rule for nuclear accidents seems premature, as States have consistently embraced the rule in such important documents as the Rio Declaration on Environment and Development (Rio Declaration) and in major international treaties such as the Convention on Biological Diversity (Biodiversity Convention) and the United Nations Framework Convention on Climate Change (UNFCCC).

As for the standard of liability, this question also obviously remains unresolved. Some scholars argue for strict or absolute liability, because nuclear energy is an ultra-hazardous activity. The 1972 Space Liability Convention, for example, makes the launching State "absolutely liable to pay compensation for damage caused by its space object on the surface of the earth or to aircraft in flight" [Space Liability Convention at art. II]. Similarly, in the civil liability (CL) conventions described below, the standard is one of strict liability.

Others have argued for a due diligence standard regarding nuclear accidents, in which liability would arise for a State in whose territory an accident occurred only if the State acted negligently in the development, application, and monitoring of appropriate safety standards. Adherents of this view look to Chernobyl as an incident *not* causing a breach of due diligence, pointing out that the plant in question was built according to national standards set by the Soviet Union. Though these standards may not rise to the level of the plants built in the West, the argument goes, this does not necessarily mean that the Soviet Union acted negligently.

Striving for coherence in the aftermath of Chernobyl, the IAEA created a Standing Committee on Nuclear Liability, which in attempting to revise the Vienna Convention on Civil Liability for Nuclear

Damage (Vienna Nuclear Liability Convention) continues to discuss the issue of SR. However, with a number of nuclear powers rejecting the notion, it now appears unlikely that any form of SR for nuclear accidents will make its way into that treaty. On the other hand, the 1994 Convention on Nuclear Safety asserts in the preamble that responsibility for nuclear safety rests with the state having jurisdiction over a particular nuclear installation. This is to be contrasted with Article 9 of the same Convention, which holds that prime responsibility lies with the operator of an installation. The result is a double-tiered program of responsibility under this treaty, with the State's duty one of regulation and monitoring, and the operator's one of stringent compliance.

ii. Civil Liability (CL)

With no global regime in place for SR, the international community has relied largely on civil liability (CL to assign responsibility for nuclear damage. Prior to 1997, CL for nuclear damage was defined by two separate conventions, the Convention on Third Party Liability in the Field of Nuclear Energy (Paris Nuclear Liability Convention) and the Vienna Nuclear Liability Convention. The two conventions share a number of characteristics, including strict liability for the operator, compulsory insurance, and a monetary limit on compensation for damage. In considering these one should keep in mind that the former U.S.S.R. was not a party to either convention, and so neither could be invoked in the case of Chernobyl. One should also be aware of the existence of another treaty—the Convention on the Liability of Operators of Nuclear Ships, which creates similar obligations but, because it has limited acceptance and scope, is not discussed further [*Convention on the Liability of Operators of Nuclear Ships*, May 25, 1962 (entered into force July 15, 1975), 57 A.J.I.L. 268].

Because the Paris Nuclear Liability Convention and the Vienna Nuclear Liability Convention were signed by different parties and at times expressed contradictory mandates, it was necessary to agree upon which treaty should apply in any given case of nuclear damage. This issue was addressed in the 1988 Joint Protocol Relating to the Application of the Vienna Convention and the Paris Convention [*Joint Protocol Relating to the Application of the Vienna Convention and the Paris Convention*, Sept. 21, 1988 (entered into force Apr. 27, 1992), 42 Nuclear Law Bulletin 56]. Under the 1988 Protocol, which is now in force, the convention ratified by the installation State governs liability for damage incurred by a party to the other convention [*Id.* at arts. II & IV]. In addition, each convention applies to each incident to the exclusion of the other [*Id.* at art. III]. Though offering a more unified approach, the 1988 Protocol only points out the necessity of completing negotiations for a global convention that would uniformly deal with CL for nuclear damage.

iii. 1960 Paris Convention on Third Party Liability in the Field of Nuclear Energy (Paris Nuclear Liability Convention)

Created under the auspices of the OECD, the Paris Nuclear Liability Convention strove to unify CL rules for nuclear damage in Western Europe. Nearly all Western nuclear States in the region are parties, including France, Germany, and the United Kingdom. The Paris Nuclear Liability Convention channels all liability to the operator of the nuclear installation for "damage to or loss of life of any person" and "damage to or loss of any property" [Paris Nuclear Liability Convention at art. 2]. Whether this includes environmental damage remains unclear. The convention does cover transport of nuclear substances to or from the installation, for which the operator in charge remains liable and not the carrier [*Id.* at art. 4]. If an incident occurs, the operator's liability is strict rather than absolute, though the Convention actually only exempts responsibility in the few cases of armed conflict, hostilities, civil war, insurrection, or grave natural disasters of an exceptional character [*Id.* at art. 9].

To pay for any liability, each operator must carry insurance in the amount specified under the Paris Nuclear Liability Convention [*Id.* at art. 10]. However, the details of the amount, type, and provisions of the insurance are left to each national government's discretion, and are not governed by the Convention. The liability remains limited—an important feature of this convention—to 15 million

Special Drawing Rights (SDR) as defined by the International Monetary Fund (IMF) [*Id.* at art. 7] (As of January 2017, one unit of SDR approximately equals $1.35 U.S. dollars). In fact, under the Paris Nuclear Liability Convention, a party may even set the liability limit as low as 5 million SDR. As the parties quickly perceived, however, a maximum of 15 million SDR would not cover an accident of any magnitude, and so they adopted the 1963 Brussels Convention Supplementary to the 1960 Convention on Third Party Liability in the Field of Nuclear Energy (Brussels Convention) [*Brussels Convention Supplementary to the 1960 Convention of Third Party Liability in the Field of Nuclear Energy*, Jan. 31, 1963, 2 I.L.M. 685].

The Brussels Convention, which has been updated by later Protocol, leaves the operator's liability at the same level and establishes a supplementary system of public funding [*Id.* at art. 3]. Thus, in the event of an accident in its territory, a party must provide up to an additional 170 million SDR to compensate worthy claimants. Furthermore, should the damage exceed that amount, the other parties to the Convention would provide up to 125 million SDR, according to a formula based on thermal power and gross national product [*Id.* at art. 12]. This party contribution limit was further defined in the Convention on Supplementary Compensation for Nuclear Damage, which is open to all States regardless of their party status in the Paris Nuclear Liability Convention [*Convention on Supplementary Compensation for Nuclear Damage,* 12 Sept. 1997, 36 I.L.M. 1473]. In total, accident liability under the amended Paris Nuclear Liability Convention was limited to 300 million SDR. On the other hand, if the damage results from fault by the operator, the party in whose territory the installation exists may pass legislation allowing both itself and other contracting parties recourse against that operator [*Id.* at art. 5(b)].

In 2004, parties to the amended Paris Nuclear Liability Convention signed a new Protocol, again revising liability limits upwards to accommodate the high costs of nuclear damage. Under that Protocol, liability will be limited to 700 million Euros for operators, 500 million Euros for public funds from the installation State, and a collective party contribution of 300 million Euros. Consequently, the new total liability for nuclear accidents will be 1.5 billion Euros. The Protocol will come into force once it has been ratified by two-thirds of the signatory States, which has not yet occurred as of this writing.

In general, jurisdiction over nuclear incidents lies with the courts of the party in whose territory the nuclear incident occurred [Paris Nuclear Liability Convention at art. 13(a)], and final judgments must be honored and enforced by all the contracting parties [*Id.* at art. 13(d)]. Moreover, though a State may actually be the installation operator in many cases, no party may invoke jurisdictional immunities to avoid actions [*Id.* at art. 13(e)].

iv. 1983 IAEA Vienna Convention on Civil Liability for Nuclear Damage (Vienna Nuclear Liability Convention)

The Vienna Nuclear Liability Convention closely resembles the Paris Nuclear Liability Convention, and was amended in 1997 to modernize its provisions in the Protocol to Amend the Vienna Convention (1997 Protocol) [*Protocol to Amend the Vienna Convention* (Sept. 12, 1996), 36 I.L.M. 1462 (hereinafter 1997 Protocol)]. As the most comprehensive and up-to-date instrument currently dealing with CL for nuclear damage, it has the potential to emerge as a unified global convention on the issue. At the moment, however, only 40 States are parties, either by ratification or accession, to the Vienna Nuclear Liability Convention (most of which do not possess significant nuclear industries, with the exception of Russia, which deposited ratification in 2005). Only four parties have also ratified the 1997 Protocol, which contains, *inter alia,* a better definition of nuclear damage (now also addressing the concept of environmental damage and preventive measures), extends the geographical scope of the Vienna Nuclear Liability Convention, and extends the period during which claims may be brought for loss of life and personal injury. The 1997 Protocol also provides for jurisdiction of coastal States over actions incurring nuclear damage during transport. Taken together, the two instruments should substantially enhance the global framework for compensation well beyond that foreseen by existing conventions.

Prior to the 1997 Protocol, the Vienna Nuclear Liability Convention, like the Paris Nuclear Liability Convention, covered damage to persons and property but made no mention of environmental damage, though the Paris Nuclear Liability Convention did allow national courts expansive interpretive power in providing for "nuclear damage" [Paris Nuclear Liability Convention at art. I(k)(ii)]. Under the 1997 Protocol, the definition of "nuclear damage" is expanded to encompass "the costs of measures of reinstatement of impaired environment," "loss of income derived from an economic interest in any use or enjoyment of the environment, incurred as a result of significant impairment of that environment," and "the costs of preventive measures" [1997 Protocol at art. 2, 2(k)iv–vi]. Liability for such damage extends to radiation emitted by any nuclear installation, including from waste produced by those installations.

The Vienna Nuclear Liability Convention's standards for operator liability, award limits, and jurisdiction generally mirror those of the Paris Nuclear Liability Convention. Unlike the OECD regime, however, the Vienna Nuclear Liability Convention contains no provision for supplemental funding by the parties themselves. Instead, the Vienna Nuclear Liability Convention sets the floor for operator liability at $5 million (value in gold on April 29, 1963). An upper ceiling is not fixed for operator liability, leaving open the possibility of massive awards directly from the operator. This is in conflict with the Paris Nuclear Liability Convention's formula of operator, state, and contracting party contributions. For the Vienna Nuclear Liability

Convention to become the global instrument on CL that the IAEA envisions, the future parties must resolve this inconsistency. Given the recent attention that has been paid to the precise amounts allowable under the Paris Nuclear Liability Convention's formula, it is likely that compensation amounts on a global treaty will follow that scheme, instead of the Vienna Nuclear Liability Convention.

f. Fusion Energy

Civil nuclear energy and military weapons research has historically centered on nuclear fission, as opposed to nuclear fusion. A fission device harnesses the energy released when a large atomic nucleus (like that of uranium) is broken apart, while a fusion device harnesses the energy released when two light atomic nuclei (e.g. deuterium and tritium) fuse together into heavier ones (like helium). Fusion energy offers an attractive alternative to fission, as it avoids many of the dangers and is more environmentally acceptable. Importantly, the process does not produce radioactive waste, nor emit greenhouse gasses (GHGs). However, the development of such devices has been met with limited success.

In an effort to establish the scientific and economic viability of fusion reactors, the International Thermonuclear Experimental Reactor (ITER) project was initiated in 1985 as a research and development collaboration between the U.S., Japan, the EU (by way of EURATOM), and the former Soviet Union. The engineering design of a large-scale fusion reactor was completed in 2001, and a site in southern France was finally chosen for its construction in 2005. Construction on the site began in 2010, and as of this writing over 2,000 people are collaborating to build the world's most advanced tokamak magnetic confinement fusion experiment [International Thermonuclear Experimental Reactor (ITER), *available at* http://www.iter.org/ (last visited Apr. 2017)]. In 2006, members of the project entered into the Agreement on the Establishment of the ITER International Fusion Energy Organization for the Joint Implementation of the ITER Project [*Agreement on the Establishment of the ITER International Fusion Energy Organization for the Joint Implementation of the ITER Project*, Nov. 21, 2006, International Atomic Energy Agency] In addition to outlining the role of the International Fusion Energy Organization, for which the IAEA will act as depository, the Agreement insists that materials developed for the project are employed only for peaceful purposes, and that care be taken for the non-proliferation of any materials that might be used for the development of nuclear weapons [*Id.* at art. 20].

D. CONCLUSIONS

The dangers to human health and the environment from the use of nuclear materials—both military and civilian—are significant. Full nuclear disarmament continues to be unlikely, and projections for nuclear power continue to show increases—particularly since nuclear power may represent an alternative to fossil fuels in a world concerned about climate change. The international agreements in this regime cover a wide range of subjects, ranging from nuclear safety, nuclear security, safeguards and non-proliferation, as well as CL for nuclear damage. In order to protect the world from nuclear damage, these agreements must continue to develop, with the IAEA playing an important role in establishing legally binding international rules.

CHAPTER EIGHTEEN
THE FUTURE OF INTERNATIONAL ENVIRONMENTAL LAW (IEL)

We have seen how an expanding international environmental law (IEL) patrols an increasingly interconnected and interdependent world. It is a world in which practitioners and judges, at many levels of international and national law, are coming alive to the impact and import of IEL. Not surprisingly, IEL is now an established subject, firmly ensconced in the law school curriculum, and is addressed by a burgeoning scholarly literature.

What of the future? Understanding the present must pave the way for even the most faltering prognostication, and we begin by taking a synoptic view of the present status of IEL. In so doing, this chapter does not venture to re-conceptualize the subject in conformity with the authors' own ideas of success or failure. Rather, the chapter looks objectively and realistically at what is. It begins by examining the greatest challenge presently facing IEL—that of meeting global energy demand within the framework of sustainable development (SD)—and proceeds thereafter to examine foundational and systemic norms of IEL: SD and the common law of humankind. It then reviews other primary rules and principles.

A. THE CHALLENGE OF SUSTAINABLE ENERGY

The manner and extent to which increasing global energy demand can be met within the framework of SD presents the greatest global environmental challenge of the 21st century. This extraordinary challenge is predicated on four widely recognized phenomena.

1. INCREASING GLOBAL ENERGY CONSUMPTION

Today's current primary global power consumption of about 550 quadrillion Btu will increase to 629 quadrillion Btu in 2020, and then to 815 quadrillion Btu in 2040—a 48% increase [U.S. Energy Information Administration (EIA), *International Energy Outlook 2016* (2016) (hereinafter EIA 2016)]. The major part of this projected increase in energy demand will occur in developing countries, which rely primarily upon the combustion of fossil fuels, such as coal, to produce the electricity necessary to meet their energy needs [*Id.*]. As a result, despite lower per capita energy consumption levels than industrialized nations, the volume and quantity of carbon dioxide (CO_2) emissions from developing countries have already exceeded emissions of industrialized nations. Energy-related CO_2 emissions rise from about 32 billion metric tons in 2012, to 36 billion metric tons in 2020, and then to 43 billion metric tons in 2040—a 34% increase [*Id.*]. The percentage of energy consumed by nations who are not members of the Organizations for Economic Cooperation and

Development (OECD), non-OECD nations, rose from 57% in 2012 to 65% in 2014 [*Id.*]. During this period non-OECD Asia accounted for 55% of the world increase in energy use and 65% of CO_2 emissions [*Id.*]. Indeed, China has overtaken the U.S. as the world's largest emitter of greenhouse gases (GHGs) [Union of Concerned Scientists, *Each Country's Share of CO₂ Emissions* Elisabeth Rosenthal, *China Increases Lead as World's Largest Emitter*, THE NEW YORK TIMES (Jun. 14, 2008)]. Developing country energy demand must be met, but doing so with fossil fuels compounds the gravity of the energy crisis.

2. ENVIRONMENTAL CONSEQUENCES OF FOSSIL FUEL RELIANCE

The environmental consequences of using fossil fuels to produce energy are formidable. Apart from the fact that fossil fuels are responsible for GHGs that cause anthropogenic climate change, the entire fossil fuel energy cycle of production, mining, transportation, refinement, use, and emissions are fraught with daunting environmental and public health problems [The Center for Health and the Global Environment, Harvard Medical School, *Oil: A Life Cycle Analysis of Its Health and Environmental Impacts* Paul R. Epstein & Jesse Selber eds. (2001)].

3. RESEARCH AND DEVELOPMENT OF RENEWABLE ENERGY

The search for smart energy that is plentiful, efficient, and accessible to replace or supplement our present environmentally damaging fossil fuel sources will involve new technological developments and creative assumptive frameworks dealing, *inter alia*, with energy production, distribution, delivery, storage, conversion, end-uses, and environmental protection. These technologies and assumptive frameworks need to be assessed and expressed in a manner that facilitates and secures global, national, and multinational corporate responses. There are no showstoppers waiting in the wings. Development and deployment of sustainable energy technologies on an unprecedented scale is needed.

The growing challenges presented by energy and environmental problems necessitate new treaty arrangements that change the way in which nations behave. For example, the 2015 Paris Agreement on climate change attempts to cut down emissions of GHGs, but fails to give primacy to research and development of renewable energy. The world relies on fossil fuels because of the non-viability of alternatives. It is imperative to embark on the kind of research and development undertaken by the Breakthrough Coalition led by Bill Gates, that is investing in new technologies to find better, more efficient, and cheaper energy sources. In order to provide reliable and affordable power without contributing to climate change, the Breakthrough Coalition is committed to addressing emissions in five key areas: electricity, transportation, agriculture, manufacturing, and buildings [Breakthrough Energy, *Reliable, Affordable Energy for the World: Investing in a Carbonless Future* (2017), *available at* http://www.b-t.energy (last visited Apr. 2017)].

B. FOUNDATIONAL AND SYSTEMIC NORMS

Primary rules and principles are those obligations found either in treaty or customary law. Our examination of primary rules is followed by a quick survey of the secondary rules of State responsibility (SR) and the legal phenomena created by a developing international civil society. We have resisted the urge to offer utopian blueprints for future action, but have settled instead for some modest, pragmatic, and incremental suggestions for future developments. Overall, we paint a mottled yet generally optimistic picture of IEL.

1. SUSTAINABLE DEVELOPMENT (SD)

As noted in Chapter 2, IEL is part of a historical continuum and we use the Plan of Implementation of the World Summit on Sustainable Development (WSSD Implementation Plan) and the Rio Declaration on Environment and Development (Rio Declaration) as our baseline to focus on SD.

SD—the syncopated foundational concept of IEL—appears to have softened its environmentalism and placed even greater emphasis on development. In Chapter 2, we noted how the Rio Declaration retreated from the high-watermark of environmental protection embodied in the Stockholm Declaration of the United Nations Conference on the Human Environment (Stockholm Declaration). The WSSD Implementation Plan also continues to drift away from certain kinds of environmentalism.

What is most striking about the re-articulation of SD at WSSD is that it introduces a third element of social development into the definition of SD. Hitherto unseen, social development has now been unveiled as a full-grown concept. This change is significant, because previously SD only consisted of two components (economic development and environmental protection), but SD has now been invested with a third component (social development). Viewed differently, the two-sticks of SD has now become a three-stick triangle.

The emphasis on economic development and the eradication of poverty may effectively have diminished the importance of certain kinds of environmentalism, and this development has been disquieting to commentators who have argued that the Rio Declaration institutionalized a preeminent right to economic development that enfeebled and attenuated the imperative of SD [Marc Pallemaerts, *International Environmental Law in the Age of Sustainable Development: A Critical Assessment of the UNCED Process*, (1996) 15 J. L. & COM. at 623 & 630–35].

However, SD as we have known it, has undergone a paradigm change. As we have seen in Chapter 2, the sustainable development goals (SDGs), which replaced the millennium development goals (MDGs), emphasized the extent to which SDGs need to be established at national and local levels. Therefore, the responsibility for taking action would be shifted primarily to developing countries.

It is important to emphasize the extent to which this conceptualization of the SDGs is different from SD as hitherto accepted. Up to this time, every formulation of SD in legal and political documents had given primary emphasis to economic and social development that eradicated poverty. A dramatically different picture now emerges. First, there is a new iteration of SD emphasizing global public goals (GPGs), discussed in Chapters 2 and 6. GPGs are distinct from the eradication of poverty found in the MDGs based on individual economic growth. Second, developing countries now assume greater responsibility for SD. Previously, SD had been premised on the legal and political principle of common but differentiated responsibilities (CBDR) embodied in the United Nations Framework Convention on Climate Change (UNFCCC), which insisted on the overriding responsibility of developed countries to help developing countries. The SDGs instead place significant responsibility on national states, the large majority of whom consist of developing countries.

The Paris Agreement gives flesh and form to SDG13. It claims that it is enhancing the implementation of UNFCCC and SD [Paris Agreement at art. 2(1)] and will be implemented to reflect equity and the principle of CBDR [Id. at art. 2(3)]. However, the singular focus of the Paris Agreement is GHG mitigation and adaptation, which is inconsistent with the priority given to economic and social development in the UNFCCC. Moreover, despite its invocation of CBDR, developing country parties are still required to take costly actions to reduce GHGs. The Paris Agreement does not contain any provisions similar to Article 4(3) of UNFCCC, under which the developed countries agreed to pay the full cost of climate action taken by developing countries, or those found in Article 4(7) of the UNFCCC, stating that its implementation would depend on the extent to which developed countries met their financial obligations.

The Paris Agreement does contain some provisions dealing with financial assistance and technology transfer. However, in contrast to the core of the UNFCCC where economic and social development takes primacy, the core of the Paris Agreement gives primacy to GHG reductions. In the Paris Agreement, financial and technical assistance obligations are pushed out to the peripheries.

The costs of climate action required by the Paris Agreement raises a central question. It is estimated the costs of implementing the Paris Agreement will amount to $1,100 billion per year [EurActiv, *Infographic: Not All SDGs Were Created Equal* (Oct. 19, 2015), *available at* http://www.euractiv.com/ sections/development-policy/infographic-not-all-sdgs -were-created-equal-318558 (last visited Apr. 2017)]. Another commentator estimates that the Paris Agreement will cost between $1 to 2 trillion dollars per year and cost $100 trillion by the end of the century [Marc Morano, *Statistician: UN Climate treaty will cost $100 trillion—To Have No Impact— Postpone warming by less than four years by* 2100, Climate Depot (Jan. 17, 2017), *available at* http:// www.climatedepot.com/2017/01/17/danish-

statistician-un-climate-treaty-will-cost-100-trillion-
to-postpone-global-warming-by-less-than-four-year-
by-2100/ (last visited Apr. 2017)].

These estimates are many times higher than the
total costs of achieving all of the SDGs (1 through 8)
dealing with the economic and social dimensions of
SD. Given the massive expenditure on climate action,
the unanswered question is whether these expenses
will be incurred at the cost of poverty reduction and
economic and social development. [Lakshman
Guruswamy, GLOBAL ENERGY JUSTICE: LAW &
POLICY (2016) at 75–83]. In the absence of enormous
increases in assistance from developed countries to
developing countries, it appears that the answer is
yes.

2.   THE COMMON LAW OF HUMANKIND

At the international level, the assumption of
common responsibility for climate change by
developing countries may point to the development of
an environmental common law of humankind. This
may also be the case on a comparative level. A review
of the environmental laws of various nations that
make up the international community reveals the
extent to which environmental problems—whether
arising from air and water pollution, land use, or
exploitation—are omnipresent. Uniform biophysical
reactions caused by pollution are part of nature's
writ, and the laws of nature, which ignore
geophysical boundaries, give rise to identical
challenges and common reactions in different parts
of the world. If, for example, the receiving medium is

air, discharges of wastes or residuals from coal powered power plants, whether in Los Angeles, Liverpool, Düsseldorf, or Auckland, lead to pollution. Common biophysical reactions take place regardless of where in the world the environment is abused. If the necessary conditions exist, sulfur dioxide (SO_2) and nitrogen oxide (NOx) will react and result in acid rain in the Ruhr, Northern England, or in the Raquette, Lake area of New York. If polychlorinated biphenyls (PCBs) are released into the air and water, they act to case cancers in West Virginia the same way as they do in Newcastle upon Tyne, United Kingdom or Colombo, Sri Lanka.

In responding to these common problems, States have often arrived at common regulatory ways of dealing with them. Time does not permit any systematic exploration of the compass of comparative environmental law, but we know from the examples of acid rain and PCBs that, when faced with this common problem, States generally act to protect the health of their people, and they seldom deny the deleterious effects or decide to ignore them. The actions States take, of course, are dependent upon their state of economic development and national priorities. While recognizing the evil of pollution, States may be economically unable to take action to remedy these evils whether in the form of technological, emission, or ambient standards placed on industry or with other restrictions placed on the consumers or society at large. Such action may, therefore, be postponed while States remain cognizant of what is required, and may even solicit international assistance to do so.

National boundaries do not constitute biophysical or chemical boundaries, and pollution sometimes migrates from one State to another causing transboundary legal problems that fall within the province of international, not national law. The customary IEL principle prohibiting a State from using its property so as to injure that of another responds to these phenomena, reflects the climate of world opinion, and symbolizes the confluence of national and international law. It is restated in numerous declarations and treaties founded upon a universal appreciation of the need to control damage caused by pollution. These articulations recognize a principle, rooted as much in national law as in international comity, which has become part of the common law of humankind.

Hersch Lauterpacht authenticated the extent to which international law is molded by domestic sources, analogies, and experience [*see* Hersch Lauterpacht, PRIVATE LAW SOURCES AND ANALOGIES OF INTERNATIONAL LAW (1970)]. He also demonstrated how Article 38 of the Statute of the International Court of Justice (ICJ) directs the ICJ to apply the "general principles of law recognized by civilized nations" [*Id.* at 69]. By "general principles" he referred to principles of law expressing rules "of uniform application in all or in the main systems of private jurisprudence" [*Id.*]. While Lauterpacht applied his reasoning to private law analogies, the principle underlying his thesis, on a parity of reasoning, is equally applicable to domestic public and regulatory law analogies. The general principles of environmental law universally recognized by

States enables us clearly to see that the formidable body of IEL, dealing both with global and non-global problems, is itself part of the greater universal rubric of the common law of humankind—a system of law that the international community and judicial tribunals are obliged to recognize and embrace.

In this context, a fecund recommendation of Agenda 21 is worthy of exploration. It urges that non-governmental organizations (NGOs) be given the opportunity of vindicating treaty rights in national forums [Agenda 21 at ¶¶ 27.10 & 27.13]. In addition, the Rio Declaration provides that "[s]tates shall develop national law regarding liability and compensation for the victims of pollution and other environmental damage" [Rio Declaration at principle 13]. These expressions of international consensus underscore the importance of giving: (1) national courts jurisdiction; and (2) individual plaintiffs' access and standing in national courts to pursue environmental rights and duties created by treaty. We have seen in Chapter 3 that such remedies are unusual, and effectively remain confined to the subjects of nuclear and oil pollution.

We have already reviewed the shortcomings of international judicial remedies in Chapter 3, and are confronted with having to deal with the stubborn political fact that in the absence of strained political relationships, States do not generally take each other to court. Whether based on self-interest arising from the mutual vulnerability of a State to actions by others, or a desire not to offend friendly States, the crop of cases has been meager. While we have noted the lack of progress of international accountability, it seems that on this occasion national liability may be a functional and practical way to develop the concept of liability for environmental harm.

On the other hand, environmental litigation in national courts is proliferating, and it makes sense to use national courts to advance international remedies. The Convention on the Law of the Non-navigational Uses of International Watercourses (Convention on International Watercourses) (*see* Ch. 3) recognizes the importance of national remedies in a curiously named Article on "Non-discrimination" [Convention on International Watercourses at art. 32]. The Non-discrimination Article prohibits States from discriminating on the basis of nationality or residence in granting judicial remedies to any natural or juridical person who has suffered appreciable harm. Although this principle has not been accepted by States, either by enacting national legislation *en masse* or agreeing to an international treaty, the fact that it has received some acceptance in the Rio Declaration and Agenda 21 is evidence of an evolving "soft" law. As we have seen, the Convention on the Protection of the Environment between Denmark, Finland, Norway and Sweden (Nordic Convention) establishes this principle and it is to be hoped that it could be built upon through implementing mechanisms of other treaties.

C. PRIMARY RULES AND PRINCIPLES

1. PRINCIPLES

We have already seen that environmental skepticism has not stood in the way of a rising environmental common law of humankind. As we have observed earlier, the SDGs require all countries to take actions to mitigate climate change. The prevention of transboundary harm and conservation are two critical areas of increased environmental protection. The resilience and dynamism of the principles applicable to these areas helps to confirm that environmental protection still remains an important component of SD.

The prohibition on transboundary pollution, which we have referred to above, was codified by Principle 21 of the Stockholm Declaration. This principle is now entrenched in numerous provisions of pre-Rio treaties and declarations, and has received such strong support through the practice and *opinio juris* of States that it has become a principle of customary international law (*see* Ch. 1). The attempt in the Rio Declaration to undermine the illegality of transboundary pollution by emphasizing the suzerainty of developmental policies, fails to overcome the overwhelming body of law that mirrors Principle 21 of the Stockholm Declaration, and defines it as an environmental wrong.

Furthermore, Principle 21 of the Stockholm Declaration, and not Principle 2 of the Rio Declaration, is reaffirmed in Article 3 of the Convention on Biological Diversity (Biodiversity

Convention)—a post-Rio treaty. The significance of this fact is that an instrument of hard law, the Biodiversity Convention, is normatively superior to the non-legal Rio Declaration. The Biodiversity Convention's prohibition on transboundary pollution makes no exceptions for transboundary pollution arising from developmental policies.

The principle of conservation asserts the equality of environmental protection, not its subordination to development, within the dynamic of SD. We have seen how the Biodiversity Convention has sought to strike this balance (*see* Ch. 5). Moreover, post-Rio developments, such as the 1995 Agreement for the Implementation of Provisions of the United Nations Convention on the Law of the Sea Relating to the Conservation and Management of Straddling Fish Stocks and Highly Migratory Fish Stocks Agreement (SFSA) and other instruments discussed in Chapter 13, have reiterated the importance of conservation.

However, it is necessary to reinforce the importance of conservation by moving toward a World Forestry Convention—something that was repudiated at the United Nations Conference on Environment and Development (UNCED), or Earth Summit. A World Forestry Convention should protect old forests, particularly tropical forests that are home to up to 50% of the plant and insect biodiversity of the world. It is necessary that the world be presented with such a plan to save its tropical forests and conserve the gene banks of the planet. The United Nations (UN) Programme on Reducing Emissions from Deforestation and Forest

Degradation has made an effort to address this problem by conserving and properly managing tropical forests to preserve biodiversity and to preserve their character as carbon sinks in an effort to sustainably deal with climate change [United Nations Programme on Reducing Emissions from Deforestation and Forest Degradation (UN-REDD), FRAMEWORK DOCUMENT (Jun. 20, 2008) at 1–2].

Given the foundational character of SD, it may well be that the principle of CBDR, found in Principle 7 of the Rio Declaration and Article 4 of the UNFCCC, has now become part of customary law. It is difficult to accept the equitable and distributional thrust of SD without the need for CBDR. Such a conclusion is reinforced by the fact that numerous treaties institutionalize CBDR and establish financial mechanisms for doing so, while institutions such as the Global Environmental Facility (GEF) (*see* Appendix § C) were reinvented to better act as a mechanism for implementing CBDR.

2. RULES

While we have covered a host of treaties and conventions, there is little doubt that climate change dominates the attention given to IEL. Consequently, we will focus on the primary obligations governing climate change and observe how they have been implemented. The Kyoto Protocol, which binds industrialized (Annex I) countries to reduce their emissions of CO_2 from 5% to 7% below their 1990 levels between 2008 and 2012 [Kyoto Protocol at art. 3], has been the subject of interminable news, discussion, and debate. Kyoto Protocol duties constitute primary rules of obligation. We have noted in Chapter 6 that the U.S. has refused to ratify Kyoto, and that it appears most States that have ratified the Protocol will not be able to meet their obligations. For the reasons stated in Chapter 6, the Kyoto Protocol is a moribund agreement.

The ability to harness energy is a prerequisite to SD. Worldwide, almost 3 billion people have little or no access to modern energy for cooking, heating, illumination, or basic mechanical needs. Instead, the "Energy Poor" generally must rely on burning biomass—such as wood, animal dung, and crop residues—with serious consequences for their health and the environment [Lakshman Guruswamy, ed., *International Energy and Poverty: The Emerging Contours,* (2016) Routledge]. Energy poverty exacerbates ill health and economic hardship, and reduces educational opportunities [*Id.*]. In fact, apart from SDG7, which ensures access to affordable, reliable, and sustainable energy for all, many of the other SDGs are not achievable without major improvements in the quality and quantity of energy services available to the world's Energy Poor.

In a welcome response to this issue, the UN embraced the need for universal access to energy and declared 2012 the "International Year of Sustainable Energy for All," with the predominant objective of providing electricity for those lacking access to it [United Nations Foundation, *2012 International Year of Sustainable Energy for All* (2011), *available at* http://seforall.org/ (last visited Apr. 2017)]. SDG7 gives expression to the need for energy for all. But, as we have observed, the world should also focus on alternative sources of energy. New sources of energy are desperately needed in the developing world, and such an effort will form an integral and essential component of SD.

3.   EMBRYONIC RULES AND PRINCIPLES

There are a number of embryonic primary principles of soft law that could develop either into widely accepted legislative treaties or into customary IEL. This would transform them from being aspirational and hortatory norms into legal obligations. Candidate principles begin with the precautionary principle, which according to some is already a principle of customary international law.

Such a conclusion is difficult to justify for a number of reasons. First, the Dispute Settlement Body of World Trade Organization (WTO), after examining the evidence, expressed doubt as to whether the precautionary principle was in fact a principle of customary international law or a general principle of law under Article 38(c) of the Statute of the ICJ [World Trade Organization (WTO), *Appellate Body Report on EC Measures Concerning Meat and Meat Products (Hormones),* WT/DS48/AB/R, (Jan. 16, 1998) at ¶ 123].

Second, the precautionary principle does not admit to any workable definition. While there is no authoritative legal definition of the "Precautionary Principle," the concept of precaution, as a distinct legal norm or term of art, is recognized in a small number of broadly adopted international instruments, and a larger number of more restricted regional legal instruments. The broadly adopted international instruments include the following provisions: Principle 15 of the Rio Declaration ("precautionary approach") [Rio Declaration at Principle 15]; Chapter 17.22 in the Report of the UNCED (1992) ("preventive, precautionary and anticipatory approaches") [UNCED at Chapter 17.22]; the preamble to the Cartagena Protocol on Biosafety to the Convention on Biological Diversity (Cartagena Protocol) ("precautionary approach") [Cartagena Protocol at pmbl.]; the preamble and Articles 1, 8, and 9 in the Stockholm Convention on Persistent Organic Pollutants (Stockholm POPs Convention) ("precaution," "precautionary manner") [Stockholm POPs Convention at art. pmbl., 1, 8, & 9]; and Article 3 in the UNFCCC ("precautionary measures") [UNFCCC at art. 3].

The indeterminacy of the precautionary principle makes it an inappropriate and ineffective regulatory decision-making tool. The precautionary principle provides no guidance on any of the fundamental questions that are faced in making any risk decision. It is ambiguous as to what level of risk is acceptable, what role costs should play in risk decisions, what quantum of scientific evidence is sufficient for making decisions, and how potential risk-risk tradeoffs should be addressed. Proponents of the precautionary principle disagree not only on these important questions, but also on whether the precautionary principle should apply in the risk assessment process, the risk management process, in both risk assessment and risk management processes, or as a substitute for the current risk assessment/risk management paradigm.

Third, the precautionary principle, at least as defended by some of its strongest proponents, would appear to be directed at hazard, as opposed to risk. These advocates call for precautionary measures whenever there is a hazard. Yet every substance or product has the intrinsic potential for some hazard, which may or may not translate into real-world risks of concern. Because hazard potential is ubiquitous, basing regulatory decisions on hazard alone creates the potential for arbitrary, unfair, and inefficient regulations.

Finally, there is a paucity of practice and *opinio juris* supporting the precautionary principle, and therefore it does not rise to the level of customary law. This does not preclude the evolution of a more refined and restricted version of the precautionary principle which could emerge as principle of customary international law.

The polluter pays principle, as articulated, for example, in Principle 16 of the Rio Declaration, encourages States to continue "to promote the internalization of environmental costs and these of economic instruments, taking into account the approach that the polluter should, in principle, bear the costs of pollution" [Rio Declaration at principle 16]. However, the objections based on indeterminacy and lack of *opinio juris* directed at the precautionary principle apply equally to the polluter pays principle.

4. CLASH OF PRIMARY OBLIGATIONS

While trade, as an instrument of economic growth, is another component of SD, the clash between environmental and trade norms has assumed an importance that warrants separate treatment. The reliance on free trade to achieve economic growth—a foundational premise of post-World War II international development strategies—appears to have been strongly endorsed in the Rio Declaration. Articles 4, 11, and 12 lean toward interpreting SD as economic development [*Id.* at art. 4, 11, & 12]. Article 12, for example, is strongly supportive of "an open international economic system that would lend itself to economic growth and sustainable development" [*Id.* at art. 12]. It goes on to state, "unilateral actions to deal with environmental challenges outside the jurisdiction of the importing country should be avoided" [*Id.*]. The WSSD Implementation Plan devotes all of Section V to "sustainable development in a Globalizing World" and emphasizes the importance of free trade [*see* WSSD Implementation Plan at Section V]. The General Agreement on Tariffs and Trade (GATT) institutionalized the universality of free trade, while the WTO established an international organization to implement it. Advocates perceive the GATT and WTO together as semi-constitutional treaties aimed at eliminating interference and intrusion in international trade.

The tension between free trade and environmental protection is an important aspect of this dispute between economic growth and environmental protection, and requires resolution within the conceptual framework of SD. The future of IEL will be critically affected by how this conflict is settled. A potential clash may well hinge on the extent to which the restrictions on trade in genetically modified organisms (GMOs) that are consistent with SD are also consistent with the GATT regime.

The WTO and the Agreement on Sanitary and Phytosanitary Measures (SPS Agreement) are part of the GATT. To the extent that a decision to ban GMOs obstructs free trade, the SPS Agreement requires that such decisions be justified on principles of scientific risk assessment. The Cartagena Protocol, on the other hand, focuses on environmental protection, not free trade. It allows States pursuing biosafety to ban GMOs by using the precautionary principle, even where strict scientific proof may be lacking.

Any judicial dispute over this issue will fall within the jurisdiction of the Dispute Settlement bodies of the WTO, because neither the Biodiversity Convention nor the Cartagena Protocol creates binding dispute settlement procedures. Environmentalists, including one of the authors, have justifiably been suspicious about the judicial machinery of the WTO. To assuage such fears, it is necessary that any decisions taken by the judicial bodies of the WTO be based on the international customary law principles of fairness and reasonableness [see Lakshman D. Guruswamy, *Sustainable Agriculture: Do GMO's Imperil Biosafety?* 9 IND. J OF GLOBAL LEGAL STUDIES 461 (2002)].

D. SECONDARY RULES AND STATE RESPONSIBILITY (SR)

Chapter 3 dealt somewhat extensively with the International Law Commission (ILC) codification of SR in the *Draft Articles on Responsibility of States for Internationally Wrongful Acts* (Draft Articles on SR). The jural status of this codification could rest: (a) on customary law, (b) a treaty, or on (c) both. It remains to be seen as to what extent this codification is treated as an expression of existing customary law, and/or the extent to which it generates or leads to the growth of customary law. If institutionalized in a treaty, it is binding on the parties as a treaty. It becomes equally binding if it is considered a restatement of existing customary law. In any event, an authoritative codification will serve as a reference point for any elucidation of SR, and this is a major step forward for IEL.

What the Draft Articles on SR has done is to fill a big hiatus in international treaty law. Many treaties embodying primary obligations do not provide for the consequences of the breach of these obligations. Where there is a breach, the absence of particularized relief or remedies often has parties groping for ways of implementing the convention. The Draft Articles on SR fill this gap by stipulating the responsibility of the parties and the nature of the remedies. Admittedly, it does not create a new system of compulsory dispute resolution, but given the undeveloped stage of the international legal system, rules of SR signal a significant advance.

E. THE ACTORS IN INTERNATIONAL ENVIRONMENTAL LAW (IEL)

World actors are changing from State actors to others, such as NGOs, businesses, and a variety of other non-governmental entities. While the 1648 Treaty of Westphalia ushered in the nation-state, which then became the sole subject of international law and policy, we now perceive a return to a pre-Westphalian world centered around a more global civil society. The concept of civil society has a long political genealogy. It originated in the works of Thomas Paine and George Hegel in the late 18th century. After lying dormant for almost 200 years, the Marxist theorist Antonio Gramsci resuscitated the concept in the post World War II era [Thomas Carothers, *Civil Society*, FOREIGN POL'Y, 18, 18–19, (2000)].

In essence, civil society is a domain parallel to, but separate from, the State in which citizen actors associate and coalesce according to their own interests and needs. It encompasses political parties and interest groups that include both for-profit as well as not-for-profit groups. Civil society thus encompasses labor unions, professional associations, chambers of commerce, ethical and religious groups, corporations, and environmental NGOs.

Domestically and internationally, NGOs work at gaining considerable expertise on a topic, then urge governments and businesses to act on the basis of their findings and conclusions. Their efforts sometimes result in "soft law," as opposed to treaties and agreements. Environmental NGOs aggressively try to keep governments accountable through protest and debate.

It is almost obvious that IEL needs to develop innovative means of overcoming the deficiencies of a sovereignty-based system of international governance. Global environmental problems do not have to be solved within a consensual legal system of sovereign States that alone are empowered to make legal and political decisions. Legal or economic theories support the plain fact that States act in their own best interests and not that of the global community. While they might act to save the global commons where their own self-interest is affected, their actions are premised on individual, not community needs. Not surprisingly, there are many situations in which the cries for legal measures to arrest or avert environmental perils are left unanswered.

Despite attempts to re-conceptualize international legal society along different lines, there is little evidence to support a fundamental change of the present sovereignty-based legal system. The suggestions for reform we propose accept that sovereignty will remain the basis of decision-making, and are of an incremental and functional nature premised on what appears possible. Even so, it is perfectly feasible for the present sovereignty-based system to give better status and delegate more functions to NGOs.

As we have seen, NGOs are a fact of international life and they have long played an active role in IEL (*see* Appendix). As such, it does not take a big leap to institutionalize them as actors entitled to contribute in the law-making and implementing processes. This has already been done by the International Labor Organization (ILO) (*see* Appendix § F) and it is achievable for the various international organizations to take measures to accord NGOs a similar status in their deliberations. We have also taken note in Chapter 2 of the key role played by NGOs at the WSSD. There will, of course, be some problems concerning selection and accountability, but these are not insurmountable obstacles, and could be resolved along the same lines as the ILO. We have also already seen how that the Commission on Sustainable Development entertains reports from NGOs. Since such a move was based on consensus, it is well within reach to hope that other organizations created by treaty will do likewise. In addition, Agenda 21 envisions a greater role for NGOs and calls on the UN system to give them increased administrative and financial support [Agenda 21 at ¶ 27.12]. It further calls on the UN system to enhance the contribution of NGOs to decision-making, implementation, and evaluation of its projects [*Id.* at ¶ 27.9 (a)]. The infusion of people power into the law-making and implementing process will help to reduce the "democratic deficit" in international law-making and implementation.

APPENDIX

A. COMMISSION ON SUSTAINABLE DEVELOPMENT (CSD)

The Commission on Sustainable Development (CSD) is a functional commission of the United Nations Economic and Social Council (ECOSOC), established in 1992 at the request of the United Nations (UN) General Assembly. The CSD facilitates and reviews the progress of commitments made under the final documents of the UN Conference on Environment and Development (UNCED), known as Earth Summit, by promoting dialogue between governments and seeking to build partnerships and facilitate projects that further sustainable development. Many important conferences and meetings are held each month in New York City, which seek to bring governmental officials together to work towards implementing protection for biodiversity, reducing global warming, and managing and conserving the world's forests. The CSD also provides written policy guidance on implementing Earth Summit's principle documents. Five years after Earth Summit, the Special Session of the General Assembly adopted a document entitled Programme for the Further Implementation of Agenda 21, which was prepared by the CSD.

The CSD has 53 members who are elected for three-year terms of office by the ECOSOC from UN Member States. States that are not represented, UN organizations, and accredited inter-governmental and non-governmental organizations (NGOs) can also observe CSD sessions when they meet each year for two to three weeks. To learn more about the CSD, see https://sustainabledevelopment.un.org/csd.html.

B. FOOD AND AGRICULTURE ORGANIZATION (FAO)

The Food and Agriculture Organization (FAO) is a UN intergovernmental organization working to alleviate hunger and poverty through agricultural development, improved nutrition, and the pursuit of food security. Since the FAO was founded in 1945, food production has increased dramatically, and has kept up with the growing population of the world. The FAO seeks to meet the needs of both present and future generations by developing long-term strategies for sustainable agricultural and rural development. To reach this aim, the FAO provides practical assistance to developing countries, advises governments, provides a neutral forum for conflicts between countries, and serves as the collector and disseminator of information about nutrition, food, agriculture, forestry, and fisheries. The FAO hosted the World Food Summit in both 1996 and 2002, where hundreds of countries gathered to pledge alliance to end hunger. The World Summit on Food Security took place in 2009. The FAO consists of 191 Member States plus the European Union (EU) and the Faroe Islands, which are associate members.

C. GLOBAL ENVIRONMENTAL FACILITY (GEF)

The Global Environmental Facility (GEF) is a funding institution jointly created by the World

Bank, the United Nations Environment Programme (UNEP), and the United Nations Development Programme (UNDP). It was formed in 1990, initially with $1.2 billion to be used to fund environmental protection efforts. The GEF is designed to aid developing countries with six primary environmental issues: (1) climate change, (2) stratospheric ozone depletion, (3) loss of biological diversity, (4) pollution of international waters, (5) land degradation, and (6) persistent organic pollutants (POPs).

The Convention on Biological Diversity (Biodiversity Convention) and the UN Framework Convention on Climate Change (UNFCCC) designate the GEF as their financial mechanism [Biodiversity Convention at art. 39; UNFCCC at art. 11]. Pursuant to the restructuring agreed to in Agenda 21, the GEF was partially reinvented in order to enhance methods of governance and guarantee a more balanced and equitable division of resources between the interests of developing and donor (developed) countries [Agenda 21 at Ch. 33.14(a)(ii)]. To summarize the restructured GEF, the entity now has both a Council and an independent Secretariat. The Council employs a voting method known as "the double-weighted majority," in which affirmative decisions require a 60% majority of the total number of participants as well as a 60% majority of the total contributions. UNEP monitors GEF projects to ensure they have been brought into conformity with other international environmental agreements and projects, while the UNDP provides the GEF with expertise on institution building and personnel training. Because of the GEF's broad and important environmental goals, and the careful attention given to it by Earth Summit and other environmental organizations, the GEF has been reshaped to play an important role in future efforts to protect the environment.

Administratively, the GEF Secretariat is located in the World Bank, which also oversees the disbursement of GEF funds.

D. INTERNATIONAL ATOMIC ENERGY AGENCY (IAEA)

The International Atomic Energy Agency (IAEA) was established by the Statute of the International Atomic Energy Agency in 1957 [*Statute of the International Atomic Energy Agency*, Oct. 26, 1956, 276 U.N.T.S. 3 (entered into force July 29, 1957)]. It is the product of a compromise following the failure of a U.S. proposal for an international body to manage and supervise all civilian nuclear operations. It is an independent intergovernmental organization that has close associations with the UN but has not been given specialized agency status. It is comprised of 151 Member States that meet annually and a Board of Governors of 35 Member States, including 10 of those most advanced in atomic energy technology.

According to its Statute, the main purpose of the IAEA is to encourage the research, development. and application of atomic energy for peaceful purposes, and to ensure through safeguards that nuclear materials are not used for military purposes [*Id.* at art. III(1) & (5)]. It was also required "where appropriate" to establish health and safety standards [*Id.* at art. III(6)]. The Chernobyl accident transformed this marginal safety mandate into a central mission, though the standards do not have the force of law and States are not obliged to comply with them.

Despite their non-legal character, IAEA standards, regulations, codes of practice, and guides cover all aspects of radiation protection and radioactive waste disposal, and are widely followed. Under the Treaty of the Non-Proliferation of Nuclear Weapons (NPT) (*see* Ch. 17), which was extended indefinitely in 1995, non-proliferation safeguards are made obligatory through bilateral agreements with the IAEA, and periodic compulsory inspections by the IAEA are also mandated. In the result, the IAEA has assumed the role of an important international environmental organization.

However, some critics say that the 2011 nuclear accidents in Fukushima, Japan have revealed that the nuclear industry lacks sufficient oversight. This has led to renewed calls to redefine the mandate of the IAEA so that it can better police nuclear power plants worldwide.

E. INTERNATIONAL COURT OF JUSTICE (ICJ)

The International Court of Justice (ICJ) hears disputes between nation-states that have accepted its jurisdiction and provides advisory opinions to international organizations authorized to request them. The ICJ, located in The Hague, Netherlands, was established by the Charter of the UN [*Charter of the United Nations*, June 26, 1945, 1 U.N.T.S. xvi (entered into force Oct. 24, 1945)] and the Statute of the ICJ [*Statute of the International Court of Justice*, June 26, 1945, 59 Stat. 1031 (entered into force Oct. 24, 1945)].

The ICJ consists of 15 judges who each are appointed for 9-year terms that can be renewed, however there cannot be more than one judge of any nationality. Sixty-six states have accepted the compulsory jurisdiction of the ICJ (often with reservations), and 20 international organizations have the authority to request advisory opinions on legal questions that arise in the scope of their activities. However, the UN General Assembly and the Security Council can request an advisory opinion from the ICJ on any legal question.

In July 1993, the ICJ established a seven-member Chamber for Environmental Matters to aid in the formulation of an international environmental jurisprudence. But the ICJ's impact on international environmental law (IEL) begins much earlier in cases (*see* Ch. 2), and it continues to play a significant role in the development of IEL (*see* Ch. 17). Though reticent at times to flex its power, the ICJ has provided authoritative restatements on many aspects of international law that have an important bearing on environmental matters.

F. INTERNATIONAL LABOR ORGANIZATION (ILO)

The International Labor Organization (ILO), located in Geneva Switzerland, was established in 1919 as an independent international body associated with the League of Nations. Currently, the ILO is a UN intergovernmental organization. The ILO promotes social justice and works to improve labor conditions and living standards. Substantively, the ILO's work has focused on nuclear hazards, carcinogenic substances, construction safety, and occupational health services. In a consortium with the World Health Organization (WHO) and the UNDP, the ILO established an intergovernmental forum on chemical safety at the 1994 Stockholm International Convention on Chemical Safety. Additionally, the ILO was one of six intergovernmental organizations that finalized and adopted International Basic Safety Standards for Protection Against Ionizing Radiation.

An outstanding feature of the ILO is its tripartite character, consisting of government, employers, and employees. Each Member State is represented in the ILO by a delegation made up of two members from government, one from the employers, and one from the employees. Delegates vote independently, and a resolution requires a two-thirds majority.

One of the principle achievements of the ILO is its conventions (treaties) dealing with a variety of safeguards, which Member States are obliged to implement. The ILO requires such compliance with a unique supervisory system, annual reports, and a complaint system granting any member the right to complain about non-observance of any ILO convention.

G. INTERNATIONAL LAW COMMISSION (ILC)

The International Law Commission (ILC), comprised of eminent jurists from various countries, was created by the UN General Assembly in 1947 to help the progressive development and codification of international law. It currently has thirty-four members, each representing a different country. "Progressive development" is defined as "the preparation of draft conventions on subjects which have not yet been regulated by international law or . . . not yet been sufficiently developed in the practice of states" [ILC Draft Articles at art. 15]. The ILC's first priority is acting upon requests by the General Assembly for legal work. In reality, this rarely takes place. The ILC customarily initiates Draft Articles, which are sent to Member States, who are then requested to make comments. This preparatory work meets the definition of "progressive development," and is intended to lead to codification and the eventual formation of customary international law. The ILC is involved in various projects traversing IEL. These projects include the Convention on the Law of the Non-Navigational Uses of International Watercourses (Convention on International Watercourses), the Draft Articles on Responsibility of States for Internationally Wrongful Acts (Draft Articles on SR), the Draft Articles on International Liability, Draft Articles on Prevention of

Transboundary Harm from Hazardous Activates, and its current project on International Liability for Injurious Consequences Arising out of Acts Not Prohibited by International Law.

H.   INTERNATIONAL MARITIME ORGANIZATION (IMO)

The International Maritime Organization (IMO) was established in March 1948 by the UN Maritime Conference, and adopted its current name in May 1982. The IMO fosters international cooperation and exchange of information on technical matters among Member States affecting international merchant shipping, encourages the general adoption of maritime safety standards, and works to prevent and control maritime pollution. The IMO makes recommendations upon issues presented to it by Member States and convenes international conferences on other matters within its competence.

The IMO worked towards the prohibition on the dumping of low-level radioactive substances at sea, which was adopted by amendment to the 1972 Protocol to the Convention on the Prevention of Marine Pollution by Dumping Wastes and Other Matters (London Protocol) that also bans the dumping or incineration of industrial wastes at sea. The IMO has also been involved in strengthening the requirements of the International Convention for the Prevention of Pollution from Ships (MARPOL). In 1994, the IMO, with $5.5 Million from the GEF and the World Bank, began the Wider Caribbean Initiative for Ship-Generated Waste in an effort to reduce vessel pollution in the Caribbean.

The IMO has aided in the establishment of major IEL conventions designed to protect the environment, including the Convention on Safety of Life at Sea 1974; the International Regulations for Preventing Collisions at Sea 1972; Standards of Training, Certification, and Watchkeeping 1978; Prevention of Pollution from Ships 1973–1978; the Establishment of an International Fund for Compensation for Oil Pollution Damage 1969; and the International Convention on Oil Pollution Preparedness, Response, and Cooperation 1990.

The IMO consists of an Assembly, a Council, a Maritime Safety Committee, a Secretariat, and small subsidiary bodies created to address specific issues, such as the Legal Committee or the Facilitation Committee. Currently, the organization has 169 Member States and three associate members, and its headquarters are in Geneva, Switzerland.

I.   ORGANISATION FOR ECONOMIC CO-OPERATION AND DEVELOPMENT (OECD)

The Organisation for Economic Co-operation and Development (OECD) was established as the Organization for European Economic Co-operation on April 16, 1948 to administer U.S. aid granted under the Marshall Plan and the Economic Co-operation Administration. In 1960—after Europe had attained economic recovery—it was transformed into the OECD. Attempts to strengthen the organizational structure of the OECD to create a stronger institution have not been successful; it lacks supra-national legal powers, which results in members acting merely on a voluntary basis.

Article 2 of the OECD constitution requires it "to promote the efficient use of the [member] resources" [OECD Constitution at art. 2]. Under this mandate, the OECD fosters sustainable economic growth and economic development, and contributes to sound economic expansion and the expansion of world trade on a multilateral, non-discriminatory basis. The OECD began addressing environmental concerns in 1970 with the creation of the Environment Committee, which is affiliated with the OECD's Executive Committee. The Environment Committee evaluates the impact of international exchanges on the environment. The OECD was the first organization to legally define pollution, and, in 1972, the OECD was among the first to develop the influential "polluter-pays principle."

The OECD's Headquarters are in Paris. It is comprised of 34 members, including European states, Canada, the U.S., and Japan. The administration of the OECD includes of a Council, an Executive Committee, a secretariat, and various committees. Membership in the OECD is open to any government.

J.   ORGANIZATION OF AMERICAN STATES

The Organization of American States is an intergovernmental organization whose origin dates back to 1890, beginning with a series of conferences called the International Union of American Republics, a conference that met for commercial purposes. The OAS charter was signed in Bogota in 1948 and entered into force in 1951. The charter has since been amended many times, most recently in 1996.

The Organization of American States has a history of promoting environmental awareness, dating back to 1938 with the Convention on Nature Protection and Wildlife Preservation in the Western Hemisphere, and most recently in the creation of an Inter-American System of Nature Conservation.

The Organization of American States strengthens the peace and security of the Western Hemisphere and its Member States; seeks the solution of political, juridical and economical issues; and promotes economic, social, and cultural development.

The Organization of American States meets annually and has 35 Member States. Cuba's present government has been excluded from participation since 1962, but remains a member as a national entity.

K.   SOUTH PACIFIC REGIONAL ENVIRONMENT PROGRAMME (SPREP)

The South Pacific Regional Environment Programme (SPREP) was founded jointly by UNEP and the South Pacific Commission in 1982. Originally under the auspices of the Regional Seas Programme, it is now an autonomous organization promoting the environmental protection of the region. It helps countries form environmental policies, educates the general population about environmental issues, conducts tests and experiments on pollution, and works on protected area management. It consists of 25 members, most of which are Pacific island countries, but also including Australia, France, New Zealand, and the U.S.

L. UNITED NATIONS (UN)

The United Nations (UN) has a membership of 192 States. Article 7 of the UN Charter creates seven "principal organs": (1) the General Assembly; (2) the Security Council; (3) the Economic Council; (4) the Social Council; (5) the Trusteeship Council; (6) the ICJ (*see* Appendix E); and (7) the Secretariat [UN Charter at art. 7]. It also maintains 13 specialized agencies: (1) the ILO (*see* Appendix F); (2) the FAO (*see* Appendix C); (3) the UN Educational, Scientific and Cultural Organization (UNESCO) (*see* Appendix O); (4) the WHO (*see* Appendix T); (5) the World Bank (*see* Appendix R); (6) the International Monetary Fund (IMF); (7) the International Civil Aviation Organization; (8) the Universal Postal Union; (9) the World Meteorological Organization (WMO) (*see* Appendix U); (10) the IMO (*see* Appendix I); (11) the World Intellectual Property Organization (WIPO); (12) the International Fund for Agricultural Development (IFAD); and (13) the UN Industrial Development Organization (*see* Appendix Q). Two other important agencies are affiliated with the UN and cooperate with its various organs, but are structured as independent organizations—the IAEA (*see* Appendix D) and the World Trade Organization (WTO) (*see* Appendix V). The UN has no specialized agency committed to the protection of the international environment, although many specialized agencies carry out functions that impact upon the environment adversely as well as beneficially. The UNDP (*see* Appendix N), though not a specialized agency, has played a vital role. The UNEP coordinates UN environmental activities and assists developing countries in implementing environmentally sound policies and practices (*see* Appendix P). The UN has also supported major environmental conferences, including the Stockholm Conference in 1972 and Earth Summit in 1992.

M. UNITED NATIONS CONFERENCE ON TRADE AND DEVELOPMENT (UNCTAD)

The United Nations Conference on Trade and Development (UNCTAD) was created by the UN General Assembly as a one-time conference, but was later established as a permanent organ. The UNCTAD encourages international trade to stimulate economic growth and development. It also formulates procedures and policies on international trade, and makes proposals to place those procedures and policies into effect. In 1992 UNCTAD adopted "A New Partnership for Development," a program that seeks to foster economic development and environmental protection through "proper management of natural resources with a view to achieving sustainable development."

The UNCTAD has 191 Member States, drawn from the UN or its specialized agencies, and the IAEA.

N. UNITED NATIONS DEVELOPMENT PROGRAMME (UNDP)

The United Nations Development Programme (UNDP) was formed by the UN General Assembly in 1965 from the UN Expanded Program of Technical Assistance and the UN Special Fund. UNDP's environmental efforts have primarily filled the role of strengthening existing programs and institutions.

For example, UNDP played a major role in the development of the GEF. As its listed goals, UNDP works to advance human development and to serve as a consultative resource in efforts to eliminate poverty, regenerate the environment, create jobs, and advance the role of women. UNDP also helps developing countries increase the efficient use of human and natural resources. Towards its goal of ensuring environmental sustainability, UNDP hopes, by the year 2015, to cut the number of people without access to safe drinking water by half. It could emerge as an important agency for advancing sustainable development in the future.

O.   UNITED NATIONS EDUCATIONAL, SCIENTIFIC, AND CULTURAL ORGANIZATION (UNESCO)

Founded in 1946, the United Nations Educational, Scientific, and Cultural Organization (UNESCO)—a subsidiary organization of the UN—advances peace through the promotion of education, science, and culture. UNESCO has played an important role in IEL in that it has attempted to influence public opinion in environmental matters. For example, UNESCO initiated the Man and Biosphere Program in 1970 and the Intergovernmental Oceanographic Commission in 1960. It also aided in the formulation of and acts as a secretariat for the 1971 Ramsar Convention and the 1972 World Heritage Convention. In addition, UNESCO works to eliminate illiteracy through worldwide elementary education programs. It also safeguards world culture, books, and art, encouraging Member States to cooperate and provide access to their intellectual and cultural enterprises.

UNESCO maintains a General Conference, an Executive Board and a Secretariat. It has 193 members, and its main office is located in Paris, France.

P. UNITED NATIONS ENVIRONMENT PROGRAMME (UNEP)

The United Nations Environment Programme (UNEP) was founded in 1972 as a result of recommendations made at the Stockholm Conference on the Human Environment. It may be seen as the "environmental conscience" of the UN. UNEP coordinates solutions of different countries and agencies to environmental problems, addressing on a global scale such issues as ecology, sustainable development, methods of connecting development with environmental problems, and environmental management. UNEP seeks partnerships with other UN agencies, private businesses, non-governmental organizations, scientists, and all others who might have something to contribute to environmental solutions.

One of UNEP's major functions is the maintenance of information systems. The Global Environmental Monitoring System is a worldwide effort to keep track of changes in the terrestrial ecosystem. The Global Resource Information Database is a global network that maintains information referenced by the Global Environmental Outlook, which has produced the State of the Environment Report since 1994.

Environment and Natural Resource Information Networking coordinates local institutions, creating regional and national state-of-the-environment reports, which keep those regions updated on important environmental changes.

UNEP has helped to formulate programs and treaties. For instance, UNEP was involved in the Regional Seas Programme, encompassing more than thirty environmental agreements, the Zambezi Agreement and Action Plan, the Vienna Convention on Ozone, the Montreal Protocol, the Basel Convention, the Stockholm Convention on POPs, the Rotterdam Convention, and the Biodiversity Convention. The World Summit on Sustainable Development was a milestone for UNEP. Moreover, the UNEP provides supportive functions as well as Secretariat functions in many of these treaties.

UNEP's Headquarters are maintained in Nairobi, Kenya. Policies are directed by its Governing Council, whose 58 members are elected to four year terms by the UN General Assembly.

Q. UNITED NATIONS INDUSTRIAL DEVELOPMENT ORGANIZATION

The United Nations Industrial Development Organization is a specialized agency of the United Nations system, headquartered in Vienna, Austria. Its primary objective is the promotion and acceleration of industrial development in developing countries and countries with economies in transition, and the promotion of international industrial cooperation. Under the leadership of its charismatic

Director General Dr. Kandeh Yumkella, the agency has developed a transformative energy and environmental dimension. It believes that the provision of reliable and affordable energy is a necessary prerequisite for industrial development and greater economic and social prosperity. Furthermore, it strives to strike a balance between its growing demand for energy and the urgent need to mitigate its impact on the environment and the global climate. The environmental activities of the UN Industrial Development Organization aim to prevent the creation of industrial waste and industrial pollution, and to manage residuals that may be created, in an integrated manner.

R. WORLD BANK

The World Bank began with the formation of the International Bank for Reconstruction and Development (IBRD) at the UN Monetary and Financial Conference held at Bretton Woods in 1944. The World Bank's original purpose was the rebuilding of post-WWII Europe. Today, the World Bank provides funds and expertise for the improvement of developing nations. The World Bank is a group composed of five organizations: (1) the International Bank for Reconstruction and Development (IBRD—established in 1944), (2) the International Development Association (established in 1960), (3) the International Finance Corporation (IFC—established in 1956), (4) the Multilateral Investment Guarantee Agency (established in 1988), and (5) the International Centre for Settlement of Investment Disputes (established in 1966). In the

1980's, the World Bank responded to environmental concerns by creating an Environment Department and Operational Directives that addressed involuntary resettlement, indigenous people, the involvement of non-governmental organizations, and environmental assessments. Moreover, it operates the Tropical Forest Action Plan with the World Resources Institute and the GEF, which assists developing countries in offsetting costs incurred from adopting environmental measures.

S. WORLD CONSERVATION UNION (IUCN)

The World Conservation Union (IUCN), founded in 1948, is a non-governmental organization whose broad capabilities include the development of conservation strategies. The IUCN seeks "to influence, encourage and assist societies throughout the world to conserve the integrity and diversity of nature and to ensure that any use of natural resources is equitable and ecologically sustainable." The IUCN has over 1,000 members, which include both governments and non-governmental organizations. Although it has played an important role in the formulation of IEL jurisprudence, its resolutions are non-binding. It has helped formulate a Convention on Biological Diversity (Biodiversity Convention), the 1972 Convention Concerning the Protection of the World Cultural and Natural Heritage (World Heritage Convention), the 1973 Convention on Trade in Endangered Species and Wild Fauna and Flora (CITES), the 1971 Convention on Wetlands of International Importance (Ramsar Convention), and the 1979 Convention on

Conservation of Migratory Species of Wild Animals (Bonn Convention). The IUCN has established an Environmental Law Program, which seeks to "lay the strongest possible legal foundation at the international, regional and national levels for environmental conservation in the context of sustainable development." The Environmental Law Program's activities are administered by the Commission on Environmental Law (comprised of over 975 volunteering environmental law specialists) and the Environmental Law Centre (comprised of 15 highly skilled legal and information specialists).

T.   WORLD HEALTH ORGANIZATION (WHO)

The World Health Organization (WHO), formed in 1948, is affiliated with ECOSOC. The WHO is a directing and coordinating authority on health issues, establishing international collaboration while assisting governments as they strengthen health services and promote medical research and training.

WHO's environmentally related activities stem from the 1992 Earth Summit's declaration that countries should implement development in a sustainable fashion. It recognizes that a safe environment is a sustainable basis for human health. Since then, the WHO has assisted a number of countries in incorporating health and environmental concerns in their development plans. In 1994 the WHO created "Africa 2000" in an effort to universally provide water and sanitation services on the continent. Together with the UNEP, WHO maintains air quality monitoring devices in more than 60 countries, and the WHO has also contributed to the study of the ozone layer and climate change. In 1993, the WHO requested the ICJ to issue an advisory opinion on the Legality of the Threat or Use of Nuclear Weapons. Currently, the WHO is planning a meeting to address the impact of climate change on human health.

The WHO is given authority to promote conventions on the international health issues, often in consort with other organizations. One hundred ninety-three governments are members.

U. WORLD METEOROLOGICAL ORGANIZATION (WMO)

The World Meteorological Organization (WMO), which came into existence in 1950, became a specialized member of the UN in the same year. The WMO establishes international networks that work together to monitor the atmosphere and standardize measurements and statistics. The WMO has a number of programs, including the World Climate Programme. As part of the World Climate Programme, the WMO and the UNEP established the Intergovernmental Panel on Climate Change (IPCC) in 1988, which has become the platform for leading authorities on the climate change issue. WMO is developing the World Hydrological Cycle Observation System, which will work towards the reduction of desertification and tempering the effects of drought.

The WMO has 187 members and is comprised of an Executive Council, a Congress, and a Secretariat.

V. WORLD TRADE ORGANIZATION (WTO)

The World Trade Organization (WTO) is a permanent institution, established in 1995 as a result of the Uruguay Round trade negotiations and the Marrakesh Declaration. It is a centralized international agency for promoting free trade. The WTO is at once a platform for international trade relations, a provider of framework trade legislation, an overseer of trade policies, and a forum for the resolution of trade disputes. In a tentative and hesitant attempt to incorporate an environmental dimension in its policies, a WTO General Council Committee on trade and the environment reported to the WTO ministerial conference at Singapore in December of 1996. While the WTO has no specific agreement dealing with the environment, a number of WTO agreements include provisions dealing with environmental concerns. Indeed, the preamble to the Agreement Establishing the WTO identifies sustainable development and environmental protection as part of its objectives. Currently the WTO has 153 members.

W. WORLD WILDLIFE FUND (WWF)

The World Wildlife Fund (WWF) is a non-governmental, public, and charitable organization that was established by a group of scientists and public relations experts, and was closely aligned with the World Conservation Union (IUCN). Originally, the WWF was a fund, established through charitable fund raising, that donated money to conservation efforts throughout the world. Today, WWF is an organization that also works directly with government and business to focus attention on key environmental issues like energy conservation, climate change, habitat destruction, and education. The WWF's mission is "to reverse the destruction of the Earth's natural environment and build a future in which humans can live in harmony with nature."

INDEX

References are to Pages

GLOBAL CLIMATE CHANGE

GLOBAL ENVIRONMENT FACILITY

GREENHOUSE GASES

GREENPEACE INTERNATIONAL

HAZARDOUS ACTIVITIES

HAZARDOUS SUBSTANCES

HAZARDOUS WASTE

INDIVIDUALS

INTERGOVERNMENTAL PANEL ON CLIMATE CHANGE (IPCC)

INTERNATIONAL ATOMIC ENERGY AGENCY (IAEA)

PRECAUTIONARY PRINCIPLE

PROTOCOL

PUBLIC INTERNATIONAL LAW

PUBLICISTS

RADIATION

REMEDIES

REPARATIONS

RESEARCH